Simulation-based Inference in Econometrics

This substantial volume has two principal objectives. First it provides an overview of the statistical foundations of simulation-based inference. This includes the summary and synthesis of the many concepts and results extant in the theoretical literature, the different classes of problems and estimators, the asymptotic properties of these estimators, as well as descriptions of the different simulators in use. Second, the volume provides empirical and operational examples of SBI methods. Often what is missing, even in existing applied papers, are operational issues. Which simulator works best for which problem and why. This volume will explicitly address the important numerical and computational issues in SBI which are not covered comprehensively in the existing literature. Examples of such issues are: comparisons with existing tractable methods, number of replications needed for robust results, choice of instruments, simulation noise and bias as well as efficiency loss in practice.

Professor Roberto Mariano is based at the University of Pennsylvania. Dr. Til Schuermann is based at A.T. and T. Bell Laboratories. Dr. Melvyn Weeks is based at the University of Cambridge.

T0339926

Simulation-based Inference in Econometrics

Methods and Applications

ROBERTO MARIANO,
TIL SCHUERMANN, AND
MELVYN J. WEEKS

CAMBRIDGE
UNIVERSITY PRESS

CAMBRIDGE UNIVERSITY PRESS
Cambridge, New York, Melbourne, Madrid, Cape Town, Singapore, São Paulo, Delhi

Cambridge University Press
The Edinburgh Building, Cambridge CB2 8RU, UK

Published in the United States of America by Cambridge University Press, New York

www.cambridge.org
Information on this title: www.cambridge.org/9780521591126

First published 2000
This digitally printed version 2008

A catalogue record for this publication is available from the British Library

Library of Congress Cataloguing in Publication data

Mariano, Roberto S.
    Simulation-based inference in economics: methods and applications
  / Roberto Mariano, Til Schuermann, and Melvyn J. Weeks.
        p. cm.
    Includes index
    ISBN 0-521-59112-0
    1. Econometric models. 2. Economics–Simulation methods.
  I. Schuermann, Til. II. Weeks, Melvyn. III. Title.
  HB141.M353 1999
  330'.01'5195–dc21   98-35993
                                                            CIP

ISBN 978-0-521-59112-6 hardback
ISBN 978-0-521-08802-2 paperback

Contents

Part III Time series methods and models

Part IV Other areas of application and technical issues

Contributors

ERIC T. BRADLOW	*Assistant Professor of Marketing and Statistics* *The Wharton School of the University of Pennsylvania*
BRYAN W. BROWN	*Hargrove Professor of Economics* *Rice University* *Houston*
FABIO CANOVA	*Universitat Pompeu Fabra and University of Southampton*
BENT JESPER CHRISTENSEN	*School of Economics and Management* *University of Aarhus, Denmark* *Bjchristensen@econ.au.dk*
JOHN GEWEKE	*University of Iowa*
VASSILIS HAJIVASSILIOU	*Department of Economics* *London School of Economics*
MIKE KEANE	*Department of Economics* *University of Minnesota and* *Department of Economics* *New York University*
PER KRUSSELL	*University of Rochester, Institute for International Economic Studies and CEPR.*
ROBERTO S. MARIANO	*Professor of Economics and Statistics* *University of Pennsylvania*
LEE OHANIAN	*Department of Economics, UCLA and Research Department, Federal Reserve Bank of Minneapolis*

ADRIAN PAGAN

Economics Program
Australian National University

JOSE-VICTOR RIOS-RULL

University of Pennsylvania, CEPR and
NBER

PETER ROSSI

School of Business
University of Chicago

STEVEN STERN

Department of Economics
University of Virginia

TANIZAKI

Associate Professor
Department of Economics
Kobe University, Japan

NIZAR TOUZI

Centre de Recherche en Mathematiques
Statistique et Economie Mathematique
Universite Paris Pantheon-Sorbonne

GIOVANNI L. VIOLANTE

Department of Economics
University of London

WEI ZHANG

Department of Economics
National University of Singapore

Foreword

Under the influence of recent and ongoing major advances in computing technology, applied econometrics is undergoing a quiet revolution. Using simulation techniques practical solutions (classical as well as Bayesian) are beginning to emerge for many difficult and analytically intractable problems. Although many of the basic principles behind simulation techniques are well known, the application of these techniques to econometric problems is less familiar. The subject matter is highly technical and relatively new. There are only few texts that directly deal with the application of simulation techniques. Most available texts are primarily concerned with general concepts and principles of stochastic simulation and do not adequately address the practical issues involved in the application of these techniques to econometric problems. This has been particularly true of the use of simulation techniques in maximum likelihood and generalized method of moment estimation, developed in the pioneering contributions of McFadden (1989) and Pakes and Pollard (1989). Other applications of stochastic simulation techniques to solving nonlinear stochastic intertemporal optimization problems, to computing probability forecasts, to testing non-nested models, and to carrying out Bayesian inference using Gibbs sampling are also scattered in working papers and technical journals and are not readily accessible.

This volume represents a first step towards filling this vacuum. It provides an excellent overview of simulation-based techniques, and collects in one place a number of important contributions covering a variety of fields in applied econometrics. The book is in four parts and covers both microeconometric and time series applications. Each part starts with a short introduction by one of the editors, which provides a useful summary and places the contributions in proper perspectives. Theoretical problems in classical and Bayesian estimation, inference and decision making are addressed, but throughout the emphasis is on operational issues. For me the strength of the book lies in its detailed treatment of concrete applied problems and how stochastic simulation techniques are likely to help.

The importance of stochastic simulation techniques as a general tool is now widely recognized. What is lacking is a detailed discussion of scope and limitations of these techniques in different areas of applied econometrics. Given the relatively large fixed costs associated with the use of simulation techniques, potential entrants to the field would want to know under what conditions these techniques actually work. When is the use of stochastic simulation techniques preferable to the use of numerical analysis techniques? Under what conditions are stochastic simulation techniques stable? How sensitive are the outcomes to the number of replications and to the particular way that the simulation techniques are implemented? The precise answers to these and many other related questions are likely to be problem-dependent. But contributions such as the ones collected in this volume will provide the readers with a wealth of valuable experience.

With fast expanding computing power and large economic data sets becoming increasingly available it is hard to imagine how future applied research in economics could be conducted without the help of numerical analysis and stochastic simulation techniques. It is with this in mind that this volume is a particularly welcome addition to the literature.

M. Hashem Pesaran
December 1999
Los Angeles

Part I

Simulation-based inference in econometrics: methods and applications

Part I

Simulation-based inference in econometrics: methods and applications

Introduction

Melvyn Weeks

Although simulation-based inference (SBI) is a relatively new field in econometrics, the discipline has a long and rich history where simulation has provided a valuable methodological tool. The recent growth in the use of SBI stems from the seminal work of Lerman and Manski (1981), who proposed a computationally intensive procedure to circumvent the dimensionality problem common to estimation problems involving evaluation of high dimensional integrals. Although the method was in many ways pioneering, a number of problems with this procedure have prompted analysts to develop improved simulators. Key contributions by McFadden (1989) and Pakes and Pollard (1989) have resulted in the development of a wide range of simulation-based estimators with better finite sample properties.

In the wake of these developments, a substantial literature has emerged in the form of published and unpublished papers. At this juncture, it is dominated by discrete choice and limited dependent variable models, which deal with either cross-section or panel data. Some work has emerged in the time series literature, especially in the area of non-linear filtering, as well as Bayesian econometrics. The common thread that ties this body of work together is the estimation of behavioral models which contain numerically intractable conditional expectations. These conditional expectations are therefore simulated in order to estimate the underlying intractable expectations. This is in fact the essence of SBI.

In terms of pragmatics we wish to make what we feel is a critical distinction between the availability of this new technology and its productive use in a research setting. Keane (1992) was probably the first to allude to such a distinction in the context of a study involving the multinomial probit model. The distinction here is between the ability to simulate multivariate probabilities, thus solving the dimensionality problem common to a class of limited dependent variable (LDV) models, and the subsequent practical use in maximum likelihood and conditional moment estimation. As a result, this volume will emphasize the use of simulation in an applied context. Subsequently the type of questions that will be addressed will reflect this. Under what conditions might SBI be useful or even necessary? How does SBI work? How would one implement it? How well does it work and what are some of its limitations? What are some of its pitfalls, theoretical and operational? What are some examples in the literature?

This volume has two principal objectives. First, we provide an overview of the statistical and probabilistic foundations of SBI. In so doing we summarize and synthesize the many concepts and results in the theoretical body of the literature. This includes the different classes of problems and estimators, the asymptotic properties of these estimators, as well as descriptions of the different simulators in use. The objective is to provide a focused motivation for the use of simulation-based methods. While the flavor will be more pedagogic than proposition-proof, an outline of proofs for important results and theorems is provided. For detailed treatment of the proofs, references to appropriate papers are given.

Second, we provide empirical and operational examples of the methods. We do not wish to restrict ourselves to mere applied examples. Often what is missing even in the existing applied papers are operational issues. Which simulator works best for which problem and why? This volume explicitly addresses in detail the important numerical and computational issues in SBI which are not covered comprehensively in the existing literature. Examples of such issues are: choice of non-linear optimization routine, comparisons with existing tractable methods, number of replications needed for robust results, choice of instruments, importance of starting values, simulation noise and bias, as well as efficiency loss in practice.

The volume will be an invaluable resource for a number of identifiable groups. First, given that the volume synthesizes a broad and complex body of literature, it provides a useful reference tool for graduate students in econometrics and statistics. Currently advanced courses in econometrics which introduce the fundamentals of SBI do so by referring to published papers, and a limited number of special references such as van Dijk, Montfort and Brown (1995). Although that mode of learning should not be dismissed, this volume fills a gap in the literature by including a systematic overview of the statistical foundations that underpin simulation methodology. One of the other main objectives of this volume is, through the use of empirical examples, to emphasize the operational aspects of SBI. In general these issues receive limited attention in published works. Subsequently, this volume provides an excellent reference source for the applied econometrician/statistician who wishes to incorporate simulation techniques in applied analysis.

There are four distinct parts to the volume. Part I, "Simulation-based inference in econometrics: methods and applications," serves as an introduction to simulation-based methodology, covering motivation and an overview of estimation techniques, simulators, and asymptotic properties. Parts II, III, and IV contain applications for LDV and time series models, as well as other areas of application. In general, each chapter in these parts highlights a substantive application of SBI and the main issues involved in the application and in numerical implementation. Below we summarize the contents of each part.

The first part of this book provides a comprehensive overview of simulation techniques with the primary focus being Monte Carlo integration. The chapter by Stern begins with a general discussion of the intractability of many non-linear stochastic models and the use of simulation techniques to circumvent the problem. A number of estimation techniques are discussed in detail including the method of simulated moments and simulated maximum likelihood. For each method, the mechanics, intuition for how it works, properties, and references for further reading are provided. This is followed by an overview of various multivariate probability simulators including the pedagogically convenient crude frequency simulator, the smooth conditioning simulator, and Gibbs sampling. The chapter closes with a Monte Carlo comparison of smooth simulators with and without antithetic acceleration.

In part II we focus upon "Microeconometric methods." Since the seminal work in SBI drew much of its impetus from the difficulties faced by analysts estimating high dimensional discrete choice models, this area of the literature is particularly active. The first contribution by Weeks sets the scene by providing an overview of simulation-based methods in microeconometrics. Next, Richard and Zhang focus upon the application of simulation techniques to dynamic latent variable models, proposing a simple weighted least squares procedure for the construction of optimal importance samplers. Here the emphasis is placed upon the generic nature of the method and that the additional computing cost is more than compensated for by the large efficiency gains that accrue. Application to a stochastic volatilty model indicates that it is possible to obtain highly accurate ML estimators and posterior means with only a small number of replications even when sample size is large.

Next Hajivassiliou provides a general overview of simulation-based estimation of limited dependent variable models, and in particular compares the theoretical and computational attributes of simulated maximum likelihood and the method of simulated moments. A number of practical issues are also considered including the relationship between speed and convergence, dimensionality, and the number of replications. These issues have generally received scant attention in the literature but are obviously important for applied econometricians.

In the chapter by Geweke and Keane the authors present a method for Bayesian inference with regard to the structural parameters of dynamic discrete choice models. The principal advantages of their approach is that the analyst is not required to solve the agents' optimization problem, or make strong assumptions about how agents form expectations. In terms of implementation, the approach is useful in that the data requirements are minimal, beyond the partial observability of the payoff functions. Next, Weeks uses simulation techniques to test binomial and multinomial choice models using Cox's non-nested test. By focusing upon a number of asymptotically equivalent procedures for estimating the Kullback–Leibler measure of closeness and the variance of the test statistic, a number of variants of the computationally intensive Cox test are compared. Results suggest that in relatively large samples, a number of methods which do not require simulation (of either the numerator or denominator) exhibit reasonable performance. The chapter by McCulloch and Rossi examines the multinomial probit model within the confines of Bayesian analysis. The authors demonstrate that the use of informative and non-informative priors, various forms of heterogeneity, non-normal mixing distributions, and multiperiod models, can all be accommodated through the use of a Gibbs sampling strategy in which a Markov chain is constructed. Practical issues such as the rate of convergence of the Gibbs sampler are also discussed.

In part III we consider "Time series methods and models." Schuermann provides an introduction and motivation for why SBI is useful for time series analysis. The chapter by Christensen and Kiefer addresses a problem in empirical finance, namely that conventional option pricing methods make the false assumption of complete markets with no arbitrage, especially in the presence of stochastic volatility. They develop a simulation-based method for computing the appropriate incomplete markets stochastic volatility option pricing operator. Next, Diebold and Schuermann describe a generic procedure of estimating observation-driven models by exact maximum likelihood. By decomposing the sample likelihood into conditional and marginal densities, where the marginal likelihood implicitly conditions on pre-sample information, they develop a simulation-based non-parametric solution to enable exact as opposed to approximate MLE.

In the chapter by Mariano and Tanizaki the authors apply non-linear/non-normal filtering techniques to testing the permanent income hypothesis. A general non-linear state-space model for unobserved permanent consumption is constructed, and the simultaneous impact of transitory consumption, variable interest rates, and non-linearity of the Euler equation are examined. As a consequence of the complexities in the model, stochastic simulations are used to obtain numerical maximum likelihood estimates of unknown model parameters. Using data from the US and Japan, results clearly reject the permanent income hypothesis.

Pagan and Martin present a method for computing parameters of latent multi-factor models within the paradigm of indirect estimation. The approach circumvents many of the difficulties associated with direct estimation of this class of models using MLE.

Finally, Geweke provides a thorough overview of Bayesian methods in econometric time series models. After arguing for the advantages of using Bayesian methods for forecasting and decision and policy making in economics, he demonstrates the analytical intractability of Bayesian inference problems and their simulation-based solutions. Applications in multivariate ARMA, ARCH, and stochastic volatility models are given.

While the cross-section and time series taxonomy in econometrics indeed seems natural, not all applications can be thus classified. The last part of this book, "Other areas of application and technical issues," provides the reader with technical aspects and applications which do not fall naturally into either of the first two categories. Mariano scans this vast area of research and provides a broad motivation within the context of simulation for multiple integral evaluation and Monte Carlo experimentation.

In the first chapter, Bradlow applies Gibbs sampling with a Metropolis step to posterior inference in hierarchical models for customer satisfaction data. Next, Gourieroux, Renault, and Touzi discuss the small-sample properties of the indirect inference procedure – a simulation-based estimator which has been studied mostly from an asymptotic point of view. Through Edgeworth expansions, the authors show that the indirect inference estimator, just like the bootstrap, automatically operates a second-order bias correction.

The chapter by Ohanian, Violante, Krusell, and Rios-Rull uses stochastic integration, indirect inference, and simulated pseudo-maximum likelihood to estimate an aggregate non-linear production function. This is then used to evaluate the extent to which different substitution possibilities between skilled labor and capital, and unskilled labor and capital, can account for wage inequality. In the following chapter Canova and Ortega utilize simulation-based approaches to test calibrated general equilibrium models. The authors further compare these simulation procedures with more standard methods for testing the fit of non-linear dynamic equilibrium models.

Finally, Brown examines the distinction between bootleg and simulation errors arising from the use of bootstrap test procedure in parametric and semiparametric models. He shows that simulation replication requirements can be reduced considerably through a control variate approach based on limiting distributions.

We want to thank all the contributing authors for their patience in assembling this comprehensive volume. We want to extend a special word of thanks to John Geweke and the Minneapolis Federal Reserve Bank for organizing a conference of all the authors.

References

Dijk, van H.K., A. Montfort, and B. Brown, eds., (1995), *Econometric Inference Using Simulation Techniques*, Wiley.

Keane, M. (1992), "A Note on Identification in the Multinomial Probit Model," *Journal of Business and Economic Statistics*, 10, 193–200.

Lerman, S. and C. Manski (1981), "On the Use of Simulated Frequencies to Approximate Choice Probabilities," in C. Manski and D. McFadden (eds.), *Structural Analysis of Discrete Data with Econometric Applications*, Cambridge, MA: MIT Press.

McFadden, D. (1989), "A Method of Simulated Moments for Estimation of Discrete Response Models with Numerical Integration," *Econometrica*, 57, 995–1026.

Pakes, A. and D. Pollard (1989), "Simulation and the Asymptotics of Optimization Estimators," *Econometrica*, 57, 1027–1058.

1 Simulation-based inference in econometrics: motivation and methods

Steven Stern

1 Introduction

Over the last few years, major advances have occurred in the field of simulation. In particular, McFadden (1989) and Pakes and Pollard (1969) have developed simulation methods to simulate expected values of random functions and have shown how to use those simulators in econometric estimation routines. Important applications where these techniques have been used include patent renewal in Pakes (1986), retirement in Berkovec and Stern (1991), market entry in Berry (1992), dynamic programming problems in Hotz, *et al.* (1994), exchange rates in Bansal, *et al.* (1995), and automobile pricing in Berry, Levinsohn, and Pakes (1995). Also, for example, Geweke (1989), Chib (1993), and McCulloch and Rossi (1994, 1996) have shown how to use simulation methods to solve previously unsolvable Bayesian econometrics problems. An and Liu (1996) and Diebold and Schuermann (1999) use simulation to solve initial conditions problems in survival models and ARCH models respectively that otherwise seem to have no tractable solution.

Simulation provides an attractive solution for dealing with problems of the following type. Let U be a random variable with density $f(.)$, and let $h(U)$ be some function of U. Then

$$Eh(U) = \int h(u)f(u)du. \tag{1}$$

Most econometrics problems including all method of moments problems and many maximum likelihood problems require one to evaluate equation (1) as part of an estimation strategy for estimating a set of parameters θ. There are many cases where $Eh(U)$ cannot be evaluated analytically or even numerically with precision. But we usually can simulate $Eh(U)$ on a computer by drawing R "pseudo-random" variables from $f(.)$, $u^1, u^2, \ldots, u^R$, and then constructing

$$\hat{E}h(U) = \frac{1}{R} \sum_{r=1}^{R} h(u^r). \tag{2}$$

Equation (2) provides an unbiased simulator of $Eh(U)$ which, for most of the methods discussed later, is enough to provide consistent estimates (or estimates with small bias) of θ.

This chapter provides some examples to motivate the problem. The first example is the multinomial probit problem, the second is a problem with unobserved heterogeneity, and the third is a Monte Carlo experiment. Next, the chapter describes a set of simulators that improve upon the most naive simulator in equation (2). Improvement is in terms of variance reduction, increased smoothness, and reduced computation cost. Then the most common simulation estimators are described. Finally, it evaluates the performance of the various simulators and estimation methods.

1.1   Multinomial probit

The first example is the multinomial probit problem. Consider a model where y_j^* is the value to a person of choosing choice j for $j = 1, 2, \ldots, J$ (a person index is suppressed). For example, j might index whether to drive a car, ride in someone else's car, take a bus, or take a train to get to work ($J = 4$); it might index whether to work full time, part time, or retire ($J = 3$); or it might index whether an elderly person lives independently, in a nursing home, with a family member, or with paid help ($J = 4$). It is assumed that the person chooses the choice j with the greatest value; j is chosen iff $y_j^* > y_k^*$ for all $k \neq j$. Furthermore, it is assumed that y_j^* is a linear function of a set of observed variables and an error

$$y_j^* = X_j \beta + u_j, j = 1, \ldots, J. \tag{3}$$

Let $u = (u_1, u_2, \ldots, u_J)'$ be the vector of errors, and assume that the covariance matrix of u is Ω. The errors sometimes represent variation in values due to unobserved variables, and sometimes they represent variation in βs across people. Let $y_j = 1$ if choice j is chosen; $y_j = 1$ iff $y_j^* > y_k^*$ for all $k \neq j$.

Usually in data, we observe the covariates X and $y = (y_1, y_2, \ldots, y_J)'$ but not $y^* = (y_1^*, y_2^*, \ldots, y_J^*)'$. In order to estimate β and Ω, we need to evaluate the probability of observing y conditional on X or the moments of y conditional on X. First, note that, since y_j is binary

$$E(y_j | X) = \Pr[y_j = 1 | X]$$

$$= \Pr[y_j^* > y_k^* \, \forall k \neq j | X]. \tag{4}$$

If we assume that $u_j \sim iid$ extreme value, then the probability in equation (4) has the analytical form

$$PR[y_j = 1 \mid X] = \exp\{X_j\beta\} / \sum_k \exp\{X_k\beta\}. \tag{5}$$

Such a model is called multinomial logit. The problem with multinomial logit is that the independence assumption for the errors is very restrictive. One can read a large literature on the independence of irrelevant alternatives problem caused by the independence of errors assumption (see, for example, Anderson, De Palma, and Thisse (1992)).

Alternatively, we could assume that $u \sim N[0,\Omega]$ where Ω can be written in terms of a small number of parameters. When we assume the error distribution is multivariate normal, the resulting choice probabilities are called multinomial probit. For this case, the parameters to estimate are $\theta = (\beta,\Omega)$.[1] The choice probabilities are

$$PR[y_j = 1 \mid X] = \int_{u_1} \cdots \int_{u_j} 1[X_j\beta + u_j > X_k\beta + u_k \; \forall k \neq j] dF(u \mid \Omega) \tag{6}$$

where $1[\bullet]$ is an indicator function equal to 1 if the condition inside is true and equal to 0 otherwise and $F(u \mid \Omega)$ is the joint normal distribution of u with covariance matrix Ω (with individual elements ω_{jk}). Let $u_{jk}^* = u_k - u_j$ for all $k \neq j$, and let $u_j^* = (u_{j1}^*, u_{j2}^*, \ldots, u_{jj-1}^*, u_{jj+1}^*, \ldots, u_{jJ}^*)'$. Then the J-dimensional integral in equation (16) can be written as a $J-1$-dimensional integral

$$Pr[y_j = 1 \mid X] = \int_{u_{1j}^*} \cdots \int_{u_{Jj}^*} 1[X_j\beta - X_k\beta > u_{jk}^* \; \forall k \neq j] dF(u_j^* \mid \Omega_j^*) \tag{7}$$

where $F^*(u_j^* \mid \Omega^*)$ is the joint normal distribution of u_j^*: $u_j^* \sim N[0,\Omega_j^*]$ where $\omega_{jkl}^* = E(u_k - u_j)(u_l - u_j) = \omega_{kl} - \omega_{kj} - \omega_{jl} + \omega_{jj}$ for each element ω_{jkl}^* of Ω_j^*. Equation (7) can be written as

$$Pr[y_j = 1 \mid X] = Pr[u_j^* < V_j] \tag{8}$$

where V_j is a vector with the kth element equal to $V_{jk} = X_j\beta - X_k\beta$. Note that equation (8) can be written as $Eh(U)$ in equation (1) with $h(U) = 1[X_j\beta - X_k\beta > u_{jk}^* \; \forall k \neq j]$, the integrand in equation (7).

In order to make progress in estimating θ, we need to be able to evaluate equation (8) for any Ω_j^* and any V_j. For example, the MLE of θ maximizes

$$\frac{1}{N} \sum_i y_{ij} \log Pr[u_{ij}^* < V_{ij}] \tag{9}$$

where i indexes observations, $i = 1, 2, \ldots, N$. If $J = 3$, then equation (8) involves evaluating a bivariate normal probability; most computers have library routines to perform such a calculation. If $J = 4$, then equation (8)

[1] Some restrictions are required for Ω for identification. See, for example, Bunch (1991).

involves a three-dimension integral. One can evaluate such an integral using Gaussian quadrature (see Butler and Moffitt (1982)) or the numerical algorithm in Hausman and Wise (1978). But, if $J > 4$, numerical routines will be cumbersome and frequently imprecise.

Simulation provides an alternative method for evaluating equation (8). The simplest simulator of equation (8) is

$$\frac{1}{R} \sum_{r=1}^{R} 1(u_j^{*r} < V_j) \tag{10}$$

where u_j^{*r} is an *iid* drawn from $N[0,\Omega_j^*]$. Essentially, the simulator in equation (10) draws a random vector from the correct distribution and then checks whether that random vector satisfies the condition, $u_j^* < V_j$. The simulator in equation (10) is called a frequency simulator. It is unbiased and bounded between 0 and 1. But its derivative with respect to θ is either undefined or 0 because the simulator is a step function; this characteristic makes it difficult to estimate θ and to compute the covariance matrix of $\hat{\theta}$. Also, especially when $\Pr[y_j = 1 | X]$ is small, the frequency simulator has a significant probability of equaling zero; since MLE requires evaluating a $\log \Pr[y_j = 1 | X]$, this is a significant problem. The simulators discussed in section 2 suggest ways to simulate $\Pr[y_j = 1 | X]$ with small variance, with derivatives, and in computationally efficient ways.

1.2 Unobserved heterogeneity

The second example involves unobserved heterogeneity in a non-linear model. Let y_{it} be a random count variable; i.e., $y_{it} = 0,1,2,\ldots$, with $i = 1,2, \ldots,N$ and $t = 1,2,\ldots,T$. Assume that $y_{it} \sim$ Poisson (λ_{it})

$$f(y_{it}|\lambda_{it}) = \exp\{-\lambda_{it}\}\lambda_{it}^{y_{it}}/y_{it}! \tag{11}$$

and that

$$\log\lambda_{it} = X_{it}\beta + u_i + e_{it} \tag{12}$$

where $u_i \sim iidG(.|\alpha_G)$, $G(.|\alpha_G)$ is a specified distribution up to a set of parameters α_G

$$e_{it} = \rho e_{it-1} + \varepsilon_{it} \tag{13}$$

$\varepsilon_{it} \sim iidH(.|\alpha_H)$, $H(.|\alpha_H)$ is a specified distribution up to a set of parameters α_H.[2] For example y_{it} might be the number of trips person i takes in period t, the number of patents firm i produces in year t, or the number of industrial accidents firm i has in year t. Adding the unobserved heterogeneity u_i

---

[2] One might want to specify a different distribution for e_{i0} because of an initial conditions problem.

and serially correlated error e_{it} allows for richness frequently necessary to explain the data. The goal is to estimate $\theta = (\beta, \rho, \alpha_G, \alpha_H)$. The log likelihood contribution of observation i is

$$L_i = \log \int\limits_{u_i} \int\limits_{\epsilon_{i1}} \cdots \int\limits_{\epsilon_{iT}} \prod_{t=1}^{T} [\exp\{-\lambda_{it}\}\lambda_{it}^{y_{it}}/y_{it}!dH(\epsilon_{it}|\alpha_H)]dG(u_i/\alpha_G \quad (14)$$

where $\lambda_i = (\lambda_{i1}, \lambda_{i2}, \ldots \lambda_{iT})'$ depends upon $X_{it}\beta$, u_i, and $\epsilon_i = (\epsilon_{i1}, \epsilon_{i2}, \ldots \epsilon_{iT})'$ through equations (12) and (13). When there is no serial correlation term e_{it}, the integral in equation (14) can be solved analytically for well-chosen $G(u_i|\alpha_G)$.[3] But for general $G(.|\alpha_G)$ and $H(.|\alpha_H)$, the integral can be evaluated neither analytically nor numerically.

Simulating the integral is quite straightforward. Let ϵ_i^r be an *iid* pseudo-random draw of ϵ_i, $r = 1, 2, \ldots, R$. Similarly, let u_i^r be an *iid* random draw of u_i, $r = 1, 2, \ldots, R$. Then L_i can be simulated by evaluating the integrand for each draw r and taking an average

$$\hat{L}_i = \log\left\{\frac{1}{R}\sum_{r=1}^{R}\left[\prod_{t=1}^{T}\exp\{-\lambda_{it}^r\}(\lambda_{it}^r)^{y_{it}}/y_{it}!\right]\right\} \quad (15)$$

where λ_{it}^r is evaluated using the pseudo-random draws of ϵ_i and u_i in equation (12). The maximum simulated likelihood estimator of θ maximizes $\sum_i \hat{L}i$. Note that even though $\exp\{\hat{L}_i\}$ is unbiased, $\hat{L}_i$ is biased for fininte R (because $\{\hat{L}i$ is a non-linear function of $\exp\{\hat{L}_i\}$). This will cause $\hat{\theta}$ to be inconsistent unless $R \to \infty$ as $NT \to \infty$. However, Monte Carlo results discussed later show that the asymptotic bias is small as long as "good" simulators are used.

1.3 *Monte Carlo experiments*

The last example is a Monte Carlo experiment. Let U be a vector of data and $s(U)$ be a proposed statistic that depends upon U. The statistic $s(U)$ may be an estimator or a test statistic. In general, the user will want to know the distribution of $s(U)$. But, for many statistics $s(.)$, deriving the small sample properties of $s(U)$ is not possible analytically. Simulation can be used to learn about the small sample properties of $s(U)$. All moments of $s(U)$ can be written in the form of $Eh(U)$.[4] Medians and, in fact, the whole distribution of $s(U)$ can be written in the form of $Eh(U)$. Monte Carlo experiments are powerful tools to use in evaluating statistical properties of $s(U)$. However care must be taken in conducting such experiments. In

---

[3] See Hausman, Hall, and Griliches (1984).
[4] For $Es(U)$, $h(U) = s(U)$, and for var $[s(U)]$, $h(U) = [s(U) - Es(U)]^2$.

particular, one must be careful in generalizing Monte Carlo results to cases not actually simulated; a Monte Carlo experiment really only provides information about the specific case simulated. Also, one must be careful not to attempt simulating objects that do not exist. For example, simulating the expected value of a two-stage least squares (2SLS) estimator of a just identified equation would provide an answer (because any particular draw of $s(U)$ is finite) but it would be meaningless because 2SLS estimators of just identified equations have no finite moments. See Hendry (1984) for more on Monte Carlo experiments.

2   Simulators

This section discusses various simulation methods. Throughout, the goal will be to simulate $Eh(U)$ or, in some special cases, $\text{PR}[y_j = 1 | X]$. The first requirement of a simulation method is to simulate U from its distribution F. In general, if $Z \sim$ uniform $(0,1)$, then $F^{-1}(Z) \sim F$.[5] For example, the exponential distribution is $F(x) = 1 - \exp\{-\lambda x\}$. Thus, $-\log(1 - Z)/\lambda \sim F$. If F is standard normal, then F^{-1} has no closed form, but most computers have a library routine to approximate F^{-1} for the standard normal distribution. Truncated random variables can be simulated in the same way. For example, assume $U \sim N[\mu,\sigma^2]$ but let it be truncated between a and b. Then, since

$$F(u) = \left[\Phi\left(\frac{u - \mu}{\sigma}\right) - \Phi\left(\frac{a - \mu}{\sigma}\right) \right] / \left[\Phi\left(\frac{b - \mu}{\sigma}\right) - \Phi\left(\frac{a - \mu}{\sigma}\right) \right] \quad (16)$$

where Φ is the standard normal distribution function, U can be simulated by letting $F(u) = Z$ in equation (16) and solving equation (16) for U as

$$\sigma\Phi^{-1}\left\{ Z\left[\Phi\left(\frac{b - \mu}{\sigma}\right) - \Phi\left(\frac{a - \mu}{\sigma}\right) \right] + \Phi\left(\frac{a - \mu}{\sigma}\right) \right\} + \mu. \quad (17)$$

This idea can be applied with a small twist to discrete random variables. Assume $U = i$ with probability p_i for $i = 1,2,\ldots,n$. Let $P_i = \Pr[U \le i] = \Sigma_{j=1}^{i} p_j$. Let $Z \sim$ uniform $(0,1)$, and let $U = i$ iff $P_{i-1} < Z \le P_i$ (where $(P_0 = 0)$). Then U is distributed as desired.

Random variables frequently can be simulated by using a composition formula. For example, since a binomial random variable is the sum of independent Bernoulli random variables, we can simulate a binomial random variable by simulating independent Bernoullis and then adding them up. A more useful example is simulating multivariate $U \sim N[\mu,\Omega]$. Let $Z \sim N[0,I]$,

---

[5] Most computers have a library routine to generate standard uniform random variables. See, for example, Ripley (1987) for a discussion of standard uniform random number generators.

and let C be any matrix such that $CC' = \Omega$ (e.g., the Cholesky decomposition of Ω). Then it is easy to verify that $CZ + \mu \sim N[\mu, \Omega]$. So we can simulate U by simulating Z and then transforming it.

In some cases, it will be necessary to simulate a random variable conditional on some event where the inverse conditional distribution has no analytical form (or good approximation). There are a number of acceptance–rejection methods available for many such cases. Assume (U,Z) have joint distribution $F(u,z)$ and that it is straightforward to draw (U,Z) from its joint distribution. Further, assume we want to draw U conditional on $Z \epsilon S$ where S is a subset of the support of Z. The simplest acceptance–rejection simulation method is:

(a) Draw (U,Z) from F.

(b) If $Z \notin S$, go to (a).

(c) If $Z \in S$, keep.

There are more sophisticated methods that reduce the expected number of draws (U,Z) needed (see, for example, Devroye (1986), Ripley (1987), or Tierney (1994)), but all acceptance–rejection simulation methods suffer from (a) a potentially large number of draws needed and (b) the lack of differentiability of $Eh(U)$ with respect to parameter vector θ.[6] Thus, for the most part, they should be avoided. For the remainder of the chapter, it will be assumed one can simulate U.

The most straightforward simulator for $Eh(U)$ is

$$\hat{E}h(U) = \frac{1}{R} \sum_{r=1}^{R} h(u^r) \tag{18}$$

where u^r, $r = 1, 2, \ldots, R$, are R iid pseudo-random draws of U. When simulating $\Pr[y_j = 1 \mid X]$, equation (18) becomes equation (10). If h is continuous and differentiable with respect to θ, then $\hat{E}h(U)$ will be continuous and differentiable. Equation (18) is unbiased, and its variance is $\mathrm{var}[h(U)]/R$. Note that, as $R \to \infty$, the variance of the simulator $\to$ zero.

2.1 Importance sampling

Several methods allow us to improve the performance of a simulator significantly either in terms of reduced variance, better smoothness properties, and/or better computation time properties. For example, the multinomial probit problem in Borsch-Supan, *et al.* (1992) and the production function estimation problem in Ohanian, *et al.* (1999) work with simulation only with the use of good importance sampling simulators. The rest of this section describes the most popular simulation methods. The first method is

---

[6] Differentiability is important for most estimation procedures. An exception is Gibbs sampling or, more generally, Monte Carlo Markov chain estimation methods.

importance sampling. Consider $Eh(U)$ in equation (1) where it is either difficult to draw U from F or where h is not smooth. In some cases, one can rewrite equation (1) as

$$Eh(U) = \int \frac{h(u)f(u)}{g(u)} g(u)du \qquad (19)$$

where $g(u)$ is a density with the following properties:
(a) it is easy to draw U from g,
(b) f and g have the same support,
(c) it is easy to evaluate $h(u)f(u)/g(u)$ given u, and
(d) $h(u)f(u)/g(u)$ is bounded and smooth over the support of U.
Note that equation (19) is $E[h(U)f(U)/g(U)]$ where $U \sim g$. Then the importance sampling simulator for $Eh(U)$ is

$$\hat{E}h(U) = \frac{1}{R} \sum_{r=1}^{R} \frac{h(u^r)f(u^r)}{g(u^r)} \qquad (20)$$

where $u^r, r = 1,2,\ldots,R_1$ are R iid draws from g. The purpose of conditions (a) and (c) are to increase computational speed. The purpose of condition (d) is variance bounding and smoothness.

Consider simulating $\Pr[y_j = 1 \mid X]$ for the multinomial probit problem. Equation (8) can be written as

$$\int_{u_j^* < V_j} f(u_j^*)du_j^* = \int_{u_j^* < V_j} [f(u_j^*)/g(u_j^*)]g(u_j^*)du_j^* \qquad (21)$$

for some multivariate density g satisfying conditions (a) through (d). Consider g where the kth element of u_j^* is distributed independently truncated normal with upper truncation point V_{jk} and variance Ω_{jkk}^* for each k. The candidate g satisfies conditions (a), (b), and (c), and $h(u)f(u)/g(u)$ is smooth over the support $u_j^* < V_j$. But $h(u)f(u)/g(u)$ is not bounded especially when Ω_j^* has large off-diagonal terms. Thus, this choice of g may be problematic. In fact, in general it is the boundedness condition that is difficult to satisfy. For the multinomial probit problem, the Geweke–Keane–Hajivassiliou (GHK) and decomposition simulators discussed below both can be thought of as importance sampling simulators that satisfy conditions (a) through (d). The simulators described in Danielsson and Richard (1993) and Richard and Zhang (1999) are more sophisticated importance sampling simulators.

2.2   GHK simulator

The GHK simulator, developed by Geweke (1991), Hajivassiliou (1990), and Keane (1994), has been found to perform very well in Monte Carlo studies (discussed later) for simulating $\Pr[u_j^* < Vj]$. The GHK algorithm switches back and forth between computing univariate, truncated normal probabilities, simulating draws from univariate normal distributions, and computing normal distributions conditional on previously drawn truncated normal random variables. Since each step is straightforward and fast, the algorithm can decompose the more difficult problem into a series of feasible steps. The algorithm is as follows:

(a) Set $t = 1$, $\mu = 0$, $\sigma^2 = \Omega_{jtt}^*$, and $\hat{P} = 1$.

(b) Compute $p = \Pr(u_{jt}^* < V_{jt})$ analytically, and increment $\hat{P} = \hat{P} * p$.

(c) Draw u_{jt}^* from a truncated normal distribution with mean μ, variance σ^2, and upper truncation point V_{jt}.

(d) If $t < J - 1$, increment t by 1; otherwise go to (g).

(e) Compute (analytically) the distribution of u_{jt}^* conditional on u_{j1}^*, u_{j2}^*, $\dots, u_{jt-1}^*$. Note that this is normal with an analytically computable mean vector μ and variance σ^2.

(f) Go to (b).

(g) $\hat{P}$ is the simulator.

The algorithm relies upon the fact that normal variables conditional on other normal random variables are still normal. The GHK simulator is strictly bounded between 0 and 1 because each increment to $\hat{P}$ is strictly bounded between 0 and 1. It is continuous and differentiable in θ because each increment to $\hat{P}$ is continuous and differentiable. Its variance is smaller than the frequency simulator in equation (10) because each draw of $\hat{P}$ is strictly bounded between 0 and 1 while each draw of the frequency simulator is either 0 or 1.

The GHK simulator is an importance sampling simulator. Consider the case where $J = 3$. Then the probability to simulate can be written as

$$\Pr[u < V] = \Phi(V_1, V_2) \int_{-\infty}^{V_1} \int_{-\infty}^{V_2} \Phi(V_3 | u_1, u_2) \frac{\phi(u_2 | u_1)\phi(u_1)}{\Phi(V_1, V_2)} du_2 du_1 \quad (22)$$

where $\Phi(V_1, V_2) = \Pr[u_1 < V_1, u_2 < V_2]$, $\Phi(V_3 | u_1, u_2) = \Pr[u_3 < V_3 | u_1, u_2]$, $\phi(u_2 | u_1)$ is the conditional density of u_2 given u_1, $\phi(u_1)$ is the marginal density of u_1. Equation (22) can be written in the form of equation (19) by letting

$$h(u) = \Phi(V_1, V_2)\Phi(V_3 | u_1, u_2),$$

$$f(u) = \frac{\phi(u_2 | u_1)\phi(u_1)}{\Phi(V_1, V_2)} 1(u_1 < V_1, u_2 < V_2),$$

$$g(u) = \frac{\phi(u_1)\phi(u_2 | u_1)}{\Phi(V_1)\Phi(V_2 | u_1)} \quad (23)$$

where $g(u)$ reflects the GHK algorithm's method of simulation. Because it is an importance sampling simulator, GHK is unbiased.

A minor modification of the algorithm provides draws of normal random variables u_j^* conditional on $u_j^* \leq V_j$. Other minor modifications are useful for related problems.

2.3 Decomposition simulators

Next, two decomposition simulators are described. The Stern (1992) simulator uses the property that the sum of two normal random vectors is also normal. The goal is to simulate $\Pr[u_j^* < V_j]$. Decompose $u_j^* = Z_1 + Z_2$ where $Z_1 \sim N[0,\lambda]$, $Z_2 \sim N[0,\Omega_j^* - \lambda]$, Z_1 and Z_2 are independent, and λ is chosen to be a diagonal matrix as large as possible such that $\Omega_j^* - \lambda$ is positive definite.[7] Then equation (8) can be written as

$$\int \Pr[Z_1 < V_j - z_2] g(z_2) dz_2$$

$$= \int \prod_k \Phi\left(\frac{V_{jk} - z_{2k}}{\lambda_k}\right) g(z_2) dz_2 \tag{24}$$

where $g(.)$ is the joint normal density of Z_2. Equation (24) can be simulated as

$$\frac{1}{R} \sum_{r=1}^{R} \prod_k \Phi\left(\frac{V_{jk} - z_{2k}^r}{\lambda_k}\right) \tag{25}$$

where Z_{2k}^r, $k = 1, 2, \ldots, J - 1$, are pseudo-random draws of Z_2. The Stern simulator has all of the properties of the GHK simulator, So which one performs better is an empirical matter left to later discussion.

Another decomposition simulator, suggested by McFadden (1989), changes the specification of equation (3) to

$$y_j^* = X_j\beta + u_j + \tau e_j, j = 1, \ldots, J \tag{26}$$

where τ is a small number and $e_j \sim iid$ extreme value. In the limit, as $\tau \to 0$, $\Pr[y_j = 1 \mid X]$ converges to a multinomial probit probability. But for any $\tau \to 0$

$$\Pr[y_j = 1 \mid X] = \int \exp\left\{\frac{X_j\beta + u_j}{\tau}\right\} \Big/ \sum_k \exp\left\{\frac{X_k\beta + u_k}{\tau}\right\} f(u) du \tag{27}$$

which is the multinomial logit probability conditional on $u = (u_1, u_2, \ldots, u_J)$ integrated over f. Equation (27) can be simulated as

---

[7] An easy way to pick λ is to set each diagonal element of λ equal to the smallest eigenvalue of Ω_j^* minus a small amount.

$$\frac{1}{R}\sum_{r=1}^{R}\left[\exp\left\{\frac{X_{j\beta}+u_j^r}{\tau}\right\}\bigg/\sum_k\exp\left\{\frac{X_k\beta+u_k^r}{\tau}\right\}\right] \tag{28}$$

where u^r are pseudo-random draws of u. The idea in McFadden (1989) is to think of equation (26) as a kernel-type approximation of equation (3) for small τ. However, assuming equation (26) is the true structure (where τ is a parameter that can sometimes be estimated) takes away no flexibility and frequently eases simulation. Multivariate normality is a desirable assumption because of its flexible covariance matrix. But there are very few applications where theory dictates that the error in equation (3) should be multivariate normal. Berkovec and Stern (1991) and Berry, Levinsohn, and Pakes (1995) use the McFadden specification as the "true" specification in a structural model of retirement behavior.

2.4 Antithetic acceleration

Antithetic acceleration is a powerful variance reduction method (see Geweke (1988)). In any simulation method, there is some probability that the pseudo-random draws will be unusually large (or small). Antithetic acceleration prevents such events from occurring and thus reduces the variance of the simulator. Consider the general problem of simulating $Eh(U)$ where $U \sim F$. Let $Z \sim$ uniform $(0,1)$. Then $H(F^{-1}(Z))$ is a simulator of $Eh(U)$. But $h(F^{-1}(1-Z))$ is also a simulator of $Eh(U)$ (because $1-Z \sim$ uniform $(0,1)$ also). The antithetic acceleration simulator of $Eh(U)$ is

$$\hat{E}h(u) = \frac{1}{2R}\sum_{r=1}^{R}[h(F^{-1}(z^r)) + h(F^{-1}(1-z^r))] \tag{29}$$

where z^r is a pseudo-random draw of Z. When F is $N[0,\sigma^2]$, equation (29) becomes

$$\hat{E}h(u) = \frac{1}{2R}\sum_{r=1}^{R}[h(u^r) + h(-u^r)] \tag{30}$$

where u^r is a pseudo-random draw of U. For any symmetric F, if h is linear, the variance of $\hat{E}h(U)$ is 0. For monotone h, the variance of $\hat{E}h(U)$ with R draws and antithetic acceleration is smaller than the variance of $\hat{E}h(U)$ with $2R$ draws and no antithetic acceleration. If $\hat{E}h(U)$ is being simulated to estimate a parameter θ with N observations and h is monotone, then the increase in $\text{var}(\hat{\theta})$ due to simulation when antithetic acceleration is used is of order $(1/N)$ times the increase in $\text{var}(\hat{\theta})$ due to simulation when antithetic acceleration is not used. The value of this is discussed more in the next section.

There are simulation problems where antithetic acceleration does not help. For example, let $U \sim N[0,\sigma^2]$, and let $h(U) = U^2$. Then var$[\hat{E}h(U)]$ with antithetic acceleration and R draws is greater than that without antithetic acceleration and $2R$ draws. This is because $h(-U) = h(U)$ which means that equation (30) becomes equation (15); the variance is twice as great as with no antithetic acceleration and $2R$ draws. In general, deviations from monotone h will diminish the performance of antithetic acceleration. But Hammersly and Handscomb (1964) suggest generalizations of antithetic acceleration that will reduce variance for more general h.

A related method is the use of control variates. Let $\hat{E}h(U)$ be a simulator of $Eh(U)$, and let $\hat{k}(U)$ be some other simulator with known expected value $Ek(U)$. Then

$$\tilde{E}h(U) = \hat{E}h(U) - \hat{k}(U) + Ek(U) \tag{31}$$

has expected value $Eh(U)$ and variance

$$\text{var}[\tilde{E}h(U)] = \text{var}[\hat{E}h(U)] + \text{var}[\hat{k}(U)] - \text{cov}[\hat{E}h(U),\hat{k}(U)]. \tag{32}$$

If $\text{cov}[\hat{E}h(U),\hat{k}(U)] > \text{var}[\hat{k}(U)]/2$, then $\text{var}[\tilde{E}h(U)] < \text{var}[\hat{E}h(U)]$. This idea can be used effectively in Monte Carlo testing and covariance matrix estimation (where it is easy to find a simulator $\hat{k}(U)$ with known expected value). In fact, it can be used to increase the rate of convergence of such estimators (see, for example, Hendry (1984) or Brown and Newey (1999)).

3   Estimation methods

The goal of this section is to use the simulators developed in the last section in some estimation problems. Four different estimation methods are discussed: method of simulated moments (MSM), maximum simulated likelihood estimation (MSL), method of simulated scores (MSS), and Monte Carlo Markov chain methods (with emphasis on Gibbs sampling). Each method is described, and its theoretical properties are discussed.

3.1   Method of simulated moments

Many estimation problems involve finding a parameter vector θ that solves a set of orthogonality conditions

$$Q'h(y,X|\theta) = 0 \tag{33}$$

where Q is a set of instruments with dimension equal to the dimension of θ.[8] Such estimators are called method of moments (MOM) estimators. All Least squares methods are special cases of equation (33), and many prob-

---

[8] When the dimension of Q is greater than the dimension of θ, the problem can be generalized to a GMM problem.

lems usually estimated as MLE can be recast as MOM estimators. For example, Avery, Hansen, and Hotz (1983) suggest how to recast the multinomial probit problem as a MOM problem where $h(y,X|\theta)$ is the vector $y - E(y|X)$ in the multinomial probit problem of section 1 with the jth element given by equation (4).

In many MOM problems, the orthogonality condition cannot be evaluated analytically. For example, in the multinomial probit problem, evaluating $E[y|X]$ involves evaluating equation (4). MSM replaces $h[y,X|\theta]$ with an unbiased simulator $\hat{h}(y,X|\theta)$ and then finds the θ that solves

$$Q'\hat{h}(y,X|\theta) = 0. \tag{34}$$

The θ that solves equation (34) is the MSM estimator of θ, $\hat{\theta}$. McFadden (1989) and Pakes and Pollard (1989) show that, as long as $\hat{h}(y,X|\theta)$ is an unbiased simulator of $h(y,X|\theta)$, deviations between $\hat{h}$ and h will wash out by the law of large numbers because equation (34) is linear in $\hat{h}$ and plim $(\hat{\theta}) = \theta$ as the sample size $N \to \infty$ even for small R.[9]

Consider the multinomial probit problem in more detail. As in section 1, let y_i be the vector of dependent variables for observation i, $i = 1,2,\ldots,N$, where $y_{ij} = 1$ iff choice j is chosen by i. The probability of i choosing j conditional on X_i is given in equation (8), and its frequency simulator is given in equation (10). The frequency simulator should be replaced by one of the simulators discussed in section 2, but for now we will use the frequency simulator for ease of presentation. As was discussed earlier, $E[y_{ij}|X_i] = \Pr[y_{ij} = 1|X_i]$. Let P_i be a J-element vector with $\Pr[y_{ij} = 1|X_i]$ in the jth element of P_i, and let $\varepsilon_i = y_i - P_i$. Then $E[\varepsilon_i|X_i] = 0$ and

$$E\sum_i Q_i'\hat{\varepsilon}_i = 0 \tag{35}$$

for any set of exogenous instruments Q_i. Thus, conditional on a chosen $Q = (Q_1,Q_2,\ldots,Q_N)$, the $\theta = (\beta,\Omega)$ that satisfies $\Sigma_i Q_i'\varepsilon_i = 0$ is the MOM estimator of θ. Let $\hat{P}_i$ be an unbiased simulator of P_i, and let $\hat{\varepsilon}_i = y_i - \hat{P}_i$. Then the θ that solves

$$\sum_i Q_i'\hat{\varepsilon}_i = 0 \tag{36}$$

is the MSM estimator of θ.

To find a reasonable Q, consider the log likelihood contribution for the multinomial probit model

$$L_i = \sum_j y_{ij}\log P_{ij}. \tag{37}$$

---

[9] Extra conditions are found in McFadden (1989) and Pakes and Pollard (1989).

The score statistics for θ can be written as

$$\partial L_i / \partial\theta = \sum_j y_{ij} \frac{\partial P_{ij}/\partial\theta}{P_{ij}}$$

$$= \sum_j \frac{\partial P_{ij}/\partial\theta}{P_{ij}}(y_{ij} - P_{ij} + P_{ij})$$

$$= \sum_j \frac{\partial P_{ij}/\partial\theta}{P_{ij}}(y_{ij} - P_{ij}) + \sum_j \frac{\partial P_{ij}}{\partial\theta} \tag{38}$$

where the last term equals zero because the $\sum_j P_{ij} = 1$. Thus, one can write

the score statistics in the form of equation (36). With an initial estimate θ, one can construct $(1/P_{ij})(\partial P_{ij}/\partial\theta)$ for θ and all j and use it as an instrument matrix Q_i for each i. It is likely that the instruments Q will need to be simulated (e.g., if the elements of Q_i are $(1/P_{ij})(\partial P_{ij}/\partial\theta)$). This presents no significant problems as long as the pseudo-random variables used to simulate Q_i are independent of those used in the estimation process (to ensure exogeneity). For any exogenous Q, the $\hat\theta$ that solves equation (36) is a consistent estimate of θ. Thus, once θ is estimated, Q can be updated using $\hat\theta$ and then used to find a new $\hat\theta$ that solves equation (36).

For any exogenous Q, the covariance matrix of $\hat\theta$ has two terms: a term due to random variation in the data and a term due to simulation. As long as $\hat P_i$ is an exogenous, unbiased simulator of P_i, one can write

$$\hat P_i = P_i + \xi_i \tag{39}$$

where ξ_i is a random variable caused by simulation with zero mean independent of ϵ_i, the deviation between y_i and P_i. Thus, the covariance matrix of $\hat\varepsilon_i$ can be written as $E\varepsilon\varepsilon' + E\xi\xi'$. If $\hat P_i$ is the frequency simulator of P_i, then ξ is just an average of R independent pseudo-random variables each with the same covariance matrix as ε. Thus, the covariance matrix of $\hat\varepsilon$ is the covariance matrix of ε times $[1 + R^{-1}]$. The asymptotic covariance matrix of $\hat\theta$ is a linear function of the covariance matrices for $\hat\varepsilon_i$, $i = 1,2,\ldots,N$ (McFadden (1989, p. 1006)). Note that for any $R \geq 1$, $\hat\theta$ is consistent; that as $R \to \infty$, the MSM covariance matrix approaches the MOM covariance matrix (which is efficient when the two-step procedure described above is used); and that the marginal improvement in precision declines rapidly in R. If an alternative simulator with smaller variance is used, then the loss of precision due to simulation declines. For example, if antithetic acceleration is used, then the loss in precision becomes of order $(1/N)$ (see Geweke (1988)) which requires no adjustment to the asymptotic covariance matrix.

Below is a road map for using MSM to estimate multinomial probit parameters:

(a) Choose an identifiable parameterization for Ω and initial values for $\theta = (\beta, \Omega)$. Make sure that the initial guess results in probabilities reasonably far from zero or one.

(b) Choose a simulator.

(c) Simulate $2NJR$[10] standard normal random variables. Store NJR of them in an instruments random number file and NJR in an estimation random number file. These random numbers will be used throughout the estimation process and never changed.

(d) Given the initial guess of θ and the instruments random number file, simulate Q. Store the simulated instruments.

(e) Given the initial guess of θ, the simulated Q, and the estimation random number file, solve equation (36) for θ. This is an MSM estimator of θ.

(f) Given the initial MSM estimator, reperform steps (d) and (e) once.

Solving equation (36) requires using an optimization algorithm to find the θ that minimizes

$$\sum_i \hat{\varepsilon}_i' Q_i Q_i' \hat{\varepsilon}_i. \tag{40}$$

The derivatives of $\hat{P}_i$ are well behaved, so derivative-based optimization routines should be used. At each guess of θ, the standard normal pseudo-random numbers in the estimation random number file are used to create a new set of $N[0,\Omega]$ random numbers using the method described in section 2. Thus, even though the standard normal random numbers never change, one is always using random numbers from the correct normal distribution.

Consider the unobserved heterogeneity count problem described in equations (11) through (13). Let y_{it} be the number of events for i at time t. $E[y_{it}|\lambda_{it}]$ is λ_{it}, but the covariance matrix of y_i has no closed form. Let v_i be a vector of residuals with $[T + T(T+1)/2]$ elements. The first T elements of v_i are $y_{it} - E\lambda_{it}$ for $t = 1,2,\ldots,T$ where the expectation is over e_{it} and u_i in equation (12). The last $T(T+1)/2$ elements corresponded to "covariance residuals." A representative element would be

$$(y_{it} - E\lambda_{it})(y_{is} - E\lambda_{is}) + C_{its} \tag{41}$$

for two periods, t and s, where C_{its} is the $\text{cov}(y_{it}, y_{is})$. The MOM estimator of $\theta = (\beta, \rho, \sigma_G, \sigma_H)$ solves

$$\sum_i Q_i' v_i = 0 \tag{42}$$

given a set of instruments Q. Since both $E\lambda_{it}$ and C_{its} cannot be evaluated analytically,[11] the MOM estimator is not feasible. But $E\lambda_{it}$ and C_{its} can be simulated. Let $\hat{y}_{it}^r$ be a simulated count variable. We can simulate e_{it} and u_i

---

[10] Remember that N = sample size, J = number of choices, and R = number of draws.

[11] Under special assumptions about the distribution of u_i and e_{it} described in Hausman, Hall, and Griliches (1984), the moments have analytical forms.

and therefore λ_{it}. Conditional on the simulated λ_{it}, we can simulate y_{it} either directly or by using the relationship between Poisson random variables and exponential random variables.

Applications using MSM include a retirement problem in Berkovec and Stern (1992), a market entry problem in Berry (1992), a dynamic programming problem in Hotz, *et al.* (1994), and an automobile pricing model in Berry, Levinsohn, and Pakes (1995).

3.2   *Maximum simulated likelihood*

A common estimation method with good optimality properties is maximum likelihood (ML) estimation. The basic idea is to maximize the log likelihood of the observed data over the vector of estimated parameters. ML estimators are consistent and efficient for a very large class of problems. Their asymptotic distribution is normal for a slightly smaller class of problems. However there are many likelihood functions that cannot be evaluated analytically. In many cases, they can be thought of as expected values of some random function that can be simulated.

Consider again the multinomial probit problem. The log likelihood contribution for observation i is defined in equation (37). Note that only one element of y_i is not zero, so only one probability needs to be computed. This is a significant advantage of maximum simulated likelihood (MSL) over MSM. Still, to evaluate the log likelihood function, one must be able to evaluate or simulate P_{ij} for the choice chosen. The MSL estimator of θ is the value of θ that maximizes

$$L = \sum_{i=1}^{N} \sum_{j} y_{ij} \ln \hat{P}_{ij} \tag{43}$$

where $\hat{P}_{ij}$ is the simulated value of P_{ij}.

A significant problem with MSL is that the log likelihood function is not linear in $\hat{P}$. Thus, unlike MSM, the simulation errors, $\hat{P}-P$, will not wash out asymptotically as $N \to \infty$ unless $R \to \infty$ also. Lerman and Manski (1981) suggested using MSL with a frequency simulator. They found that R needed to be quite large to deal with this problem. However, Börsch-Supan and Hajivassiliou (1993) show in Monte Carlo studies that, if better simulators are used, in particular smooth, smaller variance simulators bounded away from 0 and 1, then the bias caused by finite R is small for moderate sized R. In fact, in their study, MSL performs better than MSM.

Consider the unobserved heterogeneity model described in equations (11) through (13). The log likelihood contribution for observation i is given in equation (14). The argument of the log is the expected value of

$$\prod_{t=1}^{T}[\exp\{-\lambda_{it}\}\lambda_{it}^{y_{it}}/y_{it}!] \tag{44}$$

over the distribution of the errors determining λ_{it}. One can simulate λ_{it} for each i and t and therefore the expected value of the term in equation (44). Since the simulator of L_i is the log of this term, it is biased, and the bias disappears only as $R \to \infty$. But the simulator of equation (44) is smooth, and antithetic acceleration can be used to significantly reduce the variance. Thus the asymptotic bias associated with simulating the log likelihood function should be small.

Applications of MSL include a patent renewal model in Pakes (1986), a long-term care model in Börsch-Supan, et al. (1992), and the production function model in Ohanian, et al. (1999).

3.3   Method of simulated scores

A property of maximum likelihood is that the score statistic, the derivative of the log likelihood function, should have an expected value of 0 at the true value of θ. This idea is the motivation behind the method of simulated scores (MSS). Hajivassiliou and McFadden (1990) use MSS in a model of external debt crises. The potential advantage of MSS is to use an estimator with the efficiency properties of ML and the consistency properties of MSM. MSM is asymptotically efficient if the proper weights are used (those that turn the moment condition into a score statistic). MSS ensures that the proper weights are used. The difficulty in this method is to construct an unbiased simulator of the score statistic. The problems this causes will become clear in the multinomial probit example. The log likelihood contribution of observation i is given in equation (37), and its derivative is

$$\partial L_i / \partial\theta = \Sigma_j y_{ij} \frac{\partial P_{ij}/\partial\theta}{P_{ij}}$$

$$= \frac{\partial P_{ij}/\partial\theta}{P_{ij}}. \tag{45}$$

For the j corresponding to the chosen alternative. The goal is to construct an unbiased simulator for equation (45) so that the problem can be turned into a MSM problem. While it is straightforward to construct an unbiased simulator for both the numerator and denominator in equation (45), the ratio will not be unbiased as long as the denominator is random.

Consider constructing an unbiased simulator of the ratio. Suppressing the i subscript, equation (45) can be written as

$$\frac{\partial P_j / \partial \theta}{P_j} = \frac{\partial}{\partial \theta} \int\limits_{A_j} f(y^*) dy^* / P_j \tag{46}$$

where $y^* = (y_1^* y_2^*, \ldots, y_J^*)$, f is the joint density of y^*, and A_j is the subset of the support of y^* where $y_j^* > y_k^*$ for all $k \neq j$. This equals

$$\frac{\partial P_j / \partial \theta}{P_j} = \int\limits_{A_j} \frac{\partial f(y^*) / \partial \theta}{f(y^*)} f(y^*) dy^* / P_j$$

$$= E\left[\frac{\partial}{\partial \theta} \ln f(y^*) | y_i = 1 \right] \tag{47}$$

where the expectation is with respect to the joint density of y^*. One usually can simulate the expectation in equation (47) (e.g., using the GHK simulator) and thus get an unbiased estimator of the ratio. Hajivassiliou and Ruud (1994) show that this method of simulating the score generalizes for all limited dependent variable problems.

3.4   Monte Carlo Markov chain methods

The last estimation procedure discussed is quite different than the others in that it is a Bayesian estimator. In general, we have a model specified up to a set of parameters θ, some data $\{(y_i, X_i)\}_{i=1}^N$, and a prior distribution for θ. The goal is to use the data to update the prior distribution to get a posterior distribution for θ. Computing the posterior involves using Bayes rule which usually involves solving a difficult integral, thus making it an intractable problem. Consider a general problem where $\pi(z)$ is a known density function and $p(z^{n+1} | z^n)$ is a transition density function such that

$$\pi(z) = \int p(z|z') \pi(z') dz'. \tag{48}$$

Then Markov chain theory tells us that repeated application of the transition density to an arbitrary density $\varphi(z)$ will asymptote to $\pi(z)$

$$\pi(z) = \int p^n(z|z') \varphi(z') dz' \tag{49}$$

where

$$p^n(z|z') = \int p^{n-1}(z|z'') p(z''|z') \varphi(z'') dz''$$

$$p^1(z|z') = p(z|z'). \tag{50}$$

The idea in Monte Carlo Markov chain (MCMC) methods is to simulate from $p(z^{n+1} | z^n)$ repeatedly and to thus generate a sample from $\pi(z)$. A popular MCMC method is Gibbs sampling (possibly with data augmentation). Continuing with our general notation, assume that there is natural way to partition z into $(z_1, z_2, \ldots z_k)$ such that the conditional densities, $\pi(z_1, |z_1, z_2, \ldots, z_{i+1}, \ldots, z_k)$ are easy to simulate from for all i. Then the Gibbs sampling algorithm is:

(a) Initialize $z^0 = (z_1^0, z_2^0, \ldots, z_k^0)$ and set $n = 0$.

(b) Simulate $z_1^{n+1} \sim \pi(z_1^{n+1} | z_2^n, z_3^n, \ldots, z_k^n);$

$$z_2^{n+1} \sim \pi(z_2^{n+1} | z_1^{n+1}, z_3^n, \ldots, z_k^n);$$

$$z_3^{n+1} \sim \pi(z_3^{n+1} | z_1^{n+1}, z_2^{n+1} z_4^n, \ldots, z_k^n) \ldots$$

$$z_k^{n+1} \sim \pi(z_k^{n+1} | z_1^{n+1}, z_2^{n+1}, \ldots, z_{k-1}^{n+1}) \ldots$$

(c) Set $n = n + 1$, and return to (b).

MCMC theory shows that this procedure will generate a sample $\{z^n\}_{n=N_0}^{N_1}$ from $\pi(z)$ where N_0 is chosen to give any effects due to initialization of z^0 an opportunity to die out. Sometimes, while it is difficult to simulate from all of the conditional densities $\pi(z_i | z_1, z_2, \ldots, z_{i-1}, z_{i+1}, \ldots, z_k)$, there is a way to augment the data with a latent variable so that all of the new conditional densities can be simulated from; such an approach is called Gibbs sampling with data augmentation.

Returning to our Bayesian estimation problem, let us define $\{y_i^*\}_{i=1}^N$ that has the following properties:

(a) the posterior distribution of y_i^* given (y_i, θ) is easy to simulate from, and

(b) the posterior distribution of θ given (y_i^*, y_i) and the prior distribution of θ is easy to compute and simulate from.

Assume there is a $\{y_i^*\}_{i=1}^N$ that satisfies these two conditions. Then the Gibbs sampling with data augmentation algorithm draws $\{y_i^*\}_{i=1}^N$ given $\{y_i\}_{i=1}^N$ and θ, then draws θ given new $\{y_i^*, y_i\}_{i=1}^N$, and repeats this process over and over again. The draws of θ provide information about the posterior distribution of θ. The algorithm is:

(a) Assume a prior distribution for θ. Choose R_0 such that the first R_0 draws will not count and R_1 such that the process will stop after R_1 draws. Set $r = 0$.

(b) Simulate one draw of θ from its posterior distribution.

(c) If $r > R_0$, store the draw of θ as draw $r - R_0$.

(d) If $r = R_1$, then go to (g).

(e) Simulate one draw of $\{y_i^*\}_{i=1}^N$ conditional on $(\{y_i\}_{i=1}^N, \theta)$.

(f) Evaluate analytically the posterior distribution for θ given $\{(y_i, y_i^*)\}_{i=1}^N$. Increment $r = r + 1$. Go to (b).

(g) Use the $R_1 - R_0$ draws of θ as a random sample of draws of θ and compute any sample characteristics desired.

Markov chain theory implies that the Gibbs sampling algorithm described above will produce a distribution of draws of θ corresponding to the posterior distribution of θ conditional on $\{(y_i, X_i)\}_{i=1}^N$. See, for example, Casella and George (1992), Gelfand and Smith (1990), Geman and Geman (1984), and Tanner and Wong (1987) for more about Markov chains.

Consider how Gibbs sampling with data augmentation can be applied to the multinomial probit problem.[12] To simplify exposition, assume we know Ω and only need to estimate β. Assume $\beta_1 = 0$ as a normalizing factor. For step (a), we need a prior distribution for $\{\beta_j\}_{j=2}^J$. If we pick R_0 big enough and the prior with a large enough variance, then the choice of prior will become irrelevant. Thus, pick the prior to be diffuse. The diffuse prior makes it easy to compute posterior distribution for $\{\beta_j\}_{j=2}^J$. Next, let y_i^* be the latent variable associated with y_i.

$$y_{ik}^* = X_i\beta_k + u_{ik}, \ k = 1, 2, \ldots, J, \ i = 1, 2, \ldots, N \tag{51}$$

where $u_i \sim N[0, \Omega]$.

For step (b), we need to simulate β from its posterior distribution. Since, at any iteration of the algorithm, β is normal, we can simulate β using the method described in section 2.

For step (e), we need to simulate $\{y_i^*\}_{i=1}^N$ conditional on $(\{y_i\}_{i=1}^N, \beta)$. Since the observations are independent, we need only simulate y_i^* conditional on (y_i, β) for each $i = 1, 2, \ldots, N$ separately, Let j be the chosen choice. Then

$$X_i\beta_j + u_{ij} > X_i\beta_k + u_{ik} \ \forall k \neq j \tag{52}$$

or

$$u_{ijk}^* < X_i(\beta_j - \beta_k) \ \forall k \neq j \tag{53}$$

where $u_{ijk}^* = u_{ik} - u_{ij}$. The errors $u_{ijk}^* \forall k \neq j$ can be simulated using the GHK algorithm, and the y_{ik}^* can be constructed $\forall k \neq 1$[13] as

$$y_{ik}^* = X_i\beta_k + u_{ijk}^* - u_{ij1}^*. \tag{54}$$

Alternatively, we can use an acceptance–rejection simulator.

For step (f), we need to evaluate the posterior distribution of β given $\{y_i^*\}_{i=1}^N$. Since $u_{ij} \sim N(0, \omega_{jj})$ for each i and j, $y_{ij}^* \sim N[X_i\beta_j, \omega_{jj}]$ which means that computing a posterior distribution for β involves running an OLS regression of y^* on X.

For step (g), the sample of $R_1 - R_0$ draws of β are distributed from the distribution of β conditional on the data (including the dependent variables $\{y_i\}_{i=1}^N$). A few notes of caution are in order here. First, the draws of β are not independent even though any dependence dies out as the number of draws between two draws becomes large. Thus, we must not compute any statistics that depend upon the ordering of the draws. Second, the draws are conditional on $\{y_i\}_{i=1}^N$. This is quite different than what we would expect in

---

[12] This is described in much more detail in McCulloch and Rossi (1995).
[13] Recall that choice 1 is the base choice.

classical statistical analysis (where we would condition on only the exogenous variables). The effect of this is that the researcher does not know how the estimator would have behaved had a different realization of the data been observed. This is a fundamental difference between classical estimators and Bayesian estimators. There are other reasonable (and perhaps better) choices for implementing the Gibbs sampler to the multinomial probit problem. The real issues involve also estimating Ω. See McCulloch and Rossi (1994, 1995) or Albert and Chib (1993) for a much more extensive discussion.

The unobserved heterogeneity count problem is also easily adaptable to Gibbs sampling. The data should be augmented with $\{\lambda_{it}\}_{t=1,i=1}^{T,N}$ and its prior should be normal. Steps (b) and (f) are the same as in the multinomial probit problem. Step (e) involves simulating λ_{it} conditional on (y_{it},β) which is not as straightforward. The density of λ_{it} conditional on (y_{it},β) is

$$f(\lambda_{it}|y_{it},\beta) = C(y)e^{-\lambda_{it}}\lambda_{it}^{y_{it}-1}\phi\left(\frac{\log\lambda_{it} - X_{it}\beta}{\sigma_\lambda}\right) \tag{55}$$

where σ_λ is the standard deviation of the composite error in equation (12), ϕ is the standard normal density function, and $C(y)$ is a proportionality constant chosen so that equation (55) integrates to 1. One can evaluate the integral of equation (55) numerically for each value of $y = 0,1,\dots$ for a finite number of points: $\delta,2\delta,\dots,K\delta$ for some small δ. Figure 1.1 draws the approximate distribution curves for $y = 0,1,\dots,5$, $\delta = 0.01$, and $K = 1,000$. Then one can use the discretized distribution as an approximation to draw λ from. This is equivalent to drawing a random point on the vertical axis of figure 1.1 (e.g., point A), drawing a horizontal line to the curve corresponding to y (e.g., B when $y = 4$) and choosing λ to be the horizontal component of the curve at that vertical point (e.g., point C).

A generalization of Gibbs sampling is the Metropolis–Hastings (MH) algorithm described in, for example, Chib and Greenberg (1994). Returning to our general notation, let $p(z^{n+1}|z^n)$ be the density we want to simulate from so that we can generate a sample with density $\pi(z)$, but assume it is difficult to simulate from $p(z^{n+1}|z^n)$ directly. Let $q(z^{n+1}|z^n)$ be a "candidate density" chosen according to criteria described in Chib and Greenberg (1994). Then the MH algorithm is:

(a) Initialize z^0 and set $n = 0$.

(b) Simulate z^{n+1} from $q(z^{n+1}|z^n)$ and keep it with probability $\alpha(z^{n+1}|z^n)$ where

$$\alpha(z^{n+1},z^n) = \begin{cases} \min\left[1, \dfrac{\pi(z^{n+1})q(z^n|z^{n+1})}{\pi(z^n)q(z^{n+1}|z^n)}\right] & \text{if } \pi(z^n)q(z^{n+1}|z^n) > 0 \\ 1 & \text{otherwise.} \end{cases} \tag{56}$$

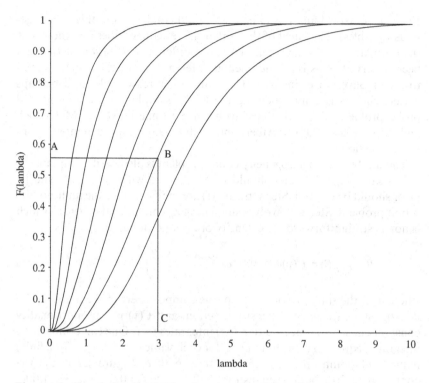

Figure 1.1 Cumulative distribution functions $(y = 0,1,\dots,5)$

(c) Set $n = n + 1$ and return to (b).

The MH algorithm is essentially a sophisticated acceptance–rejection method. The acceptance probability $\alpha(z^{n+1},z^n)$ oversamples transitions where $\pi(z^{n+1})/\pi(z^n)$ is high relative to $q(z^{n+1}|z^n)/q(z^n|z^{n+1})$. Gibbs sampling is a special case of the MH algorithm for $q(z^{n+1}|z^n)$ being the conditional density and $\alpha(z^{n+1},z^n) = 1$. The difficult part of implementing the MH algorithm is choosing the candidate density $q(z^{n+1}|z^n)$. One wants a $q(z^{n+1}|z^n)$ that moves around fast enough so that the whole support of $\pi(z)$ is sampled but slow enough so that $\alpha(z^{n+1},z^n)$ is not too small. Also, it is worthwhile to have a candidate density such that $q(z^{n+1}|z^n) = q(z^n|z^{n+1})$.[14] Chib and Greenberg suggest using candidate densities of the form $q(z^{n+1}|z^n) = q_1(z^{n+1} - z^n)$ or $q(z^{n+1}|z^n) = q_2(z^{n+1})$. They also provide an example estimating an ARMA model with regressors using the MH algorithm.

---

[14] This simplifies evaluation of $\alpha(z^{n+1},z^n)$ among other things.

3.5 Empirical comparison of methods

A number of studies have compared the performance of various simulators and estimation methods especially for the multinomial probit problem. This section summarizes the results of four of those studies and presents some new results focusing on questions that are neglected in the other studies.

Börsch-Supan and Hajivassiliou (1993) compare the GHK simulator to the Stern simulator and a frequency simulator. They present convincing evidence that the GHK simulator has a significantly smaller standard deviation than the other two simulators. They further show that the standard deviation of the GHK simulator is small enough so that it can be used in an MSL estimation routine providing parameter estimates with small root mean squared errors (RMSEs). Having a good simulator with a small standard deviation for MSL is important because, unlike MSM, MSL does not provide consistent estimates for fixed R.

Hajivassiliou, McFadden, and Ruud (1994) compare ten different simulators (including the Stern simulator, a Gibbs sampler, and a kernel smoothed simulator) in terms of the RMSE of the multinomial probit probability and its derivatives. They consider a large class of V_js and Ω_j^*s. They find that the GHK simulator performs the best overall. In particular, it performs well relative to the alternatives when Ω_j^* displays high correlation terms. They provide no results concerning parameter estimates.

Geweke, Keane, and Runke (1994a) compare MSM using GHK, MSL using GHK, Gibbs sampling, and kernel smoothing. In an unrestricted estimation procedure (including covariance parameters), MSM-GHK and Gibbs sampling dominated MSL-GHK. Kernel smoothing was dominated by all methods. In various restricted models, the performances of MSL-GHK improved. In general, as more restrictions were placed on the model, the performance of MSM-GHK, MSL-GHK, and Gibbs sampling converged. But Gibbs sampling seemed to dominate other methods overall.

Geweke, Keane, and Runkle (1994b) compare MSM-GHK, MSL-GHK, and Gibbs sampling in the related multinomial multiple period probit model. They find that Gibbs sampling dominates and MSM-GHK is second. Estimated standard errors are good for Gibbs sampling and MSM-GHK but are downward biased for MSL-GHK.

None of these methods compares the computational cost of the alternatives. Computational cost is important because the simulators are essentially a method to reduce computation time; if time was not an issue, we could compute the relevant integrals numerically using arbitrarily precise approximation methods or we could simulate them letting R be an arbitrary large number. If one method takes twice as much time as another for a given

Table 1.1. *Monte Carlo estimation results*

Method	w/Antithetic acceleration		wo/Antithetic acceleration	
	Avg RMSE	Avg time	Avg RMSE	Avg time
Results for diagonal covariance matrix (N = 500)				
MSM-GHK	0.299	3559.0	0.257	3373.8
MSM-Stern	0.270	1047.0	0.288	1097.0
MSL-GHK	0.247	1571.0	0.246	1598.8
MSL-Stern	0.254	654.9	0.252	674.7
Gibbs			0.263	16119.9
Results for diagonal covariance matrix (N = 1,000)				
MSM-GHK	0.181	6470.9	0.167	6283.1
MSM-Stern	0.173	1911.4	0.186	2006.0
MSL-GHK	0.158	1951.5	0.161	1889.9
MSL-Stern	0.161	802.0	0.163	853.0
Gibbs			0.170	29746.9
Results for non-diagonal covariance matrix (N = 1,000)				
MSM-GHK	0.267	7192.1	0.201	6782.8
MSM-Stern	0.358	2422.5	0.420	2565.2
MSL-GHK	0.175	2194.8	0.192	2010.0
MSL-Stern	0.180	1114.3	0.195	1174.0

Notes:
There are 200 Monte Carlo draws per experiment.
There are 6 choices and 5 explanatory variables per choice.
For experiments with AA, $R = 5$, and for experiments without AA, $R = 10$.
All experiments are performed on an IBM RS6000 model 390.
Gibbs sampling results are based on 10,000 draws after skipping 2,000 draws; i.e.,
   $R_0 = 2,000$ and $R_1 = 12,000$

R, then a fair comparison requires using different R for each method to produce comparable times. Also none of the methods considers the effect of using antithetic acceleration (AA) despite Geweke's strong theoretical results.

Table 1.1 presents the results of a small Monte Carlo study. Its results should be interpreted as suggestive of where more work needs to be done. The methods that are compared are MSM-GHK, MSM-Stern, MSL-GHK, MSL-Stern, Gibbs sampling (with acceptance–rejection), and MSM-KS (kernel smoothing). Three different models are used: (a) Ω is diagonal and N (sample size) = 500, (b) Ω is diagonal and $N = 1,000$, and

(c) Ω corresponds to an $AR(1)$ process with $\rho = 0.9$ and $N = 1,000$. Except for Gibbs sampling, results are reported with and without AA. RMSE results and average times per estimation procedure are reported.

Kernel smoothing methods performed poorly in terms of RMSE of the simulated multinomial probit probabilities. Also, more importantly, its derivatives with respect to parameters were poorly behaved in that if the bandwidth parameter was small, the derivatives were very volatile (and therefore derivative-based optimization algorithms for estimation behaved poorly), and if it was large, parameter bias was very large. Thus kernel smoothing method results are not reported. In terms of RMSE, Gibbs sampling estimators behave reasonably well. But the amount of time involved is an order of magnitude greater than for the MSM and MSL estimates.[15] Thus, there are only limited results reported for the Gibbs samplers.

The remainder of the discussion focuses on MSM, MSL, GHK, Stern, and AA. First, it is clear that MSL dominates MSM in these examples. It provides smaller RMSEs and it requires less computation time. GHK dominates Stern in terms of RSME, but Stern is significantly faster. One might consider using Stern with twice as large R. Unreported Monte Carlo experiments suggest that for the examples used here the standard deviation of the multinomial probit probabilities is about twice as large for the Stern simulator as for the GHK simulator when $R = 10$. This would suggest that doubling R for the Stern simulator (relative to the GHK simulator) would make the GHK simulator more efficient by a factor of $\sqrt{2}$. Thus, these results are consistent with Börsch-Supan and Hajivassiliou, suggesting that MSL-GHK provides estimates with the smallest RMSEs even after controlling for variation in computation time. Based on results in Börsch-Supan and Hajivassiliou and Hajvassiliou, McFadden, and Ruud, it probably performs even better for pathological cases with highly correlated errors or small multinomial probit probabilities.

The poor performance of AA is striking. AA almost uniformly improves the performance of the Stern simulator. But it behaves poorly for the GHK simulator. However, table 1.2 shows that AA significantly reduces the standard deviation of the simulated multinomial probit probabilities for GHK, Stern, and kernel smoothing. This apparent paradox occurs because of the small sample properties of method of moments (MOM) and maximum likelihood (MLE). In other words, the RMSE of MOM and MLE dominate any extra randomness caused by simulation. This is verified by unreported results showing that when R is increased to 50, MSL-GHK and MSL-Stern RMSEs converge to each other with or without AA and they

---

[15] It should be noted that in these Monte Carlo experiments, I am conditioning on the true value of Ω. It might be the case that the Gibbs sampler performs better relative to the other methods when Ω also is estimated.

Table 1.2. *Probability simulations*

	wo/AA	w/AA
GHK	−0.00050	−0.00269
	(0.033)	(0.021)
Stern	−0.00266	−0.00086
	(0.059)	(0.023)
Kernel smoothing	0.00000	0.00000
	(0.077)	(0.063)

Notes:
AA is antithetic acceleration.
First row for each simulation method is a sample mean, and
   second row (in parentheses) is a sample standard deviation.
There are 3,000 Monte Carlo draws per experiment.
There are 6 choices and 5 explanatory variables per choice.
For experiments with AA, $R = 5$, and for experiments without
   AA, $R = 10$.
All experiments are performed on an IBM RS6000 model 390.

are similar to RMSEs for the case when $R = 5$ with AA or $R = 10$ without AA. The bottom line is that for MSM and MSL, the choice of simulation method has a second-order effect on RMSE relative to RMSE caused by the underlying estimation method. This further suggests that computation time issues should be given high priority.

References

Albert, J. and S. Chib (1993), "Bayesian Analysis of Binary and Polychotomous Data," *Journal of the American Statistical Association*, 88, 669–679.

An, Mark Y. and Ming Liu (1996), "Structural Analysis of Labor Market Transitions Using Indirect Inference," Unpublished manuscript, Duke University.

Anderson, S.P., A. de Palma, and J.F. Thisse (1992), *Discrete Choice Theory of Product Differentiation*, Cambridge, MA: MIT Press.

Avery, Robert, Lars Hansen, and V. Joseph Hotz (1983), "Multiperiod Probit Models and Orthogonality Condition Estimation," *International Economic Review*, 24(1), 21–35.

Bansal, Ravi, A. Ronald Gallant, Robert Hussey, and George Tauchen (1995), "Non-parametric Estimation of Structural Models for High Frequency Currency Market Data," *Journal of Econometrics*, 66, 251–287.

Berkovec, J. and S. Stern (1991), "Job Exit Behavior of Older Men," *Econometrica*, 59(1), 189–210.

Berry, Steven (1992), "Estimation of a Model of Entry in the Airline Industry," *Econometrica*, 60(4), 889–917.

Berry, Steven, James Levinsohn, and Ariel Pakes (1995), "Automobile Prices in Market Equilibrium," *Econometrica*, 63(4), 841–890.

Börsch-Supan, Axel and Vassilis A. Hakivassiliou (1993), "Smooth Unbiased Multivariate Probability Simulators for Maximum Likelihood Estimation of Limited Dependent Variable Models," *Journal of Econometrics*, 58, 347–368.

Börsch-Supan, Axel, Vassilis A. Hakivassiliou, Lawrence Kotlikoff, and John Morris (1992), "Health, Children, and Elderly Living Arrangements: A Multiperiod-Multinomial Probit Model with Unobserved Heterogeneity and Autocorrelated Errors," in David Wise (ed.), *Topics in the Economics of Aging*, Chicago: University of Chicago Press.

Brown, Brian and Whitney Newey (1999), "Simulation-Based Inference in Semiparametric Procedures," in Roberto S. Mariano, Melvyn Weeks, and Til Schuermann (eds.), *Simulation-Based Inference in Econometrics: Methods and Applications*, Cambridge University Press.

Bunch, David (1991), "Estimability in the Multinomial Probit Model," *Transportation Research, Part B, Methodological*, 25B, 1–12.

Butler, J.S. and Robert Moffit (1992), "A Computationally Efficient Quadrature Procedure for the One-Factor Multinomial Probit Model," *Econometrica*, 50, 761–764.

Casella, G. and E. George (1992), "Explaining the Gibbs Sampler," *American Statistician*, 46, 167–174.

Chib, Siddhartha (1993), "Bayes Regression with Autoregressive Errors: A Gibbs Sampling Approach," *Journal of Econometrics*, 58(3), 347–368.

Chib, Siddhartha and Edward Greenberg (1994), "Understanding the Metropolis-Hastings Algorithm," Washington University, St Louis, manuscript.

Danielsson, J. and J.F. Richard (1993), "Accelerated Gaussian Importance Sampler with Application to Dynamic Latent Variable Models," *Journal of Applied Econometrics*, 8, 153–173.

Devroye, L. (1986), *Non-Uniform Random Variate Generation*, New York: Springer.

Diebold, Francis X. and Til Schuermann (1999), "Exact Maximum Likelihood Estimation of Observation-Driven Econometric Models," in Roberto S. Mariano, Melvyn Weeks, and Til Schuermann (eds.), *Simulation-Based Inference in Econometrics: Methods and Applications*, Cambridge University Press.

Gelfand, A. and A. Smith (1990), "Sampling-Based Approaches to Calculating Marginal Densities," *Journal of the American Statistical Association*, 85, 398–409.

Geman, S. and D. Geman (1984), "Stochastic Relaxation, Gibbs Distributions and the Bayesian Restoration of Images," *IEEE Transactions on Pattern Analysis and Machine Intelligence*, 6, 721–741.

Geweke, John F. (1988), "Antithetic Acceleration of Monte Carlo Integration in Bayesian Inference," *Journal of Econometrics*, 38, 73–89.

(1989), "Bayesian Inference in Econometric Models Using Monte Carlo Integration." *Econometrica*, 57(6), 1317–1339.

(1991), "Efficient Simulation from the Multivariate Normal and Student Distributions Subject to Linear Constraints," *Computer Science and Statistics: Proceedings of the Twenty-Third Symposium on the Interface*, 571–578.

Geweke, J., M. Keane, and D. Runkle (1994a), "Alternative Computational Approaches to Inference in the Multinomial Probit Model," Federal Reserve Bank of Minneapolis, Staff Report 170.

(1994b), "Statistical Inference in the Multinomial Multiperiod Probit Model," Federal Reserve Bank of Minneapolis, Staff Report 177.

Hajivassiliou, Vassilis (1990), "Smooth Simulation Estimation of Panel Data LDV Models," Unpublished paper.

Hajivassiliou, Vassilis and Daniel McFadden (1990), "The Method of Simulated Scores with Application to Models of External Debt," Cowles Foundation Discussion Paper No. 967.

Hajivassiliou, V., D. McFadden, and P. Ruud (1994), "Simulation of Multivariate Normal Rectangle Probabilities and their Derivatives: Theoretical and Computational Results," Cowles Foundation Discussion Paper No. 1021R.

Hammersly, J.M. and D.C. Handscomb (1964), *Monte Carlo Methods*, London: Methuen.

Hausman, Jerry, Bronwyn Hall, and Zvi Griliches (1984), "Econometric Models for Count Data with an Application to the Patents R & D Relationship," *Econometrica*, 52, 903–938.

Hausman, Jerry A. and David A. Wise (1978), "A Conditional Probit Model for Qualitative Choice: Discrete Decisions Recognizing Interdependence and Heterogenous Preferences," *Econometrica*, 46(2), 403–426.

Hendry, David F. (1984), "Monte Carlo Experimentation in Econometrics," *Handbook of Econometrics*, vol. II, Amsterdam: North-Holland.

Hotz, V. Joseph, Robert Miller, Seth Sanders, and Jeffrey Smith (1994), "A Simulation Estimator for Dynamic Models of Discrete Choice," *Review of Economic Studies*, 61, 265–289.

Keane, Michael P. (1994), "A Computationally Practical Simulation Estimator for Panel Data," *Econometrica*, 62(1), 95–116.

Lerman, Steven and Charles Manski (1981), "On the Use of Simulated Frequencies to Approximate Choice Probabilities," in Charles Manski and Daniel McFadden (eds.), *Structural Analysis of Discrete Data with Econometric Applications*, Cambridge, MA: MIT Press.

McCulloch, Robert and Peter Rossi (1994), "An Exact Likelihood Analysis of the Multinomial Probit Model," *Journal of Econometrics*, 64, 207–240.

(1995) "Value of Household Purchase History Information," Unpublished paper.

McFadden, Daniel (1989), "A Method of Simulated Moments for Estimation of Discrete Response Models without Numerical Integration," *Econometrica*, 57(5), 995–1026.

Ohanian, Lee, Giovanni L. Violante, Per Krusell, and José-Victor Ríos-Rull. (1999), "Simulation-Based Estimation of a Non-linear, Latent Factor Aggregate Production Function," in Roberto S. Mariano, Melvyn Weeks, and Til Schuermann (eds.), *Simulation-Based Inference in Econometrics: Methods and Applications*, Cambridge University Press.

Pakes, Ariel (1986), "Patents on Options: Some Estimates of the Value of Holding European Patent Stocks," *Econometrica*, 54(4), 755–784.

Pakes, Ariel and David Pollard (1989), "Simulation and the Asymptotics of Optimization Estimators," *Econometrica*, 57(5), 1027–1057.

Richard, J.F. and Wei Zhang (1996), "Accelerated Monte Carlo Integration: An Application to Dynamic Latent Variable Models," in Roberto S. Mariano, Melvyn Weeks, and Til Schuermann (eds.), *Simulation-Based Inference in Econometrics: Methods and Applications*, Cambridge University Press.

Ripley, Brian (1987), *Stochastic Simulation*, New York: John Wiley and Sons.

Stern, Steven (1992), "A Method for Smoothing Simulated Moments of Discrete Probabilities in Multinomial Probit Models," *Econometrica*, 60(4), 943–952.

Tanner, T. and W. Wong (1987), "The Calculation of Posterior Distribution by Data Augmentation," *Journal of the American Statistical Association*, 82, 528–549.

Tierney, L. (1994), "Markov Chains for Exploring Posterior Distributions." *Annals of Statistics*, 22(4), 1701–1762.

Part II

Microeconometric methods

Introduction

Melvyn Weeks

Although microeconometric models have many advantages over macro-econometric models, they have some disadvantages that stem from the characteristics of the available data. Of particular relevance here is the dichotomy between the information which is observed by the individual decision maker and the information available to the investigator, often referred to as the observational rule. For example, many models of individual choice are predicated on an underlying continuous random variable representing utility. However, in many instances the revealed preference of the agent provides only discrete indicators signaling, as an example, the preferred brand, occupation, or model choice.

If we consider a single equation then we may view the progression from the least squares model with continuous regressors, to the censored, truncated, and discrete choice models, as one of progressive information loss. This information loss is manifest in the need for more complex econometric models. In a multivariate setting the consequences of non-observability for estimation are considerably greater, and have provided much of the impetus for the developments in simulation-based inference.

It is instructive to consider the recent developments in simulation-based inference in a historical context. At any given point analysts may face the trade-off between a preferred modeling strategy and what is tractable given computer technology. If we examine the development of microeconometric models this trade-off is very much apparent. For the sake of exposition it is convenient to consider three stages.[1]

Up until the early 1970s computational constraints were such that for an estimator to be tractable exact analytical expressions were required, in terms of both the criterion function and first-order conditions. During this period the linear model dominated with the majority of empirical studies centered around ordinary least squares, two-stage least squares and seemingly unrelated regression.

---

[1] The following discussion is based upon a series of lectures given by Christian Gourieroux.

41

From the early 1970s the increase in computer power coupled with the growth of numerical optimization techniques, resulted in the emergence of a class of estimator where, although an analytical form for the criterion function was required, it was not necessary to be able to write down analytical expressions for the first-order conditions. At this time the applied econometrician was able to gain access to a much broader class of model, with particular developments in microeconometric models. Estimators defined by non-linear equations could now be accessed in a routine manner. Noteworthy growth areas were limited dependent variable models, duration analysis, and discrete choice models. With regard to the latter, significant contributions by McFadden (1974) and Domenich and McFadden (1975) saw the emergence of the binary logit and probit model as a powerful modeling tool, utilized in a number of diverse fields from bioassay, transport, economics, and psychology.

The study by Lerman and Manski (1981) heralded a new era in the historical development of economic modeling by proposing an innovative estimator for the multinomial probit model (MNP). The MNP model belongs to a class of models where both the criterion function and first-order conditions are without a simple analytical form. In this particular case the maximization of the likelihood function requires the evaluation of a multidimensional integral for each sample point. The attendant "curse of dimensionality" (see Bellman (1957)) is recurrent in a wide range of models as demonstrated by the diverse applications featured in this volume. Within the context of classical econometric methods Lerman and Manski, building upon the simulated frequency Monte Carlo approach (see Hammersley and Handscomb (1964)) and superseded by the work of McFadden (1989) and Pakes and Pollard (1989), advocated a procedure which through the use of simulation, reconstructs the conditional probability density function, thereby avoiding explicit evaluation of multiple integrals. In Bayesian analysis of the MNP model a simulation approach is used to provide an indirect simulator for the posterior distribution.

Up until the emergence of this powerful modeling tool analysts have circumvented the curse of dimensionality by the use of "approximate" models, trading off flexibility in being able to model a wide range of individual behavior with tractability. The predominance of the multinomial logit model and other variants of the Generalized Extreme Value (GEV) family during this period is a case in point. McFadden (1981) noted that "the primary difficulty in the application of the MNP model is the lack of practical, accurate methods for approximating the choice probabilities when the number of alternatives is large." However, since the emergence of simulation-based inference, the dominance of GEV models is now being questioned. Geweke, Keane, and Runkle (1994) state that: "Recently the method of simulated moments and Gibbs sampling with data augmentation have shown promise of making the required computations in the multinomial probit model practical."

It is worth noting that in part IV of this volume, Gourieroux, Renault, and Touzi examine the finite sample properties of the indirect inference procedure. This procedure neatly demonstrates the relationship between the maximum and pseudo-maximum likelihood estimator and in addition how "approximate" models may be utilized to recover the parameters of more complex models. Indirect inference is based upon the notion that *correct* inference can be based upon an *incorrect* criterion function, allowing a set of consistent (indirect) estimates to be obtained from the incorrect criterion function.

Progress in the development and use of specification tests may also be linked to the availability of computer resources. This is particularly evident in the problems faced in the use of Cox's non-nested test, the principal problem being due to the fact that a key component of the test statistic is the pseudo-true value. Just as analysts have utilized approximate models when the optimal modeling strategy was infeasible, it is also the case that in certain instances the construction of an optimal test statistic is infeasible owing to a dimensionality constraint. For example, given the similarity between the independent probit (IP) and MNL models, a number of analysts have utilized a classical nested test of IP against MNP as an approximate test of MNL against MNP (see Hausman and Wise (1978)). However, used in this way the test is only a convenient short cut since the underlying distributions are different, and as such there are no asymptotic grounds for the use of this test.

Recent contributions by Pesaran and Pesaran (1993, 1995) and Weeks (1996), have seen the use of simulation methods to operationalize Cox's non-nested test. The use of simulation in this context may be thought of as an application of a simple crude frequency simulator.

In this section Richard and Zhang examine an application involving dynamic latent variable models. Emphasis is placed upon the specifics of simulation technology, and in particular how accurate estimates of model parameters can be obtained with a small number of replications. In this context the benchmark is not approximate models but rather other, less efficient simulation methods. Research in this highly technical area is critical given that the applied econometrician will inevitably base any decision as to the feasibility of simulation-based estimators on both the question of accuracy and the time required to complete a given estimation run. However, the availability of easily used software as a determinant of the widespread use of these methods should not be overlooked.

The paper by Hajivassiliou, containing a transparent overview of a number of practical issues in simulation, continues in a similar vein with the focus upon simulation technology. A number of issues are explored including the use of a two-stage procedure to recapture the efficiency property of simulated maximum likelihood (SML), and the introduction of simulation principles to devise classical hypothesis tests free of simulation noise. Evidence on the impact of dimensionality and the number of simulations upon SML bias is provided. In addition a modified new simulator is suggested, which by incorporating antithetic variance reduction is shown to be superior to previous best practice.

The chapter by Geweke and Keane presents a method which enables the estimation of the structural parameters of dynamic discrete choice models. The authors consider a class of model where agents choose from a set of mutually exclusive alternatives, and must choose between them over a number of time periods. The general intractability of this type of model is again linked to the issue of information content, and specifically that the mapping from the observed data (in this instance choices and payoffs) to the posterior distribution of the structural parameters is in most cases intractable. It is worth emphasizing that the coupling of Bayesian inference in a discrete, dynamic framework gives rise to a number of additional problems which are not present in a pure discrete choice model.

The chapter by Weeks examines the finite sample performance of a number of variants of the Cox test for both binomial and multinomial choice models. Again it is instructive to consider the role of simulation methods as a tool which extends the list of feasible modeling strategies and, in the case of the Cox test, provides a formal way of evaluating the performance of these new models against more tractable but less flexible alternatives.

The chapter by McCulloch and Rossi continues the Bayesian theme by focusing upon the MNP model, suggesting that under certain conditions the Bayesian approach to inference offers an improvement over classical econometric methods. In an analysis of the binary model, Zellner and Rossi (1984) utilize standard numerical integration. However, in a Bayesian setting, the principal computational constraint to inference in the multinomial model, is the problem of evaluating moments of the posterior distribution as the size of the choice set increases. The authors discuss how the Bayesian method may be extended to incorporate a number of extensions including random coefficients models used with panel data and autocorrelated latent regression errors. Two basic approaches to specifying priors on the covariance matrix of latent errors are also examined.

References

Bellman, R. (1957), *Dynamic Programming*, Princeton: Princeton University Press.

Domenich, T. and D. McFadden (1975), *Urban Travel Demand: A Behavioural Analysis*, Amsterdam: North-Holland.

Geweke, J., M. Keane, and D. Runkle (1994), "Alternative Computational Approaches to Inference in the Multinomial Probit Model," Research Dept., Federal Reserve Bank of Minneapolis.

Hammersley, J. and D. Handscomb (1964), *Monte Carlo Methods*, London: Methuen.

Hausman, J. and D. Wise (1978), "A Conditional Probit Model for Qualitative Choice: Discrete Decisions Recognizing Interdependence and Heterogeneous Preferences," *Econometrica*, 46, 403–426.

Lerman, S. and C. Manski (1981), "On the Use of Simulated Frequencies to Approximate Choice Probabilities," in C. Manski and D. McFadden (eds.), *Structural Analysis of Discrete Data with Econometric Applications*, Cambridge, MA: MIT Press.

McFadden, D. (1974), "The Measurement of Urban Travel Demand," *Journal of Public Economics*, 3, 303–328.

(1981), *Econometric Models of Probabilistic Choice*, Cambridge, MA: MIT Press.

(1989), "A Method of Simulated Moments for Estimation of Discrete Response Models without Numerical Integration," *Econometrica*, 57, 995–1026.

Pakes, A. and D. Pollard (1989), "Simulation and the Asymptotics of Optimization Estimators," *Econometrica*, 57, 1027–1058.

Pesaran, M. and B. Pesaran (1993), "A Simulation Approach to the Problem of Computing Cox's Statistic for Testing Non-Nested Models," *Journal of Econometrics*, 57, 377–392.

(1995), "A Non-Nested Test of Level Differences Versus Log-Differenced Stationary Models," *Econometric Reviews*, 14(2), 213–227.

Weeks, M. (1996), "Testing Binomial and Multinomial Choice Models Using Cox's Non-Nested Test," in *Papers and Proceedings of the American Statistical Association, 1995.*

Zellner, A. and P. Rossi (1984), "Bayesian Analysis of Dichotomous Quantal Response Models," *Journal of Econometrics*, 25(3), 365–393.

2 Accelerated Monte Carlo integration: an application to dynamic latent variables models

Jean-François Richard and Wei Zhang

1 Introduction

Economists are well aware of the fact that the behavior of economic agents often is critically conditioned by latent (unobservable) variables. It is, therefore, hardly surprising that latent variable models have received increased attention over recent years (made possible by impressive advances in computing power). A few references are Aigner *et al.* (1983), Heckman (1981), Heckman and McCurdy (1980), McFadden (1989), and Pakes and Pollard (1989).

Estimation of latent variable models requires the elimination of the latest variables by marginalization, i.e., by integration of the joint sampling density of the observables and unobservables, in the case of continuous variables. Analytical solutions for such integrals generally are not available (with the important exception of linear Gaussian models for whose evaluation there exist analytical recurrence relationships).

In general one has to rely upon numerical integration. The problem is further complicated by the fact that latent variables often are inherently dynamic to the effect that their elimination requires *interdependent* (high-dimensional) numerical integration.

Until recently high-dimensional numerical integration could not be evaluated with sufficient numerical accuracy at any level of generality. This explains why a number of techniques had been developed over the years which circumvent this problem. For expository purposes we can usefully regroup these contributions into three broad categories:

(1) Autocorrelation: the dynamics of the model are captured in the form of autocorrelated errors which can lead to operational likelihood

Paper prepared for the conference on Simulation-Based Methods in Econometrics, Federal Reserve Bank of Minneapolis November 17–18, 1995. Financial support from NSF Grant SES-9223365 is acknowledged. Contact address: Dept. of Economics, Forbes Quad 4D12, University of Pittsburgh, Pittsburgh, PA 15260, e-mail: fantin+@pitt. edu functions (see, e.g., Laffont and Monfort (1979) for an innovative example in the context of disequilibrium models);

(2) Proxies: unobserved latent variables are replaced (or approximated) by observable proxies. Typical examples are the use of price-adjustment equations in disequilibrium models (see Quandt (1982, 1988) or Maddala (1983)) or the use of "fixed-effects" formulation as in Heckman and McCurdy (1980);

(3) Simulated moments: even though the likelihood functions associated with dynamic latent variables (hereafter DLV) models may be intractable, the models themselves often are amenable to *joint* simulation of the latent *and* observable processes. Such simulations are instrumental to the method of simulated moments, as discussed, for example, by McFadden (1989) or Pakes and Pollard (1989), which are applicable to DLV models. A key difference with the approach which is discussed here lies in the fact that likelihood evaluation requires simulations which are *conditional* upon observables (see Hendry and Richard (1992) for further discussion).

One of the most important numerical developments in recent years has been the increasing usage of Monte Carlo (MC) simulation techniques as a *numerical* method for evaluating large-dimensional analytically intractable integrals (see Klock and van Dijk (1978) or, for more recent developments, Geweke (1989, 1994) and Richard (1995)). The numerical accuracy of MC methods critically depends upon the choice of the *auxiliary* sampler (the "importance function") which is used for the random selection of the points at which the integrand has to be evaluated. Unfortunately, "natural" importance samplers (by which we mean samplers that are direct by-products of the model specification) often are so "inefficient" that they are inherently incapable of producing accurate estimates of likelihood function for DLV models (see, e.g., the comments in McFadden (1989) or Pakes and Pollard (1989) to that effect).

Conventional "acceleration" techniques, as discussed for example in Hendry (1984) or Geweke (1994) can help but generally do not solve the problem as they leave the initial sampler unaffected. Danielsson and Richard (1993), hereafter DR, proposed an algorithm for the construction of efficient samplers in high-dimensional problems but their technique is restricted to Gaussian samplers and requires iterations. Richard and Zhang (1995), hereafter RZ, proposed a more general non-iterative algorithm which is applicable to a broad class of (sequential) samplers and only requires solving auxiliary weighted least squares problems. The object of the present chapter is to discuss the application of their technique to DLV models.

The chapter is organized as follows: section 2 discusses simulated likelihood functions; accelerated importance sampling is introduced in section 3; its implementation is discussed in section 4, first in the context of a simple stochastic volatility model (section 4.1) and then at a more general level (section 4.2); numerical and statistical accuracy are discussed in section 5; results are offered in section 6 and section 7 concludes.

2   Simulated likelihood function

Let $y_t \in \mathbb{R}^n$ denote a vector of random variables observable at time t and $\lambda_t \in \mathbb{R}^p$ a vector of unobservable or latent variables. A sample of size T is available in the form of a matrix $Y' = (y_1, \ldots, y_T)$. The matrix of unobservables is $\Lambda' = (\lambda_1, \ldots, \lambda_T)$. Initial conditions are represented by the matrices Y_0 and Λ_0 respectively. For the ease of exposition we shall assume that Y_0 has been observed.[1]

Let $Y_t' = (Y_0', y_1, \ldots, y_t)$ and $\Lambda_t' = (\Lambda_0', \lambda_1, \ldots, \lambda_t)$. DLV models are typically expressed in the form of a sequence of conditional density functions[2] $\phi(\cdot)$ for (y_t, λ_t) given $(Y_{t-1}, \Lambda_{t-1}, \theta)$, where θ denote a vector of unknown parameters. Let $\phi(y_0, \lambda_0 | \theta)$ denote an assumed density function for $y_0 = \text{vec} Y_0$ and $\lambda_0 = \text{vec} \Lambda_0$. The likelihood function associated with the $(T + \ell).n$ matrix Y_T is given by

$$L(\theta; Y_T) = \int \phi(Y_T, \Lambda_T | \theta) d\Lambda_T \tag{1}$$

where $\phi(Y_T, \Lambda_T | \theta)$ denotes the joint sampling density of Y_T and Λ_T and is given by

$$\phi(Y_T, \Lambda_T | \theta) = \prod_{t=0}^{T} \phi(y_t, \lambda_t | Y_{t-1}, \Lambda_{t-1}, \theta). \tag{2}$$

Note that ϕ is used as a generic notation for all sampling density functions associated with the model under consideration. Assumptions relative to the dynamic structure of the model are generally formulated in terms of one of the following two additional factorizations[3]

$$\phi(y_t, \lambda_t | Y_{t-1}, \Lambda_{t-1}, \theta) = \begin{cases} \phi(y_t | Y_{t-1}, \Lambda_t, \theta) \cdot \phi(\lambda_t | Y_{t-1}, \Lambda_{t-1}, \theta) & (3) \\ \phi(y_t | Y_{t-1}, \Lambda_{t-1}, \theta) \cdot \phi(\lambda_t | Y_{t-1}, \Lambda_t, \theta). & (4) \end{cases}$$

---

[1] If Y_0 were unknown, it would have to be treated in the same way as Λ_0, i.e., it would have to be integrated out along with the λs.

[2] For the ease of notation, we shall only consider here continuous random variables. Our analysis trivially extends to discrete or mixed random variables.

[3] A cursory look through the literature suggests that factorization (3) prevails. In particular, it applies to cases where a "state space" representation of the latent process is paired with a (stochastic) "measurement equation" (see, e.g., Harvey (1990) for details).

In general it is not possible to derive from equations (3) and/or (4) operational expressions for the distribution of $\lambda_t | \Lambda_{t-1}, Y_T, \theta$ (except for the obvious and rather uninteresting case where λ_t does not "cause" y_t in the sense of Granger (1969), i.e., where y_t is independent of Λ_{t-1}, conditionally on Y_{t-1}). This is precisely why the integral in (1) has to be numerically evaluated.

In order to evaluate (1) by Monte Carlo (MC) we first have to construct an *auxiliary*[4] sampler for the λs say

$$p_0(\Lambda_T | Y_T, \theta) = \prod_{t=0}^{T} p_t^0(\lambda_t | \Lambda_{t-1}, Y_T, \theta). \tag{5}$$

Based upon the factorizations in (3) and (4) two "natural" choices for p_t^0 are $\phi(\lambda_t | Y_{t-1}, \Lambda_{t-1}, \theta)$ or $\phi(\lambda_t | Y_t, \Lambda_{t-1}, \theta)$ though, as illustrated by the example discussed in section 4.1 below, other (possibly more "efficient") choices may be available. The "remainder function" g_0 associated with the sampler p_0 is defined as $g_0 = \phi/p_0$ and is partitioned conformably with ϕ and p_0

$$g_0(\Lambda_T, Y_T, \theta) = \prod_{t=0}^{T} g_t^0(\Lambda_t; Y_T, \theta) \tag{6}$$

where

$$g_t^0(\Lambda_t; Y_T, \theta) = \frac{\phi(y_t, \lambda_t | Y_{t-1}, \Lambda_{t-1}, \theta)}{p_t^0(\lambda_t | \Lambda_{t-1}, Y_T, \theta)}. \tag{7}$$

It follows that $L(\theta, Y_T)$, as defined in equation (1), can be rewritten as

$$L(\theta; Y_T) = \int g_0(\Lambda_T; Y_T, \theta) \cdot p_0(\Lambda_T | Y_T, \theta) d\Lambda_T. \tag{8}$$

An "initial" MC estimate of $L(\theta; Y_T)$ (for a pre-assigned value of θ) is given by

$$\bar{L}_S^0(\theta; Y_T) = \frac{1}{S} \sum_{i=1}^{S} g_0(\tilde{\Lambda}_{Ti}^0; Y_T, \theta) \tag{9}$$

where $\{\tilde{\Lambda}_{Ti}^0; i: 1 \to S\}$ denotes a set of S independent random draws from the initial sampler p_0. In practice, the λ_{ti}s are drawn conformably with the sequential factorization of p_0, as given in equation (5), to the effect that $\tilde{\lambda}_{ti}$ denotes a draw from the conditional density $p_t^0(\lambda_t | Y_{t-1}, \tilde{\Lambda}_{t-1,i}^0, \theta)$. The MC sampling variance of $\bar{L}_S^0$ is given by

$$\text{var}[\bar{L}_S^0(\theta; Y_T)] = \frac{1}{S} \text{var}_{p0}[g_0(\Lambda_T; Y_T, \theta)]. \tag{10}$$

---

[4] p_0 is "auxiliary" in the sense that it differs from $\phi(\Lambda_T | Y_T, \theta)$, the *actual* sampling distribution of $\Lambda_T | Y_T, \theta$.

It is now well documented that for a broad range of applications the MC sampling variance of g_0 is so large that accurate MC estimation of $L(\theta; Y_T)$ and by-products thereof is utterly impractical (see e.g., McFadden (1989) or Pakes and Pollard (1989)). This explains the growing popularity of alternative methods of estimation and, in particular, of the method of simulated moments (MSM) which, relative to inference procedures based upon simulated likelihood, is computationally simpler but potentially *statistically* inefficient.

The object of the present chapter is to demonstrate that it is possible to construct accurate MC estimates of the likelihood function itself, at the cost of replacing the numerically inefficient initial MC sampler p_0 by a more efficient one, obtained by application of the generic acceleration principle proposed by RZ.

3 Accelerated importance sampling

In this section we discuss how to efficiently evaluate the integral in (8) for *given* values of Y_T and θ.[5] In order to simplify notation, let $\delta = (\theta; Y_T)$. Equation (5) is rewritten as

$$L(\delta) = \int \phi(\Lambda_T; \delta) d\Lambda_T \tag{11}$$

with

$$\phi(\Lambda_T; \delta) = g_0(\Lambda_T; \delta) \cdot p_0(\Lambda_T | \delta). \tag{12}$$

In our experience, p_0 often is so dramatically inefficient that conventional acceleration techniques, as discussed, e.g., in Hendry (1984) or Geweke (1994), are incapable of delivering sufficient efficiency gains. The only remedy consists of the replacement of p_0 by a more efficient sampler p_*.

For obvious practical reasons, the search for p_* is restricted to a pre-assigned class of samplers, the choice of which will be discussed in section 4 below. Therefore, let M denote a class of MC samplers indexed by an auxiliary parameter vector $\alpha \in A$

$$M = \{m(\Lambda_T | \alpha); \alpha \in A\}. \tag{13}$$

In practice we shall partition m comfortably with p_*. However, for expository purposes we present the proposed acceleration principle at a "global" level first and discuss its sequential application next.

---

[5] Such calculations will have to be repeated for different values of θ as provided, for example, by an ML optimization algorithm and, possibly also, for different values of Y_T, in the context of an MC simulation of the finite sample (statistical) properties of the relevant estimator of θ.

3.1   General principle

For any arbitrary value $\alpha \in A$, we can rewrite the integral in (11) as

$$L(\delta) = \int \frac{\phi(\Lambda_T;\delta)}{m(\Lambda_T \mid \alpha)} \cdot m(\Lambda_T \mid \alpha) d\Lambda_T \tag{14}$$

$$= \int g_0(\Lambda_T;\delta) \cdot \omega(\Lambda_T;\alpha,\delta) \cdot m(\Lambda_T \mid \alpha) d\Lambda_T \tag{15}$$

where

$$\omega(\Lambda_T;\alpha,\delta) = \frac{p_0(\Lambda_T \mid \delta)}{m(\Lambda_T \mid \alpha)}. \tag{16}$$

The corresponding MC estimate of $L(\delta)$ is given by

$$\hat{L}_S(\delta;\alpha) = \frac{1}{S} \sum_{i=1}^{S} g_0(\tilde{\Lambda}_{Ti};\delta) \cdot \omega(\tilde{\Lambda}_{Ti};\alpha,\delta) \tag{17}$$

where $\{\tilde{\Lambda}_{Ti}; i:1 \to S\}$ denotes a set of S independent random draws from m. As shown in RZ, its MC sampling variance is given by

$$V_S(\delta;\alpha) = \frac{1}{S} \cdot \left[\int \frac{\phi^2(\Lambda_T;\delta)}{m(\Lambda_T \mid \alpha)} d\Lambda_T - L^2(\delta) \right] \tag{18}$$

$$= \frac{1}{S} \cdot L(\delta) \cdot \int h[d(\Lambda_T;\delta,\alpha)] \cdot \phi(\Lambda_T;\delta) d\Lambda_T \tag{19}$$

where

$$d(\Lambda_T;\delta,\alpha) = \ln\left[\frac{\phi(\Lambda_T;\delta)}{L(\delta) \cdot m(\Lambda_T \mid \alpha)} \right] \tag{20}$$

$$h(d) = e^d + e^{-d} - 2. \tag{21}$$

If, in particular, there existed $\alpha_0 \in A$ such that

$$m(\Lambda_T \mid \alpha_0) \equiv \frac{\phi(\Lambda_T;\delta)}{L(\delta)} \tag{22}$$

then $V_S(\delta;\alpha_0) \equiv 0$. More generally we should aim at finding values of α such that $m(\Lambda_T \mid \alpha)$ closely "mimics" $\phi(\Lambda_T;\delta)$ in Λ_T. However, there do not appear to exist easy ways of directly minimizing $V_S(\delta;\alpha)$ with respect to α. We propose instead to replace $h(d)$ in equation (19) by d^2 on grounds that its Taylor series expansion around zero is given by

$$h(d) = 2 \cdot \sum_{i=1}^{\infty} \frac{d^{2i}}{(2i)!} \tag{23}$$

and that we expect d to remain close to zero for "efficient" choices of α. A more formal argument to that effect can be found in RZ. Hence, we propose to solve the following minimization problem

$$\alpha^*(\delta) = \underset{\alpha \in A}{\arg\min} [Q(\delta;\alpha)] \tag{24}$$

where

$$Q(\delta;\alpha) = \int [\ln\phi(\Lambda_T;\delta) - \ln L(\delta) - \ln m(\Lambda_T|\alpha)]^2 \cdot \phi(\Lambda_T;\delta)d\Lambda_T. \tag{25}$$

In practice we can use the *initial* sampler p_0 to construct the following MC estimate of $Q(\delta;\alpha)$

$$\hat{Q}_N(\delta;\alpha) = \frac{1}{N}\sum_{i=1}^{N}[\ln\phi(\tilde{\Lambda}_{Ti}^0;\delta) - \ln L(\delta) - \ln m(\tilde{\Lambda}_{Ti}^0|\alpha)]^2 \cdot g_0(\tilde{\Lambda}_{Ti}^0;\delta) \tag{26}$$

where $\{\tilde{\Lambda}_{Ti}^0; i:1 \to N\}$ denotes a set of N independent random draws from p_0. Whence our proposed "efficient" importance sampler is given by

$$p^*(\Lambda_T|\delta) = m(\Lambda_T|\hat{\alpha}_N(\delta)) \tag{27}$$

where

$$\hat{\alpha}_N(\delta) = \underset{\alpha \in A}{\arg\min}[\hat{Q}_N(\delta;\alpha)]. \tag{28}$$

In other words $\hat{\alpha}_N(\delta)$ is obtained by application of a weighted (non-linear) least squares (W(NL)LS) procedure applied to an auxiliary data set constructed with random draws from p_0. The constant $\ln L(\delta)$ in equation (26) is to be treated as an *unconstrained* intercept since p_0 cannot produce an accurate estimate of the $\ln L(\delta)$ itself.[6] Our final (efficient) MC estimate of $L(\delta)$ is given by

$$\bar{L}_S^*(\delta) = \frac{1}{S}\sum_{i=1}^{S}g_0(\tilde{\Lambda}_{Ti}^*;\delta) \cdot \omega(\tilde{\Lambda}_{Ti}^*;\delta) \tag{29}$$

where

$$\omega(\tilde{\Lambda}_{Ti}^*;\delta) = \frac{p_0(\tilde{\Lambda}_{Ti}^*;\delta)}{p_*(\tilde{\Lambda}_{Ti}^*;\delta)} \tag{30}$$

and $\{\tilde{\Lambda}_{Ti}^*; i:1 \to S\}$ denotes a set of S independent random draws from p_*.

---

[6] We could construct a two-step estimate of $\alpha^*(\delta)$ as follows: the first step consists of the procedure we just described with unconstrained intercept; The second step reruns the W(NL)LS procedure replacing $L(\delta)$ in equation (26) by its (accurate) first step MC estimate. As discussed in RZ, the efficiency gains are produced by this second step appear to be negligible.

3.2   Sequential acceleration

In the context of DLV models all densities are given in sequential form as in equation (1). Let, therefore, partition $m(\Lambda_T|\alpha)$ conformably

$$m(\Lambda_T|\alpha) = \prod_{t=0}^{T} m_t(\lambda_t|\Lambda_{t-1},\alpha_t) \tag{31}$$

with $\alpha' = (\alpha'_0 \ldots \alpha'_T)$. The corresponding partitionings for the functions ϕ, p_0, and g_0 are found in equations (1), (5), and (7) respectively. For the ease of exposition we shall keep using the shorthand notation introduced in section 3.1. The correspondence between the two sets of notation is found in the following equations

$$\phi_t(\Lambda_t;\delta) = \phi(y_t,\lambda_t| Y_{t-1},\Lambda_{t-1},\theta) \tag{32}$$

$$g_t^0(\Lambda_t;\delta) = g_t^0(y_t|\Lambda_t; Y_T,\theta) \tag{33}$$

$$p_t^0(\lambda_t|\Lambda_{t-1},\delta) = p_t^0(\lambda_t|\Lambda_{t-1}, Y_T,\theta). \tag{34}$$

In order to provide heuristic support for the sequential version of our acceleration technique, lets first provide the sequential counterpart of condition (22) for an "ideal" MC sampler.

   Theorem 1   Condition (22) holds if and only if there exist $\{\alpha_t^0; t:0 \rightarrow T\}$ such that

$$m_t(\lambda_t|\Lambda_{t-1},\alpha_t^0) = \frac{k_t(\Lambda_t;\delta)}{\chi_t(\Lambda_{t-1};\delta)} \tag{35}$$

where the k_ts and χ_ts are given by the backward recursion

$$\chi_{T+1}(\Lambda_T;\delta) \equiv 1 \tag{36}$$

$$k_t(\Lambda_t;\delta) = \phi_t(\Lambda_t;\delta) \cdot \chi_{t+1}(\Lambda_t;\delta) \tag{37}$$

$$\chi_T(\Lambda_{t-1};\delta) = \int k_t(\Lambda_t;\delta) d\lambda_t \tag{38}$$

whence

$$\chi_0(\cdot;\delta) \equiv L(\delta). \tag{39}$$

   Proof
(i) Sufficiency: Under conditions (36) to (38) we have

$$\phi(\Lambda_T;\delta) = \prod_{t=0}^{T} \left[\frac{k_t(\Lambda_t;\delta)}{\chi_{t+1}(\Lambda_t;\delta)} \right]$$

$$= \chi_0(\cdot\,;\delta) \cdot \prod_{t=0}^{T}\left[\frac{k_t(\Lambda_t;\delta)}{\chi_t(\Lambda_{t-1};\delta)}\right]$$

$$= L(\delta) \cdot m(\Lambda_T|\alpha_0)$$

with $\alpha_0 = \{\alpha_t^0; t : 0 \to T\}$.

(ii) Necessity obtains by backward induction: See RZ for details.

In words which are familiar to Bayesians k_t, as defined in (37), is a "density kernel" for m_t and χ_t is its integrating constant (w.r.t. λ_t only). The following notation will be used

$$m_t(\lambda_t|\Lambda_{t-1},\delta) \propto k_t(\Lambda_t;\delta). \tag{40}$$

In practice we do not expect formula (35) to hold. Nevertheless, it unambiguously suggests that it would be suboptimal to require that m_t individually "mimics" ϕ_t for $t : T \to 0$. The point is that the integrating constant of ϕ_t with respect to λ_t depends on Λ_{t-1}, while that of m_t does not (being equal to 1 by definition). It follows that the sequential construction of an efficient sampler inherently requires backward transfer of appropriate integration constants, in line with formula (35).

Note that it would be impractical to transfer back integrating constants for the ϕ_ts, as these are not analytically available. In contrast, the χ_ts will have analytical expressions for a broad range of sequential samplers. Hence, theorem 1 provides the key insight for the construction of a *sequential* sampler based upon an *operational* backward transfer rule for integrating constants.

Let M_t denote a parametric class of sequential sampler

$$M_t = \{m_t(\lambda_t|\Lambda_{t-1};\alpha_t); \ \alpha_t \in A_t\}. \tag{41}$$

Let K_t denote the corresponding set of density kernels

$$K_t = \{k_t(\Lambda_t;\alpha_t); \ \alpha_t \in A_t\}. \tag{42}$$

The correspondence between M_t and K_t is characterized by the identity

$$m_t(\lambda_t|\Lambda_{t-1};\alpha_t) = \frac{k_t(\Lambda_t;\alpha_t)}{\chi_t(\Lambda_{t-1};\alpha_t)} \tag{43}$$

where

$$\chi_t(\Lambda_{t-1};\alpha_t) = \int k_t(\lambda_t|\Lambda_{t-1},\alpha_t)d\lambda_t. \tag{44}$$

Note that in formula (43) we can multiply k_t and χ_t by an arbitrary function $\tau(\Lambda_{t-1})$ without changing m_t (which, as we just discussed, is a key component of sequential "matching" between ϕ and m). It follows that equation (43) defines an equivalence relationship on K_t, whose equivalence classes regroup all density kernels associated with a common density m_t in M_t.

In line with formula (37), the proposed sequential version of our acceleration principle consists of the (backward) search for a sequence of α_ts such that

$$\frac{k_t(\Lambda_t;\alpha_t)}{\chi_{t+1}(\Lambda_t;\alpha_{t+1})} \text{ "mimics" } \phi_t(\Lambda_t;\delta) \tag{45}$$

for $t: T \searrow 0$, where the χ_ts are given by (44). This condition is tantamount to requiring that k_t/χ_{t+1} could serve as an "efficient" sampler for ϕ_t in the auxiliary integral[7]

$$J_t(\delta) = \int \phi_t(\Lambda_t;\delta) \cdot \prod_{s=0}^{t-1} p_s^0(\lambda_s|\Lambda_{s-1},\delta) d\Lambda_t. \tag{46}$$

Application of the general principle introduced in section 3.1 leads to the following sequence of (low-dimensional) optimization problems

$$\hat{\alpha}_{t,N}(\delta) = \underset{\alpha_t \in A_t}{\arg\min} [\hat{Q}_{t,N}(\delta;\alpha_t)] \tag{47}$$

where

$$\hat{Q}_{t,N}(\delta;\alpha_t) = \frac{1}{N} \sum_{i=1}^{N} [\ln\phi_t(\tilde{\Lambda}_{ti}^0;\delta) + \ln\chi_{t+1}(\tilde{\Lambda}_{ti}^0;\hat{\alpha}_{t+1,N}(\delta))$$
$$- \ln k_t(\tilde{\Lambda}_{ti}^0;\alpha_t)]^2 g_t^0(\tilde{\Lambda}_{ti}^0;\delta). \tag{48}$$

Note that, following equation (46), the $\tilde{\Lambda}_{ti}^0$s all are subsets of a *common* set of $\{\tilde{\Lambda}_{Ti}^0; i: 1 \rightarrow N\}$ independently drawn from the initial sampler p_0. The corresponding sequence of "efficient" samplers is given by

$$\hat{p}_t(\lambda_t|\Lambda_{t-1},\delta) = \frac{k_t(\Lambda_t;\hat{\alpha}_{t,N}(\delta))}{\chi_t(\Lambda_t;\hat{\alpha}_{t,N}(\delta))} \tag{49}$$

where χ_t is the (analytical) integration constant of the density kernel k_t, as defined in equation (44).

The "sequential" version of our acceleration principle cannot be expected to be as efficient as its "global" counterpart. On the other hand, it consists of a sequence of $T+1$ low dimensional W(NL)LS optimization problems in the individual α_ts while the global algorithm requires *joint* optimization in $\alpha' = (\alpha'_0 \dots \alpha'_T)$ and is, therefore, expected to be prohibitively expensive to run for large Ts.

---

[7] Note that we do not expect to have an analytical expression for the integrating constant of k_t/χ_{t+1}. This is irrelevant since we do not propose to actually evaluate $J_t(\delta)$, whose only role is that of providing a formal validation for the algorithm which follows.

Our current experience, which is based upon such applications as that described in sections 4.1 and 5 below, unequivocally suggests that our sequential algorithm can produce highly accurate MC estimates of likelihood functions (and their by-products) for DLV models at reasonable computing costs even for very large Ts (1,500 to 2,000$^+$).

4   Implementation

In order to motivate additional technical assumptions that lead to a particularly operational version of our sequential algorithm in the context of a broad range of DLV models, we first discuss its application to a simple dynamic stochastic volatility model.

4.1   A dynamic stochastic volatility model

Let y_t denote a (univariate) observable return variable and $\lambda_t > 0$ a latent (stochastic) "volatility" variable. The bivariate model we propose to analyze consists of a static measurement process

$$y_t | \lambda_t \sim N(0, \lambda_t) \tag{50}$$

and of a dynamic latent process for λ_t. As for the latter, a broad variety of specifications can be found in the literature. Early contributions, where λ is interpreted as a "mixing" variable, often assumed independence in order to preserve numerical tractibility.[8] See, for example, Clark (1973), Epps and Epps (1976), or Tauchen and Pitts (1983). Dynamic equations for λ_t predominantly appear in the form of GARCH processes whereby λ_t is assumed to be a *non-stochastic* function of past λs and/or y^2s (in which case the evaluation of $L(\theta; Y_T)$ requires no integration at all).

A few references are Engle (1982), Bollerslev (1986), Nelson (1991), or Friedman and Laibson (1989). Dynamic *stochastic* equations for λ_t have been estimated by the method of moments. See, for example, Taylor (1986), Melino and Turnbull (1990), or Duffle and Singleton (1989). Danielsson and Richard (1993), hereafter DR, apply an accelerated Gaussian importance sampler (AGIS), which in many ways is a precursor to the more general procedure proposed here, to a simple bivariate model for daily S&P 500 data ($T = 2,022$).

In the present chapter we shall assume that $\lambda_t | \lambda_{t-1}$ has an inverted-gamma (IG) distribution. There are several reasons for introducing that assumption: (i) first and foremost (inverted) gamma distributions are

---

[8] When λ_ts are assumed to be independent over time, the integral in (1) reduces to a product of univariate integrals for which there exists a broad range of efficient evaluation procedures.

widely used in statistics to model non-negative random variables (see for example Cox and Oakes (1984) or Kalbfleisch and Prentice (1980));[9] (ii) it serves to illustrate the applicability of the proposed algorithm to non-normal distributions; and (iii) it produces a particularly simple version of our algorithm.

Let

$$\lambda_t | \lambda_{t-1}, \theta \sim IG(\gamma + \tau\lambda_{t-1}, \nu) \tag{51}$$

where $\theta' = (\gamma, \tau, \nu)$ and $IG(s, \nu)$ represents an inverted gamma distribution with density function[10]

$$h_{ig}(\lambda | s, \nu) = \left[\left(\frac{s}{2} \right)^{\frac{1}{2}\nu} \Big/ \Gamma\left(\frac{1}{2}\nu \right) \right] \lambda^{-\frac{1}{2}(\nu+2)} \exp -\frac{s}{2\lambda} \tag{52}$$

for $\lambda > 0$, $s > 0$ and $\nu > 0$. Properties for the IG distribution and selection of a distribution for λ_0 are discussed in an appendix. For the ease of exposition, all constants which have no bearing on the actual computations – such as those which are included between brackets in equation (52) – are deleted from the notation in the sequel to our discussion.

The function ϕ_t associated with equations (50) and (51) is given by

$$\phi_t(\Lambda_t; \delta) \propto (\gamma + \tau\lambda_{t-1})^{\frac{1}{2}\nu} \cdot \lambda_t^{-\frac{1}{2}(\nu+3)} \cdot \exp\left[-\frac{1}{2\lambda_t}(\gamma + y_t^2 + \tau\lambda_{t-1}) \right]. \tag{53}$$

Our first task is that of factorizing ϕ_t into a (sequential) initial sampler p_t^0 and a remainder function g_t^0. A "natural" choice for p_t^0 would be the latent process itself, as given in equation (51). In the present case, however, examination of ϕ_t immediately suggests using for p_t^0 an IG distribution with parameters $(\gamma + y_t^2 + \tau\lambda_{t-1}, \nu + 1)$, whence

$$p_t^0(\lambda_t | \lambda_{t-1}, \delta) \propto (\gamma + y_t^2 + \tau\lambda_{t-1})^{\frac{1}{2}(\nu+1)} \cdot \lambda_t^{-\frac{1}{2}(\nu+3)} \cdot \exp\left[-\frac{1}{2\lambda_t}(\gamma + y_t^2 + \tau\lambda_{t-1}) \right]$$

$$\tag{54}$$

$$g_t^0(\Lambda_t; \delta) \propto (\gamma + \tau\lambda_{t-1})^{\frac{1}{2}\nu} \cdot (\gamma + y_t^2 + \tau\lambda_{t-1})^{-\frac{1}{2}(\nu+1)}. \tag{55}$$

It also appears that K_t, the set of density kernels from which an "efficient" kernel will be selected, should itself consist of IG density kernels (we shall argue in section 4.2 below that it generally helps to select for K_t a set of density kernels which comprises the latent process itself). We do not choose

---

[9] Bayesians, in particular, would immediately recognize that an Inverted Gamma distribution for λ_t constitutes a "natural" complement to equation (50). Such distributions are widely used as "Natural Conjugate" priors for unknown variances in regression models (see, for example, Zellner (1971)).

[10] The implied restriction that $\gamma + \tau\lambda_{t-1} > 0$ is "non-binding" for *all* calculations which are reported in section 4.

a specific parametric representation of K_t at this stage of the discussion as an operational characterization thereof naturally emerges from our subsequent analysis.

(i) **Period T** Note that ϕ_T already is in the form of an IG density kernel with parameters $(\gamma + y_T^2 + \tau\lambda_{T-1}, \nu+1)$. Therefore, no optimization is required and an efficient choice for k_T is given by

$$k_T(\Lambda_T; \delta) \equiv \phi_T(\Lambda_T; \delta). \tag{56}$$

It follows immediately that, except for irrelevant constants, χ_T is given by

$$\chi_T(\Lambda_{T-1}; \delta) \propto g_T(\Lambda_{T-1}; \delta) \tag{57}$$

where g_T has been defined in equation (55).

(ii) **Period t** $(t: T-1 \searrow 0)$ It will appear by recursion that $\chi_{t+1}(\Lambda_t; \delta)$ only depends on λ_t (and δ). Furthermore, as mentioned earlier, ϕ_t is in the form of an IG density kernel. Finally, products of IG density kernels are themselves IG density kernels. These considerations immediately suggest parametrizing k_t in the following way

$$k_t(\Lambda_t; \alpha_t) \equiv \phi_t(\Lambda_t; \delta) . \kappa_t(\lambda_t; \alpha_t) \tag{58}$$

where[11]

$$k_t(\lambda_t; \alpha_t) = \lambda^{-\frac{1}{2}a_t} . \exp\left[-\frac{1}{2}\left(b_t + \frac{c_t}{\lambda_t} \right) \right] \tag{59}$$

with $\alpha_t' = (a_t, b_t, c_t)$. This specific characterization of k_t offers the advantage that, as we substitute equation (58) into equation (48), ϕ_t immediately cancels out! We are then left with a particularly simple expression for the objective function $\hat{Q}_{t,N}$ which is given by

$$\hat{Q}_{t,N}(\delta; \alpha_t) = \frac{1}{N} \sum_{i=1}^{N} [\ln \chi_{t+1}(\tilde{\lambda}_{ti}^0; \hat{\alpha}_{t+1,N}^*(\delta))$$
$$- \ln \kappa_t(\tilde{\lambda}_{ti}^0; \alpha_t)]^2 . g_t(\tilde{\lambda}_{t,i}^0; \delta) \tag{60}$$

where g_t and κ_t have been defined in equation (55) and (59) respectively. As for χ_t it is obtained by integration of k_t, as given in (58), with respect to λ_t

$$\chi_t(\lambda_{t-1}; \alpha_t) \propto (\gamma + \tau\lambda_{t-1})^{\frac{1}{2}\nu} . (\gamma + c_t + y_t^2 + \tau\lambda_{t-1})^{-\frac{1}{2}(\nu+a_t+1)}. \tag{61}$$

[11] The motivation for introducing b_t in equation (59) originates from the fact that, as discussed earlier, we have to include an unconstrained intercept in the WLS regression associated with equation (48).

In summary, the two simple steps are required in order to produce an efficient sequential sampler are:

(i) We use the initial sampler $\{p_t^0\}$, as defined in equation (54) to produce a set of N *iid* draws $\{\tilde{\Lambda}_{ti}^0; i: 1 \to N\}$;

(ii) We run the following $T+1$ weighted *linear* LS regression problems for $t: T \backslash 0$

dependent variable: $\ln \chi_{t+1}(\tilde{\lambda}_{ti}^0, \hat{\alpha}_{t+1,N}^*(\delta))$

regressors: constant, $\dfrac{1}{\tilde{\lambda}_{ti}^0}$, $\ln \tilde{\lambda}_{ti}^0$

weights $g_t(\tilde{\lambda}_{ti}^0, \delta)$

with $i: 1 \to N$.

Note that these calculations have to be rerun for all relevant values of θ as produced, for example, by an ML optimization routine. As discussed in RZ – see also McFadden (1989), or Pakes and Pollard (1989) – all calculations are run under a set of common random numbers (CRNs) in order to "smooth" the simulated likelihood function. In other words, our $\{\tilde{\Lambda}_{ti}^0\}$ are all obtained from a common set of $(T+1).N$ uniform draws by "inversion" of the distribution function of our *IG* sampler.[12]

Numerical results will be presented in section 5 below. The example we just discussed is particularly simple. In general we do not expect ϕ_t to belong to K_t. Nevertheless, a weaker form of equation (58) applies to a broad class of DLV models and serves as the basis of the algorithm which is discussed in section 4.2 below.

In order to introduce this more general case, consider how the computation we just described would be affected if we chose the latent process itself, as given in (51), as our initial sampler instead of p_t in equation (54). Equations (54) and (55) would be replaced by

$$\tilde{p}_t^0(\lambda_t | \lambda_{t-1}, \delta) \propto (\gamma + \tau \lambda_{t-1})^{\frac{1}{2}\nu} \cdot \lambda_t^{-\frac{1}{2}(\nu+2)} \cdot \exp\left[-\frac{1}{2\lambda_t}(\gamma + \tau \lambda_{t-1})\right] \quad (62)$$

$$\tilde{g}_t^0(\Lambda_t; \delta) \propto \lambda_t^{-\frac{1}{2}} \exp\left(-\frac{y_t^2}{2\lambda_t}\right). \quad (63)$$

If for some reason (related, for example, to the availability of a preprogrammed algorithm) we were to recognize that $\tilde{p}_t^0$ is in the form of an *IG* kernel, while ignoring that this is also true for $\tilde{g}_t^0$, we might replace k_t in equation (58) by

---

[12] As discussed, for example, in Devroye (1986), "inversion" constitutes a (relatively) inefficient technique for the generation of *IG* random variables. In our experience this inefficiency is more than compensated for by the gain in the smoothness of the simulated likelihood function and, furthermore, can be greatly reduced by judicious usage of interpolation applied to a precomputed table of auxiliary fractiles.

$$\tilde{k}_t(\Lambda_t;\tilde{\alpha}_t) \equiv \tilde{p}_t^0(\Lambda_t;\delta)\kappa_t(\lambda_t;\tilde{\alpha}_t) \tag{64}$$

where κ_t has been defined in (59). Under these changes ϕ_t no longer cancels out in equation (48), but $\tilde{p}_t^0$ does. Therefore, we would now use a weighted linear LS with dependent variable $\ln[\chi_{t+1}.\tilde{g}_{t}^0]$, same regressors as before, and weights $\tilde{g}_t^0$. Since, however, $\tilde{g}_t^0$ actually is in the form of an IG kernel, it will be the case that the optimal values $\hat{\alpha}_t$ in the initial regression and $\hat{\tilde{\alpha}}_t$ in the modified one will be related in the following way

$$\tilde{a}_t = \hat{a}_t + 1 \qquad \tilde{b}_t = \hat{b}_t \qquad \tilde{c}_t = \hat{c}_t + y_t^2 \tag{65}$$

Actual MC estimates would differ in finite samples owing to the change of initial sampler and weight function. In other words, except for MC small samples fluctuations, the optimal kernel k_t and its integrating constant χ_t inherently are invariant relative to the change from p_t to $\tilde{p}_t$. In practice p_t turns out to be more "efficient" than $\tilde{p}_t$ in delivering a close approximation to the optimal sampler under (very) small Ns.

4.2   An operational algorithm

The example we just discussed indicates that the simplicity of the proposed algorithm depends upon the choice of K_t, the class of density kernels from which an efficient sampler is to be selected. The following two conditions play a useful role in our design:

(1) We should aim at selecting K_ts which contain kernels that are good functional approximations to the ϕ_ts themselves. More specifically, it ought to be the case that, for relevant values of δ, there exist $\alpha_t^1(\delta)$s in A_t such that

$$\phi_t(\Lambda_t;\delta) = k_t(\Lambda_t;\alpha_t^1(\delta)) \cdot \Gamma_t(\Lambda_t;\delta) \tag{66}$$

where Γ_t are as "simple" functions of Λ_t as possible. (If, in particular $\phi_t \in K_t$, as in the example we discussed above, then $\Gamma_t \equiv 1$.) More generally, there exist a broad class of models which can be factorized according to equation (4) and for which the "measurement" process which transforms the latent λ_ts into observable y_ts takes (very) simple forms. Under such circumstances we should select K_ts which contain the latent process itself and define k_t and Γ_t accordingly as

$$k_t(\Lambda_t;\alpha_t^1(\delta)) = \phi(\lambda_t|Y_{t-1},\Lambda_{t-1},\theta) \tag{67}$$

$$\Gamma_t(\Lambda_t;\delta) = \phi(y_t|Y_{t-1},\Lambda_t,\theta) \tag{68}$$

(2) K_t should be "closed under multiplication" in the sense of DeGroot (1970, section 9.3).

Definition 1 A class $K = \{k(\cdot;\alpha); \alpha \epsilon A\}$ of density kernels is closed under multiplication if and only if, for any two α_1 and α_2 in A, there exists an α_3 in A such that

$$k(\cdot;\alpha_3) \propto k(\cdot;\alpha_1) . k(\cdot;\alpha_2). \tag{69}$$

We shall use the following notation to represent the operator which maps (α_1, α_2) into α_3 via transformation (69)

$$\alpha_3 = \alpha_1 * \alpha_2. \tag{70}$$

Definition 1 plays a central role in Bayesian statistics as the cornerstone of the concept of "natural conjugate" prior density. It is satisfied for a broad range of distributions from the exponential family.[13] If K_t is closed under multiplication and if equation (66) holds, we can factorize the approximating kernel k_t in equation (45) as

$$k_t(\Lambda_t; \alpha_t^*(\delta)) = k_t(\Lambda_t; \alpha_t^1(\delta)) \cdot k_t(\Lambda_t; \alpha_t^0). \tag{71}$$

It follows that $k_t(.; \alpha_t^1(\delta))$ cancels out in the objective function (48). Our "efficient" choice for α_t^* is then given by

$$\hat{\alpha}_{t,N}^*(\delta) = \alpha_t^1(\delta) * \hat{\alpha}_{t,N}^0(\delta) \tag{72}$$

$$\hat{\alpha}_{t,N}^0(\delta) = \underset{\alpha_t^0 \epsilon A_t}{\arg\min} [\hat{Q}_{t,N}(\delta; \alpha_t^0)] \tag{73}$$

$$\hat{Q}_{t,N}(\delta; \alpha_t^0) = \frac{1}{N} \sum_{i=1}^{N} [\ln\Gamma_t(\tilde{\Lambda}_{ti}^0; \delta) + \ln\chi_{t+1}(\tilde{\Lambda}_{ti}^0; \hat{\alpha}_{t+1,N}^*(\delta))$$
$$- \ln k_t(\tilde{\Lambda}_{ti}^0; \alpha_t^0)]^2 g_t^0(\tilde{\Lambda}_{ti}^0; \delta) \tag{74}$$

where the $\tilde{\Lambda}_{ti}^0$s are subsets of a common set $\{\tilde{\Lambda}_{Ti}^0; i: 1 \to N\}$ of *iid* draws from p_0, and χ_{t+1} denotes the integrating constant of k_t as given by equation (44).

As illustrated by the example discussed in section 4.1 and by the numerical results which are provided in section 5 below, the algorithm described by equations (72)–(74) is easy to program, fast, and very efficient, in particular for DLV models characterized by a simple measurement process.

The algorithm we just described differs from that proposed by DR in two key respects: (1) It is not restricted to Gaussian samplers, and; (2) the objective function used by DR differs from equation (74) in that it does *not* include the factors χ_{t+1} and g_t^0.

---

[13] As shown, e.g., by DeGroot (1970, section 9.3), if the family of density kernels $\{f_n(\cdot|\omega); \omega\epsilon\Omega\}$ has a sufficient statistic T_n of fixed dimension, i.e., if there exists a function ν_n such that

$$f_n(x_1, \ldots, x_n | \omega) \propto \nu_n[T_n(x_1, \ldots, x_n); \omega]$$

and if ν_n is integrable w.r.t. t, then there exists a density function $g(\cdot|t,n)$ on Ω such that

$$g(\omega|t,n) \propto \nu_n(t;\omega)$$

and the family consisting of all such gs is closed under multiplication.

As discussed in greater details in RZ, the omission of χ_{t+1} from equation (74) is inconsequential for *Gaussian* samplers as χ_{t+1} itself is in the form of a Gaussian kernel for λ_t. In general, however, it will not be the case that $\chi_{t+1} \in K_t$, which precisely is why the DR algorithm cannot be generalized as such to a broader class of samplers.

The omission of g_t^0 implies that the DR algorithm is not as efficient as ours in its search for an optimized sampler (for the very same reason as OLS estimates are inefficient relative to GLS estimates in the presence of heteroskedasticity) which is why it requires several rounds of computation. In contrast our algorithm produces an efficient MC sampler in a single round of computation (though a second round might occasionally prove useful when the initial sampler p_0 is particularly inefficient and N is very small).

5   Numerical and statistical standard deviations

There are a broad range of classical and Bayesian techniques which require (numerical) evaluation of the likelihood function. In the present paper we restrict our attention to maximum likelihood (ML) estimation. A simulated ML estimator is one which maximizes the (log) likelihood function, as defined in equation (29). We shall draw a clear distinction between the actual (not feasible) ML estimator $\hat{\theta}(Y_T)$ and its simulated counterpart $\hat{\theta}_S(Y_T)$, respectively defined as

$$\hat{\theta}(Y_T) = \operatorname*{argmin}_{\theta \in \Theta} L(\theta; Y_T) \tag{75}$$

$$\hat{\theta}_S(Y_T) = \operatorname*{argmin}_{\theta \in \Theta} \bar{L}_S^*(\theta; Y_T) \tag{76}$$

where $\bar{L}_S^*$ has been defined in equation (29).

It is common practice in the literature to treat $\hat{\theta}_S(Y_T)$ as an estimate of θ itself. As discussed in Richard (1995), such practice confuses the issue of assessing the *statistical properties of* $\hat{\theta}(Y_T)$ as an *estimator of* θ with that of evaluating the *numerical accuracy of* $\hat{\theta}_S(Y_T)$ as an *estimate of* $\hat{\theta}(Y_T)$.

Therefore, in the application which follows (as well as in future applications of our techniques) we propose to compute two distinct standard deviations for simulated ML estimators: (1) an MC standard deviation, whereby $\hat{\theta}_S(Y_T)$ is treated as a function of the auxiliary MC samples and Y_T is kept fixed and; (2) an estimate of the statistical standard deviation of $\hat{\theta}(Y_T)$ obtained by treating $\hat{\theta}_S(Y_T)$ as a function of Y_T under a fixed set of common random numbers.

Asymptotic formulas for these two sets of standard deviations can be found in RZ (1995). However, their evaluation requires a fair amount of (additional) programming work. We find it easier (and often more relevant) to compute finite sample standard deviations based upon additional auxiliary MC simulations.

MC standard deviations are obtained by keeping Y_T fixed and rerunning our *entire* algorithm (including the search for an efficient sampler) under different sets of random draws for Λ_T accounting, thereby, for the overall MC uncertainty induced by our procedure.

MC estimates of the statistical standard deviations of $\hat{\theta}(Y_T)$ are obtained by generating auxiliary Y_T samples from the model itself and each time rerunning the entire algorithm under a *common* set of random numbers for the Λs.[14]

As we shall illustrate below, such auxiliary simulations are far less computer intensive than one might expect in light of the high efficiency of our algorithm. More importantly, they only require minor adjustments to the base line algorithm.

6   Numerical illustration

In order to evaluate the performance of our algorithm we use it to compute simulated ML estimates for the parameters of the stochastic volatility model defined by equations (50) and (51), using a fairly large data set ($T = 1,447$) consisting of IBM daily stock price changes for the period from January 9, 1982 to March 31, 1987.

All calculations are based upon ten MC replications only ($N = S = 10$) which, as we shall see below, suffices to produce accurate MC estimates under "efficient" sampling at least.

Each "run of computation" which is reported in tables 2.1 and 2.2 consists of the search for a simulated ML estimate and includes, therefore, as many likelihood evaluations as necessitated for convergence. Each run is based upon a single $10 \times 1,447$ matrix $\tilde{U}$ of uniform random draws from which inverted gamma CRNs are obtained by "inversion." Calculation of MC standard deviations requires using a different $\tilde{U}$ for each.

In table 2.1, we report ML estimates obtained by maximization of the simulated likelihood given by equation (9), together with MC standard deviations.[15] (Statistical standard deviations were not computed as the

---

[14] Specifically we compute a different "efficient" sampler for each auxiliary Y_T, θ. The corresponding sets of $\tilde{\Lambda}_{ti}$ are all obtained by inversion of a common set of random numbers. We find this procedure to be preferable (by far) to one whereby a common sampler would be used for all Y_Ts. Our procedure secures maximal numerical efficiency at all stages of the auxiliary MC simulations (as we shall illustrate below, statistical standard deviations far exceed MC standard deviations).

[15] Actually, these MC standard deviations are underestimated since we did set -0.0001 as a lower bound for τ and 67.0 as an upper bound for ν, in order to avoid numerical problems.

Table 2.1. *Simulated ML estimates with natural sampling*

	γ	τ	ν	$\gamma/(\nu-2)$	$\tau/(\nu-2)$
	0.011410	−0.0001	66.8655	0.0001759	0.00000
	0.007142	−0.1658	42.2482	0.0001774	0.00412
	0.007056	0.7178	42.2537	0.0001753	0.01783
	0.004975	3.8307	33.5841	0.0001575	0.12129
	0.007033	1.7653	44.0172	0.0001674	0.04201
	0.005206	3.3973	34.0815	0.0001623	0.10590
	0.011482	−0.0001	67.0000	0.0001766	0.00000
	0.005621	−0.0001	33.5000	0.0001784	0.00000
	0.010521	5.5777	67.0000	0.0001619	0.08581
	0.007225	−0.0001	42.5622	0.0001781	0.00000
mean	0.007767	1.5454	47.3112	0.0001711	0.03769
MC s.d.	0.002353	1.9262	13.4033	0.0000076	0.04602

Note: $N = S = 10$; $T = 1,447$.

reported results are useless anyway.) These results confirm the frequent impracticability of "natural" importance sampling evaluation of likelihood functions, as documented in the literature – see, e.g., McFadden (1989). Moreover, the regression coefficient of λ_t on λ_{t-1}, which equals $\tau.(\nu-2)^{-1}$ is dramatically as well as significantly downward biased (as seen by comparison with the more accurate results in table 2.2 or with results found in the literature for similar models). Each run of computation in table 2.1 requires of the order of 14 minutes of CPU on a UNIX DEC 5000/240 workstation.

In table 2.2, we report ML estimates obtained from an "efficient" sampler obtained by application of the algorithm described in section 4.1. (The results are similar whether we draw the "initial" sample $\{\tilde{\Lambda}_{ti}^0\}$ from p_t^0 or from $\tilde{p}_t^0$ as defined in equations (54) and (62), respectively.) Note that, in spite of the small number of replications ($N = S = 10$), the simulated ML estimates are numerically quite accurate (particularly those of ν, τ, and τ. $(\nu-2)^{-1}$ which are the key coefficients of our model). We could easily achieve greater accuracy by increasing S. We did not do so since statistical standard deviations already are at least three times as large as MC standard deviations.

In addition to the fact that the results in table 2.2 are far more accurate than those in table 1, their evaluation only requires of the order of 23 minutes of CPU time for each run (i.e., the net "cost" of implementing our efficient procedure of 9 minutes only of CPU time for each run).

Table 2.2. *Simulated ML estimates with efficient sampling*

	γ	τ	ν	$\gamma/(\nu-2)$	$\tau/(\nu-2)$
	0.000722	42.4865	48.6306	0.0000155	0.91113
	0.000767	42.3839	48.8696	0.0000164	0.90429
	0.000920	42.2840	49.7925	0.0000192	0.88474
	0.000954	42.3479	49.9800	0.0000199	0.88262
	0.000868	42.3597	49.4187	0.0000183	0.89331
	0.000806	42.3741	48.9732	0.0000172	0.90209
	0.000819	42.3691	49.4016	0.0000173	0.89383
	0.000990	42.1223	48.9770	0.0000211	0.87537
	0.000962	42.4506	49.9309	0.0000201	0.88566
	0.000931	42.4504	49.9848	0.0000194	0.88466
	0.000887	42.3376	49.9124	0.0000185	0.88365
	0.000722	42.1088	47.9635	0.0000157	0.91614
	0.000810	42.4976	49.3935	0.0000171	0.89670
	0.001066	42.3289	50.6304	0.0000219	0.87042
	0.000584	42.4080	47.4255	0.0000121	0.93357
	0.001138	42.2803	50.9828	0.0000232	0.86317
	0.000565	42.4864	47.6824	0.0000124	0.93004
	0.000736	41.9340	48.7493	0.0000157	0.89700
	0.000685	42.0434	48.3735	0.0000148	0.90663
	0.000814	42.1450	49.4697	0.0000171	0.88783
mean	0.000835	42.2599	49.2271	0.0000176	0.89514
MC s.d.	0.000148	0.3006	0.9063	0.0000028	0.01781
St s.d	0.000459	3.1054	2.6845	0.0000089	0.05968

Note: $N = S = 10$; $T = 1,447$.

Similar results are reported in DR (1993) and RZ (1995) which fully support the high efficiency of our new algorithm.

7   Conclusion

The results presented in this chapter fully confirm similar findings in DR (1993) and RZ (1995). They unequivocally indicate that, contrary to current wisdom, accurate MC estimates of the likelihood functions of DLV models can be obtained with very small numbers of replications (as low as 10) *provided* one uses efficient samplers, such as the ones produced by our algorithm.

The methods we propose offer three key advantages:
(1) Programming cost is minimum, as it essentially consists of the imple-

mentation of a sequence of simple weighted least squares problems which are applied to artificial data generated from an "initial" sampler (typically the latent process itself).

(2) Relatedly, the algorithm is highly generic. Its base structure does not depend on specific classes of samplers (beyond the requirement that the class under consideration be closed under multiplication which, as we discussed, contributes to the simplicity of our method). Changes in the statistical formulation of the model under scrutiny can easily be accommodated as they only require minor programming adjustments (For example, in RZ (1995), we re-estimate the stochastic volatility model presented in section 4.1 under different distributional assumptions at the cost of minor modifications of our FORTRAN code).

(3) The additional computing cost required for the evaluation of an efficient sampler is small and, moreover, is more than compensated for by the large efficiency gains it produces.

In short, our new acceleration procedure paves the way for routine application of a broad range of (classical *and* Bayesian) likelihood-based inference techniques to DLV models even when sample size is (very) large. It does not render alternative estimation techniques such as the MSM obsolete but it does imply that the choice of an inference procedure no longer is dominated by computational considerations and can be based instead on more fundamental statistical issues (robustness, statistical efficiency, etc.).

Appendix

The inverted-gamma distribution introduced in equation (52) has the following moments (centered at zero)

$$E(\lambda^r) = \frac{\Gamma(\frac{1}{2}\nu - r)}{\Gamma(\frac{1}{2}\nu)} \cdot \left(\frac{s}{2}\right)^r \quad \text{(for } \nu > 2r)$$

whence

$$E(\lambda) = \frac{s}{\nu - 2}\text{(for } \nu > 2), \text{ and } E(\lambda^2) = \frac{s^2}{(\nu - 2)(\nu - 4)}\text{(for } \nu > 4).$$

The first- and second-order conditional moments of $\lambda_t | \lambda_{t-1}$ according to equation (51) are

$$E(\lambda_t | \lambda_{t-1}) = \frac{\gamma + \tau\lambda_{t-1}}{\nu - 2}$$

$$E(\lambda_t^2 | \lambda_{t-1}) = \frac{(\gamma + \tau\lambda_{t-1})^2}{(\nu - 2)(\nu - 4)}$$

whence the stationary first- and second-order moments of λ_t satisfy the equation

$$\mu_1 = \frac{\gamma + \tau\mu_1}{\nu - 2} \text{ if } \nu - 2 > \tau$$

$$\mu_2 = \frac{\gamma^2 + 2\gamma\tau\mu_1 + \tau^2\mu_2}{(\nu - 2)(\nu - 4)} \text{ if } (\nu - 2)(\nu - 4) > \tau^2$$

whence

$$\mu_1 = \frac{\gamma}{\nu - \tau - 2}$$

$$\mu_2 = \frac{\nu + \tau - 2}{(\nu - 2)(\nu - 4) - \tau^2} \cdot \gamma^2.$$

However, the stationary distribution of λ_t is *not* an inverted gamma. Nevertheless (in light of the large sample size) the final results are unaffected if, instead of generating λ_0 from its actual stationary distribution, we generate it from an inverted gamma with parameters s_1 and ν_1 chosen in such a way that

$$\frac{s_1}{\nu_1 - 2} = \mu_1 \text{ and } \frac{s_1^2}{(\nu_1 - 2)(\nu_1 - 4)} = \mu_2.$$

References

Aigner, D.J., C. Hsiao, A. Kapteyn, and T. Wansbeek (1983), "Latent Variables Models in Econometrics," in Z. Griliches and M.D. Intriligator (eds.), *The Handbook of Econometrics*, vol. II, Amsterdam: North-Holland, chapter 23, pp. 1321–1393.

Bollerslev, T. (1986), "Generalized Autoregressive Conditional Heteroskedasticity," *Journal of Econometrics*, 31, 307–327.

Clark, P. (1973), "A Subordinated Stochastic Process Model with Finite Variance for Speculative Process," *Econometrica*, 41, 135–155.

Cox, D.R. and D. Oakes (1984), *Analysis of Survival Data*, London: Chapman and Hall.

Danielson, J. and J.F. Richard (1993), "Accelerated Gaussian Importance Sampler with Application to Dynamic Latent Variable Models," *Journal of Applied Econometrics*, 8, 153–173.

DeGroot, M.H. (1970), *Optimal Statistical Decisions*, New York: McGraw-Hill.

Devroye, L. (1986), *Non-Uniform Random Variate Generation*, New York: Springer Verlag.

Duffie, D. and K.J. Singleton (1989), "Simulated Moments Estimation of Markov Models of Asset Prices", Stanford University mimeo.

Engle, R.F. (1982), "Autoregressive Conditional Heteroskedasticity with Estimates of the Variance of UK Inflation," *Econometrica*, 50, 987–1008.

Epps, T.W. and M.L.O. Epps (1976), "The Stochastic Dependence of Security Price Changes and Transaction Volumes: Implications for the Mixture-of-Distributions Hypothesis," *Econometrica*, 44, 305–321.

Friedman, B.M. and D.I. Laibson (1989), "Economic Implications of Extraordinary Movements in Stock Prices," Brookings Papers on Economic Activity, 2189, 137–189.

Geweke, J. (1989), "Bayesian Inference in Econometric Models using Monte Carlo Integration," *Econometrica*, 57, 1317–1339.

(1994), "Monte Carlo Simulation and Numerical Integration," Federal Reserve Bank of Minneapolis, Working paper no. 526.

Granger, C.W.J. (1969), "Investigating Causal Relations by Econometric Models and Cross-spectral Methods," *Econometrica*, 37, 424–438.

Harvey, A.C. (1990), *Forecasting, Structural Time Series Models and the Kalman Filter*, Cambridge University Press.

Heckman, J.J. (1981), "Statistical Models for Discrete Panel Data," in C.F. Manski and D. McFadden (eds.), *Structural Analysis of Discrete Data with Economic Applications*, Cambridge: MIT Press, chapter 3.

Heckman, J.J. and T.F. McCurdy (1980), "A Life Cycle Model of Female Labor Supply," *Review of Economic Studies*, 47, 47–74.

Hendry, D.F. (1984), "Monte Carlo Experimentation in Econometrics," in Z. Griliches and M.D. Intriligator (eds.), *The Handbook of Econometrics*, vol. II, Amsterdam: North-Holland, chapter 16, pp. 937–976.

Hendry, D.F. and J.F. Richard (1992), "Likelihood Evaluation for Dynamic Latent Variables Models," in H.M. Amman, D.A. Belsley, and L.F. Pau (eds.), *Computational Economics and Econometrics*, Dordrecht: Kluwer Academic, chapter 1.

Kalbfleisch, J.D. and A. Monfort (1979), *The Statistical Analysis of Failure Time Data*, New York: John Wiley.

Kloek, T. and H.K. Van Dijk (1978), "Bayesian Estimates of Equation System Parameters: an Application of Integration by Monte Carlo," *Econometrica*, 46, 1–19.

Laffont, J.J. and A. Monfort (1979), "Disequilibrium Econometrics in Dynamic Models," *Journal of Econometrics*, 11, 353–361.

Maddala, G.S. (1983), "Disequilibrium, Self-selection and Switching Models," in Z. Griliches and M.D. Intriligator (eds.), *The Handbook of Econometrics*, vol. III, Amsterdam: North-Holland, chapter 28, pp. 1633–1688.

McFadden, D. (1989), "A Method of Simulated Moments for Estimation of Discrete Response Models Without Numerical Integration," *Econometrica*, 57, 995–1026.

Melino, A. and S. Turnbull (1990), "Pricing Foreign Currency for Estimation of Discrete Response Models Without Numerical Integration," *Econometrica*, 45, 239–265.

Nelson, D.B. (1991), "Conditional Heteroskedasticity in Asset Returns: A New Approach," *Econometrica*, 59, 347–370.

Pakes, A. and D. Pollard (1989), "Simulation and the Asymptotics of Optimization Estimators," *Econometrica*, 57, 1027–1058.

Quandt, R.E. (1988), *The Econometrics of Disequilibrium*, New York: Basil Blackwell.

(1988), "Econometric Disequilibrium Models," *Econometric Review*, 1, 1–96 (with comments by D.F. Hendry, A. Montfort, and J.-F. Richard).

Richard, J.F. (1995), "Simulation Techniques," in L. Matyas and P. Sevestre (eds.), *The Econometrics of Panel Data Handbook of Theory and Applications*, 2nd edn., Boston: Kluwer Academic.

Richard, J.F. and W. Zhang (1996), "Accelerated Importance Sampling," University of Pittsburgh mimeo.

Tauchen, G.E. and M. Pitts (1983), "The Price Variability-Volume Relationship on Speculative Markets," *Econometrica*, 51, 485–505.

Taylor, S. (1986), *Modelling Financial Time Series*, Chichester: John Wiley.

Zellner, A. (1971), *An Introduction to Bayesian Inference in Econometrics*, New York: John Wiley.

3 Some practical issues in maximum simulated likelihood

Vassilis A. Hajivassiliou

1 Introduction

Estimation of econometric models is often hampered by computational complexity. The likelihood and moment functions that characterize an estimator cannot be computed with sufficient speed and accuracy to make the iterative computational search for the estimator feasible. Recent research has developed a marriage of simulation and estimation methods to overcome these computational obstacles. Generally, such methods sacrifice the efficiency of classical estimators for consistency, with simulation noise causing the efficiency loss. In order to make simulation an attractive technique the number of replications of the simulations must be restricted to small values. Otherwise the repeated computations of the functions required for the iterative solution of the estimators remain unmanageable.

After presenting an overview of simulation-based estimation of limited dependent variable models (LDV) in section 2, this chapter explores methods of recapturing the efficiency property of estimators that rely on simulation in section 3. The techniques exploit estimation methods that do not require iterative computation, which are already familiar from classical applications. The leading example is linearized maximum likelihood estimation (LMLE) discussed in subsection 3.1, which computes an asymptotically efficient estimator from an initial $\sqrt{N}$-consistent estimator. Because simulation methods for estimation do offer such initial estimators, one can apply the LMLE technique. In addition, because the LMLE does not require iteration, one can apply simulation with relatively high numbers of replications to reduce the simulation noise to potentially negligible levels. In section 3.2, I discuss the optimal determination of the number of simulations to employ in practice for this type of estimators.

In section 4, I first explain some practical computational advantages of maximum simulated likelihood (MSL) over the method of simulated

Some ideas in this paper developed after long discussion with Paul Ruud.

moments (MSM) and then construct in 4.2 a diagnostic test for adequacy of number of simulations employed to guarantee negligible bias for the MSL. In section 4.3, I provide some evidence on the computational speed of the GHK simulator as a function of (a) the dimension of the problem and (b) the number of simulations employed in a vectorized context. I outline how one can derive a similar approach for checking the adequacy of the number of Gibbs resamplings in simulation estimation methods that employ this technique.

Given the computation of estimators, classical hypothesis test statistics typically do not involve iterative computation either. Therefore, I also show in section 5 how to suitably introduce simulation into classical hypothesis testing methods and provide test statistics (simulated Wald, Lagrange multiplier, and likelihood ratio tests in 5.1–5.3) that are free of influential simulation noise. This provides improvements in power comparable to the improvements in efficiency of estimators. Examples are given in subsection 5.4 for hypotheses of major interest in LDV models.

Finally, I explain in section 6 how simulation-variance-reduction techniques, most notably antithetics, can improve even further the practical performance of the GHK simulator. Section 7 concludes.

2   Estimation in LDV models

2.1   The computational complexity of LDV models

Consider the problem of maximum likelihood estimation given the N observations on the vector of random variables y drawn from a population with cumulative distribution function (c.d.f.) $F(\theta, Y) = \Pr\{y \le Y\}$.[1] Let the corresponding density function with respect to Lebesgue measure be $f(\theta, y)$. The density f is a parametric function and the parameter vector θ is unknown, finite-dimensional, and $\theta \epsilon \Theta$, where Θ is a compact subset of $\mathbf{R}^K$. Estimation of θ by maximum likelihood (ML) involves the maximization of the log likelihood function $\ell_N(\theta) \equiv \Sigma_{n=1}^N \log f(\theta; y_n)$ over Θ. Often, finding the root of a system of normal equations $\nabla_\theta \ell_N(\theta) = 0$ is equivalent. In the limited dependent variable models that I consider here, F will be a mixture of discrete and continuous distributions, so that f may consist of non-zero probabilities for discrete values of y and continuous probability densities for intervals of y. These functions are generally difficult to compute because they involve multivariate integrals that do not have closed forms, accurate approximations, or rapid numerical solutions. As a result, estimation of θ by classical methods is effectively infeasible.

[1] The discussion in this section follows closely the exposition in Hajivassiliou and Ruud (1994). See that study for a deeper and more extensive theoretical analysis of the problem.

In general, and particularly in LDV models, one can represent the data generating process for y as an "incomplete data" or "partial observability" process in which the observed data vector y is an indirect observation on a latent vector y^*. In such a case, y^* cannot be recovered from the *censored* random variable y. Let Y^* be a random variable from a population with c.d.f. $F(Y^*)$ and support $\mathbf{A}$. Let $\mathbf{B}$ be the support of the random variable $Y = \tau(Y^*)$ where $\tau: \mathbf{A} \rightarrow \mathbf{B}$ is not invertible. Then Y is a *censored* random variable.

In LDV models, τ is often called the "observation rule"; and though it may not be monotonic, τ is generally piece-wise continuous. An important characteristic of censored sampling is that no observations are missing. Observations on y^* are merely abbreviated or summarized, hence the descriptive term "censored." Let $\mathbf{A} \subseteq \mathbf{R}^M$ and $\mathbf{B} \subseteq \mathbf{R}^J$.

The latent c.d.f. $F(\theta, Y^*)$ for y^* is related to the observed c.d.f. for y by the integral equation

$$F(\theta; Y) = \int_{\{y^* \mid \tau(y^*) \le Y\}} dF(\theta; y^*). \tag{1}$$

The p.d.f. for y is the function that integrates to $F(\theta; Y)$. In this chapter, integration refers to the Lebesgue–Stieltjes integral and the p.d.f. is a generalized derivative of the c.d.f. This means that the p.d.f. has discrete and continuous components. Everywhere in the support of Y where F is differentiable, the p.d.f. can be obtained by ordinary differentiation

$$f(\theta; Y) = \frac{\partial^J F(\theta; Y)}{\partial Y_1, \dots, \partial Y_J}. \tag{2}$$

In the LDV models I consider, F generally has a small number of discontinuities in some dimensions of Y so that F is not differentiable everywhere. At a point of discontinuity Y^d, I can obtain the generalized p.d.f. by partitioning Y into the elements in which F is differentiable, $\{Y_1, \dots, Y_{J'}\}$ say, and the remaining elements $\{Y_{J'+1}, \dots, Y_J\}$ in which the discontinuity occurs. The p.d.f. then has the form

$$f(\theta; Y) = \frac{\partial^{J'}}{\partial Y_1, \dots, \partial Y_{J'}} \cdot [F(\theta; Y) - F(\theta; Y - 0)]$$

$$= f(\theta; Y_1, \dots, Y_{J'}) \cdot \Pr\{Y_j = Y_j^d; j > J' \mid \theta; Y_1, \dots, Y_{J'}\} \tag{3}$$

where the discrete jump $F(\theta; Y) - F(\theta; Y - 0)$ reflects the non-trivial probability of the event $\{Y_j = Y_j^d; j > J'\}$.[2]

---

[2] The height of the discontinuity is denoted by
$$F(\theta; Y) - F(\theta; Y - 0) \equiv \lim_{\epsilon \downarrow 0} F(\theta; Y) - F(\theta; Y - \epsilon).$$

It is these probabilities, the discrete components of the p.d.f., that pose computational obstacles to classical estimation.One must carry out multivariate integration and differentiation in (1)–(3) to obtain the likelihood for the observed data – see the examples in Hajivassiliou and Ruud (1994) for a clear illustration of this problem. Because accurate numerical approximations are unavailable, this integration is often handled by such general purpose numerical methods as quadrature. But the speed and accuracy of quadrature is inadequate to make the computation of the MLE practical except in special cases.

2.2   Score functions

For models with censoring, the score for θ can be written in two ways which I will use to motivate two approaches to approximation of the score by simulation

$$s(\theta;y) \equiv \nabla_\theta \ln f(\theta;y) = \frac{\nabla_\theta f(\theta;y)}{f(\theta;y)} \tag{4}$$

$$= E[\nabla_\theta \ln f(\theta;y^*)|y] \tag{5}$$

where ∇_θ is an operator that represents partial differentiation with respect to the elements of θ. The ratio expression in (4) is simply the derivative of the log likelihood and simulation can be applied to the numerator and denominator separately. The second expression (5), the conditional expectation of the score of the latent log likelihood, can be simulated as a single expectation if $\nabla_\theta \ln f(\theta;y^*)$ is tractable. Ruud (1986), van Praag and Hop (1987), and Hajivassiliou and McFadden (1997) have noted alternative ways of writing score functions for the purpose of estimation by simulation.

2.3   Simulation-based estimation of LDV models

I begin with the application of simulation to approximating the log likelihood function. Next, I consider the simulation of moment functions. Because of the simulation biases that naturally arise in the log likelihood approach, the unbiased simulation of moment functions and the method of moments is an alternative approach. Finally, I discuss simulation of the score function. Solving the normal equations of ML estimation is a special case of the method of moments and simulating the score function offers the potential for efficient estimation.

Throughout this section, I will assume that we are working with models for which the maximum likelihood estimator is well behaved. In particular, I suppose that the usual regularity conditions are met, ensuring that the ML estimator is the most efficient CUAN estimator.

2.3.1   Simulation of the log-likelihood function

One of the earliest applications of simulation to estimation was the general computation of multivariate integrals in such likelihoods as that of the multinomial probit by Monte Carlo integration. Crude Monte Carlo simulation can approximate the probabilities of the multinomial probit to any desired degree of accuracy, so that the corresponding *maximum simulated likelihood* (MSL) estimator can approximate the ML estimator.

Definition 1 (Maximum simulated likelihood) Let the log likelihood function for the unknown parameter vector θ given the sample of observations $(y_n, n = 1, \ldots, N)$ be

$$\ell_N(\theta) \equiv \sum_{n=1}^{N} [\log f(\theta; y_n)]$$

and let $\hat{f}(\theta; y, \omega)$ be an unbiased simulator so that $f(\theta; y) = E_\omega[\hat{f}(\theta; y, \omega)|y]$ where ω is a simulated vector of R random variates. The maximum simulated likelihood estimator is

$$\hat{\theta}_{MSL} \equiv \arg \max_\theta \tilde{\ell}_N(\theta)$$

where

$$\tilde{\ell}_N(\theta) \equiv \sum_{n=1}^{N} [\log \hat{f}(\theta; y_n, \omega_n)]$$

for some given simulation sequence $\{\omega_n\}$.

It is important to note that the MSL estimator is conditional on the sequence of simulators $\{\omega_n\}$. For both computational stability and asymptotic distribution theory, it is important that the simulations do not change with the parameter values (see McFadden (1989) and Pakes and Pollard (1989) for an explanation of this point).

Note also that unbiased simulation of the likelihood function is neither necessary nor sufficient for consistent MSL estimation. Because the estimator is a non-linear function (through optimization) of the simulator, the MSL estimator will generally be a biased simulation of the MLE even when the criterion function of estimation is simulated without bias because

$$E[\tilde{\ell}(\theta)] = \ell(\theta) \not\Rightarrow E[\arg \max_\theta \tilde{\ell}(\theta)] = \arg \max_\theta \tilde{\ell}(\theta).$$

Note also that while unbiased simulation of the likelihood function is often straightforward, unbiased simulation of the *log* likelihood is generally infeasible. The logarithmic transformation of the intractable function introduces a non-linearity that cannot be overcome simply. However, to obtain an estimator with the same *probability limit* as the MLE, a sufficient characteristic of a simulator for the log likelihood is that its sample average converges to the same limit as the sample average log likelihood. Only by reducing the error of a simulator for the log likelihood function to zero at a sufficiently rapid rate with sample size can one expect to obtain a consistent estimator.

For LDV models with censoring, the generic likelihood simulator $\tilde{f}(\theta;y_n,\omega_n)$ is the average of R replications of one of the simulation methods described elsewhere

$$\tilde{f}(\theta;y_n,\omega_n) \equiv \frac{1}{R}\sum_{r=1}^{R}\tilde{f}(\theta;y_n,\omega_{nr}).$$

The simulation error will generally be $O_P(1/R)$. Thus, a common approach to approximating the log likelihood function with sufficient accuracy is increasing the number of replications per observation R with the sample size N. This statistical approach is in contrast to a strictly numerical approach of setting R high enough to achieve a specified numerical accuracy independent of sample size.

2.3.2   Simulation of moment functions

The simulation of the log likelihood is an appealing approach to applying simulation to estimation, but this approach must overcome the inherent simulation bias that forces one to increase R with the sample size. Instead of simulating the log likelihood function, one can stimulate moment functions. When they are linear in the simulations, moment functions can be simulated easily without bias. The direct consequence is that the simulation bias in the limiting distribution of an estimator is also zero, making the need to increase the number of simulations per observation with sample size unnecessary. This was a key insight of McFadden (1989) and Pakes and Pollard (1989).

Method of moments (MOM) estimators have a simple structure. Such estimators are generally constructed from "residuals" that are the differences between observed random variables y and their conditional expectations. These expectations are known functions of the conditioning variables x and the unknown parameter vector θ to be estimated, let $E(y|x,\theta) \equiv \mu(\theta;x)$. Moment equations are built up by multiplying the residuals by various weights or instrumental variable functions, z_n, and specifying the estimator as the parameter values which equate the sample average of these products with zero. The MOM estimator $\hat{\theta}_{MOM}$ is defined by

$$\frac{1}{N}\sum_{n=1}^{N}z_n(X,\hat{\theta}_{MOM})[y_n - \mu(\hat{\theta}_{MOM};x_n)] = 0. \tag{6}$$

Simulation has an affinity with the MOM. Substituting an unbiased, finite-variance simulator for the conditional expectation $\mu(\theta;x_n)$ does not alter the essential convergence properties of these sample moment equations. I therefore consider the class of estimators generated by the *method of simulated moments* (MSM).

Definition 2 (Method of simulated moments) Let $\tilde{\mu}(\theta;x,\omega) = 1/R\sum_{r=1}^{R}\mu(\tilde{\theta};x_n,\omega_r)$ be an unbiased simulator so that $\mu(\theta;x) = E[\tilde{\mu}(\theta;x,\omega)|x]$ where ω is a simulated random variable. The method of simulated moments estimator is

$$\hat{\theta}_{MSM} \equiv \arg\min \|\tilde{s}_N(\theta)\|$$

where

$$\tilde{s}_N(\theta) \equiv 1/N\sum_{n=1}^{N}z_n(\theta)[y_n - \tilde{\mu}(\theta;x_n,\omega_n)] \tag{7}$$

for some sequence $\{\omega_n\}$.

2.3.3 Simulation of the score function

Interest in the efficiency of estimators naturally leads to attempts to construct an efficient MSM estimator. The obvious way to do this is to simulate the score function as a set of simulated moment equations. Within the LDV framework however, unbiased simulation of the score with a finite number of operations is not possible with simple censored simulators; the efficient weights are non-linear functions of the objects that require simulation. Nevertheless, it may be possible with the aid of simulation to construct good approximations that offer improvements in efficiency over simpler MSM estimators.

There is an alternative approach based on truncated simulation. It was shown in Hajivassiliou and Ruud (1994) that every score function can be expressed as the expectation of the score of a latent data generating process taken conditional on the observed data. In the particular case of normal LDV models, this conditional expectation is taken over a truncated multivariate normal distribution and the latent score is the score of a multivariate normal distribution. Simulations from the truncated normal distribution can replace the expectation operator to obtain unbiased simulators of the score function.

I define the *method of simulated scores* as follows,[3]

Definition 3 (Method of simulated scores) Let the log likelihood function for the unknown parameter vector θ given the sample observations

---

[3] The term was coined by Hajivassiliou and McFadden (1998).

$(y_n, n = 1, \ldots, N)$ be $\ell_N(\theta) \equiv \sum_{n=1}^{N} \log f(\theta; y_n)$.   Let $\tilde{\mu}(\theta; y_n, \omega_n) =$
$1/R \sum_{r=1}^{R} \tilde{\mu}(\theta; y_n, \omega_{nr})$ *be an asymptotically (in R) unbiased simulator of the*
score function $s(\theta; y) \equiv \nabla \ln f(\theta; y)$ where ω is a simulated random variable. The
method of simulated scores *estimator is* $\theta_{MSS} \equiv \arg \min_{\theta \in \Theta} \| \tilde{s}_N(\theta) \|$ *where*
$\tilde{s}_N(\theta) \equiv 1/N \sum_{n=1}^{N} \tilde{\mu}(\theta; y_n, \omega_n)$ *for some sequence* $\{ \omega_n \}$.

Truncated simulation of the score The truncated simulation methods provide unbiased simulators of the LDV score (4). Such simulation would be ideal, because R can be held fixed, thus leading to fast estimation procedures. The problem is that these truncated simulation methods pose new problems for the MSS estimators that use them.

The accept/reject (A/R) method provides simulations that are discontinuous in the parameters. A/R simulation delivers the first element in a simulated sequence that falls into a region which depends on the parameters under estimation. As a result, changes in the parameter values cause discrete changes as to which element in the sequence is accepted (see Hajivassiliou and McFadden (1997) and McFadden and Ruud (1992) for treatments of the special asymptotic distribution theory for such simulation estimators). Briefly described, this distribution theory requires a degree of smoothness in the estimator with respect to the parameters that permits such discontinuities but allows familiar linear approximations in the limit (see Ruud (1991) for an illustrative application).

The Gibbs resampling simulation method can also be used here. This method is continuous in the parameters provided that one uses a continuous univariate truncated normal simulation scheme. But this simulation method also has a drawback: strictly applied, each simulation requires an infinite number of resampling rounds. In practice, Gibbs resampling is truncated and applied as an approximation. The limited Monte Carlo evidence that I have seen suggests that such approximation is reliable.

3   Statistically efficient simulation-based estimation

In this section, I discuss various approaches to obtaining statistically fully efficient simulation estimators that are computationally feasible. Often, simulation estimation methods sacrifice the efficiency of classical estimators for consistency, with simulation noise causing the efficiency loss. I show how one can recapture the efficiency property for estimators that rely on simulation by exploiting two-step estimation methods that are familiar in classical applications. A critical issue is the selection of a value of the number of replications to attain a negligible level of asymptotic efficiency loss due to simulation.

3.1   Two-step estimators

In LMLE, the score and the information need only be evaluated once (or very few times). This is in contrast to obtaining the simulation estimators themselves through some iterative scheme, which requires the repeated evaluation of simulated functions. Whenever functions to be simulated only need to be evaluated once, then a large number of replications, R, can be used in the simulation. This implies, of course, that the additional noise contributed by simulation can be negligible (assuming that, as is typically the case, the simulators are consistent, as R grows without bound, for the true (expressions). As a result, all the standard asymptotic properties of estimators and test statistics *not based on simulation* still hold.

Hence, an efficient estimation procedure can be outlined as follows: in step 1, I obtain a consistent but inefficient estimator of θ_0, using MSM for example. In step 2, a LMLE step is carried out, using the optimal score expressions corresponding to full-information maximum likelihood, using a very high number of operations in approximating these score expressions. "Operations" in this context means number of simulations if the MSL version of the scores is used, and Gibbs resamplings if the MSS version is used. This is computationally appealing, since the second-step (intractable) optimal scores need to be approximated only once.   •

Let us explain this approach in greater detail. When the MLE $\hat{\theta}_N$ is the root of the score equations

$$E_N[s(\hat{\theta}_N,y,x)] = 0$$

$\hat{\theta}_N$ is consistent, asymptotically normal, and statistically efficient under standard regularity conditions. Given an initial $\sqrt{N}$-consistent estimator $\check{\theta}_N$, the LMLE $\check{\theta}_N$

$$\check{\theta}_N \equiv \check{\theta}_N + \bar{H}_N^{-1}E_N[s(\check{\theta}_N,y,x)]$$

is an asymptotically equivalent estimator, where $\bar{H}_N$ is a consistent estimator of the information matrix $E\{\text{var}[s`(\theta,y,x)|x]\}$. Two estimators are popular. When

$$\bar{H}_N = \text{var}_N[s(\check{\theta}_N,y,x)]$$

the LMLE is often called the *Gauss–Newton two-step estimator*. When

$$\bar{H}_N = - E_N[\nabla_\theta s(\check{\theta}_N,y,x)]$$

the LMLE is called the *Newton–Raphson two-step estimator*. Subject to standard regularity conditions (see, for example, Newey and McFadden (1994)) both two-step estimators are asymptotically equivalent to $\hat{\theta}_N$ in the sense that plim $\sqrt{N}(\check{\theta}_N - \hat{\theta}_N) = 0$. Hence, these two estimators share the consistency and efficiency properties of $\hat{\theta}_N$, even though they are considerably more tractable computationally given that they are based on the inefficient but simple-to-calculate preliminary estimator $\bar{\theta}_N$ and evaluate only once the (intractable) scores of $\hat{\theta}_N$.

This result is readily transportable to estimation by simulation. Let the tractable but inefficient estimator be MSM, and the intractable but efficient one be MSS. Since the score expressions need only be evaluated once at the MSM estimate, one can afford to base this calculation on a huge number of replications, R. Since this implies that the simulated score expressions only add negligible simulation noise since R is very large, no modification of the standard asymptotic theory for estimation without simulation is necessary.

3.2   Choosing the number of simulations R

I now discuss a method for choosing the level of R. This is essentially a sampling design question, where one is asking how many replications are needed to get a certain level of statistical precision. First, estimate the simulation noise contribution to the variance. Second, determine R to reduce this to γ per cent of the sampling variance of the classical estimator. Note that a similar analysis can be developed for choosing an acceptable value of Gibbs resampling rounds for calculating the MSS/Gibbs estimator.

Let the covariance matrix of an MSM estimator be written

$$\text{var}(\hat{\theta}) = \Omega_C + \frac{1}{R}\Omega_S$$

where Ω_C represents the covariance matrix for the classical estimator that the MSM estimator approximates, and Ω_S represents the covariance matrix contributed by simulation noise. In the special case where the simulation process and data generating process are the same (except for parameter values), $\Omega_C = \Omega_S$ and one can choose R easily to reduce the contribution of simulation to a fraction considered negligible, say 1 per cent.

In general, $\Omega_C \neq \Omega_S$ and the problem of choosing R is less transparent. I suggest a method based on bounding the contribution of simulation in least favorable circumstances. It is convenient to consider variances of all linear combinations of the parameters to be estimated and ensure that the variance of the most variable linear combination contains no more than a tolerable fraction of simulation variance, say ϵ. Formally, one can choose R so that

$$\frac{1}{R}\max_a \frac{a'\Omega_S a}{\text{var}(a'\hat{\theta})} \leq \epsilon, \epsilon > 0.$$

To make this analytically convenient, note that

$$a'\left(\Omega_C+\frac{1}{R}\Omega_S\right)a>a'\Omega_C a$$

so that

$$\frac{a'\Omega_S a}{var(a'\hat{\theta})}\leq\frac{a'\Omega_S a}{a'\Omega_C a}$$

and a conservative solution can be obtained from find R such that

$$\frac{1}{R}\max_a\frac{a'\Omega_S a}{a'\Omega_C a}\leq\epsilon,\epsilon>0.$$

The maximization problem has a (presumably) well-known solution. The first-order conditions state that

$$a'\Omega_C a\cdot\Omega_S a-a'\Omega_S a\cdot\Omega_C a=0$$

$$\Leftrightarrow\left(\Omega_C^{-1}\Omega_S-\frac{a'\Omega_S a}{a'\Omega_C a}I\right)a=0$$

so that a must be proportional to an eigenvector of $\Omega_C^{-1}\Omega_S$. Restricting attention to eigenvectors

$$a'\Omega_C^{-1}\Omega_S a=\frac{a'\Omega_S a}{a'\Omega_C a}$$

so that the possible values for the objective function are the eigenvalues of $\Omega_C^{-1}\Omega_S$ and the largest value of the objective function is the largest such eigenvalue, call it λ^*. I conclude that one should set $R=\lambda^*/\epsilon$.

4   Improving the performance of MSL

Let us begin with a preliminary computational issue that, though very simple and potentially extremely important, does not appear to be widely recognized in practice. I am referring to the fact that the tails of the multi-variate normal density function die out very rapidly indeed. For example, the standard normal c.d.f. $\Phi(q)$ is less than about $1.e-14$ for q approximately less than -12. What this means is that in practice the calculation of multivariate normal rectangle probabilities will cause underflows (implying severe problems in evaluating their logarithms) unless the arguments of these functions remain not too far from the center of the distribution. In the canonical model in our context where the probabilities of interest are of the form.

$$\text{prob}(a<Z<b),\quad Z\sim N(X\beta,\Omega)$$

it will typically be very useful to first standardize the Xs[4] to 0 sample mean and 1 sample variance, calling the standardized regressors X^*. Then the analysis is carried out with X^* as the regressors, thus alleviating some of the computational problems with the trial arguments of the prob($\cdot$) expressions getting too far out in the tails. Given the simple linearity of the transformation of the standardization operation, remapping from the estimates corresponding to the X^* regressors to those corresponding to the original X is obvious.

With this practical suggestion in mind, let us proceed to some computational characteristics of the MSL and MSM estimators. The fact, stated in the previous section, that consistency and asymptotic normality of the MSL estimator requires that R grow without bound faster than $\sqrt{N}$ begs several questions. First, one needs to ask why use MSL that is biased for finite R as opposed to MSM that is CUAN for any (finite) R. The answer is given in subsection 4.1. Subsection 4.2 develops a diagnostic test for simulation bias, thus enabling one to adopt the following two-step strategy: (1) compute an MSL estimator which is biased, but computationally attractive and (2) test for magnitude of bias and re-estimate if necessary.

4.1   Computational attractiveness of MSL over MSM

Researchers have noted that the MSM can be numerically unstable (Geweke, *et al.* (1997) and McFadden and Ruud (1992)), whereas MSL is relatively straightforward (Börsch-Supan and Hajivassiliou (1993) and Hajivassiliou and Ruud (1994)). The MSM estimation criterion function is constructed from a set of moment equations. In this sense, the MSM estimation criterion function is an artificial construct: the distance function. The MSL criterion function has the properties of a log-likelihood function, giving MSL an inherently more tractable criterion function. The computational differences between MSM and MSL are analogous to the differences in identification between the classical MOM and MLE. For the former, identification is a more difficult exercise.

I can give some concreteness to the nature of some of the problems encountered in estimation with simulation by examining the simple binary probit as an example. In this model, one can write the log likelihood function as

$$\ell(\beta) = y \log \Phi(x'\beta) + (1 - y) \log[1 - \Phi(x'\beta)].$$

The MLE avoids regions of the parameter space in which the fitted probability values are near zero, because the contribution of such terms to the log

---

[4] Except for the intercept.

likelihood function approaches negative infinity. The score function for binary probit is often written as

$$s(\theta;y,x) = x\frac{\phi(x'\beta)}{\Phi(x'\beta)[1 - \Phi(x'\beta)]}[y - \Phi(x'\beta)]$$

$$= x\begin{cases} \dfrac{\phi(x'\beta)}{\Phi(x'\beta)} & \text{if } y = 1 \\ \dfrac{-\phi(x'\beta)}{[1 - \Phi(x'\beta)]} & \text{if } y = 0 \end{cases}$$

and the information matrix is

$$J(\theta;x) = \frac{\phi(x'\beta)^2}{\Phi(x'\beta)[1 - \Phi(x'\beta)]}xx'.$$

These expressions have familiar MOM interpretations. The denominator $\Phi(x'\beta)[1 - \Phi(x'\beta)]$ reflects the heteroskedasticity in the residual $y - \Phi(x'\beta)$ and the numerator $\phi(x'\beta)$ captures the non-linearity of the regression function $\Phi(x'\beta)$. On balance, the MLE is largely driven to avoid poor in-sample predictions of the sample outcomes in y.

The noise in the instrumental variables employed by MSM estimators can easily obscure this efficient weighting. One typically constructs the MSM estimator by replacing all of the analytical p.d.f. and c.d.f. terms with unbiased simulations. In this way, one attempts to approximate the efficient score. For example, a particular simulated moment function could be

$$g(\theta;y,x,\omega) = x\frac{f(x'\beta,\omega_1)}{F(x'\beta,\omega_1)[1 - F(x'\beta,\omega_1)]}[y - F(x'\beta,\omega_2)] \tag{8}$$

where the ωs are simulations and f and F are chosen so that

$$E_\omega[F(z,\omega)] = \Phi(z)$$

$$E_\omega[f(z,\omega)] = \phi(z).$$

Care must be taken to ensure that ω_1 and ω_2 are independently distributed, otherwise the MSM estimator is inconsistent because the residual $y - F(x'\beta,\omega_2)$ will be correlated with the simulated weighting term. An MSM estimator then seeks to minimize a distance function

$$\hat{\beta}_{MSM} = \arg\min_{\beta} \| E_N[g(\theta;y,x,\omega)] \|.$$

The operator E_N denotes the empirical expectation over the sample observations.

But the MSM restriction on the ωs has an important side effect. It vitiates the intimate relationship between the regression function and the weighting function so that poor in-sample predictions are no longer as costly as in the log likelihood function. In practice, one frequently finds an MSM searching in regions of the parameter space where the weights are diminished rather than the residuals. The result of this failure is that in small samples, the MSM estimator can be very poorly behaved, wandering into unlikely regions of the parameter space.

The noise in the instrumental variables employed by MSL estimators does not have this effect. In the MSL, one solves the quasi-maximum likelihood problem.

$$\hat{\beta}_{MSL} = \arg \max_{\beta} \mathrm{E}_N \, y \log F(x'\beta, \omega_1) + (1 - y) \log [1 - F(x'\beta, \omega_1)]$$

so that (8) is altered by equating $\omega_1 = \omega_2$ and $f(z, \omega) = dF(z, \omega)/dz$ yielding the alternative moment function

$$g(\theta; y, x, \omega) = x \frac{f(x'\beta, \omega_1)}{F(x'\beta, \omega_1)[1 - F(x'\beta, \omega_1)]} [y - F(x'\beta, \omega_1)]$$

$$= x \left\{ \begin{array}{ll} \dfrac{f(x'\beta, \omega_1)}{F(x'\beta, \omega_1)} & \text{if } y = 1 \\[2ex] \dfrac{-f(x'\beta, \omega_1)}{[1 - F(x'\beta, \omega_1)]} & \text{if } y = 0 \end{array} \right\}.$$

Like the MLE, the MSL estimator will avoid regions of the parameter space that yield poor in-sample predictions. Even for crude simulators, this yields optimization problems that do not lead numerical algorithms to the edges of the parameter space.

It is well understood that this stability comes at the cost of inconsistency in the MSL estimator. But experience shows that the magnitude of the inconsistency is frequently small. With a modest R, an estimator that is *practically* consistent can be constructed by MSL. Given the computational attractiveness of the MSL estimator, I suggest a diagnostic test for whether the magnitude of the inconsistency is important in inference.

4.2   A diagnostic test for simulation bias

Given the MSL estimator $\hat{\theta}$, where

$$\hat{\theta} = \arg \max_{\theta \in \Theta} \ell_N(\theta; y, x, \omega) \Leftrightarrow g(\hat{\theta}; y, x, \omega) = 0,$$

we know that bias arises from the condition

$$\mathrm{E}[g(\theta_0; y, x, \omega)] \neq 0.$$

As R grows, this expectation approaches zero and the inconsistency disappears. Under the hypothesis that the MSL is consistent

$$E[g(\theta;y,x,\omega)|\omega, \ \theta=\theta_0]=0$$

$$\text{var}[g(\theta;y,x,\omega)|\omega, \ \theta=\theta_0]=E\{g[\theta_0;y,x,\omega]g[\theta_0;y,x,\omega)'|\omega\}.$$

The basis for a test of consistency is to check the necessary condition that

$$E[g(\theta;y,x,\omega)|\omega, \ \theta=\hat\theta]=0.$$

For any R and $\hat\theta$, we can easily compute the expectation and variance of the MSL score function. Let $y(\theta)$ denote a simulation of the data generating process for y at θ conditional on x, where this additional simulation is independent of ω, and let E_S denote the empirical expectation of functions of $y(\theta)$ over S replications of $y(\theta)$. Then

$$m\equiv E_S\{g[\hat\theta;y(\hat\theta),x,\omega]\}$$

and

$$V\equiv var_s \ \{g[\hat\theta;y(\hat\theta),x,\omega]\}$$

are unbiased simulators of $E\{g[\theta;y,x,\omega]|x, \omega, \theta=\hat\theta\}$ and var $\{g[\theta;y,x,\omega]|x,$ $\omega, \theta=\hat\theta\}$. Under the hypothesis that the MSL estimator is consistent

$$[E_N(V)]^{-\frac{1}{2}}\sqrt{SN}E_N(m)\xrightarrow{d}\mathcal{N}(0,I)$$

as $N\to\infty$. Thus a simple specification test, similar in spirit to the Hausman (1978) specification test, can be constructed from the Wald statistic

$$W=SN\cdot[E_N(m)]'[E_N(V)]^{-1}[E_N(m)]$$

evaluating the moments at the particular θ of interest, $\hat\theta$. Under the null hypothesis of MSL consistency, W has an asymptotic distribution that is central chi-square with K degrees of freedom, where K is the dimension of θ.

We interpret an insignificant statistic as evidence that the variation in the estimator is large relative to the simulation bias. Therefore, if the precision of the MSL estimator is satisfactory, there is negligible inconsistency in the MSL estimator itself. The statistic W measures the difference in bias correction between the MSL estimator and a one-step estimator as advanced by McFadden and Ruud (1992). In cases where the test statistic W is considered to be non-negligible, the researcher can inspect a local estimate of the bias in the MSL estimator. If $E(m)\neq0$, then the first-order approximation of the MSM estimator that solves

$$E_N(g[\theta;y,x,\omega]-E_S\{g[\theta;y(\theta),x,\omega]\})=0$$

is

$$\hat\delta=J \, m$$

where

$$J \equiv [\nabla_\theta E_N(g[\hat{\theta};y,x,\omega] - E_S\{g[\hat{\theta};y(\hat{\theta}),x,\omega]\})]^{-1}$$

The precision in the estimated bias $\hat{\delta}$ can be evaluated using the estimated covariance matrix $J E_N V J'$. Although testing whether $\hat{\delta}$ is significantly different from zero is equivalent to W, looking at the outcome in the parameter space rather than the moment space may be more meaningful.

Keep in mind that this analysis is conditional on W, treating the simulated score as an exact function. Another way to look at this approach is to think of $\tilde{\theta}$ as a potentially misspecified MLE, as in White (1982). This diagnostic has the same spirit as White's information test, except one is conducting the test based on first, rather than second, moments. This is possible because the entire data generating process is specified in the MSL setting, permitting us to draw from that DGP given θ.

If the MSL estimator fails to pass this test, the statistic can also be used to compute the level of R that will yield an acceptable estimator. The researcher can experiment with increasing R until the W statistic is acceptably small. Having found such a level, he can return to reapply the MSL at this higher value.

4.3   Investigating the computational speed of the GHK simulator

The leading simulator for multivariate normal rectangle probabilities of the form encountered in ML estimation of LDV models is the Geweke–Hajivassiliou–Keane approach. See Hajivassiliou, *et al.* (1996) for extensive Monte Carlo evidence that this simulator is to be preferred over all other known simulators for this problem. To outline this method, define $q(u, a, b) \equiv \Phi^{-1}(\Phi(a) \cdot (1 - u) + \Phi(b) \cdot u)$, where $0 < u < 1$ and $-\infty \le a < b \le \infty$. Then q is a mapping that takes a uniform $(0,1)$ random variate into a truncated standard normal random variate on the interval $[a,b]$.

Proposition 1 Consider the multivariate normal $M \times 1$ random vector $Y \sim N(X\beta, \Omega)$ with Ω positive definite, the linear transformation $Z = FY \sim N(FXB, \Sigma)$, with F non-singular and $\Sigma = F\Omega F'$, and the event $B \equiv \{a^* \le Z = FY \le b^*\}$, with $-\infty \le a^* < b^* \le +\infty$. Define $P \equiv \int_B n(z; FX\beta, \Sigma) dz$, $a \equiv a^* - FX\beta$, $b \equiv b^* - FXB$, and let L denote the lower-triangle Cholesky factor of Σ. Let $(u_1, \ldots, u_M)$ be a vector of independent uniform $(0,1)$ random variates. Define recursively for $j = 1, \ldots, M$:

$$e_j = q(u_j, (a_j - L_{j1}e_1 - \ldots - L_{j,j-1}e_{j-1})/ \\ L_{jj}, (b_j - L_{j1}e_1 - \ldots - L_{j,j-1}e_{j-1})/L_{jj}), \tag{9}$$

$$Q_j \equiv \Phi((b_j - L_{j1}e_1 - \ldots - L_{j,j-1}e_{j-1})/L_{jj}) \\ - \Phi((a_j - L_{j1}e_1 - \ldots - L_{j,j-1}e_{j-1})/L_{jj}). \tag{10}$$

Define $e \equiv (e_1, \ldots, e_M)'$, $\tilde{Y} \equiv X\beta + F^{-1}Le$, *and* $Q(e) \equiv Q_1, \ldots, Q_M$. *Then* $\tilde{Y}$ *is a random vector on* **B**, *and the ratio of the densities of* $\tilde{Y}$ *and* Y *at* $y = X\beta + F^{-1}$ *Le, where* e *is any vector satisfying* $a \le Le \le b$, *is* $P/Q(e)$.

Proof Börsch-Supan and Hajivassiliou (1993) and Hajivassiliou and McFadden (1998)

These studies also show that by combining proposition 1 about the GHK simulator together with importance-sampling arguments, one can show that GHK is a smooth, unbiased, and consistent simulator for the likelihood contributions P_i and their derivatives $P_{\theta i}$ and a smooth, asymptotically unbiased, and consistent simulator for the logarithmic derivatives of the $P(\cdot)$ expressions.

It is instructive to give here a complete implementation of the GHK simulator in the GAUSS computer matrix language.[5]

```
proc l=ghk(m,mu,w,wi,c,a,b,r,u);
local j,ii,ta,tb,tt,wgt,v,p;
j=1;
ii=1;
ta=cdfn(((a[1,1]-mu[1,1])/(c[1,1]+1.e-100))*ones(1,r);
tb=cdfn(((b[1,1]-mu[1,1])/(c[1,1]+1.e-100))*ones(1,r);
tt=cdfinvn(u[1,.].*ta+(1-u[1,.].*tb);
wgt=tb-ta;
do while j<m;
  j=j+1
  ta=cdfn(((a[j,1]-mu[j,1])*ones(1,r)-c[j,ii]*tt)/(c[j,j]+1.e-100));
  tb=cdfn(((b[j,1]-mu[j,1])*ones(1,r)-c[j,ii]*tt)/(c[j,j]+1.e-100));
  tt=tt|cdfinvn(u[j,.].*ta+(1-u[j,.]).*tb);
  ii=ii|j;
  wgt=wgt.*(tb-ta);
endo;
v=c*tt;
tt=(ones(m,1)*wgt).*v;
p=sumc(wgt')/r;
retp(p);
endp;
```

---

[5] The inputs to the routine are: m = dimension of multivariate normal vector Z; mu = EZ; $w = V(Z)$; $wi = w^{-1}$; c = cholesky factor of w; the restriction region is defined by $a < Z < b$; r = number of replications; u = an $m \times r$ matrix of *iid* uniform [0,1] variates.

To guard against possible division by 0, a very small positive number $(1.e - 100)$ is added to denominators.

cdfn = standard normal c.d.f. function and *cdfinvn* = inverse of the standard normal c.d.f. function.

Table 3.1. *Computational speed of GHK: effects of dimensionality and number of simulations*

	M = 4[a]	M = 8	M = 16	M = 32	M = 64
R = 20[b]	1[c]	3	2	3	5
R = 50	2	4	3	4	11
R = 100	3	5	4	8	11
R = 250	4	6	8	16	33
R = 500	5	7	17	27	76
R = 1000	8	16	33	72	176
R = 2500	16	38	82	181	444
R = 5000	38	77	165	429	1,022

Notes:
[a] $M \equiv$ dimension of $Z \sim N(0,\Omega)$.
[b] Number of replications in GHK simulator.
[c] Time in $1/100th$ seconds.
[d] $\Omega = Toeplitz$ matrix with $\rho = 0.5$.
Restricted region considered is the orthant $Z_i > 0. \ \forall i$.

As can be seen from the timing experiments reported in table 3.1 and Figures 3.1 and 3.2, the computational time of the GHK simulator is almost linear in the dimension of the multivariate vector Z given the number of simulations employed, as well as approximately linear in the number of simulations given the dimension. This is an extremely convenient feature of this method, making it applicable even for problems of very high dimensionality without making the implied computational burden intractable.[6]

5   Simulation-based diagnostic tests

In this section I discuss the use of the simulation estimation principles introduced above to devise classical hypothesis testing methods that are free of influential simulation noise. These test also rely on the fact that whenever intractable expressions do not need to be calculated repeatedly, one can afford to employ a huge number of simulations, thus eliminating the impact of additional noise introduced by the simulations. I illustrate the ideas by developing several new diagnostic tests for popular econometric models.

[6] Some slight non-linearities observed are primarily caused by the fact that due to limitations with random-access-memory workspace at high $M \times R$ values, virtual memory is employed, involving disk-reading and writing. As is well known, virtual disk-based memory is orders of magnitude slower than real RAM.

Time in 1/100th seconds

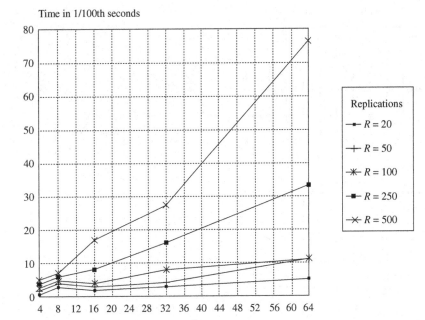

Figure 3.1a Time versus dimension M, given replications R

Consider the classical problem of testing a nested hypothesis (possibly non-linear) against a sequence of local alternatives

$$H_0 : g(\theta^*) = 0$$
$$H_1 : g(\theta^*) = \frac{\delta}{\sqrt{N}} \tag{11}$$

where $g(\cdot)$ is a function $\Re^p \to \Re^r$ defining the r restrictions on the unknown p-dimensional parameter vector θ^*. Under H_1, the unconstrained maximum likelihood estimator

$$\hat{\theta}_N \equiv \arg\max_\theta \ell_N(\theta) \tag{12}$$

is asymptotically efficient, while under H_0 the constrained MLE

$$\bar{\theta}_N \equiv \arg\max_\theta \ell_N(\theta) \text{ s.t. } g(\theta) = 0 \tag{13}$$

is efficient. I use the definitions

$$J = \mathrm{E}[\ell_\theta(x \mid \theta^*) \cdot \ell_\theta(x \mid \theta^*)'] = -\mathrm{E}[\ell_{\theta\theta}(x \mid \theta^*)] \tag{14}$$

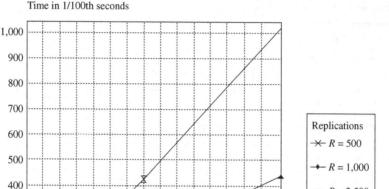

Figure 3.1b Time versus dimension M, given replications R

and

$$\hat{J}_{1N} = \sum_{i=1}^{N}[\ell_\theta(x_i|\hat{\theta}_N)\cdot\ell_\theta(x_i|\hat{\theta}_N)'], \bar{J}_{1N} = \sum_{i=1}^{N}[\ell_\theta(x_i|\bar{\theta}_N)\cdot\ell_\theta(x_i|\bar{\theta}_N)'],$$

$$\hat{J}_{2N} = -\sum_{i=1}^{N}\ell_{\theta\theta}(x_i|\hat{\theta}_N), \bar{J}_{2N} = -\sum_{i=1}^{N}\ell_{\theta\theta}(x_i|\bar{\theta}_N) \qquad (15)$$

where $\ell_\theta(\cdot) \equiv \dfrac{\partial\ell(\cdot)}{\partial\theta}$ and $\ell_{\theta\theta}(\cdot) \equiv \dfrac{\partial^2\ell(\cdot)}{\partial\theta\partial\theta'}$. Note that by the local nature of the deviations from H_0, all four estimators for the true J are consistent under local H_1 as well, because even though $\sqrt{N}(g(\hat{\theta}_N) - g(\theta^*))$ converges in distribution to a normal random vector with a non-zero mean under H_1, the unnormalized by $\sqrt{N}$ quantity $g(\hat{\theta}_N) - g(\theta^*)$ converges in probability to 0. (The same holds for $\bar{\theta}_N$.)

It should be noted that linear and non-linear hypotheses of interest typically involve restrictions on the coefficients of explanatory variables, as well as restrictions on the elements of the variance–covariance matrix of the latent variable vector. For example, in the context of discrete choice models, special hierarchical structures correspond to certain correlations among

Time in 1/100th seconds

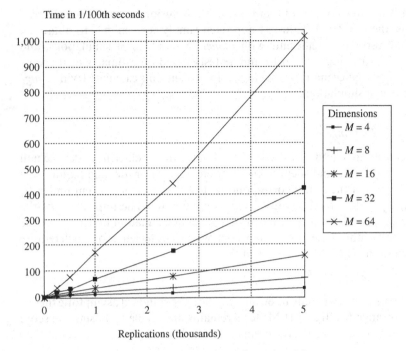

Figure 3.2 Time versus replications R, given dimension M

the elements of the unobservable utilities being zero. I will give explicit examples of such hypotheses in subsection 5.4 below.

5.1   Wald tests

As I explained in the Introduction, simulation estimators that are asymptotically equivalent to the unconstrained maximum likelihood estimator $\hat{\theta}_N$ can be obtained by several methods, notably two-step methods beginning from consistent but inefficient estimates (e.g., MSM or MSL tested for bias). Once such an estimator is available, one can define the familiar Wald test statistic for (11) as

$$W_N \equiv g(\hat{\theta}_N)'[\hat{g}_\theta' \cdot \hat{J}_N^{-1} \cdot \hat{g}_\theta]^{-1} g(\hat{\theta}_N). \tag{16}$$

As is well known, this statistic converges to a $\chi^2(r)$ distribution under either H_0 and to a non-central $\chi^2(r)$ with non-centrality parameter $\lambda = \delta' g_\theta(\theta^*)' \cdot J^{-1} \cdot g_\theta(\theta^*)\delta$ under local H_1. Since the calculation of W_N will be done only at $\hat{\theta}_N$, a very large number of simulations can be used in evaluating the quantities $g(\cdot)$, $g_\theta(\cdot)$, and $J(\cdot)$, thus introducing only negligible simulation noise.

It is useful to point out that for tests of exclusion or other linear restrictions, the simulated Wald test approach simply corresponds to obtaining the unrestricted coefficients with *moderate* numbers of simulations, and then constructing standard t and χ^2 tests based on estimates of the variance–covariance matrix of the regression coefficients calculated with a *huge* number of simulations.

5.2   *Lagrange multiplier tests*

Such tests are based on the CUAN estimator that is efficient under the null hypothesis (i.e., equivalent to the restricted estimator $\bar{\theta}_N$), and requires the evaluation of the scores corresponding to the estimator efficient under H_1 (i.e., equivalent to the unrestricted estimator $\hat{\theta}_N$). The imposition of the restrictions will frequently mean that efficient estimation under H_0 will be tractable without the use of simulation, while the efficient scores will require simulation. The LM statistic is of the form

$$LM_N \equiv \ell_{N\theta}(\bar{\theta}_N)' \bar{J}_N^{-1} \ell_{N\theta}(\bar{\theta}_N). \tag{17}$$

Since the scores will only be evaluated once, the standard asymptotic theory of Lagrange Multiplier (LM) tests remains applicable by basing the score calculations on a very large number of simulations.

5.3   *Likelihood ratio tests*

The familiar LR statistic

$$LR_N \equiv 2 \cdot [\ell_N(\hat{\theta}_N) - \ell_N(\bar{\theta}_N)], \tag{18}$$

which is asymptotically equivalent to W_N and LM_N under both H_0 and local H_1, is computationally more burdensome than either test since it requires one to obtain efficient estimators under both H_0 and H_1. The same basic principle is still applicable, however, namely that the calculation of the two components of LR_N can be based on a very large number of simulations, thus obviating the need for the development of special asymptotic results to allow for simulation noise. This fact makes the application of LR_N tests very appealing, because they do not require the derivation of possibly complicated expressions like $\ell_{N\theta}(\cdot)$, $g_\theta(\cdot)$, or $J(\cdot)$, but only the evaluation of the log likelihood function at two points. Analogously to the concluding remarks in the simulated Wald section, the simulated LR test for simple restrictions corresponds to obtaining the restricted and unrestricted parameter estimates based on moderate R, and then employing a huge R for the two restricted and unrestricted likelihood function evaluations that are needed for the LR statistic.

Table 3.2

Version	Description	Restrictions on Ω
P1	General MNP	none
P2	MNP with nested hierarchical structure	off-diagonal blocks of 0
P3	Independent but heteroskedastic MNP	$\omega_{\ell m} = 0$, for all $\ell \neq m$
P4	Independent and homoskedastic MNP	$\omega_{\ell m} = 0$, for all $\ell \neq m, \omega_{\ell\ell} = c$ for all ℓ

5.4   Testing hypotheses in discrete choice models

As examples, I discuss here two discrete choice models to illustrate concretely the main issues involved with simulation-based testing.

5.4.1   The multinomial probit model
The MNP model is defined as

$$y_i = \arg\max_k \{y_{i1}^*, \ldots, y_{ik}^*, \ldots, y_{iJ}^*\} \tag{19}$$

where $y_i^* \sim N(X_i\beta, \Omega_i)$ denotes the $J \times 1$ vector of latent utilities of the J alternatives.

The cases listed in table 3.2 have been identified in the literature as being particularly useful for modeling discrete choice settings in practice. Let $\omega_{\ell m}$ be the (ℓ, m)th element of the variance-covariance matrix Ω_i.

All three classical testing approaches discussed above are applicable in these cases. Of special usefulness are the Wald and LR tests because all hypotheses under test involve estimating the model with and without equality restrictions imposed, and letting the final round of calculations be based on a very large number of simulations.

In terms of computation, P4 and P3 are extremely straightforward since they correspond to likelihood contributions that are products of $J - 1$ univariate normal c.d.f.s ($g(z)$) integrated over the normal p.d.f. of the normalizing utility. Since this integral is of the form $\int_{-\infty}^{+\infty} g(z)\exp(-z^2/2)dz$, Hermite Gaussian quadrature can be used. Alternatively, though not necessary, one could always use simulation estimation. This would provide a good test of the accuracy of simulation-based versus quadrature-based estimation. Models P2 and P1 require simulation-based estimation.

5.4.2   The multinomial ordered probit model
As with the MNP model, individual i chooses alternative k that offers the highest utility y_{ik}^*. The analyst, however, observes the full ranking of the J alternatives in terms of the utility they yield, i.e., the analyst observes the J-dimensional vector of indices

$$y_i \equiv (k_1, \ldots, k_J)'$$

such that

$$y^*_{ik_1} \le y^*_{ik_2} \le \ldots \le y^*_{ik_J}. \tag{20}$$

If such information is available, the resulting estimators will be, in general, much better behaved than the ones from the MNP model, since, as Keane (1992) shows, the informational content of the MNP model can be quite low in view of the severity of the MNP filtering.

6   Antithetics

Antithetics is one of the leading "variance-reduction" simulation techniques and can be explained as follows: suppose we want to approximate a function $g(u)$ by using the average over $2R$ simulations

$$S_{na,2R} = \frac{1}{2R} \sum_{r=1}^{2R} g(u_r)$$

where u_r are *iid* draws from the appropriate distribution. As a result, simulator $S_{na,2R}$ with no-antithetics and $2R$ simulations has variance $\frac{1}{4R^2} 2R \cdot V(g(u)) = \frac{1}{2R}(g(u))$. To introduce antithetics, we define the estimator based on only R *iid* u_r draws defined by

$$S_{a,R} = \frac{1}{R} \sum_{r=1}^{R} \frac{1}{2}[g(u_r) + g(-u_r)]$$

i.e., for each u_r we average $g(\cdot)$ both at u_r and at $-u_r$. This simulator has variance $\frac{1}{4R^2} \sum_{r=1}^{R}[2 \cdot V(g(u)) + 2\text{cov}(g(u_r), g(-u_r))] = \frac{1}{2R}(V(g(u)) + \text{cov}(g(u), g(-u)))$. Depending on whether or not $g(\cdot)$ is monotonic, the covariance term will be negative, implying that the variance of the simulator that employs antithetics with R simulations will be lower than the basic simulator with $2R$ independent simulations. In addition, $S_{a,R}$ may offer also computational advantages over the $S_{na,2R}$ simulator, if the relative savings in drawing R fewer u_rs (R versus $2R$) are substantial relative to performing the same number of $g(\cdot)$ evaluations in the two cases ($Rg(u)$s plus ($Rg(-u_r)$s versus $2R\, g(u)$s).

For more extensive discussion of the use of antithetics in further improving the GHK simulator, see Andrews and Hajivassiliou (1995). Tables 3.2a–3.2c below summarize the results from the same set of 84 Monte Carlo experiments analyzed in Hajivassiliou, et al. (1996). That study did not investigate antithetic variance reduction and concluded that the best

Table 3.2a. *Relative MSE efficiency: GHK versus GHKA*

Quantity simulated	Simulator	Relative MSE efficiency[a]
$P(Z \in \mathbf{B})^b$	GHKA	0.8783
$P(Z \in \mathbf{B})^b$	GHK	0.7283
$\partial P / \partial \mu_1$	GHKA	0.9904
$\partial P / \partial \mu_1$	GHK	0.4532
$\partial P / \partial \mu_2$	GHKA	0.9900
$\partial P / \partial \mu_2$	GHK	0.4160
$\partial P / \partial \Omega_{11}$	GHKA	0.9395
$\partial P / \partial \Omega_{11}$	GHK	0.6857
$\partial P / \partial \Omega_{12}$	GHKA	0.9692
$\partial P / \partial \Omega_{12}$	GHK	0.5653
$\partial P / \partial \Omega_{22}$	GHKA	0.9508
$\partial P / \partial \Omega_{22}$	GHK	0.6209
Avg. for all linear derivs.	GHKA	0.9680
Avg. for all linear derivs.	GHK	0.5482
$\partial \ln P / \partial \mu_1$	GHKA	0.9889
$\partial \ln P / \partial \mu_1$	GHK	0.4714
$\partial \ln P / \partial \mu_2$	GHKA	0.9895
$\partial \ln P / \partial \mu_2$	GHK	0.4455
$\partial \ln P / \partial \Omega_{11}$	GHKA	0.9378
$\partial \ln P / \partial \Omega_{11}$	GHK	0.6983
$\partial \ln P / \partial \Omega_{12}$	GHKA	0.9705
$\partial \ln P / \partial \Omega_{12}$	GHK	0.5828
$\partial \ln P / \partial \Omega_{22}$	GHKA	0.9475
$\partial \ln P / \partial \Omega_{22}$	GHK	0.6509
Avg. for all logarithmic derivs.	GHKA	0.9668
Avg. for all logarithmic derivs.	GHK	0.5698

Notes:

[a] Relative Mean-Squared Error efficiency of simulator S averaged over 84 experiments $\equiv$.

$$\frac{1}{84} \sum_{i=1}^{84} \frac{\text{Lowest MSE for a specific experiment}}{\text{MSE of simulator } s \text{ for experiment } i}.$$

[b] Number of simulations for each simulator selected so as to require equal amounts of CPU time.

Bivariate random vector $Z \sim N(\mu, \Omega)$. Fourteen rectangular regions $\mathbf{B}$ and six correlation structures for Ω analyzed as described in Hajivassiliou, *et al.* (1996).

Table 3.2b. *Relative MSE efficiency: PCF versus GHKA*

Quantity simulated	Simulator	Relative MSE efficiency[a]
$P(Z \epsilon \mathbf{B})$[b]	PCF	0.2685
$P(Z \epsilon \mathbf{B})$[b]	GHKA	0.9621
$\partial P / \partial \mu_1$	PCF	0.3622
$\partial P / \partial \mu_1$	GHKA	0.8693
$\partial P / \partial \mu_2$	PCF	0.2993
$\partial P / \partial \mu_2$	GHKA	0.9303
$\partial P / \partial \Omega_{11}$	PCF	0.6477
$\partial P / \partial \Omega_{11}$	GHKA	0.6947
$\partial P / \partial \Omega_{12}$	PCF	0.5730
$\partial P / \partial \Omega_{12}$	GHKA	0.7961
$\partial P / \partial \Omega_{22}$	PCF	0.4784
$\partial P / \partial \Omega_{22}$	GHKA	0.8595
Avg. for all linear derivs.	PCF	0.4721
Avg. for all linear derivs.	GHKA	0.8300
$\partial \ln P / \partial \mu_1$	PCF	0.4474
$\partial \ln P / \partial \mu_1$	GHKA	0.8687
$\partial \ln P / \partial \mu_2$	PCF	0.4481
$\partial \ln P / \partial \mu_2$	GHKA	0.8732
$\partial \ln P / \partial \Omega_{11}$	PCF	0.6959
$\partial \ln P / \partial \Omega_{11}$	GHKA	0.6948
$\partial \ln P / \partial \Omega_{12}$	PCF	0.6426
$\partial \ln P / \partial \Omega_{12}$	GHKA	0.7813
$\partial \ln P / \partial \Omega_{22}$	PCF	0.6737
$\partial \ln P / \partial \Omega_{22}$	GHKA	0.7312
Avg. for all logarithmic derivs.	PCF	0.5815
Avg. for all logarithmic derivs.	GHKA	0.7898

Notes:
See table 3.2a.

Table 3.2c. *Relative MSE efficiency: GHK versus PCF versus GHKA*

Quantity simulated	Simulator	Relative MSE efficiency[a]
$P(Z \in \mathbf{B})^b$	PCF	0.2499
$P(Z \in \mathbf{B})^b$	GHK	0.7738
$P(Z \in \mathbf{B})^b$	GHKA	0.8418
$\partial P/\partial \mu_1$	PCF	0.3614
$\partial P/\partial \mu_1$	GHK	0.4299
$\partial P/\partial \mu_1$	GHKA	0.8685
$\partial P/\partial \mu_2$	PCF	0.2981
$\partial P/\partial \mu_2$	GHK	0.4523
$\partial P/\partial \mu_2$	GHKA	0.9288
$\partial P/\partial \Omega_{11}$	PCF	0.6470
$\partial P/\partial \Omega_{11}$	GHK	0.5201
$\partial P/\partial \Omega_{11}$	GHKA	0.6942
$\partial P/\partial \Omega_{12}$	PCF	0.5730
$\partial P/\partial \Omega_{12}$	GHK	0.4872
$\partial P/\partial \Omega_{12}$	GHKA	0.7961
$\partial P/\partial \Omega_{22}$	PCF	0.4748
$\partial P/\partial \Omega_{22}$	GHK	0.6063
$\partial P/\partial \Omega_{22}$	GHKA	0.8441
Avg. for all linear derivs.	PCF	0.4709
Avg. for all linear derivs.	GHK	0.4992
Avg. for all linear derivs.	GHKA	0.8263
$\partial \ln P/\partial \mu_1$	PCF	0.4443
$\partial \ln P/\partial \mu_1$	GHK	0.4447
$\partial \ln P/\partial \mu_1$	GHKA	0.8635
$\partial \ln P/\partial \mu_2$	PCF	0.6254
$\partial \ln P/\partial \mu_2$	GHK	0.4283
$\partial \ln P/\partial \mu_2$	GHKA	0.8690
$\partial \ln P/\partial \Omega_{11}$	PCF	0.6926
$\partial \ln P/\partial \Omega_{11}$	GHK	0.5320
$\partial \ln P/\partial \Omega_{11}$	GHKA	0.6894
$\partial \ln P/\partial \Omega_{12}$	PCF	0.6396
$\partial \ln P/\partial \Omega_{12}$	GHK	0.4972
$\partial \ln P/\partial \Omega_{12}$	GHKA	0.7763
$\partial \ln P/\partial \Omega_{22}$	PCF	0.6712
$\partial \ln P/\partial \Omega_{22}$	GHK	0.5226
$\partial \ln P/\partial \Omega_{22}$	GHKA	0.7268
Avg. for all logarithmic derivs.	PCF	0.6146
Avg. for all logarithmic derivs.	GHK	0.4850
Avg. for all logarithmic derivs.	GHKA	0.7850

Notes:
See table 3.2a.

method overall was the GHK simulator, followed by the parametric cylinder function simulator (PCF) under certain conditions. In the experiments here, the simulators considered were GHK and PCF as well as GHKA, which is the GHK method with antithetics built into it. The improvements in terms of mean-squared-error performance controlled for computational requirements in terms of CPU time are quite uniform and substantial. Given how simple it is to program the antithetic modification into the GHK method, the results here suggest that GHKA should supplant the basic GHK as the simulator of choice for routine applications.

7   Conclusions

In this chapter, I explored ways of recapturing the efficiency property for estimators that rely on simulation. In particular, I showed how this can be achieved by exploiting two-step maximum simulated likelihood (MSL) estimation methods that are familiar in classical applications. I also constructed a diagnostic test for adequacy of number of simulations employed to guarantee negligible bias for the MSL and provided some evidence on the computational requirements of the Geweke–Hajivassiliou–Keane (GHK) simulator as a function of (a) the dimension of the problem and (b) the number of simulations employed in a vectorized context.

This chapter also showed how to suitably introduce simulation into classical hypothesis testing methods and provide test statistics (simulated Wald, Lagrange multiplier, and likelihood ratio tests) that are free of influential simulation noise.

Finally, I explained how simulation-variance-reduction techniques can improve substantially the practical performance of the GHK simulator and presented extensive Monte Carlo evidence confirming this.

References

Andrews, D. and V. Hajivassiliou (1995), "Antithetics for Simulation of Multivariate Normal Rectangle Probabilities," Cowles Foundation Working paper, Yale University.

Börsch-Supan, A. and V. Hajivassiliou (1993), "Smooth Unbiased Multivariate Probability Simulators for Maximum Likelihood Estimation of Multinomial Probit Models," *Journal of Econometrics*, 58(3), 347–368.

Geweke, J., M. Keane, and D. Runkle (1997), "Comparing Simulation Estimators for the Multinomial Probit Model," *Journal of Econometrics*, 80(1) (September), 125–166.

Hajivassiliou, V. and D. McFadden (1998), "The Method of Simulated Scores for Estimating Limited Dependent Variable Models," *Econometrica*, 66(4), 863–896.

Hajivassiliou, V., D. McFadden, and and P. Ruud (1996), "Simulation of Multivariate Normal Rectangle Probabilities and Derivatives: Theoretical and Computational Results," *Journal of Econometrics*, 72(1&2), 85–134.

Hajivassiliou, V. and P. Ruud (1994), "Classical Estimation Methods for LDV Models Using Simulation," in R. Engle and D. McFadden (eds.), *Handbook of Econometrics*, vol. IV. Amsterdam: North-Holland.

Hausman, J.A. (1978), "Specification Tests in Econometrics," *Econometrica*, 46 (November), 1251–1271.

Keane, M. (1992), "A Note on Identification in the Multinomial Probit Model," *Journal of Business and Economic Statistics*, 10, 193–200.

McFadden, D. (1989), "A Method of Simulated Moments for Estimation of Discrete Response Models," *Econometrica*, 57(5) (September), 995–1026.

McFadden, D. and P. Ruud (1992), "Estimation by Simulation," University of California at Berkeley Working paper.

Newey, W.K. and D.L. McFadden (1994), "Estimation in Large Samples," in Rob Engle and D. McFadden (eds.), *Handbook of Econometrics*, vol. IV, Amsterdam, North-Holland, chapter 40, pp. 2383–2441.

Pakes A. and D. Pollard (1989), "Simulation and the Asymptotics of Optimization Estimators," *Econometrica*, 57, 1027–1057.

Ruud, O. (1991), "Extensions of Estimation Methods Using the EM Algorithm," *Journal of Econometrics*, 49, 305–341.

(1984), "Tests of Specification in Econometrics," *Econometric Reviews*, 3(2), 211–242.

(1986), "On the Method of Simulated Moments for the Estimation of Limited Dependent Variable Models," mimeo, University of California at Berkeley.

van Praag, B.M.S. and J.P. Hop (1987), "Estimation of Continuous Models on the Basis of Set-Valued Observations," Erasmus University Working paper.

White, Halbert (1982), "Maximum Likelihood Estimation of Misspecified Models," *Econometrica*, 50(1), 1–25.

4 Bayesian inference for dynamic discrete choice models without the need for dynamic programming

John F. Geweke and Michael P. Keane

1 Introduction

This chapter presents a method for Bayesian inference with regard to the structural parameters of dynamic discrete choice models. The method does not require the econometrician to solve the agents' optimization problem, or make strong assumptions about how agents form expectations. It is implemented using a Gibbs sampling-data augmentation algorithm (Gelfand and Smith (1990), Tanner and Wong (1987)). We first describe the generic discrete choice model framework, describe our method for Bayesian inference, and then present some results obtained by applying the method to trial problems.

We consider models in which agents choose from among a set of J mutually exclusive alternatives, and make choices repeatedly over T periods. such models can usually be written in the form:

$$V_{ijt}(S_i(t)) = P_{ijt}(S_i(t)) + \delta E_t[V(S_i(t+1))|S_i(t),d_{ijt}=1] \tag{1}$$

$$S_i(t+1) = M[S_i(t),d_{it}] \tag{2}$$

where $S_i(t)$ is the state of agent i at time t, $V_{ijt}(S_i(t))$ is the value to agent i of choosing alternative j at time t, $P_{ijt}(S_i(t))$ is the time t payoff to agent i from choosing alternative j, δ is the discount factor, E_t is the expectation operator, $V(S_i(t+1))$ is the value of being in state $S_i(t+1)$, d_{ijt} is an indicator equal to 1 if alternative j is chosen at time t and zero otherwise, d_{it} is the $J*1$ vector of the J choice indicators, and M is a random function that maps $S_i(t)$ and d_{it} into $S_i(t+1)$.

Equation (1) says that the value of choosing alternative j at time t is the immediate payoff plus a "future component" equal to the discount factor times the expected value of the state the agent attains at time $t+1$ given the

Geweke's work on this project was supported in part by National Science Foundation Grants SBR-9210070 and SBR-9514865, and Keane's work was supported in part by National Science Foundation Grant SBR-9511186. Dan Houser provided excellent research assistance.

current state $(S_i(t))$ and current choice. Since $S_i(t+1)$ is determined by the random function $M[S_i(t), d_{it}]$, the expectation is taken over realizations from M.

We consider situations in which the econometrician is willing to assume parametric functional forms for the payoff functions $P_{ijt}(S_i(t))$ and the law of motion for the state variables (equation (2)), and in which the econometrician observes at least some information about payoffs (e.g., the value of a payoff $P_{ijt}(S_i(t))$ may be observed if and only if $d_{ijt} = 1$).

The econometrician is interested in learning about the structural parameters that enter the payoff functions. However, the econometrician is either unwilling to make strong assumptions about the process by which expectations are formed, or lacks the necessary computational power to calculate the $E_t[V(S_i(t+1))|S_i(t), d_{ijt} = 1]$ functions given such assumptions. As an example of the latter case, suppose that a rational expectations assumption is invoked. Then, solving for the future components of the value functions requires that the agents' optimization problem be solved via dynamic programming. This will be an extremely computationally burdensome process for all but the most simple model structures (see Keane and Wolpin (1994) or Rust (1995) for a discussion).

If it were feasible to solve for the $E_t[V(S_i(t+1))|S_i(t), d_{ijt} = 1]$ functions rather quickly via dynamic programming, then classical inference with regard to the structural parameters would be feasible. But, even then, Bayesian inference would likely remain infeasible. This is because the $E_t[V(S_i(t+1))|S_i(t), d_{ijt} = 1]$ functions are themselves complex non-linear functions of the deep structural parameters. Thus, the mapping from the observed data (choices and payoffs) to the posterior distribution of the structural parameters will typically be intractably complex. (Recently, Lancaster (1996) has shown that the mapping is quite tractable in the simple infinite horizon job search model, but this special case is unusual.)

The idea behind our approach to Bayesian inference for dynamic discrete models is that much can be learned about the future components of the value functions just by looking at observed choices and payoffs – without the need to assume an expectations formation mechanism or solve agents' optimization problem. Suppose that agents in a particular state usually choose alternative 1, despite the fact that their observed payoffs are relatively low as compared to those of other agents in the same state who choose alternative 2. This suggests that the future component of the value function associated with choice of alternative 1 is greater than that associated with 2 (e.g., the fact that young people often choose to go to school, despite the fact that immediate payoffs in terms of income would be greater if they chose to work, suggests that future component of the value function associated with the school choice is greater than that associated with the work choice for many young people). Of course, if payoffs are only partially observable, such inferences about the future components of the value functions will hinge on functional form assumptions for the payoff functions.

Following the above intuition, our approach is to specify a flexible functional form for the future component of the value function $\delta E_t[V(S_i(t+1)) | S_i(t), d_{ijt} = 1]$, expressing it as a polynomial in the state variables. Then, given assumed functional forms for the payoff functions, and given some information about actual payoffs, it is possible to learn both about the parameters of the payoff functions and the structure of expectations. Using a Gibbs sampling-data augmentation algorithm, it is straightforward to simulate the joint posterior distribution of the structural parameters of the payoff functions and the parameters characterizing expectations. We illustrate this approach in section 2.

It is worth noting that our approach is somewhat related to that of Hotz and Miller (1993), who also develop a method for estimating dynamic discrete choice models without the need for dynamic programming. If agents solve a dynamic programming problem to arrive at their decision rules, then $E_t[V(S_i(t+1)) | S_i(t), d_{ijt} = 1]$ in (1) takes the form:

$$E_t[V(S_i(t+1)) | S_i(t), d_{ijt} = 1] = E_t[\max_k (V_{ikt}(S_i(t+1)) | S_i(t), d_{ijt} = 1)] \quad (3)$$

where the expectation is taken over realizations for $S_i(t+1)$ determined by the random function M. Given the definition in (3), equation (1) becomes the Bellman equation (Bellman (1957)). In this case, Hotz and Miller point out that $E_t[V(S_i(t+1)) | S_i(t), d_{ijt} = 1]$ can be written as a function of agents' choice probabilities in periods $t+1$ through T, conditional on every state that may be occupied from $t+1$ through T, and the current payoff functions for each alternative in those states. Thus, the future components of the value functions can be calculated, given data on choice probabilities *conditional on all possible states*, and assumed functional forms for the payoff functions. Given such calculations, it is not necessary to solve a dynamic programming problem to construct the future components of the value functions in (1).

In practice, of course, the econometrician will not typically have access to data on the conditional choice probabilities at every point in the state space. Suppose one has a panel data set on choices over time for a set of individuals. One can only construct the choice frequencies at the subset of state points actually observed in the data. To these one can apply nonparametric smoothing techniques to obtain estimated conditional choice probabilities at all state points. The predicted conditional choice probabilities are then used to form the $E_t[V(S_i(t+1)) | S_i(t), d_{ijt} = 1]$ functions.

The Hotz–Miller procedure suffers from a number of limitations. First, the data requirements are heavy. For large state-space problems, the ratio of observed choices to state points will tend to be small unless one has access to an enormous data set. Thus, as Rust (1995) has observed, the results may be very sensitive to the choice of non-parametric smoothing technique. Second, a strong stationarity assumption is required. Panel data sets typically only contain data collected over a fraction of each individual's life. Therefore, the choice frequencies for periods far in the future that are used in estimating the future component of an agent's value function will typically be the choice frequencies that were observed for much older cohorts of agents. The implicit assumption that a younger cohort's choice probabilities will be identical to those of older cohorts, when they reach the same state points, rules out regime changes over time. Third, unobserved heterogeneity is ruled out, since conditional choice frequencies for *all* agents are used to calculate the choice probabilities of all agents in the same observed state.

A related approach to the problem is that of Manski (1993), who assumes that agents form the $E_t[V(S_i(t+1))|S_i(t),d_{ijt}=1]$ functions by looking at the life histories of payoffs for older agents who at some past date were in the state $S_i(t)$ and made the choice $d_{ijt}=1$. This again entails a strong stationarity assumption.

Our approach to inference in dynamic discrete choice models has important advantages over these other approaches. It does not require the assumption of stationarity in the economic environment across cohorts, since the method could be applied to a single cohort observed over a fraction of the planning period $t=1,T$. Our approach can admit unobserved heterogeneity provided the econometrician specifies the manner in which the unobservable affects the payoff functions. And our approach does not make heavy data requirements, other than that the payoffs be at least partially observable. We do need to place some structure on the future component of the value function $\delta E_t[V(S_i(t+1))|S_i(t),d_{ijt}=1]$, although this can be a flexible functional form such as a high-order polynomial in the state variables. And we do need to assume functional forms for the current payoff functions, but this is true of the other approaches as well.

Given substitution of a flexible functional form for the future components of the value function, the dynamic discrete choice model takes a form similar to a static Roy (1951) model augmented to include non-wage influences on choice, as in Heckman and Sedlacek (1985). The difference is that (1) and (2) imply restrictions on the form of the non-wage component that are not typically invoked in estimation of static selection models (i.e., the parameters of the non-wage component are the same for all alternatives, while the values of the regressors in the non-wage component differ in a systematic way across alternatives). Nevertheless, classical estimation of our model would, from a computational standpoint, proceed similarly to classical estimation of a static selection model. But Bayesian inference introduces two interesting complications: (1) the posterior is not analytically tractible, so that a Markov chain–Monte Carlo method must be used to explore it, and (2) unlike pure discrete choice models (e.g. multinomial probit), in which conditional posterior densities for all model parameters typically take a simple analytical form, the conditional posteriors for unobserved payoffs in the selection model typically take a complex form that cannot be handled analytically (i.e., they cannot easily be drawn from using inverse CDF methods). While substantial evidence is now available indicating that the Gibbs sampling data augmentation algorithm works well in discrete choice models, our work provides new evidence on the performance of this method in selection type models.

2   An illustrative application

In this section we present an illustrative application of our method of Bayesian inference for dynamic discrete choice models. Consider a homogeneous population of agents who choose between two occupations in each of T periods. Wages in each occupation are determined by the functions

$$\ln W_{i1t} = \beta_{01} + \beta_{11}X_{i1t} + \beta_{21}X_{i1t}^2 + \beta_{31}X_{i2t} + \beta_{41}X_{i2t}^2 + \epsilon_{i1t} \tag{4}$$

$$\ln W_{i2t} = \beta_{02} + \beta_{12}X_{i2t} + \beta_{22}X_{i2t}^2 + \beta_{32}X_{i1t} + \beta_{42}X_{i1t}^2 + \epsilon_{i2t} \tag{5}$$

where X_{ijt} is experience of agent i in occupation j at time t, and

$$\epsilon_{it} \equiv (\epsilon_{i1t}, \epsilon_{i2t})' \sim N(0_2, \Sigma_\epsilon). \tag{6}$$

The ϵ_{it} are assumed to be serially independent. We also assume that each alternative has associated with it a non-pecuniary benefit ν_{ijt}, where $\nu_{it} \equiv (\nu_{i1t}, \nu_{i2t})' \sim N(0_2, \Sigma_\nu)$. In this model, the state of agent i at time t is

$$S_i(t) = (X_{i1t}, t, \epsilon_{it}, \nu_{it}). \tag{7}$$

Note that it is redundant to include the occupation 2 experience level in the state space, since $X_{i1t} + X_{i2t} = t$.

Notice that while the state variables X_{i1t} and t evolve deterministically (i.e., $X_{i1,t+1} = X_{i1t} + 1$), the state variables ϵ_{it} and ν_{it} are serially independent. Thus, the future component of the value function $\delta E_i[V(S_i(t+1))|S_i(t), d_{ijt} = 1]$, is a function of only $X_{i1,t+1}$ and t. In writing the value functions, we will suppress the argument $S_i(t)$ and instead subscript by i so as to keep the notation more compact.

The value functions associated with each alternative are

$$V_{i1t} = W_{i1t} + \nu_{i1t} + F(X_{i1t} + 1, t) \tag{8}$$

$$V_{i2t} = W_{i2t} + v_{i2t} + F(X_{i1t}, t) \tag{9}$$

where $F(X_1, t)$ is the expected present value of arriving at time $t+1$ with X_1 as the occupation 1 experience level. Note that this formulation assumes that utility is linear in consumption, so that agents solve a wealth maximization problem. This simplifies the problem, but is not essential. Houser (1998) extends the framework to a utility maximization setting.

Since choices depend only on the differences, rather than the levels, of the value functions, we define

$$
\begin{aligned}
Z_{it} &\equiv V_{i1t} - V_{i2t} \\
&= W_{i1t} - W_{i2t} + v_{i1t} - v_{i2t} + F(X_{i1t}+1, t) - F(X_{i1t}, t) \\
&= W_{i1t} - W_{i2t} + \eta_{i1t} + f(X_{i1t}+1, t) \tag{10}
\end{aligned}
$$

where $\eta_{i1t} = v_{i1t} - v_{i2t} \sim N(0, \sigma_\eta^2)$, and $f(X_{i1t}+1, t) = F(X_{i1t}+1, t) - F(X_{i1t}, t)$.

We assume that the value functions V_{i1t} and V_{i2t}, as well as the value function differences Z_{it} that determine choices, are unobserved by the econometrician. The econometrician only observes the agents' choices d_{i1t} and d_{i2t} for $t = 1, T$, and the wage for the chosen alternative (i.e., W_{ijt} is observed if and only if $d_{ijt} = 1$). Thus, payoffs are never completely observed, both because wages are censored and because the non-pecuniary components of the payoffs v_{i1t} and v_{i2t} are never observed. Nevertheless, given observed choices and partially observed wages, along with the functional form assumptions about the payoff functions, it is possible to learn something about the $F(X_1, t)$ function and the structural parameters of the payoff functions without making strong assumptions about how agents form expectations.

Rather than making strong assumptions about how agents form the $F(X_1, t)$ function, we will simply allow it to be a polynomial function of the state variables X_1 and t. For example, a 3rd-order polynomial would be

$$
\begin{aligned}
F(X_1, t) &= \pi_0 + \pi_1 X_1 + \pi_2 X_1^2 + \pi_3 X_1^3 + \pi_4 X_1 t + \pi_5 X_1^2 t + \pi_6 X_1 t^2 \\
&\quad + \pi_7 t + \pi_8 t^2 + \pi_9 t^3. \tag{11}
\end{aligned}
$$

In this case we would have

$$
\begin{aligned}
f(X_{i1t}+1, t) &= \pi_1 + \pi_2(2X_{i1t}+1) + \pi_3(3X_{i1t}^2 + 3X_{i1t} + 1) + \pi_4 t + \\
&\quad \pi_5(2X_{i1t}+1)t + \pi_6 t^2. \tag{12}
\end{aligned}
$$

Notice that the terms involving the parameters π_0, π_7, π_8, and π_9 drop out of the $f(X_{i1t}+1, t)$ function after differencing. This is because these terms capture influences on the level of the $F(X_1, t)$ function that do not depend on the level X_1. Since these terms are the same regardless of whether alternative 1 or 2 is chosen, they drop out when the future component is differenced. Also notice that the number of regressors is $P(P+1)/2$, where P is the order of the polynomial. With the 4th-order polynomial, additional terms would be

$$(4X_{i1t}^3 + 6X_{i1t}^2 + 4X_{i1t} + 1),\ (3X_{i1t}^2 + 3X_{i1t} + 1)t,\ (2X_{i1t} + 1)t^2, t^3$$

while the 5th-order polynomial would add the terms

$$(5X_{i1t}^4 + 10X_{i1t}^3 + 10X_{i1t}^2 + 5X_{i1t} + 1),\ (4X_{i1t}^3 + 6X_{i1t}^2 + 4X_{i1t} + 1)t,$$
$$(3X_{i1t}^2 + 3X_{i1t} + 1)t^2, (2X_{i1t} + 1)t^3, t^4$$

and a 6th-order polynomial adds the terms

$$(6X_{i1t}^5 + 15X_{i1t}^4 + 20X_{i1t}^3 + 15X_{i1t}^2 + 6X_{i1t} + 1),$$
$$(5X_{i1t}^4 + 10X_{i1t}^3 + 10X_{i1t}^2 + 5X_{i1t} + 1)t,$$
$$(4X_{i1t}^3 + 6X_{i1t}^2 + 4X_{i1t} + 1)t^2,\ (3X_{i1t}^2 + 3X_{i1t} + 1)t^3,\ (2X_{i1t} + 1)t^4, t^5.$$

In our Monte Carlo results reported below, we use 6th-order polynomials. Writing the model in matrix notation, we have

$$\ln W_{ijt} = X_{ijt}\beta_j + \epsilon_{ijt} \qquad j = 1, \ldots, 2 \quad t = 1, \ldots, T \tag{13}$$

and

$$f(X_{i1t} + 1, t) = S_{i1t}\pi \qquad t = 1, \ldots, T \tag{14}$$

where S_{i1t} is the row vector of functions of state variables that appear in the equation for $f(X_{i1t} + 1, t)$ and π is the corresponding column vector of coefficients. Equation (14) highlights the fact that the polynomial function $f(X_{i1t} + 1, t)$ is linear in the unknown parameters π.

The first step in a Bayesian analysis of this model via a Gibbs sampling data augmentation algorithm is to form the "complete data" likelihood function. That is, we consider the likelihood function that could be formed if we had data on N individuals observed over T periods each, and we observed the value function differences $Z = \{Z_{it}, i = 1, N; t = 1, T\}$ and the complete set of wages $W = \{(W_{i1t}, W_{i2t}), i = 1, N; t = 1, T\}$ for all alternatives. This is

$$\mathcal{L}(W, Z \mid \beta_1, \beta_2, \Sigma_\epsilon, \sigma_\eta, \pi)$$
$$= \prod_i \prod_t (2\pi)^{-1} |\Sigma_\epsilon|^{-1} W_{i1t}^{-1} W_{i2t}^{-1} \exp\left\{ -\frac{1}{2} \begin{pmatrix} \ell n W_{i1t} - X_{i1t}\beta_1 \\ \ell n W_{i2t} - X_{i2t}\beta_2 \end{pmatrix}' \Sigma_\epsilon^{-1} \right.$$
$$\left. \begin{pmatrix} \ell n W_{i1t} - X_{i1t}\beta_1 \\ \ell n W_{i2t} - X_{i2t}\beta_2 \end{pmatrix} \right\}$$

$$\cdot (2\pi)^{-1/2} \sigma_\eta^{-1} \exp\left\{ -\frac{1}{2} (Z_{it} - W_{i1t} + W_{i2t} - S_{i1t}\pi)^2 / \sigma_\eta^2 \right\}$$

$$\cdot I[Z_{it} \geq 0 \text{ if } d_{i1t} = 1, \quad Z_{it} < 0 \text{ if } d_{i1t} = 0]. \tag{15}$$

Given flat priors, the joint posterior density of the structural parameters $(\beta_1, \beta_2, \Sigma_e, \sigma_\eta)$, the parameters characterizing expectations π, the unobserved wages $\{W_{ijt}$ when $d_{ijt} = 0$ for $i = 1, N, j = 1, 2, t = 1, T\}$, and the value function differences $\{Z_{it}, i = 1, N; t = 1, T\}$, are proportional to the likelihood in (15).

It is not feasible to construct this posterior density analytically, because of the high dimensional integrations over the unobserved wages and value function differences that are involved. For instance, to form the joint posterior of the parameters of interest $(\beta_1, \beta_2, \Sigma_e, \sigma_\eta, \pi)$, we must perform an $N*T*2$ dimensional integration over the unobserved wages and value function differences.

But it is possible to simulate draws from the posterior using a Gibbs sampling-data augmentation algorithm. To implement this algorithm, we factor the joint posterior density (15) into a set of conditional densities, each of which can be drawn from easily. Then, we repeatedly cycle through these conditionals, drawing from each one in turn. As the number of cycles grows large, the draws so obtained converge in distribution to that of the complete joint posterior (see Gelfand and Smith (1990) or Geweke (1995b) for a discussion of convergence conditions).

Our Gibbs sampling data augmentation algorithm consists of six steps or "blocks." To start the algorithm off, we need an initial guess for the model parameters $(\beta_1, \beta_2, \Sigma_e, \sigma_\eta, \pi)$, and for the unobserved wages. Then, the six steps are:

(S1) Draw the value function differences $\{Z_{it}, i = 1, N; t = 1, T\}$
(S2) Draw the unobserved wages $\{W_{ijt}$ when $d_{ijt} = 0$ for $i = 1, N; j = 1, 2, t = 1, T\}$
(S3) Draw (β_1, β_2)
(S4) Draw (Σ_e)
(S5) Draw π
(S6) Draw σ_η
Return to step (S1).

Each loop steps (S1) through (S6) is referred to as a "cycle" of the Gibbs sampler. We now describe the steps in detail.

Step 1

With everything else known, the Z_{it} have a simple truncated normal distribution. We have

$$Z_{it} \sim T^+ N(-W_{i1t} + W_{i2t} - S_{i1t}\pi, \sigma_\eta^2) \text{ if } d_{i1t} = 1$$

$$Z_{it} \sim T^- N(-W_{i1t} + W_{i2t} - S_{i1t}\pi, \sigma_\eta^2) \text{ if } d_{i1t} = 0$$

where T^+ indicates that the normal is truncated from below at 0, while T^-

indicates that the normal is truncated from above at 0. It is straightforward to draw from these distributions using an inverse CDF method.

Step 2

With everything else known, the unobserved wages still have a rather complex distribution. Suppose W_{i1t} is unobserved. The kernel of its density is

$$g(W_{i1t}) = W_{i1t}^{-1} \exp\{-\tfrac{1}{2}(\ln W_{i1t} - X_{i1t}\beta_1 - \lambda_{it})^2\}/\sigma_*^2 \exp\{-\tfrac{1}{2}(Z_{i1t} - W_{i1t} + W_{i2t} + S_{i1t}\pi)^2/\sigma_\eta^2\}$$

where $\lambda_{it} \equiv \sigma_{\epsilon_1\epsilon_2}\epsilon_{i2t}/\sigma_{\epsilon_2}^2$ and $\sigma_*^2 \equiv \sigma_{\epsilon_1}^2(1 - (\sigma_{\epsilon_1\epsilon_2}/\sigma_{\epsilon_1}, \sigma_{\epsilon_2})^2)$. Notice that the appearance of log wages on the left-hand side of the wage functions and the level of wages in the payoff functions creates a density that is difficult to draw from (because the inverse CDF must be constructed using quadrature methods).

Rather than using an inverse CDF method, we draw from this density using a more efficient acceptance/rejection (A/R) method described in Geweke (1995a). In this case, $g(W_{i1t})$ is the "target" density kernel. The "sampling" density kernel is

$$h(W_{i1t}) = W_{i1t}^{-1} \exp\{-\tfrac{1}{2}(\ln W_{i1t} - X_{i1t}\beta_1 - \lambda_{it})^2/\sigma_*^2\}.$$

Note that one can draw wages from this density simply by drawing log wages from the normal density kernel $\exp\{-\tfrac{1}{2}(\ln W_{i1t} - X_{i1t}\beta_1 - \lambda_{it})^2/\sigma_*^2\}$ and then taking the anti-log. The acceptance probability in the A/R algorithm is

$$\{\max_w g(W)/h(W)\}^{-1} g(W_{i1t})/h(W_{i1t}).$$

Note that the first term in the acceptance probability is a normalizing factor that sets the maximum acceptance probability, which occurs at the point where the $g(W)/h(W)$ ratio is greatest, equal to one.

To examine the acceptance probabilities more closely in our case, define $\mu_{i1t} = Z_{it} + W_{i2t} - S_{i1t}\pi$. Then the ratio of the target to the sampling density kernel is

$$g(W_{i1t})/h(W_{i1t}) = \exp\{-\tfrac{1}{2}(W_{i1t} - \mu_{i1t})^2/\sigma_\eta^2\}.$$

If $\mu_{i1t} > 0$ then this is maximized at $W_{i1t} = \mu_{i1t}$, the normalizing factor $\{\max_w g(W)/h(W)\}^{-1}$ is simply 1 (since the sampling density kernel is always at least as great as the target density kernel), and the acceptance probability is $g(W_{i1t})/h(W_{i1t})$. If, on the other hand, $\mu_{i1t} \leq 0$ then, given the constraint that wages must be positive, the ratio $g(W)/h(W)$ approaches its maximum $\exp\{-\mu_{i1t}^2/2\sigma_\eta^2\}$ as $W \to 0$. Thus, the acceptance probability is $\exp\{\mu_{i1t}^2/2\sigma_\eta^2\} g(W_{i1t})/h(W_{i1t})$. Finally, note that $\mu_{i1t} = W_{i1t} + \eta_{i1t}$, so that negative values will be a rather rare event provided that σ_η^2 is small relative to $\sigma_{\epsilon_1}^2$.

Step 3

With everything else known, the density of (β_1, β_2) is just

$$\prod_i \prod_t (2\Pi)^{-1} |\Sigma_\epsilon|^{-1} \exp\left\{-\frac{1}{2}\begin{pmatrix} \ln W_{i1t} - X_{i1t}\,\beta_1 \\ \ln W_{i2t} - X_{i2t}\,\beta_2 \end{pmatrix}' \Sigma_\epsilon^{-1} \begin{pmatrix} \ln W_{i1t} - X_{i1t}\,\beta_1 \\ \ln W_{i2t} - X_{i2t}\,\beta_2 \end{pmatrix}\right\}.$$

Note that, as a function of (β_1, β_2), this is just the kernel of a multivariate normal density. This can be constructed by estimating a seemingly unrelated regression (SUR) system in which the first equation is the $\ln W_{i1t}$ equation and the second is the $\ln W_{i2t}$ equation. Since Σ_ϵ is known we apply a GLS transformation. Then (β_1, β_2) is distributed according to the standard GLS formula

$$\beta \sim N(X'\Sigma^{-1}X)^{-1}X'\Sigma^{-1}\ln W, (X'\Sigma^{-1}X)^{-1}$$

where $\beta \equiv (\beta_1, \beta_2)'$, $\Sigma \equiv \Sigma_\epsilon \otimes I_{NT}$, X is defined as a matrix with the X_{i1t} in the upper left block, X_{i2t} in the lower right block, and zeros in the upper right and lower left blocks, and $\ln W$ is defined as a vector with the $\ln W_{i1t}$ stacked on top and $\ln W_{i2t}$ on the bottom. It is straightforward to draw (β_1, β_2) from this bivariate normal density

Step 4

With everything else known, Σ_ϵ^{-1} has a Wishart distribution. Define $e_{ijt} = \ln W_{i1t} - X_{ijt}\beta_j$. Then Σ_ϵ^{-1} has the distribution

$$\Sigma_\epsilon^{-1} \sim W[\sum_i \sum_t (e_{i1t}e_{i2t})'(e_{i1t}e_{i2t}), NT].$$

It is straightforward to draw from the bivariate Wishart, and then invert the draw for Σ_ϵ^{-1} to obtain a draw for Σ_ϵ.

Step 5

With everything else known, π has the density

$$\prod_i \prod_t (2\pi)^{-1/2}\sigma_\eta^{-1}\exp\{-\frac{1}{2}(Z_{it} - W_{i1t} + W_{i2t} - S_{i1t}\pi)/\sigma_\eta^2\}.$$

Note that, as a function of π, this is the kernel of a multivariate normal density. This can be constructed by running a regression with the $Z_{it} - W_{i1t} + W_{i2t}$ as the dependent variable and the S_{i1t} as the independent variables. Then π is distributed according to the standard OLS formula

$$\pi \sim N((S'S)^{-1}S'Z^*, \sigma_\eta^2(S'S)^{-1})$$

where S is the matrix consisting of the stacked S_{ilt} vectors and Z^* is the column vector consisting of the stacked $Z_{it} - W_{ilt} + W_{i2t}$ values. It is straightforward to draw from this using a multivariate normal random number generator.

Step 6

With everything else known, σ_η has an inverted gamma distribution. Since $\eta_{it} = Z_{it} - W_{ilt} + W_{i2t} - S_{ilt}\pi$, we have that

$$\sum_i \sum_t \eta_{it}^2/\sigma_\eta^2 \sim \chi^2(NT)$$

To draw σ_η, just draw a χ^2 random variable with NT degrees of freedom, set this equal to the quantity $\sum_i \sum_t \eta_{it}^2/\sigma_\eta^2$, and choose σ_η accordingly.

3   Experimental design

In order to evaluate the performance of the method described in sections 1 and 2, we have performed several Monte Carlo experiments. In these experiments, we generated data from the occupation choice model in equations (4)–(6), using the following parameter values

$$\ln W_{ilt} = 9.425 + 0.033X_{ilt} - 0.0005X_{ilt}^2 + 0.000X_{i2t} + 0.0000X_{ilt}^2 + \epsilon_{ilt}$$

$$\ln W_{i2t} = 9.000 + 0.67X_{i2t} - 0.0010X_{i2t}^2 + 0.022X_{ilt} + 0.0005X_{ilt}^2 + \epsilon_{i2t}$$

$$\begin{pmatrix} \epsilon_{ilt} \\ \epsilon_{i2t} \end{pmatrix} \sim \left(\begin{pmatrix} 0 \\ 0 \end{pmatrix}, \begin{pmatrix} 0.0400 & 0.0000 \\ 0.0000 & 0.0625 \end{pmatrix} \right)$$

$$\sigma_\eta = 400.$$

We set N, the number of individuals, equal to 500, and T, the number of time periods, equal to 40.

We generated data from this model using two different assumptions about how agents form their expectations. In one case, we assume that agents solve a dynamic programming (DP) problem to generate the optimal decision rule, using a discount factor of $\delta = 0.95$. Since there are only two alternatives, and given the simplicity of the state space, it is straightforward to solve this DP problem analytically. The DP solution gives us the future components of the value functions associated with each alternative in each state in each time period. That is, we obtain

$$F(X_{ilt} + d_{ilt}, t) = \delta E_t[V(S_i(t+1))|S_i(t), d_{ilt}]$$

for $X_{ilt} = 0, t - 1, d_{ilt} = 0, 1$, and $t = 1, T = 1$. Given these objects, we can form the optimal decision rule (10). Then, by drawing values of the stochastic terms $\{\epsilon_{i1t}, \epsilon_{i2t}, \eta_{it}\}, t = 1, T, i = 1, N$, we simulate lifetime occupational choice and wage paths.

A problem with using data generated in this way is that in our Gibbs sampling algorithm we constrain the $f(X_{i1t} + 1, t)$ functions to lie in a space spanned by finite order polynomials. But if the agents in the artificial data are solving a DP problem to form optimal decision rules, then neither the future components of the value functions $F(X_{i1t} + d_{i1t}, t)$, nor their differences across choices $f(X_{i1t} + 1, t)$, will lie in a space spanned by finite order polynomials. Thus, we have a misspecification of the true data generating process.

It is of interest to see how the algorithm performs when the data generating process is correctly specified. Thus, we also generated data under the assumption that agents use a decision rule in which the future component is a polynomial in the state variables. To construct this polynomial, we regressed the $f(X_{i1t} + 1, t)$ functions obtained from solving the DP problem on a 6th-order polynomial in the state variables. The form of the polynomial is given in equation (12) and the subsequent discussion. We then used the fitted values from this regression as the $f(X_{i1t} + 1, t)$ functions in the decision rule (10).

We find that the 6th-order OLS fitted polynomial approximation to the future components gives a very good approximation to the optimal decision rule in two senses. First, the R^2 from the regression is 0.932. Second, and more importantly, we determined that agents' wealth losses from using the suboptimal decision rule based on the polynomial future component rather than the optimal rule obtain by solution of the DP problem are trivial.

To determine the wealth loss from using the suboptimal decision rule we constructed two types of artificial data sets, each with $N = 500$ and $T = 40$. In one, agents used the optimal decision rule while in the other they used a decision rule based on the 6th-order polynomial approximation to the $f(X_{i1t} + 1, t)$ functions. The results are reported in table 4.1. The data sets labeled 1 through 5 were constructed using five independent sets of draws for the $\epsilon_{i1t}, \epsilon_{i2t}$ and η_{it}. But for each set of draws we constructed two artificial data sets. In one agents use the optimal decision rule based on the future components obtained from solution of the DP problem. Henceforth we call these data sets 1-EMAX through 5-EMAX. In the other agents use the polynomial approximation to the future components to form a decision rule. Henceforth we call these data sets 1-POLY through 5-POLY, Any differences in choices between the corresponding EMAX and POLY data sets result only because the future components of the value functions differ. Across the five experiments, the average wealth loss among the set of agents using the suboptimal rule is 8.8 hundredths of 1 per cent. The finding that

Table 4.1. *Quality of the OLS estimated polynomial approximation to the true future component*

Error set	1	2	3	4	5
Mean* wealth** with true future component	354534.72	354912.59	356430.12	355723.35	355438.58
Mean* wealth** with polynomial approximation	354404.31	354401.22	356092.88	355612.60	354926.21
Mean* dollar loss	130.43	511.37	337.24	110.75	512.37
Mean* percent loss	0.03%	0.14%	0.09%	0.03%	0.14%
Percent agreement in choices	92.40	92.80	90.60	93.20	92.80
Aggregate (by age)	%	%	%	%	%
1	97.60	97.80	95.00	96.20	96.80
2	98.00	98.80	97.40	97.20	98.20
3	98.60	98.40	97.60	98.60	98.20
4	96.60	96.60	95.40	97.40	97.20
5	94.40	95.20	93.20	96.00	97.00
10	90.40	88.60	89.80	91.40	87.20
20	91.20	93.00	91.20	92.60	92.40
30	91.80	92.20	91.40	94.60	93.60
40	92.60	93.40	90.60	93.20	92.80

Notes:
* Mean is taken over 500 agents that live for exactly 40 periods.
** "Wealth" is defined as the discounted stream of ex-post lifetime earnings.

wealth losses from using a simple polynomial approximation to the optimal decision rule are small is consistent with the findings of Krussell and Smith (1996).

Table 4.2 reports on various characteristics of the artificial data sets. For data sets 1-EMAX and 1-POLY we report the fraction of agents who choose alternative 1 at each age, and the mean accepted wage in occupations 1 and 2 at each age. With these parameter values, occupation 1 can be thought of as "unskilled labor" while occupation 2 is "skilled labor." The mean of the offer wage distribution for inexperienced workers is higher in occupation 1, but in occupation 2 wages rise more quickly with experience. It is also the case that experience in occupation 1 raises offer wages in occupation 2, but not vice-versa. Together, these features create an "occupational ladder" in which workers have some tendency to shift from 1 to 2 as they get older.

Table 4.3 reports the results from applying the Gibbs sampling algorithm described in section 2 to the POLY data sets. For starting values, we set the wage function intercepts and error standard deviations equal to the means and standard deviations of accepted log wages, set σ_η at 1,000, set π_0 at a value that roughly equated predicted and actual choice frequencies at the initial parameter values ($-3,100$), and set all other parameters at zero. After a sufficient number of "burn-in" cycles so as to achieve convergence (with the criteria to be discussed below), we used the next 2,000 cycles to simulate the joint posterior distribution. The column labeled "True" in table 4.3 contains the data generating values for the structural parameters ($\beta_1, \beta_2, \Sigma_\epsilon, \sigma_\eta$) and the 21 polynomial coefficients π that capture expectations. The column labeled "Mean" contains the posterior means, followed in the next column by the posterior standard deviation (see Geweke and Keane (1996) for additional results).

Overall, the results in table 4.3 are quite impressive. For instance, in the runs on the 1-POLY data, 2-POLY, and 4-POLY data sets, the posterior means for all the wage equation parameters are all within two posterior standard deviations of the data generating values, and most are well within one standard deviation. The posterior mean for the wage error correlation is slightly more than two posterior standard deviations above the data generating value in the run on the 3-POLY data set, while the posterior mean for the occupation 2 wage error variance is slightly more than two posterior standard deviations above the data generating value in the run on the 5-POLY data set.

Table 4.4 contains OLS regressions of accepted log wages on experience, ignoring the dynamic selection bias that is generated by agents' decision rule, for the 1-POLY through 5-POLY data sets. These estimates show substantial biases for all the wage equation parameters. Thus, it is clear that the

Table 4.2. *Choice contributions and mean accepted wages in the data generated with true and OLS polynomial future components*

	Data set 1–EMAX			Data set 1–POLY		
	Percent	Mean accepted wage		Percent	Mean accepted wage	
Period	in Occ. 1	Occ. 1	OCC. 2	in Occ. 1	Occ. 1	OCC. 2
1	68.20%	13518.95	10157.72	65.80%	13582.70	10090.85
2	64.20%	14075.90	10333.34	62.20%	14143.49	10270.84
3	63.60%	14259.73	10412.94	62.60%	14273.48	10410.98
4	61.60%	14711.21	10720.55	60.20%	14722.20	10736.39
5	57.80%	15149.64	11265.89	56.60%	15126.34	11352.12
6	53.40%	15074.74	11386.17	52.40%	15024.08	11511.15
7	51.20%	15873.34	12043.19	49.80%	15916.81	12104.61
8	53.60%	16110.32	12483.63	50.60%	16366.56	12351.35
9	46.80%	16435.97	12807.57	44.40%	16580.96	12849.18
10	45.40%	16880.64	13191.99	43.40%	17012.38	13276.41
11	43.20%	17147.20	13546.29	40.20%	17178.43	13654.06
12	44.80%	17228.21	14193.09	40.40%	17349.29	14210.80
13	37.80%	17581.22	15073.76	36.20%	17702.36	15086.65
14	37.80%	17434.20	15696.70	34.40%	17389.17	15704.33
15	36.80%	17880.31	16124.57	35.20%	17708.52	16266.96
16	32.60%	18237.00	16864.88	31.60%	18031.73	16956.84
17	31.80%	18776.79	17215.52	29.60%	18524.06	17288.61
18	33.00%	18915.48	18427.82	31.80%	18754.68	18460.48
19	32.40%	18929.04	18692.19	30.40%	19070.55	18728.53
20	26.60%	19465.56	19474.62	26.20%	19173.03	19581.50
21	30.20%	20174.20	20024.03	29.60%	20105.41	20154.48
22	30.80%	19771.71	20891.76	29.80%	19752.06	21014.38
23	28.20%	19931.67	21044.38	28.20%	19888.64	21126.76
24	27.20%	19612.29	22108.70	27.00%	19896.59	22160.10
25	27.40%	20484.94	22476.02	27.60%	20275.29	22661.92
26	26.80%	19880.57	23026.35	26.00%	19946.60	22899.08
27	26.40%	21125.67	23990.42	25.60%	21112.75	23911.17
28	27.00%	20889.27	23755.55	28.20%	20743.88	23989.04
29	25.40%	20784.30	25539.36	24.60%	20844.08	25487.78
30	26.60%	21159.77	25761.60	25.20%	21157.22	25691.86
31	25.60%	21421.28	26887.25	25.60%	21302.05	26904.03
32	24.40%	21271.78	26857.47	23.80%	21276.90	26786.20
33	24.00%	20470.71	27392.54	22.80%	20497.13	27373.38
34	23.20%	22078.95	27592.74	22.20%	22101.79	27459.55
35	24.80%	21493.14	27957.00	22.80%	22002.08	27700.57
36	23.40%	21680.03	27799.76	22.20%	22047.80	27706.19
37	23.80%	21546.08	28819.30	22.20%	21896.35	28533.66
38	22.20%	21255.37	29480.34	21.00%	21475.40	29466.02
39	21.20%	20816.65	29277.87	20.80%	20892.50	29241.84
40	22.00%	21680.48	28889.35	20.60%	21976.99	28583.09

Table 4.3. *Descriptive statistics for final 2000 Gibbs sampler parameter draws for several different data sets generated using polynomial future component*

Parameter	True	1-Polynomial		2-Polynomial		3-Polynomial		4-Polynomial		5-Polynomial	
		Mean	SD	Mean	SD	Mean	SD	Mean	SD	Mean	SD
Occ. 1 Int.	9.42500	9.42581	0.00480	9.42975	0.00472	9.42433	0.00463	9.42540	0.00499	9.42477	0.00470
Occ. 1 Own Exp.	0.03300	0.03262	0.00074	0.03182	0.00076	0.03339	0.00076	0.03293	0.00078	0.03296	0.00076
Occ. 1 Own Exp. Sq.	-0.00050	-0.00049	0.00002	-0.00047	0.00002	-0.00050	0.00002	-0.00050	0.00002	-0.00050	0.00002
Occ. 1 Other Exp.	0.00000	0.00102	0.00099	0.00036	0.00088	0.00179	0.00105	0.00130	0.00118	0.00076	0.00104
Occ. 1 Other Exp. sq.	0.00000	-0.00005	0.00003	-0.00001	0.00004	-0.00006	0.00004	-0.00007	0.00004	-0.00004	0.00004
Occ. 1 Error Var.	0.04000	0.03873	0.00084	0.03960	0.00072	0.03923	0.00062	0.03956	0.00088	0.03985	0.00069
Occ. 2 Int.	9.00000	9.00645	0.00662	9.01192	0.00649	9.00963	0.00596	8.99729	0.00725	8.99958	0.00605
Occ. 2 Own Exp.	0.06700	0.06763	0.00100	0.06585	0.00081	0.06695	0.00087	0.06876	0.00092	0.06761	0.00092
Occ. 2 Own Exp. Sq.	-0.00100	-0.00102	0.00003	-0.00098	0.00002	-0.00101	0.00003	-0.00104	0.00003	-0.00101	0.00003
Occ. 2 Other Exp.	0.02200	0.01960	0.00139	0.02205	0.00122	0.02210	0.00135	0.02076	0.00136	0.02077	0.00127
Occ. 2 Other Exp. sq.	-0.00050	-0.00043	0.00005	-0.00051	0.00005	-0.00054	0.00005	-0.00051	0.00007	-0.00047	0.00005
Occ. 2 Error Var.	0.06250	0.06245	0.00087	0.06087	0.00087	0.06177	0.00091	0.06154	0.00089	0.06464	0.00089
Error Covariance	0.00000	-0.00154	0.00119	0.00073	0.00085	0.00264	0.00073	-0.00174	0.00135	-0.00103	0.00072
Error Correlation	0.00000	-0.03122	0.02400	0.01494	0.01721	0.05376	0.01502	-0.03505	0.02682	-0.02031	0.01404
SD Eta	400.00	877.92	89.37	626.78	79.67	365.07	23.43	674.58	113.83	594.25	128.49
PI1	-2861.22	-2569.51	219.86	-2831.80	187.41	-2770.31	233.39	-2536.40	198.81	-2823.83	217.86
PI2	-717.03	-2789.23	590.09	-1238.40	619.12	-1247.45	634.46	-1899.82	597.81	-1374.43	547.50
PI3	2285.40	3883.24	497.74	3026.43	504.76	2322.31	458.09	3274.53	541.34	3054.51	531.96
PI4	-790.83	-1181.06	187.77	-1021.39	152.72	-667.07	159.63	-1142.62	227.35	-1038.84	189.35

Table 4.3. (*cont.*)

Parameter	True	1-Polynomial		2-Polynomial		3-Polynomial		4-Polynomial		5-Polynomial	
		Mean	SD	Mean	SD	Mean	SD	Mean	SD	Mean	SD
PI5	108.03	146.48	29.91	127.16	19.56	79.06	23.52	153.39	39.35	133.97	27.80
PI6	-5.24	-6.57	1.62	-5.44	0.93	-3.51	1.21	-7.11	2.19	-6.00	1.48
PI7	137.86	1483.24	376.34	1029.23	397.84	425.65	468.02	278.15	419.08	845.36	388.94
PI8	-5757.05	-6719.48	767.26	-6936.46	655.01	-5055.43	682.36	-5916.11	780.33	-6881.36	747.04
PI9	2835.75	2897.92	403.07	3098.48	246.50	2158.62	306.03	3034.69	495.56	3233.48	339.08
PI10	-437.15	-429.25	79.04	-415.57	39.49	-305.88	50.34	-459.75	98.94	-458.84	64.93
PI11	21.28	20.94	4.82	17.25	2.52	14.22	2.98	21.68	5.84	20.34	4.37
PI12	3763.28	3612.86	403.40	3907.54	328.78	3160.24	318.48	3833.76	460.40	4110.59	324.99
PI13	-2986.69	-2773.78	386.38	-2845.31	204.96	-2267.32	285.97	-3270.66	446.07	-3191.07	270.15
PI14	479.48	485.97	92.89	357.96	58.12	353.01	76.52	520.19	98.28	436.44	87.82
PI15	-20.18	-24.70	6.48	-9.82	4.88	-15.51	5.81	-22.55	6.26	-14.51	7.28
PI16	897.49	882.39	153.68	802.56	110.10	704.08	121.60	1025.35	146.49	930.51	120.27
PI17	-88.54	-161.07	49.31	7.72	42.97	-80.92	52.39	-110.93	41.10	-10.34	60.63
PI18	-4.20	6.95	4.63	-11.02	4.35	0.18	4.77	-0.55	3.60	-10.70	5.70
PI19	-57.82	-22.99	15.22	-81.97	14.31	-38.75	12.65	-56.08	10.77	-91.47	14.01
PI20	8.92	2.58	1.84	9.22	1.67	4.37	1.44	6.34	1.31	10.36	1.66
PI21	-0.74	0.00	0.20	0.00	0.16	0.00	0.09	-0.01	0.16	-0.02	0.19

Table 4.4. OLS wage equation parameter estimates for data generated with polynomial future component (standard deviations in parentheses)*

| | Occupation 1 | | | | | Occupation 2 | | | | | Wage error SDs | |
| | Own | | | Other | | Own | | | Other | | | |
Data set	Intercept	Own exp.	exp. squared	Other exp.	exp. squared	Intercept	Own exp.	exp. squared	Other exp.	exp. squared	Occ. 1	Occ. 2
Actual	9.42500	0.03300	−0.00050	0.00000	0.00000	9.00000	0.06700	−0.00100	0.02200	−0.00050	0.20000	0.25000
1-POLY	9.51154	0.02621	−0.00039	0.01970	−0.00049	9.17053	0.05818	−0.00083	0.01124	0.00012	0.17728	0.22841
	(0.00459)	(0.00071)	(0.00002)	(0.00104)	(0.00005)	(0.00616)	(0.00088)	(0.00003)	(0.00148)	(0.00007)		
2-POLY	9.51300	0.02633	−0.00040	0.01991	−0.00050	9.17570	0.05665	−0.00079	0.01210	0.00011	0.17662	0.22648
	(0.00466)	(0.00077)	(0.00002)	(0.00103)	(0.00004)	(0.00620)	(0.00087)	(0.00003)	(0.00163)	(0.00008)		
3-POLY	9.51180	0.02707	−0.00041	0.02029	−0.00053	9.16835	0.05781	−0.00082	0.01306	0.00008	0.17806	0.22836
	(0.00463)	(0.00073)	(0.00002)	(0.00104)	(0.00005)	(0.00619)	(0.00087)	(0.00003)	(0.00157)	(0.00008)		
4-POLY	9.51410	0.02648	−0.00040	0.02039	−0.00051	9.16211	0.05899	−0.00084	0.01213	0.00007	0.17732	0.22673
	(0.00460)	(0.00072)	(0.00002)	(0.00102)	(0.00004)	(0.00623)	(0.00088)	(0.00003)	(0.00161)	(0.00008)		
5-POLY	9.51402	0.02696	−0.00041	0.01999	−0.00053	9.17109	0.05834	−0.00082	0.00881	0.00031	0.17676	0.23088
	(0.00472)	(0.00077)	(0.00002)	(0.00101)	(0.00004)	(0.00625)	(0.00089)	(0.00003)	(0.00170)	(0.00009)		

Note:
* Results from simple OLS regression using only observed wages and experience.

Gibbs sampling algorithm is doing an impressive job implementing the appropriate dynamic selection correction.

The results in table 4.3 also indicate that there is difficulty in pinning down σ_η, the standard deviation of the non-pecuniary component of payoffs. In the runs on data sets 1-POLY, 2-POLY, and 4-POLY, the posterior means for σ_η are well above the data generating value. However, some investigation revealed that choices are quite insensitive to rather large changes in σ_η. Recall that the true value of σ_η is 400. In an experiment we regenerated one of the artificial data sets using the same sets of draws for the ϵ_{i1t}, ϵ_{i2t}, and η_{it}, but scaling σ_η up to 600. In that case, 97.4 per cent of choices remained identical. When we scaled σ_η down to 200, 97.4 per cent of choices also remained identical. Thus, it is not surprising that σ_η is hard to identify.

Finally, we note that for the most part the algorithm does a good job of uncovering the true values of the polynomial coefficients π that capture expectations. But a close examination reveals that we tend to do better on the lower order polynomial terms. In particular, the draws for π_{21}, the coefficient on the 6th-order experience term, are usually too high. This suggests we may have some trouble capturing the future components that agents assign to choices near the end of the life cycle. (Some evidence to this effect is reported below).

More interesting is an analysis of how the algorithm performs in the case where agents do in fact use the optimal decision rule. Table 4.5 reports the results for artificial data sets 1-EMAX through 5-EMAX. The column labeled "True" still contains the data generating values of the structural parameters. However, for the π coefficients we simply reproduce the coefficients from the OLS regression of the $f(X_{i1t} + 1, t)$ functions obtained by solving the DP problem on a 6th-order polynomial in the state variables. Thus, these π values are only reported so that we can gauge the extent to which the Gibbs sampling algorithm obtains a polynomial fit to the future components that looks similar to the OLS fit.

The results in table 4.5 are again quite impressive. There are a few instances in which the structural parameters in the wage equations are (slightly) more than two posterior standard deviations away from the data generating values. These include: (1) the occupation 2 own-experience linear and quadratic terms in data set 1-EMAX, (2) the occupation 2 cross-experience linear and quadratic terms in data sets 1-EMAX and 5-EMAX, and (3) the occupation 1 cross-experience linear and quadratic terms in data set 3-EMAX. But these three instances are not of much concern, because in each case where the linear term in the quadratic function is too big (small), the quadratic term is also too big (small). Such problems in pinning down the exact curvature of quadratic functions are common in

Table 4.5. *Descriptive statistics for final 2,000 Gibbs sampler parameter draws for several different data sets generated using true future component*

Parameter	True	1-EMAX Mean	SD	2-EMAX Mean	SD	3-EMAX Mean	SD	4-EMAX Mean	SD	5-EMAX Mean	SD
Occ. 1 Int.	9.42500	9.42126	0.00484	9.42768	0.00486	9.42285	0.00454	9.42747	0.00491	9.42501	0.00476
Occ. 1 Own Exp.	0.03300	0.03262	0.00070	0.03196	0.00078	0.03311	0.00073	0.03221	0.00075	0.03326	0.00075
Occ. 1 Own Exp. Sq.	−0.00050	−0.00049	0.00002	−0.00047	0.00002	−0.00050	0.00002	−0.00048	0.00002	−0.00051	0.00002
Occ. 1 Other Exp.	0.00000	0.00019	0.00084	0.00099	0.00100	0.00173	0.00081	0.00095	0.00105	0.00116	0.00091
Occ. 1 Other Exp. sq.	0.00000	−0.00005	0.00003	−0.00005	0.00004	−0.00008	0.00003	−0.00007	0.00004	−0.00006	0.00003
Occ. 1 Error Var.	0.04000	0.04072	0.00082	0.03958	0.00063	0.03977	0.00063	0.04023	0.00084	0.03947	0.00073
Occ. 2 Int.	9.00000	8.99625	0.00689	9.00681	0.00659	9.00106	0.00636	8.99930	0.00675	9.00383	0.00614
Occ. 2 Own Exp.	0.06700	0.06978	0.00112	0.06658	0.00096	0.06839	0.00111	0.06884	0.00101	0.06845	0.00093
Occ. 2 Own Exp. Sq.	−0.00100	−0.00107	0.00003	−0.00100	0.00003	−0.00105	0.00003	−0.00105	0.00003	−0.00103	0.00003
Occ. 2 Other Exp.	0.02200	0.01803	0.00138	0.02183	0.00150	0.02162	0.00155	0.02074	0.00162	0.01861	0.00139
Occ. 2 Other Exp. sq.	−0.00050	−0.00041	0.00005	−0.00055	0.00006	−0.00052	0.00006	−0.00050	0.00007	−0.00041	0.00006
Occ. 2 Error Var.	0.06250	0.06346	0.00089	0.06132	0.00083	0.06264	0.00088	0.06099	0.00088	0.06379	0.00088
Error Covariance	0.00000	−0.00256	0.00104	−0.00139	0.00126	0.00114	0.00074	−0.00280	0.00130	0.00007	0.00097
Error Correlation	0.00000	−0.05026	0.02026	−0.02807	0.02551	0.02288	0.01479	−0.05648	0.02603	0.00154	0.01929
SD Eta	400.00	412.45	90.60	932.32	86.61	376.46	47.28	1144.95	79.45	743.69	54.89
PI1	−2861.22	−2275.14	163.01	−2466.07	196.85	−1944.13	240.25	−1706.04	233.52	−2254.28	202.82
PI2	−717.03	−2515.66	721.67	−1209.73	694.31	−3566.42	632.92	−3784.52	818.64	−2534.70	751.72
PI3	2285.40	4402.92	589.58	3829.17	613.10	5104.83	580.72	5253.57	734.46	4384.96	669.77
PI4	−790.83	−1783.01	178.52	−1792.41	214.09	−1972.37	193.83	−2210.30	240.23	−1805.12	225.74

Table 4.5. (cont.)

Parameter	True	1-EMAX Mean	SD	2-EMAX Mean	SD	3-EMAX Mean	SD	4-EMAX Mean	SD	5-EMAX Mean	SD
PI5	108.03	270.88	21.85	287.78	31.49	300.46	27.10	348.53	32.68	277.95	32.42
PI6	−5.24	−13.73	1.02	−14.91	1.64	−15.50	1.38	−18.08	1.60	−14.21	1.68
PI7	137.86	455.12	565.73	−38.20	461.49	401.09	444.25	21.51	536.85	277.55	434.78
PI8	−5757.05	−6780.05	628.35	−7533.96	858.56	−6515.94	821.56	−6457.47	882.95	−6844.18	739.95
PI9	2835.75	4184.87	253.29	4826.89	391.18	4065.07	306.68	4865.96	346.21	4314.75	358.08
PI10	−437.15	−747.73	51.73	−842.73	72.96	−770.07	57.24	−931.15	64.32	−757.24	77.59
PI11	21.28	40.73	3.85	44.52	4.61	44.39	3.84	52.34	4.27	40.23	5.30
PI12	3763.28	4108.51	304.92	4801.36	387.29	4114.05	272.16	4425.14	360.98	4279.90	341.38
PI13	−2986.69	−4432.14	226.42	−4888.25	365.90	−4512.99	275.15	−5819.93	371.54	−4543.45	371.71
PI14	479.48	897.15	88.34	898.91	102.49	1019.16	87.81	1209.70	110.46	829.44	117.22
PI15	−20.18	−50.66	7.71	−46.37	8.02	−63.35	7.12	−68.59	8.70	−41.67	9.26
PI16	897.49	1455.56	84.79	1468.11	178.55	1523.18	135.72	2055.85	183.49	1438.60	165.12
PI17	−88.54	−316.72	63.99	−244.07	66.98	−441.26	62.32	−413.97	77.98	−186.41	74.59
PI18	−4.20	17.16	6.42	9.44	7.03	30.27	6.03	20.22	7.69	2.29	7.02
PI19	−57.82	−22.86	18.34	−45.38	24.53	16.73	17.44	−53.15	27.66	−78.93	20.38
PI20	8.92	2.61	2.08	4.59	3.33	−1.80	2.12	6.28	3.43	9.31	2.41
PI21	−0.74	−0.01	0.18	0.17	0.52	−0.03	0.22	−0.09	0.61	−0.14	0.43

data sets of this size, even when the data generating process is correctly specified. The posterior mean for the wage error correlation is also slightly more than two posterior standard deviations below the data generating value in data sets 1-EMAX and 4-EMAX.

Table 4.6 contains OLS regressions of accepted log wages on experience, ignoring the dynamic selection bias that is generated by agents' decision rule, for the 1-EMAX through 5-EMAX data sets. These estimates again show substantial biases for all the wage equation parameters. Thus, the Gibbs sampling algorithm continues to do an impressive job of implementing a dynamic selection correction despite the fact that agents' decision rule is misspecified due to the 6th-order polynomial approximation.

Returning to table 4.5, we see that we again have difficulty in pinning down σ_η, just as with the POLY data sets. It's posterior mean is well above the data generating value in the runs on data sets 2-EMAX, 4-EMAX, and 5-EMAX. But again, it appears that choices are little affected by changes in the magnitude of σ_η on the order we observe here.

Figure 4.1 contains the simulated posterior densities for a subset of the structural parameters, using data set 3-EMAX. In each figure, a vertical bar indicates the true data generating value of the parameter. The marks along the horizontal axis indicate the posterior mean and points one and two posterior standard deviations away from the mean. Except for the cross-experience and cross-experience squared coefficients in occupation 1, the posterior means are all very close to the data generating values. An interesting feature is the bimodal density for σ_η.

Returning to table 4.5, a comparison of the posterior means of the π parameters with the OLS estimates obtained by regression of the actual $f(X_{i1t} + 1, t)$ functions on a 6th-order polynomial in the state variables reveals many substantial differences. Thus, the polynomial approximation to the future components in the agents' optimal decision rule generated by the Gibbs algorithm appears (superficially) to be quite different from that generated by OLS regression.

Table 4.7 contains an analysis of how well the approximation to agents' decision rule obtained by the Gibbs algorithm matches the agents' optimal decision rule. The following experiment was performed. For each of the data sets 1-EMAX through 5-EMAX, we formed the polynomial approximation to the $f(X_{i1t} + 1, t)$ function implied by the posterior means for the π parameters obtained from the respective runs. We then used these polynomial approximations to the $f(X_{i1t} + 1, t)$ functions to form an approximate versions of agents' decision rule (10). We then regenerated each of the five data sets, using the exact same draws for the ϵ_{i1t}, ϵ_{i2t}, and η_{it}, but with the polynomial approximations replacing the optimal $f(X_{i1t} + 1, t)$ functions in (10). The average wealth loss across the five data sets if agents use these

Table 4.6. *OLS wage equation parameter estimates for data generated with true future component (standard deviations in parentheses)*

| | Occupation 1 | | | | | Occupation 2 | | | | | Wage error SDs | |
| | | Own | | Other | | | Own | | Other | | | |
Data set	Intercept	Own exp.	exp. squared	Other exp.	exp. squared	Intercept	Own exp.	exp. squared	Other exp.	exp. squared	Occ. 1	Occ. 2
Actual	9.42500	0.03300	−0.00050	0.00000	0.00000	9.00000	0.06700	−0.00100	0.02200	−0.00050	0.20000	0.25000
1-EMAX	9.50638	0.02627	−0.00039	0.02123	−0.00054	9.17518	0.05938	−0.00086	0.00796	0.00031	0.17981	0.22853
	(0.00470)	(0.00074)	(0.00002)	(0.00107)	(0.00005)	(0.00635)	(0.00094)	(0.00003)	(0.00169)	(0.00009)		
2-EMAX	9.50716	0.02662	−0.00038	0.02098	−0.00053	9.17877	0.05829	−0.00083	0.00907	0.00024	0.17890	0.22594
	(0.00475)	(0.00074)	(0.00002)	(0.00104)	(0.00005)	(0.00648)	(0.00095)	(0.00003)	(0.00188)	(0.00011)		
3-EMAX	9.49973	0.02763	−0.00040	0.02251	−0.00059	9.17000	0.05893	−0.00086	0.01066	0.00017	0.17999	0.22882
	(0.00469)	(0.00071)	(0.00002)	(0.00106)	(0.00005)	(0.00658)	(0.00095)	(0.00003)	(0.00183)	(0.00010)		
4-EMAX	9.50622	0.02653	−0.00039	0.02164	−0.00054	9.16782	0.06002	−0.00088	0.00962	0.00023	0.18052	0.22606
	(0.00474)	(0.00072)	(0.00002)	(0.00106)	(0.00005)	(0.006414)	(0.000945)	(0.00003)	(0.00177)	(0.00010)		
5-EMAX	9.50534	0.02773	−0.00042	0.02081	−0.00055	9.17511	0.05929	−0.00085	0.00808	0.00025	0.17916	0.22986
	(0.00475)	(0.00074)	(0.00002)	(0.00100)	(0.00004)	(0.00629)	(0.00094)	(0.00003)	(0.00169)	(0.00009)		

Note:

* Results from simple OLS regression using only observed wages and experience.

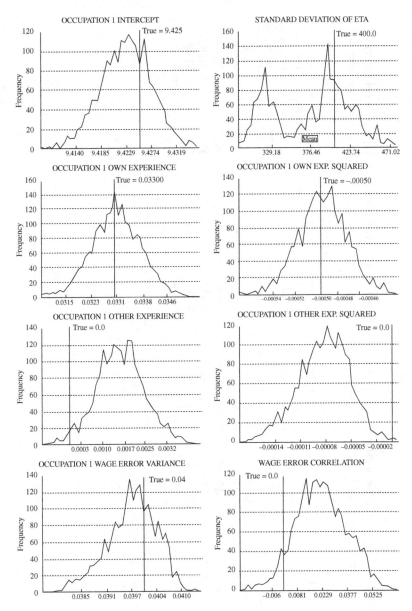

Figure 4.1 Empirical posterior distributions of selected structural parameters.
Notes: * Based on last 2,000 draws of the data set 3-EMAX estimation routine.
** Each horizontal axis contains five marks; the middle indicates the posterior mean and the others one and two standard deviations from mean.

Table 4.7. *Analysis of wealth loss when estimated polynomial approximation is used in place of true future component**

Data set	Using true EMAX**	Using approximate EMAX**						
	Mean wealth***	Mean wealth***	Mean dollar loss	Mean percent loss	Aggregate choice agreement	Percent with 0–35 agreements	Percent with 36–39 agreements	Percent choosing same path
1-EMAX	354534.72	354345.25	189.47	0.05%	94.10%	9.60%	39.40%	51.00%
2-EMAX	354912.59	354529.61	382.98	0.11%	94.60%	7.20%	38.40%	54.40%
3-EMAX	356430.12	356175.54	254.58	0.07%	93.90%	10.20%	39.20%	50.60%
4-EMAX	355723.35	355589.21	134.14	0.03%	95.00%	6.80%	35.80%	57.40%
5-EMAX	355438.58	354984.04	454.54	0.12%	93.90%	8.60%	39.00%	52.40%

Notes:

* Polynomial parameter values are set to the mean of their respective empirical posterior distributions.

** Each simulation includes 500 agents that live for exactly 40 periods.

*** "Mean wealth" is the equal-weight sample average of discounted streams of *ex-post* lifetime earnings in $.

suboptimal decision rules is 7.6 hundredths of 1 per cent. This is actually slightly smaller than the average wealth loss of 8.8 hundredths of 1 per cent obtained when OLS estimates of the π parameters were used (see table 4.1).

Figures 4.2 and 4.3 compare the true values and polynomial approximations to the $f(X_{i1t} + 1,t)$ – the difference between the future component associated with choice of occupation 1 and that associated with choice of 2. Figure 4.2a plots the true values of the $f(X_{i1t} + 1,t)$ at various state points that arise in periods 1 through 10, while figure 4.2b plots the polynomial approximation. The horizontal axis shows the level of occupation 1 experience at each state point.

For example, in period 1 the only possible state is zero experience in occupation 1. That point is indicated by a box in figures 4.2a and 4.2b. In that state, the true value of $f(X_{i1t} + 1,t) = f(1,1)$ is minus \$2,653. The value is negative because the return to experience is less in occupation 1 than in occupation 2. The polynomial approximation is minus \$2,524.

In period 2 there are two possible states – either one or zero periods of experience in occupation 1. These two points are indicated by shaded boxes in figures 4.2a and 4.2b. When occupation 1 experience is zero, the true value of $f(X_{i1t} + 1,t) = f(1,2)$ is minus \$3,022. The polynomial approximation is minus \$2,945. When occupation 1 experience is one, the true value of $f(X_{i1t} + 1,t) = f(2,2)$ is minus \$2,805. The polynomial approximation is minus \$2,837.

Overall, figures 4.2 and 4.3 show that the Gibbs sampling algorithm does an excellent job of uncovering agents' expectations. As figure 4.2c indicates, the polynomial approximations to the $f(X_{i1t} + 1,t)$ functions are generally within a few hundred dollars of the true values at state points that may arise over the first several periods. Figure 4.2c also shows that the accuracy of the approximation deteriorates over certain regions of the state space that may arise in later periods.

This pattern, whereby the inferences about the future components of the value functions deteriorate with age, is to be expected for two reasons. First, since in later periods there are more possible states, the data will tend to contain fewer agents at each state point. Thus, there are less data to pin down the $f(X_{i1t} + 1,t)$ functions at those less frequently observed state points. Second, as agents age they tend to specialize in either occupation 1 or 2. As a result of human capital accumulation, the current payoff function realizations for that occupation in which an agent specializes come more and more to dominate those for the alternative occupation. Thus, with age, choices become less influenced by the future components, and the data therefore contain less information about them.

Despite the fact that our inferences about the future components of the value functions tend to deteriorate with age (at least over certain regions of

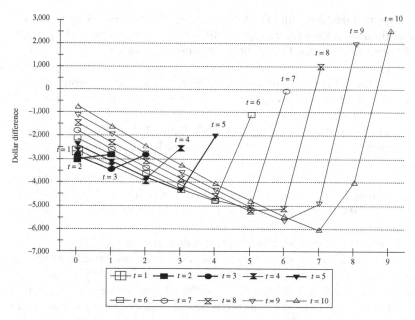

Figure 4.2a True future component differences at all states in first ten periods

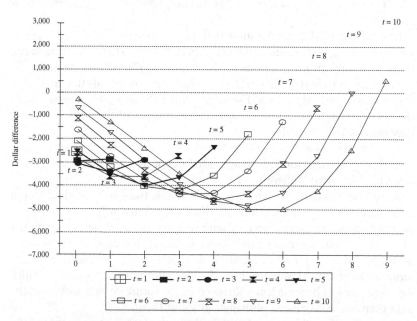

Figure 4.2b Estimated future component difference at all states in first ten periods
Note: From 3-EMAX estimation.

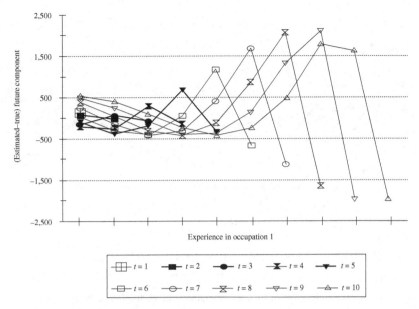

Figure 4.2c Dollar error in estimated difference of future components at all states
of first ten periods
Note: From 3-EMAX estimation.

the state space), figures 4.3a and 4.3b indicate that the Gibbs sampling algorithm does a good job of picking up the overall shape of the $f(X_{i1t}+1,t)$
functions over the whole life cycle.

Finally, figure 4.4 contains graphical evidence on convergence of the
Gibbs sampling algorithm for data set 3-EMAX. To gauge convergence we
used such graphical evidence. Specially, we constructed charts of the draws
by cycle and the posterior means by cycle, and let the Gibbs sampler run
until it appeared that the distribution was stationary. We found that from
5,000 to 18,000 cycles were necessary to achieve convergence, with substantial variation across runs. For data set 3-EMAX, we concluded that
convergence had been achieved after 18,000 cycles. Each cycle required
approximately 12.6 seconds on an IBM RISC 6000 model 360. That is
0.0252 seconds per person, and 0.00063 seconds per person-year.

4   Conclusion

In this chapter we have illustrated a method for Bayesian inference in
dynamic discrete choice models that does not require the econometrician
to make strong assumptions about how agents form expectations, or to

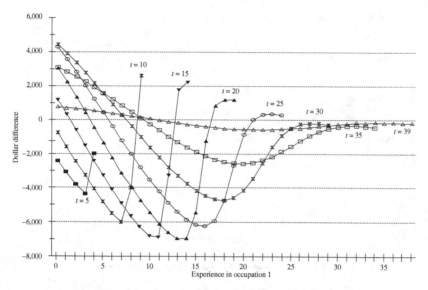

Figure 4.3a True difference in future components at various state points

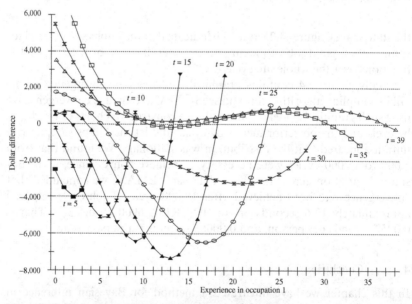

Figure 4.3b Estimated difference in future components at various state points
Note: From 3-EMAX estimation.

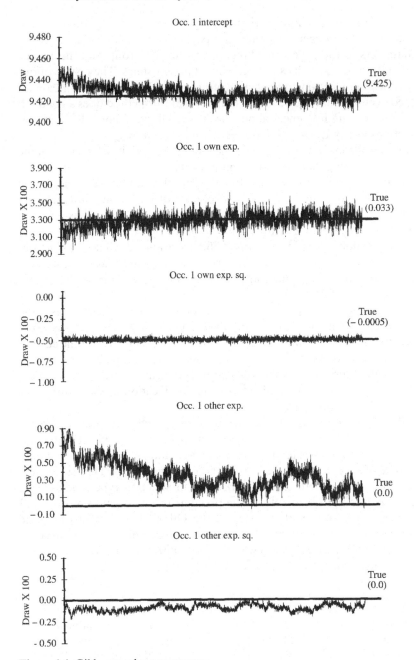

Figure 4.4 Gibbs sampler convergence
Note: Results for selected parameters from data set 3-EMAX estimation routine.

solve the agents' dynamic optimization problem. In this method, we use observed data on agents' choices and payoffs to infer both the structural parameters of the payoff functions that agents confront, and the agents' expectations of the values of occupying different states. The results of our numerical application to artificial data generated from a human capital-based occupational choice model indicate that the method does a good job both of drawing inferences about the structural parameters of the payoff functions and of drawing inferences about expectations.

Our results indicate that misspecification of agents' decision rules, in the form of assuming that the future components of the value functions follow a 6th-order polynomial when in fact they are the discounted values of the EMAX functions that come from a solution of a dynamic programming problem, is a "second-order" problem in two senses. First, it has a negligible effect on inferences with regard to the structural parameters of the payoff functions. Second, the misspecified decision rule that we infer from the data is very close to the optimal rule – in the sense that if agents were to use our suboptimal rule rather than the optimal rule it would lead to trivial wealth losses.

In future work, we plan to investigate how our method performs if the current payoff functions are misspecified. Then, we will compare this to the performance of full solution methods under misspecification of the current payoff functions. We conjecture that in statistical inference for dynamic optimization models the misspecification of the current payoff functions is a "first-order" problem relative to the misspecification of the future component of the value functions.

The Gibbs sampling data augmentation approach to Bayesian inference that we have used here has previously been successfully applied to inference in static discrete choice models in work by McCulloch and Rossi (1994) and Geweke, Keane, and Runkle (1994, 1997), among others. The results here indicate that the method also works well in selection type models. This outcome was not obvious from the previous results because of potential problems associated with the step of the Gibbs algorithm in which the unobserved wages are drawn. As we have described, this step is significantly more complex than the step in which latent utilities are drawn in a pure discrete choice framework without observed payoffs.

References

Bellman, R. (1957), *Dynamic Programming*, Princeton: Princeton University Press.

Gelfand, A.E. and A.F.M. Smith (1990), "Sampling Based Approaches to Calculating Marginal Densities," *Journal of the American Statistical Association*, 85, 389–409.

Geweke, J. (1995a), "Priors for Macroeconomic Time Series and Their Application," Working paper, Federal Reserve Bank of Minneapolis.

(1995b), "Simulation Based Bayesian Inference for Economic Time Series," Working paper, Federal Reserve Bank of Minneapolis.

Geweke, J. and M. Keane (1996), "Bayesian Inference for Dynamic Discrete Choice Models without the need for Dynamic Programming," Working paper 564, Federal Bank of Minneapolis.

Geweke, J., M. Keane, and D. Runkle (1994), "Alternative Computational Approaches to Inference in the Multinomial Probit Model," *Review of Economics and Statistics*, XX, 609–632.

(1997), "Statistical Inference in the Multinomial Multiperiod Probit Model," *Journal of Econometrics*, 80(1), 125–165.

Heckman, J. and G. Sedlacek (1985), "Heterogeneity, Aggregation and Market Wage Functions: An Empirical Model of Self-Selection in the Labor Market," *Journal of Political Economy*, 93, 1077–1125.

Hotz, V.J. and R.A. Miller (1993), "Conditional Choice Probabilities and the Estimation of Dynamic Programming Models," *Review of Economic Studies*, 60, 497–530.

Houser, D. (1998), "Bayesian Analysis of a Dynamic Stochastic Model of the Labor Supply and Savings," Ph.D. dissertation, Dept. of Economics, University of Minnesota.

Keane, M. and K. Wolpin (1994), "Solution and Estimation of Discrete Choice Dynamic Programming Models by Simulation and Interpolation: Monte Carlo Evidence," *Review of Economics and Statistics*, 76(4), 648–672.

Krussel, P. and A.A. Smith Jr. (1996), "Rules of Thumb in Macroeconomic Equilibrium: A Quantitative Analysis," *Journal of Economic Dynamics and Control*, 20(4), 527–558.

Lancaster, T. (1997), "Exact Structural Inference in Optimal Job Search Models," *Journal of Business and Economic Statistics*, 15(2): 165–179.

Manski, C. (1993), "Dynamic Choice in Social Settings," *Journal of Econometrics*, 58, 121–136.

McCulloch, R. and P. Rossi (1994), "An Exact Likelihood Analysis of the Multinomial Probit Model," *Journal of Econometrics*, 64(1), 207–240.

Roy, A.D. (1951), "Some Thoughts on the Distribution of Earnings," *Oxford Economics Papers*, 3, 135–146.

Rust, J. (1995), "Structural Estimation of Markov Decision Processes," in R. Engle and D. McFadden (eds.), *Handbook of Econometrics*, vol. IV, Amsterdam: North-Holland, chapter 51, pp. 3081–3143.

Tanner, M.A. and W.H. Wong (1987), "The Calculation of Posterior Distributions by Data Augmentation," *Journal of the American Statistical Association*, 82, 528–550.

5 Testing binomial and multinomial choice models using Cox's non-nested test

Melvyn Weeks

1 Introduction

The proliferation of random effects is one of the most troublesome characteristics of the multinomial probit (MNP) model. Given recent developments in simulation based inference (see McFadden (1989), Hajivassiliou and Ruud (1994), and Weeks (1994)), the original "curse of dimensionality," a characteristic of many limited dependent variable models, has been partially lifted. Monte Carlo simulation is now commonly used to estimate analytically intractable integrals. Further, in much of the emerging literature considerable space has been devoted to a discussion of simulation-based estimation, to the relative neglect of specification testing. Although it must be said that studies in this area will logically follow the development of reliable and consistent estimation techniques, it would appear that at this juncture there is a relative neglect of model evaluation.

The focus of this chapter is twofold. First, we extend the recent work of Pesaran and Pesaran (1993) by implementing and attempting to evaluate the Cox non-nested test for binomial and multinomial choice models. To our knowledge this represents the first study of this type. Second, focusing upon a number of asymptotically equivalent procedures for estimating the Kullback–Leibler (KL) measure of closeness and the variance of the test statistic, we compare a number of variants of the computationally intensive Cox test statistic. The variants considered are based upon asymptotically equivalent procedures for estimating the numerator and denominator of the Cox test statistic.

The outline of the chapter is as follows. In section 2 we present a brief overview of some key issues in the testing of multinomial choice models. In section 3 we examine the structure of the Cox test and develop notation. We also demonstrate the asymptotic equivalence of a class of Cox test statistics. In section 4 we outline the experimental design upon which a series of

I would like to thank Chris Orme and Les Godfrey for constructive comments.

Monte Carlo experiments are based. In section 5 we present a simple example which is illustrative of the calculations involved and in section 6 compare our findings with those of Pesaran and Pesaran (1995) using the same insurance choice data. In section 7 we present the results of a small Monte Carlo study. In section 8 we utilize the Cox test procedure to test multinomial probit and multinomial logit (MNL) specifications of a discrete choice model of labor force status.

2   Issues in the testing of multinomial choice models

The specification of an error structure that is consonant with the underlying data generating process (DGP) is a key component of any (stochastic) economic model. In the case of the MNP model the importance of this is magnified since misspecification of the error structure can seriously affect the estimation of model parameters and choice probabilities. For example, if an incorrect specification resulted in simple efficiency loss, as in the familiar linear regression model, then the computational ease with which the MNL model (and other variants of the generalized extreme value family) may be estimated would most likely have resulted in fewer resources being directed toward the development of multivariate probability simulators. The fact that the specification of the stochastic component does influence estimation of mean equation parameters (as well as affecting the efficiency of model estimates) provides the motivation for much of the recent work in simulation-based inference.

The importance and need for specification testing may also be viewed in the context of a paper by Bunch and Kitamura (1989). In surveying a large number of empirical studies in multinomial choice models, the authors found that over half contained notable misspecification errors. Further, although the importance of specification analysis in the MNP model is recognized, the dearth of studies in this area is itself a direct consequence of the formidable barriers that still exist in terms of parameter estimation. Moreover, an early study by Davidson and MacKinnon (1984) which proposed regression-based Lagrange Multiplier (LM) tests for the binary logit and probit models, highlighted a similar dearth for these simpler models.[1] The reason stems from the fact that estimators for these types of models are typically of the maximum likelihood (ML) variety. Thus, relative to linear models they impose a computational burden. However, over the last ten years, computational power available to the average investigator has increased to such an extent that now ML estimation of probit, logit, and

---

[1] As an example, the authors observe that the extensive survey article on qualitative response models by Amemiya (1981) contains no reference to LM-based tests.

related models is commonplace. As a result, there has been a similar increase in studies devoted to testing, with the particular prominence of the Lagrange multiplier (LM) test. Godfrey (1988) presents an extensive review of this literature.

In one of the few examples of specification testing in multinomial choice models, Hausman (1984) notes that in order to construct a specification test for MNL, the MNP model does not represent a viable alternative because of its inherent complexity. As a consequence, the author focuses upon two tractable tests based upon two distinct test procedures. The first, an application of the Hausman (1978) specification test, partitions the choice set into a complete (F) and restricted (R) set of alternatives. The test statistic is based upon the difference between the two sets of parameter estimates and relies on both being consistent under the null. This is a particularly logical test of the MNL model since the predominant characteristic of the model, the independence of irrelevant alternatives (IIA), states that the ratio of two probabilities depends only upon the attributes and characteristics of the two alternatives considered. Thus, the ratio is independent of the number of alternatives in the choice set and the curse of dimensionality does not apply. The advantage of this test is that it does not require the specification of an alternative model, and therefore does not require specialized software. A disadvantage is that the choice of the partition of F is arbitrary, and as a result test conclusions (i.e., power) may vary dependent upon which alternatives are excluded. Fry and Harris (1993) note that there exist a number of variants of this test, including a likelihood-ratio (LR) test of the difference of the respective maximized log likelihoods.

An alternative to the partitioning of the choice set is to utilize classical (nested) test procedures and thereby consider the MNL logit model against one or more nested models. Both Hausman (1984) and Fry and Harris (1993) employ the nested logit model as an alternative specification since MNL is a special case of this more general model. Following recent developments in simulation-based inference, it is now possible to utilize the MNP as an alternative to MNL. Although these two models are at first glance non-nested, a restricted model (independent probit (IP)) where all covariance parameters are fixed at zero and variances fixed at one, does allow an approximate test of the IIA assumption given the virtual equivalence of MNL and identity probit (see Hausman and Wise (1978) and Duncan and Weeks (1997)).[2]

---

[2] Since the underlying distributions are different, there are no asymptotic grounds for the use of this test, and therefore the test can only be considered a convenient approximation.

2.1   Non-nested tests

The problem with the above test strategies is that they both involve arbitrary decisions by the analyst. In the case of Hausman tests the analyst must decide on the form of the partitioning, and the use of classical tests requires decisions as to the form of the nesting. In both cases, these decisions may affect the outcome of the test.[3] An alternative approach is provided by the work of Cox (1961) and later Atkinson (1970), who formulated a series of non-nested tests based upon an adjusted log likelihood ratio statistic. The key trade-off here is between the application of general tests which have reasonable power against a wide range of departures from a null model and highly specific tests exhibiting high power for a specific form of departure. Davidson and MacKinnon (1981) have proposed a similar set of tests which are easier to implement and asymptotically equivalent.

When two DGPs are nested it is well known that the KL measure of closeness has zero expectation and, as a result, the use of standard asymptotic theory (i.e., the use of nominal critical values) requires no mean adjustment. For non-nested models this is not the case. To circumvent this problem, Cox proposed a "mean-adjusted" test statistic. The computational problem that such an adjustment creates stems from the fact that a key component of the test statistic is the pseudo-true value. One of a number of ways of overcoming this problem is to apply stochastic simulation in an analogous fashion to that used in simulation-based estimation. In fact the application of simulation here may be thought of as a simple crude frequency simulator as discussed in Hajivassiliou and Ruud (1994).

Within the field of discrete choice modeling one of the few applications of the Cox test is provided by Pesaran and Pesaran (1993). The reason for the dearth of applications follows from the same line of reasoning underlying the dominance of MNL over MNP – namely the calculation of the numerator in the Cox statistic presents a considerable computational burden. Pesaran and Pesaran (1993) show how the use of stochastic simulation circumvents the necessity to evaluate complex integrals. Although the authors utilize simulation methods to calculate the Cox statistic to test a simple binary probit model against a binary logit, it is also possible to utilize simulation techniques to provide a consistent estimator of model parameters for MNP and to construct the Cox statistic facilitating a non-nested test of MNP against the MNL model. Although the MNP model is characterized by the intractability of probability expressions for greater than four alternatives, the log likelihood function has a relatively simple

---

[3] For example, in the case of nested models there exists the possibility that a test statistic may exhibit low power against a specific, incorrect, alternative model.

structure. As a consequence, once an estimator has been found for the pseudo-true value, the Cox test statistic has a closed-form representation (see Pesaran and Pesaran (1993)).

3   The structure of the Cox test statistic

The essence of the Cox non-nested test is that the mean adjusted ratio of the maximized log likelihoods of two non-nested models has a well-defined limiting distribution under the null hypothesis. However, as recent papers by Orme (1994) attest, the existence of a large number of asymptotic equivalent variants of the Cox test statistic represents a formidable menu of choices for the applied econometrician. In the case of the numerator, various test statistics are based upon the use of different consistent estimators of the Kullback–Leibler measure of closeness. Further, as shown below, the asymptotic equivalence (hereafter AE) of these particular variants depends upon the AE of various consistent estimators of the pseudo-true value.

An additional set of variants of the Cox test statistic depend upon the existence of a number of AE ways of estimating the variance of the test statistic. Orme (1994) presents a detailed analysis of these variants. In this chapter we estimate the variance using three methods. First, we employ an outer product of the gradient (OPG) variant. This estimator, which is computationally simple to implement, is based upon an artificial regression where the regressand is the observed log likelihood ratio, and the regressors are the matrix of first derivatives of the log likelihood evaluated at the MLE plus a constant term. We compare this estimator with one which uses the observed Hessian, and following Pesaran and Pesaran (1995), an estimator which ignores variation due to uncertainty of parameter estimates under the null.[4]

3.1   Notation

Since the various AE approaches to consistently estimating the KL measure of closeness depends critically upon the estimation of the pseudo-true value, in developing notation we begin by focusing upon a number of standard results based upon familiar law of large numbers (LLN) type arguments applied to the true and pseudo-true values.

First, we let $H_f: f(y,\theta)$ and $H_g: g(y,\lambda)$ denote the conditional densities for two non-nested models. Both $f(.)$ and $g(.)$ define a family of distributions over the respective parameter spaces, Θ and Λ; $f(y,\theta_0)$, $g(y,\lambda_0)$ are the respective true and alternative models. $l_f(y_i,\theta), l_g(y_i,\lambda)$ represent the log-like-

---

[4] We note that although the test statistic based upon this method is correctly centered in large samples, the variance is asymptotically invalid.

lihood components for observation i for the respective true and alternative models. Assuming an independent and identically distributed sample of n observations, the log likelihood for the respective samples may be written

$$l_f(y,\theta) = \sum_{i=1}^{n} l_f(y_i,\theta) \text{ and } l_g(y,\lambda) = \sum_{i=1}^{n} l_g(y_i,\lambda).$$

For all the variants of the numerator in Cox's test statistic we rely on a standard consistency result for the maximum likelihood estimator (MLE), $\hat{\theta}_n$, which may be written

$$p\lim_{n\to\infty} \hat{\theta}_n = \theta_0. \tag{1}$$

The consistency property for the pseudo-MLE is a little more difficult to show. Three consistent estimators for λ_0, or perhaps more appropriately $\lambda(\theta)$ given the dependence upon θ_0 (under H_0), are detailed below.

1 White (1982) and White (1994) demonstrates that the observed pseudo-maximum likelihood estimator (PMLE), $\hat{\lambda}(\theta)$, is consistent for $\lambda(\theta_0)$ such that

$$p\lim_{n\to\infty} \hat{\lambda}(\theta) = \lambda(\theta_0). \tag{2}$$

2 Pesaran and Pesaran (1993) utilize stochastic simulation to construct a consistent estimator of the pseudo-true value. This estimator we denote by $\lambda^R(\hat{\theta}_n) = 1/R \sum_{i=1}^{R} \lambda^r(\hat{\theta}_n)$, where $\lambda^r(\hat{\theta}_n)$ represents the solution to the problem

$$\max_{\lambda} \sum_{i=1}^{n} \log g(\lambda, y_i^r(\hat{\theta}_n)) \tag{3}$$

in which $y_i^r(\hat{\theta}_n)$ represents the ith component of the rth simulated sample conditional upon $\hat{\theta}_n$. If we now repeat the maximization in (3) R times and apply a LLN to the *number of simulations*, then for any given θ we may write

$$p\lim_{R\to\infty} \lambda^R(\hat{\theta}_n) = \lambda(\hat{\theta}_n). \tag{4}$$

Given (1), we may apply a LLN argument to both sides of (4), giving

$$p\lim_{n\to\infty} \lambda(\hat{\theta}_n) = p\lim_{n\to\infty}[p\lim_{R\to\infty} \lambda^R(\hat{\theta}_n)] = \lambda(\theta_0). \tag{5}$$

The juxtaposition of two LLN in (5) neatly illustrates the trade-off between sample size and simulation noise.[5] Obviously as n becomes large, such that the probability mass in the tails of the sampling distribution of $\hat{\theta}_n$ disappears as the variance approaches zero, the extent of sampling error in the individual terms in $\lambda^R(\hat{\theta}_n)$ is small. Thus, there is less need to

[5] Brown (1998) examines this distribution in analysing the trade-off between simulation and bootstrap approximation in the context of bootstrap test procedures.

increase R which, given that the errors have mean zero, ensures that errors will average out in the summation. This trade-off is further illustrated in section 5. Orme (1995) demonstrates this relationship in the construction of simulated conditional moment tests.

3 An alternative consistent estimator for $\lambda(\theta_0)$, which we denote $\bar{\lambda}$, may be obtained by maximizing what Kent (1986) refers to as the "fitted" log likelihood

$$E_f[\log g(y,\lambda)] = n^{-1} \sum_{i=1}^{n} \int \log g(y_i,\lambda) f(y_i,\hat{\theta}_n)) dy \qquad (6)$$

where the subscript on the expectations operator indicates that expectations are taken with regards to the null model. the consistency of $\bar{\lambda}$ once again follows from (1) such that $plim_{n\to\infty}\bar{\lambda}(\hat{\theta}_n) = \lambda(\theta_0)$.

Using the notation set out above we may write the numerator of the Cox test statistic as

$$T_f = \bar{l}_f - \bar{l}_g - C(\hat{\theta}_n,\tilde{\lambda}) \qquad (7)$$

where $\bar{l}_f = 1/n \sum_{i=1}^{n} l_f(y_i,\hat{\theta})$ and $\bar{l}_g = 1/n \sum_{i=1}^{n} l_g(y_i,\hat{\lambda})$ are the observed means of the log-likelihood and the pseudo-log likelihood evaluated at the respective maximum likelihood and pseudo-maximum likelihood estimates. The last term on the right-hand side of (7), $C(\hat{\theta},\tilde{\lambda})$, represents a consistent estimator of $C(\theta_0,\lambda(\theta_0))$, the KL measure of closeness of $f(.)$ and $g(.)$. This may be written as $C(\hat{\theta},\tilde{\lambda}) = E_f[\bar{l}_f - \bar{l}_g]$, and is an estimator of the difference between the expected value of the two maximized log likelihoods under the distribution given by $f(.)$; $\tilde{\lambda}$ is any consistent estimator for $\lambda(\theta_0)$. Focusing solely upon the numerator of the Cox test statistic in (7), we distinguish between three variants which are derived from three AE estimators for the KL measure, which in turn depend upon $\tilde{\lambda} = \{\hat{\lambda}, \lambda^R(\hat{\theta}_n), \hat{\lambda}\}$.

In passing we note that the test procedure for non-nested (or nested) hypothesis developed by Gourieroux, Montfort, and Trognon (1984) exploits the consistency of a number of alternative estimators for the pseudo-true value. In particular they examine the difference between the PMLE, here $\hat{\lambda}$, and an estimator for the pseudo-true value based upon the MLE for the null model, here $\hat{\lambda}(\hat{\theta}_n)$ and $\bar{\lambda}$. As MacAleer (1987) notes, if the null is true then the observed PMLE should be similar to what is expected given a true null.

In examining the variance of the limiting distribution of $\sqrt{n}T_f$ under H_f, denoted $v_f^2(\theta_0,\lambda_0)$, we utilize a decomposition employed by Orme (1994)

$$v_f^2 = \text{var}(M) - \text{cov}(D,U)(\text{var}(U))^{-1}\text{cov}(D,U)' \qquad (8)$$

where $\text{var}(M)$ represents the variance of the observed log likelihood ratio.

Expressions for D and U are

$$D = l_f(y, \theta_0) - l_g(y, \theta_0) \tag{9}$$

$$U = \frac{\partial}{\partial \theta} l_f(y, \theta_0). \tag{10}$$

As Pesaran and Pesaran (1995) note, the second term on the right-hand side of (8) represents the sampling uncertainty associated with the parameters estimated under the null. In an application of the Cox test procedure to a test linear and log linear models, the authors consider three AE versions of v_f^2. Two of these exploit the information equality: an outer-product estimator calculating the variance of U using

$$E_f \left[\left\{ \frac{\partial}{\partial \theta} \log f(y, \theta_0) \frac{\partial}{\partial \theta} \log f(y, \theta_0)' \right\} \right]; \tag{11}$$

and an estimator using

$$- E_f \left\{ \frac{\partial^2}{\partial \theta \partial \theta'} \log f(y, \theta_0) \right\} \right]. \tag{12}$$

The advantage of (11) is that it only requires evaluation of the vector of scores (for each sample point). This is particularly important in the case of the MNP model where the evaluation of the matrix of second derivatives of the log likelihood is especially burdensome. In addition, many optimization routines that are commonly used in these models (i.e., Berndt, *et al.* (1974)) rely solely upon the gradient of the log likelihood. The disadvantage of this method is the well-known poor finite sample properties of variance estimators based upon the outer product of the gradient (see Davidson and MacKinnon (1981)).

A third AE of the variance of the Cox test statistic utilizes only the first term in (8), and thus ignores the variance component due to the sampling uncertainty of the estimated parameters under the null model. Hereafter we refer to this estimator as ISV. In the comparison of the performance of the Cox test using these three different estimators for the variance, Pesaran and Pesaran find that this particular version exhibits superior performance relative to estimators based upon an OPG and an observed Hessian estimator.

4   Experimental design

In this section we present the experimental design to be used in the Monte Carlo study. For both the binomial and multinomial discrete choice models we simulate artificial data sets based upon probit and logit specifications.

For the multinomial models we simulate a trinomial discrete choice model similar to that used by Börsch-Supan and Hajivassiliou (1993), where the deterministic component of choice is parameterized using a single alternative specific attribute. For the probit model the stochastic component is distributed trivariate normal, and we impose conditions that reflect the existence of correlation between two of the alternatives (choices 1 and 2), and impose zero correlation between each of the first two choices and the third. In the vernacular of discrete choice modeling, this variant is often referred to as conditional probit and is common in transport studies of modal choice (see Daganzo (1979)). For the logit model the stochastic component is distributed multivariate logistic and involves no unknown parameters.

Dropping the individual subscript and using the notation outlined above, we write the data generating process as additive in a deterministic and stochastic component

$$y_1^* = x_1\theta_1 + \varepsilon_1$$
$$y_2^* = x_2\theta_1 + \varepsilon_2$$
$$y_3^* = x_3\theta_1 + \varepsilon_3 \qquad (13)$$

where y_j^* is an unobserved latent variable for alternative j, x_j is a single alternative specific attribute, and ε_j is the stochastic component of choice. For the probit model the covariance matrix is given by

$$\Sigma = \begin{bmatrix} \theta_2 & \theta_3 & \theta \\ \theta_3 & 1 & 0 \\ 0 & 0 & 1 \end{bmatrix} \qquad (14)$$

such that the true error process embodies both heteroskedastic errors (over choices) and interalternative correlation. The mean equation parameter is constant across the choice set and we draw three independent normal regressors with mean $(1,0,0)$ and covariance matrix $2 \cdot I_3$, where I_3 denotes a 3*3 identity matrix. The regressors are fixed in repeated sampling.

For the binomial probit and logit models we assume the same structure for the mean equation over two choices drawing two independent normal regressors with mean $(1,0)$. However, in both cases no elements of the error covariance matrix are separately identified.

5   An illustrative case

Prior to examining a full set of Monte Carlo results, we examine the performance of the various Cox test statistics outlined in the above for a single replication with varying number of observations. The rationale for this is simply to present an introduction to the type of calculations involved and to illustrate in a cursory manner the asymptotic equivalence of the various test statistics.

Table 5.1 presents parameter estimates, log likelihoods, and Cox test statistics obtained by applying the MNP and MNL model to a trinomial probit DGP as set out in (13) and (14). We utilize three variants of the numerator based upon three methods of calculating the pseudo-true value: White's (W), the fitted estimator (F), and the simulated estimator (S). The three variants of the denominator are based upon using the observed Hessian (H), an OPG estimator (O), and the ISV estimator (X).

The first four columns record results for the MNP model. As sample size increases, we observe an increase in the accuracy of our estimates, and reasonable performance observed for $N = 500$ and $N = 2,000$. Columns 5–7 present parameter estimates for the three estimators of the pseudo-true value in $\tilde{\lambda}$ using the MNL model: $\hat{\lambda}$ is the pseudo-maximum likelihood estimator, $\hat{\lambda}(R)$ and $\tilde{\lambda}$ are respectively estimators of the pseudo-type value based upon simulation and maximizing the fitted log likelihood. Due to small sample fluctuations we note differences between these estimators for sample sizes 200–500. For $N = 2,000$ we observe convergence of parameter estimates.

The relationship between the components of $\tilde{\lambda}$ is further illustrated by figure 5.1. For each sample size, we plot the simulated pseudo-true value for $R = 1 \rightarrow 150$ simulations against $\hat{\lambda}$ and $\tilde{\lambda}$. In each case as R becomes large, fluctuations in $\hat{\lambda}(R)$ die out, with minimal variation after 50 replications. Further, the trade-off between sample size and R is evident in that as we increase sample size convergence of $\hat{\lambda}(R)$ is achieved for fewer simulations. This result confirms previous findings of Pesaran and Pesaran (1993). In an application of the Cox test to a test of binomial probit and logit models, they found that the simulated Cox test statistic settles down very quickly. Here we focus upon the convergence properties of the simulated pseudo-true value, since, for a given variance estimator, this will account for any fluctuations in the test statistic.

A corollary of the asymptotic equivalence of the elements of $\tilde{\lambda}$ is given by similar behavior of the nine Cox test statistics in table 5.1. We note that despite differences due to small samples, for a single replication all versions of the test statistic do not reject the null. Further, as with members of $\tilde{\lambda}$, all nine test statistics, with the exception of those based upon the ISV variance estimator, are almost identical as sample size becomes large. This result is not unexpected given that the ISV variant of the Cox test statistic produces a variance which is too large (asymptotically), and thus the resulting test statistic is undersized. This form of test statistic belongs to the Durbin (1970) class of naive tests.

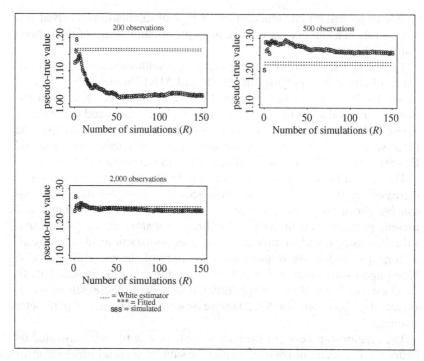

Figure 5.1 Pseudo-true values: White, Fitted, and simulated

Turning to the variation in test statistics due to different variance estimators it is evident that unlike the case of the binomial DGP (results not
reported), there exist considerable small sample differences between the
associated test statistics. This particular finding, although based upon a
single replication, is likely to be a function of the increased dimensionality
of the Hessian in multinomial models when the assumed DGP has a multivariate normal error structure. This result is further evident in the extended
Monte Carlo study.

6   Some previous findings

Prior to presenting results from the Monte Carlo experiments we first
demonstrate that our procedures (including computational algorithms) are
consistent with previous work. To do this we utilize the insurance choice
data set which was employed by Pesaran and Pesaran (1995). The data set
records whether or not 1,331 single-person households at or below the age
of 65 in New South Wales purchased health insurance, and includes standard conditioning variables such as sex, age, and income. Utilizing the same

Table 5.1. *Data generating process: trinomial probit*

	Null model (probit)			Alternative model (logit)			
β	σ^2	σ_{12}	l_f	$\hat{\lambda}$	$\hat{\lambda}(R)$	$\bar{\lambda}$	l_g
			$N = 200$				
1.196	4.723	1.609	-99.9	1.161	1.269	1.166	-105.5
(0.254)	(2.324)	(0.645)					
			$N = 500$				
0.959	1.799	0.881	-245.9	1.236	1.285	1.244	-254.2
(0.108)	(0.881)	(0.228)					
			$N = 2,000$				
1.000	1.903	0.789	-951.7	1.264	1.269	1.262	-972.4
(0.056)	(0.341)	(0.131)					

Truth: $\beta = 1$, $\sigma^2 = 2$, $\sigma_{12} = 0.7$

Cox test statistics

	Sample size		
	200	500	2,000
$C_{WH}(\hat{\lambda})$	0.161	0.749	-0.297
$C_{WO}(\hat{\lambda})$	0.246	0.973	-0.298
$C_{WX}(\hat{\lambda})$	0.081	0.277	-0.132
$C_{SH}(\hat{\lambda}^r(\hat{\theta}))$	0.127	0.678	-0.284
$C_{SO}(\hat{\lambda}^r(\hat{\theta}))$	0.252	0.826	-0.286
$C_{SX}(\hat{\lambda}^r(\hat{\theta}))$	0.079	0.188	-0.072
$C_{FH}(\bar{\lambda})$	0.160	0.750	-0.297
$C_{FO}(\bar{\lambda})$	0.240	0.982	-0.298
$C_{FX}(\bar{\lambda})$	0.082	0.280	-0.133

form for the mean equation, our results for testing univariate logit versus univariate probit are presented in table 5.2. Incomplete experiments are denoted NA. In keeping with the exposition in section 5, we report nine test statistics based upon the different methods of calculating the numerator and denominator of the Cox test statistic. The results reported by Pesaran and Pesaran are denoted P&P.

In comparing our simulated test statistics with those of P&P we first focus on the test of probit versus logit, where probit is the null model (result A in table 5.2). Only very small differences are observed and they are negligible as the number of simulations is increased. However, more noteworthy is the fact that we also observe a high degree of similarity

Table 5.2. *Trivedi insurance data*

Numerator/denominator	H_f: Probit H_g: Logit Hessian	OPG	ISV
Results A			
White	− 2.161	− 2.125	− 1.791
Fitted	− 2.066	− 2.031	− 1.711
Simulated			
$R = 100$	− 2.133	− 2.097	− 1.766
$R = 200$	− 2.088	− 2.053	− 1.729
$R = 500$	− 2.094	− 2.060	− 1.735
Simulated (P&P)			
$R = 100$	NA	−2.078	NA
$R = 200$	NA	−2.052	NA
$R = 500$	NA	−2.059	NA
Results B			
White	1.569	1.529	1.289
Fitted	1.664	1.621	1.366
Simulated			
$R = 100$	1.573	1.531	1.290
$R = 200$	1.625	1.583	1.340
$R = 500$	1.646	1.603	1.350
Simulated (P&P)			
$R = 100$	NA	1.567	NA
$R = 200$	NA	1.602	NA
$R = 500$	NA	1.598	NA

between the alternate methods of estimating the Cox test statistic, with the exception of the substantially smaller test statistic which ignores any sampling variation under the null (ISV). Both the White and Fitted method for the numerator are comparable with the computationally intensive simulated version, independent of whether the denominator is an OPG or Hessian variant. These findings also apply when we switch the roles of the probit and logit model as in results B. Although these results are not unexpected given the relatively large sample size, they do provide important empirical validation of the asymptotic equivalence of these alternate versions of the Cox test statistic.

Table 5.3. *Data generating process: binomial probit
rejection probabilities (0.05-level test)*

	H_f: Probit	H_f: Logit
# obs = 200		
C_{WH}	0.194	0.426
C_{WH}	0.204	0.432
C_{WX}	0.158	0.380
C_{FH}	0.198	0.418
C_{FO}	0.204	0.422
C_{FX}	0.154	0.362
C_{SH}^{30}	0.050*	0.262
C_{SO}^{30}	0.054*	0.262
C_{SX}^{30}	0.048*	0.260
# obs = 500		
C_{WH}	0.164	0.440
C_{WO}	0.164	0.440
C_{WX}	0.142	0.418
C_{FH}	0.168	0.432
C_{FO}	0.164	0.434
C_{FX}	0.144	0.414
# obs = 2,000		
C_{WH}	0.062*	0.636
C_{WO}	0.064*	0.636
C_{WX}	0.062*	0.632
C_{FH}	0.060*	0.630
C_{FO}	0.064*	0.631
C_{FX}	0.062*	0.620
C_{SH}^{2}	0.060*	0.631
C_{SO}^{2}	0.060*	0.630
C_{SX}^{2}	0.056*	0.628

7   Monte Carlo results

In this section we utilize Monte Carlo experiments to examine the performance of the various Cox test statistics applied to binomial and multinomial probit and logit discrete choice models. We utilize data sets of size
200, 500, and 2,000, with the latter employed to examine behavior under a
large sample. In many microeconomic applications data sets of this size are
not uncommon. In all cases experiments are based upon 500 replications.

Table 5.3 presents results given that the true model is binomial probit.
Rejection probabilities under the true and false model are given under the

Table 5.4. *Data generating process: binomial logit rejection probabilities (0.05-level test)*

	H_f: Probit	H_f: Logit
# obs = 200		
C_{WH}	0.154	0.242
C_{WH}	0.150	0.238
C_{WX}	0.124	0.212
C_{FH}	0.138	0.240
C_{FO}	0.142	0.238
C_{FX}	0.110	0.204
C_{SH}^{30}	0.218	0.056*
C_{SO}^{30}	0.221	0.058*
C_{SX}^{30}	0.194	0.054*
# obs = 500		
C_{WH}	0.106	0.190
C_{WO}	0.100	0.192
C_{WX}	0.090	0.176
C_{FH}	0.096	0.190
C_{FO}	0.090	0.190
C_{FX}	0.080	0.178
# obs = 2,000		
C_{WH}	0.276	0.063*
C_{WO}	0.276	0.058*
C_{WX}	0.258	0.056*
C_{FH}	0.264	0.061*
C_{FO}	0.264	0.065
C_{FX}	0.244	0.054*

columns headed H_f: Probit and H_f: Logit respectively. Table 5.4 presents results when the true DGP is binomial logit. For sample size equal to 500 and 2,000 we report results based upon the White and Fitted method for numerator estimation, and the three methods for estimating the variance of the Cox test statistic. For sample size equal to 200 we also report results for the simulation estimator, setting the number of replications equal to 30.

In tables 5.3 and 5.4 cases we observe rather disappointing results. For example size equal to 200 and 500 both the test statistics computed using the White and the Fitted estimator are similar, with the exception of the fitted estimator using the ISV method for computing the variance. Further, relative to the Hessian (H), the use of the OPG term in the variance accords slightly inferior performance. In contrast the use of the simulation estimator, although restricted to a single experiment and with R set at only 30, produced much better results. If we increase sample size to 2,000 then under both H_f: Probit and H_f: Logit the results are much better with no significant difference between nominal and empirical size. We also note that for a large sample, the simulation estimator produces reasonable results for only two draws. This is the empirical analogue of the statement that statistics based upon simulation methods are consistent for a single draw.

Although these results are preliminary given both the number of replications and the relative simplicity of the assumed mean equations, a notable result is the apparent asymmetry for rejecting a false null across the two models. The systematic lower probability of rejecting a false alternative when the true DGP is logit requires further investigation.

Tables 5.5 and 5.6 report some *preliminary* results for the multinomial models. In table 5.6 we provide rejection frequencies based upon a trinomial probit model given by (14) and (15); and in table 5.6 we do the same when the true model is trinomial logit. Given the computational burden, we do not utilize the simulation estimator. In the case of the three variance estimators we observe a wider dispersion in rejection frequencies, which is most prominent when the true DGP is trinomial probit. Focusing upon table 5.5, we note the especially poor performance of the OPG estimator for sample size 200 and 500. In contrast the performance of the Cox test using the Hessian and the ISV variance estimator is considerably superior.

One similarity with the results obtained from binomial models is the pronounced asymmetry between test performance under the two true models. When the true model is probit, results are suggestive that for sample size 500 and 2,000 the Cox test statistic has, with the exception of the ISV variant, appropriate size and reasonable power. However, when the true DGP is logit, we observe systematic lower power and also failure of size even in large samples.

8   Application: a multinomial model of labor force status

We now turn our attention to a real data set and introduce an empirical model of labor force status of married women in the UK. We use this to illustrate the application of the Cox test to the problem of testing a MNP and MNL model of labor force status. The model is discrete in that we allow for three states: non-workers supplying zero hours of work; part-time workers whose weekly supply is between 0 and 30 hours; and full-time workers supplying more than 30 hours. We consider a number of alternative model

Table 5.5. *Data generating process: trinomial probit rejection probabilities (0.05-level test)*

	H_f: Probit	H_f: Logit
#obs = 200		
C_{WH}	0.081	0.837
C_{WH}	0.145	0.845
C_{WX}	0.033	0.791
C_{FH}	0 078	0.821
C_{FO}	0.113	0.856
C_{FX}	0.024	0.765
#obs = 500		
C_{WH}	0.079	0.835
C_{WO}	0.149	0.838
C_{WX}	0.046*	0.821
#obs = 2,000		
C_{WH}	0.057*	0.904
C_{WO}	0.057*	0.912
C_{WX}	0.000	0.886
C_{FH}	0.058*	0.835
C_{FO}	0.058*	0.838
C_{FX}	0.001	0.821

specifications by focusing upon the stochastic component of choice. To date, with the exception of Bingley and Walker (1995), the tractability of the multinomial logit model has provided a convenient framework for the estimation of discrete choice models of labor supply (see Zabalza, Pissarides, and Barton (1980) and Blau and Robbins (1988)).

We construct a discrete choice model of labor force status by utilizing a $J \times 1$ vector of unobserved utilities, where J denotes the number of labor supply states. The utility for state J may be written

$$y_j^* = \alpha_j + x_{jk}\beta_k + v_t\theta_{jt} + \varepsilon_j \ (j = 1, \ldots, J) \tag{15}$$

where $y^* = \{y_j^*\}$ is the $J \times 1$ vector of utilities; $x = \{x_{jk}\}$ is a $J \times K$ matrix of non-stochastic components of utility, whose rows contain the K *alternative specific* attributes of alternative J; $v = \{v_t\}$, on the other hand, is a $T \times 1$ vector of *alternative invariant* individual characteristics; $\alpha = \{\alpha_j\}$, $\beta = \{\beta_k\}$, and $\theta = \{\theta_{jt}\}$ are respectively $(J \times 1)$, $(K \times 1)$, and $(J \times 1)$ arrays of unknown parameters. The stochastic component of the model $(\varepsilon = \{\varepsilon_j\})$ is a $J \times 1$ vector of disturbance terms whose distribution is known, possibly up to a

Table 5.6. *Data generating process: trinomial logit rejection probabilities (0.05-level test)*

	H_f: Probit	H_f: Logit
# obs = 200		
C_{WH}	0.181	0.405
C_{WH}	0.158	0.406
C_{WX}	0.038	0.388
C_{FH}	0.161	0.106
C_{FO}	0.152	0.114
C_{FX}	0.116	0.081
# obs = 500		
C_{WH}	0.269	0.307
C_{WO}	0.231	0.310
C_{WX}	0.097	0.302
C_{FH}	0.247	NA
C_{FO}	0.224	NA
C_{FX}	0.107	NA
# obs = 2,000		
C_{WH}	0.762	0.139
C_{WO}	0.787	0.141
C_{WX}	0.721	0.139

knowledge of a further set of unknown variance and covariance parameters. Thus (15) may be compactly written $y^* = \alpha + x\beta + \theta v + \varepsilon = D + \varepsilon$ where $D = \{D_j\} = \{\alpha_j + x_{jk}\beta_k + v_t\theta_{jt}\}$. A given individual chooses alternative if

$$y_j^* = \text{argmax}(y_j^*) \quad i = 1,\dots,J. \tag{16}$$

In this study the probability of observing the jth labor force state depends upon a vector, v, of individual varying (state invariant) characteristics such as education, marital status, and age; and a single attribute, X, imputed income, which varies across labor force states and individuals.

We exploit the flexibility of the MNP model and examine the impact of different error structures. Given that we have only a single cross-section we focus on the impact of contemporaneous correlation of unobserved attributes and random coefficients due to unobserved taste variation across individuals.[6] By decomposing the stochastic component we may isolate each of these random components and in doing so rewrite (15) as

$$y_{ij}^* = V_{ij} + x_{ij}(\beta + \beta_i') + u_{ij}. \tag{17}$$

For the sake of exposition (17) assumes a single attribute, X. V_{ij} denotes the linear combination of observed individual characteristics of state J, β is the mean coefficient for the attribute, and β_i' is a coefficient which captures the deviations of the ith individual's tastes from the mean. If we assume that β_i is constant then this implies that individuals with the same characteristics have identical tastes with regard to the observed attributes of alternatives. If there is variation in tastes (beyond that measured by observable characteristics) then we would expect variation in the β parameters. If we place a distribution on β_i' this facilitates a model which allows for random taste variation. Forcing homogeneous tastes is therefore a form of misspecification. u_{ij} is an additive disturbance which, dependent upon the imposed distributional assumptions, may be used to capture unobserved attributes of the choice set which may be both heteroskedastic and exhibit cross-alternative correlation.

If we now write (17) as $y_{ij}^* = D_{ij} + \varepsilon_{ij}$ where $D_{ij} = V_{ij} + x_{ij}\beta$ and $\varepsilon_{ij} = x_{ij}\beta_i' + u_{ij}$, we observe a highly general specification. For β_i' constant for all individuals, we have a model which allows for contemporaneous correlation but implicitly assumes that observed individual characteristics capture any heterogeneous preferences. Similar if u_{ij} is independent and identically distributed across alternatives and β_i' is non-constant then we have the random coefficient model, first considered by Hausman and Wise (1978).

In a three-state model there are $J(J+1)/2$ unique covariance parameters in the matrix Σ_u. However, only $(J(J-1)/2) - 1$ are identifiable.[7] This is analogous to the identification of mean equation parameters and follows from the fact that the probability of a given individual choosing any of the alternatives can be estimated in terms of utility differences. In this study we allow one free parameter which represents the contemporaneous covariance of omitted attributes and individual characteristics for the part-time and full-time states.

The data we use for our empirical analysis – a random sample of 1,971 women living with employed men – are drawn from the 1993 *Family Expenditure Survey* (FES). We choose to condition our labor supply model on wage rates, net incomes at various hours levels, and the following sociodemographic characteristics: age of the women, age of the youngest child,

---

[6] Chesher and Silva (1995) propose an extension to the multinomial logit model which is able to incorporate taste variation both across individuals and for the attribution of alternatives.

[7] Weeks (1993) presents a more detailed analysis of the identification of covariance parameters.

number of children, level of formal education, and marital status (whether married or cohabiting).[8]

8.1   Results

Table 5.7 presents results based upon the estimation of four different discrete choice models of labor supply. We denote Model A as MNP with a stochastic structure that allows for both contemporaneous correlation and heterogeneous preferences; model B accommodates heterogeneous preferences but assumes that the additive disturbance term is *iid* across both alternatives and individuals; C is independent probit and D is multinomial logit. An additional set of parameter estimates are included under the column heading "Adj. D". This set of estimates are the adjusted logit parameters based upon a modification of the 1.6 rule as used in binary models.

Our dependent variable in each case is a three-state variable which distinguishes non-participants (category 1), part-time workers between 1 and 30 hours (category 2), and full timers working in excess of 30 hours (category 3). The reference group for each discrete choice model is the non-participation category; hence, in reading the economic significance of the parameter estimates, a negative coefficient represents a decrease in the likelihood of working either part time or full time relative to not working. Which comparison is appropriate is identified for each parameter estimate in table 5.7 by the indicators in the second column (marked compare).

Socio-demographic, wage and income influences on full-time and part-time labor market participation are generally in line with previous studies (see Duncan and Weeks (1997) and Bingley and Walker (1995)). Most noticeably, the presence of young children in the household negatively affects both the probability of labor market participation and the choice between part-time and full-time work. We also find clear empirical support for the introduction of random preference heterogeneity, operating in this case through the income term (see income (var) in table 5.7).

From a cursory glance at the values of the respective log likelihoods it would appear that model A indicates the best fit. However, if we want to test whether the log likelihood for model B (MNP with heterogeneous preferences) is significantly different from the same for model D (MNL) we may utilize the Cox non-nested test. We do this below.

Table 5.8 presents the results of an application of the Cox test to the choice between the MNL model D and the MNP models (A, B and C) of labor force status. In the case of model B we demonstrate the application of

---

[8] See Duncan and Weeks (1997) for further discussion.

Table 5.7. *Labour supply estimates: constant attribute model*

Variable	Compare	Multinomial probit			Multinomial logit	
		A	B	C	D	Adj.D
Constant	3/1	− 1.1554	− 1.3112	− 1.8045	− 1.4842	− 0.8265
		(0.4413)	(0.5226)	(0.4692)	(0.6266)	
	2/1	− 0.5622	− 0.0593	0.1241	− 0.0421	− 0.0234
		(0.2181)	(0.4439)	(0.4263)	(0.5224)	
Youngest child	3/1	− 0.8201	− 1.1057	− 1.0730	− 1.3302	− 0.7408
aged 0–2		(0.2476)	(0.2948)	(0.2817)	(0.3624)	
	2/1	− 0.5502	− 0.2990	− 0.1919	− 0.3994	− 0.2224
		(0.1238)	(0.2537)	(0.2605)	(0.3215)	
Youngest child	3/1	− 0.6626	− 1.1722	− 1.3094	− 1.5726	0.8758
aged 3–4		(0.3115)	(0.3514)	(0.3426)	(0.4462)	
	2/1	− 0.0023	0.4252	0.3463	0.3779	0.2105
		(0.2201)	(0.3034)	(0.3160)	(0.3899)	
Youngest child	3/1	0.1641	− 0.2772	− 0.4279	− 0.3743	− 0.2084
aged 5–10		(0.2424)	(0.2911)	(0.2823)	(0.3736)	
	2/1	0.5581	1.1038	0.8916	1.239	0.6866
		(0.1422)	(0.2474)	(0.2563)	(0.3088)	
Youngest child	3/1	0.3946	0.2542	0.0980	0.2933	0.1634
aged 11–16		(0.1936)	(0.2326)	(0.2212)	(0.3001)	
	2/1	0.5398	0.9798	0.7341	1.1199	0.6237
		(0.0852)	(0.1922)	(0.1970)	(0.2379)	
Number of	3/1	− 0.3117	− 0.3618	− 0.3556	− 0.4587	− 0.2555
children		(0.0894)	(0.1101)	(0.1057)	(0.1364)	
	2/1	− 0.2615	− 0.2761	− 0.2021	− 0.3343	− 0.1862
		(0.0409)	(0.0946)	(0.0980)	(0.1192)	
Age	3/1	− 0.6015	− 0.8633	− 0.9317	− 1.1477	− 0.6392
		(0.1442)	(0.1651)	(0.1589)	(0.2120)	
	2/1	− 0.3297	− 0.0678	− 0.0412	− 0.1828	− 0.1018
		(0.0887)	(0.1436)	(0.1453)	(0.1769)	
Education	3/1	0.1382	0.2102	0.2069	0.2700	0.1504
		(0.1416)	(0.1709)	(0.1604)	(0.2106)	
	2/1	0.0949	0.0501	0.0302	0.0721	0.0401
		(0.0471)	(0.1411)	(0.1430)	(0.1712)	
Cohabitee	3/1	0.3146	0.5865	0.6601	0.7772	0.4328
		(0.2503)	(0.2897)	(0.2719)	(0.3635)	
	2/1	− 0.007	− 0.4544	− 0.4146	− 0.5393	− 0.3003
		(0.1249)	(0.2851)	(0.2831)	(0.3670)	
Log of predicted	3/1	1.2386	1.7279	1.6102	2.0694	1.1524
wage		(0.2884)	(0.3321)	(0.2881)	(0.3873)	
	2/1	0.8525	0.5971	0.3451	0.7759	0.4321
		(0.1470)	(0.2707)	(0.2523)	(0.3123)	
Income (mean)		0.1530	0.1959	0.1616	0.2624	0.1461
		(0.0320)	(0.0443)	(0.0282)	(0.0415)	
Income (var)		0.0662	0.0738	NA	NA	NA
		(0.0274)	(0.0639)			
Log likelihood		− 1430.84	− 1434.70	− 1439.37	− 1434.86	

Table 5.8. *Non-nested statistics:*
constant attribute model

	H_f: Probit H_g: Logit	H_f: Logit H_g: Probit
Model A		
C_{WH}	NA	-2.945
C_{WH}	-1.862	-2.946
C_{WH}	-1.772	-2.862
Model B		
C_{WH}	NA	-1.119
C_{WO}	-3.955	-1.197
C_{WX}	-1.397	-1.169
C_{SH}^{30}	NA	-1.238
C_{SO}^{30}	-2.254	-1.235
C_{SX}^{30}	-1.687	-1.203
Model C		
C_{WH}	-3.944	2.624
C_{WO}	-3.924	2.585
C_{WX}	-3.666	2.257

the simulation-based estimator first proposed by Pesaran and Pesaran (1993), with the number of replications set equal to 30. Given the large sample size we also utilize White's (1982) estimator for the pseudo-true value in the construction of the numerator of the test statistic. Weeks (1996) showed that in large samples the size of properties of this computationally convenient method for constructing the numerator is comparable to the simulation estimator. We utilize the three variants of the denominator introduced in section 5. Replications are set equal to 30.

In the test of the independent probit (model C) against multinomial logit (model D) we reject both models. The result is not unusual and serves to emphasize that the application of the Cox test involves a choice between only two of all the possible data generating process. Although in testing a null model against a particular alternative it is only the null which is being tested, and thus on the basis of the available data we can only accept or reject the null model, we may utilize the information content of the *direction or rejection*. For example, in this instance we reject the probit model in the direction of logit, and reject the logit model in a direction opposite to probit (see the discussion in Fisher and McAleer (1979) and Dastoor (1981)).

Table 5.9. *Likelihood ratio test statistics: constant attribute model*

	Restricted model: independent probit	Unrestricted model MNP	
		A	B
Log likelihood	− 1439.37	− 1430.83	− 1434.70
Likelihood ratio statistics		17.08	9.34
P-value		0.000	0.002

In testing model A (MNP with both contemporaneous correlation and heterogeneous preferences) against MNL we accept probit and reject logit. However, in the test of model B (MNP with heterogeneous preferences) and B1 (MNP with contemporaneous correlation) against MNL we accept both models.[9] Overall the results provide clear evidence that in the specification of the discrete choice model of labor force status, there are considerable gains from a careful consideration of the stochastic component. Both models which impose an *iid* specification (C and D) are clearly rejected.

In table 5.9 we utilize a likelihood ratio test to test the independent probit model against the three non-*iid* multinomial probit models. A classical testing framework is permissible since the independent probit is a special case of each of the more general MNP models given appropriate parameter restrictions. The results provide further confirmation of the superiority of the general probit models. Given the similarity between the IP model and MNL, a number of analysts have utilized this procedure as an approximate test of MNL against MNP (see Hausman and Wise (1978)).

9   Conclusion

The emergence of a broad class of consistent simulation-based estimators has expanded the menu of models available to the modeler. Within the microeconometrics literature this development has resulted in the choice between models which are non-nested due to differences in the distribution of the stochastic term. In this study we have begun to explore the potential of utilizing the Cox non-nested test procedure for testing binomial and multinomial choice models. Our results suggest that simulation-based test statistics exhibit a superior performance in small samples, with the convergence of per-

---

[9] Note that we base our conclusions on the C_{WX} and C_{SX}^{30} test statistics. The well-known oversized characteristic of the OPG variant seems to be evident in our results.

formance measures for simulation and non-simulation tests in large samples. The extent to which our Monte Carlo results are specific to the admittedly small set of experiments can only be determined by further analysis.

References

Amemiya, T. (1981), "Qualitative Response Models: A Survey," *Journal of Economic Literature*, 19, 483–536.

Atkinson, A. (1970), "A Method for Discriminating Between Models," *Journal of the Royal Statistical Society, Series B*, 32, 323–353.

Berndt, E., B. Hall, R. Hall, and J. Hausman (1974), "Estimation and Inference in Nonlinear Structural Models," *Annals of Economic and Social Measurement*, 3, 653–666.

Bingley, P. and I. Walker (1995), "Labour Supply, Unemployment and Participation in in-work Transfer Programmes," Discussion paper, Institute for Fiscal Studies.

Blau, D. and P. Robbins (1988), "Child-Care Costs and Family Labour Supply," *Review of Economics and Statistics*, 70, 474–481.

Börsch-Supan, A. and V. Hajivassiliou (1993), "Smooth Unbiased Multivariate Probability Simulators for Maximum Likelihood Estimation in Limited Dependent Variable Models," *Journal of Econometrics*, XX pp. 347–368.

Brown, B.W. (1999), "Simulation Variance Reduction for Bootstrapping," this volume.

Bunch, D. and R. Kitamura (1989), "Multinomial Probit Estimation Revisited: Testing of New Algorithms and Evaluation of Alternative Model Specifications for Trinomial Models of Household Car Ownership," Discussion paper Research Report UCD-TRG-RR-4., Transportation Research Group, University of California, Davis, CA.

Chesher, A. and J. Silva (1995), "Taste Variation in Discrete Choice Models," Discussion paper no. 95/936, Department of Economics, University of Bristol.

Cox, D. (1961), "Tests of Separate Families of Hypothesis," *Proceedings of the Fourth Berkeley Symposium on Mathematical Statistics and Probability*.

Daganzo, C. (1979), *Multonomial Probit: The Theory and Its Application to Demand Forecasting*, Place: Academic Press.

Dastoor, N. (1981), "A Note on the Interpretation of the Cox Procedure for Non-Nested Hypothesis," *Economic Letters*, 8, 113–119.

Davidson, R. and J. MacKinnon (1981), "Several Tests for Model Specification in the Presence of Alternative Hypothesis," *Econometrica*, 49, 781–793.

(1984), "Convenient Specification Tests for Logit and Probit Models," *Journal of Econometrics*, 25, 241–262.

Duncan, A. and M. Weeks (1997), "Non-Nested Models of Labour Supply with Discrete Choices," Discussion paper no. 97/20, Department of Applied Economics, University of Cambridge.

Durbin, J. (1970), "Testing for Serial Correlation in Least Squares Regression When Some of the Regressors are Lagged Dependent Variables," *Econometrics*, 38, 410–421.

Fisher, G. and M. McAleer (1979), "On the Interpretation of the Cox Test in Econometrics," *Economic Letters*, 4, 145–150.

Fry, T. and M. Harris (1993), "A Monte Carlo Study of Tests for the Independence of Irrelevant Alternatives Property," Discussion paper 8/93, Department of Econometrics, University of Monash.

Godfrey, L. (1988), *Misspecification Tests in Econometrics: The Lagrange Multiplier Principle and Other Approaches*, Cambridge University Press.

Gourieroux, C., A. Montfort, and A. Trognon (1984), "Pseudo-Maximum Likelihood Methods," *Econometrica*, 52, 681–700.

Hajivassiliou, V. and P. Ruud (1994), "Classical Estimation Methods for LDV Models Using Simulation," in R.F. Engle and D. McFadden (eds.), *Handbook of Economics*, vol. IV, Amsterdam: North-Holland, chapter 40, pp. 2385–2441.

Hausman, J. (1978), "Specification Tests in Econometrics," *Econometrica*, 46, 1251–1271.

(1984), "Specification Tests for the Multinomial Logit Model," *Econometrica*, 52, 1219–1239.

Hausman, J. and D. Wise (1978), "A Conditional Probit Model for Qualitative Choice: Discrete Decisions Recognising Interdependence and Heterogeneous Preferences," *Econometrica*, 46, 403–426.

Kent, J. (1986), "The Underlying Structure of Non-nested Hypothesis Tests," *Biometrika*, 7, 333–343.

McAleer, M. (1987), *Specification Tests for Separate Models: A Survey*, London: Routledge and Kegan Paul.

McFadden, D. (1989), "A Method of Simulated Moments for Estimation of Discrete Response Models Without Numerical Integration," *Econometrica*, 57, 995–1026.

Orme, C. (1994), "Non-Nested Tests for Discrete Choice Models," Discussion paper, University of York.

(1995), "Simulated Conditional Moment Tests," *Economic Letters*, 49, 239–245.

Pesaran, M.H. and B. Pesaran (1993), "A Simulation Approach to the Problem of Computing Cox's Statistic for Testing Non-Nested Models," *Journal of Econometrics*, 57, 377–392.

(1995), A Non-nested Test of Level Differences Versus Log-Differenced Stationary Models," *Econometric Reviews*, 14(2), 213–227.

Weeks, M. (1993), "The Multinomial Probit Model Revisited: A Discussion of Parameter Estimability, Identification and Specification Testing," *Journal of Economic Surveys*, 11(3), 297–320.

(1994), "Probit Versus Logit: Some New Evidence," Discussion paper 94/21, Department of Economics, University of York.

(1996), "Testing the Binomial and Multinomial Choice Models Using Cox's Non-Nested Test," *Papers and Proceedings of the American Statistical Association*, 105, 519–530.

White, H. (1982), "Regularity Conditions for Cox's Test of Non-nested Hypotheses," *Journal of Econometrics*, 19, 301–318.

(1994), *Estimation, Inference and Specification Analysis*, Cambridge University Press.

Zabalza, A., C. Pissarides, and M. Barton (1980), "Social Security and the Choice between Full-time work, Part-time work and Retirement," *Journal of Public Economics*, 14, 245–276.

6 Bayesian analysis of the multinomial probit model

Robert E. McCulloch and Peter E. Rossi

1 Introduction

In this chapter, we discuss Bayesian analysis of the multinomial probit model (MNP) using Markov chain Monte Carlo methods. Although the MNP model has been in the econometrics and psychology literature for some 60 years, it is only recently that estimation and inference methods have made it feasible to analyze MNP models with more than two or three response categories. Classical sampling theoretic approaches to estimation of the MNP model have recently been proposed in the econometrics literature (see Hajivassiliou (1994) for an excellent overview of these methods). All of these classical econometric methods rely on asymptotic approximations to conduct inference about the probit model parameters. McCulloch and Rossi (1994) show that is possible to conduct exact, likelihood-based inference for the MNP model by using a Bayesian simulation method which complements the work by Albert and Chib (1993) on the binomial probit model (see Zellner and Rossi (1984) for a non-simulation approach to Bayesian inference in the binomial setting). Evidence in McCulloch and Rossi (1994) and Geweke, Keane, and Runkle (1994) shows that the asymptotic approximations used in the classical approaches can be inaccurate and that the improved inference available in the Bayesian approach is no more computationally demanding than the classical simulation-based approaches.

Our Bayesian method can easily be extended to handle hierarchical or random coefficient models used with panel data, autocorrelated latent regression errors, and non-normal random coefficient distributions all within the same hierarchical framework. Below we outline approaches for each of these important extensions. All of these extensions build on the basic hierarchical model structure laid out in McCulloch and Rossi. A critical component of the Bayesian approach to inference in the MNP is a prior on the covariance matrix of the latent regression errors. We review two

158

basic approaches to specifying these covariance matrix priors. We also review the approach of the Barnard, McCulloch, and Meng (1995) and show how this very flexible class of covariance matrix priors can be used in this situation.

2   The MNP model and identification

2.1   The model

To begin, we briefly review the notation for the MNP model. Let Y be a multinomial random variable which takes on one of the possible values, $\{1, \ldots, p\}$. In many econometric applications, Y denotes the choice made by economic agents between p alternative goods. We observe Y conditional on information contained in the matrix Z $(p \times k')$. The conditional distribution of $Y|Z$ is specified via a latent regression system

$$U = Z\delta + v \text{ where } v \sim N(0, \Omega). \tag{1}$$

We do not observe U directly but instead observe the index of the maximum W

$$Y = i \text{ if } \max_i(U) = U_i. \tag{2}$$

Here $\max(U)$ means the maximal element of $U' = (U_1, U_2, \ldots, U_p)'$.

U is often interpreted in the choice context as the system of latent utilities associated with p choice alternatives. Agents choose among the mutually exclusive p choice alternatives so as to maximize utility but the econometrician is unable to observe the utility levels and must make inferences about utility using choice information alone.

(1) and (2) define the sampling model $Y|Z, \delta\Sigma$. Typically, we observe the set of observations (Y_i, Z_i) and assume that they are *iid* according to the sampling model. In many applications, choice data are obtained by observing a panel of consumers and the *iid* assumption requires modification. In section 7 below, we elaborate the model to accommodate a panel structure.

At this point, we can readily appreciate two problems associated with inference in this model. First, the model is specified in (1) and (2) is not identified. Second, the likelihood of $\delta, \Sigma | Y, Z$ requires the evaluation of the conditional multinomial choice probabilities which require integration of a p-dimensional normal distribution over sets of the form $\{U|Y(U) = i\}$. These sets are cones over which the normal distribution is difficult to integrate. Much of the research on the MNP model has been devoted to the development of methods for computing these integrals which would allow for fast evaluation of the likelihood function or moment conditions.

2.2   *Identification*

As is well known, the model specified by (1) and (2) is not identified. The distribution of $Y|Z$ is unchanged adding a scalar random variable to all components of U or by scale shifts. The location invariance problem is solved by differencing the system with respect to some base choice alternative (which we assume is alternative 1).

$$W_i = U_{i+1} - U_1, \ i = 1,\ldots,p = 1,$$

$$w_i' = z_{i+1}' - z_1'.$$

If there are intercept terms in the Z matrix for each choice alternative, then the differencing of the rows of Z exposes each of the intercepts as differences with respect to the first choice alternative. Thus, to achieve identification we customarily set the first element of δ to zero. From this point on, we will call this vector, β. The sampling model can now be written as

$$W = X\beta + \varepsilon \quad \varepsilon \sim N(0,\Sigma)$$
$$Y = \begin{cases} 0 \text{ if } \max(W) < 0 \\ i \text{ if } \max(W) = W_i > 0. \end{cases}$$

W is $p-1$, X $((p-1) \times k)$, and Σ $((p-1) \times (p-1))$.

While differencing the system removes the location invariance problem, we still face the problem of scale invariance. This problem arises from the fact that $Y(cW) = Y(W)$ for all $c > 0$. Since $cW = c(X\beta + \varepsilon) = X(c\beta) + c\varepsilon$, we can see that $Y|X,\beta,\Sigma = Y|X,c\beta,c^2\Sigma$ and thus that $L(\beta,\Sigma) = L(c\beta,c^2\Sigma)$.

In the classical literature, it is common to fix an element of Σ (e.g., set σ_{11} = 1.0) (cf. Dansie (1985)). Another possibility would be to fix an element of the β vector which would require *a priori* knowledge of the sign of the element. In the Bayesian approach, it is not straightforward to adopt a prior with $\sigma_{11} = 1.0$ since this requires putting a prior on the set of covariance matrices with fixed 1,1 element. As we show below, this is possible but it requires non-standard, non-conjugate priors.

3   The MCMC approach to Bayesian inference in the MNP

To conduct Bayesian inference in the MNP, we must summarize information given by the posterior distribution of the model parameters

$$p(\beta,\Sigma \,|\, Y,X) \propto p(\beta,\Sigma) p(Y|X,\beta,\Sigma).$$

Generally, we want to compute the moments of the posterior and make various probability statements about the likely range of parameter values.

If the likelihood function could be evaluated at low computational cost, we could use standard numerical integration methods as in Zellner and Rossi (1984). Even with more modern methods of approximating the probabilities needed to evaluate the likelihood function, direct numerical integration procedures would be computationally infeasible for all except the smallest models. In addition, approximation error in computation of the multinomial probabilities would have to be held to a minimum so as not to affect the properties of the direct numerical integration methods such as importance sampling.

3.1   Gibbs samplers for the MNP

Our approach to the problem of posterior inference for the MNP model is to construct a method which provides the equivalent of an indirect simulator from the posterior distribution. We construct a Markov chain whose invariant or equilibrium distribution is the posterior distribution. Thus, we can simply run this Markov chain forward from some starting point to generate sequences of draws which can be used to estimate any desired feature of the posterior distribution. This idea of constructing a Markov chain is an indirect posterior simulator is called Markov chain Monte Carlo (MCMC) and has been fruitfully applied to many important problems in Bayesian statistics and econometrics.

In the analysis of the MNP model, we use a particular MCMC method called the Gibbs sampler (introduced by Geman and Geman (1984) and Tanner and Wong (1987)). The Gibbs sampler relies on the remarkable result that iterative, recursive sampling from the full set of conditional distribution results in a Markov chain with equilibrium distribution equal to the point of distribution. In the case of the MNP model, if we *augment* the parameters (β, Σ) with the vector of all latent utilities, W, then we can break the full set of parameters into three groups and draw these groups successively to form the Gibbs sampler. This strategy relies on the fact that, conditional on W, the Bayesian analysis of the MNP reduces to standard linear model results. The three groups of conditional distributions are defined as follows

(i) $w|\beta, G = \Sigma^{-1}, y, X$ where $w' = (W'_1, \ldots, W'_N), y' = (Y'_1, \ldots, (Y'_N),$

$$X = \begin{bmatrix} X_1 \\ \vdots \\ X_N \end{bmatrix},$$

(ii) $\beta|w, X, G,$
(iii) $G|\beta, W.$

To implement the Gibbs sampler, we start with the values of β and G. We then draw w from (i), β from (ii) using the new value of W, and, finally, G

from (iii) using the new values of w and β. This process is repeated to produce a sequence of draws of (w,β,G). Note that since this simple version of the MNP model is *iid*, we can draw the w vector in conditional (i) above, one observation at a time and then piece the W_i together.

The distribution of $W_i | \beta, G, Y_i$ is a $p-1$ dimensional normal distribution truncated to a cone. For example, if $Y_i = j$ then $W_{i,j} > \max(W_{i,-j}, 0)$ where $W_{i,-j}$ is the $p-2$ dimensional vector of all of the components of W excluding $W_{i,j}$. We avoid this problem of drawing from a truncated multivariate normal distribution by using a sub-chain Gibbs sampler to draw from the truncated univariate conditional distributions, $W_{i,j} | W_{i,-j}, \beta, \Sigma, Y_i, X_i$. The truncation point of this univariate normal distribution can readily be calculated from the definition of implied regions in $\Re^{p-1}$. The moments of these univariate normal distributions can readily be calculated from the multivariate normal distribution of $W_i | \beta, G, X_i \sim N(X_i\beta, G)$. To make draws from the truncated univariate normal distribution, we use a rejection strategy (see McCulloch and Rossi (1994, p. 212)).

The second conditional distribution, $\beta | G, w$, is a simple matter to draw from if the prior on β is multivariate normal. $\beta \sim N(\bar{\beta}, A^{-1})$.

Let $G = C\,C'$

$$\beta | w, X, G \sim N(\hat{\beta}, \Sigma_\beta) \quad \Sigma_\beta = (X'_* X_* + A)^{-1}; \hat{\beta} = \Sigma_\beta (X'_* w_* + A\bar{\beta})$$
$$w_* = \iota_N \otimes C' w; X_* = \iota_N \otimes C' X.$$

The method by which we draw the conditional posterior distribution of G depends critically on the prior adopted. In this chapter, we develop three different sorts of priors for G, each with a different draw strategy which we introduce in sections 4, 5, and 6 below.

To summarize, we use various Gibbs samplers to construct a Markov chain which enables us to estimate via simulation any required posterior quantity. Given sufficient computer resources, we can achieve a very high degree of accuracy in these estimates of posterior quantities. Thus, while our inferences do not rely on asymptotics in the sense of arbitrarily large sample sizes, we do require large simulation sizes to achieve a high degree of accuracy in the estimates of posterior quantities. We take the basic view that asymptotic approximations are more relevant and useful when the investigator has control over the sample size.

3.2   *Practical considerations for the MNP Gibbs sampler*

The theory of MCMC and, in particular, the Gibbs sampler shows that under very mild conditions, the Gibbs sampler Markov chain will converge in distribution to the posterior distribution at a geometric rate (see

McCulloch and Rossi (1984) and Tierney (1991)). While these theoretical results assure the eventual convergence of the MNP Gibbs samplers, this theory offers little practical guidance. There are two important practical considerations: (1) How long must the Gibbs sampler be run in order to be confident that the effect of initial conditions have dissipated? (2) What is the information content of a given sequence of Gibbs draws from the stationary distribution?

These practical convergence considerations can only be answered empirically. To assess the rate at which the initial conditions are dissipated, we conduct an analysis of the sensitivity of the estimated posterior distributions to various, widely dispersed initial conditions (see Gelman and Rubin (1992)). For each initial condition, we "burn-in" or run out the Gibbs sampler for a large number of draws (typically at least 5,000 draws) and then use the remaining draws in the sequence to estimate the posterior distribution. If we have chosen an adequate burn-in series length T^*, then the estimated posteriors should all be about the same for all starting points. McCulloch and Rossi (1994) report a series of experiments in which the algorithm specified in section 3 below is tested with a wide variety of initial conditions. The sampler appears to converge rapidly from any initial condition. Our experience with more complicated samplers affirms this general finding of insensitivity to initial conditions (Nobile (1995) documents a possible exception which can occur using informative priors, see section 4 for details).

If we feel comfortable that the "burn-in" periods of T^* draws is sufficient, we then use the remaining $T - T^*$ draws to estimate posterior quantities. It is important to remember that the Gibbs sampler is a non-*iid* simulation method and, therefore, the draws can exhibit dependence. In the first applications of the Gibbs sampler to linear models, this dependence in the draw sequence was never a severe problem and quite short runs could be made. However, our experience with the MNP model is that the draw sequence can be highly autocorrelated, necessitating long runs of the sampler to achieve good accuracy in the estimates of posterior quantities. Given even relatively modest computing resources, it is possible to make very long runs of the MNP Gibbs samplers even for relatively large samples and high dimensional (e.g., $p > 4$ and $N > 2,000$) problems. Our usual approach is to make a "burn-in" run and then start short runs on a number of workstations, starting from the "burned-in" values of the parameters (including the latent variables). These short runs are pieced together to form the draw sequence which is used for inference. In this manner, we can solve most problems in no more than one day of computing.

4   An algorithm with non-identified parameters

As discussed in section 2.2, the model parameters (β, Σ) are not identified. The identified parameters are functions of these unidentified parameters

$$\tilde{\beta} = \beta / \sqrt{\sigma_{11}}; \tilde{\Sigma} = \Sigma / \sigma_{11}.$$

If we desire informative priors, it would seem most convenient to put these priors directly on the identified parameters $(\tilde{\beta}, \tilde{\Sigma})$. This requires a prior on the space of covariance matrices conditional on $\sigma_{11} = 1.0$. One approach to this problem taken in McCulloch and Rossi (1994) is to specify a prior on the full set of parameters (β, Σ). This induces a prior on the identified parameters. For a given choice of the prior hyperparameters, we then examine the implied prior on the identified parameters. With some trial and error we can hope to find prior parameter settings that will appropriately reflect our views on the identified parameters. In practice, this approach is most useful for specifying relatively diffuse or uniformative priors.

To define the Gibbs sampler in this case, we use the approach outlined in 3.1 and specify a conditionally conjugate Wishart prior on G.

$$p(G|v,V) \propto |G|^{\frac{v-p-1}{2}} \operatorname{etr}\left\{-\frac{1}{2}GV\right\}.$$

The posterior of G is also in the Wishart form

$$G \bigg| \beta, w, X \sim \mathrm{W}\left(v+N, V+\sum_{i=1}^{N} \varepsilon_i \varepsilon_i'\right).$$

If we combine this Wishart draw with the draws from the conditional posterior of β and the draws of w specified in section 3.1, we define a Gibbs sampler that navigates in the full parameter space of unidentified parameters (Fortran code for this algorithm can be obtained at ftp://gsbper.uchicago.edu in the directory pub/rossi/mnp).

Our approach in most applications of this sampler is to specify proper but fairly diffuse priors on G and β. We investigate the induced prior over the identified parameters to insure that it reflects a proper level of diffusion. We then run the Gibbs sampler to indirectly simulate from the joint posterior of (β, Σ, w). We report the *marginal* posterior distribution of the identified parameters. It should be emphasized that it does not matter whether we first marginalize the prior and conduct the analysis only on the identified parameters or marginalize the posterior since the likelihood depends only on the identified parameters.

This Gibbs sampler navigates freely in the non-identified parameter space, constrained only on the non-identified directions by the proper priors. Nobile (1995) has constructed some examples in which this algorithm can take a very long time to dissipate the initial conditions. These examples involve informative priors on the space of non-identified priors. These priors "flatten" down the likelihood ridge in certain regions of the parameter space and make it difficult for the algorithm to find the region of high posterior value. The priors Nobile considers are informative about non-identified parameters. It is hard to imagine how such prior information could arise in normal circumstances. Nobile proposes a hybrid MCMC method which accelerates convergence.

5 An algorithm with fully identified parameters

An alternative to the non-identified algorithm would be to specify a prior directly on the identified parameters $(\tilde{\beta},\tilde{\Sigma})$, in such a way as we can easily draw from the appropriate conditional posteriors. McCulloch, Polson, and Rossi (1993) introduce a computationally attractive prior for $\tilde{\Sigma}$.

We define this prior by first reparameterizing Σ. According to the basic model, $\varepsilon_i \sim N(0,\Sigma)$. Write $\varepsilon_i' = \{\varepsilon_{i,1},(\varepsilon_{i,2},\ldots,\varepsilon_{i,p-1})\} = \{U_i,e_i'\}$. We can then write the joint distribution of ε_i as the marginal distribution of U_i and the conditional distribution, $e_i|U_i$. Let $\gamma = E[U_i e_i]$ and $\Sigma_e = E[e_i e_i']$. We then can write the marginal distribution of U and the conditional distribution of $e_i|U_i$

$$U_i \sim N(0,\sigma_{11})$$

$$e_i|U_i \sim N\left(\frac{\gamma}{\sigma_{11}}U_i, \Sigma_z - \gamma\gamma'/\sigma_{11}\right).$$

Let $\Phi = \Sigma_z - \gamma\gamma'/\sigma_{11}$. Then we can reparameterize Σ in terms of σ_{11}, γ, and Φ

$$\Sigma = \begin{bmatrix} \sigma_{11} & \gamma' \\ \gamma & \Phi + \gamma\gamma'/\sigma_{11} \end{bmatrix}.$$

Hence, we can put a prior on $\{\Sigma|\sigma_{11}=1\}$ by setting $\sigma_{11}=1$ and putting priors on γ and Φ.

For convenience, we use the following priors

$$\gamma \sim N(\bar{\gamma},B^{-1})$$

and

$$\Phi^{-1} \sim W(\kappa,C).$$

To obtain draws from $(\gamma,\Phi)|\beta,w,X$, we note that we "observe" (U_i,e_i). γ and Φ are simply the parameters of a multivariate regression of e_i on U_i. Standard results from Bayes linear models provide the conditional posteriors.

$$\gamma|\Phi,\beta,w,X \sim N(A_\gamma((\text{vec}(\Phi^{-1}E'U) + \beta\gamma),A\gamma)$$

where $A_\gamma = (U'U\Phi^{-1} + B)^{-1}$; $U' = (U_1,\ldots,U_N)$; $E' = (e_1,\ldots,e_N)'$ and

$$\Phi^{-1}|\gamma,\beta,w,X \sim W\left(\kappa + N, C + (E - U\gamma')'(E - U\gamma')\right).$$

The Gibbs sampler for the identified parameter case is defined as the following sequence of conditional draws:

(i) $w|\tilde{\beta},\tilde{\Sigma},X,y$,

(ii) $\tilde{\beta}|\tilde{\Sigma},w,X$,

(iii) $\tilde{\Sigma}|\tilde{\beta},w,X$ which is achieved via

$$\gamma|\Phi^{-1},\tilde{\beta},w,X \text{ and } \Phi^{-1}|\gamma,\tilde{\beta},w,X.$$

This Markov chain navigates in a lower (by one) dimensional space that the MNP sampler for non-identified parameters. In addition, the one-shot draw of the covariance matrix is broken down into two conditional draws which may introduce an additional source of autocorrelation into the Markov chain. It should be noted, however, that with the natural conjugate prior of the multivariate regression framework (see Zellner (1971), chapter VIII) we can draw $\tilde{\Sigma}$ in one shot by drawing from the marginal posterior $\Phi^{-1}|\tilde{\beta},w,X$ instead of the posterior conditional on γ.

Some care has to be used in assessing the prior hyperparameters in this set-up. The relative diffusion of the prior on γ and Φ is important. To see this, consider the case of $p = 3$

$$\tilde{\Sigma} = \begin{bmatrix} 1 & \gamma \\ \gamma & \phi + \gamma^2 \end{bmatrix}$$

and

$$\text{corr}(\varepsilon_1,\varepsilon_2) = \frac{\gamma}{\sqrt{\phi + \gamma^2}}.$$

If the prior on γ is relatively more diffuse that the prior on Φ, then the joint prior will put most mass near high correlations.

The advantages of the prior on identified parameters is twofold: (1) improper diffuse priors are possible and (2) informative priors for $\tilde{\beta}$ are more easily assessed than for the method which uses the full non-identified parameterization. In many applications, we have prior information on the likely values of $\tilde{\beta}$. In the prior set-up for the non-identified parameters, we do not directly assess a prior on the identified slope coefficients but must induce a complicated prior instead (see McCulloch, Polson, and Rossi (1993) for an analysis of the implied marginal distribution of $\tilde{\beta}$ for this prior).

One might ask the legitimate question of whether or not it is possible to assess a prior on the identified parameters via the method of section 4 which is similar to the prior introduced in this section. In McCulloch,

Polson, and Rossi (1993) the marginal distributions of γ and Φ are derived under the non-identified prior. While the priors on the identified parameters are not identical for the two methods in sections 4 and 5, it is possible to assess very similar priors by careful equating of moments.

6   Other informative priors for the covariance matrix

Experience with actual and simulated data has shown that it is very difficult to make precise inferences about the covariance parameters in the MNP. Keane (1992) notes that there are situations in which these covariance parameters are nearly unidentified. Our experience is that the relative variances σ_{ij}/σ_{11} are well identified by the data, but that the correlations may require a great deal of information to make relatively precise inferences. Thus, in many situations, it may be desirable to inject prior information about the correlation patterns in the data via exact restrictions on covariance structure or via informative priors.

6.1   Variance components approaches

To discuss the variance component approach, it is useful to return to the notation for the undifferenced system of latent variables

$$U = Z\delta + v \quad v \sim N(0,\Omega).$$

If we start with an independence ($\Omega = D$, a diagonal matrix), then the differenced system errors will show an equi-correlated structure

$$\text{var}(\varepsilon = v_{-1} - v_1) = \begin{bmatrix} d_2 + d_1 & d_1 & \cdots & d_1 \\ & d_3 + d_1 & \ddots & \vdots \\ & & \ddots & d_1 \\ & & & d_{p-1} + d_1 \end{bmatrix}.$$

If $D = dI$, we would have an equi-correlated structure with a correlation of 0.5.

Patterns of correlation can be most easily introduced by using a variance components structure. For the purpose of interpretation, we find it more intuitive to introduce the variance components in the undifferenced system. We can think of grouping the p choice alternatives into G groups, each of which has some common, unobservable component of utility. For example, if the alternatives are different brands of a consumer product, then the high-priced products might all enjoy a higher perceived quality in the eyes of certain consumers. This would introduce a variance component for quality perceptions for the higher-priced brands.

We break the p alternatives into G groups. Let $g(j)$ be an indicator index function for group g. $g(j) = 1$ if $j \epsilon$ indices for group g, $g = 1, \ldots, p$.

$$v_j = w_j + \sum_{g=1}^{G} g(j) r_g$$

$w_j \sim iidN(0, \sigma_w^2)$; $r_g \sim N(0, \sigma_g^2)$; $\{r_g\}$ are independent.

This parameterizes the Ω matrix with $G + 1$ variance component parameters. We note that because of the restricted structure of this parameterization of Ω, differencing is not required for identification purposes. We still must impose some restriction on the covariance parameters for identification. If we restrict $\sigma_w^2 = 1$, this will achieve identification.

We can easily define a Gibbs strategy for this variance component structure by introducing the $\{r_g\}$ as additional latent variables. If we group together the components of each v_i vector corresponding to group g, then the conditional posterior of r_g is a normal mean problem. Our MNP Gibbs sampler for the variance component problem replaces the draw of Σ or $\tilde{\Sigma}$ with the following sets of conditional draws

$$r_{g,i} | v_i, \sigma_g$$

$$\sigma_g | \{r_{g,i}\}.$$

6.2   More general priors on the correlation matrix

The variance component approach to specifying an information prior on the covariance structure is appealing because of its parsimony and usefulness in cases in which the alternatives can be grouped into similar groups. However, the covariance structure generated from the variance component model is restrictive in that it only affords positive covariances. In addition, a prior information on grouping may not be available. A more general approach would be to put an informative prior on the matrix of correlations which "shrinks" the correlation toward some base case such as the equi-correlated case produced by a scalar independence probit.

Barnard, McCulloch, and Meng (1995) introduce a general class of priors for covariance matrices that can be applied fruitfully here. To introduce this prior, it is most convenient to return to the differenced system. The Barnard, et al. approach is to reparameterize the covariance matrix in terms of the standard deviations and the correlation matrix and then put independent priors on each.

$$\Sigma = \Lambda R \Lambda \quad \text{where } \Lambda \text{ is a diagonal matrix with } \lambda_{ii} = \sigma_{ii}.$$

The prior considered in Barnard, et al. is

$$p(\Lambda,R) = p(\Lambda)p(R); \quad p(R) \propto 1; \quad \log(\lambda_i) \sim iid\, N(\mu_i, \sigma_i).$$

The emphasis in Barnard, *et al.* is on the prior for the variances with the primary motivation stemming from a location shrinkage application. Here we might prefer to be very diffuse on the variances and more informative on R.

In this general framework, we put a prior on Σ by simply specifying $p(\Lambda)$ and $p(R)$. We set $\lambda_1 = 1$ for identification purposes, and let the log-normal priors on remaining elements of Λ be very diffuse (or even improper). We then must choose an appropriate prior on R. The region of support of the prior on R is a subset of the hypercube with side $(-1,1)$. This region becomes more restricted further from the origin due to the constraints implied by positivity of the R matrix. This implies the "non-informative" uniform prior on R is actually informative owing to the nature of the restricted support. For $p > 2$, the marginal prior distributions of each r_{ij} element is non-uniform and becomes more concentrated near zero as the dimension (p) increases. If we wanted to "center" the prior over the independent scalar Probit model (this is the probit analogue of the multinomial logit model), we would have to use a prior which puts mass around 0.5. One such prior with reasonably slow damping tails might be

$$p(R) \propto \exp\left\{ -\eta \sum_{i=1}^{p-1} \sum_{j=i+1}^{p-1} \left| r_{ij} - 0.5 \right| \right\}.$$

The task of drawing from the conditional posterior, $\tilde{\Sigma}|\tilde{\beta},w,X$, might seem formidable because of the reparameterization of Σ, the non-conjugate nature of the prior, and the restricted region of support. The un-normalized conditional posterior density can be written

$$p(\tilde{\Sigma}|\tilde{\beta},w,X) = p(\tilde{\Sigma}|E) = p(\Lambda,R|E) \propto$$

$$\text{etr}\{-0.5(\Lambda R\Lambda)^{-1}EE'\}p(R)\prod_{i=2}^{p-1} p(\lambda_i)$$

$$E = (\varepsilon_1,\ldots,\varepsilon_N).$$

Direct draws from this density are not possible. A very general solution to this problem is to define a sub-Gibbs sampler and draw the elements of Λ and R one by one, conditional on the others. This one-by-one method also allows one to compute the region of support for each r_{ij} given all of the other elements. Still, the conditional distributions are in very non-standard forms. A highly effective solution to this problem is to adopt a "griddy" Gibbs strategy (Ritter and Tanner (1992)). The griddy Gibbs sampler uses a discrete approximation to the conditional distributions used in the sub-Gibbs sampler. We choose a grid of points in the support of the prior and simply compute the multinomial approximation to the conditional distribution by evaluating the conditional posterior density at each of the grid points. It should be emphasized that the griddy Gibbs sampler does not suffer from the curse of dimensionality that would afflict a standard discrete approximation to the joint posterior. We only evaluate the conditional posteriors, one by one, and never have to evaluate the joint posterior at a grid of points designed to fill the entire parameter space. Furthermore, the grids can be adaptive so that we only put points in regions where there is high posterior mass. Barnard, *et al.* report effective use of the griddy Gibbs method for up to 10×10 covariance matrices.

7 Bayesian random coefficient or hierarchical models for panel data

As we have discussed, reasonably precise inferences about the MNP model parameters, particularly correlation and covariance parameters, may require a large number of observations. It is rare to observe only one economic agent making choices between the same set of alternatives on many different occasions. Large samples are obtained in MNP applied work by observing the choices made by a large number of agents. Frequently, these choices are observed in a panel setting in which a large number of entries are observed for a relatively short period of time. In these panel settings, it is important that the MNP model be able to accommodate differences between entries. From this point on, we will refer to the economic entities as households even though they could just as easily be firms.

Differences between households in model coefficients or "heterogeneity" has received a good deal of attention in the econometric literature. The standard approach to this problem of accommodating heterogeneity with large N and small T is to use a random coefficient model. In the MNP literature, we typically see heterogeneity modeled as a random coefficient model for the intercepts (cf. Börsch-Supan and Hajivassiliou (1990)). There is no particular reason to believe that heterogeneity is restricted to the intercepts (for example, it is entirely reasonable that different households might display different sensitivities to choice characteristics such as price). In addition, a distinction is often made between "observable" heterogeneity (differences which are linked to observable attributes of households) and "unobservable" heterogeneity which is only revealed by choice behavior. Therefore, it is imperative that our approach to modeling heterogeneity accommodates differences in all MNP regression coefficient parameters as well as incorporating observable and unobservable heterogeneity.

7.1   A hierarchical approach to modeling heterogeneity

To fix the notation, we consider a panel of N households observed over T_h periods for each household

$$w_{h,t} = X_{h,t}\beta_h + \varepsilon_{h,t} \quad \varepsilon_{h,t} \, iid \, N(0,\Sigma)$$

$$h = 1,\ldots,H \quad t = 1,\ldots T_h.$$

We model the household heterogeneity via an additional regression model

$$\beta_h = \Delta z_h + v_h \quad v_h \sim N(0,V_\beta).$$

z_h contains a vector of d household characteristic ("demographic") variables. Thus, each MNP regression coefficient is related to a vector of characteristics and an unobservable component v. The unobservable component has a general covariance structure over households. Since we typically do not want to fix Δ and V_β as known, we introduce priors for these common parameters. This is a good example of a hierarchical Bayesian model in which the sampling model and set of priors is built up from a series of conditional distributions.

The complete model is specified as follows:

(i) $y_{h,t} | w_{h,t}$,
(ii) $w_{h,t} | X_{h,t}, \beta_h, \Sigma$,
(iii) $\beta_h | z_h, \Delta, V_\beta$,
(iv) $\Sigma | v, V$,
(v) $\Delta | \bar{\Delta}, A, V_\beta$,
(vi) $V_\beta | v_\beta, V_0$.

$\bar{\Delta}, A, V_\beta, V_0$ are hyper-parameters of the priors for Δ and V_β. The conditionals (i) and (ii) specify what most consider the "sampling" model. Conditional (iii) specifies what econometricians call the "random coefficient" model. In our Bayesian hierarchical approach, the conditionals (iii)–(vi) specify a joint prior over the set of $\{\beta_h\}$. Rossi, McCulloch, and Allenby (1995) discuss the specific form of these priors using the conditionally conjugate families.

The prior on V_β is is especially important in determining how much information is shared or "borrowed" across households in performing inference about the $\{\beta_h\}$. If the prior for V_β is tight around a small value, then there will be extensive shrinkage and the $\{\beta_h\}$ will differ little. More diffuse priors on V_β will induce less shrinkage. It is important to note that this prior must be proper in order for the joint posterior in this model to be proper. Thus, even with very diffuse settings, the prior on V_β must be influential. By making this a proper prior, we are asserting that there is some commonality among the $\{\beta_h\}$.

Given the basic framework outlined for the fixed coefficient MNP model outlined in section 3 above, it is a simple matter to elaborate the Gibbs sampler to include conditional posterior draws of the Δ and V_β which are in well-known multivariate normal and Wishart form (see Rossi, *et al.* (1996) for details). Our experience with this more elaborate sampler is that the sampler converges rapidly to a stationary distribution but that the draw sequences can be highly autocorrelated, necessitating long runs for accurate results.

In some problems, it may be useful to make inferences about the draw of β_h for a specific household. In the Bayesian hierarchical approach, we require the marginal posterior distribution of β_h

$$p(\beta_h|\text{data}) \propto \int p(\beta_h, \Delta, V_\beta|\text{data})d\Delta dV_\beta.$$

Fortunately, we can easily marginalize on β_h using the sequence of Gibbs draws produced as a by-product of our procedure. Rossi *et al.* (1996) make explicit use of these household-level parameter inferences to solve various targeted marketing problems which involve customizing promotional offers at the household level. The β_h draws can also be used as the basis of an informal diagnostic procedure for the form of the prior or mixing distribution. The assumption $\beta_h \sim N(\Delta z_h, V_\beta)$ is only the form of the prior for each household. The individual household data can shape the posterior for household h to a different form. If we lump together all draws across households and look at this distribution, we can assess whether the normal prior is appropriate to characterize the distribution of β_h over households. For example, if we see a multimodal distribution, this might suggest that we should investigate more flexible priors.

In a classical random coefficient model, the likelihood is averaged over the mixing distribution and inference is only made about the common parameters of the mixing distribution. On the other hand, the Bayesian approach combines the smoothing advantages of the frequentist random effects model with the richness of the fixed effects approach. In the Bayesian approach, there is no real distinction between fixed and random effects only between independent priors ("fixed" effects) and dependent priors (hierarchical or random coefficient models).

7.2   Extensions

7.2.1   Normal mixtures
The normal mixing model used in section 7.1 as the first stage of the hierarchical prior can be criticized as insufficiently flexible. In many situations, we might want to specify a prior structure that would allow for some grouping or clustering of households into more homogeneous sub-populations.

One way of achieving this would be to specify a mixture of normals as the prior. To illustrate how this might be achieved, we will simplify the model of section 7.1 to remove the household characteristics vector, z_h. In this model, we would simply have a normal prior with a fixed mean vector, $\beta_h \sim N(\bar{\beta}, V_\beta)$. We can replace this normal distribution with a mixture of normals

$$p(\beta_h | \lambda, \{\bar{\beta}_j\}, \{V_{\beta,j}\}) = \sum_{j=1}^{J} \lambda_j \varphi(\beta_h, | (\bar{\beta}_j, V_{\beta,j})) \quad \sum_{j=1}^{J} \lambda_j = 1.$$

We would have to introduce a prior for the λ_j mixture probabilities, and it would be most convenient to use a standard natural conjugate Dirichlet prior. The mixture of normals model could be easily handled in the Gibbs sampler via the introduction of latent indicator variables which switch on for each of the J components in the mixture. The indicator variables would have a conditional multinomial distribution. Given the component indicator variables, inference about the parameters of each component in the mixture can be done using standard normal theory.

7.2.2   Multiperiod probit models

In many panel applications, the assumption of independence of the model errors across time for the same households is questionable. It is straightforward to extend the MNP samplers to handle error terms which follow an AR(p) process. To illustrate this idea, consider a binomial multiperiod probit model. Geweke, Keane, and Runkle (1994) consider a Gibbs sampling approach to the multinomial multiperiod probit model and conduct extensive comparisons with the methods of simulated likelihood.

The latent variables set up for the binomial multiperiod probit is given as follows

$$w_{h,t} = x_{h,t}' \beta_h + \varepsilon_{h,t} \quad \text{where } \varepsilon_{h,t} = \Gamma_p(B)\varepsilon_{h,t} + u_{h,t}; \text{ var}(u_{h,t}) = 1.$$

The AR polynomial is parameterized by p autoregressive coefficients which we denote by the vector ϕ. The $u_{h,t}$ are assumed to be independent across time and households. We must introduce priors for the $\varepsilon_{h,0}$ and ϕ. To implement the Gibbs sampler, we must modify our strategy for drawing w and append two sets of conditionals to the Gibbs structure. Thus Gibbs sampler consists of the following set of conditionals

$$w | \beta, \varphi, \varepsilon_0, y, X$$

$$\beta | w, \varphi, \varepsilon_0, X$$

$$\varphi | w, \beta, \varepsilon_0, X$$

$$\varepsilon_0 | w, \varphi, \beta, X.$$

Here β, ε_0,w,y, and X are stacked vectors (matrices) of household parameters and data. The draw of w proceeds using the same strategy as before except that the autocorrelation structure changes the univariate normal conditional distribution of $w_{h,t}|w_{h,t-1}$. In addition, the conditional posterior of β is computed as before except on the orthogonalized regression system (pre-multiplied by the Cholesky root of the correlation structure which is available since we are conditioning on ϕ).

8   Conclusions

In this chapter, we illustrate how Bayesian inference can be achieved for a number of variants of the multinomial probit model. In particular, we consider various informative and non-informative priors on the model parameters, accommodating heterogeneity of various forms, non-normal mixing distributions, and multiperiod models. All of these situations can be handled via a Gibbs sampling strategy in which a Markov chain is constructed with the posterior distribution as its invariant distribution. Extensions of the basic model are handled in a unified framework by appending additional distributions to the base Gibbs sampler.

Our experience to date with the MNP model with both actual and simulated data suggests that there is much promise in this line of research. All of the data sets we have analyzed strongly support a rejection of the IIA property which is at the core of the multinomial logit model. The MNP model provides a great deal of flexibility at the expense of a complicated and high-dimensional parameterization. Our own experience is that it is difficult to make precise inferences about the covariance structure of the latent variable errors. This suggests that future successful modeling approaches will rely on restricted MNP models or informative priors.

Finally, Bayesian methods offer an alternative to the recent classical methods of simulated moments, simulated scores, and simulated maximum likelihood. These methods provide the basis for finite sample inferences at approximately the same order of computation demands as these classical alternatives. In addition, our methods provide a natural and flexible method for modeling heterogeneity and provide household-level parameter inferences should these be needed. The chief practical concern in the application of our methods is the rate of convergence of the Gibbs sampler. Our experience is that convergence is rapid enough for reliable practical application.

References

Albert, J. and S. Chib (1993), "Bayesian Analysis of Binary and Polychotomous Data," *Journal of the American Statistical Association*, 88, 669–679.
Barnard, J., R.E. McCulloch, and X. Meng (1995), "Shrinkage Priors for Covariance Matrices," Working paper, University of Chicago.

Börsch-Supan, A. and V. Hajivassiliou (1990), "Health, Children, and Elderly Living Arrangements: A Multiperiod-multinomial Probit Model with Unobserved Heterogeneity and Autocorrelated Errors," in D. Wise (ed.), *Topics of the Economics Aging*, Cambridge: NBER, 79–107.

Dansie, B. (1985), "Parameter Estimability in the Multinomial Probit Model," *Transportation Research -B*, 19B:6, 526–528.

Gelman, A. and D. Rubin (1992), "Inference from Iterative Simulation Using Multiple Sequences," *Statistical Science*, 7, 457–511.

Gemen, S. and D. Gemen (1984), "Stochastic Relaxation, Gibbs Distributions, and the Bayesian Restoration of Images," *IEEE Transactions on Pattern Analysis and Machine Intelligence*, 6, 721–741.

Geweke, J., M. Keane, and D. Runkle (1994), "Alternative Computational Approaches to Statistical Inference in the Multinomial Probit Model," *Review of Economics and Statistics*, 76, 609–632.

(1994), "Statistical Inference in the Multinomial, Multiperiod Probit Model," forthcoming, *Journal of Econometrics*, 80(1), 125–165.

Hajivassiliou, V.A. and P. Ruud (1994), "Classical Estimation for LDV Models Using Simulation," in Eagle and McFaddens, eds., *Handbook of Econometrics*, vol. IV, Amsterdam: North-Holland, chapter 40, 2384–2438.

Keane, M. (1992), "A Note on Identification in the Multinomial Probit Model," *Journal of Business and Economic Statistics*, 10, 193–200.

McCulloch, R.E., N.G. Polson, and P.E. Rossi (1993), "A Bayesian Analysis of the Multinomial Probit Model with Fully Identified Parameters," Working paper, Graduate School of Business, University of Chicago.

McCulloch, R.E. and P.E. Rossi (1994), "An Exact Likelihood Analysis of the Multinomial Probit Model," *Journal of Econometrics*, 64, 207–240.

Nobile, A. (1995), "A Hybrid Markov Chain for Bayesian Analysis of the Multinomial Probit Model," Working paper, Institute of Statistics and Decision Sciences, Duke University.

Ritter, C. and M.A. Tanner (1992), "Facilitating the Gibbs Sampler: the Gibbs Stopper and the Griddy-Gibbs Sampler," *Journal of the American Statistical Association*, 48, 276–279.

Rossi, P., R. McCulloch, and G. Allenby (1996), "The Value of Purchase History Data in Target Marketing," *Marketing Science*, 15, 32–340.

Tanner, M. and W. Wong (1987), "The Calculations of Posterior Distributions by Data Augmentation," *Journal of the American Statistical Association*, 82, 528–549.

Tierney, L. (1991), "Markov Chains for Exploring Posterior Distributions," Technical Report No. 560, School of Statistics, University of Minnesota.

Zellner, A. (1971), *An Introduction to Bayesian Inference in Econometrics*, New York: Wiley.

Zellner, A. and P.E. Rossi (1984), "Bayesian Analysis of Dichotomous Quantal Response Models," *Journal of Econometrics*, 25, 365–393.

Part III

Time series methods and models

Introduction

Til Schuermann

The simulation-based inference literature grew out of problems faced by microeconometricians in estimating discrete choice models in cross-sections. The classic problem is the multinomial probit model which encounters the computational barrier if there are more than four alternatives. Generically the problem is one of evaluating highly complex conditional expectations no matter what the data structure. Not surprisingly, time series econometricians have recently made increased use of the simulation-based techniques to solve some computational issues of their own. Some themes which emerge are the modeling of highly non-linear financial instruments, conditioning on pre-sample information and the evaluation of posterior distributions in a Bayesian context. This section presents several examples from this rapidly growing literature.

Many of the applications are in the area of empirical finance and macroeconometrics. The first chapter in this section by Christensen and Kiefer is a poignant example. Their contribution is a great step forward toward bridging the gap between recent developments in theoretical finance and econometric modeling. The finance theoretical point of departure is a probability measure under which suitably discounted security price processes are martingales. Knowledge of this equivalent martingale measure allows one to simulate long realizations of the theoretical price process whose moments can be matched to the empirical moments. Specifically, when evaluating option prices empirically, the analyst is forced to make the false assumption of complete markets with no arbitrage in order to make the problem tractable. Christensen and Kiefer solve this problem by outlining a simulation-based method of moments approach for computing the appropriate incomplete markets stochastic volatility option pricing operator.

Next, Diebold and Schuermann address an open question in econometrics: the possibility of exact maximum likelihood estimation of many observation-driven models. This follows the useful distinction made initially by Cox (1981) and again by Shephard (1995) between observation and parameter-driven models, the former describing the model directly in terms of observables, the latter separating out the observation and "deep" dynamic equations. Within the observation-driven world, we write down time series likelihood functions by taking the Schweppe decomposition and separating out that part of the likelihood which conditions on pre-sample information. Then, often only approximate maximum likelihood estimation is attempted because the unconditional density needed for exact estimation is not known in closed form. Using simulation and non-parametric density estimation techniques that facilitate empirical likelihood evaluation, they develop an exact maximum likelihood procedure and provide an illustrative application to the estimation of ARCH models in which they compare the sampling properties of the exact estimator to those of several competitors. Perhaps not surprisingly they find that both bias and variance are reduced, especially in situations of small samples and high persistence, i.e., in precisely those situations when pre-sample information is likely to matter most.

The third chapter by Mariano and Tanizaki deals with an important part of time series econometrics: filtering and prediction. Their point of departure is the Kalman filter which is well defined when the observation or measurement equation is linear. If one wishes to relax this assumption the problem quickly becomes quite complex. Mariano and Tanizaki present simulation-based methods to solve this problem and illustrate their solution by measuring permanent consumption in the US and Japan. They set up a general non-linear state-space model for unobserved permanent consumption, extending the literature on this celebrated topic to a simultaneous consideration of transitory consumption, variable interest rates and non-linearity of the Euler equation derived from utility maximization by the representative agent. Because of the non-linear complexities in the model, stochastic simulations are used to obtain numerical maximum likelihood estimates of the unknown model parameters.

In the spirit of separating the model to be estimated from the model used for estimation, Pagan and Martin outline a method for computing the parameters of latent multifactor models within the paradigm of indirect estimation. As they point out, direct estimation via maximum likelihood of model parameters in macroeconomic models is frequently quite difficult. It is this difficulty which motivated Gourieroux, Montfort, and Renault (1993) and Gallant and Tauchen (1996) to propose estimating an indirect parameter π instead of the deep parameter θ, so long as there is a relationship between them. To do so can be computationally costly but possible using simulation techniques. They provide us with two examples: a two-factor model of a long series of US stock returns where the factor is a descriptor of volatility; and a multifactor model to estimate the term structure of interest rates in the tradition of Cox, Ingersoll, and Ross (1985).

Finally Geweke provides us with a thorough review of Bayesian methods in time series econometrics. Because Bayesian methods require the full specification of the posterior distribution of the model and because these distributions are often highly complex, simulation-based inference techniques seem like a natural place to turn for a solution. The first application of Monte Carlo integration of posterior densities can be found as far back as 1978 in an *Econometrica* paper by Kloek and van Dijk (1978). Geweke discusses the gamut of topics: from the choice of priors and model averaging, hypothesis testing, latent variable models, forecasting, and signal extraction. He then presents several common examples such as vector autoregression, time-varying volatility models like GARCH and stochastic volatility models, changing regime and Markov switching models. He outlines the three steps of a Bayesian econometrician: (1) be explicit about assumptions, including distribution of ones priors; (2) condition on available information; and (3) use posterior simulators to report the logical implications of (1) and (2).

References

Cox, D.R. (1981), "Statistical Analysis of Time Series: Some Recent Developments," *Scandinavian Journal of Statistics*, 8, 93–115.

Cox, J.C., J.E. Ingersoll, and S.A. Ross (1985), "A Theory of the Term Structure of Interest Rates," *Econometrica*, 53, 385–407.

Gallant, A. and G. Tauchen (1996), "Which Moments to Match," *Econometric Theory*, 12, 657–681.

Gourieroux, C., A. Montfort, and E. Renault (1993), "Indirect Inference," *Journal of Applied Econometrics*, 8, S85–S118.

Kloek, T. and H.V. van Dijk (1978): "Bayesian Estimation of Equation System Parameters: An Application of Integration by Monte Carlo," *Econometrica*, 46, 1–19.

Shephard, N. (1995), "Statistical Aspects of ARCH and Stochastic Volatility," Discussion paper, Nuffield College Oxford.

7 Simulated moment methods for empirical equivalent martingale measures

Bent Jesper Christensen and Nicholas M. Kiefer

1   Introduction

In this chapter we introduce a new simulation methodology for the empirical analysis of financial market data. The purpose of the new methodology is to build a bridge between the theoretical developments in recent years in mathematical finance and the econometric models employed in empirical finance. The powerful theoretical concepts we explore center around the idea of an equivalent martingale measure, as introduced by Harrison and Kreps (1979) and Harrison and Pliska (1981), i.e., a probability measure under which suitably discounted security price processes are martingales. The existence of an equivalent martingale measure allows convenient contingent claims pricing without reference to the mean return or drift parameters. For our purposes, this implies that simulation under the equivalent martingale measure can be accomplished without specifying the drifts of the price processes.

   Given the emphasis on simulation, the econometric framework we consider is cast in terms of the method of moments, where the unbiasedness of simulators as approximations to expectations is most readily exploited. However, our methodology does not merely amount to integration by simulation in the method of moments. Rather, we use simulation as a tool to operationalize the advances in theoretical finance associated with the martingale pricing model.

   The chapter is organized as follows. In section 2, the simulation methodology is introduced and discussed. Numerous advantages of the new methodology are listed in section 3. Thus, the lack of need to estimate drift

We are grateful to participants at the Conference on Simulation-Based Econometrics: Methods and Applications in Minneapolis, November 1995, and at the Sixth Annual Derivative Securities Conference at Queen's University, April 1996, and to Yacine Ait-Sahalia (the discussant) and other participants at the North-American Econometric Society Meetings in New Orleans, January 1997, for useful comments, and to N.R. Prabhala for providing the data. The first author acknowledges research support from the Centre for Analytical Finance, Aarhus; the Centre for Nonlinear Modelling in Economics, Aarhus; and the Network for Mathematical Finance, Denmark.

parameters is taken up in section 3.1. In section 3.2 it is emphasized that, with the particular simulator in question, a single pseudo-random draw per observation suffices for the asymptotic properties of the estimation and inference procedures. The methodology is robust to missing data situations, as detailed in section 3.3. In addition, the procedure leads to an efficiency gain in the estimation of the volatility parameters that are so important in all contingent claim pricing, and this is discussed in section 3.4. Section 3.5 builds tests of the martingale pricing model that involve specified maintained hypotheses and thus serve as complements to the conventional moment method tests against unspecified alternatives. Finally, in the new simulation methodology, parameter estimation and testing of the martingale model may take place without necessarily computing a very precise version of the option pricing formula implied by the model, an issue discussed in section 3.6. In section 4 we go on to compare the new methodology with existing techniques. First, the representative agent equilibrium model based on a specified utility function is considered in section 4.1. Pros and cons of the utility-based model versus the martingale model are discussed, as well as a test of the utility model against the more general martingale model. The potential roles of finite difference solutions to partial differential equations and binomial approximations are considered in section 4.2, and the differences between our methodology and those of Engle and Mustafa (1992) and Duffie and Singleton (1993) are pointed out in sections 4.3 and 4.4, respectively. A numerical illustration in the context of stock index options is offered in section 4.5, and concluding comments are relegated to section 5.

2   The new simulation methodology

In this section we outline the main ideas of the new methodology. Consider a security price process of the continuous time diffusion type typically considered in mathematical finance

$$dS_t = \mu(S_t,t)dt + \sigma(S_t,t)dZ_t \tag{1}$$

where S_t denotes the security price at time t, μ denotes the drift and σ the volatility, and Z_t is a standard Wiener process or Brownian motion, i.e. dZ_t / dt is white noise. We assume that the coefficients satisfy sufficient regularity (e.g., Lipschitz and growth) conditions for the Ito stochastic differential equation (1) to possess a strong solution.

Perhaps the most important result in mathematical finance is that the absence of arbitrage opportunities in the market place in wide generality is equivalent to the existence of an equivalent martingale measure. Thus, if we have a filtered probability space $(\Omega, \mathcal{F}, \{\mathcal{F}_t\}_t, P)$ satisfying the usual conditions, with $\{Z_t\}_t$ adapted to $\{\mathcal{F}_t\}_t$ and P a probability measure defined on $(\Omega, \mathcal{F})$ under which the security price dynamics are as indicated in (1), and if for simplicity we consider the situation where a riskless bond paying a constant interest rate r exists and thus follows the deterministic price process

$$dB_t = rB_t dt, \tag{2}$$

then an equivalent martingale measure is a probability measure Q defined on $(\Omega, \mathcal{F})$ with the same null sets as P such that under Q, the discounted security price process S_t/B_t is a martingale. Hence, market prices admit no arbitrage opportunities, as for instance in any equilibrium, if and only if under an equivalent martingale measure Q there is a white noise, say dW_t/dt, such that the security price dynamics take the form

$$dS_t = rS_t dt + \sigma(S_t, t)dW_t. \tag{3}$$

In other words, while the volatility is unchanged from (1), the instantaneous rate of return now coincides with that of the riskless bond (2).

An equivalent martingale measure is particularly convenient in relation to contingent claim pricing. Consider a derivative security selling for C_t at time t and paying $g(S_\tau)$ at some specified expiration date $\tau > t$, where g is a known function. For example, in the case of a European call option with strike price K, $g(S) = (S - K)^+$. The objective is to determine the fair value of C_t. The martingale approach allows the solution

$$C_t = e^{-r(\tau - t)} E_t^Q g(S_\tau) \tag{4}$$

where E_t^Q indicates conditional expectation under Q, given information available up to time t. This valuation formula is free of the security specific drift parameters in μ from (1) since the expectation is with respect to the distribution under Q, in which only r enters the drift.

The objective in the empirical methodology that we now introduce is to estimate the parameters that matter for contingent claim pricing, such as $\theta = (r, \sigma)$, and to test the validity of the model (4), without reference to the parameters in μ. We achieve this essentially by constructing an appropriate estimating function $h_t(\theta)$ such that $E_t h_t(\theta_0) = 0$ and therefore $Eh_t(\theta_0) = 0$ at the true parameter value θ_0, whereas $Eh_t(\theta) \neq 0$ for $\theta \neq \theta_0$. This is the idea in the method of moments, and we shall build on Hansen (1982). The difference is that if data are used on S_τ in (4) then such observations are drawn under the physical probability measure $P = P(\theta_0, \mu_0)$, not the equivalent martingale measure $Q = Q(\theta_0)$, and this runs counter to our purpose. Therefore, we do not use data on S_τ, but instead a simulated value S_τ^*, and the simulation is performed under Q and thus without reference to any value of μ. Of course, to get the conditioning right, the simulation is conditional on the observed value of S_t, and at the trial value θ of the interest parameters these dependencies are indicated by writing $S_\tau^*(\theta;S_t)$. With data $X_t = (S_t,C_t)$, the basic idea is therefore to use the estimating function

$$h_t(\theta) \equiv h(\theta;X_t) \equiv C_t - e^{-r(\tau-t)}g(S_\tau^*(\theta;S_t)). \qquad (5)$$

Thus, C_t may be expressed as an expectation, albeit under a new probability measure, and expectations can be simulated, even when no analytical form is known, as is the case for most options. This use of simulation to approximate the fair value of C_t is in line with Boyle (1977). Of course, we may on a given date have an entire array of options written on the same underlying security, with distinct values of (τ,K) and other contractual terms, and these can all be included in the analysis by appropriately interpreting C_t and associated variables as vectors in what follows.

When verifying $Eh_t(\theta_0) = 0$, the expectation is under $R \equiv P \times Q$. In particular

$$E^R h_t(\theta_0) = E^P E_t^Q h_t(\theta_0) = E^P\{C_t - e^{-r_0(\tau-t)}E_t^Q g(S_\tau^*(\theta_0;S_t))\} = E^P\{C_t - C_t\} = 0. \qquad (6)$$

To get a more precise simulator, multiple pseudo-random draws $S_\tau^{*m}(\theta;S_t)$, $m = 1,\ldots,M$ per observation X_t may be used, so when we make statements about the above estimating function, they may in practice refer to the version

$$h_t(\theta) = C_t - e^{-r(\tau-t)}\frac{1}{M}\sum_{m=1}^{M}g(S_\tau^{*m}(\theta;S_t)).$$

Importantly, this is linear in the simulated objects $g(S_\tau^{*m}(\theta;S_t))$, $m = 1,\ldots,M$, and this has consequences for the required value of M in applications, as we shall return to.

In practice, some mild regularity conditions, such as stationarity and ergodicity (Hansen (1982)) or certain mixing properties (e.g., Gallant (1987)) should be satisfied by $\{X_t,h_t\}$ to ensure desirable properties of the resulting estimator, and since S_t and therefore C_t in many specifications can be explosive processes it is often convenient to apply a transformation and look instead at the equation obtained, for example, by dividing through by S_t. If the transformed process, say $Y_t \equiv C_t/S_t$, satisfies the regularity condition, then so does the relevant conditional expectation divided by S_t, and hence the new estimating function. A simple case is the at-the-money call ($K = S_t$) where the transformed estimating function is

$$\tilde{h}_t(\theta) \equiv Y_t - e^{-r(\tau-t)}(R_\tau^*(\theta;S_t) - 1)^+ \qquad (7)$$

and $R_\tau^*(\theta;S_t) = S_\tau^*(\theta;S_t)/S_t$ is recognized as a return that typically will be, for example, stationary and ergodic.

Importantly, the procedure allows for a zero conditional mean error structure beyond what is implied by (4). For instance, let m_t denote the measurement error due to, for example, non-synchronicities in data on option prices C_t and the underlying security S_t, such that

$$C_t = e^{-r(\tau-t)}E_t^Q g(S_\tau) + m_t$$

and assume that $E_t^P m_t = 0$. When verifying (2.6) we now get $E^P\{C_t - (C_t + m_t)\} = 0$, and the mechanics of what follows are unaltered.

As usual, we may expand the estimating function using instruments $z_t \in \mathcal{F}_t$ and consider $f_t(\theta) = h_t(\theta) \otimes z_t$. In any case, this must be done if it is necessary to ensure that $\dim f \geq \dim \theta$. The moment condition still holds, i.e.

$$E^R f_t(\theta_0) = E^P[E_t^Q h_t(\theta_0) \otimes z_t] = E^P[(E_t^P m_t) \otimes z_t] = 0.$$

If z_t summarizes important information available at t, then the information loss stemming from the reliance only on vanishing unconditional (as opposed to conditional) expectations is reduced.

By convention we indicate time points as $t = 1, \ldots, T$ when the mechanism for handling intervals that are for example shorter or not equidistant is obvious. Thus, with observations $\{X_t, z_t\}_{t=1}^T$, the empirical moment $g_T(\theta) = \Sigma_t f(\theta; X_t, z_t)/T$ is formed, and the estimator is chosen to solve the estimating equation $g_T(\theta) = 0$ if $\dim f = \dim \theta$. If $\dim f > \dim \theta$, the estimator is chosen to minimize $J_T^A(\theta) = Tg_T(\theta)' A_T g_T(\theta)$ for a suitable metric $A_T > 0$. In this case, an initial consistent estimate $\tilde{\theta}_T$ is obtained by letting $A_T = I_{\dim f}$, the identity. The optimal weights are then estimated as $V_T = \Sigma_j K_T(j) \gamma_T(j)$, using the sample autocovariances $\gamma_T(j) = \Sigma_t f_t(\tilde{\theta}_T) f_{t-j}(\tilde{\theta}_T)/T$ along with the kernel $K_T(j)$, e.g. $K_T(j) = (1 - |j|/\sqrt{T})^+$, and the final estimator $\hat{\theta}_T$ is constructed by letting $A_T = V_T^{-1}$ in the objective function. The approximating normal distribution for $\hat{\theta}_T$ is $N(\theta_0, \frac{1}{T}(F' V^{-1}F)^{-1})$, where V is estimated consistently by V_T and F by $\frac{1}{T}\Sigma_t \delta f_t(\tilde{\theta}_T)/\delta\theta'$. These derivatives, in turn, should be approximated as $(f_{it}(\tilde{\theta}_{iT})) - (f_{it}(\tilde{\theta}_T))/\varepsilon$ in the ith coordinate, where $\tilde{\theta}_{iT}$ is obtained from $\tilde{\theta}_T$ by adding a small number ε to the ith coordinate, or a similar two-sided approximation could be adopted, in either case to account for the fact that shifting θ has an effect not only through the straight partial of f_t (e.g., through the derivative of $\exp(-r(\tau - t))$ in (5) with respect to r), but also because different parameters imply different simulated values of future prices S_τ^* and hence different approximated expectations.

The estimated parameter $\hat{\theta}_T$ implies an estimate of the equivalent martingale measure, $\hat{Q}_T = Q(\hat{\theta}_T)$, which we label an empirical equivalent martingale measure (EEMM). The martingale pricing model (4) may be tested by treating $J_T^V(\hat{\theta}_T)$ as a $\chi^2(\dim f - \dim \theta)$ variate, and we refer to this as an EEMM test.

3   Advantages of the new methodology

3.1   No drift parameters

A main theoretical advantage of working with the equivalent martingale measure is that contingent claim pricing may be performed without reference to the security drifts μ. Our methodology allows extension of this idea to empirical work. The parameters θ that matter for contingent claim pricing may be estimated without any attempt to estimate μ. This is the essence of the empirical equivalent martingale measure $\hat{Q}_T$. Further, the martingale pricing model may be subjected to an EEMM test as outlined in the previous section, again without first estimating μ. This means that no particular equilibrium (determining the form of μ) need be specified, and the analysis can rely purely on no arbitrage.

Apart from the theoretical appeal and the close link to mathematical finance, a substantial advantage of this is that the drift μ typically is the most difficult parameter to estimate in stochastic differential equation models. Thus, if the asymptotics are established for a sampling interval of fixed total length, with the time between observations tending to zero, then there is usually no consistent estimator for μ, but σ may still be estimated consistently, and in our framework so may $\theta = (r, \sigma)$. In other words, the EEMM methodology provides a means of isolating as the parameters of economic interest those that are most tractable from a statistical viewpoint.

Finally, to be sure, note that with many securities or complicated models, μ may contain many parameters, whereas r is always a scalar, common across securities, so the improvement also involves a strict reduction in dimensionality. As the EEMM methodology operationalizes the mathematical finance theory and reduces dimensionality, it provides far more than mere integration by simulation in the method of moments.

3.2   A single draw per observation suffices

In our methodology, the estimating function is an expectation and so lends itself to simulation. This is not changed by the fact that the expectation in question is taken under the equivalent martingale measure. In particular, the relevant moment conditions are linear in the simulated quantities $g(S_\tau^{*m})$. In consequence, a single draw per observation suffices for the asymptotics. This is the virtue of the original simulation estimators due to McFadden (1989) and Pakes and Pollard (1989). In contrast, if a non-linear function of an expectation must be approximated by simulation, a large number of draws, of the order $\sqrt{T}$, is necessary. For example, a discrete choice probability is plainly the expectation of an obvious experiment with outcomes $\{0,1\}$, and the outcome itself is thus an unbiased simulator for the probability, but if the log probability (a non-linear function of the "expectation") must be simulated, for example, in the process of performing maximum simulated likelihood estimation, then alternative methods are called for, in particular to avoid taking log of zero for some of the outcomes. A simple but costly way out is to take a very large number of draws to get the probability right before taking logs (Lerman and Manski (1981)). Thus, discrete choice problems where probabilities must be simulated lend themselves to simulated moment estimation rather than maximum simulated likelihood.

Similarly, thinking of maximum likelihood as the case where the estimating function is the score, the problem is that this is not conveniently expressed as the expectation of a simulation experiment. Rather, simulators for both the density derivative in the numerator and the density in the denominator must be employed, again involving a non-linear function of averages. Exceptions are particular latent variable models where the explicit functional form of the score contributions may be recognized as expectations of latent variables which in turn may be simulated (Ruud (1986)), but in other discrete models (and in continuous models) an increasing number of draws per observation are again required for the asymptotics.

The non-linearity of the contingent claim payoff functions in the EEMM methodology (such as $g(S) = (S - K)^+$ in the call option case) does not lead to a similar problem since our simulator is for the expectation of the non-linear function ($E(g)$ is approximated, not ($g(E)$)).

3.3 No missing data issue

Our methodology applies even if no security price data are available at the expiration date, i.e., if S_τ is unobserved. Typical examples would be that the financial instruments in question are very long-term issues, perhaps warrants, all expiring years out in the future, or have very short terms to expiration. In the former case $\tau >> T$, and in the latter $t < \tau < t + 1$. In either case we may easily simulate S_τ. In fact, though, even if for example the option whose price C_t is observed at time t expires at $\tau = t + 1$ where we do have the observation S_{t+1}, we would not in any way condition the simulation of S_{t+1} ...S_τ (more precisely, of $S_\tau^*(\theta;S_t)$) on S_{t+1} or in general on any observations between t and τ. The only conditioning is on S_t. The reason is that the observed S_{t+1} in a sense is "drawn" from the true probability measure $P = P(\theta_0,\mu_0)$, whereas the virtue of our methodology is that $S_\tau^*(\theta;S_t)$ is drawn from $Q(\theta)$ (conditional on S_t). It is seen that the spacing of expiration dates τ relative to the observation times $\{1,...,T\}$ is utterly irrelevant to the EEMM methodology.

3.4   Efficiency gain in volatility estimation

As already noted, σ is a parameter that may typically be estimated directly from the stochastic differential equation model, without invoking contingent claim theory or data. Nonetheless, the estimating equations we propose may be used in conjunction with such standard methods to produce an efficiency gain. That is, in addition to the estimator based on the estimating function f_t above, we may study the extended approach based on $a_t = (f_t, b_t)$, combining f_t with the estimating function b_t generating the standard estimator. In a simple model, the moment condition based on b_t would generate the sample standard deviation. Consider now the portion $(F'F)^{-1}$ of the asymptotic variance of our estimator stated previously. Here, we have absorbed $V^{-1/2}$ in the definition of F. The corresponding term for the standard estimator based on b_t is of the form $(B'B)^{-1}$, and for the combined estimator based on a_t we get $(F'F + B'B)^{-1}$, which is less than both the individual variances. Of course, this argument is only indicative of the efficiency gain that generally will arise. Thus, the expressions take f_t and b_t to be asymptotically uncorrelated. Also, for this to indicate the asymptotic variance of the estimator for σ only, which is where the efficiency gain occurs, we either take r as given or interpret $(F'F)^{-1}$ as the submatrix corresponding to σ only, not r, and likewise take $(B'B)^{-1}$ to be the submatrix of the relevant variance matrix associated with b_t that corresponds to σ only, not μ, if the latter is estimated in the standard scheme under consideration. Generally, though, adding the option data $\{C_t\}_t$ and considering $\{X_t\}_t = \{S_t, C_t\}_t$ in an EEMM procedure will improve efficiency compared to classical methods based on $\{S_t\}_t$ only.

3.5   EEMM tests for structure

In the set-up from subsection 3.4, it is possible to derive alternative tests of the martingale pricing model that may serve as useful complements to the model test in section 2. Thus, in section 2 the null was that $E^R f_t = 0$, and the alternative then obviously that $E^R f_t \neq 0$. With the added conditions based on b_t we may consider the joint null $E^R a_t = 0$ (recall that $a_t = (f_t, b_t)$), but for the purpose of testing the martingale model there is no reason to consider the possibility that the standard model with estimating function b_t is misspecified, so we let the alternative be given by the maintained hypothesis $E^P b_t = 0$. Say the standard method in question involves estimation of both σ and μ (if μ is not estimated it may be left out in the following). Then the full parameter vector is $\pi = (r, \sigma, \mu)$. Let $\hat{\pi}_T^a$ be the joint estimator based on the estimating function a_t, corresponding to the null, and let $(\hat{\sigma}_T^b, \hat{\mu}_T^b)$ be the standard estimator associated with the alternative, based on b_t. We consider two alternative EEMM tests, both with null $E^R a_t = 0$ and specified alternative $E^P b_t = 0$. The first test is based on the statistic

$$TJ_T^a(\hat{\pi}_T^a) - TJ_T^b(\hat{\sigma}_T^b, \hat{\mu}_T^b) \tag{8}$$

where J_T^a is defined in analogy with J_T^V earlier, but with a_t replacing f_t. Analogously, J_T^b is calculated by replacing f_t by b_t, but in this case taking care that the metric is compatible with that defining J_T^a. Writing $A_T = (V_T^a)^{-1}$ for the latter, the metric $(V_T^b)^{-1}$ is employed in J_T^b, with V_T^b the submatrix of V_T^a corresponding to b_t. Under the null, the test statistic is asymptotically $\chi^2(\dim f - 1)$ and so is distributed on more degrees of freedom than the previous test from section 2.

The second EEMM test of $E^R a_t = 0$ against the specified alternative $E^P b_t = 0$ is derived as a Hausman (1978) test based on the efficiency gain of the previous subsection, i.e., the test statistic is

$$(\hat{\sigma}_T^b - \hat{\sigma}_T^a)' W_T^-(\hat{\sigma}_T^b - \hat{\sigma}_T^a) \tag{9}$$

where by slight abuse of notation $\hat{\sigma}$ indicates a column consisting of estimates of the parameters that enter the function σ, and with W_T^- indicating the generalized inverse of the weighting matrix $W_T = \text{var}(\hat{\sigma}_T^b) - \text{var}(\hat{\sigma}_T^a)$. If asymptotically the rank of W_T is constant when $E^R a_t = 0$, then the test statistic may be treated as an asymptotic $\chi^2(\text{rank } W_T)$ statistic under the null. If many instruments z_t are used in forming f_t (precisely, if $(\dim f - 1)$ is more than twice the number of parameters to be estimated in σ), then this statistic is distributed on fewer degrees of freedom than the test from section 2. A complementary interpretation of this test is of course that it is a test of whether the efficiency gain alluded to in the previous subsection indeed applies.

Thus, the two alternative statistics of this subsection add substantially to the spectrum of EEMM testing procedures. They allow an increase or decrease the degree of freedom in a meaningful manner, and, in particular, they are tests of structure. That is, a logical sequential testing procedure is to first identify a (maintained) hypothesis that is not rejected in a test based on b_t. This first step is used to isolate a stochastic differential equation model such as (1) which is not at odds with the data at hand. The second step is then to implement one of the EEMM tests of this subsection in order to test the additional structural hypothesis that the financial market mechanism works to ensure that, given the underlying security price process (1), contingent claims are priced according to (4). Under mild regularity conditions, the two steps are asymptotically independent, so significance levels may be computed as already indicated.

3.6   No numerical solution of pricing formula necessary

If the number of draws per observation tends to infinity, then the simulated average converges to the true expectation, and so at the true parameter point to the exact contingent claim price, i.e.

$$h_t(\theta_0) \to 0, \quad \text{a.s.} < Q_t(\theta_0) >.$$

This is a much stronger condition than

$$g_T(\theta_0) \to 0, \quad \text{a.s.} < R(\theta_0) >$$

and it implies that we have calculated the exact option pricing formula, i.e., for given S_t and parameters θ_0 we can construct C_t. The particular numerical procedure employed in this construction is simulation with a large number of draws. However, the EEMM methodology allows parameter estimation and testing of the martingale pricing model without ever calculating this exact option pricing formula. Thus, with a single or a fixed and finite number of draws per observation we do not have anything close to the exact formula from (4), but the asymptotic inference works regardless. Similarly, as noted earlier, the condition $g_T(\theta_0) \to 0$ permits conditional mean zero but otherwise fairly general measurement errors m_t, for example, due to non-synchronicities between data on the option and the underlying security, whereas such errors would lead to a violation of the condition $h_t(\theta_0) \to 0$.

From an academic research perspective it will usually be of main interest to test for the general validity of the underlying pricing relationships, i.e., for (4) holding in a statistical sense, but not necessarily to calculate the exact pricing formula that gives a precise contingent claim price for a given argument (S_t, θ). The EEMM methodology is tailored to these research purposes, not necessarily to on-line trading.

4   Comparison of the new methodology with existing techniques

4.1   Specified representative agent utility function

The main theoretical advantage of the martingale methodology is that no particular equilibrium need be specified: pricing is purely by no arbitrage, a necessary condition in any equilibrium. Nonetheless, for the sake of comparison we consider the alternative situation where a particular representative agent equilibrium pricing relationship based on a specified utility function is postulated. The resulting pricing relationship is of the type introduced by Rubinstein (1976) and also corresponds to the stochastic Euler equations of Lucas (1978). For concreteness, consider

$$C_t = e^{-\delta(\tau-t)} E_t^P \left\{ \frac{u'(c_\tau)}{u'(c_t)} g(S_\tau) \right\} \tag{10}$$

as an alternative to (4), with δ the subjective discount rate, u the period utility function (u' is the marginal utility), and c_t aggregate consumption. To turn this into a useful empirical model we assume rational expectations on the part of the representative agent, i.e., the expectation is taken under P. Comparing (4) and (10), the density or likelihood ratio process of the equivalent martingale measure Q with respect to the true measure P is given by

$$e^{-(\delta-r)(\tau-t)} \frac{u'(c_\tau)}{u'(c_t)}. \tag{11}$$

With data on (S_t, C_t, c_t) and with the new restriction that expiration dates τ coincide with sampling dates t, the estimating function is constructed by replacing the expectation in (10) by its empirical analogue. No simulation is needed since the theoretical and sampling probabilities now coincide. Parameters to estimate include δ and the parameters of the utility function, say η. A common specification in applications is that of a constant relative risk aversion (CRR) η, such that $u(c) = (c^{1-\eta} - 1)/(1 - \eta)$, and so $u'(c_\tau)/u'(c_t) = (c_t/c_\tau)^\eta$. Logarithmic preferences obtain as the limiting case $\eta \to 0$ by appeal to l'Hôpital rule. Considering again the at-the-money call we take in analogy with (7)

$$\tilde{k}_t(\lambda) \equiv Y_t - e^{-\delta(\tau-t)} U_\tau (R_\tau - 1)^+ \tag{12}$$

with $\lambda = (\delta, \eta)$ for the basic estimating function. In specific cases this would allow verifying sufficient regularity of $Y_t = C_t/S_t, R_\tau = S_\tau/S_t$, and the variable $U_\tau = u'(c_\tau)/u'(c_t)$ which captures the way in which consumption enters (e.g., in the CRR case the regularity of U_τ would follow from that of consumption growth c_τ/c_t).

The usual method of moments estimation and testing procedure now follows the steps outlined in section 2. Using $\tilde{k}_t$ in place of $\tilde{h}_t$, the analogues in the present model of the quantities f_t, g_T, etc. from section 2 are formed, but this time no simulation is called for. As outlined here, both methods appear to share the advantage that the option pricing model may be tested without having to estimate the drift parameters μ. However, firstly, once a specific utility function is adopted, the option pricing model being tested is much more narrow, and so the advantage of the simulation methodology is that it allows testing the general model that merely assumes absence of arbitrage opportunities. A second difference is that the utility-based approach imposes common parameters λ across all securities, and σ need not be estimated, whereas in the martingale approach separate estimates of σ for the individual securities are admitted.

A third issue is that the martingale approach applies even if the expiration dates τ do not coincide with sampling dates. If this is the situation in the representative agent approach, then a natural solution with inspiration from the martingale approach is to calculate the relevant conditional expectation by simulation rather than by employing an empirical analogue. Thus, given the observed (S_t, c_t), pseudo-random draws of (S_τ, c_τ) are generated. The drawbacks of this method relative to our methodology are that in addition to prices also aggregate consumption must be simulated, and in particular that in this representative agent simulation procedure the parameters that must be estimated in addition to λ are both μ and σ, as well as the corresponding drift and volatility parameters for consumption. The reason that μ must be estimated is that it is needed in the simulation which must be under P, not Q. Similarly, the consumption process parameters must be estimated since they are needed for the consumption simulation. All in all, the martingale model, though theoretically the most general, is vastly better suited for simulation-based estimation and inference than the utility-based model.

Of course, the fact that the martingale model is more general than the utility model suggests that if the martingale is not rejected in the testing procedure of section 2, then in the next step a particular utility model could be tested as a further restriction on the martingale model. To be sure, the usual χ^2 test of the overidentifying restrictions associated with (12) is available for testing the utility model against an unspecified alternative, but as in section 3.5 we may complement this basic test with variations based on specified alternatives. In this case, the maintained hypothesis is that the martingale model applies, and the null is that the particular utility function in question generates the correct martingale measure. In fact, it is appropriate to specify the alternative when conducting the test of the null if indeed the indicated alternative was not rejected in the previous test (if the standard stochastic differential equation model is not rejected in 3.5, respectively if the martingale model is not rejected in the present section).

Thus, with the alternative we now associate the estimating function a_t from 3.5, yielding estimators for μ, σ, and r. If μ is not desired, for example, if in the given setup it cannot be estimated consistently, then we consider the estimating function f_t and parameters σ and r. With the null we associate these estimating functions along with $d_t = \tilde{k}_t \otimes z_t$, and the parameters are those from the alternative plus $\lambda = (\delta, \eta)$. Following section 3.5, the test comparing the minimized objective functions under the null and the alternative is under the null approximately $\chi^2(\dim d - \dim \lambda)$. Since there are no common parameters in a_t and d_t, the degrees of freedom are the same as in the basic test against an unspecified alternative, but the present test is likely to have superior inferential properties since λ is estimated more efficiently from (a_t, d_t) than from d_t alone unless a_t and d_t happen to be uncorrelated, an unlikely event since they both depend heavily on C_t.

Still following 3.5, we may in addition consider the test of efficiency gain under the null, given consistency under both the null and maintained hypotheses. In 3.5 we considered the test based on the parameter σ common to both the standard and the martingale model, but could have expanded with μ if this too was estimated under both hypotheses. In the present situation no parameters are common to both the utility and the martingale model, but we could again base the test on σ, and if desired r, since these are estimated both under the null and the alternative. We could add μ if this is estimated under both hypotheses, too, but λ is not a candidate, since it is only estimated under the null.

The number of parameters being compared indicates the degrees of freedom, at least in case of a strict efficiency gain, which still requires that a_t and d_t are not uncorrelated. In general, they are only so if the utility-based model operates a local cut in the full model (Christensen and Kiefer (1994)), and in this case there is inferential separation between the comparison parameters and λ.

In short, our methodology allows analysis of the conventional utility-based equilibrium model as a special case, and tests for this particular form of martingale measure may be considered, but many general advantages to a focus on an arbitrage-based EEMM analysis have been noted.

4.2   Finite difference and binomial tree methods

It is well known that a contingent claim price such as (4) satisfies a certain partial differential equation with boundary conditions, and that such equations may be solved with respect to the pricing operator by finite difference methods. Similarly, the pricing operator may be approximated by the known operator in an approximating binomial tree model that converges weakly to the true model (4). Either approach provides a means of constructing the relevant contingent claim price C_t as a function of S_t and parameters. Furthermore, neither approach requires μ in the construction of this function. Thus, the possibility exists to define the estimating equation directly in terms of the numerical option pricing formula obtained by the finite difference or binomial method, and avoid simulation. However, in this case it is necessary for the validity of the resulting statistical method to perform a detailed and costly numerical analysis and actually produce functions that are very close to the true relationship, i.e., the virtue of the simulation methodology discussed in 3.6 is lost. The reason is that while the averaging involved in the definition of the estimation procedure works to counteract the lack of precision in the individual simulators as approximations to the respective expectations, this is not so for the finite difference and binomial approximations to the same expectations. In particular, the latter approximations may not be unbiased, the error committed when ending the numerical work at a too rough approximation potentially being systematic. When building a precise formula for trading and other commercial purposes, finite difference and binomial schemes may compete with simulators with many draws, but for research purposes there is no close substitute for the EEMM methodology for which just a few draws suffice.

4.3   The Engle and Mustafa (1992) implied ARCH method

In this very young area of research, Engle and Mustafa (1992) is an important early contribution, and so it is important to clarify the additional contributions. The authors compare empirical and theoretical option prices and also simulate the latter. However, rather than adopting a direct (e.g., Euler, see below) approximation to the stochastic differential equation, they replace it by a GARCH(1,1) model in the simulation. This is motivated by a focus on stochastic volatility models for S_t, but the same approach cannot be transferred to other models for the underlying security. Secondly, stochastic volatility introduces a market incompleteness and thus non-uniqueness of Q that requires special handling. The authors choose to make assumptions that essentially remove the effect of stochastic volatility on the option pricing mechanism (i.e., volatility risk is unpriced).

The econometrics are different from ours, too, i.e., they adopt a nonlinear SUR framework rather than a moment approach, thus implying that a large number of simulations per observation are required. The SUR assumes serially uncorrelated and homoskedastic errors. Our methodology is more robust and applies for far more general stochastic structures. In particular, the EEMM methodology is required to get consistent standard errors for parameter estimates and theoretical option prices in the face of serial dependencies and heteroskedasticity, even if only for the measurement errors. In addition, unlike Engle and Mustafa, we provide a means of combining information on the interest parameters from both option and underlying data, achieving an efficiency gain over any model focusing only on one of the subsets of data, and a means of testing the option model against the pure underlying model.

It is seen that the Engle and Mustafa (1992) procedure is more specifically geared toward backing out implied GARCH(1,1) models from the options data and less toward testing general versions of the martingale pricing theory than ours, and given this difference in purposes it makes sense that the mechanics of the methodologies differ, too.

4.4   The Duffie and Singleton (1993) simulated moment method

In Duffie and Singleton (1993), simulation was used in conjunction with moment methods, but in a different way and for a different purpose. Consider an estimating function k_t that does not require simulation. The moment method rests on the condition $Ek_t = 0$. If this condition cannot be verified for a function k_t that for some other reason is desirable for the definition of the method, then an alternative is to consider the modified estimating function $k_t - E^*k_t$, where E^*k_t is an approximation to the true but supposedly unknown mean, in this case obtained by simulation. The role of g_T from section 2 is now played by the construct $\frac{1}{T}\sum_{t=1}^{T}k(\psi;X_t)$ $-\frac{1}{D}\sum_{j=1}^{D}k(\psi;X_j^*)$, with k a known function, ψ the parameter to be estimated, X_t the observed ergodic series, and X_j^* a corresponding simulated series of length D, drawn from the distribution for X_t corresponding to parameter ψ. It is immediate that the second term is a simulator for the unconditional expectation of the first sum, and a moment procedure applies. A precise simulator is obtained by letting $D \gg T$, i.e., the second sum may be much longer than the first and in that case is simply based on a very long run of consecutive draws from the process in question.

In our methodology, the pseudo-random draws are conditional on the observed data, and there is no run of the type just considered. For example, we may for each observation X_t, say, draw a single future security price from a distribution that is conditioned on X_t. If the expectation yielding the theoretical value corresponding to the observed contingent claim price C_t is approximated using p pseudo-random draws instead of one, these p draws are independent, given X_t. The Duffie and Singleton (1993) approach consists of drawing variables that mimic the observations and then typically operating the same function $k(\psi; \cdot)$ on both observed and generated data, whereas our approach involves drawing variables that do not correspond to any observations, and then operating the functions $g(\cdot)$ specifying the contingent claim on the generated variables, but of course never on the observed data (such as the given option prices).

Thus, the mechanics of the two procedures are clearly different, and the procedures serve different purposes. Finally, note that the draws in the Duffie and Singleton (1993) mechanism are from the supposed true distribution, i.e., from P, whereas ours are from Q, the equivalent martingale measure.

4.5   A numerical example

We now turn to a numerical illustration of the methodology. We consider an extended constant elasticity of variance (CEV) diffusion

$$dS_t = \mu(S_t,t)dt + (\sigma S_t + \omega S_t^\gamma)dZ_t \qquad (13)$$

for asset prices S_t, and the pricing of call options, i.e., $g(S) = (S - K)^+$. No analytical option pricing formula is known for this model. In the special cases (i) $\omega = 0$ (the geometric Brownian motion or log-normal diffusion case, Black and Scholes (1973)), (ii) $\sigma = 0$, $\gamma < 1$ (the CEV case, Cox (1975)), and (iii) $\sigma = \gamma = 0$ (the arithmetic Brownian motion case, Cox and Ross (1976)), analytical formulas are known, but we shall not restrict ourselves to these cases, and hence the importance of the simulation approach.

Black (1976) argued that because of a leverage effect, the conditional standard deviation of the stock return should be a decreasing function of the level of the stock price. The Black–Scholes model rules this out, and the Cox and Cox–Ross specifications restrict the standard deviation to be of the form $\omega S_t^{\gamma-1}$. Our extended CEV (ECEV) specification allows adding an intercept σ to this functional form, viz.

$$\mathrm{var}_t\left(\frac{dS_t}{S_t}\right)^{1/2} = \sigma + \omega S_t^{\gamma-1}.$$

Consider a data set of the form $\{X_t, Z_t\}_t$, with $X_t = (S_t, C_t)$ the asset price and the corresponding option price at time t, and $Z_t = (K_t, \tau_t, r_t)$ the required regressors, namely the strike price and expiration date for the option, and the interest rate. We shall employ the relationship (4), treating the parameter r as known and equal to the observed r_t in time period t. Under the equivalent martingale measure, the price dynamics take the form (3), but to ensure positive prices in the simulation, we apply Ito's lemma and rewrite the equation as

$$d\log S_t = \left(r - \frac{1}{2}\frac{\sigma(S_t,t)^2}{S_t^2}\right)dt + \frac{\sigma(S_t,t)}{S_t}dW_t.$$

Based on this, and for trial parameter values $\theta = (\sigma, \gamma, \omega)$, we simulate according to the Euler scheme

$$S_t^{i+1} = S_t^i \exp\left\{\left(r - \frac{1}{2}\frac{\sigma(S_t^i,t_i)^2}{(S_t^i)^2}\right)\Delta + \frac{\sigma(S_t^i,t_i)}{S_t^i}\Delta^{1/2}\varepsilon_{i+1}\right\}$$

where Δ indicates the length of the time step, $t_i = t + i\Delta$, and $\{\varepsilon_i\}_i$ are pseudo-random draws of *iid* $N(0,1)$ variates. In the ECEV model this scheme takes the form

$$S_t^{i+1} = S_t^i \exp\left\{\left(r_t - \frac{1}{2}(\sigma + \omega(S_t^i)^{\gamma-1})^2\right)\Delta + (\sigma + \omega(S_t^i)^{\gamma-1})\Delta^{1/2}\varepsilon_{i+1}\right\}.$$

With N steps, $\Delta = (\tau_t - t)/N$. The iterations are started at $S_t^0 = S_t$, the observed asset price, and $S_{\tau_t}^*(\theta;S_t) = S_t^N$ is recorded for use in (5). If the scheme is repeated M times, starting at S_t each time and producing $S_{\tau_t}^{*m}(\theta;S_t)$ in the mth repetition, then (5) is replaced by

$$h_t(\theta) = C_t - e^{-r_t(\tau_t - t)}\frac{1}{M}\sum_{m=1}^{M} g_t(S_{\tau_t}^{*m}(\theta;S_t))$$

where $g_t(S) = (S - K_t)^+$.

We consider monthly data on S&P 100 index (OEX) options. The data span the period from November 1983, when these options started trading on the Chicago exchange (CBOE), to May 1995, for a sample size of 139. Thus, C_t is the option price in month t, immediately after the expiration of the $(t-1)$th option, and S_t is the contemporaneous level of the S&P 100 index. We consider the one-month, at-the-money OEX option, i.e., $\tau_t = 1$, $K_t = S_t$, and to complete the data set, we use the one month LIBOR – the interbank borrowing rate in the Eurodollar market – for r_t. For the instruments z_t, we use the most recent returns on the index and the option, i.e., $(S_t - S_{t-1})/S_{t-1}$ and $(C_t - C_{t-1})/C_{t-1}$, the increment in the interest rate $r_t - r_{t-1}$, and the squares of these three variables. We use $N = 20$ in the simulations, a figure roughly corresponding to the number of trading dates during a month. The estimation procedure of section 2 is implemented, simulating the relevant moments using the Euler scheme and minimizing their norm over parameters. In this example, dim $f = 6$ and dim $\theta = 1, 2, 3$ and 1 for the Cox–Ross, Cox, ECEV, and Black–Scholes models, respectively. A lag length of 10 is employed in the construction of the final weights in the objective function.

The results from using $M = 1, 10$, and 100 repetitions appear in panels A, B, and C of table 7.1. The point estimates of σ, ω, γ are reported, with asymptotic standard errors in parentheses, and the EEMM test based on the minimized objective appears in the last column. The first thing to note is that standard errors drop as M is increased. Nonetheless, neither point estimates nor standard errors are completely off even with only a single draw per observation, and certainly not with 10, as judged by the benchmark results for $M = 100$.

On the substantive side, the Black–Scholes, Cox–Ross, and Cox models are consistently rejected by the data, whereas the ECEV model cannot be rejected (except in the case $M = 1$ at, e.g., the 5 per cent level). This is evidence in favor of the model extension here considered, although the parameter estimates in the extended model apparently are much less precise than in the straight CEV (Cox) model. Of course, if the latter model is indeed invalid, as the test statistics indicate, then the associated standard errors are inconsistent. We note that in the ECEV estimation with $M = 100$ all parameters are significant, including the new parameter σ that represents our extension beyond CEV. Furthermore, the elasticity parameter γ

Table 7.1. *Empirical equivalent martingale measure applications*

Model	σ	ω	γ	df	χ^2_{df}
Panel A: 1 draw per observation					
Black–Scholes	0.148			5	19.0
	(0.072)				
Cox–Ross		40.7		5	25.5
		(5.65)			
Cox		0.786	0.793	4	12.3
		(0.026)	(0.032)		
ECEV	0.081	0.311	0.796	3	8.2
	(0.041)	(0.146)	(0.320)		
Panel B: 10 draws per observation					
Black–Scholes	0.159			5	16.3
	(0.045)				
Cox–Ross		44.8		5	23.7
		(4.09)			
Cox		0.790	0.817	4	11.8
		(0.020)	(0.024)		
ECEV	0.073	0.390	0.764	3	6.44
	(0.031)	(0.113)	(0.259)		
Panel C: 100 draws per observation					
Black–Scholes	0.153			5	16.0
	(0.042)				
Cox–Ross		42.4		5	22.6
		(3.99)			
Cox		0.819	0.803	4	12.1
		(0.015)	(0.024)		
ECEV	0.081	0.397	0.725	3	6.7
	(0.030)	(0.093)	(0.129)		

may be distinguished from unity (the Black–Scholes case), although barely so, but not from the value one-half. In other words, the options data indicate that the index process is at least as close to a square-root model similar to the Cox, Ingersoll, and Ross (1985) model of interest rates as to the popular log-normal or geometric Brownian Motion specification.

As a further illustration, the Hausman (1978)-style EEMM test against a specified alternative is considered next. In what follows, the calculations are done with $M = 100$, and only the CEV and ECEV models are considered. For the maintained hypothesis we first specify that an unbiased esti-

Table 7.2. *Empirical equivalent*
martingale measure tests

Model	df	χ^2_{df}
Panel A: QML alternative		
Cox	2	20.30
ECEV	3	9.44
Panel B: MEE alternative		
Cox	2	8.14
ECEV	3	6.21
Panel C: EMM alternative		
Cox	2	11.90
ECEV	3	7.05

mating function b_t is given by the quasi-score function corresponding to a suitable quasi-likelihood function. In the ECEV case, the exact likelihood function is unknown, although in the CEV case it is known and indeed has been used in empirical work on pure asset (i.e., no options) data by Gibbons and Jacklin (1988) (MacBeth and Merville (1980) is an early contribution adopting approximate criteria involving both stocks and options). The quasi-likelihood function takes the conditional distribution of S_{t+1} given S_t to be normal with mean $S_t + \mu(S_t,t) = (1 + \mu)S_t$ (μ is a scalar) and standard deviation $\sigma S_t + \omega S_t^\gamma$, imposing $\sigma = 0$ in the CEV case. The resulting QML estimators may under the null of structure (i.e., the martingale pricing model holds) be improved upon by expanding the estimating function using f_t underlying table 7.1. The test for structure (or for whether the efficiency gain from adding the options data applies) is reported in table 7.2, panel A. It rejects in both the Cox and ECEV cases. The first model was actually rejected also in table 7.1, so we have no indication that a particular procedure based on pure index data would be likely to fail to reject it (so that the EEMM test against such an alternative would be of interest). The model is included here for comparison since in table 7.1 it was not rejected as outright as the Black–Scholes and Cox–Ross.

The reason that the test also rejects in the ECEV case may of course not be lack of structure (the ECEV was not rejected in table 7.1), but rather that the maintained hypothesis itself is violated. Thus, the approximation involved in the QMLE may not be warranted. The obvious remedy against the key problem, namely that the QML estimating function b_t in fact is biased, would be transform it to an O_A-optimal estimating function in the sense of Godambe and Heyde (1987). However, in practice it typically suffices to subtract the compensator from b_t to leave it a martingale estimating equation (MEE), and following Bibby and Sørensen (1995) this is accomplished by simulating the conditional mean and variance of S_{t+1} given S_t instead of using the above QML approximations to these, for example, $\Sigma_{m=1}^{M} S_{t+1}^{*m}(\theta;S_t)/M$ replaces $(1+\mu)S_t$. The results appear in panel B. Indeed, the change compared to panel A is substantial, thus indicating the importance of testing against a valid alternative. In particular, the ECEV is no longer rejected at the 5 per cent level, and this result is in agreement with table 7.1. The Cox model is still rejected.

The idea of turning a misspecified estimating equation (say, a quasi-score equation) into a useful device by simulation also underlies the techniques of indirect inference (II) by Gourieroux, Montfort, and Renault (1993) and efficient method of moments (EMM) by Gallant and Tauchen (1996). Rather than using simulation to make b_t a martingale as in MEE, these approaches replace the observed data in b_t with data simulated for a given θ, then choose θ to make the simulated data imply a QMLE as close as possible to that obtained in the observed data. Closeness is literally in a minimum distance sense in II, but is understood more indirectly in the EMM, where the estimator is selected as the θ for which the simulated data bring $\Sigma_{t=1}^{T} b_t(\hat{\theta}_T^b)/T$ as close to zero as possible (if necessary in a GMM sense), $\hat{\theta}_T^b$ here indicating the estimator from the observed data.

Thus, II and EMM are similar, and we focus on the latter, again using the Euler scheme to perform the simulations. In the present case dim $b = $ dim θ, so no GMM weighting is called for in the definition of $\hat{\theta}_T^b$, the estimator under the alternative, but weighting does take place (and in the usual way) when combining with the options data and the estimating equations from table 7.1 to form $\hat{\theta}_T^a$. The results of the EEMM tests are exhibited in panel C. Qualitatively, they agree with those in panel B, thus supporting the notion that EMM (and presumably II) may be effective alternatives to MEE for mitigating the QML bias. The efficiency gains of EEMM relative to MEE and EMM are about the same. Generally, standard errors (not reported) are about one third to one half in the EEMM, relative to MEE and EMM.

On the substantive side, we have added further evidence that ECEV may be a candidate for an index model, that index options are priced in accordance with this, and that adding them to the data set produces an efficiency gain. This supports the notion that volatility estimation should not ignore the observations that are most sensitive to – and therefore most informative about – volatility, namely, the options, and this is where the EEMM methodology plays its key role.

5   Conclusion

We have outlined a new simulation methodology that furnishes a fruitful combination of recent developments in mathematical finance and econometrics. The advantages associated with the lack of need to specify a particular equilibrium in the theoretical model and the lack of dependence on drift parameters in the resulting contingent claim pricing relationships are operationalized in the simulation methodology, and the same reductions in dimensionality are exploited in simplifying simulation, estimation, and inference. Reduction in missing data issues and efficiency gains are among the benefits of the new methodology. Some numerical experience with the technique in the context of stock index options was reported. In on-going research, the methodology is applied to larger data sets, and the validity of the asymptotics are assessed in sampling experiments.

References

Bibby, B.M. and M. Sørensen (1995), "Martingale Estimating Functions for Discretely Observed Diffusion Processes," *Bernoulli*, 1, 17–39.

Black, F. (1976), "Studies of Stock Price Volatility Changes," *Proceedings of the 1976 Meetings of the American Statistical Association*.

Black, F. and M. Scholes (1973), "The Pricing of Options and Corporate Liabilities," *Journal of Political Economy*, 81, 637–659.

Boyle, P.P. (1977), "Options: A Monte Carlo Approach," *Journal of Financial Economics*, 4, 323–338.

Christensen, B.J., and N.M. Kiefer (1994), "Local Cuts and Separate Inference," *Scandinavian Journal of Statistics*, 21, 389–402.

Cox, J.C. (1975), "Notes on Option Pricing I: Constant Elasticity of Variance Diffusions," Working paper, Stanford University.

Cox, J.C. and S.A. Ross (1976), "The Valuation of Options for Alternative Stochastic Processes," *Journal of Financial Economics*, 4, 145–166.

Cox, J.C., J.E. Ingersoll, and S.A. Ross (1985), "A Theory of the Term Structure of Interest Rates," *Econometrica*, 53, 385–408.

Duffie, D. and K.J. Singleton (1993), "Simulated Moments Estimation of Markov Models of Asset Prices," *Econometrica*, 61, 929–952.

Engle, R.F. and C. Mustafa (1992), "Implied ARCH Models from Options Prices," *Journal of Econometrics*, 52, 289–311.

Gallant, A.R. (1987), *Nonlinear Statistical Models*, New York: Wiley.

Gallant, A.R. and G. Tauchen (1996), "Which Moments to Match?" *Econometric Theory*, 12(4), 657–681.

Gibbons, M. and C. Jacklin (1988), "CEV Diffusion Estimation," Working paper, Stanford University.

Godambe, V.P. and C.C. Heyde (1987), "Quasi-likelihood and Optimal Estimation," *International Statistical Review*, 55, 231–244.

Gourieroux, C., A. Montfort, and E. Renault (1993), "Indirect Inference," *Journal of Applied Econometrics*, 8, S85–S118.

Hansen, L.P. (1982), "Large Sample Properties of Generalized Method of Moments Estimators," *Econometrica*, 50, 1029–1054.

Harrison, J.M. and D. Kreps (1979), "Martingales and Arbitrage in Multiperiod Securities Markets," *Journal of Economic Theory*, 20, 381–408.

Harrison, J.M. and S. Pliska (1981), "Martingales and Stochastic Integrals in the Theory of Continuous Trading," *Stochastic Processes and Their Applications*, 11, 215–260.

Hausman, J.A. (1978), "Specification Tests in Econometrics," *Econometrica*, 46, 1251–1272.

Lerman, S.R. and C.F. Manski (1981), "On the Use of Simulated Frequencies to Approximate Choice Probabilities," in C.F. Manski and D. McFadden (eds.), *Structural Analysis of Discrete Data with Econometric Applications*, Cambridge, MA: MIT Press.

Lucas, R. (1978), "Asset Prices in an Exchange Economy," *Econometrica*, 46, 1429–1445.

MacBeth, J.D. and L. Merville (1980), "Tests of the Black–Scholes and Cox Call Option Pricing Models," *Journal of Finance*, 35, 285–300.

McFadden, D. (1989), "A Method of Simulated Moments for Estimation of Discrete Response Models Without Numerical Integration," *Econometrica*, 57, 995–1026.

Pakes, A. and D. Pollard (1989), "The Asymptotics of Simulation Estimators," *Econometrica*, 57, 1027–1058.

Rubinstein, M. (1976), "The Valuation of Uncertain Income Streams and the Pricing of Options," *Bell Journal of Economics*, 7, 407–425.

Ruud, P. (1986), "On the Method of Simulated Moments for the Estimation of Limited Dependent Variable Models," Working paper, University of California, Berkeley.

8 Exact maximum likelihood estimation of observation-driven econometric models

Francis X. Diebold and Til Schuermann

1   Introduction

Cox (1981) makes the insightful distinction between observation-driven and parameter-driven models. A model is observation driven if it is of the form

$$y_t = f(y^{(t-1)}, \varepsilon_t)$$

and parameter driven if it is of the form

$$y_t = h(\phi_t, \nu_t)$$

$$\phi_t = g(\phi^{(t-1)}, \eta_t)$$

where superscripts denote past histories, and ε_t, ν_t, and η_t are white noise. If, moreover, the relevant part of $y^{(t-1)}$ is of finite dimension, we will call an observation driven model finite ordered, and similarly if the relevant part of $\phi^{(t-1)}$ is of finite dimension, we will call a parameter-driven model finite ordered.

Of course the distinction is only conceptual, as various state-space and filtering techniques enable movement from one representation to another, but the idea of cataloging models as observation or parameter driven facilitates interpretation and provides perspective. The key insight is that observation-driven models are often easy to estimate, because their dynamics are defined directly in terms of observables, but they are often hard to manipulate. In contrast, the non-linear state-space form of parameter-driven models makes them easy to manipulate but hard to estimate.

This is a revised and extended version of our earlier paper, "Exact Maximum Likelihood Estimation of ARCH Models." Helpful comments were provided by Fabio Canova, Rob Engle, John Geweke, Werner Ploberger, Doug Steigerwald, and seminar participants at Johns Hopkins University and the North American Winter Meetings of the Econometric Society. All errors remain ours alone. We gratefully acknowledge support from the National Science Foundation, the Sloan Foundation, the University of Pennsylvania Research Foundation, and the Cornell National Supercomputer Facility.

A simple comparison of ARCH and stochastic volatility models will clarify the concepts.[1] Consider the first-order ARCH model

$$y_t = \sigma_t \varepsilon_t$$

$$iid$$
$$\varepsilon_t \sim N(0,1)$$

$$\sigma_t^2 = \alpha_0 + \alpha_1 y_{t-1}^2,$$

so that

$$y_t | y_{t-1} \sim N(0, \alpha_0 + \alpha_1 y_{t-1}^2).$$

The model is finite ordered and observation driven and, as is well known (e.g., Engle (1982)), it is easy to estimate by (approximate) maximum likelihood. Alternatively, consider the first-order stochastic volatility model

$$y_t = \sigma_t \nu_t$$

$$iid$$
$$\nu_t \sim N(0,1)$$

$$\ln \sigma_t^2 = \delta_0 + \delta_1 \sigma_{t-1}^2 + \eta_t$$

$$iid$$
$$\eta_t \sim N(0,1)$$

so that

$$y_t | \sigma_{t-1} \sim N(0, \exp(\delta_0 + \delta_1 \sigma_{t-1}^2 + \eta_t)).$$

The model is finite ordered but parameter driven and, as is also well known, it is very difficult to construct the likelihood because σ_t is unobserved.

In this chapter we study finite-ordered observation-driven models. This of course involves some loss of generality, as some interesting models (like the stochastic volatility model) are not observation driven and/or finite ordered, but finite-ordered observation-driven models are nevertheless tremendously important and popular. Autoregressive models and ARCH models, for example, satisfy the requisite criteria, as do many more complex models. Moreover, observation-driven counterparts of parameter-driven models often exist, such as Gray's (1995) version of Hamilton's (1989) Markov switching model.

Observation-driven models are often easy to estimate. The likelihood may be evaluated by prediction-error factorization, because the model is stated in terms of conditional densities that depend only on a finite number

---

[1] This example draws upon Shephard's (1995) insightful survey.

of past observables. The initial marginal term is typically discarded, however, as it can be difficult to determine and is of no asymptotic consequence in stationary environments, thereby rendering such "maximum likelihood" estimates *approximate* rather than *exact*. Because of the potential for efficiency gains, particularly in small samples with high persistence, exact maximum likelihood estimation may be preferable.

We will develop an exact maximum likelihood procedure for finite-ordered observation-driven models, and we will illustrate its feasibility and examine its sampling properties in the context of ARCH models. Our procedure makes key use of simulation and non-parametric density estimation techniques to facilitate evaluation of the exact likelihood, and it is applicable quite generally to any finite-ordered observation-driven model specified in terms of conditional densities.

In section 2, we briefly review the exact estimation of the AR(1) model, which has been studied extensively. In that case, exact estimation may be done using procedures more elegant and less numerically intensive than ours, but those procedures are of course tailored to the AR(1) model. By showing how our procedure works in the simple AR(1) case, we provide motivation and intuitive feel for it, and we generalize it to much richer models in section 3. In sections 4 and 5, we use our procedure to obtain the exact maximum likelihood estimator for an ARCH model, and we compare its sampling properties to those of three common approximations. We conclude in section 6.

2 Exact maximum likelihood estimation of autoregressions revisited

To understand the methods that we will propose for the exact maximum likelihood estimation of finite-ordered observation-driven models, it will prove useful to sketch the construction of the exact likelihood for a simple Gaussian AR(1) process.

The covariance stationary first-order Gaussian autoregressive process is

$$y_t = \rho y_{t-1} + \varepsilon_t$$
$$iid$$
$$\varepsilon_t \sim N(0, \sigma^2)$$

where $|\rho| < 1$, $t = 1, \ldots, T$. The likelihood may be factored into the product of $T-1$ conditional likelihoods and an initial marginal likelihood. Specifically

$$L(\theta) = l_T(y_T | \Omega_{t-1}; \theta) \, l_{T-1}(y_{T-1} | \Omega_{T-2}; \theta) \ldots l_2(y_2 | \Omega_1; \theta) \, l_1(y_1; \theta)$$

where $\theta = (\rho, \sigma^2)'$ and $\Omega_t = \{y_t, \ldots, y_1\}$. the initial likelihood term $l_1(y_1; \theta)$ is known in closed form; it is

$$l_t(y_t; \theta) = (2\pi)^{-1/2} \sqrt{\frac{1-\rho^2}{\sigma^2}} \exp\left[-\frac{1-\rho^2}{2\sigma^2} y_1^2\right].$$

The remaining likelihood terms are

$$l_1(y_1 | \Omega_{t-1}; \theta) = (2\pi\sigma^2)^{-1/2} \exp\left[-\frac{1}{2\sigma^2}(y_t - \rho y_{t-1})^2\right]$$

$t = 2, \ldots, T$.

Beach and MacKinnon (1978) show that small sample bias reduction and efficiency gains are achieved by maximizing the exact likelihood, which includes the initial likelihood term, as opposed to the approximate likelihood, in which the initial likelihood term is either dropped or treated in an *ad hoc* manner. Moreover, they find as ρ increases, the relative efficiency of exact maximum likelihood increases.

Now let us consider an alternative way of performing exact maximum likelihood. The key insight is that the initial likelihood term, for any given parameter configuration, is simply the unconditional density of the first observation, evaluated at y_1, which can be estimated to any desired degree of accuracy using well-known techniques of simulation and consistent non-parametric density estimation.

We proceed as follows. At any numerical iteration (the jth, say) en route to finding a maximum of the likelihood, a current "best guess" of the parameter vector exists; call it $\theta^{(j)}$. Therefore, we can simulate a very long realization of the process with parameter $\theta^{(j)}$ and estimate its unconditional density at y_1; denote it $\hat{l}_1(y_1; \theta^{(j)})$. The estimated density at y_1 is the first observation's contribution to the likelihood for the particular parameter configuration $\theta^{(j)}$. Then we construct the Gaussian likelihood

$$L(\theta^{(j)}) \approx \hat{l}_1(y_1; \theta^{(j)}) \prod_{t=2}^{T} \sigma^{-1} \exp\left[-\frac{1}{2\sigma^2}(y_t - \rho y_{t-1})^2\right]$$

and we maximize it with respect to θ using standard numerical techniques. The approximation error goes to zero – that is, $\hat{l}_1(y_1; \theta^{(j)}) \to l_1(y_1; \theta^{(j)})$, so we obtain the exact likelihood function – as the size of the simulated sample whose density we consistently estimate goes to infinity.

Obviously, it would be wasteful to adopt the simulation-based approach outlined here for exact estimation of the first-order autoregressive model, because the unconditional density of y_1 is known in closed form. In other important models, however, the unconditional density is *not* known in closed form, and in such cases our procedure provides a solution. Thus, we turn now to a general statement of our procedure, and then to a detailed illustration.

3 Observation-driven models with arbitrary conditional density

The observation-driven form

$$y_t = f(y^{(t-1)}, \varepsilon_t)$$

usually makes it a simple matter to find the conditional density

$$y_t | y^{(t-1)} \sim D(y^{(t-1)}; \theta)$$

where the form of the conditional density D depends on $f(.)$ and the density of ε_t. Many observation-driven models are in fact specified directly in terms of the conditional density D, which is typically assumed to be a member of a convenient parametric family. The likelihood is then just the product of the usual conditional densities and the initial joint marginal D^* (which is p-dimensional, say)

$$L(y_T, \ldots, y_1; \theta^{(j)}) = D^*(y_1, \ldots, y_p; \theta^{(j)}) \prod_{t=(p+1)}^{T} D(y^{(t-1)}; \theta^{(j)}).$$

The difficulty of constructing the exact likelihood function stems from the fact that the unconditional density D^* is typically not known in closed form, even when a large amount of structure (e.g., normality) is placed on the conditional density D. In a fashion that precisely parallels the above AR(1) discussion, however, we can consistently estimate D^* from a long simulation of the model, resulting in

$$L(y_T, \ldots, y_1; \theta^{(j)}) \approx \hat{D}^*(y_1, \ldots, y_p; \theta^{(j)}) \prod_{t=(p+1)}^{T} D(y^{(t-1)}; \theta^{(j)}).$$

As in the AR(1) case, the approximation error is under the control of the investigator, regardless of the sample size T, and it can be made arbitrarily small by simulating a long enough realization.

A partial list of observation-driven models for which exact maximum likelihood estimation may be undertaken using the techniques proposed here includes Engle's (1982) ARCH model, models of higher-order conditional dynamics (e.g., time-varying conditional skewness or kurtosis), Poisson models with time-varying intensity, Hansen's (1994) autoregressive conditional density model, Cox's (1981) dynamic logit model, and Engle and Russell's (1995) conditional duration model. Moreover, the conditional density need not be Gaussian, and the framework is not limited to pure time series models. It applies, for example, to regressions with disturbances that follow observation-driven processes.

4   Exact maximum likelihood estimation of ARCH models

Volatility clustering and leptokurtosis are routinely found in economic and financial time series, but they elude conventional time series modeling techniques. Engle's (1982) ARCH model and its generalizations are consistent with volatility clustering by construction and with unconditional leptokurtosis by implication; hence their popularity. ARCH models are now widely used in the analysis of economic time series and are implemented in popular computer packages like Eviews and PC-GIVE. Applications include modeling exchange rate, interest rate, and stock return volatility, modeling time-varying risk premia, asset pricing (including options), dynamic hedging, event studies, and many others.[2]

Engle's (1982) ARCH process is a classic and simple example of a model amenable to exact estimation with the techniques developed here. The known conditional probability structure of ARCH models facilitates approximate maximum likelihood estimation by prediction-error factorization of the likelihood. *Exact* maximum likelihood estimation has not been attempted, however, because the unconditional density l_p is not known in closed form. The prevailing view (namely, that exact maximum likelihood estimation is effectively impossible) is well summarized by Nelson and Cao (1992, p. 232), who assert that

in practice (for example in estimation) it is necessary to compute [the conditional variance] recursively . . . assuming arbitrary fixed values for $\{\varepsilon_0^2, \ldots, \varepsilon_{-p+1}^2; \theta\}$.[3]

In short, the issue of exact maximum likelihood estimation is, without exception among the hundreds of published studies using ARCH techniques, skirted by conditioning upon *ad hoc* assumptions about l_p. Although the treatment of l_p is asymptotically inconsequential, it may be important in small samples, particularly when conditional variance persistence is high. With this in mind, we construct the exact likelihood function of an ARCH process using the procedure outlined earlier.

Consider the sample path $\{\varepsilon_t\}_{t=1}^T$ governed by the pth-order ARCH process

$$\varepsilon_t = \sigma_t \eta_t$$

$$\sigma_{t-1}^2 = \omega + \alpha_1 \varepsilon_{t-1}^2 + \ldots + \alpha_p \varepsilon_{t-p}^2$$

$$\eta_t \overset{iid}{\sim} N(0,1),$$

---

[2] See Diebold and Lopez (1995).
[3] Their notation has been changed to match ours.

where $\sum_{i=1}^{p} \alpha_i < 1$, $\omega > 0$, $\alpha_i \geq 0$, $\forall i = 1, \ldots, p$.[4] Let $\theta = (\omega, \alpha_1, \ldots, \alpha_p)'$. The exact likelihood for a sample of size T is the product of the $T - p$ conditional point likelihoods corresponding to observations $(p + 1)$ through T, and the unconditional joint likelihood for observations 1 through p. That is

$$L(\varepsilon_T, \ldots, \varepsilon_1; \theta) = l_T(\varepsilon_T | \Omega_{T-1}; \theta) \, l_{T-1}(\varepsilon_{T-1} | \Omega_{T-2}; \theta) \ldots$$

$$\ldots l_{p+1}(\varepsilon_{p+1} | \Omega_p; \theta) \, l_p(\varepsilon_p, \ldots, \varepsilon_1; \theta).$$

We simulate a very long realization of the process with parameter $\theta^{(j)}$ and consistently estimate the height of the unconditional density of the first p observations, evaluated at $\{\varepsilon_1, \ldots, \varepsilon_p\}$; denote it $\hat{l}_p(\varepsilon_1, \ldots, \varepsilon_p; \theta^{(j)})$. We substitute this estimated p-dimensional unconditional density into the likelihood where the true unconditional density appears, yielding the full conditionally Gaussian likelihood

$$L(\varepsilon_T, \ldots, \varepsilon_1; \theta^{(j)}) \approx \hat{l}_p(\varepsilon_1, \ldots, \varepsilon_p; \theta^{(j)}) \prod_{t=(p+1)}^{T} \left[\sigma_t^{-1}(\theta^{(j)}) \right.$$

$$\left. \exp\left(\frac{-1}{2\sigma_t^2(\theta^{(j)})} \varepsilon_t^2 \right) \right]$$

which we maximize using standard numerical techniques.

5 Comparative finite-sample properties of exact and approximate maximum likelihood estimators of ARCH models

For purposes of illustration, we study a conditionally Gaussian ARCH(1) process with unit unconditional variance

$$\varepsilon_t | \varepsilon_{t-1} \sim N(0, \sigma_t^2)$$

$$\sigma_t^2 = (1 - \alpha) + \alpha \varepsilon_{t-1}^2.$$

The stark simplicity of this data generating process is intentional. Although the model is restrictive, all the points that we want to make can be made within its simple context, and the simplicity of the model (in particular, the one-dimensional parameter space) renders it amenable to Monte Carlo analysis. Moreover, the ARCH(1) *is* sometimes used in practice; the popular PC-GIVE software, for example, permits only ARCH(1) estimation. It should be kept in mind that our procedure is readily applied in

---

[4] We adopt the conditional normality assumption only because it is the most common. Alternative distributions, such as the Student's t advocated by Bollerslev (1987), could be used with no change in our procedure.

higher-dimensional situations, even though the associated increased computational burden makes Monte Carlo analysis not feasible.

The Monte Carlo experiments were done in vectorized FORTRAN 77 at the Cornell National Supercomputer Facility. We report the results of nine experiments, corresponding to $\alpha = 0.9, 0.95, 0.99$, and $T = 10, 25, 50$, each with 1,000 Monte Carlo replications performed. the non-parametric estimation of the initial likelihood term is done by the kernel method, using a standard normal kernel, fit to a simulated series of length 1,000. The bandwidth is set to $\hat{\gamma}(1,000)^{-1/5}$, where $\hat{\gamma}(\alpha^{(j)}) = (\sum_{i=1}^{1,000} x_i^2 \ (\alpha^{(j)})/1,000)^{1/2}$ and $x_i(\alpha^{(j)}), i, \ldots, 1,000$, is the simulated sample.[5] The same random numbers are used to construct the simulated sample at each evaluation of the likelihood and across Monte Carlo replications.

Because the effect of initial conditions is central to this small sample exercise, we take care to let the process run for some time before sampling. Specifically, each Monte Carlo sample is taken as the last T elements of a vector of length $500 + T$, thus eliminating any effects that the starting value (0) might have.

The calculation of the likelihood for observations 2 through T is the same for the exact and approximate methods; the methods differ only in the calculations of the initial likelihood. Our exact method, specialized to the case at hand, yields

$$\hat{l}_1(\varepsilon_1; \alpha) = \frac{1}{1,000 \ \hat{\gamma}(\alpha^{(j)})(1,000)^{-1/5}} \sum_{i=1}^{1,000} K\left(\frac{\varepsilon_1 - x_i(\alpha^{(j)})}{\hat{\gamma}(\alpha^{(j)})(1,000)^{-1/5}}\right)$$

where $K(\cdot)$ is the $N(0,1)$ density function, and $x_i, i = 1, \ldots, 1,000$ is a simulated ARCH(1) process with parameter α.

Three approximations to the initial likelihood are considered;

(A1) We simply set $l_1(\varepsilon_1; \alpha) = 1$. this is of course a perfectly well-defined likelihood, but it does not make full use of all the information contained in the sample.

(A2) The functional form of $l_1(\varepsilon_1; \alpha)$ is assumed (incorrectly) to be Gaussian, as with all of the conditional densities, and the unconditional variance (1) is substituted for the unavailable ε_0^2, which yields $l_1(\varepsilon_1; \alpha) = \exp(-\varepsilon_1^2/2)$.

(A3) The functional form of $l_1(\varepsilon_1; \alpha)$ is assumed (incorrectly) to be Gaussian, and the unconditional mean (0) is substituted for the unavailable ε_0, which yields

---

[5] Silverman (1986) advocates the use of such a bandwidth selection procedure, and it satisfies the conditions required for consistency of the density estimator. More sophisticated "optimal" bandwidth selection procedures may of course be employed if desired.

$$l_1(\varepsilon_1; \alpha) = (1 - \alpha)^{-1/2} \exp\left(-\frac{1}{2}\left(\frac{\varepsilon_1^2}{1-\alpha}\right)\right).$$

To be certain that global maxima are found, we maximize the exact and approximate likelihoods using a grid search over the relevant parameter space (in this case, the unit interval). The grid mesh is of width 0.01, and it is reduced to 0.002 when the distance from either boundary is less than or equal to 0.05, and when the distance from the true parameter value is less than or equal to 0.05.

The exact and approximate estimators' biases, variances, and mean-squared errors are displayed in table 8.1. Efficiency of all methods increases with T and α. The exact method, however, consistently outperforms all approximate methods, especially for small T and large α. The mean-squared error reductions afforded by the exact estimator typically come from both variance and bias reductions. In figure 8.1, we graphically high-light the results for small samples ($T = 5, 10, 15, 20$) with high persistence ($\alpha = 0.99$); the efficiency gains from exact maximum likelihood are immediately visually apparent.

Our results are consistent with existing literature. Beach and MacKinnon (1978), in particular, report efficiency gains from exact maximum likeli-hood estimation in autoregressive processes. But ARCH processes *are* autoregressions in squares; that is, if ε_t is an ARCH(p) process

$$\varepsilon_t | \varepsilon_{t-1} \ldots, \varepsilon_{t-p} \sim N(0, \sigma_t^2)$$

$$\sigma_t^2 = \omega + \alpha(L)\varepsilon_t^2,$$

where $\alpha(L) = \sum_{i=1}^{p} \alpha_i L^i$, $\omega > 0$, $\alpha_i \geq 0 \ \forall i$, and $\alpha(1) < 1$, then ε_t^2 has the covari-ance stationary autoregressiveness representation

$$\varepsilon_t^2 = \omega + \alpha(L)\varepsilon_t^2 + \nu_t$$

where $\nu_t = \varepsilon_t^2 - \sigma_t^2$ is the difference between the squared innovation and the conditional variance at time t.[6]

6   Summary and directions for future research

We have proposed an exact estimator for finite-ordered observation-driven models. The exact estimator is more efficient than commonly used approx-imate estimators. Our methods are computationally intense but neverthe-less entirely feasible, even accounting for the "curse of dimensionality"

[6] See Diebold and Lopez (1995) for additional discussion.

Table 8.1. *Exact and approximate maximum likelihood estimation*

		Exact	A1	A2	A3
	$\alpha = 0.9$				
	Bias	0.01822	0.04967	0.04628	0.05147
	Var.	0.01640	0.02327	0.02218	0.02593
	MSE	0.01674	0.02573	0.02432	0.02858
	$\alpha = 0.95$				
	Bias	0.00843	0.03028	0.02662	0.03241
$T = 10$	Var.	0.00570	0.01010	0.00807	0.01229
	MSE	0.00577	0.01102	0.00878	0.01334
	$\alpha = 0.99$				
	Bias	0.00258	0.00923	0.00831	0.01119
	Var.	0.00152	0.00226	0.00219	0.00339
	MSE	0.00153	0.00234	0.00225	0.00351
	$\alpha = 0.9$				
	Bias	0.00699	0.02372	0.02228	0.01959
	Var.	0.00398	0.00685	0.00685	0.00682
	MSE	0.00403	0.00741	0.00735	0.00720
	$\alpha = 0.95$				
	Bias	0.00339	0.01425	0.01328	0.01199
$T = 25$	Var.	0.00121	0.00268	0.00273	0.00294
	MSE	0.00122	0.00288	0.00290	0.00307
	$\alpha = 0.99$				
	Bias	0.0019	0.00432	0.00308	0.00293
	Var.	9.72E-5	2.15E-4	1.88E-4	2.49E-4
	MSE	9.72E-5	2.26E-4	1.98E-4	2.57E-4
	$\alpha = 0.9$				
	Bias	0.00122	0.00940	0.00801	0.00914
	Var.	0.00129	0.00226	0.00165	0.00252
	MSE	0.00129	0.00235	0.00171	0.00261
	$\alpha = 0.95$				
	Bias	0.00024	0.00532	0.00426	0.00493
$T = 50$	Var.	0.00032	0.00074	0.00046	0.00074
	MSE	0.00032	0.00077	0.00047	0.00076
	$\alpha = 0.99$				
	Bias	0.00003	0.00122	0.00101	0.00114
	Var.	1.23E-5	3.52E-5	1.96E-5	3.38E-5
	MSE	1.23E-5	3.67E-5	2.06E-5	3.51E-5

Notes:
The data are generated as an ARCH(1) process; α is the ARCH
parameter and T is the sample size. Three estimators are compared:
exact maximum likelihood ("Exact"), and three approximations ("A1,"
"A2," and "A3"). We report the bias, variance and mean-squared error
for each estimator ("Bias," "Var.," and "MSE"). See the text for details.

MSE

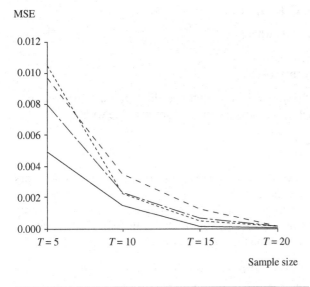

Figure 8.1 MSE comparison, $\alpha = 0.99$
Notes: The data are generated as an ARCH(1) process; α is the ARCH parameter and T is the sample size. We show the mean-squared error (MSE) of three estimators of α as a function of T: exact maximum likelihood ("Exact method"), and three approximations ("A1," "A2," and "A3"). See the text for details.

associated with higher-dimensional situations, due to the fact that the simulation sample size may be made very large.

Our "exact" estimator, like its approximate competitors, is in fact an approximation, but with the crucial difference that the size of the approximation error is under the control of the investigator. In real applications, a very large simulation sample size can be used in order to guarantee that the approximation error is negligible. Similarly, more sophisticated methods of band width selection and likelihood maximization may be used.

In closing, let us sketch a potentially fruitful direction for future research – application of our likelihood evaluation technique to panel data, the time series dimension of which is often notoriously small. Consider, for example, a simple dynamic model for panel data[7]

---

[7] For background on such models, see Bhargava and Sargan (1983), Sevestre and Trognon (1992), and Nerlove (1996).

$$y_{it} = \rho y_{i,t-1} + x'_{it}\beta + \mu_i + \varepsilon_{it}$$

$i = 1, \ldots, N$ and $t = 1, \ldots, T$, where

$$E(\varepsilon_{it}\varepsilon_{js}) = \sigma_\varepsilon^2, j = i, t = s$$
$$= 0 \text{ otherwise.}$$

In a fixed effects model, μ_i is an individual-specific parameter, whereas in a random-effects model μ_i is a zero-mean random variable with

$$E(\mu_i\mu_j) = \sigma_\mu^2 \text{ for } i = j$$
$$= 0 \text{ otherwise.}$$

Assume that the densities of ε_{it} and μ_i are Gaussian, and that the regressors x_{it} are *iid* over space and time.[8]

Because of the independence across i, the complete likelihood is simply the product of the likelihoods for the N individuals. In an obvious notation, the ith likelihood for either the fixed or random coefficient model is

$$L(Y_i, X_i, \mu_i; \theta) = l_T(y_{iT}, x_{iT}, \mu_i | y_{i,T-1}, \theta) l_{T-1}(y_{i,T-1}; x_{i,T-1}, \mu_i | y_{i,T-2}; \theta) \ldots$$
$$\ldots l_2(y_{i2}, x_{i2}, \mu_i | y_{i1}; \theta) \, l_1(y_{i1}, x_{i1}, \mu_i; \theta).$$

This is our familiar likelihood factorization. As before, the only complication is evaluation of the unconditional likelihood of the initial observation, and as before we simply stimulate a long realization of y_{it} from which we can estimate the unconditional density at y_{i1}. At iteration j the model is

$$y_{it} = \rho^{(j)} y_{i,t-1} + x'_{it}\beta^{(j)} + \mu_i + \varepsilon_{it}.$$

If we estimate a fixed effects model, we also have $\mu_i^{(j)}$ at iteration j; under random effects we instead have $\sigma_\mu^{2(j)}$. Thus the only barrier to performing the required simulation is the set of regressors, x_{it}. But the regressors are uncorrelated over space and time; thus we can sample with replacement from the observed set of NT regressors. The likelihood evaluation algorithm is as follows. At iteration j

(1) Initialize y_{i0}
(2) Draw $\varepsilon_{it} \sim N(0, \sigma_\varepsilon^{2(j)}), t = 1, \ldots, R$.
(3) Draw x_{it} by sampling with replacement from $X_{[N \times T]}, t = 1, \ldots, R$.
(4) If random effects, draw $\mu_i \sim N(0, \sigma_\mu^{2(j)})$; else if fixed effects, let $\mu_i = \mu_i^{(j)}$.
(5) Generate $y_{it} = \rho^{(j)} y_{i,t-1} + x'_{it}\beta^{(j)} + \mu_i + \varepsilon_{it}, t = 1, \ldots, R$.
(6) Estimate the unconditional density (likelihood) of y_{it} at the initial observation y_i.
(7) Form the complete likelihood for individual i.
(8) Repeat for $i = 1, \ldots, N$ and form the complete likelihood.

[8] A challenging extension will be to allow for serial dependence and spatial heterogeneity in the regressors.

The separability of the likelihood across i makes for simple likelihood evaluation. In particular, the dimension of the required density estimation for each i is only as large as the order of serial dependence, just as in the univariate time series case. Thus, for the prototype model at hand, evaluation of the likelihood requires only one-dimensional density estimates.

References

Beach, C.M. and J.G. MacKinnon (1978), "A Maximum Likelihood Procedure for Regression with Autocorrelated Errors," *Econometrica*, 46, 51–58.

Bhargava, A. and J.D. Sargan (1983), "Estimating Dynamic Random Effects Models from Panel Data Covering Short Time Periods," *Econometrica*, 51, 1635–1659.

Bollerslev, T. (1987), "A Conditional Heteroskedastic Time Series Model for Speculative Prices and Rates of Return," *Review of Economics and Statistics*, 69, 542–547.

Cox, D.R. (1981), "Statistical Analysis of Time Series: Some Recent Developments," *Scandinavian Journal of Statistics*, 8, 93–115.

Diebold, F.X. and J. Lopez (1995), "Modeling Volatility Dynamics," in Kevin Hoover (ed.), *Macroeconometrics: Developments, Tensions and Prospects*, Boston: Kluwer Academic, 427–472.

Engle, R.F. (1982), "Autoregressive Conditional Heteroskedasticity with Estimates of the Variance of United Kingdom Inflation," *Econometrica*, 50, 987–1007.

Engle, R.F. and J. Russell (1995), "Forecasting Transaction Rates: The Autoregressive Conditional Duration Model," Manuscript, Department of Economics, University of California, San Diego.

Gray, S.F. (1995), "Modeling the Conditional Distribution of Interest Rates as a Regime-Switching Process," Manuscript, Fuqua School of Business, Duke University.

Hamilton, James D. (1989), "A New Approach to the Economic Analysis of Nonstationary Time Series and the Business Cycle," *Econometrica*, 57, 357–384.

Hansen, B.E. (1994), "Autoregressive Conditional Density Estimation," *International Economic Review*, 35, 705–730.

Nelson, D.B. (1991), "Conditional Heteroskedasticity in Asset Returns: A New Approach," *Econometrica*, 59, 347–370.

Nelson, D.B. and C.Q. Cao (1992), "Inequality Constraints in the Univariate GARCH Model," *Journal of Business and Economic Statistics*, 10, 229–235.

Nerlove, M. (1996), *Econometrics for Applied Economists*, San Diego: Academic Press.

Sevestre, P. and A. Trognon (1992), "Linear Dynamic Models," in L. Matyas and P. Sevestre (eds.), *Econometrics of Panel Data: Handbook of Theory and Applications*, Amsterdam: Kluwer.

Shephard, N. (1995), "Statistical Aspects of ARCH and Stochastic Volatility," Nuffield College, Oxford, Economics Discussion Paper No. 94.

Silverman, B.W. (1986), *Density Estimation*, New York: Chapman and Hall.

9 Simulation-based inference in non-linear state-space models: application to testing the permanent income hypothesis

Roberto S. Mariano and Hisashi Tanizaki

1 Introduction

Non-linear filtering has been developed in various directions beyond the classic linear/normal filtering theory of Kalman (1960) and Kalman and Bucy (1961).

One approach is to apply a Taylor series expansion to linearize the non-linear measurement and transition equations. The linear recursive algorithm is then applied to this modified system. Procedures in this genre – such as the extended Kalman filter and the second-order non-linear filter – are discussed in Wishner, Tabaczynski, and Athans (1969), Sorensen and Alspach (1971), Alspach and Sorenson (1972), Gelb (1974), Anderson and Moore (1979), and Tanizaki and Mariano (1996).

Proceeding in another direction, others have sought to avoid normality assumptions by working on recursive algorithms for updating probability density functions. Kitagawa (1987) and Kramer and Sorenson (1988) evaluate densities through numerical integration. Alternatively, simulation techniques are a natural tool for evaluating these densities. Monte Carlo integration with Gibbs sampling is explored in Carlin, Polson, and Stoffer (1992). Monte Carlo integration with importance sampling in this context is discussed in Tanizaki (1993), Tanizaki and Mariano (1994), and Mariano and Tanizaki (1995). Further modifications of these procedures – using rejection sampling – are discussed also in Tanizaki and Mariano (1998).

In this chapter, we consider the application of these non-linear/non-normal filtering techniques to testing the permanent income hypothesis. Numerous papers have revisited this celebrated hypothesis. Flavin (1981), Hall and Mishkin (1982), and Campbell and Mankiw (1987) examined this issue taking transitory consumption into account. Hayashi (1985a, 1985b)

Presented at the Conference on Simulation-Based Inference in Econometrics, Minneapolis Federal Reserve Bank, Minnesota, November 17–18, 1995.

introduced liquidity constraints and durable goods in testing this hypothesis while Mankiw (1981) and Muelbauer (1983) introduced variable interest rates into the model. Here, for our analysis of the permanent income hypothesis as proposed by Hall (1978), we set up a non-linear state space model for unobserved permanent consumption, which simultaneously takes into account transitory consumption, variable interest rates, and non-linearity of the Euler equation. With our approach – of formulating a non-linear state-space model of permanent consumption – the permanent income hypothesis can be stated in terms of unknown parameters in the model. Because of non-linearities in the model, non-linear filtering techniques based on stochastic simulations are used to perform two major steps in the analysis:

estimate unknown model parameters and calculate likelihood ratio tests of the permanent income hypothesis, and

estimate unobserved permanent consumption over the sample period.

Thus, our approach differs from earlier studies in two significant aspects. First, our analysis copes at the same time with these issues of the presence of transitory consumption, variability of interest rates, and non-linearity of first-order conditions. Secondly, stochastic simulation plays a key role in the empirical implementation of the analysis because of non-linear complexities in the model.

Annual data for the US and Japan are used in these calculations. Filters are also used to estimate permanent consumption in the US and Japan. Difference in permanent consumption as a percent of total are observed for these two countries showing differences in degree of rationality in consumer behavior.

Before going into this application, we provide a brief overview of filtering in non-linear state space models. A more complete discussion is in Tanizaki and Mariano (1994, 1995).

2   Non-linear state-space models and non-linear filtering

Consider the following non-linear state-space model:

measurement equation

$$y_t = h_t(\alpha t, \epsilon_t) \tag{1}$$

transition equation

$$\alpha_t = f_t(\alpha_{t-1}, \eta_t). \tag{2}$$

The vector y_t is observed over the sample period $t = 1, 2, \ldots, T$ while α_t is a vector of unobserved "state" variables. The vector functions h_t and f_t are specified known functions. The disturbances (ϵ_t, η_t) are assumed to have zero means and to be jointly independent over time. Their probability distributions are known and are not necessarily normal.

Given the sample $\{y_t : t = 1, 2, \ldots, T\}$, the main problem is to evaluate $E(\alpha_r | I_s)$, where

$$I_s = \text{information at time } s$$
$$= \{y_1, y_2, \ldots, y_s\}. \tag{3}$$

Standard terminology refers to the problem as:

prediction – if $r > s$,
filtering   – if $r = s$,
smoothing – if $r < s$. $\hspace{3cm}$ (4)

In addressing this problem, we first consider determination of the conditional probability density function of α_r given I_s, namely, $P(\alpha_r | I_s)$ and then work on the evaluation of

$$E(\alpha_r | I_s) = \int \alpha_r P(\alpha_r | I_s) d\alpha_r. \tag{5}$$

The recursive calculation of $P(\alpha_r | I_s)$ proceeds from basic principles in probability theory, e.g., see Harvey (1989). For prediction, we have

$$P(\alpha_{t+k} | I_{t-1}) = \int P(\alpha_{t+k}, \alpha_{t+k-1} | I_{t-1}) d\alpha_{t+k-1} \tag{6}$$

$$= \int P(\alpha_{t+k} | I_{t-1}, \alpha_{t+k-1}) \cdot P(\alpha_{t+k-1}, | I_{t-1}) d\alpha_{t+k-2} \tag{7}$$

$$= \int P(\alpha_{t+k} | \alpha_{t+k-1}) \cdot P(\alpha_{t+k-1}, | I_{t-1}) d\alpha_{t+k-1}. \tag{8}$$

Note that (8) follows from the time independence of (ϵ_t, η_t).

For filtering, first let $k = 0$ in the prediction formula, to get

$$P(\alpha_t | I_{t-1}) = \int P(\alpha_t | \alpha_{t-1}) \cdot P(\alpha_{t-1} | I_{t-1}) d\alpha_{t-1}. \tag{9}$$

Consequently, we have

$$P(\alpha_t | I_t) = P(\alpha_t | I_{t-1}, y_t) = P(\alpha_t, y_t | I_{t-1}) / P(y_t | I_{t-1})$$
$$= P(y_t | \alpha_t, I_{t-1}) \cdot P(\alpha_t | I_{t-1}) / P(y_t | I_{t-1})$$
$$= P(y_t | \alpha_t) \cdot P(\alpha_t | I_{t-1}) / P(y_t | I_{t-1}). \tag{10}$$

The denominator in (10) is obtained by integrating the numerator with respect to α_t. $P(y_t | \alpha_t)$ is obtained directly from the measurement equation with the function h_t and the distribution of ϵ_t both specified. Finally, $P(\alpha_t | I_{t-1})$ comes from the prediction algorithm in (9). Formulas (9) and (10)

Table 9.1. *Recursive algorithm for non-linear prediction and filtering*

Observations		Measurement equation		Filter/ prediction		Transition equation
y_1	$\rightarrow$	$P(y_1\mid\alpha_1)$	$\rightarrow$	$P(\alpha_1\mid I_1)$	$\leftarrow$	$P(\alpha_1\mid\alpha_0)$
				$\downarrow$		
				$P(\alpha_2\mid I_1)$	$\leftarrow$	$P(\alpha_2\mid\alpha_1)$
				$\downarrow$		
y_2	$\rightarrow$	$P(y_2\mid\alpha_2)$	$\rightarrow$	$P(\alpha_2\mid I_2)$		
				$\downarrow$		
				$P(\alpha_3\mid I_2)$	$\leftarrow$	$P(\alpha_3\mid\alpha_2)$
				$\downarrow$		
y_3	$\rightarrow$	$P(y_3\mid\alpha_3)$	$\rightarrow$	$P(\alpha_3\mid I_3)$		
				$\downarrow$		
				etc.		

provide the recursive algorithm (as summarized in table 9.1) for prediction and filtering, starting from initial conditions, say α_0, for the state variables.

Next, we move on to the calculation of $P(\alpha_{t+1}\mid I_t)$ and $P(\alpha_t\mid I_t)$. As we pointed out earlier, Kitagawa (1987) and Kramer and Sorenson (1988) used numerical integration in their calculations.

Monte Carlo simulation with importance sampling proceeds as follows. Denote the importance density on α_t by $P^*(\alpha_t)$. Then we can write

$$P(\alpha_{t+1}\mid I_t)=\int [P(\alpha_{t+1}\mid\alpha_t)\cdot P(\alpha_t\mid I_t)/P^*(\alpha_t)]\cdot P^*(\alpha_t)d\alpha_t \tag{11}$$

and, for n random draws from $P^*(\alpha_t)$, say $\{\tilde{\alpha}_{it}:i=1,2,\ldots,N\}$, we obtain the following approximations to (9) and (10)

$$\hat{P}(\alpha_{t+1}\mid I_t)=\sum_i P(\alpha_{t+1}\mid\tilde{\alpha}_{it})\cdot w_{t\mid t}(\alpha_{it})/n \tag{12}$$

$$\hat{P}(\alpha_t\mid I_t)=P(y_t\mid\alpha_t)\cdot \hat{P}(\alpha_t\mid I_{t-1})/\hat{D}_t \tag{13}$$

$$\hat{D}_t=\sum_i P(y_t\mid\tilde{\alpha}_{it})\cdot w_{t\mid t-1}(\tilde{\alpha}_{it})/n \tag{14}$$

$$w_{t\mid t}(\hat{\alpha}_{it})=\hat{P}(\tilde{\alpha}_{it}\mid I_t)/P^*(\tilde{\alpha}_{it}) \tag{15}$$

$$w_{t\mid t-1}(\tilde{\alpha}_{it})=\hat{P}(\tilde{\alpha}_{it}\mid I_{t-1})/P^*(\tilde{\alpha}_t). \tag{16}$$

Recursion formulas for $w_{t\mid t}$ and $w_{t\mid t-1}$ are given in Tanizaki and Mariano (1998).

The above formulas also give us a recursive approximation to the likelihood of the observations. This is particularly useful for a numerical maximization of the likelihood function

$$P(I_T) = \prod_{t=1}^{T} P(y_t|I_{t-1})$$

$$= \prod \int P(y_t|\alpha_t) \cdot P(\alpha_t|I_{t-1}) d\alpha_t$$

$$\approx \left((1/n)^T\right) \prod_t \sum_i P(y_t|\tilde{\alpha}_{it}) \cdot w_{t|t-1}(\tilde{\alpha}_{it}). \tag{17}$$

As before, the $\tilde{\alpha}_{it}$ are random draws from the importance density $P^*(\alpha_t)$.

A modified simulation approach, using rejection sampling as proposed in Tanizaki and Mariano (1996) gets random draws $\tilde{\alpha}_{ir|s}$ from $P(\alpha_r|s)$. For prediction, we then have

$$\hat{P}(\alpha_{t+1}|I_t) \approx \sum P(\alpha_{t+1}|\tilde{\alpha}_{i,t|t})/n. \tag{18}$$

This is because of (9) where

$$P(\alpha_{t+1}|I_t) = E_{\alpha_t|I_t} P(\alpha_{t+1}|\alpha_t).$$

Given $\tilde{\alpha}_{i,t|t}$ we can generate $\tilde{\alpha}_{i,t+1|t}$ by

$$\tilde{\alpha}_{i,t+1|t} = f_{t+1}(\tilde{\alpha}_{i,t|t}; \tilde{\eta}_{i,t+1}). \tag{19}$$

For any integrable function g, we get

$$\hat{E}(g(\alpha_{t+1})|I_t) = \sum_i g(\tilde{\alpha}_{i,t+1|t}). \tag{20}$$

For filtering, how do we generate $\tilde{\alpha}_{i,t|t}$? The formulas are

$$P(\alpha_t|I_{t-1}) = \int P(\alpha_t, \alpha_{t-1}|I_{t-1}) d\alpha_{t-1}$$
$$= \int P(\alpha_t|\alpha_{t-1}) \cdot P(\alpha_{t-1}|I_{t-1}) d\alpha_{t-1}. \tag{21}$$

This implies that, from (10)

$$P(\alpha_t|I_t) = N_t / \int N_t d\alpha_t$$

where

$$N_t = \int P(y_t|\alpha_t) \cdot P(\alpha_t|\alpha_{t-1}) \cdot P(\alpha_{t-1}|I_{t-1}) d\alpha_{t-1}. \tag{22}$$

Thus, $P(\alpha_t|I_t)$ is proportional to N_t, which, in turn, can be approximated by

$$N_t \approx \sum_i P(y_t|\alpha_t) \cdot P(\alpha_t|\tilde{\alpha}_{i,t-1|t-1})/n. \tag{23}$$

To get draws recursively from this approximate filtering density in (23), apply the following "rejection" sampling scheme:

1 Given $(\tilde{\alpha}_{i,t-1|t-1}, \ldots, \tilde{\alpha}_{n,t-1|t-1})$, choose one of these randomly and get, say $\tilde{\alpha}_{*,t-1}$.

2 Sample $P(\alpha_t|\tilde{\alpha}_{t-1})$ to get α_t calculated as

$$\alpha_t = f_t(\tilde{\alpha}_{t-1}, \tilde{\eta}_t). \tag{24}$$

3 Calculate $w(\alpha_t, y_t)$, where we construct w_t such that

$$0 \le w(\alpha_t, y_t) \le 1,$$
$$w(\alpha_t, y_t) \propto P(y_t|\alpha_t).$$

4 Include α_t in the draw from $P(\alpha_t|I_t)$ with probability calculated in step 3 and denote this by $\tilde{\alpha}_{1,t|t}$.

5 Continue doing this until you get n draws $\tilde{\alpha}_{i,t|t}$.

6 Finally, calculate

$$\hat{E}(g(\alpha_t)|I_t) = \sum g(\tilde{\alpha}_{i,t|t})/n. \tag{25}$$

3 Testing the permanent income hypothesis

To test the permanent income hypothesis, we now consider the following state-space model:

measurement equation

$$C_t = C_t^p + C_t^* + \epsilon_t \tag{26}$$

transition equation

$$\beta R_{t-1} \left(\frac{C_t^p}{C_{t-1}^p}\right)^{-1} = 1 + \eta_t \tag{27}$$

where $\epsilon t, \eta_t$ are bivariate normal, independent over time, with mean zero and covariance matrix

$$\begin{pmatrix} \sigma_\epsilon^2 Y_t^2/L_t & 0 \\ 0 & \sigma_\eta^2 \end{pmatrix}. \tag{28}$$

The above model is driven by the behavior of the representative agent, with the following definitions:

C = per capita total consumption

C^p = per capita permanent consumption

C^* = consumption component independent of the permanent income hypothesis

$\epsilon = C^T$, per capita transitory consumption, assumed random with zero mean

R = gross rate of return on savings between t and $t + 1$

Y = per capita disposable income

L = population size

η = random disturbance term in the transition equation.

C_t^p and C_t^T are unobservable, while C_t, Y_t, L_t, R_t are observed. C_t^p is treated as the state variable. This is estimated by non-linear filtering; in the process, we can thus estimate permanent and transitory consumption separately. A more detailed discussion of this model follows.

3.1   Measurement equation

The measurement equation is simply the identity that total consumption is the sum of permanent consumption, transitory consumption, and a part of consumption which is independent of the permanent income hypothesis.

The assumption on transitory consumption is based on earlier authors' treatment of the subject. In a cross-sectional framework

$$\sum_i C_{it}^T = 0$$

is assumed by Friedman (1974), where C_{it}^T denotes transitory consumption of the ith household at time t. Furthermore, Friedman (1957) assumed that C_{it}^T is independent of the permanent income, transitory income, and permanent consumption – see Branson (1979). Aggregate transitory consumption is represented as

$$C_t^T = \sum_i C_{it}^T / L_t.$$

Assuming that C_{it}^T are identically and independently distributed with mean zero and variance $(\sigma_\epsilon Y_t)^2$ for all i and t, the transitory consumption of the representative agent (i.e., C_t) is given by a random shock with mean zero and variance $(\sigma_\epsilon Y_t)^2 / L_t$. It might be plausible to assume that the transitory consumption increases (decreases) as the income level increases (decreases).

C_t^* represents an exogenous part of consumption which does not depend on the permanent income hypothesis proposed by Hall (1978). It is well known that variables other than lagged consumption appear to play a significant role in the determination of current consumption (see Diebold and Nerlove (1989)). Accordingly C_t^* is a part of consumption which depends on other variables such as income. Therefore, it is assumed in this chapter that C_t^* is a function of income, i.e.

$$C_t^* = \gamma_1 \hat{Y}_t + \gamma_2 Y_{t-1} \tag{29}$$

where γ_1 and γ_2 are unknown parameters to be estimated. Under the permanent income hypothesis, $C_t^* = 0$, which is equivalent to $\gamma_1 = \gamma_2 = 0$ in (29). $\hat{Y}_t$ denotes an instrument variable of Y_t, because Y_t is correlated with η_t.[1]

In this section, to test whether the permanent income hypothesis holds, we use the likelihood ratio test for the null hypothesis

$$H_0: \gamma_1 = \gamma_2 = 0. \tag{30}$$

3.2   Transition equation

The transition equation corresponds to the Euler equation, which is derived as follows. Consider the problem of choosing a consumption sequence $\{C_t^p\}$ by the representative agent which maximizes the following expected utility

$$E_t\left(\sum_t \beta^t u(C_t^p)\right)$$

subject to

$$A_{t+1} = R_t(A_t + W_t - C_t)$$
$$C_t = C_t^p + C_t^* + C_t^T \tag{31}$$

where A_0 is given. The representative utility function $u(.)$ is twice continuously differentiable, bounded, increasing, and concave. A_{t+1} is the stock of assets at the beginning of time $t+1$, W_t is non-capital or labor income at t, and R_t is the gross rate of return on savings between t and $t+1$. $E_t(\cdot)$ denotes the mathematical expectation, given information known at t. β is the discount rate. It might be plausible in empirical studies that the discount rate β is less than one. However, Kocherlakota (1990) showed that well-behaved competitive equilibria with positive interest rates may exist in infinite horizon growth economies even though individuals have discount factors larger than one, which implies that when per capita consumption is growing over time, it is possible for equilibria to exist in representative consumer endowment economies even though $\beta > 1$. Therefore, we do not have to pay much attention to the possibility of the discount rate being greater than one.

Thus, under the above set-up, maximizing the expected utility with respect to the permanent consumption sequence $\{C_t^p\}$,[2] we obtain the Euler equation,

---

[1] Since Y_t is correlated with C_t, we use a proxy variable of Y_t as $\hat{Y}_t$ to exclude correlation between Y_t and C_t. In this chapter, the instrument variable $\hat{Y}_t$ is taken as the predicted value of Y_t regressed on a constant term, a time trend, Y_{t-1}, and C_{t-1}.

[2] Usually, the utility function is maximized with respect to total consumption C_t, not permanent consumption C_t^p. We assume that the utility function depends on C_t as well as μ_t, where μ_t denotes a sum of the transitory consumption and the other part of consumption independent of the permanent income hypothesis, i.e., $\mu_t = C_t^* + C_t^T$ in this chapter. Taking the utility function as $u(C_t - \mu_t)$, we obtain the Euler equation (32).

$$\left(\frac{\beta R_{t-1} u'(C_t^p)}{u'(C_{t-1}^p)}\right) = 1 + \eta_t \tag{32}$$

where the error term η_t is assumed to be truncated normal.[3] $u'(\cdot)$ represents the first derivative of the underlying utility function.

Taking the utility function as

$$u(C_t^p) = \log(C_t^p) \tag{33}$$

the Euler equation corresponding to this particular form of the utility function reduces to the transition equation in (27).

4   Estimation results

The likelihood function of the innovation form is maximized by a simple grid search with respect to the unknown parameters (i.e., γ_1, γ_2, σ_ϵ, β, and σ_η).

We test the permanent income hypothesis (i.e., the null hypothesis $H_0 : \gamma_1 = \gamma_2 = 0$) and estimate permanent consumption for both Japan and the US.

4.1   Data

Annual data from 1955 to 1993 are used for Japan and the US, and the estimation period is from 1957 to 1993.

For Japanese Data, C_t, Y_t, P_t, and L_t denote per capita final consumption expenditure of households (Japanese yen at 1985 prices, annual data, per capita data divided by number of population), per capita national disposable income of households (Japanese yen at 1985 prices, annual data, per capita data divided by number of population), implicit price deflator of final consumption expenditure of households (1985 = 1.00), and number of population, taken from *Annual Report on National Accounts* (Economic Planning Agency, Government of Japan). The gross rate of return on savings (R_t) is defined as $R_t = (1 + r_t / 100) P_t / P_{t+1}$, where r_t is installment savings of banks (annual rate, percent).

For the US data, C_t, Y_t, P_t, and L_t denote per capita personal consump-

---

[3] Note that we have $1 + \eta_t > 0$. Therefore, the exact distribution of η_t is represented as

$$P_\eta(\eta_t) = \frac{(2\pi\sigma_\eta^2)^{-1/2} \exp\left(-\frac{1}{2\sigma_\eta}\eta_t^2\right)}{\int_{-1}^{\infty} (2\pi\sigma_\eta^2)^{-1/2} \exp\left(-\frac{1}{2\sigma_\eta^2}\eta_t^2\right) d\eta_t}.$$

$-1/\sigma_\eta$ is small enough. Accordingly, we approximate the density function of η_t as the normal density, i.e., $\eta_t \sim N(0, \sigma_\eta^2)$.

Table 9.2. *Extended Kalman filter*

	β	σ_η	γ_1	γ_2	σ_ϵ	log L
	1.060	0.0415	—	—	41.5	-435.322
Japan	1.065	0.0714	0.596	—	33.2	-411.017
	1.059	0.0685	0.317	0.317	68.3	-409.503
	0.989	0.0269	—	—	26.9	-251.419
US	0.992	0.0734	0.720	—	13.6	-231.589
	0.994	0.0789	0.506	0.246	49.3	-230.316

Table 9.3. *Numerical integration filter*

	β	σ_η	γ_1	γ_2	σ_ϵ	log L
	1.051	0.0405	—	—	40.5	-435.149
Japan	1.039	0.0687	0.586	—	30.3	-410.193
	1.040	0.0674	0.311	0.298	66.2	-409.056
	0.986	0.0270	—	—	26.5	-251.805
US	0.965	0.0738	0.717	—	7.5	-230.458
	0.974	0.0828	0.495	0.232	43.6	-229.781

tion expenditure (US dollars at 1987 prices, annual data, per capita data divided by number of population), per capita national disposable income (US dollars at 1987 prices, annual data, per capita data divided by number of population), implicit price deflator of personal consumption expenditure (1987 = 1.00), and number of population, from *Economic Report of the President*. The gross rate of return on savings (R_t) is defined as $R_t = (1 + r_t/100)P_t/P_{t+1}$, where r_t is Aaa (annual rate percent).

In tables 9.2–9.6, each parameter is estimated by a simple grid search method, i.e., the log likelihood function is maximized by changing the parameter value by 0.001 for β, by 0.0001 for σ_η, 0.001 for γ_1 and γ_2 and 0.1 for σ_ϵ, respectively. Log L in table 9.2 denotes the maximized log likelihood function.

4.2   Non-linear filtering technique

We estimate the state-space model (26) and (27) by five non-linear filtering methods: extended Kalman filter in table 9.2 and figure 9.1, numerical integration filter in table 9.2 and figure 9.2, importance sampling filter in table 9.4 and figure 9.3, density-based Monte Carlo filter in table 9.5 and

Table 9.4. *Importance sampling filter*

	β	σ_η	γ_1	γ_2	σ_ϵ	$\log L$
	1.051	0.0407	—	—	42.4	−436.070
Japan	1.035	0.0722	0.602	—	20.3	−408.768
	1.031	0.0684	0.323	0.323	65.4	−409.117
	0.985	0.0272	—	—	27.4	−251.313
US	0.965	0.0735	0.718	—	8.2	−231.813
	0.958	0.0809	0.509	0.248	45.6	−231.234

Table 9.5. *Density-based Monte-Carlo filter*

	β	σ_η	γ_1	γ_2	σ_ϵ	$\log L$
	1.061	0.0414	—	—	41.4	−446.788
Japan	1.064	0.0713	0.597	—	33.1	−421.532
	1.058	0.0685	0.318	0.317	68.3	−420.637
	0.989	0.0269	—	—	26.9	−258.077
US	0.992	0.0733	0.720	—	13.6	−237.904
	0.993	0.0789	0.506	0.246	49.3	−237.388

Table 9.6. *Rejection sampling filter*

	β	σ_η	γ_1	γ_2	σ_ϵ	$\log L$
	1.060	0.0414	—	—	41.5	−446.784
Japan	1.065	0.0714	0.596	—	33.0	−421.430
	1.058	0.0686	0.316	0.317	68.3	−420.418
	0.982	0.0269	—	—	26.9	−258.233
US	0.992	0.0734	0.719	—	13.6	−237.432
	0.994	0.0789	0.506	0.246	49.3	−236.925

figure 9.4, and rejection sampling filter in table 9.6 and figure 9.5. The parameter estimates are similar for tables 9.2–9.6.

In the extended Kalman filter, the transition equation (27) is approximated by the first-order Taylor series expansion and applied to the standard Kalman filter algorithm, i.e., the linear recursive algorithm.

In the numerical integration filter, we take $n = 200$. The first half of n nodes (i.e., m nodes) are obtained from $[a^*_{t|t-1} - 4\sqrt{\Sigma^*_{t|t-1}}, a^*_{t|t-1} + 4\sqrt{\Sigma^*_{t|t-1}}]$

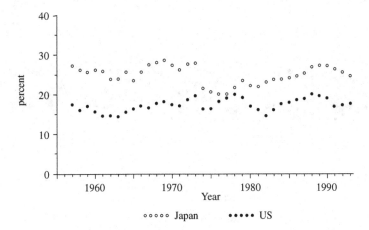

Figure 9.1 Ratio of permanent consumption: case $\gamma_1 \neq 0$ and $\gamma_2 \neq 0$

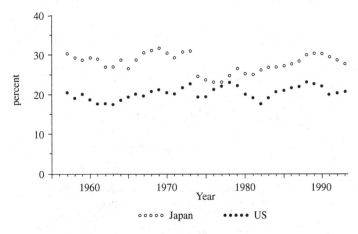

Figure 9.2 Ratio of permanent consumption: case $\gamma_1 \neq 0$ and $\gamma_2 \neq 0$
   Numerical integration filter

and the second half of n nodes (i.e., $n - m$ nodes) are from $[a^*_{t|t} - 4\sqrt{\Sigma^*_{t|t}}, a^*_{t|t} + 4\sqrt{\Sigma^*_{t|t}}]$. For both intervals, the distance between two nodes is equal. That is, m nodes are from

$$a^*_t|_t + 4\frac{2i - 1 - m}{m}\sqrt{\Sigma^*_{t|t}}$$

and $n - m$ nodes are from

$$a^*_t|_{t-1} + 4\frac{2i - 1 - m}{m}\sqrt{\Sigma^*_{t|t-1}}$$

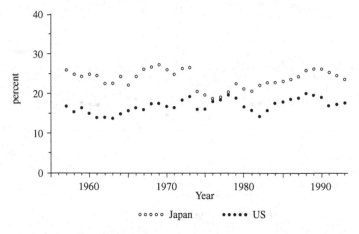

Figure 9.3 Ratio of permanent consumption: case $\gamma_1 \neq 0$ and $\gamma_2 \neq 0$
Importance sampling filter

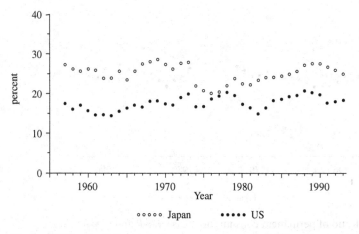

Figure 9.4 Ratio of permanent consumption: case $\gamma_1 \neq 0$ and $\gamma_2 \neq 0$
Density-based Monte Carlo filter

where $i = 1, \ldots, m$ and $m = 100$ is taken. $a_{t|t-1}^*$, $\Sigma_{t|t-1}^*$, $a_{t|t}^*$ and $\Sigma_{t|t}^*$ are obtained from the extended Kalman filter algorithm.

In the importance sampling filter, $n = 200$ random draws are generated from the following importance density

$$P_t(\alpha_t) = \frac{1}{2}N(a_{t|t-1}^*, 4\Sigma_{t|t-1}^*) + \frac{1}{2}N(a_{t|t}^*, 4\Sigma_{t|t}^*)$$

where $a_{t|t-1}^*$, $\Sigma_{t|t-1}^*$, $a_{t|t}^*$ and $\Sigma_{t|t}^*$ are obtained from the extended Kalman filter algorithm.

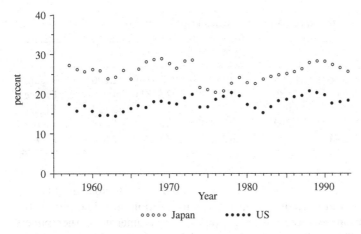

Figure 9.5 Ratio of permanent consumption: case $\gamma_1 \neq 0$ and $\gamma_2 \neq 0$
Rejection sampling filter

For density approximation, the importance density should have broader tails than the prediction density and the filtering density (see Tanizaki (1993), Tanizaki and Mariano (1994), and Mariano and Tanizaki (1995)). Therefore, for the importance density, we choose a larger variance than the variance obtained from the extended Kalman filter.

In the density-based Monte Carlo filter, $n = 10,000$ random draws are generated from the transition equation (27).

In the rejection sampling filter, the random draws are generated from the transition equation (27), where the number of random draws is taken as $n = 1,000$. The acceptance probability is given by the exponential part of the normal density obtained from the measurement equation (26), i.e.

$$w(\alpha_t; y_t) = \exp\left(-\frac{1}{2(\sigma_\epsilon Y_t)^2/L_t}(C_t - C_t^p - C_t^*)^2\right).$$

Under the above set up of each non-linear filter, the unknown parameters (i.e., β, σ_η, γ_1, γ_2, and σ_ϵ) are estimated in tables 9.2–9.6. The parameter estimates are similar for all the tables.

For each country in each table, we have three estimation results, i.e., (i) $\gamma_1 = 0$ and $\gamma_2 = 0$, (ii) $\gamma_1 \neq 0$ and $\gamma_2 = 0$, and (iii) $\gamma_1 \neq 0$ and $\gamma_2 \neq 0$. For all the estimation methods and both the countries, the hypothesis $H_0: \gamma_1 = \gamma_2 = 0$ is rejected according to the likelihood ratio test.[4]

The likelihood ratio statistics are given in table 9.7. This indicates that

---

[4] Note that the likelihood ratio test statistic of the hypothesis $H_0: \gamma_1 = \gamma_2 = 0$ is asymptotically distributed as a Chi-squared random variable with two degrees of freedom. The critical values of a Chi-squared distribution with two degrees of freedom are given by 5.99 for 0.05 percent and 9.21 for 0.01 percent, respectively.

Table 9.7. *Likelihood ratio test statistics* (H_0: $\gamma_1 = \gamma_2 = 0$)

Japan	US	Figure
2(435.322 − 409.503) = 51.638	2(251.419 − 230.316) = 42.206	Figure 1
2(435.149 − 409.056) = 52.186	2(251.805 − 229.781) = 44.048	Figure 2
2(436.070 − 409.117) = 53.906	2(251.313 − 231.234) = 40.158	Figure 3
2(446.788 − 420.637) = 52.302	2(258.077 − 237.388) = 41.378	Figure 4
2(446.784 − 420.418) = 52.732	2(258.233 − 236.925) = 42.616	Figure 5

the permanent income hypothesis does not hold for both Japan and the US. This test takes into account transitory consumption, non-linearity of the Euler equation, and the variable interest rate. Numerous earlier papers testing the permanent income hypothesis consider some of these three issues, but none of them deals with all three issues simultaneously. Our result shows that even if all three issues are included in the model, we still find significant evidence against the permanent income hypothesis.

Next, in figures 9.1–9.5, we plot the ratio of estimated permanent consumption relative to total consumption, i.e., $100 C_{t|t}^p / C_t$, where $C_{t|t}^p$ denotes the filtering estimate of per capita permanent consumption at time t, for Japan and the US. A high ratio of permanent consumption implies that a large amount of people behave under the permanent income hypothesis. In the US, about 15–20 percent of consumption is based on the permanent income hypothesis during the estimation period. The ratio is almost constant over time although it is slightly lower in 1974 and 1981, the years of the two oil crises. The ratio in Japan is larger than that in the US for all the periods. Around 25 percent of total consumption is permanent consumption over the whole sample period except for the first oil crisis. During the first oil shock, the ratio of permanent consumption to total consumption fell to about 20 percent in Japan. For the US, however, there was hardly any downward adjustment in the ratio. These numerical results indicate that Japan behaves somewhat more rationally than the US and the experience in the first oil crisis indicates that this occurs even more so in a recessionary period.

In Japan, the first oil shock brought on a serious recession – with inflation and wage increases ranging between 23 percent and 25 percent in 1974. From this experience, the Japanese economy learned quickly and managed to steer a more stable course in the second oil shock. In 1981, wage and price increases in Japan were kept at a normal rate of 5 percent. Consequently, as figures 9.1–9.5 show, there was hardly any adjustment in Japanese permanent consumption as the second oil shock took place.

5 Summary

In this chapter, for both Japan and the US, we have formulated a non-linear state-space model to test the permanent income hypothesis. The state-space model is based on the Euler equation derived from a utility maximization by a representative agent. A contribution of the chapter to the wide literature on this celebrated topic comes from the fact that our approach simultaneously takes into account the presence of transitory consumption, non-linearity of the Euler equation, and the effects of variable interest rates. A second contribution of the chapter shows how stochastic simulations, applied to non-linear filtering, are utilized not only to calculate numerical maximum likelihood estimates of model parameters but also to estimate unobserved permanent consumption over the sample period.

Annual consumption data from 1955 to 1993 are used for both Japan and the US. All the filtering techniques used here produced similar results. Taking into account transitory consumption, non-linearity of the Euler equation and the variable interest rate simultaneously, our results reject the permanent income hypothesis and point to differences in degree of rationality in consumer behavior in the US and Japan.

References

Alspach, D.L. and H.W. Sorenson (1972), "Nonlinear Bayesian Estimation Using Gaussian Sum Approximations," *IEEE Transactions on Automatic Control*, AC-17 (4), 439–448.

Anderson, B.D.O. and J.B. Moore (1979), *Optimal Filtering*, New York: Prentice-Hall.

Branson, W.H. (1979), *Macroeconomic Theory and Policy*, 2nd edn., New York: Harper & Row.

Campbell, J.Y. and N.G. Mankiw (1987), "Are Output Fluctuations Transitory?" *Quarterly Journal of Economics*, 102, 857–880.

Carlin, B.P., N.G. Polson, and D.S. Stoffer (1992), "A Monte Carlo Approach to Nonnormal and Nonlinear State Space Modeling," *Journal of the American Statistical Association*, 87, 493–500.

Diebold, F.X. and M. Nerlove (1989), "Unit Roots in Economic Time Series: A Selective Survey," in *Advances in Econometrics*, vol. VIII, Place: JAI Press, pp. 3–69.

Flavin, M.A. (1981), "The Adjustment of Consumption to Changing Expectations about Future Income," *Journal of Political Economy*, 89(5), 974–1009.

Friedman, M. (1957). *A Theory of the Consumption Function*, Princeton: Princeton University Press.

Gelb, A. (1974), *Applied Optional Estimation*, Cambridge, MA: MIT Press.

Hall, R.E. (1978), "Stochastic Implications of the Life Cycle-Permanent Income Hypothesis: Theory and Evidence," *Journal of Political Economy*, 86(6), 971–987.

(1990), *The Rational Consumer*, Cambridge, MA. MIT Press.

Hall, R.E. and F.S. Mishkin (1982), "The Sensitivity of Consumption to Transitory Income: Estimates from Panel Data on Households," *Econometrica*, 50(2), 461–481.

Harvey, A.C. (1989), *Forecasting, Structural Time Series Models and the Kalman Filter*, Cambridge University Press.

Hayashi, F. (1985a), "The Effects of Liquidity Constraints on Consumption: A Cross-sectional Study," *Quarterly Journal of Economics*, 100, 183–206.

(1985b), "The Permanent Income Hypothesis and Consumption Durability: Analysis Based on Japanese Panel Data," *Quarterly Journal of Economics*, 100, 1083–1113.

Kalman, R.E. (1960), "A New Approach to Linear Filtering and Prediction Problems," *Journal of Basic Engineering, Transactions ASME*, Series D, 92, 35–45.

Kalman, R.E. and R.S. Bucy (1961), "New Results in Linear Filtering and Prediction Theory," *Journal of Basic Engineering, Transactions ASME*, Series D, 83, 95–108.

Kitagawa, G. (1987), "Non-Gaussian State-Space Modeling of Nonstationary Time Series" (with discussion) *Journal of the American Statistical Association*, 82, 1032–1063.

Kocherlakota, N.R. (1990), "On the 'Discount' Factor in Growth Economies," *Journal of Monetary Economics*, 25, 43–48.

Kramer, S.C. and H.W. Sorenson (1988), "Recursive Bayesian Estimation Using Piece-wise Constant Approximation," *Automatica*, 24(6), 789–801.

Mankiw, N.G. (1981), "The Permanent Income Hypothesis and The Real Interest Rate," *Economics Letters*, 7, 307–311.

Mariano, R.S. and H. Tanizaki (1995), "Prediction of Final Data with Use of Preliminary and/or Revised Data," *Journal of Forecasting*, 14(4), 351–380.

Muellbauer, J. (1983), "Surprise in the Consumption Function," *Economic Journal* (Supplement), 34–50.

Sorenson, H.W. and D.L. Alspach (1971), "Recursive Bayesian Estimation Using Gaussian Sums," *Automatica*, 7, 465–479.

Tanizaki, H. (1993), *Nonlinear Filters: Estimation and Applications* (Lecture Notes in Mathematical Economics and Systems, No. 400), Place: Springer-Verlag.

Tanizaki, H. and Mariano, R.S. (1994), "Prediction, Filtering and Smoothing in Nonlinear and Nonnormal Cases Using Monte-Carlo Integration," *Journal of Applied Econometrics*, 9(2), 163–179.

(1996), "Nonlinear Filters Based on Taylor Series Expansions," *Communications in Statistics, Theory and Methods*, 25, 1261–1282.

(1998), "Nonlinear and Nongaussian State-Space Modeling with Monte-Carlo Stochastic Simulation," *Journal of Econometrics*, 83, 263–290.

Wishner, R.P., J.A. Tabaczynski, and M. Athans (1969), "A Comparison of Three Non-Linear Filters," *Automatica*, 5, 487–496.

10 Simulation-based estimation of some factor models in econometrics

Vance L. Martin and Adrian R. Pagan

1 Introduction

Although never as popular in econometrics as in fields such as sociology or psychology, there has always been some interest in the application of factor models to economic data. This interest has been heightened in the past two decades by the rise of quantitative finance, where thinking in factor terms has been found to be very useful, with one representation, the arbitrage pricing theory of Ross (1976), becoming a key approach in the modeling of asset returns. Some of the lack of enthusiasm for factor models might be explained by a concern that the factors were unobservable, and such a qualification would naturally lead to a clear preference for identifying influences upon economic variables from forces that were capable of being directly measured. In this respect things have changed a good deal in many parts of economics, nowhere more so than in macroeconomics. Today unobserved factors such as technology shocks are prominent in many models, while the common trends apparent in many time series have become the basis of the expanding literature on cointegration between them.[1]

Section 2 of the chapter sets out in more detail various applications of factor models. Such a review emphasizes the common structure underlying these models, making it possible to consider estimation issues from a general perspective, rather than through the extant specialized approaches. As we describe, direct estimation of the parameters of such models, θ, is frequently very difficult, and this leads us to propose the indirect estimation methods of Gourieroux, Monfort, and Renault (1993) and Gallant and Tauchen (1996) as good ways of finding estimates of θ at reasonable computational

We would like to thank participants at the conference on Simulation-Based Inference in Econometrics: Methods and Applications, November 1995, held at the University of Minnesota. All computer programs are written in GAUSS and are available from Martin, Economics Department, University of Melbourne, Parkville, Australia, 3052.
[1] It should be noted here that factors such as technology shocks are unobserved and are only represented by "Solow residuals" if a particular model is employed that enables them to be backed out of time series.

cost. The beauty of the indirect estimation technology is the demarcation of the model to be estimated from the model to be used for estimation. Provided the parameters of the latter, π, have a relationship with the former, θ, it may be preferable to recover $\hat{\theta}$ indirectly from $\hat{\pi}$ than to attempt direct estimation of θ. Such is the situation with most factor models.

The advantages of indirect estimation methods are highlighted in sections 3 and 4 of the chapter where two applications of the methodology are discussed. The first applies Hamilton's (1989) model to a long series of US stock returns; this model involves a single factor that takes two values determining whether volatility is high or low. Whilst this application is illustrative, a range of possible extensions to the model can be entertained. For example, generalizations to multivariate problems with non-normal error structures and more elaborate switching processes can be considered provided that the model can be easily simulated. The second application derives from the term structure literature and is a good vehicle for illustrating many other features of the approach as well as demonstrating its advantages over direct estimation methods including maximum likelihood methods. In particular, issues concerning estimation of multivariate continuous time models with discrete data, complications arising from models with singular latent factor structures, and variance processes exhibiting levels effects which do not admit closed-form solutions for the distributions of factors, are overcome with indirect estimation. This is in direct contrast with estimation based on maximum likelihood methods which are at best computationally difficult and *ad hoc*, while at worst infeasible. Section 5 concludes.

2   Some factor models in econometrics

Many econometric models, particularly in finance applications, can be thought of as factor models in which a set of N variables, collected in an ($N \times 1$) vector, $Y_t = (y_{1,t}, \ldots, y_{N,t})$, are linearly explained by a set of K factors, $f_{1,t}, \ldots, f_{K,t}$, gathered in the ($K \times 1$) vector F_t, i.e.

$$Y_t = A(\theta) + B(\theta)F_t \tag{1}$$

where the ($N \times 1$) and ($N \times K$) matrices A and B might be functions of a smaller number of parameters θ. A regression model is of course a factor model in which ($K - 1$) of the factors are observable and one, namely the error term, is unobservable. More structure can be placed upon the multivariate processes involved by requiring that F_t follow some autoregressive process, say

$$F_t = C + DF_{t-1} + V_t^{1/2}(\mathcal{F}_t)\epsilon_t \tag{2}$$

where $V_t(\mathcal{F}_t)$ is the conditional variance of F_t, ϵ_t is a $(K \times 1)$ martingale difference with conditional variance I_K, both being defined relative to $\mathcal{F}_t$, and C and D are respectively $(K-1)$ and $(K-K)$ matrices of parameters. The description of $\mathcal{F}_t$ will vary according to circumstances. In discrete time, $\mathcal{F}_t$ could be such that the conditional variance of the jth factor depends upon the past history of that factor and (possibly) the contemporaneous values of factors other than itself. Hence $\mathcal{F}_t$ can be taken to be $(F_{t-j})_{j=0}^{\infty}$, provided the recursive structure for contemporaneous values is understood. In those instances where (2) is replaced by a stochastic differential equation, V_t will generally be a function of "contemporaneous" values of F_t. It is also quite common for V_t to be linear in F_{t-j}. Despite the linear structure in (1) it is worth observing that the method of estimation we adopt is capable of dealing with a non-linear mapping between factors and observables. In this case (1) can be replaced by

$$Y_t = g(F_t; \theta) \tag{3}$$

where $g(\cdot)$ is available either analytically or numerically.

It is useful to describe some of the models that can be summarized by (1) and (2). A simple example is provided by the basic real business cycle model in King, Plosser, and Rebelo (1988), where Y_t is a collection of variables such as consumption, investment, etc. and a single unobservable factor, technology shocks, drives these series, while θ are referred to as the "deep parameters." Technology shocks follow an autoregressive process but $V(\mathcal{F}_t)$ is generally held to be constant. An extension of this idea is the common trends, common cycles analysis of Vahid and Engle (1993), where some of the factors are integrated random variables while the others are stationary.

A particularly interesting class of macroeconomic models which sustains a factor interpretation is that proposed by Hamilton (1989). Here there are unobserved states that affect both the conditional mean and the conditional variance of a series, and we can think of these states as unobserved factors. To take a simple case, estimated later, assume that there are two factors, one of which drives the conditional variance. When $N=1$ we might have

$$y_{1,t} = a_{10} + f_{1,t} \tag{4}$$

$$f_{1,t} = (\phi_1 + \psi_{12} f_{2,t})^{1/2} \epsilon_{1t} \tag{5}$$

$$f_{2,t} = c_2 + d_{22} f_{2,t-1} + (\phi_2 + \psi_{22} f_{2,t-1})^{1/2} \epsilon_{2t} \tag{6}$$

where $c_2 = 1 - q$, $d_{22} = p + q - 1$, $\phi_2 = q(1-q)$, $\psi_{22} = p(1-p) - q(1-q)$, and $p = \text{prob}[f_{2,t} = 1 | [f_{2,t-1} = 1]$, $q = \text{prob}[f_{2,t} = 0 | [f_{2,t-1} = 0]$, a_{10}, ϕ_1 and ψ_{12} are parameters which need to be estimated. The error terms ϵ_{1t} and ϵ_{2t} are respectively $N(0,1)$ and binary random variables. The derivations in order to cast Hamilton's model in this form follow from the results set out in Hamilton (1989, p. 360–361).[2] Clearly, in this case the unobserved factor $f_{2,t}$, will be a discrete random variable while $f_{1,t}$ is continuous.

It is when one turns to finance however that these models are most popular. The factor GARCH model of Engle, Ng, and Rothschild (1990) has returns to various assets that are a function of factors represented by portfolios of assets. Diebold and Nerlove (1989) and Mahieu and Schotman (1994) take Y_t to be a vector of N exchange rate returns relative to a numeraire currency, whereupon there are $K = N + 1$ factors made up of the N items of news relating to the countries involved plus one pertaining to the numeraire country itself. Designating the latter as the $(N+1)$th factor, we have, for the change in the jth exchange rate

$$y_{jt} = b_{j,1} f_{N+1,t} + f_{j,t}, j = 2, \ldots, N. \tag{7}$$

Diebold and Nerlove assume that all factors are martingale differences and that only the common factor $f_{N+1,t}$ exhibits conditional heteroskedasticity. They implemented their procedure by making a preliminary estimate of $f_{N+1,t}$, thereby getting an estimate of V_t. In contrast, Mahieu and Schotman make all factors possess conditional volatility, of the stochastic volatility variety. Since stochastic volatility makes V_t in (2) an unobserved random variable governed by an autoregressive process, it can be treated as a factor, and therefore the model can be placed into the framework outlined earlier. King, Sentana, and Wadhwani (1994) have a similar model except that the Y_t are stock returns on different markets and there is a combination of both observable and unobservable shocks that is common to each of the markets. Their objective is to study the correlation between stock returns on various markets.

Term structure models are perhaps the major class that emphasize a factor structure. Such models abound within this literature, ranging from the one and two factor models of yields in Cox, Ingersoll, and Ross (1985) and Vasicek (1977), through forward rates in Heath, Jarrow, and Morton (1992), to the multivariate models of Chen and Scott (1993) and Duffie and Kan (1993). This literature is vast and approaches differ according to the assumptions made about the number of factors, whether they are correlated or not, and the restrictions placed upon the A and B matrices in (1). In most models the set of underlying parameters θ is quite small relative to those in A and B.

Estimating factor models has proved to be a major challenge when F_t is

---

[2] Defining $v_t = (\phi_2 + \psi_{22} f_{2,t-1})^{1/2} \epsilon_{2t}$, Hamilton shows that, conditional upon $f_{2,t-1}$ being unity, v_t takes values $1 - p$ and $-p$ with probabilities p and $1 - p$ respectively, while, conditional upon $f_{2,t-1}$ being zero, it takes values $-(1-q)$ and q with probabilities q and $1 - q$. We use this representation later in order to simulate the factors.

unobserved. Early developments, such as Joreskog (1967), assume that the factors are martingale differences with constant covariances, but this restriction is obviously at variance with the nature of economic data. Moreover, it is generally presumed that the factors are normally distributed, which would not appeal when modeling financial data. One solution to the problem has been to proxy F_t by some observable sequence. For example, in the term structure literature, a major factor is the instantaneous rate, and this is sometimes replaced by a short-term yield. Others have noted the similarity of (1) and (2) to the state space form in control engineering, and that has led to proposals to apply the Kalman filter, as the output from that filter can be used to construct the likelihood of Y_t through the "prediction error decomposition" of Schweppe (1965). Unfortunately, the resemblance fails on one crucial dimension, viz. that the Kalman filter requires that V_t be a function of observables for its operation.[3]

The central problem therefore becomes the fact that unobservables such as V_t have to be integrated out of the multivariate density in order to find the marginal density for the observables Y_t, and this has proven to be very difficult to do. Hamilton's model is a case where it is possible, since the unknown factor only takes a few states, as does V_t. Moreover, provided that V_t has a simple relation to F_t, it is sometimes possible to find the likelihood either analytically or numerically. For example, in the term structure literature featuring $K = 1$, $V_t^{1/2} = \Psi F_t^{1/2}$, and (2) a stochastic differential equation, it has been possible to find an analytical expression for the density of V_t, while simulation procedures outlined in Danielsson and Richard (1993) and Kim and Shepherd (1994) can be applied to compute the likelihood arising when the factors represent stochastic volatility.[4] This has led authors such as Diebold and Nerlove (1989) and King, Sentana, and Wadhwani (1994) to replace the mapping from V_t to $\mathcal{F}_t$ by a mapping into some observable variable. Generally, the authors recognize that their resolution of the issue is not entirely satisfactory.

Rather than attempt to provide a solution that is specific to a particular model, we wish to dwell on how one might provide estimates for the general structure. Our proposal is to engage in indirect estimation.[5] A full description of this is available elsewhere but we note that it involves two models –

---

[3] Moreover, the Kalman filter could not be applied if the observation equation was (3) rather than (1). The so-called "extended Kalman filter" can be used to handle the non-linearity but it is only approximate as it essentially linearizes the non-linearity.

[4] There are cases where one can sometimes convert the problem into the Kalman filter framework. For example Harvey and Shephard (1993) take Y_t to be the log of squared returns as this quantity depends linearly upon the stochastic volatility factor, which, in turn, is an AR(1) with constant variance. That is, V_t is a constant in the reformulated model.

[5] Others have done this for various factor models, for example, Smith (1993) for RBC models and, unknown to us when writing the first version of this chapter, Frachot, Lesne, and Renault (1995) for term structure models.

the theoretical one having parameters θ and an auxiliary (statistical) one with parameters π. From the theory of misspecified models (White (1994)), it is the case that there will be a relation connecting π and θ, $\pi = g(\theta)$, so that we might form estimates of $\hat{\theta} = g^{-1}(\hat{\pi})$ from the estimates of π obtained from fitting the statistical model. In order to get the inverse mapping we need to be able to find numerically $g^{-1}(\cdot)$. Essentially this is done by first simulating the theoretical model for given values of θ and then fitting the statistical model to the simulated data so as to produce the corresponding population values of π. Basically, the method works from the premise that, if the theoretical model is correct, the principle of encompassing maintains that it is possible to predict what the parameters of the statistical model should be. Hence, if we reverse the normal encompassing methodology, it is possible to recover estimates of the parameters of the theoretical model from those of the statistical model, and these will be consistent since $\hat{\pi} \overset{P}{\to} \pi^* = g(\theta_0)$, where θ_0 is the true value of θ and π^* is the "pseudo-true" value of π. The particular variant of indirect estimation we use is that due to Gallant and Tauchen (1996), which notes that the expected values of the scores of the log likelihood for θ, under the theoretical model, are set to zero whenever π is replaced by π^*, so that simulating the scores provides the requisite information.

In order to apply indirect estimation two items are important: it should be simple to simulate from the theoretical model and relatively easy to estimate the statistical one. It is very easy to simulate (1) and (2), thereby enabling energies to be concentrated upon getting a good statistical model of the data that may then be used to infer the parameters of (1) and (2). Apart from the division of labor exemplified by the presence of the two models, another nice feature of indirect estimation is that we can simulate data from (1) and (2) using plausible values for θ and then determine what is likely to be a good statistical model, before we actually approach the data. Perhaps the major difficulty that arises is if $K < N$, since this will mean that the predicted density of the observations on Y_t will be singular and it seems unlikely that any set of data can be exactly described in this way. The problem has caused concern in the estimation of RBC and term structure models, since a singular density would mean that the likelihood of Y_t would not be defined.[6] A number of solutions have been proposed and implemented. One is to choose N so as to equal the number of factors. Thus Pearson and Sun (1994) use only two yields when estimating a two factor model. A more popular modification is to add on idiosyncratic factors to (1), i.e., yields are assumed to be observed with error. In the RBC model

---

[6] Of course one might simply adopt a non-likelihood estimator, for example, in RBC models estimation of the parameters could be done by applying GMM with equal weights rather than the "optimal weights" that depend on the (singular) covariance matrix.

this is the approach of McGrattan (1994), while its incarnation in the term structure literature is Chen and Scott (1993) – McGrattan adds on N shocks whereas Chen and Scott augment the number of model based factors in order to make the total equal N. Formally, we could subsume these variants into the structure of (1) and (2) by re-defining the number of factors, where K of these are the model-based factors while the remainder are supplementary factors.

There is of course nothing in the indirect estimation approach which requires one to work with a higher number of factors than that coming from the model, since estimation is being performed with the density of the observed random variables and there will be no singularity in that. However, one cannot appeal to the consistency properties of the indirect estimator in this situation, since the pseudo-true value involves not only the model parameters but also parameters describing the characteristics of the errors in variables. The indirect estimator will produce an answer but it may be inconsistent. Of course, there is also a likely inconsistency from any of the strategies above, as assumptions have to be made about the errors in variables, frequently that they are discrete autoregressions with normal innovations, and there is no reason to think that this would be a good description of such errors.

3   Modeling shifts in volatility

To demonstrate how Hamilton's (1989) model can be estimated by indirect estimation methods, a two factor model of stock market returns is estimated. The data set is taken from Pagan and Schwert (1990) and consists of monthly observations on US stock returns from 1834 to 1925. Following Pagan and Schwert the returns were first regressed on a constant, ten lags of the returns, and a series of monthly dummy variables. The residuals from this regression are taken to be $y_{1,t}$.

The indirect estimator chosen is based on the strategy of Gallant and Tauchen. This proceeds from the well-known result of the theory of mis-specified models that $E[\sum_{t=1}^{T} \frac{\partial L_t}{\partial \pi}(y_{1,t}; \pi^*)] = 0$, where L_t is the contribution of the tth observation to the log likelihood of the auxiliary model, the pseudo-true value π^* is a function of θ_0, and the expectation is taken with respect to the density of the true latent variable model. Gallant and Tauchen propose estimating $E[\frac{\partial L_t}{\partial \pi}(y_{1,t}; \pi^*)]$ with $\frac{1}{S}\sum_{s=1}^{S} \frac{\partial L_t}{\partial \pi}(y_{1,t}^s; \pi^*)$, where S simulations of the latent variable model produce sequences $y_{1,t}^s, s = 1, \ldots, S$, and then replacing π^* with a consistent estimator, the MLE $\hat{\pi}$. Inspection of (4) to (6) shows that $y_{1,t}^s$ can be generated from sequences of random numbers given values of θ, provided the initial value of $f_{2,t}$, namely $f_{2,1}$, is known. As the initial value can only take two values, it follows that $E[\frac{\partial L_t}{\partial \pi}(y_{1,t}; \pi^*)]$ can be decomposed as

$$E[\frac{\partial L_t}{\partial \pi}(y_{1,t}; \pi^*)|f_{2,1} = 1] \cdot \Pr[f_{2,1} = 1] + E[\frac{\partial L_t}{\partial \pi}(y_{1,t}; \pi^*)|f_{2,1} = 0] \cdot$$

$$\Pr[f_{2,1} = 0] \qquad (8)$$

where $\Pr[f_{2,1} = 1] = (1 - q)/(1 - p + 1 - q)$. Consequently, the unconditional expectations can be evaluated by finding separate values for $y_{1,t}^s$ when $f_{2,1} = 1$ and when $f_{2,1} = 0$, subsequently using these to estimate the two conditional expectations in (8).

Specifically, the indirect estimation algorithm for estimating the model consists of the following steps:
1 Estimate an auxiliary model based on actual stock returns $y_{1,t}$. The first-order conditions of the auxiliary model satisfy

$$\sum_{t=1}^{T} \frac{\partial L_t}{\partial \pi}(y_{1,t}, \hat{\pi}) = 0 \qquad (9)$$

where L is the log likelihood function and $\hat{\pi}$ is the vector of parameter estimates of the auxiliary model.
2 Choose an initial set of parameter estimates: $\theta^{(0)} = \{p^{(0)}, q^{(0)}, \phi_1^{(0)}, \psi_{12}^{(0)}\}$.[7]
3 Generate the second factor as

$$f_{2,t}^s = 1 - q^{(0)} + (p^{(0)} + q^{(0)} - 1)f_{2,t-1}^s + v_t \qquad (10)$$

where the initial value is chosen as $f_{2,1}^s = 0$, and where v_t is an error term defined as

$$v_t = \begin{cases} -(1 - p^{(0)}): \text{if } u_{2,t} < p^{(0)} \\ -p^{(0)}: \text{if } u_{2,t} \geq p^{(0)} \end{cases}$$

when $f_{2,t-1} = 1$, and

$$v_t = \begin{cases} (1 - q^{(0)}): \text{if } u_{2,t} < q^{(0)} \\ q^{(0)}: \text{if } u_{2,t} \geq q^{(0)} \end{cases}$$

when $f_{2,t-1} = 0$. The error term $u_{2,t}$ is a uniform random number over the unit interval.
4 Generate the first factor as

$$f_{1,t}^s = (\phi_1^{(0)} + \psi_{12}^{(0)} f_{2,t}^s)^{1/2} u_{1,t} \qquad (11)$$

---

[7] No intercept term is included in the specification of the model as the unconditional mean of the data is zero; also see the empirical results reported in Pagan and Schwert (1990, p. 274).

where $u_{1,t}$ is an $\mathcal{N}(0,1)$ random number.

5 Compute the simulated returns as

$$y_{1,t}^s = f_{1,t}^s. \tag{12}$$

6 Now evaluate the scores of the auxiliary model at the MLE estimates of the parameters of that model, but using the simulated data $y_{1,t}^s$, i.e., form $\frac{\partial L_t}{\partial \pi}(y_{1,t}^s, \hat{\pi}, f_{2,1}^s = 0)$.

7 Repeat steps 3 to 6, with the initial value of the second factor chosen as $f_{2,1}^s = 1$.

8 Repeat steps 3 to 7, S times and compute an estimate of (8), $d_{\pi,t}$, from the two simulated data sets with the weights for the conditional expectations equaling the unconditional probabilities, producing

$$\hat{d}_{\pi,t} = [S^{-1}\sum_{s=1}^{S}(\frac{\partial L_t}{\partial \pi}(y_{1,t}^s; \hat{\pi})|f_{2,1} = 1)] \cdot \Pr[f_{2,1} = 1] + [S^{-1}\sum_{s=1}^{S}\frac{\partial L_t}{\partial \pi}(y_{1,t}^s; \hat{\pi})|$$

$$f_{2,1} = 0] \cdot \Pr[f_{2,1} = 0]$$

where $\Pr[f_{2,1} = 1] = (1 - q^{(0)})/(1 - p^{(0)} + 1 - q^{(0)})$ and $\Pr[f_{2,1} = 0] = 1 - \Pr[f_{2,1} = 1]$.

9 The parameter vector $\theta = \{p, q, \phi_1, \psi_{12}\}$ is calibrated to satisfy the criterion

$$\hat{\theta} = \underset{\theta}{\mathrm{argmin}}\left\{\sum_{t=1}^{T}\hat{d}'_{\pi,t}\Omega\hat{d}_{\pi,t}\right\} \tag{13}$$

where Ω is a variance–covariance matrix given in Gourieroux, Monfort, and Renault (1993).[8] The objective function in (13) is minimized using the algorithm *BFGS* in the GAUSS program *OPTMUM*.

The indirect estimation results are given in table 10.1. The number of simulation paths is set at $S = 100$. Two auxiliary models are chosen. The first, model A, consists of a constant mean, a conditional variance process which follows a GARCH(1, 1) structure, and a conditional error distribution which is student's t. The second, model B, is the same as the first except that the conditional variance is EGARCH(1, 1). A GARCH(1, 1) auxiliary model with a normally distributed innovations structure is not used, as this model only contains three parameters, i.e., $\dim(\pi) = 3$, which is not enough to identify the four parameters contained in θ. It is apparent that the use of an EGARCH model gives no gains over a GARCH model. The reason becomes clear from an analysis of simulated realizations from Hamilton's model using the parameter estimates of table 10.1. Three thousand such realizations were fitted to an EGARCH(1, 1) process and in all cases it was noticeable that the EGARCH parameter which captures an asymmetric

---

[8] If $\dim(\pi) = \dim(\theta)$, as in many of our applications, the choice of Ω is irrelevant.

Table 10.1. *Parameter estimates of Hamilton's model (stock returns data, monthly, 1834 to 1925)*

Parameter	Indirect estimates		MLE (Hamilton)
	Model A	Model B	
ϕ_1	5.8225×10^{-4}	6.1173×10^{-4}	6.1022×10^{-4}
ψ_{12}	17.7889×10^{-4}	19.9976×10^{-4}	18.5889×10^{-4}
p	0.9037	0.9017	0.9008
q	0.9613	0.9610	0.9614

Notes: Model A = Constant mean, GARCH(1,1), conditional student's t
Model B = Constant mean, EGARCH(1,1), conditional student's t

response of the conditional variance to news is close to zero and positive (around 0.02). Consequently, Hamilton's model does not replicate the leverage effect that exists in the data, whereby volatility is larger when returns are negative than when positive, and which the EGARCH model was specifically designed to capture (the equivalent parameter estimate with the data being -0.11). Moreover, using the same simulated data, it was found that Hamilton's model does imply thick tails in the estimated density of the GARCH innovations, with an estimated degrees of freedom coefficient for the student's t density of around 8.3 (and 8.6 in the data). This illustrates one of the advantages of indirect estimation alluded to earlier, viz. we can better understand the nature of the model being estimated by describing it in terms of the characteristics of the auxiliary model, as these are frequently very well documented in previous research.

For comparison the maximum likelihood estimates based on the algorithm proposed by Hamilton (1989) are also presented in table 10.1. The key result is that there is strong agreement between the direct estimates based on MLE and the indirect estimates.

4   Modeling the term structure

4.1   The CIR class

4.1.1   Theory
In this section estimation strategies for computing parameter estimates of multifactor models of the term structure of interest rates for a broad class of specifications of the stochastic differential equations (SDE) governing

the evolution of the factors, are provided.[9] The approach is to exploit the relationship that exists between factors and the term structure identified by Cox, Ingersoll, and Ross (1985) (CIR hereafter). Let $f_i(t)$, $i = 1, 2, \ldots, K$, be a set of K factors at time t. The diffusion processes governing the movement of $f_{i,t}$ over time are

$$df_i(t) = \kappa_i(\beta_i - f_i(t))dt + \sigma_i\sqrt{f_i(t)}dW_i(t) \tag{14}$$

where $W_i(t)$ is a Wiener process with the property that $dW_i(t) \sim \mathcal{N}(0, dt)$ and is independent of $dW_j(t)$, $i \neq j$.

The price of a discount bond at time t that matures at time Q, $P(t,Q)$, is determined by solving the partial differential equation

$$\frac{1}{2}\sum_{i=1}^{K}\sigma_i^2 f_i(t)\frac{\partial^2 P}{\partial f_i \partial f_j} + \sum_{i=1}^{K}(\kappa_i\beta_i - \kappa_i f_i(t) - \lambda_i f_i(t))\frac{\partial P}{\partial f_i} + \frac{\partial P}{\partial t} - rP = 0 \tag{15}$$

subject to the boundary condition that the bond pays \$1 at the time of maturity Q

$$P(Q,Q) = 1. \tag{16}$$

The term $\lambda_i f_i$ represents the risk premium, and r the instantaneous nominal rate of interest, which is also a function of the K factors.

The solution of (15) has the exponential form

$$P(t,Q) = \prod_{i=1}^{K} A_i \exp\left[-\sum_{i=1}^{K} B_i f_i(t)\right] \tag{17}$$

where

$$A_i = \left[\frac{2\gamma_i \exp[0.5\tau(\kappa_i + \lambda_i + \gamma_i)]}{2\gamma_i + (\kappa_i + \lambda_i + \gamma_i)(\exp[\gamma_i\tau] - 1)}\right]^{\frac{2\kappa_i\beta_i}{\sigma_i^2}} \tag{18}$$

$$B_i = \left[\frac{2(\exp[\gamma_i\tau] - 1)}{2\gamma_i + (\kappa_i + \lambda_i + \gamma_i)(\exp[\gamma_i\tau] - 1)}\right] \tag{19}$$

and $\tau = Q - t$, is the time to maturity, and $\gamma_i = \sqrt{(\kappa_i + \lambda_i)^2 + 2\sigma_i^2}$. Clearly, if we can simulate the factors it is possible to produce simulated prices which can then be matched with actual prices through whatever auxiliary model is chosen as the basis of indirect estimation. Notice that (14) and the logarithm of (17) correspond to (2) and (1) respectively in the general representation used in section 2.

---

[9] Although we focus upon the modeling of yields the technology could also be applied either to forward rates using the framework of Heath, Jarrow, and Morton (1992), or to spreads using the principal components structure of Knez, Litterman, and Scheinkman (1989). This later application, which is contained in a University of Melbourne discussion paper, has the advantage that it combines the CIR and the principal component factor decomposition structure into a single unifying framework; see Pagan and Martin (1996).

To compute the parameters $\theta = \{\kappa_i, \beta_i, \lambda_i, \sigma_i;\ i = 1, 2, \ldots, K\}$ by indirect estimation the following steps are adopted. In outlining the algorithm, the variables observed and simulated are taken to be yields. An alternative approach is to use either bond prices or the logarithm of bond prices, where the latter form is consistent with the transformation adopted by Chen and Scott (1993). In the case of zero coupon bonds, the relationship between the price $P_{j,t}$ and the yield $y_{j,t}$, of maturity τ_j, is simply

$$y_{j,t} = -\ln(P_{j,t})/\tau_j. \tag{20}$$

1 Estimate an auxiliary model based on a VAR for actual bond yields, $y_{j,t}$, with maturities $\{\tau_1, \tau_2, \ldots, \tau_N\}$. The first-order conditions of this model satisfy

$$\sum_{t=1}^{T} \frac{\partial L_t}{\partial \pi}(y_{j,t}, \hat{\pi}) = 0, \tag{21}$$

where $L_t()$ is the log likelihood function of the auxiliary model at time t, and $\hat{\pi}$ is the estimated vector of parameters based on fitting the auxiliary model to the actual yields.

2 Choose an initial set of parameter estimates: $\theta^{(0)} = \kappa_i^{(0)}, \beta_i^{(0)}, \lambda_i^{(0)}, \sigma_i^{(0)};\ i = 1, 2, \ldots, K$.

3 The SDEs in (14) are simulated S times using a Euler approximation

$$f_{i,t+\Delta t}^s = f_{i,t}^s + \kappa_i^{(0)}(\beta_i^{(0)} - f_{i,t}^s)\Delta t + \sigma_i^{(0)}\sqrt{f_{i,t}^s} u_{i,t}, \tag{22}$$

where $u_{i,t} \sim \mathcal{N}(0, \Delta t)$. This results in S simulated time series on the K factors, $f_{i,t}^s$, $i = 1, 2, \ldots, K$; $s = 1, \ldots, S$. The length of the time step is Δt which is chosen to be small.[10]

4 A set of $N > K$, simulated bond prices $P_{j,t}^s$, $j = 1, 2, \ldots, N$; with respective maturities $\{\tau_1, \tau_2, \tau_N\}$, are computed using (17) to (19)

$$P_{j,t}^s = \prod_{i=1}^{K} A_i^{(0)} \exp\left[-\sum_{i=1}^{K} B_i^{(0)} f_{i,t}^s\right], \tag{23}$$

where the $A_i^{(0)}$ and $B_i^{(0)}$ terms signify that the parameters in the expressions (18) and (19) respectively, are evaluated at $\theta^{(0)}$. These are converted into simulated yields using (20)

$$y_{j,t}^s = -\ln(P_{j,t}^s)/\tau_j, j = 1, 2, \ldots, N. \tag{24}$$

5 The expected value of the scores of the auxiliary model are evaluated using the parameter estimates of the auxiliary model and the simulated bond yield data $y_{j,t}^s$. That is, we form

---

[10] A natural barrier is used to ensure that $f_{i,t+\Delta t}^s \geq 0$. This is achieved by setting $f_{i,t+\Delta t}^s = k_i \beta_i$, whenever the right-hand side of (22) is negative.

$$\hat{d}_{\pi,t} = \frac{1}{S} \sum_{s=1}^{S} \frac{\partial L_t}{\partial \pi} (y_{j,t}^s, \hat{\pi}). \tag{25}$$

6 The parameters associated with the factors are calibrated to satisfy the criterion

$$\hat{\theta} = \underset{\theta}{\text{argmin}} \sum_{t=1}^{T} \hat{d}'_{\pi,t} \Omega \hat{d}_{\pi,t}, \tag{26}$$

where Ω is a variance–covariance matrix defined above. The objective function in (26) is minimized using the algorithm *BFGS* in *OPTMUM*.

4.1.2   Application
The proposed indirect estimator is now applied to estimating single ($K = 1$) and multifactor ($K > 1$) models of the term structure. For comparability with Chen and Scott's (1993) results, similar zero coupon bond rates are used; namely the three month $y_{1,t}$, six months $y_{2,t}$, five year $y_{3,t}$, and a rate equal to an unweighted average of the ten, fifteen, and twenty year yields $y_{4,t}$. Thus the maturities are $\tau = \{0.25, 0.50, 5.0, 15.00\}$. The yields are taken from McCulloch (1989). The data are monthly, beginning in December 1946 and ending in December 1987, a sample of 483 observations.

The indirect estimation results for the one-factor, two-factor, and three-factor CIR models are given in table 10.2 based on the algorithm given above. A four-variate VAR with a constant and each interest rate lagged one period is chosen as the auxiliary model. Two variants of the auxiliary model are tried: one where there is an adjustment for time-varying variances, achieved by dividing each equation by the square root of the lagged dependent variable, and another where there is no adjustment. The square root adjustment is motivated by the square root formulation of the SDE processes assumed to be driving the factors. As both auxiliary models yield similar results, only the results based on the square root adjustment are reported in table 10.2.[11] The number of simulation paths is chosen as $S = 100$, and the time interval is set at $\Delta t = 0.1$. The initial value of the factors is computed as $\min(y_{1,t}, y_{2,t}, y_{3,t}, y_{4,t}; t = 1, 2, \ldots, T)$. The standard errors are computed using a Newey–West filter with 12 lags; see Gourieroux, Monfort, and Renault (1993, pp. S112–113).[12]

---

[11] Another auxiliary model that would be appropriate would be to allow the VAR errors to exhibit a GARCH or even EGARCH structure following Pagan, Hall, and Martin (1995) and Pastorello, Renault, and Touzi (1994). This model has not been adopted at this stage as the strategy is to see how close the direct and indirect estimates are for the simplest of all auxiliary models.

[12] The weighting matrix in (267) is set at $\Omega = I$. Choosing Ω as the optimal weighting matrix results in the algorithm getting stuck. This problem possibly reflects a more general problem, namely the use of gradient optimization routines to compute indirect estimates. While the

Table 10.2. *Parameter estimates of the CIR model: yield data, December 1946 to December 1987 (abs. standard errors in brackets)*

Parameter	Indirect estimation			MLE (Chen and Scott)		
	1-factor	2-factor	3-factor	1-factor	2-factor	3-factor
κ_1	0.6979	0.7165	0.6567	0.4697	0.7660	1.6331
	(0.0300)	(0.0458)	(0.1612)	(0.0543)	(0.1513)	(0.1655)
β_1	0.0526	0.0541	0.0966	0.0618	0.0321	0.0324
	(0.0026)	(0.0194)	(0.0358)	(0.0074)	(0.0064)	(0.0029)
σ_1	0.1506	0.1493	0.1227	0.0825	0.1312	0.1373
	(0.0050)	(0.0121)	(0.0241)	(0.0018)	(0.0043)	(0.0040)
λ_1	$-0.2805)$	-0.2784	-0.2540	-0.0454	-0.1186	-0.0317
	(0.0222)	(0.0438)	(0.0723)	(0.0564)	(0.1516)	(0.1504)
κ_2		0.0050	0.0052		0.0009	0.0051
		(0.0533)	(0.0596)		(0.0617)	(0.2065)
β_2		0.0104	0.0104		0.0212	0.0108
		(0.1068)	(0.1900)		(1.4710)	(0.4366)
σ_2		0.1065	0.0468		0.0531	0.0755
		(0.0084)	(0.0220)		(0.0017)	(0.0017)
λ_2		-0.1091	-0.1032		-0.0415	-0.1530
		(0.0611)	(0.0839)		(0.0618)	(0.2072)
κ_3			0.0083			0.0062
			(0.0143)			(0.5259)
β_3			0.0082			0.0091
			(0.1517)			(0.7747)
$\sigma_3 0$			0.1452			0.1842
			(0.0147)			(0.0044)
$\lambda_3 0$			-0.0714			-0.1373
			(0.0219)			(0.5260)

Starting estimates used in the algorithm are based on the direct, MLE estimates reported by Chen and Scott (1993). For comparison these estimates are also given in table 10.2. Overall the parameter estimates of the direct and indirect procedures are very similar in terms of sign, magnitude, and statistical significance. Focusing on the one-factor results, the main difference between the two sets of parameter estimates is the estimate of the

use of a non-optimal weighting matrix causes some loss of efficiency in the parameter estimates, this loss should be small, at least for the three-factor model, where the dimension of θ is similar to the dimension of the parameter vector of the auxiliary model, namely π.

risk premium parameter (λ_1), which tends to be larger in magnitude using the indirect estimator than the direct estimator. However, inspection of the one-factor results shows that the indirect estimate of $\kappa_1 + \lambda_1$, the term which is important in pricing bonds, is $0.4174 = 0.6979 - 0.2805$, which is close to the direct estimate of $0.4243 = 0.4697 - 0.0454$.

The direct and indirect parameter estimates of the two-factor and three-factor models are especially similar. In particular, both sets of results point to a lack of additional information in the third factor. This suggests that the behaviour of the four yields used in the empirical analysis are captured quite well by at most two factors.

4.2   Extending the CIR class for levels effects

For the class of factor models proposed by CIR, analytical expressions are available to describe the relations between factors and bond prices, i.e., (17) and the simulated bond prices can be easily computed. However, this outcome depends crucially upon the nature of the SDEs generating the factors. Given that there is mounting evidence to suggest that the "square root formulation" of the conditional variance in (14) is not always consistent with the data (for example Chan, *et al.* (1992) and Pagan, Hall, and Martin (1995)), extension to allow for more general specifications of the conditional variance is desirable. The cost of adopting this generality is that no analytical expression relating the factors to bond prices is now available; however solutions can be obtained numerically by using simulation methods.[13] When this is done there will no longer be a linear relation connecting factors and observed variables, but this is not necessary for indirect estimation methods to work, although it would create difficulties for applications of the Kalman filter.[14]

The approach now is to extend the CIR factor specification given by (14) by writing the diffusion processes as

$$df_i(t) = \kappa_i(\beta_i - f_i(t))dt + \sigma_i f_i(t)^{\alpha_i}dW_i(t), \tag{27}$$

where α_i, $i = 1, 2, \dots, K$, is a set of additional parameters that need to be estimated. For the CIR class $\alpha_i = 0.5$, $\forall i$.

---

[13] An alternative approach to the simulation method adopted below is to compute prices using finite difference procedures to solve the partial differential equation. This approach is likely to be computationally intensive, especially for multifactor models.

[14] An exception is when there is no levels effect in the variance; see Jamshidian (1989). However, given that the empirical evidence for a levels effect is overwhelming, this case does not appear to be especially interesting.

Table 10.3. *Comparison of analytical and simulated solutions of CIR* $\kappa = 1.0, \beta = 0.1, \sigma = 0.1, \lambda = -0.5; \Delta\tau = 1/12; Y_0 = 0.1$

Maturity (months)	Analytical	Simulated				
		$H = 10$	$H = 100$	$H = 1,000$	$H = 10,000$	$dW = 0.0$
1	0.9915	0.9914	0.9915	0.9915	0.9915	0.9915
2	0.9828	0.9826	0.9827	0.9828	0.9828	0.9828
3	0.9738	0.9735	0.9737	0.9738	0.9738	0.9738
4	0.9647	0.9641	0.9645	0.9647	0.9646	0.9646
5	0.9553	0.9542	0.9552	0.9553	0.9552	0.9552
6	0.9458	0.9442	0.9456	0.9457	0.9457	0.9457
9	0.9163	0.9129	0.9163	0.9160	0.9162	0.9160
12	0.8859	0.8808	0.8857	0.8853	0.8856	0.8854

4.2.1   Simulating prices

While it is a simple matter to simulate the set of factors using (27) the main problem confronting the use of indirect estimation is that there is in general no analytical solution for computing bond prices that is comparable to the CIR expressions given in (17) to (19). For a one-factor model the general expression for the price is

$$P(t,Q) = E_t\left[-\exp\left(-\int_t^Q f_1(\tau)d\tau\right)\right],\tag{28}$$

where the conditional expectation is with respect to the modified diffusion process

$$df_1(t) = (\kappa_1\beta_1 - \kappa_1 f_1(t) - \lambda_1 f_1(t)^{2\alpha_1})dt + \sigma_1 f_1(t)^{\alpha_1}dW_1(t).\tag{29}$$

The approach that is adopted for computing the price is to replace the conditional expectation in (28) by the sample mean of a set of H simulated paths of equations (28)–(29). To gauge the accuracy of the simulated prices, results are given in table 10.3 for the CIR case, $\alpha_1 = 0.5$, and for values of H ranging from 10 to 10,000. These are compared with the analytical results in (17). For all maturities ranging from one month to one year, the simulated prices are at least accurate to two decimal places and in most cases accurate to three decimal places.

For the short end of the maturity spectrum it is possible to reduce the number of sample paths to one. The approach is based on noting that, if at the short end the term structure is close to being linear, Jensen's inequality can be approximated by an equality and the price computed as

$$P(t,Q) \simeq \exp\left(-\int_t^Q E_t[f_1(\tau)]d\tau\right).\tag{30}$$

From (29) the term $E_t[f_1(\tau)]$, can be simply computed from using one simulated path and by setting $dW_1(t) = 0$. The results of computing the price using (30) are given in the last column of table 10.3 headed by $dW = 0$. As can be seen, the approximation performs extremely well with the simulated prices being accurate to at least three decimal places for all maturities, while being accurate to four decimal places for maturities less than four months. Comparing the dW results with those obtained for alternative values of H shows that similar results are obtained when $H = 1,000$ is chosen.

4.2.2   Application

In this section, a one-factor model ($K = 1$) with a levels effect is estimated for a set of eight monthly interest rates ($N = 8$) on US Treasury bills, consisting of all maturities in the range from one to six months, as well as the nine month and one year rates. The data begin in January 1959 and end in February 1991, a sample of 386 observations. The auxiliary model chosen consists of a system of eight autoregressive equations, one for each interest rate, with the conditional error variance of the one-month yield being specified as an EGARCH process, while all other yields are taken to have constant conditional variance. The diffusion processes (27) and (29) are simulated with a time step of $dt = 1/12$.

The indirect estimation results of the parameters in equation (29) are given in table 10.4. The number of simulation paths to handle the continuous time nature of the factor is set to $S = 10$, and the number of simulations used to approximate the price in (28) corresponding to the eight maturities, is chosen as $H = 10$. Also given are the results using $dW = 0$. To gauge the accuracy of the numerical procedure for computing prices, the CIR model ($\alpha_1 = 0.5$) is estimated with prices computed using both the analytical expressions given by (17)–(19), and by simulation. A comparison of the parameter estimates shows that the use of simulated prices causes at most a small reduction in accuracy. In particular, the results based on $dW = 0$, tend to generate parameter estimates closer to those obtained when prices are computed analytically. The final two columns of table 10.4 give estimates of the full model allowing for a levels effect in the factor. The estimates of the levels effect, given by $\hat{\alpha}_1 = 0.7167$ ($H = 10$) and $\hat{\alpha}_1 = 0.7448$ ($dW = 0$) are somewhat higher than the value used by CIR in their models of $\hat{\alpha}_1 = 0.5$, but not as high as the estimates reported by Chan, et al. (1992).

Table 10.4. *Parameter estimates of a one-factor, levels effect model: yield data, January 1959 to February 1991 (abs. standard errors in brackets)*

		CIR		Levels effect	
Parameter	Anal.	Sim. $(H=10)$	Sim. $(dW=10)$	Sim. $(H=10)$	Sim. $(dW=10)$
κ_1	0.1885	0.1875	0.1888	0.2245	0.2310
	(0.0003)	0.0003)	(0.0002)	(0.0011)	(0.0007)
β_1	0.0671	0.0663	0.0671	0.0684	0.0694
	(0.0003)	(0.0002)	(0.0001)	(0.0002)	(0.0003)
σ_1	0.0679	0.0678	0.0679	0.1258	0.1364
	(0.0001)	(0.0001)	(0.0001)	(0.0003)	(0.0004)
λ_1	-0.3319)	-0.3518	-0.3310	-0.7948	-0.8075
	(0.0008)	(0.0009)	(0.0007)	(0.0076)	(0.0010)
α_1	0.5000	0.5000	0.5000	0.7167	0.7448
				(0.0018)	(0.0010)

5   Conclusions

This chapter has provided a general framework for estimating factor models in econometrics using the indirect estimator proposed by Gallant and Tauchen (1996) and Gourieroux, Monfort, and Renault (1993). A number of empirical examples were given. Hamilton's model was applied to monthly stock return data to characterize high and low volatility states. Two applications were made to term structure models. The first example provided a comparison between the indirect estimates of one-factor, two-factor and three-factor CIR models of the term structure with the estimates obtained by Chen and Scott (1993) using a direct, MLE estimator. The Next, a one-factor model possessing a levels effect was specified and estimated. Overall the empirical results were very encouraging.

References
Chan, K.C., G.A. Karolyi, F.A. Longstaff, and A.B. Sanders (1992), "An Empirical Comparison of Alternative Models of the Short-Term Interest Rate," *Journal of Finance*, 52, 1209–1227.

Chen, R.C. and L. Scott (1993), "Maximum Likelihood Estimation for a Multifactor Equilibrium Model of the Term Structure of Interest Rates," *Journal of Fixed Income*, December, 14–31.

Cox, J.C., J.E. Ingersoll, and S.A. Ross (1985), "A Theory of the Term Structure of Interest Rates," *Econometrica*, 53, 385–407.

Danielsson, J. and J.F. Richard (1993), "Accelerated Gaussian Importance Sampler with Application to Dynamic Latent Variable Models," *Journal of Applied Econometrics*, 8, S153–S174.

Diebold, F.X. and M. Nerlove (1989), "The Dynamics of Exchange Rate Volatility: A Multivariate Latent-Factor ARCH Model," *Journal of Applied Econometrics*, 4, 1–22.

Duffie, D. and R. Kan (1993), "A Yield-Factor Model of Interest Rates," Graduate School of Business, Stanford University.

Engle, R.F., V.K. Ng, and M. Rothschild (1990), "Asset Pricing with a Factor-ARCH Covariance Structure: Empirical Estimates for Treasury Bills," *Journal of Econometrics*, 45, 213–237.

Frachot, A., J.P. Lesne, and E. Renault (1995), "Indirect Inference Estimation of Yield Curve Factor Models," mimeo, University of Toulouse.

Gallant, A.R. and G. Tauchen (1996), "Which Moments to Match," *Econometric Theory* 12, 657–681.

Gourieroux, C., A. Monfort, and E. Renault (1993), "Indirect Inference," *Journal of Applied Econometrics*, 8, S85–S118.

Hamilton, J.D. (1989), "A New Approach to the Economic Analysis of Nonstationary Time Series and the Business Cycle," *Econometrica*, 57, 357–384.

Harvey, A.C. and N. Shephard (1993), "The Econometrics of Stochastic Volatility," mimeo, London School of Economics.

Heath, D., R. Jarrow, and A. Morton (1992), "Bond Pricing and the Term Structure of Interest Rates: A New Methodology for Contingent Claims Valuation," *Econometrica*, 60, 77–105.

Jamshidian, F. (1989), "An Exact Bond Formula Option," *Journal of Finance*, 44, 205–209.

Joreskog, K.G. (1967), "Some Contributions to Maximum Likelihood Factor Analysis," *Psychometrika*, 32, 443–482.

Kim, S. and N. Shephard (1994), "Stochastic Volatility: Likelihood Inference and Comparison with ARCH Models," mimeo, Nuffield College, Oxford.

King, R.G., C. Plosser, and S. Rebelo (1988), "Production, Growth and Business Cycles I: The Basic Neoclassical Model," *Journal of Monetary Economics*, 21, 195–232.

King, M., E. Sentana, and S. Wadhwani (1994), "Volatility and Links Between National Stock Markets," *Econometrica*, 62, 901–933.

Knez, P., R. Litterman, and J. Scheinkman (1989), "Explorations into Factors Explaining Money Market Returns," Goldman Sachs & Co., Discussion Paper series, No. 6.

Mahieu, R. and P. Schotman (1994), "Neglected Common Factors in Exchange Rate Volatility," *Journal of Empirical Finance*, 1, 279–311.

McCulloch, J.H. (1989), "US Term Structure Data, 1946–1987," in B.M. Friedman and F.H. Hahn (eds.), *Handbook of Monetary Economics*, vol I, Amsterdam: North-Holland, pp. 672–715.

McGrattan, E.B. (1994), "The Macroeconomic Effects of Distortionary Taxation," *Journal of Monetary Economics*, 33, 573–601.

Pagan, A.R., A.D. Hall, and V.L. Martin (1995), "Modelling the Term Structure," in G.S. Maddala and C.R. Rao (eds.), *Statistical Methods in Finance, Handbook of Statistics*, vol. XIII, Amsterdam: Elsevier Science.

Pagan, A.R. and V.L. Martin, (1996), "Simulation Based Estimation of Some Factor Models in Econometrics," University of Melbourne, Economics Department, Discussion Paper No. 521.

Pagan, A.R. and G.W. Schwert (1990), "Alternative Models for Conditional Stock Volatility," *Journal of Econometrics*, 45, 267–290.

Pearson, N.D. and T.S. Sun (1994), "Exploiting the Conditional Density in Estimating the Term Structure: An Application to the Cox, Ingersoll, Ross Model," *Journal of Finance*, 49, 1279–1304.

Ross, S.A. (1976), "The Arbitrage Theory of Capital Asset Pricing," *Journal of Economic Theory*, 13, 341–360.

Schweppe, F.C. (1965), "Evaluation of Likelihood for Gausian signals," *IEEE Transactions on Information Theory*, 11, 61–70.

Smith, A.A. (1993), "Estimating Nonlinear Time Series Models using Simulated Vector Autoregressions," *Journal of Applied Econometrics*, 8, S63–S84.

Vahid, F. and R. Engle (1993), "Common Trends and Common Cycles," *Journal of Applied Econometrics*, 8, 341–360.

Vasicek, O. (1977), "An Equilibrium Characterization of the Term Structure," *Journal of Financial Economics*, 5, 177–188.

White, H. (1994), *Estimation, Inference and Specification Analysis*, Econometric Society Monograph No. 22, Cambridge University Press.

11 Simulation-based Bayesian inference for economic time series

John F. Geweke

1 Introduction

Econometric time series analysis is the discipline of using data to revise beliefs about economic questions, especially about the future. These questions have a common structure. Given data resulting from past behavior, and a set of assumptions about economic behavior (or, several sets of competing assumptions), what decision or action should be taken at the present time? The decision for action might involve public economic policy, a private economic decision, or a choice between competing assumptions.

Unfortunately economic questions are rarely laid out so explicitly. Interactions between assumptions and data are studied by a group of individuals, who (following Hildreth (1963)) we may call investigators. The investigators' tasks are complicated by the facts that data sets are constantly being updated, new models are continually being introduced and old ones modified, and the complete constellation of alternative assumptions is never neatly defined. Decisions are made by another group of individuals, who (again, following Hildreth) we may call clients. An ultimate client may be a public or private sector decision making body, in the case of policy, or the scholarly community, in the case of choices among assumptions. Investigators typically have at best a vague idea who the clients are, and exactly what use clients will wish to make of their results.

This chapter surveys some recently developed methods that hold fresh promise for investigators and their clients. These methods are based on the Bayesian paradigm for the use of economic time series, and on recent advances in simulation methods for the implementation of that paradigm. The purpose is to convey these innovations and their significance for time

First draft, November 1995; final draft, August 1996. This chapter does not include additions to the literature since November 1995. References with later dates are publications of working papers available in 1995. Partial financial support from NSF grants SES-9210070 and SBR-9514865 are gratefully acknowledged. The views expressed in this paper are those of the author and not necessarily those of the Federal Reserve Bank of Minneapolis or the Federal Reserve System.

255

series econometrics, to econometricians who have not followed the relevant mathematical and applied literature. There are three substantive sections. The next section reviews aspects of Bayesian inference essential to understanding the implications of the Bayesian paradigm for time series analysis, and of posterior simulators for Bayesian econometrics. Section 3 brings the theory together with computational advances described in Geweke (1996a, 1996b), and sets forth a practical framework for Bayesian investigators to report results in a way that is immediately useful for decision making in general and forecasting in particular. Implementation in some specific time series models is taken up in section 4. The survey in this section is representative, not complete; see the surveys of Koop (1994), Chib and Greenberg (1994), and Geweke (1996b) for other models. The key points of the chapter are reviewed in the concluding section.

2   Bayesian inference

This section provides a quick review of the principles of Bayesian inference. The purpose is threefold: to set up notation for the chapter, to provide an introduction for econometricians unfamiliar with Bayesian methods, and to set forth the technical challenges that posterior simulators largely overcome. Much of the notation is standard for econometric models, but differs in some important respects from that used in non-Bayesian approaches because these approaches do not condition on observables.

The introduction here is very concise and provides only the analytic essentials for the subsequent development of posterior simulators. There are few examples and at a number of points the exposition touches lightly on concepts of great depth. Those versed in Bayesian methods at the level of Berger (1985) or Bernardo and Smith (1994) can easily skip to section 3 and use this section as a reference. Those seeking a complete introduction can consult these references, perhaps supplemented by DeGroot (1970) and Berger and Wolpert (1988) on the distinction between Bayesian and non-Bayesian methods. On Bayesian econometrics in particular, see Zellner (1971) and Poirier (1995).

The results presented in this section are not operational. In particular they all involve integrals that rarely can be evaluated analytically, and the dimensions of integration are typically greater than the four or five for which quadrature methods are practical. The balance of the chapter shows how the theory developed in this section can be implemented in applied econometrics using posterior simulators.

2.1 Basics

Inference takes place in the context of one or more models. A model describes the behavior of a $p \times 1$ vector of observables $\mathbf{y}_t$ over a sequence of discrete time units $t = 1, 2, \ldots$. The history of the sequence $\{\mathbf{y}_t\}$ at time t is given by $\mathbf{Y}_t = \{\mathbf{y}_s\}_{s=1}^t$; $\mathbf{Y}_0 = \{\varnothing\}$. A *model* is a corresponding sequence of probability density functions

$$f_t(\mathbf{y}_t \mid \mathbf{Y}_{t-1}, \theta) \tag{1}$$

in which θ is a $k \times 1$ vector of unknown parameters, $\theta \in \Theta \subseteq \mathbb{R}^k$. The function "p($\cdot$)" will be used to denote a generic probability density function (p.d.f.). The p.d.f. of $\mathbf{Y}_T$, conditional on the model and parameter vector θ, is

$$p(\mathbf{Y}_T \mid \theta) = \prod_{t=1}^T f_t(\mathbf{y}_t \mid \mathbf{Y}_{t-1}, \theta) \tag{2}$$

The *likelihood function* is any function $L(\theta; \mathbf{Y}_T) \propto p(\mathbf{Y}_T \mid \theta)$.

If the model specifies that the $\mathbf{y}_t$ are independently and identically distributed then $f_t(\mathbf{y}_t \mid \mathbf{Y}_{t-1}, \theta) = f_t(\mathbf{y}_t \mid \theta)$ and $p(\mathbf{Y}_t \mid \theta) = \prod_{t=1}^T f_t(\mathbf{y}_t \mid \theta)$. More generally, the index "t" may pertain to cross sections, to time series, or both, but time series models and language are used here for specificity. Likewise it is assumed that $\mathbf{y}_t$ is continuously distributed for specificity and brevity.

The objective of Bayesian inference can in general be expressed

$$E[g(\theta) \mid \mathbf{Y}_T] \tag{3}$$

in which $g(\theta)$ is a *function of interest*. There are several broad categories of functions of interest that between them encompass most applied econometric work. Clearly the function of interest can be a parameter or a function of parameters. Another category is $g(\theta) = L(a_1, \theta) - L(a_2, \theta)$ in which $L(a, \theta)$ is the loss function pertaining to action a, parameter vector θ, and (implicitly, through (3)) the model itself. A third category is $g(\theta) = \chi_{\Theta_0}(\theta)$ which arises when a hypothesis restricts θ to a set Θ_0. (Here $\chi(\cdot)$ is the characteristic function $\chi_s(z) = 1$ if $z \in S$, $\chi_s(z) = 0$ if $z \in S$.) Then $E[g(\theta) \mid \mathbf{Y}_T] = P(\theta \in \Theta_0) \mid \mathbf{Y}_T$. Yet another important category arises from predictive densities, taken up in detail in section 3.

The specification of the model (1) is completed with a *prior density* p(θ). It may be shown that given (1) and a density of p($\mathbf{Y}_T$) (i.e., a density for the data *unconditional* on θ) a prior density must exist; see Bernardo and Smith (1994, section 4.2). It is more direct to place the specification of the prior density on the same logical footing as the specification of (1). Thus a *complete model* specifies

$$P(\theta \in \tilde{\Theta}) = \int_{\tilde{\Theta}} p(\theta) d\theta, \ P(\mathbf{Y}_T \in \tilde{Y} \mid \theta) = \int_{\tilde{y}} \prod_{t=1}^T f_t(\mathbf{y}_t \mid \mathbf{Y}_{t-1}, \theta) d\mathbf{Y}_T \tag{4}$$

where $\tilde{\Theta}$ is any Lebesgue-measurable subset of Θ and $\tilde{Y}$ is any Lebesgue-measurable subset of R^{pT}. (To keep the notation simple, a strictly continuous prior probability distribution for θ is assumed.)

By Bayes' theorem the *posterior density* of θ is

$$p(\theta|\mathbf{Y}_T) = p(\mathbf{Y}_T|\theta)p(\theta)/p(\mathbf{Y}_T)$$
$$\propto p(\mathbf{Y}_T|\theta)p(\theta)$$
$$\propto L(\theta;\mathbf{Y}_T)p(\theta).$$

Thus

$$E[g(\theta)|\mathbf{Y}_T] = \int_{\Theta} g(\theta)p(\theta|\mathbf{Y}_T)d\theta = \frac{\int_{\Theta} g(\theta)L(\theta;\mathbf{Y}_T)p(\theta)d\theta}{\int_{\Theta} L(\theta;\mathbf{Y}_T)p(\theta)d\theta}. \tag{5}$$

In the representation (5), one may substitute for $p(\theta)$ any function $p^*(\theta) \propto p(\theta)$. The function $p^*(\theta)$ is a *kernel* of the prior density $p(\theta)$. Posterior moments in a given model are invariant to any arbitrary scaling of either the likelihood function or the prior density.

2.2   Sufficiency, ancillarity, and nuisance parameters

The vector $\mathbf{s}_T = \mathbf{s}_T(\mathbf{Y}_T)$ is a sufficient statistic in the model (2) given any of the following equivalent conditions

$$p[\mathbf{Y}_T|\mathbf{s}_T(\mathbf{Y}_T), \theta] = p[\mathbf{Y}_T|\mathbf{s}_T(\mathbf{Y}_T)] \forall \theta \epsilon \Theta; \tag{6}$$

$$p(\theta|\mathbf{Y}_T) = p[\theta|\mathbf{s}_T(\mathbf{Y}_T)] \forall \theta \epsilon \Theta \text{ for all realizations } \mathbf{Y}_T \tag{7}$$

$$p(\mathbf{Y}_T|\theta) = h[\mathbf{s}_T(\mathbf{Y}_T), \theta]r(\mathbf{Y}_T) \text{ for some } h(\cdot) \text{ and } r(\cdot). \tag{8}$$

Condition (8), the *Neyman factorization criterion*, is the condition usually verified to demonstrate sufficiency of $\mathbf{s}_T = \mathbf{s}_T(\mathbf{Y}_T)$. Sufficiency implies that one may use the (sometimes much simpler) expression $h[\mathbf{s}_T(\mathbf{Y}_T), \theta]$ in lieu of the likelihood function in (5).

If $\mathbf{s}_T(\mathbf{Y}_T)' = [\mathbf{s}_{1T}(\mathbf{Y}_T)', \mathbf{s}_{2T}(\mathbf{Y}_T)']$ and $p[\mathbf{s}_{1T}(\mathbf{Y}_T)|\theta] = p[\mathbf{s}_{1T}(\mathbf{Y}_T)]$, then $\mathbf{s}_{1T}(\mathbf{Y}_T)$ is *ancillary with respect to* θ. As a consequence, it suffices to use any function proportional to $p[\mathbf{s}_{2T}(\mathbf{Y}_T)|\theta]$ in lieu of the likelihood function in (5).

If $\theta' = (\theta_1', \theta_2')$ and $g(\theta) = g(\theta_1)$ then θ_2 is a *nuisance parameter* for the function of interest $g(\theta)$. A nuisance parameter presents no special problems in (5).

2.3   Point estimation and credible sets

Let the $q \times 1$ vector $\omega \epsilon \Omega$ represent an unknown state of the world: for example, ω could be the parameter vector θ itself, a function of interest $g(\theta)$, or a vector of future values $\mathbf{y}^* = (y_{T+1}, \ldots, y_{T+f})'$. Let $\tilde{\omega} \in \tilde{\Omega} \subseteq \Omega$ represent an estimate of ω. The *Bayes estimate of* ω corresponding to the loss function $L(\tilde{\omega}, \omega)$ is $\hat{\omega} = \arg\min_{\tilde{\omega}} E[L(\tilde{\omega}, \omega)|\mathbf{Y}_T]$. (Clearly, the estimate $\hat{\omega}$ depends on the complete model (4) as well as the loss function $L(\tilde{\omega}, \omega)$. But given the model and loss function, there is no ambiguity about the Bayes estimate.)

Three loss functions are notable for the simplicity of the Bayes estimate $\hat{\omega}$ that they imply:

given *quadratic loss* $L(\tilde{\omega}, \omega) = (\tilde{\omega} - \omega)'\mathbf{Q}(\tilde{\omega} - \omega)$ (where $\mathbf{Q}$ p.d., $\tilde{\omega} \in R^q$), $\hat{\omega}$ = $E(\omega|\mathbf{Y}_T)$;

given *quantile loss* $L(\omega, \tilde{\omega}) = c_1(\tilde{\omega} - \omega)\chi_{(-\infty, \tilde{\omega})}(\omega) + c_2(\omega - \tilde{\omega})\chi_{(\tilde{\omega}, \infty)}(\omega)$ (where $c_1 > 0$, $c_2 > 0$, $q = 1$), $\hat{\omega} = \tilde{\omega} : P(\omega \leq \tilde{\omega}|\mathbf{Y}_T = c_2/(c_1 + c_2))$ and hence if $c_1 = c_2$ the Bayes estimate of ω is the median of its posterior distribution;

given *0/1 loss* $L(\tilde{\omega}, \omega) = 1 - \chi_{N_\varepsilon(\tilde{\omega})}(\omega)$ (where $N_\varepsilon(\tilde{\omega})$ is an ε-neighborhood of $\tilde{\omega}$), as $\varepsilon \to 0$, $\hat{\omega}$ converges to the global mode of $p(\omega|\mathbf{Y}_T)$ if a global mode exists.

All three estimators are derived in most texts in Bayesian statistics, e.g., Berger (1985, section 2.4.2) or Bernardo and Smith (1994, proposition 5.2).

A $100(1 - \alpha)$ percent *credible set for* ω is any set C such that $\int_C p(\omega|\mathbf{Y}_T)d\omega = 1 - \alpha$. The credible set depends on the complete model (4) but is defined without reference to a loss function because it does not involve a Bayes action. In general a credible set can be defined with reference to any distribution for ω, not just the posterior distribution. In most cases (always, for continuous distributions) the credible set is not unique.

If $p(\omega_1|\mathbf{Y}_T) \geq p(\omega_2|\mathbf{Y}_T) \forall (\omega_1, \omega_2) : \omega_1 \in C, \omega_2 \in \Omega - C$, except possibly for a subset of Ω with posterior probability 0, then C is a *highest posterior density (HPD) credible set for* ω. It can be shown that HPD sets provide the credible sets with the smallest Lebesgue measure. Therefore the choice of a HPD set is a Bayes action if loss is proportional to the Lebesgue measure of the credible set.

Since credible sets are defined with respect to a probability measure they are invariant under one-to-one transformations: i.e., if $\nu = h(\omega)$, $h(\cdot)$ is one-to-one, and C is a $100(1 - \alpha)$ percent credible set for ω, then $D = \{\nu : \nu = h(\omega), \omega \in C\}$ is a $100(1 - \alpha)$ percent credible set for ν. However, HPD credible sets are not invariant under transformation. (The technical step involves the Jacobian of transformation. For demonstration and further discussion see Berger (1985, pp. 144–145) or Bernardo and Smith (1994, pp. 261–262).)

2.4   Prior distributions

The complete model (4) provides a representation of belief. The choice of model is always a judicious compromise between realistic richness in form and the effort required to obtain posterior moments $E[g(\theta)|\mathbf{Y}_T]$. To this end, it has proven useful to employ classes of prior densities, $p(\theta|\tau)$ where τ is an indexing parameter, just as it has proven useful to index the conditional density $f_t(\mathbf{y}_t|\mathbf{Y}_{t-1},\theta)$ by θ.

Suppose that $p(\mathbf{Y}_t|\theta), \theta\epsilon\Theta$ has sufficient statistic $\{T, s_T(\mathbf{Y}_T)\}$, where $s_T(\mathbf{Y}_T)$ is a vector whose dimension is independent of T and $\mathbf{Y}_T$. Then the *conjugate family of prior densities for θ with respect to* $p(\mathbf{Y}_T|\theta)$ is

$$\{p(\theta|\tau), \tau\epsilon\mathbf{T}; \tau_0\}$$

where

$$\mathbf{T} = \{\tau.\textstyle\int_\Theta p[s_T(\mathbf{Y}_{\tau_0}) = \tau|\theta]d\theta\} < \infty$$

and

$$p(\theta|\tau) = p[s_T(\mathbf{Y}_{\tau_0}) = \tau|\theta]/\textstyle\int_\Theta p[s_T(\mathbf{Y}_{\tau_0}) = \tau|\theta]d\theta.$$

A conjugate prior distribution for θ is thus proportional to a likelihood function composed of τ_0 observations whose sufficient statistics are given in the vector τ. Less formally, the information about θ in a conjugate prior distribution is equivalent to the information about θ in a likelihood function with τ_0 imaginary observations and sufficient statistic τ.

There is an extensive literature providing conjugate families of prior distributions corresponding to various specifications of $f_t(\mathbf{y}_t|\mathbf{Y}_{t-1},\theta)$. A strong practical reason for this effort is that in the presence of a conjugate prior distribution, the posterior distribution will retain the same mathematical tractability that characterizes $p(\mathbf{Y}_T|\theta)$ and was likely to be an important reason for the choice of $f_t(\mathbf{y}_t|\mathbf{Y}_{t-1},\theta)$ in the first place. For example, in the regular *exponential family of distributions*

$$p(\mathbf{Y}_T|\theta) = [s(\theta)]^T\textstyle\prod_{t=1}^T r(\mathbf{y}_t)\exp\{\sum_{i=1}^m c_i\phi_i(\theta)[\sum_{t=1}^T h_i(\mathbf{y}_t)]\}$$

the conjugate family for θ is

$$p(\theta|\tau) \propto [s(\theta)]^{\tau_0}\exp[\textstyle\sum_{i=1}^m c_i\phi_i(\theta)\tau_i],$$
$$\tau\epsilon\mathbf{T} = \{\tau.\textstyle\int_\Theta [s(\theta)]^{\tau_0}\exp[\sum_{i=1}^m c_i\phi_i(\theta)\tau_i] < \infty\}$$

and then

$$p(\theta|\mathbf{Y}_T) \propto [s(\theta)]^{\tau_0+T}\{\textstyle\sum_{i=1}^m c_i\phi_i(\theta)[\sum_{t=1}^T \tau_i + h_i(\mathbf{y}_t)]\}. \tag{9}$$

If $\theta' = (\theta_1', \theta_2')$ and the value of $\theta_2 = \theta_2^0$ is fixed, then one may define the *conditionally conjugate family of prior densities for θ_1 with respect to* $p(\mathbf{Y}_T|\theta_1, \theta_2^0)$

in precisely the same way. Given purely analytical approaches to Bayesian inference the use of conjugate prior distributions is almost always essential. With the advent of the numerical approaches that are the focus of this chapter conjugate prior distributions are no longer essential, but are often useful as belief representations and can simplify computation. Numerical approaches have rendered Bayesian inference practical in models so complex that conjugate prior distributions do not provide simple belief representations. In these cases, conditionally conjugate priors are often more useful and provide computational advantages, as will be seen in section 3.

The prior distribution, even if it is restricted to a conjugate family, provides a flexible representation of prior beliefs. It is tempting to characterize prior distributions by the extent to which they provide information about parameters. At one extreme, a prior distribution with all its mass at a single point $\theta^* \in \Theta$ is clearly quite informative; such a prior is said to be *dogmatic*, At the other extreme, what (if anything) constitutes an uninformative prior distribution is less clear.

The desire to work with less-informative prior distributions leads to an extension of prior distributions that can be useful if applied carefully. Consider a sequence of prior density *kernels* $p_j^*(\theta)$: i.e., $\int_\Theta p_j^*(\theta)d\theta < \infty$ and the corresponding prior density is $p_j(\theta) = p_j^*(\theta)/\int_\Theta p_j^*(\theta)d\theta$. Suppose further that $\lim_{j\to\infty} p_j(\theta) = 0$ and $\lim_{j\to\infty} p_j^*(\theta) = p^*(\theta) \forall \theta \in \Theta$, but that $\int_\Theta p^*(\theta)d\theta$ is divergent. It is often the case that $\int_\Theta L(\theta; \mathbf{Y}_T)p^*(\theta)d\theta$ and $\int_\Theta g(\theta)L(\theta; \mathbf{Y}_T)p^*(\theta)d\theta$ are convergent and furthermore

$$\lim_{j\to\infty} \frac{\int_\Theta g(\theta)L(\theta;\mathbf{Y}_T)p_j^*(\theta)d\theta}{\int_\Theta L(\theta;\mathbf{Y}_T)p_j^*(\theta)d\theta} = \frac{\int_\Theta g(\theta)L(\theta;\mathbf{Y}_T)p^*(\theta)d\theta}{\int_\Theta L(\theta;\mathbf{Y}_T)p^*(\theta)d\theta}.$$

In this case the formal use of the "prior density" $p^*(\theta)$ has an unambiguous interpretation and provides correct posterior moments. If $p^*(\theta)$ is the limit of kernels of conjugate prior densities then it generally retains the analytical advantages of the conjugate family. For example in the regular exponential family with conjugate priors, if $\tau^{(j)} = (\tau_0^{(j)}, \dots, \tau_m^{(j)}) \xrightarrow{j\to\infty} \mathbf{0}$ then the limiting posterior distribution is given by (9) with $\tau_i = 0 (i = 0, \dots, m)$. Formal analysis with $p^*(\theta) = 1$ would have led to the same result.

2.5 Model averaging

Typically one has under consideration several complete models of the form (4). For specificity suppose there are J models, and distinguish model M_j by the subscript "j"

$$P_j(\theta_j \in \tilde{\Theta}_j) = \int_{\tilde{\Theta}_j} p_j(\theta_j)d\theta_j, \ P_j(\mathbf{Y}_T \in \tilde{Y} \mid \theta_j) = \int_{\tilde{y}} \prod_{t=1}^T f_{jt}(\mathbf{y}_t \mid \mathbf{Y}_{t-1}, \theta)d\mathbf{Y}_T.$$

The J models are related by their description of a common set of observations $\mathbf{Y}_T$ and a common vector of interest ω. The number of parameters in the models may or may not be the same and various models may or may not nest one another. The vector of interest ω – e.g., the outcome of a change in policy, or actual future values of $\mathbf{y}_t$ – is substantively the same in all models although its representation in terms of θ_j may vary greatly from one model to another. Each model specifies its conditional p.d.f. for ω, $p_j(\omega|\theta_j, \mathbf{Y}_T)$. The specification of the collection of J models is completed with the prior probabilities $p_j(j=1,\dots,J)$, $\Sigma_{j=1}^{J} p_j = 1$.

There are now three levels of conditioning. Given model j and θ_j, the p.d.f. of $\mathbf{Y}_T$ is $p_j(\mathbf{Y}_T|\theta_j)$. Given only model j, the p.d.f. of θ_j is $p_j(\theta_j)$. And given the collection of models $M_1, \dots M_J$ the probability of model j is p_j. If the collection of models changes then the p_j will change in accordance with the laws of conditional probability. There is no essential conceptual distinction between model and prior: one could just as well regard the entire collection as the model, with $\{p_j, p_j(\theta_j)\}_{j=1}^{J}$ as the characterization of the prior distribution. At an operational level the distinction is usually quite clear and useful: one may undertake the essential computations one model at a time.

Suppose that the posterior moment $E[h(\omega)|\mathbf{Y}_T]$ is ultimately of interest. (This expression is just as general as (3) and encompasses the particular cases discussed there.) The formal solution is

$$E[h(\omega)|\mathbf{Y}_T] = \Sigma_{j=1}^{J} E[h(\omega)|\mathbf{Y}_T, M_j] P(M_j|\mathbf{Y}_T). \tag{10}$$

From (5),

$$E[h(\omega)|\mathbf{Y}_T, M_j] = \frac{\int_{\Theta_j} g(\theta_j) L_j(\theta_j; \mathbf{Y}_T) p_j(\theta_j) d\theta_j}{\int_{\Theta_j} L_j(\theta_j; \mathbf{Y}_T) p_j(\theta_j) d\theta_j} \tag{11}$$

with $g(\theta_j) = \int_\omega h(\omega) p_j(\omega|\theta_j, \mathbf{Y}_T) d\omega$. There is nothing new in this part of (10). From Bayes' rule

$$P(M_j|\mathbf{Y}_T) = p(\mathbf{Y}_T|M_j) P(M_j)/p(\mathbf{Y}_T)$$

$$= p_j \int_{\Theta_j} p_j(\mathbf{Y}_T|\theta_j) p_j(\theta_j) d\theta_j / p(\mathbf{Y}_T)$$

$$\propto p_j \int_{\Theta_j} p_j(\mathbf{Y}_T|\theta_j) p_j(\theta_j) d\theta_j = p_j M_{jT}. \tag{12}$$

The value M_{jT} is known as the *marginalized likelihood* of model j. The name reflects the fact that one can write

$$M_{jT} = \int_{\Theta_j} L_j(\theta_j; \mathbf{Y}_T) p_j(\theta_j) d\theta_j. \tag{13}$$

Expression (13) must be treated with caution, because the likelihood function typically introduces convenient, model-specific proportionality constants: $\int_{\hat{\mathbf{Y}}} p_j(\mathbf{Z}_T|\theta_j) d\mathbf{Z}_T = 1$ but $\int_{\hat{\mathbf{Y}}} L_j(\theta_j; \mathbf{Z}_T) d\mathbf{Z}_T \neq 1$. Whereas (11), like

(5), is invariant to arbitrary renormalizations of $p_j(\mathbf{Y}_T | \theta_j)$ and $p_j(\theta_j)$, (12) is valid only with the conditional p.d.f.s themselves, not their kernels. As a simple corollary, model averaging cannot be undertaken using improper prior distributions, a point related to Lindley's paradox described below.

Model averaging thus involves three steps. First, obtain the posterior moments (11) corresponding to each model. Second, obtain the marginalized likelihood M_{jT} from (12). Finally, obtain the posterior moment using (10) which now only involves simple arithmetic. Variation of the prior model probabilities p_j is a trivial step, as is the revision of the posterior moment following the introduction of a new model or deletion of an old one from the conditioning set of models, if (11) and (13) for those models are known.

2.6   Hypothesis testing

Formally, *hypothesis testing* is the problem of choosing one model from several. With no real loss of generality assume there are only two models in the choice set. Treating model choice as a Bayes action, let $L(i|j)$ denote the loss incurred in choosing model i when model j is true and suppose that $L(i|i) = 0$ and $L(i|j) > 0$ $(j \neq i)$. Given the data $\mathbf{Y}_T$ the expected loss from choosing model i is $P(M_j | \mathbf{Y}_T) L(i|j)$ $(j \neq i)$ and so the Bayes action is to choose model 1 if and only if

$$\frac{P(M_1 | \mathbf{Y}_T)}{P(M_2 | \mathbf{Y}_T)} = \frac{p_1 M_{1T}}{p_2 M_{2T}} > \frac{L(1|2)}{L(2|1)}.$$

The value $L(1|2)/L(2|1)$ is known as the *Bayes critical value*. The data bear on model choice only through the ratio M_{1T}/M_{2T}, known as the *Bayes factor* in favor of model 1. The term $p_1 M_{1T}/p_2 M_{2T}$ is the *posterior odds ratio* in favor of model 1. For reasons of economy an investigator may therefore report only the marginalized likelihood, leaving it to his or her *clients* – i.e., the users of the investigator's research – to provide their own prior model probabilities and loss functions. The steps of reporting marginalized likelihoods and Bayes factors are sometimes called hypothesis testing as well.

It is instructive to consider briefly the choice between two models given a sequence of prior distributions $p_{1j}(\theta_1)$ in model 1 in which $\lim_{j \to \infty} p_{1j}(\theta_1) = 0 \,\forall\, \theta_1 \in \Theta_1$. It was seen in section 2.4 that the limiting posterior moment in model 1 can be well defined in this case, and that it may be found conveniently using a corresponding sequence of convergent prior density kernels. The condition $\lim_{j \to \infty} p_{1j}(\theta_1) = 0 \,\forall\, \theta_1 \in \Theta_1$ ensures $\lim_{j \to \infty} M_{jT} = 0$, however. Therefore, if the prior distribution in model 1 is improper whereas that in model 2 is proper, the hypothesis test cannot conclude in favor of model 1.

This result is widely known as *Lindley's paradox*, after Lindley (1957) and Bartlett (1957).

As will be seen, the computation of marginalized likelihoods has been a substantial technical challenge. The reason is that in general M_{jT} cannot be cast as a special case of (5). In specific settings, however, (5) may be used to express Bayes factors. A common one is that in which models 1 and 2 have a common likelihood function and differ only in their prior densities $p_j(\theta)$. Then the Bayes factor in favor of model 1 is

$$\frac{M_{1T}}{M_{2T}} = \frac{\int_\Theta g(\theta)L(\theta;\mathbf{Y}_T)p_2(\theta)d\theta}{\int_\Theta L(\theta;\mathbf{Y}_T)p_2(\theta)d\theta} \tag{14}$$

with

$$g(\theta) = p_1(\theta)/p_2(\theta). \tag{15}$$

2.7   *Hierarchical priors and latent variable models*

A *hierarchical prior distribution* expresses the prior in two or more steps. The two-step case specifies a model

$$p_A(\mathbf{Y}_T|\theta,\psi)(\theta\epsilon\Theta,\psi\epsilon\Psi) \tag{16}$$

and a prior density for θ conditional on a *hyperparameter* ϕ

$$p_B(\theta|\phi)(\phi\epsilon\Phi). \tag{17}$$

The model is completed with a prior density for ϕ and ψ

$$p_C(\phi,\psi). \tag{18}$$

The full prior density for all parameters and hyperparameters is

$$p(\theta,\phi,\psi) = p_C(\phi,\psi)p_B(\theta|\phi). \tag{19}$$

There is no fundamental difference between this prior density and the one described in section 2.4, since

$$p(\theta,\psi) = \int_\Phi p_B(\theta|\phi)p_C(\phi,\psi)d\phi.$$

As will be seen, however, the hierarchical formulation is often so convenient as to render fairly simple problems that otherwise would be essentially impossible. Given a hierarchical prior, one may express the full posterior density

$$p(\theta,\psi,\phi|\mathbf{Y}_T)\propto p_A(\mathbf{Y}_T|\theta,\psi)p_B(\theta|\phi)p_C(\phi,\psi). \tag{20}$$

A *latent variable model* expresses the likelihood function in two or more steps. In the two-step case the likelihood function may be written

$$p_A(\mathbf{Y}_T \mid \mathbf{Z}_T^*, \psi)(\mathbf{Z}_T^* \epsilon \tilde{\mathbf{Z}}, \psi \epsilon \Psi) \tag{21}$$

where $\mathbf{Z}_T^*$ is a matrix of latent variables. The model for $\mathbf{Z}_T^*$ is

$$p_B(\mathbf{Z}_T^* \mid \phi)(\phi \epsilon \Phi) \tag{22}$$

and the prior density for ϕ and ψ is

$$p_C(\phi, \psi). \tag{23}$$

The full prior density for all parameters and unobservable variables is

$$p(\mathbf{Z}_T^*, \psi, \phi) \propto p_A(\mathbf{Y}_T \mid \mathbf{Z}_T^*, \psi) p_B(\mathbf{Z}_T^* \mid \phi) p_C(\phi, \psi) \tag{24}$$

and the full posterior density is

$$p(\mathbf{Z}_T^*, \psi, \phi \mid \mathbf{Y}_T) \propto p_A(\mathbf{Y}_T \mid \mathbf{Z}_T^*, \psi) p_B(\mathbf{Z}_T^* \mid \phi) p_C(\phi, \psi). \tag{25}$$

Comparing (16)–(20) with (21)–(25), it is apparent that the latent variable model is formally identical to a model with a two-stage hierarchical prior: the latent variables correspond to the intermediate level of the hierarchy. With appropriate marginalization of (25) one may obtain $p(\mathbf{Z}_T^* \mid \mathbf{Y}_T)$, which fully reflects uncertainty about the parameters. If one is interested only in ψ, or in ψ and ϕ, these distributions may also be obtained by marginalization of (25). In the latter case the matrix of latent variables $\mathbf{Z}_T^*$ is a group of nuisance parameters, which are treated here as described in section 2.2. Marginalization requires integration, which is generally impossible analytically. If the problem is approached using simulation methods, then marginalization simply amounts to discarding the nuisance parameters.

The duality between the hierarchical prior and latent variable models often suggests formulations that decompose more complex problems into simpler ones. For example

$$y_t \sim t(0, \sigma^2; \nu)$$

is formally equivalent to the latent variable model

$$y_t = \omega_t \varepsilon_t$$

with ω_t a latent variable $\nu / \omega_t^2 \sim \chi^2(\nu)$, and $\varepsilon_t \sim N(0, 1)$ independent of ω_t. The equivalent hierarchical prior formulation is the p.d.f. specification

$$y_t \mid (\omega_t, \sigma^2) \sim N(0, \sigma^2 \omega_t)$$

and the conditional prior distribution

$$\nu / \omega_t^2 \sim \chi^2(\nu).$$

3   Bayesian investigation and communication

The elements of the formal problem addressed by a Bayesian investigator are summarized in section 2.5, which provides the point of departure here. The essentials include a collection of complete models ($j = 1, \ldots, J$), each of which describes the joint distribution of observed data $\mathbf{Y}_T$ and vector of interest ω, conditional on a vector of parameters θ_j

$$p_j(\mathbf{Y}_T, \omega \mid \theta_j) = p_j(\omega \mid \mathbf{Y}_T, \theta_j) p_j(\mathbf{Y}_T \mid \theta_j).$$

Each model is completed with the specification of the prior density $p_j(\theta_j)$ for its parameters, and the collection is completed with the prior model probabilities $p_j(j = 1, \ldots, J)$. Within each model, $p_j(\mathbf{Y}_T \mid \theta_j) = \prod_{t=1}^{T} f_{jt}(\mathbf{y}_t \mid \mathbf{Y}_{t-1}, \theta_j)$. Section 3.1 describes some insights into model comparison, predictive densities, and forecasting that arise from this elementary relation.

Since it is required only to specify $p_j(\omega \mid \mathbf{Y}_T, \theta_j)$, the vector of interest ω is quite general. For example, it may consist of some future data, $\omega = (\mathbf{y}_{T+1}, \ldots, \mathbf{y}_{T+f})$. In this case

$$p_j(\omega \mid \mathbf{Y}_T, \theta_j) = \prod_{t=1}^{T+f} f_{jt}(\mathbf{y}_t \mid \mathbf{Y}_{t-1}, \theta_j) / \prod_{t=1}^{T} f_{jt}(\mathbf{y}_t \mid \mathbf{Y}_{t-1}, \theta_j).$$

Closed-form expressions may or may not be readily computed, but it is essentially always the case that simulations from $p_j(\omega \mid \mathbf{Y}_T, \theta_j)$ can be carried out in straightforward fashion, and as will be seen this is typically all that is required. In other cases ω may be a vector of latent variables, and then greater ingenuity may be required to simulate from $p_j(\omega \mid \mathbf{Y}_T, \theta_j)$: the problem is one of signal extraction, which for many models has been thoroughly investigated.

In a *closed investigation* all of the elements of this problem are completely specified, including models, priors, and vectors of interest. The closed investigation is completed with the specification of a reporting objective in the form of a mapping from the distribution $\omega \mid \mathbf{Y}_T$ to a real number, $R[p(\omega \mid \mathbf{Y}_T)]$. Very often this mapping may be expressed as $E[h(\omega) \mid \mathbf{Y}_T]$, for a known function $h(\omega)$. Examples include minimum mean square error forecasting, probabilities of turning points, and the evaluation of relative loss for alternative decisions. In other instances quantiles of the distribution are required, as in minimum absolute error forecasting or the reporting of an interquartile range. For simplicity of notation we proceed as if the problem is always of the form $E[h(\omega) \mid \mathbf{Y}_T]$.

Section 3.2 takes up the common elements of forecasting and signal extraction problems in a closed investigation with a single model. Their solution is general, simple and elegant – especially in comparison with non-Bayesian methods. Section 3.3 takes up the question of why this is so.

In a closed investigation with multiple models the investigator requires

$$p(\omega | \mathbf{Y}_T) = \Sigma_{j=1}^{J} P(M_j | \mathbf{Y}_T) p_j(\omega | \mathbf{Y}_T).$$

The essential incremental task is the evaluation of the marginalized likelihood, as explained in section 2.5. Some methods of evaluating the marginalized likelihood are taken up in section 3.4.

The closed investigation has two distinguishing features. First, the ultimate consumer – who, following Hildreth (1963) may be called the *client* – has provided a complete formal specification of the problem. Second, the investigator's report $E[h(\omega) | \mathbf{Y}_T]$ is formally useless if any aspect of the problem specification is changed, and typically is not then very useful in an informal way either. In an *open investigation* the investigator is missing one or more elements of the problem specification: for example, the investigator may not know the client's priors or vectors of interest, and may not know all of the models the client entertains and their associated prior probabilities. This situation is much more typical of the conditions under which investigations are carried out. Given the methods set forth in this chapter the investigator can in fact do a great deal in this situation, as described in section 3.5.

3.1 The predictive decomposition

Suppose that $\mathbf{Y}_u = \{y_s\}_{s=1}^{u}$ is available, and a single model has been completely specified. Then the *predictive density* for observations $u+1$ through t is

$$p(y_{u+1}, \ldots, y_t | \mathbf{Y}_u) = \int_{\Theta} p(\theta | \mathbf{Y}_u) \prod_{s=u+1}^{t} f_s(\mathbf{y}_s | \mathbf{Y}_{s-1}, \theta) d\theta, \qquad (26)$$

where

$$p(\theta | \mathbf{Y}_t) = p(\theta) \prod_{s=1}^{u} f_s(\mathbf{y}_s | \mathbf{Y}_{s-1}, \theta) / \int_{\Theta} \prod_{s=1}^{u} f_s(\mathbf{y}_s | \mathbf{Y}_{s-1}, \theta) d\theta. \qquad (27)$$

In this expression $(y_{u+1}, \ldots, y_t)$ is a random vector; the practical mechanics of working with its distribution are taken up in section 3.2.

Once the observations $y_{u+1}, \ldots, y_t$ are known, the *predictive likelihood* for observations $u+1$ through t is

$$\hat{p}_u^t \equiv \int_{\Theta} p(\theta | \mathbf{Y}_u) \prod_{s=u+1}^{t} f_s(\mathbf{y}_s | \mathbf{Y}_{s-1}, \theta) d\theta. \qquad (28)$$

The right-hand sides of expressions (26) and (28) are only formally identical: $(y_{u+1}, \ldots, y_t)'$ is a random vector in the former, and is fixed in the latter. the predictive likelihood is the probability density assigned to the observed $(y_{u+1}, \ldots, y_t)'$ by the posterior based on observations $1, \ldots, u$. It is a measure of the out-of-sample forecasting performance of the model – one that fully accounts for parameter uncertainty.

Since $\mathbf{Y}_0 = \{\varnothing\}$, the marginalized likelihood is

$$\hat{p}_0^T = \int_\Theta p(\theta) \prod_{s=1}^T f_s(\mathbf{y}_s | \mathbf{Y}_{s-1}, \theta) d\theta = M_T.$$

Substituting (27) in (26)

$$\hat{p}_u^t = \int_\Theta \left\{ \frac{p(\theta) \prod_{s=1}^u f_s(\mathbf{y}_s | \mathbf{Y}_{s-1}, \theta)}{\int_\Theta p(\theta) \prod_{s=1}^u f_s(\mathbf{y}_s | \mathbf{Y}_{s-1}, \theta) d\theta} \right\} \prod_{s=u+1}^t f_s(\mathbf{y}_s | \mathbf{Y}_{s-1}, \theta) d\theta$$

$$= \frac{\int_\Theta p(\theta) \prod_{s=1}^t f_s(\mathbf{y}_s | \mathbf{Y}_{s-1}, \theta) d\theta}{\int_\Theta p(\theta) \prod_{s=1}^u f_s(\mathbf{y}_s | \mathbf{Y}_{s-1}, \theta) d\theta_j} = \frac{M_t}{M_u}.$$

Hence for any $0 \le u = s_0 < s_1 < \ldots < s_q = t$

$$\hat{p}_u^t = \frac{M_{s_1}}{M_{s_0}} \cdot \frac{M_{s_2}}{M_{s_1}} \cdots \frac{M_{s_q}}{M_{s_{q-1}}} = \prod_{\tau=1}^q \hat{p}_{s_{\tau-1}}^{s_\tau}. \tag{29}$$

This decomposition has several significant implications for time series analysis.

First, specific choices of the s_τ yield

$$M_T = \hat{p}_0^T = \prod_{s=1}^T \hat{p}_{s-1}^s = \prod_{s=1}^{T/r} \hat{p}_{r(s-1)}^{rs} \tag{30}$$

where T is an integer multiple of r. This identity links the model marginalized likelihood with its out-of-sample forecasting record as embodied in the predictive likelihood. Recall that the data bear on model choice only through the marginalized likelihood (section 2.6). Therefore, (30) provides a well-defined sense in which model choice is equivalent to the comparison of out-of-sample forecast performance. In a symmetric model choice problem (balanced loss function and equal prior probabilities) the chosen model will be the one with the best out-of-sample forecasting record as indicated by the right-hand side of (30). The forecasting record can be stated in terms of all one step ahead forecasts, or in terms of non-overlapping forecasts of r successive realizations. It cannot be expressed only in terms of r step ahead forecasts. This accords well with the common experience in time series analysis, that preferred models provide superior one step ahead forecasts, but not necessarily superior r step ahead forecasts for $r > 1$.

The decomposition (28) also provides a general method of computing M_T. If M_T is cast directly in the form of (3)

$$M_T = E[g(\theta) | \mathbf{Y}_0] = \int_\Theta p(\theta) g(\theta) d\theta, \quad g(\theta) = \prod_{s=1}^T f_s(y_s | \mathbf{Y}_{s-1}, \theta),$$

the result is not useful for computation: the prior distribution is typically much more diffuse than the likelihood function $\prod_{s=1}^T f_s(y_s | \mathbf{Y}_{s-1}, \theta)$, so that draws from the prior are very inefficient, being almost always far removed from the main support of the likelihood function. On the other hand, since

$$\hat{p}_u^t = \mathrm{E}[g(\theta) \,|\, \mathbf{Y}_u] = \int_\Theta \mathrm{p}(\theta \,|\, \mathbf{Y}_u) g(\theta) d\theta, \; g(\theta) = \prod_{s=u+1}^t f_s(y_s \,|\, \mathbf{Y}_{s-1}, \theta)$$

a simulation method may provide a computationally efficient approximation of $\hat{p}_u^t$. Then, one may appeal to (30) to approximate M_T (for further details see Geweke (1994)).

A third use of the decomposition is a reporting. For all $v : u \le v < t$

$$\hat{p}_v^T = \frac{M_t}{M_v} = \frac{M_t/M_u}{M_v/M_u} = \frac{\hat{p}_u^t}{\hat{p}_u^v}.$$

Consequently a plot of $\log(\hat{p}_u^s)$ for $s = u+1, \dots, t$ is visually revealing of predictive likelihood for all subintervals.

The decomposition also provides a useful diagnostic in the comparison of models. Introduce an additional subscript "j" or "k" to denote alternative models and define the predictive Bayes factor $\hat{B}_{j|k,u}^t = \hat{p}_{ju}^t / \hat{p}_{ku}^t$; $\hat{B}_{j|k,0}^t = \hat{p}_{j0}^t / \hat{p}_{k0}^t = M_{jT} / M_{kT}$ is the Bayes factor defined in section 2.6. From (30)

$$\hat{B}_{j|k,u}^t = \hat{p}_{ju}^t / \hat{p}_{ku}^t = \prod_{\tau=1}^q \hat{p}_{js_{\tau-1}}^{s_\tau} / \prod_{\tau=1}^q \hat{p}_{ks_{\tau-1}}^{s_\tau} = \prod_{\tau=1}^q \hat{B}_{j|k,s_{\tau-1}}^{s_\tau}.$$

By considering characteristics of observations for which $\hat{B}_{j|k,s_{\tau-1}}^{s_\tau}$ is relatively larger or smaller, it is often possible to get a deeper understanding of model suitability and new models may be suggested.

3.2   *Forecasting and signal extraction*

The general forecasting and signal extraction problem can be stated as follows. Given a data set $\mathbf{Y}_T$ and a collection of models $M_j (j = 1, \dots, J)$, corresponding to each model j there is a parameter vector θ_j, a data density $\mathrm{p}(\cdot \,|\, \theta_j)$, a prior density $\mathrm{p}(\theta_j)$, and a prior model probably p_j. There is also a common vector of interest $\omega \in \Omega$, and for each model a specified density $\mathrm{p}_j(\omega \,|\, \theta_j, \mathbf{Y}_T)$, The problem is to choose a Bayes action $\mathbf{a} \in A$ to minimize

$$\mathrm{E}[C(\omega, \mathbf{a}) \,|\, \mathbf{Y}_T] = \int_\Omega C(\omega, \mathbf{a}) \mathrm{p}(\omega \,|\, \mathbf{Y}_T) d\omega$$

$$= \int_\Omega C(\omega, \mathbf{a}) \sum_{j=1}^J [\int_\Theta \mathrm{p}_j(\omega \,|\, \theta_j, \mathbf{Y}_T) \mathrm{p}_j(\theta_j \,|\, \mathbf{Y}_T) d\theta_j] \mathrm{P}(M_j \,|\, \mathbf{Y}_T) d\omega$$

where C is a loss (or "cost") function, $\mathrm{P}(M_j \,|\, \mathbf{Y}_T)$ is given by (12), and $\mathrm{p}_j(\theta_j \,|\, \mathbf{Y}_T)$ is given by Bayes theorem for each model.

In many instances the solution of the minimization problem can be expressed $\mathrm{E}[h(\omega) \,|\, \mathbf{Y}_T]$ for a known function $h(\cdot)$: the leading example is quadratic loss, discussed in section 2.3. if $g(\theta) = \int_\Omega h(\omega) \mathrm{p}(\omega \,|\, \mathbf{Y}_T.\theta) d\omega$ can be evaluated in closed form, then the forecasting and signal extraction problem is a special case of the problem set forth in section 2.1, to which the simulation methods (Geweke (1996a)) are directly addressed. This is rarely the case.

In most instances, however, simulation methods can be adapted to the approximation of $E[h(\omega)|\mathbf{Y}_T.]$ through an auxiliary simulation. To cast this method as a special case of the general treatment in Geweke (1996a), let $\tilde{\theta}' = (\omega', \theta')$, $\tilde{\theta} \epsilon \tilde{\Theta} = \Omega \times \Theta$, and $g(\tilde{\theta}) = h(\omega)$. Then

$$E[h(\omega)|\mathbf{Y}_T] = \int_{\tilde{\Theta}} g(\tilde{\theta}) p(\tilde{\theta}|\mathbf{Y}_T) d\tilde{\theta}.$$

To draw from $p(\tilde{\theta}|\mathbf{Y}_T)$, first draw θ using an appropriate simulator, and then draw ω from $p(\omega|\theta, \mathbf{Y}_T)$. The second step is generally easy: in forecasting, it amounts to simulation of the model with known parameter values; in signal extraction, it typically involves the appropriate conditional distribution, again with known parameter values. If the convergence conditions of (Geweke (1996a)) are satisfied, and if $E[h(\omega)|\mathbf{Y}_T]$ exists, then

$$\sum_{m=1}^{M} w(\theta_m) h(\omega_m) / \sum_{m=1}^{M} w(\theta_m) \rightarrow E[h(\omega)|\mathbf{Y}_T]$$

where $w(\theta_m)$ is associated with draw m from $p(\theta|\mathbf{Y}_T)$, and $\omega_m \sim p(\omega|\theta_m, \mathbf{Y}_T)$.

The class of forecasting and signal extraction problems that lead to the approximation of posterior moments of ω is interesting but not exhaustive. It includes minimum mean square error forecasting and signal extraction, taking one of a finite number of Bayes actions, and interval forecasting of the form $P(\omega \epsilon \Omega^*|\mathbf{Y}_T)$. However, solutions of quantile of 0/1 loss forecasting or signal extraction problems, and the formation of credible sets, cannot be expressed as posterior moments.

The set of forecasting and signal extraction problems that can be solved using posterior simulation methods can be widened to include most continuous loss functions using some results of Shao (1989). Shao obtained results for importance sampling algorithms. It is reasonable to conjecture that his results extend to MCMC methods, but this has not yet been shown, to the author's knowledge. Let $r(\mathbf{a}) = \int_{\Omega} C(\omega, \mathbf{a}) p(\omega|\mathbf{Y}_T) d\omega$ denote expected loss corresponding to action $\mathbf{a}$, and let $\mathbf{a}^* = \arg\min r(\mathbf{a})$ denote the (possibly set-valued) solution. Correspondingly from the posterior simulator denote

$$r_m(\mathbf{a}) = \sum_{m=1}^{M} C(\omega_m, \mathbf{a}) w(\theta_m) / \sum_{m=1}^{M} w(\theta_m)$$

and $\mathbf{a}_m = \underset{\mathbf{a} \epsilon A}{\arg\min} \, r_m(\mathbf{a})$. Shao (1989) sets forth two sets of conditions under which

$$r(\mathbf{a}_m) \rightarrow r(\mathbf{a}^*), \, r_m(\mathbf{a}_m) \rightarrow r(\mathbf{a}^*), \text{ and } \mathbf{a}_m \rightarrow \mathbf{a}^* \text{ if } \mathbf{a}^* \text{ is unique.}$$

Optimal action convergence conditions 1
(1) The action space A is compact.
(2) The loss function $C(\omega, \mathbf{a})$ is continuous in $\mathbf{a}$ for all $\omega \epsilon \Omega$.
(3) There exists a measurable function $M(\omega)$ with the properties $\underset{\mathbf{a} \epsilon A}{\sup} C(\omega, \mathbf{a}) \leq M(\omega)$ and $\int_{\Omega} M(\omega) p(\omega|\mathbf{Y}_T) d\omega < \infty$.

Optimal action convergence conditions 2

(1) A is convex and $C(\omega,\mathbf{a})$ is a convex continuous function of $\mathbf{a}$ for all $\omega \in \Omega$.

(2) For all $\mathbf{a} \in A$, $r(\mathbf{a}) < \infty$, and there exists $\mathbf{a}^* : r(\mathbf{a}^*) = \min_{\mathbf{a} \in A} r(\mathbf{a})$.

(3) Let A' denote the closure of A and $B(c) = \{\mathbf{a} \in A' : \|\mathbf{a} - \mathbf{a}^*\| = c\}$; there is non-empty $B(c)$ such that $\inf_{\mathbf{a} \in B(c)} r(\mathbf{a}) > r(\mathbf{a}^*)$.

(4) Let $N(c) = \{\mathbf{a} \in A' : \|\mathbf{a} - \mathbf{a}^*\| \leq c\}$; there exists a measurable function $M(\omega)$ such that $\sup_{\mathbf{a} \in N(c)} C(\omega,\mathbf{a}) \leq M(\omega)$ and $\int_{\Omega} M(\omega) p(\omega | \mathbf{Y}_T) d\omega < \infty$.

The second set of conditions admits the quantile loss function. A consequent corollary is that quantiles can be approximated consistently based on posterior simulator output. If the loss function is twice differentiable and it is convenient to evaluate $\partial r_m / \partial \mathbf{a}$ and $\partial^2 r_m / \partial \mathbf{a} \partial \mathbf{a}'$, then $\mathbf{a}_m$ can be computed by standard optimization algorithms, subject to the usual caveats about the local shape of the objective function.

3.3   Bayesian and non-Bayesian approaches

In the classical non-Bayesian approach to forecasting and signal extraction an action $\mathbf{a} = \mathbf{a}(\mathbf{Y}_T)$ is taken to minimize

$$E[C(\omega, \mathbf{a}) | \theta] = E\{C[\omega(\mathbf{Y}_T), \mathbf{a}(\mathbf{Y}_T)] | \theta\}. \tag{31}$$

In (31) $\mathbf{Y}_T$ is a set of random vectors whose distribution is indicated by the data density (2) and an assumed parameter vector θ. (If more than one model is being considered then the conditioning set includes one particular model as well as the parameter vector.) In the classical approach the action $\mathbf{a}(\mathbf{Y}_T)$ minimizes loss on average *over all realizations conditional on a specified model*. In the Bayesian approach the action minimizes loss on average *over all model specifications under consideration conditional on the observed data*. This contrast between *ex ante* and *ex post* approaches is the philosophical heart of the contrast between Bayesian and non-Bayesian methods; e.g., see Berger and Wolpert (1988) and Poirier (1988, 1995).

There are two hurdles that must be overcome in implementing the classical approach to forecasting and signal extraction. Each has spawned a substantial literature.

The first hurdle consists of the technical problems inherent in the minimization of the expression (31) as stated, i.e., assuming a value for θ. A seminal contribution is Granger (1969), which obtains analytical results for multistep ahead forecasts of Gaussian processes. Recent extensions of Granger's approach include Weiss and Anderson (1984) and Weiss (1991) for model selection and estimation, Diebold and Mariano (1995) for forecast evaluation, and Christoffersen and Diebold (1997) for conditional heteroskedasticity.

The latter paper proposes a numerical approach to multistep ahead forecasting,

$$a = \hat{y}_{T+h} = G(\mu_{T+h|T}, \sigma^2_{T+h|T})$$

where $\mu_{T+h|T}$ and $\sigma^2_{T+h|T}$ are the first two conditional moments and G is twice continuously differentiable. A second-order Taylor series approximation to G leads to an expression with six unknown coefficients, which are determined by means of a long simulation of $\{y_t\}$ and evaluation of the loss function. This approach requires three levels of approximation: limitation of the conditional distribution to its first two moments; a quadratic approximation to the unknown function of these moments; and the simulation error in approximating the quadratic function. In addition, $\mu_{T+h|T}$ and $\sigma^2_{T+h|T}$ must be determined analytically.

Clearly the approach of Christoffersen and Diebold (1997) can be extended to overcome all of these difficulties except simulation noise (which can be made arbitrarily small with sufficient computing). Since the forecast a is an unknown function of $\{y_{t-s}, s \geq 0\}$, the entire literature on non-parametric minimization provides a good approach. (For technical essentials see Amemiya (1985), and for an application whose essentials are similar to what is being proposed here see Smith (1991).) Thus, the first hurdle in implementing the classical approach to forecasting and signal extraction is entirely technical.

The second hurdle arises from the fact that θ is not, in fact, known. This difficulty is fundamental, not merely technical, for the minimization of (31) is conditional on fixed θ. In all but a handful of trivial problems – e.g., one-step ahead best linear unbiased forecast in a Gaussian first-order autoregression – the unknown parameter vector θ remains in the solution. As a practical matter, θ can be replaced by an estimator $\hat{\theta}$ with desirable asymptotic properties, but good results typically require modification based on an expansion of the distribution and the loss function at hand.

To highlight the fact that the conditioning on θ is the fundamental difficulty, consider the modification of the classical problem (31) in which **a** minimizes $E[C(\omega, \mathbf{a}) | \theta, \mathbf{Y}_T]$. In this problem the first technical hurdle vanishes. Conditional on the data set $\mathbf{Y}_T$, it is no longer necessary to determine the full mapping from all possible $\mathbf{Y}_T$ to the optimal a. Simulation of ω conditional on θ and $\mathbf{Y}_T$ can be employed to find a satisfactory numerical approximation of a, directly. The problem of uncertainty about θ – the second hurdle – still remains.

The technical difficulties in the classical approach to forecasting and signal extraction reflect the conditioning on a true model, and the minimization of loss averaged over all possible realizations. Problems arise because this conditioning does not reflect the information the investigator brings to the situation. The Bayesian approach conditions on the data in hand, and loss is minimized conditional on all models under consideration and the corresponding possible values of the signal or future data ω. This reflects the investigator's situation, and simulation methods provide the direct solution of the problem.

3.4   Model averaging

Posterior odds ratios are the basis of model averaging, which via (10) is fundamental to forecasting and signal extraction when more than one model is under consideration. The essential technical task in model comparison is obtaining the marginalized likelihood M_{jT} defined in (12). In describing how the marginalized likelihood can be obtained using a posterior simulator it is convenient to drop the subscript j denoting the model. For reasons discussed in section 2.5 it is essential to distinguish between probability distribution functions and their kernels in the marginalized likelihood. In what follows, $p(\theta)$ always denotes the properly normalized prior density and $p(\mathbf{Y}_T | \theta)$ the properly normalized data density.

There are three conditions that a good approach to the computation of the marginalized likelihood M_T should satisfy.

(1) Given a large number of models it is much easier to summarize the comparative evidence through the marginalized likelihood than through pairwise Bayes factors. Therefore, the approach should provide a simulation-consistent approximation of M_T alone, rather than the Bayes factor comparing two models. For example, it is sometimes easy to compute a Bayes factor using (14) and (15), but that does not meet this criterion.

(2) The development of a posterior simulator, its execution, and the organization of simulator output all require real resources. Therefore, the numerical approximation of M_T should require only the original simulator output and not any additional, auxiliary simulations.

(3) Accurate approximations are always desirable. The accuracy of the approximation of M_T should be of the same order as the approximation of posterior moments in the model. Ideally, it should be convenient to assess numerical accuracy using a central limit theorem.

For posterior simulators based on independence sampling it is generally straightforward to satisfy all three criteria. In the case of importance sampling let $j(\theta)$ denote the p.d.f. of the importance sampling distribution, not merely the kernel. Since importance sampling distributions are chosen in part with regard to the convenience of generating draws from them, their normalizing constants are generally known. So long as the support of the importance sampling distribution includes the support of the posterior distribution

$$\hat{M}_T^{(M)} = M^{-1}\sum_{m=1}^M p(\theta_m)p(\mathbf{Y}_T|\theta_m)/j(\theta_m) = M^{-1}\sum_{m=1}^M w(\theta_m)$$
$$\to \int_\Theta p(\theta)p(\mathbf{Y}_T|\theta)d\theta = M_T. \tag{32}$$

From Geweke (1989b), if

$$\int_\Theta [p(\theta)^2 p(\mathbf{Y}_T|\theta)^2/j(\theta)]d\theta = \int_\Theta w(\theta)^2 j(\theta)d\theta < \infty, \tag{33}$$

then

$$M^{1/2}(\hat{M}_T^{(M)} - M_T) \Rightarrow N(0, \sigma^2)$$

where

$$\sigma^2 = \int_\Theta [p(\theta)p(\mathbf{Y}_T|\theta)/j(\theta) - M_T]^2 j(\theta)d\theta$$

and

$$\hat{\sigma}^2 = M^{-1}\sum_{m=1}^M [p(\theta_m)p(\mathbf{Y}_T|\theta_m)/j(\theta_m) - \hat{M}_T]^2 \to \sigma^2.$$

A sufficient condition for these results is that the weight function $w(\theta)$ be bounded above, the same condition that is most useful in establishing the simulation consistency of importance sampling simulators.

This approximation to the marginalized likelihood was used in Geweke (1989a). More recently it has been proposed by Gelfand and Dey (1994); see also Raftery (1995). The pracitical considerations involved are the same as those in the approximation of posterior moments using importance sampling. For the sake of efficiency the importance sampling distribution should not be too diffuse relative to the posterior distribution. For example $j(\theta) = p(\theta)$ satisfies (33) and leads to the very simple approximation $\hat{M}_T^{(M)} = M^{-1}\sum_{m=1}^M p(\mathbf{Y}_T|\theta_m)$. But the prior distribution works well as an importance sampler only if sample size is quite small and θ is of very low dimension (Kloek and van Dijk (1978)). For an evaluation of the use of the prior in this way, see McCulloch and Rossi (1991).

Acceptance sampling from a source density $r(\theta)$ is so similar to importance sampling that exactly the same procedure can be used to produce $\hat{M}_T^{(M)}$. The ratio $p(\theta_m)p(y_T|\theta_m)/r(\theta_m)$ is needed for the acceptance probability in any event. The only additional work is to record $p(\theta_m)p(\mathbf{Y}_T|\theta_m)/r(\theta_m)$ whether the draw is accepted or not, and then to set $\hat{M}_T^{(M)} = M^{-1}\sum_{m=1}^M p(\theta_m)p(\mathbf{Y}_T|\theta_m)/r(\theta_m)$, the summation being taken over all candidate draws.

Simulation-consistent approximation of the marginalized likelihood from the output of a Markov chain Monte Carlo posterior simulator is a greater challenge, and has spawned a substantial recent literature. No method will fully meet the three criteria stipulated above, without more fundamental progress on the application of central limit theorems. Many methods are specialized to particular kinds of models and require at least two models for the computations because they provide Bayes factors rather than marginalized likelihoods. Methods have been developed for approximation of Bayes factors when the dimension of the parameter vectors in the two models is the same (Gelman and Meng (1999), Chen and Shao (1994)), or the models are nested (Chen and Shao (1995)). A more general procedure is due to Carlin and Chib (1995) but this requires simultaneous simulation of two models. The decomposition of the likelihood function set forth in section 3.1 provides a fully general approach, but in effect this requires the consideration of many models. On this approach see also Gelfand, Dey and Chang (1992), Geweke (1994), Kass and Raftery (1995, section 3.2), and Min (1995).

Many straightforward approaches yield procedures with impractically slow convergence rates. A leading example is the "harmonic mean of the likelihood function" suggested by Newton and Raftery (1994): if $g(\theta) = [p(\theta)p(\mathbf{Y}_T|\theta)]^{-1}$ then $E[g(\theta)] = M_T^{-1}$. But $g(\theta)$ generally has no higher moments and consequently numerical approximations are poor.

At this juncture the procedure for approximating the marginalized likelihood from the output of a Markov chain Monte Carlo posterior simulator that comes closest to satisfying all these criteria is a modification of the harmonic mean of the likelihood function suggested in Gelfand and Dey (1994). They observed that

$$E[f(\theta)/p(\theta)p(\mathbf{Y}_T|\theta)] = M_T^{-1} \qquad (34)$$

for any p.d.f. $f(\theta)$ whose support is contained in Θ. One can approximate (34) from the output of any posterior simulator in the obvious way, but for this approximation to have a practical rate of convergence, $f(\theta)/p(\theta)p(\mathbf{Y}_T|\theta)$ should be uniformly bounded. Gelfand and Dey (1994) and Raftery (1995) interpret this condition as requiring that $f(\theta)$ have "thin tails" relative to the likelihood function.

It is not difficult to guarantee both the boundedness and thin tail condition in (34). Consider first the case in which $\Theta = R^k$. From the output of the posterior simulator define $\hat{\theta}_M = M^{-1}\sum_{m=1}^{M}\theta_m$ and $\hat{\Sigma}_M = M^{-1}\sum_{m=1}^{M}(\theta_m - \hat{\theta}_M)$ $(\theta_m - \hat{\theta}_M)'$. (Since the posterior simulator is a Markov chain Monte Carlo algorithm, it is assumed that $w(\theta_m) = 1$. If the posterior simulator is an importance sampler, then (32) can be applied directly.) It is not essential that the posterior mean and variance of θ exist. Then take

$$f(\theta) = 2(2\pi)^{-k/2}|\hat{\Sigma}_M|^{-1/2}\exp\left[-\tfrac{1}{2}(\theta_m - \hat{\theta}_M)'\Sigma^{-1}(\theta_m - \hat{\theta}_M)\right]\chi_{\hat{\Theta}_M}(\theta),$$

$$\hat{\Theta}_M = \left\{\theta:(\theta - \hat{\theta}_M)'\Sigma^{-1}(\theta - \hat{\theta}_M) \leq \chi^2_{.5}(k)\right\}. \qquad (35)$$

If the posterior is uniformly bounded away from 0 on every compact subset of Θ, then the function of interest $f(\theta)/p(\theta)p(\theta|\mathbf{Y}_T)$ possesses posterior moments of all orders. For a wide range of regular problems, this function will be approximately constant on $\hat{\Theta}_M$, which is nearly ideal.

If $\hat{\Theta}_M$ is not included in Θ some modifications of this procedure are required. In some cases it may be easy to reparameterize the model so that $\Theta = \mathbf{R}^k$. If not, the domain of integration for the function of interest $f(\theta)/p(\theta)p(\mathbf{Y}_T|\theta)$ can be redefined to be $\hat{\Theta}_M \cap \Theta$ or a subset of $\hat{\Theta}_M \cap \Theta$, and a new normalizing constant for $f(\theta)$ can be well approximated by taking a sequence of *iid* draws $\{\theta_t\}$ from the original distribution with p.d.f. (35) and averaging $\chi_\Theta(\theta_t)$, at the cost of an additional, but simple, simulation.

In the case of the Gibbs sampler there is an entirely different procedure due to Chib (1995) that provides quite accurate evaluations of the marginalized likelihood, at the cost of additional simulations. Suppose that the output from the blocking $\theta' = (\theta'^{(1)}, \ldots, \theta'^{(B)})$ is available, and that the conditional p.d.f.s $p(\theta^{(j)}|\theta^{(i)}(i \neq j), \mathbf{Y}_T)$ can be evaluated in closed form for all j. [This latter requirement is generally satisfied.]

From the identity $p(\theta|\mathbf{Y}_T) = p(\theta)p(\mathbf{Y}_T|\theta)/M_T$, $M_T = p(\theta^*)p(\mathbf{Y}_T|\theta^*)/p(\theta^*|\mathbf{Y}_T)$ for any $\theta^* \in \Theta$. (In all cases, $p(\cdot)$ denotes a properly normalized density and not merely a kernel.) Typically $p(\mathbf{Y}_T|\theta^*)$ and $p(\theta^*)$ can be evaluated in closed form, but $p(\theta^*|\mathbf{Y}_T)$ cannot. A marginal/conditional decomposition of $p(\theta^*|\mathbf{Y}_T)$ is

$$p(\theta^*|\mathbf{Y}_T) = p(\theta^{*(1)}|\mathbf{Y}_T)p(\theta^{*(2)}|\theta^{*(1)}, \mathbf{Y}_T) \cdot \ldots \cdot p(\theta^{*(B)}|\theta^{*(1)}, \ldots,$$
$$\theta^{*(B-1)}, \mathbf{Y}_T).$$

The first term in the product of B terms can be approximated from the output of the posterior simulator because

$$M^{-1}\sum_{m=1}^{M} p(\theta^{*(1)}|\theta_m^{(2)}, \ldots, \theta_m^{(B)}, \mathbf{Y}_T) \to p(\theta^{*(1)}|\mathbf{Y}_T).$$

To approximate $p(\theta^{*(j)}|\theta^{*(1)}, \ldots, \theta^{*(j-1)}, \mathbf{Y}_T)$, first execute the Gibbs sampling algorithm with the parameters in the first j blocks fixed at the indicated values, thus producing a sequence $\{\theta_{jm}^{(j+1)}, \ldots, \theta_{jm}^{(B)}\}$ from the conditional posterior. Then

$$M^{-1}\sum_{m=1}^{M} p(\theta^{*(j)}|\theta^{*(1)}, \ldots, \theta^{*(j-1)}, \theta_{jm}^{(j+1)}, \ldots, \theta_{jm}^{(B)}, \mathbf{Y}_T) \to p(\theta^{*(j)}|\theta^{*(1)},$$
$$\ldots, \theta^{*(j-1)}, \mathbf{Y}_T).$$

Chib (1995) describes an extension to include latent variables.

3.5   *Bayesian communication*

Investigators cannot anticipate the uses to which their work will be put, or the variants on their model that may interest a client. Different uses will be reflected in different functions of interest. Variants will often revolve around changes in the prior distribution. Any investigator who has publicly reported results has confronted the constraint that only a few representative findings can be conveyed in written work.

Posterior simulators provide a clear answer to the question of what the investigator should report, and in the process remove the constraint that only a few representative findings can be communicated. What should be reported is the $M \times (k+2)$ *simulator output matrix*

$$\begin{bmatrix} \theta_1' & w(\theta_1) & p(\theta_1) \\ \vdots & \vdots & \vdots \\ \theta_m' & w(\theta_m) & p(\theta_m) \end{bmatrix}$$

by making it publicly and electronically available. In a reasonably large problem ($M = 10,000$ and $k = 100$) the corresponding file occupies about 3.2 megabytes of storage (at a current capital cost of about US\$1.40) and can be moved over the Internet in about a minute.

Given the simulator output matrix the client can compute posterior moments and solve signal extraction and forecasting problems not considered by the investigator. In signal extraction or forecasting the client simulates one (or more) values of ω corresponding to each θ_m, from the density $p(\omega | \theta_m, \mathbf{Y}_T)$. This simulation is typically much easier and faster than is the posterior simulator itself. Given the collection of simulated ω, solution of the formal problem then proceeds as described in section 3.2.

With a small amount of additional effort the client can modify many of the investigator's assumptions. Suppose the client wishes to evaluate $E[g(\theta) | \mathbf{Y}_T]$ using the client's own prior density $p^*(\theta)$ rather than the investigator's prior density $p(\theta)$. Suppose further that the support of the investigator's prior distribution includes the support of the client's prior. Then the investigator's posterior distribution may be regarded as an importance sampling distribution for the client's posterior density. The client reweights the investigator's $\{\theta^m\}_{m=1}^M$ using the function

$$w^*(\theta) = \frac{p^*(\theta | \mathbf{Y}_t)}{p(\theta | \mathbf{Y}_t)} = \frac{p^*(\theta)L(\theta | \mathbf{Y}_t)}{p(\theta)L(\theta | \mathbf{Y}_t)} = \frac{p^*(\theta)}{p(\theta)},$$

where $p^*(\theta | \mathbf{Y}_t)$ denotes the client's posterior distribution. The client then approximates posterior moment $E^*[g(\theta) | \mathbf{Y}_t]$ by

$$\bar{g}_M^* \equiv \sum_{m=1}^M w^*(\theta_m) w(\theta_m) g(\theta_m) / \sum_{m=1}^M w^*(\theta_m) w(\theta_m)$$
$$\rightarrow E^*[g(\theta) | \mathbf{Y}_t] \equiv \bar{g}^*.$$

The result $\bar{g}_M^* \to \bar{g}^*$ follows almost at once from Tierney (1994).

The efficiency of the reweighting scheme requires some similarity of $p^*(\theta)$ and $p(\theta)$. In particular, both reasonable convergence rates and the use of a central limit theorem to assess numerical accuracy essentially require that $p^*(\theta)/p(\theta)$ be bounded. Across a set of diverse clients this condition is more likely to be satisfied the more diffuse is $p(\theta)$, and is trivially satisfied for the improper prior $p(\theta) \propto$ constant if the client's prior is bounded. In the latter case the reweighting scheme will be efficient so long as the client's prior is uninformative relative to the likelihood function. This condition is stated precisely in theorem 2 of Geweke (1989b). Diagnostics described there will detect situations in which the reweighting scheme is inefficient, as will standard errors of numerical approximation. If the investigator chooses to use an improper prior for reporting, it is of course incumbent on her to verify the existence of the posterior distribution and convergence of her posterior simulator.

Including $p(\theta_m)$ in the standard simulator output file avoids the need for every client who wishes to impose his own priors to re-evaluate the investigator's prior. Of course, the $p^*(\theta)$s need not be the client's subjective priors: they may simply be devices by which clients explore robustness of results with respect to alternative reasonable priors.

The potential for clients to alter investigators' priors, update their results, and examine alternative posterior moments, exists given current technology. All that is required is for Bayesian investigators to begin making their results available in a conventional format, in the same way that many now provide public access to text and data. Once this is done, colleagues, students, and policy makers may employ the results to their own ends much more flexibly than has heretofore been possible, with modest technical requirements.

4   Some models

The innovations in methods for simulation from posterior distributions just described have made possible routine and practical applications of Bayesian methods in statistics. This section reviews the implementation of posterior simulators in a few models for economic time series. The survey concentrates on just a few models in order to provide the technical detail that is essential to the application of these methods, not just their appreciation. All of the methods presented here can be combined, used in more elaborate models, and be tailored to more specific models implied by the theory and data in a given application.

4.1 Vector autoregressions

The vector autoregression (VAR) was introduced by Sims (1980) and has subsequently been applied extensively in macroeconomics (e.g. Doan, Litterman, and Sims (1984), Blanchard and Quah (1989)) and forecasting (e.g. Litterman (1986)). The canonical model for L time series $\mathbf{y}_t = (y_{1t}, \dots, y_{Lt})$ is

$$\mathbf{y}_t = \mathbf{B}_0 \mathbf{z}_t + \sum_{s=1}^p \mathbf{B}_s \mathbf{y}_{t-s} + \varepsilon_t, \ \varepsilon_t \overset{iid}{\sim} N(\mathbf{0}, \Sigma) \ (t = 1, 2, \dots) \tag{36}$$

conditional on $(\mathbf{y}_0, \dots, \mathbf{y}_{1-p})$ and a $k \times 1$ vector of deterministic covariates $\mathbf{z}_t$. There are other, equivalent, representations of the VAR, based on alternative normalizations; these include recursive and block recursive forms, as well as error correction representations. Since these are all renormalizations, it proves convenient to treat them as functions of interest and they are described from that point of view below in section 4.1.2.

Some extension of notation reveals relationships between the VAR and other econometric models. Let

$$\underset{T \times k}{\mathbf{Z}} = \begin{bmatrix} \mathbf{z}_1' \\ \vdots \\ \mathbf{z}_T' \end{bmatrix}, \ \underset{T \times L}{\mathbf{Y}_s} = \begin{bmatrix} \mathbf{y}_1' \\ \vdots \\ \mathbf{y}_T' \end{bmatrix}, \ \underset{T \times L}{\mathbf{E}} = \begin{bmatrix} \varepsilon_1' \\ \vdots \\ \varepsilon_T' \end{bmatrix}$$

and take $\mathbf{X} = [\mathbf{Z}, \mathbf{Y}_0, \dots, \mathbf{Y}_{1-p}]$, $\mathbf{B}' = [\mathbf{B}_0, \dots, \mathbf{B}_p]$. Then

$$\underset{T \times L}{\mathbf{Y}_1} = \underset{T \times (k+pL)}{\mathbf{X}} \underset{T \times L}{\mathbf{B} + \mathbf{E}}$$

a multivariate regression (Anderson (1984)). The maximum likelihood estimator of the parameters is $\hat{\mathbf{B}} = (\mathbf{X}'\mathbf{X})^{-1}\mathbf{X}'\mathbf{Y}$, $\hat{\Sigma} = T^{-1}\mathbf{S} = T^{-1}(\mathbf{Y} - \mathbf{X}\hat{\mathbf{B}})'\mathbf{Y} - \mathbf{X}\hat{\mathbf{B}})$.

Alternatively, let $\mathbf{y} = \text{vec}(\mathbf{Y})$, $\beta = \text{vec}(\mathbf{B})$, and $\varepsilon = \text{vec}(\mathbf{E})$. Then

$$\mathbf{y} = (\mathbf{I} \otimes \mathbf{X})\beta + \varepsilon, \ \varepsilon \sim N(\mathbf{0}, \Sigma \otimes \mathbf{I}_T).$$

Thus, the VAR is a seemingly unrelated regressions model (Zellner (1962)) with the same covariates in each equation.

4.1.1 Prior distributions
Through straightforward manipulations like likelihood function for (36) can be expressed

$$|\Sigma|^{-T/2} \exp(-\tfrac{1}{2} \text{tr} \Sigma^{-1} \mathbf{S}) \tag{37}$$

$$\cdot \exp\left\{-\tfrac{1}{2}(\beta - \hat{\beta})'(\Sigma^{-1} \otimes \mathbf{X}'\mathbf{X})(\beta - \hat{\beta})\right\} \tag{38}$$

where $\hat{\beta} = \text{vec}(\hat{\mathbf{B}})$. Integrating (38) with respect to β, obtain

$$|\Sigma|^{-(T-k-pL^2)/2}\exp(-\tfrac{1}{2}\mathrm{tr}S\Sigma^{-1})$$

up to a factor of proportionality not involving Σ. The functional form in Σ^{-1} is the same as that of the Wishart distribution (26). Interpreted as a kernel in β, (38) implies $\beta \sim N[\hat{\beta}, \Sigma \otimes (X'X)^{-1}]$. Hence a fully conjugate prior distribution has the form

$$\Sigma^{-1} \sim W(\underline{S}^{-1}, \underline{\nu}), \ \beta|\Sigma \sim N(\underline{\beta}, \Sigma \otimes \underline{H}_\beta^{-1}).$$

Multiplying the kernel of the conjugate distribution by (37)–(38), after a little manipulation one obtains the kernel of the posterior distribution

$$\Sigma^{-1} \sim W[(\underline{S}+S)^{-1}, \underline{\nu}+T-k-pL^2], \ \beta|\Sigma \sim N(\overline{\beta}, \Sigma \otimes \overline{H}_\beta^{-1}).$$

with $\overline{H}_\beta = \underline{H}_\beta + X'X$ and $\overline{\beta} = (I \otimes \overline{H}_\beta^{-1}\underline{H}_\beta)\underline{\beta} + (I \otimes \overline{H}^{-1}X'X)\hat{\beta}$. Independence simulation from this posterior distribution is very fast and simple.

The fully conjugate prior distribution is often an inconvenient representation of beliefs, since uncertainty about the variance matrix and the coeffficient is linked. The prior distribution

$$\beta \sim N(\underline{\beta}, \underline{H}_\beta^{-1}), \quad \Sigma^{-1} \sim W(\underline{S}^{-1}, \underline{\nu}) \tag{39}$$

does not have this property, and leads immediately to

$$\beta|\Sigma, Y, X \sim N(\overline{\beta}, \overline{H}_\beta^{-1}) \tag{40}$$

with $\overline{H}_\beta = \underline{H}_\beta + \Sigma^{-1} \otimes X'X$, $\overline{\beta} = \overline{H}_\beta^{-1}(\underline{H}_\beta\underline{\beta} + \overline{H}_\beta\hat{\beta})$, and

$$\Sigma^{-1}|B, Y, X \sim W(\overline{S}^{-1}, \overline{\nu})$$

with $\overline{S} = \underline{S} + (Y - XB)'(Y - XB)$, $\overline{\nu} = \underline{\nu} + T$. Thus this prior distribution is conditionally conjugate. It is immediately suited to a Gibbs sampling algorithm blocked in β and Σ. The computations here are more demanding, since a linear system of order $k + pL^2$ must be solved at each step.

The prior distribution (39) as stated involves potentially a very large number of parameters simply to organize the representation of prior beliefs about $\underline{\beta}$ and Σ within the family (39) it is necessary to restrict $\underline{\beta}$ and $\underline{H}_\beta$. This can be done conveniently through a system of hierarchical priors (section 2.7). This approach has been taken by Doan, Litterman, and Sims (1984) and by Chib and Greenberg (1995) for a closely related problem in the seemingly unrelated regressions model. A common notation that captures all of these approaches is

$$\beta \sim N([\underline{\beta}(\mu), \underline{H}_\beta(\pi)^{-1}]; \ \mu \sim p_\mu(\cdot), \ \pi \sim p_\pi(\cdot).$$

Conditional on μ, π, Σ, X, and Y the distribution of β is (40). Conditional on β and Σ the posterior distribution of μ and π has kernel

$$\exp\left\{-\tfrac{1}{2}[\beta-\underline{\beta}(\mu)]'\,\underline{\mathbf{H}}_\beta(\pi)[\beta-\underline{\beta}(\mu)]\right\}\mathrm{p}_\mu(\mu)\mathrm{p}_\pi(\pi) \tag{41}$$

since μ and π do not appear directly in the likelihood function. The practicality of this procedure rests on the existence of a suitable method of drawing μ and π from (41). This is generally not difficult to achieve since μ and π are likely of low dimension. For example, in the spirit of Doan, Litterman, and Sims (1984) we might have

$$b_{1jj}|(\mu,\pi)\sim\mathrm{N}(\mu_1,\pi_1),\ b_{1ij}|(\mu,\pi)\sim\mathrm{N}(\mu_2,\pi_2)\ (i\neq j)$$
$$b_{sij}|(\mu,\pi,\tau)\sim\mathrm{N}(\mu_3,\pi_3\pi_5^{s-1}),\ b_{sij}|(\mu,\pi,\tau)\sim\mathrm{N}(\mu_4,\pi_4\pi_6^{s-1})$$
$$(s>1,i\neq j).$$

where all distributions are conditionally independent. The hierarchy might be completed by the seven independent prior distributions,

$$\mu\sim\mathrm{N}(\underline{\mu},\underline{\mathbf{H}}_\mu^{-1}),\ \underline{s}_j^2\pi_j\sim\chi^2(\underline{\nu}_j)(j=1,\dots,4),\ \pi_j\sim\mathrm{U}(0,1)(j=5,6).$$

It is straightforward to verify that conditional on $\beta,\Sigma,\mathbf{Y}$, and $\mathbf{X},\beta$ is sufficient for the distribution of μ and π; that the seven posterior distributions of μ and π; $(j=1,\dots,6)$ are conditionally independent; that the conditional distribution of μ is multivariate normal; and π_j $(j=1,\dots,4)$ is inverted gamma. The conditional distributions of π_5 and π_6 are unconventional but are easily handled through acceptance sampling along the lines described in Geweke (1996a, section 3.2).

4.1.2 Functions of interest

The properties of vector autoregressions in the population have been studied extensively. Any set of such properties may be represented through functions of interest of the form $g(\mathbf{B}_0,\dots,\mathbf{B}_p,\Sigma)$, and hence inferences about them can be carried out readily by means of posterior simulation. Examples include questions about stationarity, cointegration, spectral densities, and various decompositions of variance. Here we discuss three kinds of properties: alternative normalizations, transformations of parameters, and problems in prediction.

For many purposes, other normalizations of (36) are convenient. One such normalization is the fully recursive form

$$\mathbf{y}_t=\Sigma_{s=0}^p\mathbf{A}_s\mathbf{y}_{t-s}+\eta_t,\ \eta_t\overset{iid}{\sim}\mathrm{N}(\mathbf{0},\Phi) \tag{42}$$

in which $\mathbf{A}_0$ is lower triangular, $[\mathbf{A}_0]_{jj}=0$ $(j=1,\dots,L)$, and Φ is a diagonal matrix. The mapping from Σ and the $\mathbf{B}_s$ to Φ and the $\mathbf{A}_s$ can be constructed explicitly by letting $\mathbf{PP}'=\Sigma$ be the unique Choleski decomposition of Σ in which $\mathbf{P}$ is lower triangular and $p_{jj}>0$ $(j=1,\dots,L)$; take $\Phi=\mathrm{diag}(p_{jj}^2)$; $\mathbf{R}=\mathbf{P}\Phi^{-1/2}$; $\mathbf{A}_s=\mathbf{R}^{-1}\mathbf{B}_s$ $(s>1)$; and $\mathbf{A}_0=\mathbf{I}-\mathbf{R}^{-1}$.

Given stationarity of $\mathbf{y}$ conditional on $\mathbf{z}$ there are three other standard useful representations of multivariate time series that may be obtained as functions of interest. A necessary and sufficient condition for conditional stationarity is that the roots of

$$|\mathbf{I}_L - \Sigma_{s=1}^{p}\mathbf{B}_s z^s| = 0 \tag{43}$$

all lie outside the unit circle. Stationarity may be imposed by checking this condition directly, and discarding draws corresponding to non-stationary configurations of $\{\mathbf{B}_s\}_{s=1}^{p}$.

The moving average representation corresponding to (36) is $\mathbf{y}_t = \Sigma_{s=0}^{\infty}\mathbf{B}_s^*\mathbf{B}_0\mathbf{z}_{t-s} + \Sigma_{s=0}^{\infty}\mathbf{B}_s^*\varepsilon_{t-s}$. The sequence $\{\mathbf{B}_s^*\}_{s=0}^{\infty}$ is the inverse of $\{\mathbf{B}_s\}_{s=1}^{p}$ under convolution, i.e.

$$\Sigma_{s=0}^{\infty}\mathbf{B}_s^* z^s(\mathbf{I}_L - \Sigma_{s=1}^{\infty}\mathbf{B}_s z^s) = \mathbf{I}_L \forall z : |z| \le 1.$$

The terms $\mathbf{B}_s^*$ may be obtained through the recursion

$$\mathbf{B}_0^* = \mathbf{I}, \ \mathbf{B}_r^* = \Sigma_{j=0}^{r-1}\mathbf{B}_j^*\mathbf{B}_{r-j} \ (r = 1,2,\ldots).$$

One may obtain moving averages corresponding to other normalizations, as well. The representation $\mathbf{y}_t = \Sigma_{s=0}^{\infty}\mathbf{D}_s^*\mathbf{D}_0\mathbf{z}_{t-s} + \Sigma_{s=0}^{\infty}\mathbf{D}_s^*\zeta_{t-s}$ corresponding to (42) is given by the recursion

$$\mathbf{A}_0^* = (\mathbf{I} - \mathbf{A}_0)^{-1}, \ \mathbf{A}_r^* = \left(\Sigma_{j=0}^{r-1}\mathbf{A}_j^*\mathbf{A}_{r-j}\right)\mathbf{A}_0^* \ (r = 1,2,\ldots).$$

This representation has been used extensively to examine the impulse response functions

$$[\mathbf{D}_s^*]_{ij}(\psi_{jj})^{1/2} \ (s = 0,1,2,\ldots)$$

which trace out the effect of a typical shock of size $(\psi)_{jj}^{1/2}$ in ζ_{jt} on y_{it}. There is a substantial literature on methods for obtaining confidence bands for impulse response functions (e.g., Sims (1986), Runkle (1987), Blanchard and Quah (1989), Sims and Zha (1999), Koop (1995), Phillips (1995)). Since the impulse response function is a closed-form mapping from the parameters of the VAR, however, there really are no essential difficulties in a Bayesian approach.

The spectral density matrix corresponding to (36) is

$$\mathbf{S}_y(\lambda) = [\mathbf{I} - \Sigma_{s=1}^{p}\mathbf{B}_s \exp(-i\lambda s)]^{-1}\Sigma[\mathbf{I} - \Sigma_{s=1}^{p}\mathbf{B}_s \exp(i\lambda s)]^{-1'}.$$

At a given frequency the spectral density matrix is a closed-form function of the parameters of the VAR, and it may be computed at many frequencies. Spectral densities have been applied in a wide variety of signal extraction problems (Nerlove, Grether, and Carvalho (1979, chapters 3–4), Whittle (1983)). The frequency domain representation provides several useful adjuncts to the study of multiple time series. One is that the roots of (43) all lie outside the unit circle if and only if

$$(2\pi)^{-1}\int_{-\pi}^{\pi}\log|\mathbf{I}-\Sigma_{s=1}^{p}\mathbf{B}_{s}\exp(-i\lambda s)|^{2}d\lambda=0 \tag{44}$$

(Rozanov (1967, theorem 4.2)). For large systems it is easier to check this condition by computing $\mathbf{I}-\Sigma_{s=1}^{p}\mathbf{B}_{s}\exp(-i\lambda s)$ at many frequencies than to determine the roots of (43) directly. From (36) and (44),

$$(2\pi)^{-1}\int_{-\pi}^{\pi}\log|\mathbf{S}_{y}(\lambda)|d\lambda=\log|\Sigma|.$$

The autocovariance function of $\mathbf{y}$ conditional on z cannot be determined in closed form from the VAR parameters. Three approaches are possible, but it is not clear if any is generally more efficient than the others. Since

$$\mathbf{R}_{y}(r)=(2\pi)^{-1}\int_{-\pi}^{\pi}\mathbf{S}_{y}(\lambda)\exp(-i\lambda r)d\lambda=\Sigma_{s=r}^{\infty}\mathbf{A}_{s}\Sigma\mathbf{A}'_{s-r}$$

the autocovariance function may be approximated by computing many spectral density ordinates or terms in the moving average representation. Alternatively the Yule–Walker relations

$$\mathbf{R}_{y}(0)=\Sigma_{s=1}^{p}\mathbf{B}_{s}\mathbf{R}_{y}(-s)+\Sigma$$
$$\mathbf{R}_{y}(j)=\Sigma_{s=1}^{p}\mathbf{B}_{s}\mathbf{R}_{y}(j-s)\ (j=1,\ldots,p-1)$$

may be solved for $\mathbf{R}_{y}(j)\ (j=0,\ldots,p-1)$ through iteration to a fixed point, and then $\mathbf{R}_{y}(j)=\Sigma_{s=1}^{p}\mathbf{B}_{s}\mathbf{R}_{y}(j-s)\ (j=p,p+1,\ldots)$ may be computed iteratively.

Yet another normalization is the error-correction representation (Davidson, et al. (1978)) that has proved especially useful in the study of co-integration (Engle and Granger (1987)). Write (36) in the form

$$\Delta\mathbf{y}_{t}=\mathbf{C}_{0}\Delta\mathbf{z}_{t}+\Sigma_{s=1}^{p-1}\mathbf{C}_{s}\Delta\mathbf{y}_{t-s}+\mathbf{C}_{p}\mathbf{y}_{t-1}+\varepsilon_{t},\ \varepsilon_{t}\stackrel{iid}{\sim}\mathrm{N}(0,\Sigma) \tag{45}$$

in which $\mathbf{C}_{0}=\mathbf{B}_{0},\mathbf{C}_{j}-\Sigma_{s=j+1}^{p}\mathbf{B}_{s}(j=1,\ldots,p-1)$, and $\mathbf{C}_{p}=-(\mathbf{I}-\Sigma_{s=1}^{p}\mathbf{B}_{s})$. A necessary and sufficient condition for stationarity of $\mathbf{y}$ conditional on z is that all roots of (43) lie outside the unit circle. hence $\mathrm{rk}(\mathbf{C}_{p})=L$ is necessary for stationarity. Moreover, departures from stationarity thought likely *a priori* typically imply $\mathrm{rk}(\mathbf{C}_{p})<L$.

Interest in the literature has concentrated on the implications of $\mathrm{rk}(\mathbf{C}_{p})<L$. Let

$$\mathbf{w}_{t}=\begin{pmatrix}\mathbf{w}_{1t}\\\mathbf{w}_{2t}\end{pmatrix}=\begin{bmatrix}\mathbf{R}_{1}\\\mathbf{R}_{2}\end{bmatrix}\mathbf{y}_{t}=\mathbf{R}\mathbf{y}_{t}$$

with $\mathbf{R}$ non-singular and $\mathbf{R}_{1}\mathbf{R}'_{2}=0$. The vector $\mathbf{w}_{1t}$ is taken to be stationary while $\mathbf{w}_{2t}$ is non-stationary with no stationary linear combinations. Then (45) implies

$$\Delta \mathbf{w}_t = \mathbf{C}_0^* \mathbf{z}_t + \sum_{s=1}^{p-1} \mathbf{C}_s^* \Delta \mathbf{z}_{t-1} + \mathbf{C}_p^* \Delta \mathbf{z}_{t-1} + \varepsilon_t^*$$

where $\mathbf{C}_0^* = \mathbf{R}\mathbf{C}_0$, $\mathbf{C}_s^* = \mathbf{R}\mathbf{C}_s \mathbf{R}^{-1} (s = 1, \dots, p-1)$, and

$$\mathbf{C}_p^* \mathbf{R}\mathbf{C}_p \mathbf{R}^{-1} = \begin{bmatrix} \mathbf{R}_1 \mathbf{C}_p \\ \mathbf{R}_2 \mathbf{C}_p \end{bmatrix} \mathbf{R}^{-1}.$$

If $\mathbf{R}_1 \mathbf{C}_p$ is of full row rank and $\mathbf{R}_2 \mathbf{C}_p = \mathbf{0}$, then $\mathbf{w}_{1t}$ is stationary but $\mathbf{w}_{2t}$ is non-stationary. Imposition of this condition amounts to assuming that the last r_2 rows of $\mathbf{C}_p^*$ are zero, which is easily accomplished in the context of the Gibbs sampling posterior simulator described above.

Because of the recursive formulation of the VAR, sampling from the predictive density is straightforward. Given the parameters of the model, the data, and all future values of the deterministic process $\{\mathbf{z}_t\}$, the recursion

$$\tilde{\mathbf{y}}_t \equiv \mathbf{y}_t \ (t = 1, \dots, T)$$

$$\tilde{\mathbf{y}}_{T+j} \sim \mathrm{N}\left(\mathbf{B}_0 \mathbf{z}_{T+j} + \sum_{s=1}^{p} \mathbf{B}_s \tilde{\mathbf{y}}_{T+j-s}, \Sigma \right) \ (j = 1, 2, \dots)$$

provides a draw from the conditional distribution. Based on one or more such draws for each simulation of parameter values, forecasting problems can be attacked directly as described in section 3.2.

4.2   *Time-varying volatility models*

Models in which the volatility of asset returns varies smoothly over time have received considerable attention in recent years. (For a survey of several approaches see Bollerslev, Chou, and Kroner (1992)). Persistent but changing volatility is an evident characteristic of returns data. Since the conditional distribution of returns is relevant in the theory of portfolio allocation, proper treatment of volatility is important. Time-varying volatility also affects the properties of real growth and business cycle models.

The earliest model of time varying volatility is the autoregressive conditional heteroskedasticity (ARCH) model of Engle (1982). This was extended to the generalized ARCH (GARCH) model by Bollerslev (1986). Since then many variants of ARCH models have appeared. The distinguishing characteristic of these models is that the conditional variance of the return is a deterministic function of past conditional variances and past values of the return itself. GARCH models exhibit both time-varying volatilty and leptokurtic unconditional distributions, but the two cannot be separated: these models cannot account for leptokurtosis without introducing time-varying volatility.

Stochastic volatilty models have been examined by a series of investigators beginning with Taylor (1986). Promising Bayesian methods have been developed by Jacquier, Polson, and Rossi (1994). In these models the conditional variance of the return is a stochastic function of its own past values but is unaffected by past returns themselves. Like GARCH models they account for time-varying volatilty and leptokurtosis, but unlike GARCH models it is possible to have excess kurtosis without heteroskedasticity.

4.2.1   The GARCH model
The GARCH model of time-varying volatility may be expressed

$$y_t = \beta'\mathbf{x}_t + h_t^{1/2}\varepsilon_t$$
$$h_t = \alpha + \Sigma_{s=1}^q \gamma_s \varepsilon_{t-s}^2 + \Sigma_{j=1}^p \delta_j h_{t-j}$$
$$\varepsilon_t \overset{iid}{\sim} \mathrm{N}(0,1). \tag{46}$$

Here, y_t is the observed return at time t; $\mathbf{x}_t$ is a vector of covariates and β is the corresponding vector of coefficients; h_t is the conditional variance at time t; $\alpha > 0$, $\gamma_s \geq 0$ $(s = 1, \ldots, q)$, $\delta_j \geq 0$ $(j = 1, \ldots, p)$. The vector of covariates is typically deterministic, including a constant term and perhaps indicator variables for calendar effects on the mean of y_t.

For the discussion here, assume the GARCH $(1,1)$ model, which is (46) with $p = q = 1$. (Henceforth, we omit the subscripts on γ_1 and δ_1.) The GARCH $(1,1)$ specification has proven attractive for models of returns. It typically dominates other GARCH models using the Akaike or Schwarz Bayesian information criteria (Bollerslev, Chou and Kroner (1992)). Following the GARCH literature we treat h_1 as a known constant. Then, the likelihood function is

$$\mathrm{L}_u(\beta, \alpha, \gamma, \delta \mid Y_u) = \Pi_{s=1}^u h_s^{1/2} \exp[-(y_s - \mathbf{x}_s'\beta)^2 / 2h_s]$$

where h_s is computed recursively from (46).

For expressing prior distributions as well as for carrying out the computations it proves useful to work with $a = \log(\alpha)$ rather than α. With this reparameterization a convenient functional form of the prior distribution is

$$a \sim \mathrm{N}(\underline{a}, \underline{s}_a^2);$$

$$\beta \sim \mathrm{N}(\underline{\beta}, \underline{S}_\beta);$$

$$\pi(\gamma, \delta) = 2(\gamma \geq 0, \delta \geq 0, \gamma + \delta < 1) \tag{47}$$

and the distributions are independent. Restriction of γ and δ to the unit simplex is equivalent to the statement that the variance process is stationary.

A metropolis independence chain (Tierney (1991, 1994), Geweke (1996b)) can be constructed to produce a sequence of parameters whose unconditional limiting distribution is the posterior distribution. Let $\theta' = (\beta', a, \gamma, \delta)$, and let $p(\theta|\mathbf{Y}_T)$ denote the posterior distribution. The kernel of this distribution is the product of (46) and the three prior density kernels in (47). The mode of the log posterior kernel is easily found using analytical expressions for the gradient and Hessian and a standard Newton–Raphson algorithm. Denote the mode $\hat{\theta}$, and the Hessian at the mode by $\mathbf{H}$. Let $J(\cdot; \mu, \mathbf{V}, v)$ denote the kernel density of a multivariate student-t distribution with location vector μ, scale matrix $\mathbf{V}$, and v degrees of freedom. For the choices $\mu = \hat{\theta}$, $\mathbf{V} = -(1.2)^2\mathbf{H}^{-1}$, $v = 5$, the ratio $p(\theta|\mathbf{Y}_T)/J(\theta; \mu, \mathbf{V}, v)$ is typically bounded above.

This multivariate student-t distribution forms a proposal distribution for an independence metropolis algorithm as follows. At step m, generate a candidate θ^* from $J(\cdot; \mu, \mathbf{V}, v)$. With probability

$$p = \min\left\{\frac{p(\theta^*|Y_t)/J(\theta^*; \mu, \mathbf{V}, v)}{p(\theta^{(m-1)}|Y_t)/J(\theta^{(m-1)}; \mu, \mathbf{V}, v}, -1\right\}$$

$\theta^{(m)} = \theta^*$; and with probability $1 - p$, $\theta^{(m)} = \theta^{(m-1)}$. In applications of this proposal distribution, about half the candidate parameter vectors are typically accepted Geweke (1994)).

4.2.2   The stochastic volatility model

The stochastic volatility model taken up by Jacquier, Polson, and Rossi (1994) is

$$y_t = \beta'\mathbf{x}_i + \varepsilon_t, \quad \varepsilon_t = h_t^{1/2}u_t,$$

$$\log h_t = \alpha + \delta\log h_{t-1} + \sigma_v v_t,$$

$$\begin{pmatrix} u_t \\ v_t \end{pmatrix} \overset{iid}{\sim} N(0, \mathbf{I}_2)$$

where $|\delta| < 1$ and $\sigma_v > 0$. Following Jacquier, Polson, and Rossi, do not condition on h_1 but regard h_1 as a random variable drawn from its unconditional distribution $N(\alpha/(1-\delta), \sigma_v^2/(1-\delta^2))$. Then

$$L(\beta, \alpha, \delta, \sigma_v; \mathbf{Y}_T) = \int_0^\infty \ldots \int_0^\infty L^*(\beta, \alpha, \delta, \sigma_v, h_1, \ldots, h_u; \mathbf{Y}_T)dh_1, \ldots, dh_u$$

where

$$L^*(\beta, \alpha, \delta, \sigma_v, h_1, \ldots, h_u; \mathbf{Y}_T) =$$
$$\Pi_{s=1}^u h_s^{-3/2}\exp\left(-\Sigma_{s=1}^u \varepsilon_s^2/2h_s\right)$$
$$\exp\left[-\Sigma_{s=2}^u (\log h_s - \alpha - \delta\log h_{s-1})^2/2\sigma_v^2\right]$$
$$\cdot \exp\{[\log h_1 - \alpha/(1-\delta)]^2/[\sigma_v^2/(1-\delta^2)]\}. \tag{48}$$

The prior distributions for β and σ_v are of the forms

$$\beta \sim N(\underline{\beta},\underline{S}_\beta)$$

and

$$\underline{v}_v \underline{s}_v^2/\sigma_v^2 \sim \chi^2(\underline{v}_v)$$

respectively. The prior distribution of $(\alpha, \delta)'$ is bivariate normal, induced by independent normal prior distribution on the persistence parameter δ

$$\delta \sim N(\underline{\delta},s_\delta^2)$$

and the unconditional mean of $\log h_t$

$$\alpha/(1-\delta) \sim N(\underline{h},s_h^2).$$

A linearization of $\alpha/(1-\delta)$ yields the corresponding bivariate normal prior distribution

$$\begin{pmatrix} \alpha \\ \delta \end{pmatrix} \sim N\left(\begin{bmatrix} \underline{h}(1-\underline{\delta}) \\ \underline{\delta} \end{bmatrix}, \begin{bmatrix} s_h^2(1-\underline{\delta})^2 + \underline{h}^2 s_\delta^2 & -\underline{h}\,s_\delta^2 \\ -\underline{h}\,s_\delta^2 & s_\delta^2 \end{bmatrix} \right). \tag{49}$$

Draws from the posterior distribution may be accomplished using Markov chain Monte Carlo algorithms. To describe these procedures, let $\theta' = (\beta', \alpha, \delta, \sigma_v)$ and $\mathbf{h}' = (h_1,\ldots,h_u)$, and note that for any function of interest $g(\theta,\mathbf{h})$,

$$E[g(\theta,\mathbf{h})] = \frac{\int_\Theta \int_H g(\theta) L^*(\theta,h;Y_T)\pi(\theta)d\mathbf{h}d\theta}{\int_\Theta \int_H L^*(\theta,h;Y_T)\pi(\theta)d\mathbf{h}d\theta}$$

where $\pi(\theta)$ is the prior distribution constructed from (49).

The posterior distribution of β conditional on (α, δ), σ_v, and $\mathbf{h}$ is normal, and the posterior distribution of (α, δ) conditional on β, σ_v, and $\mathbf{h}$ is normal up to the last term of (48) which may be accommodated by acceptance sampling; and the distribution of σ_v conditional on β, (α, δ), and $\mathbf{h}$ is inverted gamma.

The non-standard part of the problem is drawing the vector of latent variables $\mathbf{h}$. The posterior distribution of h_s $(1 < s < u)$, conditional on $\{h_r, r \neq s\}$ and θ has density kernel

$$h_s^{-3/2}\exp(-\varepsilon_s^2/2h_s) \tag{50}$$

$$\cdot \exp[-(\log h_s - \mu_s)^2/2\sigma^2] \tag{51}$$

where

$$\varepsilon_s = y_s - \mathbf{x}_s'\beta,\ \mu_s = \frac{\alpha(1-\delta) + \delta(\log h_{s-1} + \log h_{s+1})}{1+\delta^2},\ \sigma^2 = \frac{\sigma_v^2}{1+\delta^2}.$$

Drawing **h** may be accomplished in a number of different ways. Jacquier, Polson, and Rossi (1994) use a metropolis chain, generating from a candidate density, and using the procedures described in section 3.4.2 to either accept or reject the draw. The term (50) is the kernel of a random variable whose inverse has a gamma distribution. Using this family to approximate (50)–(51) by matching first and second moments, and combining with the first term, yields the candidate density kernel

$$x^{-(\phi+1)}\exp(-\lambda/x);$$

$$\phi = [1 - \exp(\sigma^2)]/[1 - \exp(\sigma^2)] + 0.5,$$

$$\lambda = (\phi - 1)\exp(\mu_s + 0.5\sigma^2) + 0.5\varepsilon_s^2.$$

Alternatively (Geweke (1994)) note that the posterior conditional density kernel for $H_s = \log h_s$ is

$$\exp[-(H_s - \mu_s^*)/2\sigma^2]\exp[-\varepsilon_s^2/2\exp(H_s)]$$

where $\mu_s^* = \mu_s - 0.5\sigma^2$. One can draw efficiently from this distribution using acceptance sampling, employing a source $N(\lambda, \sigma^2)$ distribution with λ chosen optimally as described in Geweke (1994, section 3.2). For $H_1 = \log h_1$ the conditional posterior density kernel is

$$\exp[-(H_1 - \mu_1^*)/2\sigma_v^2]\exp[-\varepsilon_1^2/2\exp(H_1)]$$

where $\mu_1^* = \alpha + \delta H_2 - 0.5\sigma_v^2$. There is a symmetric expression for $H_u = \log h_u$.

This approach to stochastic volatility can be extended in several dimensions, using Markov chain Monte Carlo methods for Bayesian inference. These include leptokurtic or skewed shocks and leverage effects through correlation between u_t and v_t. A multivariate generalization of the model is

$$\underset{L \times 1}{y_t} = h_t^{-1/2}\Sigma^{1/2}\varepsilon_t,$$

$$\log h_1 = \alpha + \delta \log h_{t-1} + \sigma_v v_t,$$

$$\binom{\varepsilon_t}{v_t} \overset{iid}{\sim} N(0, I_{L+1})$$

which is also a stochastic generalization of the discount dynamic model used extensively in Bayesian forecasting (Harrison and Stevens (1976), West and Harrison (1989)). For an overview of these extensions see Jacquier, Polson, and Rossi (1995).

4.3   *Changing regime models*

Changing regime models provide one means of introducing non-linear behavior in time series, while still retaining much of the tractability of (36).

The non-linearity is introduced through a latent process $\{s_t\}$ whose range is $s_t = j(1,\ldots,J)$. If $s_t = j$, then

$$\mathbf{y}_t = \mathbf{B}_0^{(j)}\mathbf{z}_t + \sum_{s=1}^{p}\mathbf{B}_s^{(j)}\mathbf{y}_{t-s} + \boldsymbol{\varepsilon}_t, \ \boldsymbol{\varepsilon}_t \overset{iid}{\sim} \mathrm{N}(\mathbf{0},\Sigma^{(j)}) \ (t = 1,2,\ldots).$$

Much as before denote $\mathbf{B}^{(j)'} = [\mathbf{B}_0^{(j)},\ldots,\mathbf{B}_p^{(j)}]$, $\beta^{(j)} = \mathrm{vec}[\mathbf{B}^{(j)}]$, $\beta^{(1)'} = (\beta^{(1)'},\ldots, \beta^{(J)'})$. A conditionally conjugate family of priors is

$$\beta \sim \mathrm{N}(\underline{\beta},\underline{\mathbf{H}}_\beta^{-1}), \ [\Sigma^{(j)}]^{-1} \sim \mathrm{W}([\underline{S}^{(j)}]^{-1},\underline{v}^{(j)}) \ (j = 1,\ldots J)$$

where the $J + 1$ distributions are independent. The need for expression of $\underline{\beta}$ and $\underline{\mathbf{H}}_\beta$ in terms of hyperparameters, or for hierarchical priors, is once again evident.

Since the model is symmetric in the $(\beta^{(j)},\Sigma^{(j)})$, further restrictions are required for identification. These necessarily depend on the particular application. Examples include inequality restrictions on the intercept coefficient in growth rate equations, thus identifying one state as a contraction in a two-state model (McCulloch and Tsay (1994)), restriction of a particular time to a specific state, and inequality constraints on variances (Albert and Chib (1993a)). The threshold model, described below, provides yet another means of identification.

Conditional on the process $\{s_t\}$, inference can proceed much as in section 4.1.1. If the $\beta^{(j)}$ are independent *a priori*, then this amounts to applying the procedures of section 4.1.1 separately to subsamples of the form $\{t:s_t=j\}$ $(j = 1,\ldots,J)$. If not, the posterior distribution of β, conditional on the $\Sigma^{(j)}$ and $\{s_t\}$, is still multivariate normal, and the posterior distributions of the $\Sigma^{(j)}$ are conditionally inverted Wishart.

The changing regime model is completed with specification of the process determining $\{s_t\}$

$$p(s_t \mid \theta, \mathbf{y}_{t-1},\ldots,\mathbf{y}_{t-r}, s_{t-1}, t) \ (t = 1,\ldots T)$$

in which the parameter vector θ indexes the class of processes, and a prior distribution $p(\theta)$. The posterior density kernel is

$$\prod_{t=1}^{T}\Big\langle \big|\Sigma^{(st)}\big|^{-1/2}$$

$$\cdot \exp\Big\{-\tfrac{1}{2}\big[\mathbf{y}_t - \mathbf{B}_0^{(st)}\mathbf{z}_t - \sum_{s=1}^{p}\mathbf{B}_s^{(st)}\mathbf{y}_{t-s}\big]'[\Sigma^{(st)}]^{-1}$$

$$\big[\mathbf{y}_t - \mathbf{B}_0^{(st)}\mathbf{z}_t - \sum_{s=1}^{p}\mathbf{B}_s^{(st)}\mathbf{y}_{t-s}\big]\big\}\Big\rangle \tag{52}$$

$$\cdot \prod_{t=1}^{T} p(s_t \mid \theta, \mathbf{y}_{t-1},\ldots,\mathbf{y}_{t-r}, s_{t-1}, t) \tag{53}$$

$$\cdot p(\theta) \tag{54}$$

$$\cdot \prod_{j=1}^{J} p(\Sigma^{(j)}) \cdot p(\mathbf{B}_s^{(j)}) \ (s = 0,\ldots,p; (j = 1,\ldots,J)). \tag{55}$$

Conditional on all other parameters and the latent variables $\{s_t\}$, the kernel density for θ involves only (53) and (54). Thus, issues of drawing θ involve only the auxiliary model for the latent variables $\{s_t\}$. Conditional on $s_r(r \neq t)$

$$P(s_t = j) \propto f_t(s_t) \cdot p(s_t | \theta, \mathbf{y}_{t-1}, \dots, \mathbf{y}_{t-r}, s_{t-1}, t) \cdot p(s_{t+1} | \theta, \mathbf{y}_{t-1}, \dots,$$
$$\mathbf{y}_{t-r}, s, t) \tag{56}$$

where $\prod_{t=1}^{T} f_t(s_t)$ denotes (52) as a function of s_t. Thus, s_t can be drawn by evaluating (56) for $j = 1, \dots, J$. A practical issue that may arise in this procedure is serial correlation of the algorithm induced in this data augmentation. Generally serial correlation can be reduced by drawing r adjacent s_t simultaneously, at the cost of J^r rather than rJ evaluations.

Several variants of (53)–(55) have been proposed, and in fact the variety of models that can be applied has been enhanced greatly by the development of Markov chain Monte Carlo methods for Bayesian inference. Here we describe four such models. In each case we concentrate on the conditional posterior distributions of the latent variables s_t, and the conditional distribution of the parameters peculiar to the variant.

4.3.1   Markov switching models
In the Markov switching regime model the evolution of states is described by the first order Markov chain

$$P(s_t = j | \theta, t = 1) = p_{0j}(j = 1, \dots, J),$$

$$P(s_t = j | \theta, s_t = i) = p_{ij}(i, j = 1, \dots, J; t = 2, 3 \dots).$$

This model was developed and applied to macroeconomic time series by Hamilton (1989, 1990). Bayesian inference using the Gibbs sampler has been implemented by Albert and Chib (1993a), Chib (1996), and McCulloch and Tsay (1994).

The kernel of the likelihood function in the p_{ij} (53) is the product of $J + 1$ kernels of the multinomial distribution indexed by $i = 0, \dots, J$: $\prod_{j=1}^{J} p_{ij}^{n_{ij}}$ where n_{ij} is the number of transitions from the regime i to regime j in $\{s_t\}_{t=1}^{T}$. A natural conjugate prior distribution for these parameters is the Dirichlet (also known as the multivariate beta) distribution

$$p_i(p_{ij}) \propto \prod_{j=1}^{J} p_{ij}^{a_{ij}} [p_{ij} \geq 0(j = 1, \dots, J); \Sigma_{j=1}^{J} p_{ij} = 1; a_{ij} \geq -1(i = 0, \dots, J)].$$

(For further discussion see Zellner (1971, 38–9).) Hence a conditionally conjugate prior distribution for $\theta = \{p_{ij}, j = 1, \dots, J; i = 0, \dots, J\}$ is

$$p[\theta] \propto \prod_{i=0}^{J} \prod_{j=1}^{J} p_{ij}^{a_{ij}} [a_{ij} \geq 1, p_{ij} \geq 0, j = 1, \dots, J; \Sigma_{j=1}^{J} p_{ij} = 1;$$
$$(i = 0, \dots, J)]$$

and the corresponding conditional posterior density kernel is

$$p(\theta) \propto \prod_{i=0}^{J} \prod_{j=1}^{J} p_{ij}^{n_{ij}+a_{ij}} \left[p_{ij} \geq 0, j=1,\dots,J; \sum_{j=1}^{J} p_{ij} = 1; \right.$$
$$\left. (i=0,\dots,J) \right]. \tag{57}$$

There is a convenient genesis for this density (Johnson and Kotz (1972, pp. 232–233)). Construct the $J(J+1)$ independent random variables

$$d_{ij} \sim \chi^2[2(n_{ij}+a_{ij}+1)] \ (j=1,\dots,J; i=0,\dots,J).$$

Then

$$p_{ij} = d_{ij} / \sum_{k=1}^{m} d_{ik} \ (j=1,\dots,J; i=0,\dots,J)$$

has probability density kernel (57).

Conditioning to denote (52) as a function of s_t by $\prod_{t=1}^{T} f_t(s_t)$, the distribution of s_t conditional on $s_t (r \neq t)$ and all other parameters is

$$P(s_1 = j) \propto f_1(j) p_{0j} p_{j,s_2};$$
$$P(s_t = j) \propto f_t(j) p_{s_{t-1},j} p_{j,s_{t+1}} (t=2,\dots,T-1);$$
$$P(s_T = j) \propto f_T(j) p_{s_{T-1},j}.$$

This completes the set of conditional distributions needed for a Gibbs sampling algorithm for the Markov switching model. One can readily verify that Gibbs sampler convergence condition 1 applies.

The Markov switching model may be extended, by allowing transition probabilities to depend on the time of year. See Ghysels, McCulloch, and Tsay (1998) for methods, and evidence for this sort of behavior in macroeconomic time series.

4.3.2 Probit switching model

In the probit switching regime model, the evolution of the state variables is described by means of an auxiliary $J+1$ vector of latent variables $\mathbf{v}_t$,

$$(v_{1t},\dots v_{J-1,t})' \sim (\Gamma \mathbf{w}_t, \Omega)$$

where $\mathbf{w}_t$ is a subset of $\{\mathbf{y}_{t-1},\dots,\mathbf{y}_{t-r}\}$, and $v_{Jt} \equiv 0$. Then

$$P(s_t = j) = P(v_{jt} \geq v_{it} \forall i = 1,\dots,J).$$

This model has been studied by McCulloch and Tsay (1993b).

Conditional on s_t, this is a conventional multinomial probit model. If (Γ, Ω) and $(\mathbf{B}^{(j)}, \Gamma^{(j)}, j=1,\dots,J)$ are independent in the prior distribution, then the entire literature on Markov chain Monte Carlo methods for Bayesian inference in the multinomial probit model applies directly to the step of drawing Γ and Ω; e.g., see Geweke, Keane, and Runkle (1994, 1997), McCulloch and Rossi (1995), and McCulloch, Polson, and Rossi (1995). If $J=2$ there is considerable simplification: see Albert and Chib (1993b).

Once again letting $\prod_{t=1}^{T} f_t(s_t)$ denote (52) as a function of s_t, the distribution of s_t conditional on $s_t (r \neq t)$ and all parameters is

$$P(s_t = j) \propto f_t(j) \cdot P(\mathbf{v}_{jt} \geq v_{it} | \Gamma, \Omega).$$

When $J = 2$ the second probability in this expression is the c.d.f. of a univariate normal distribution. For $J \geq 3$, a recent literature on evaluation of orthant probabilities for the multivariate normal distribution can be applied; see Hajivassiliou, McFadden, and Ruud (1996) for documentation of the advantages of the GHK probability simulator due to Keane (1990), Geweke (1992), and Hajivassiliou and McFadden (1998). See Geweke, Keane, and Runkle (1995) for a description and code.

4.3.3 Threshold autoregressive model

In the threshold autoregressive model introduced by Tong (1978, 1983) and Tong and Lim (1980)

$$s_t = f(y_{t-q}, \theta).$$

The simplest leading example that has been studied from both Bayesian and non-Bayesian perspectives, is $s_t = 1$ if $y_{t-q} \leq r$, $s_t = 2$ if $y_{t-q} > r$; $\theta = (Q, r)'$. Conditional on θ the states are known. If prior distributions for the $\mathbf{B}^{(j)}$ and $\Sigma^{(j)}$ are jointly conditionally conjugate (as described at the start of section 4.1.1) then analytic marginalization of the $\mathbf{B}^{(j)}$ and $\Sigma^{(j)}$ is possible. The marginal posterior in θ can then be evaluated directly, leading to an independence sampling algorithm for the whole posterior. Examples of this approach are Geweke and Terui (1992, 1993). Alternatively the problem can be blocked into the $\mathbf{B}^{(j)}$, the $\Sigma^{(j)}$, q and r. For this approach, see Carlin, Gelfand, and Smith (1992) and McCulloch and Tsay (1995).

4.3.4 Pure break models

Perhaps the simplest changing regime model is

$$s_t = 1, t \leq b; s_t = 2, t > b,$$

as a special case of (53), together with a prior distribution for b from (53). There is a considerable non-Bayesian literature associated with this model in economics, beginning with Peron (1989). Non-Bayesian approaches are complicated by the issue of inference about b; conditioning problems similar to those discussed in section 3.3 arise. In the Bayesian formulation the parameter b is symmetric with all other parameters in the model. Bayesian inference in the context of (52)–(55), using a Gibbs sampling algorithm, is straightforward (see DeJong (1992) for an early study).

The focus in the literature has been on the comparison of models with, and without, breaks. A formal comparison using Bayesian methods has not yet been made, to the author's knowledge. In doing so, it would be important that the prior distribution for the $\mathbf{B}^{(j)}$ and $\Sigma^{(j)}$ be chosen carefully. Given improper priors for these parameters, a finding of a one-regime model would be implied by Lindley's paradox.

The pure break model is ultimately handicapped by its failure to specify a stochastic process that determines breaks. Because of this, forecasts conditional only on the data are not possible in this model, as they are in the other changing regime models considered here. As an incompletely specified model, it is not well suited to serious practical application.

5   Conclusions

The procedures described in this survey can be summarized in three steps for the Bayesian econometric analysis of time series.

(1) *Be explicit about assumptions.* This entails a formal probability distribution over all the models under consideration. As a technical matter, it means describing prior beliefs through a probability for each model and a distribution of plausible parameter values within each model.

(2) *Condition on available information.* Available information consists of the assumptions in (1), and data related to the random variables whose distribution is governed by these assumptions.

(3) *Use posterior simulators to report the logical implications of (1) and (2).* The logical implications are completely summarized by the probability distributions of models and parameters conditional on available information. These implications are drawn using the laws of probability, i.e., Bayes' theorem.

These procedures impose considerable discipline on the econometrician, in all three steps. The discipline is precisely the same as that imposed in the development of ideas in modern economic theory, and on the behavior of rational economic agents in these models. The first two steps are no more than the application of the defining paradigm of the discipline of economics, to the work that economists and econometricians do when they confront their ideas with facts about the real world.

The third step is not essential to drawing the logical implications of the first two steps. However, it has two compelling advantages. The first stems from the fact that drawing the logical implications is technically very demanding. Posterior simulators provide by far the best device currently available for completing this task. As a practical matter they are the only device in most situations. The second compelling advantage is that the output of a posterior simulator, generated by an investigator, provides a simple tool by means of which a remote client can, within reasonable limits, alter the assumptions made in (1), update the data sets used in (2), and examine implications in (3) not considered by the investigator.

The implementation of the Bayesian paradigm made possible by recent innovations in posterior simulators places the formal analysis of economic time series on the same logical footing as economic science in general, and makes the results of that analysis more accessible to scholars and policy makers. The realization of this promise is just beginning, and its pursuit should provide worthy tasks for econometricians for some time.

References

Albert, J.H. and S. Chib (1993a), "Bayes Inference via Gibbs Sampling of Autoregressive Time Series Subject to Markov Mean and Variance Shifts," *Journal of Business and Economic Statistics*, 11, 1–15.

(1993b), "Bayesian Analysis of Binary and Polychotomous Response Data," *Journal of the American Statistical Association*, 88, 669–679.

Amemiya, T. (1985), *Advanced Econometrics*, Cambridge, MA; Harvard University Press.

Anderson, T.W. (1984), *An Introduction to Multivariate Statistical Analysis* (2nd edn.), New York: Wiley.

Bartlett, M.S. (1957), "A Comment on D.V. Lindley's Statistical Paradox," *Biometrika*, 44, 533–534.

Berger, J.O. (1985), *Statistical Decision Theory and Bayesian Analysis* (2nd edn.), New York: Springer-Verlag.

Berger, J.O. and R.L. Wolpert (1988), *The Likelihood Principle* (2nd edn.), Hayward: Institute of Mathematical Statistics.

Bernardo, J.M. and A.F.M. Smith (1994), *Bayesian Theory*, New York: Wiley.

Blanchard, O.J. and D. Quah (1989), "The Dynamic Effects of Aggregate Demand and Supply Disturbances," *American Economic Review*, 79, 655–673.

Bollerslev, T. (1986), "Generalized Autoregressive Conditional Heteroskedasticity," *Journal of Econometrics*, 31, 307–327.

Bollerslev, T., R. Chou, and K.F. Kroner (1992), "ARCH Modeling in Finance," *Journal of Econometrics*, 52, 5–59.

Carlin, B. and S. Chib (1995), "Bayesian Model Choice via Markov Chain Monte Carlo," *Journal of the Royal Statistical Society*, Series, B, 57, 473–484.

Carlin, B., A. Gelfand, and A.F.M. Smith (1992), "Hierarchical Bayesian Analysis of Change Point Problems," *Applied Statistics*, 41, 389–405.

Chen, M. and Q. Shao (1994), "On Monte Carlo Methods for Estimating Ratios of Normalizing Constants," National University of Singapore Department of Mathematics Research Report No. 627.

(1995), "Estimating Ratios of Normalizing Constants for Densities with Different Dimensions," Worcester Polytechnical Institute technical report.

Chib, S. (1995), "Marginal Likelihood from the Gibbs Output, *Journal of the American Statistical Association*, 90, 1313–1321.

(1996). "Calculating Posterior Distributions and Modal Estimates in Markov Mixture Models," *Journal of Econometrics*, 75(1), 79–97.

Chib, S. and E. Greenberg (1994), "Understanding the Metropolis-Hastings Algorithm," Washington University Olin School of Business working paper.

(1995), "Hierarchical Analysis of SUR Models with Extensions to Correlated Serial Errors and Time Varying Parameter Models," *Journal of Econometrics*, 68(2), 339–360.

Christoffersen, P.F. and F.X. Diebold (1997), "Optimal Prediction Under Asymmetric Loss," *Econometric Theory*, 13, 808–817.

Davidson, J.E.H., D.F. Hendry, F. Srba, and S. Yeo (1978), "Econometric Modeling of the Aggregate Time-Series Relationship Between Consumers' Expenditure and Income in the United Kingdom," *Economic Journal*, 88, 661–692.

DeGroot, M. (1970), *Optimal Statistical Decisions*, New York: McGraw-Hill.

DeJong, D.N. (1992), "A Beyesian Search for Structural Breaks in US GNP," in T. Formby and R.C. Hill (eds.), *Advances in Econometrics: Bayesian Methods Applied to Time Series Data*, Place: JAI Press.

Diebold, F.X. and R.S. Mariano (1995), "Comparing Predictive Accuracy," *Journal of Business and Economic Statistics*, 13, 253–265.

Doan, T., R. Litterman and C.A. Sims (1984), "Forecasting and Conditional Projection Using Realistic Prior Distributions," *Econometric Reviews*, 5, 57–61.

Engle, R. (1982), "Autoregressive Conditional Heteroscedasticity with Estimates of the Variance of United Kingdom Inflation," *Econometrica*, 50, 987–100.

Engle, R.F. and C.W.J. Granger (1987), "Co-Integration and Error Correction: Representation, Estimation, and Testing," *Econometrica*, 55, 251–276.

Gelfand, A.E., D.K. Dey, and H. Chang (1992), "Model Determination Using Predictive Distributions with Implementation via Sampling-Based Methods," in J.M. Bernardo, J.O. Berger, A.P. Dawid, and A.F.M. Smith (eds.), *Bayesian Statistics*, Oxford University Press.

Gelfand, A.E. and D.K. Dey (1994), "Bayesian Model Choice: Asymptotics and Exact Calculations," *Journal of the Royal Statistical Society*, Series B, 56, 501–514.

Gelman, A. and X.L. Meng (1999), "Simulating Normalizing Constants: From Importance Sampling to Bridge Sampling to Path Sampling." *Statistical Science* (forthcoming).

Geweke, J. (1989a), "Exact Predictive Densities in Linear Models with ARCH Disturbances," *Journal of Econometrics*, 40, 63–86.

(1989b), "Bayesian Inference in Econometric Models Using Monte Carlo Integration," *Econometrica*, 57, 1317–1340.

(1992), "Evaluating the Accuracy of Sampling-Based Approaches to the Calculations of Posterior Moments," in J.O. Berger, J.M. Bernardo, A.P. Dawid, and A.F.M. Smith (eds.), *Proceedings of the Fourth Valencia International Meeting on Bayesian Statistics*, Oxford University Press, pp. 169–194.

(1994), "Bayesian Comparison of Econometric Models," Federal Reserve Bank of Minneapolis Working Paper No. 532.

(1996a), "Monte Carlo Simulation and Numerical Integration," in H. Amman, D. Kendrick, and J. Rust (eds.), *Handbook of Computational Economics*, vol. I Amsterdam: North-Holland, pp. 731–800.

(1996b), "Posterior Simulators in Econometrics," in D. Kreps and K.F. Wallis (eds.), *Advances in Economics and Econometrics: Theory and Applications*, Cambridge University Press.

Geweke, J., M. Keane, and D. Runkle (1994), "Alternative Computational Approaches to Statistical Inference in the Multinomial Probit Model," *Review of Economics and Statistics*, 76, 609–632.

(1995), "Recursively Simulating Multinomial Multiperiod Probit Probabilities," *American Statistical Association 1994 Proceedings of the Business and Economic Statistics Section*.

(1997), "Statistical Inference in Multinomial Multiperiod Probit Models," *Journal of Econometrics*, 80(1), 125–166.

Geweke, J. and N. Terui (1992), "Threshold Autoregressive Models for Macroeconomic Time Series: A Bayesian Approach," *American Statistical Association 1991 Proceedings of the Business and Economic Statistics Section*, 42–50.

(1993), "Bayesian Threshold Autoregressive Models for Nonlinear Time Series," *Journal of Time Series Analysis*, 14, 441–455.

Ghysels, E., R.E. McCulloch, and R.S. Tsay (1998), "Bayesian Inference for General Class of Periodic Markov Regime-Switching Models," *Journal of Applied Econometrics* 13(2), 129–143.

Granger, C.W.J. (1969), "Prediction with a Generalized Cost of Error Function," *Operational Research Quarterly*, 20, 199–207.

Hajivassiliou, V. and D. McFadden (1998), "The Method of Simulated Scores for the Estimation of LDV Models," *Econometrica*, 66, 863–896.

Hajivassiliou, V.A., D.L. McFadden, and P. Ruud (1996), "Simulation of Multivariate Normal Rectangle Probabilities and their Derivatives: Theoretical and Computational Results," *Journal of Econometrics*, 72(1 and 2), 85–124.

Hamilton, J.D. (1989), "A New Approach to the Economic Analysis of Nonstationary Time Series," *Econometrica*, 57, 357–384.

(1990), "Analysis of Time Series Subject to Changes in Regime," *Journal of Econometrics*, 45, 39–70.

Harrison, P.J. and C.F. Stevens (1976), "Bayesian Forecasting," *Journal of the Royal Statistical Society*, Series B, 38, 205–247.

Hildreth, C. (1963), "Bayesian Statisticians and Remote Clients," *Econometrica*, 31, 422–438.

Jacquier, E., N.G. Polson, and P.E. Rossi (1994), "Bayesian Analysis of Stochastic Volatility Models," *Journal of Business and Economic Statistics*, 12, 371–417.

——— (1995), "Stochastic Volatility: Univariate and Multivariate Extensions," mimeo.

Johnson, N.L. and S. Kotz (1972), *Distributions in Statistics: Continuous Multivariate Distributions*, New York: Wiley.

Kass, R.E. and A.E. Raftery (1995), "Bayes Factors," *Journal of the American Statistical Association*, 90, 773–795.

Keane, M. (1990), "Four Essays in Empirical Macro and Labor Economics," Unpublished Ph.D. dissertation, Brown University.

Kloek, T. and H.K. van Dijk (1978), "Bayesian Estimates of Equation System Parameters: An Application of Integration by Monte Carlo," *Econometrica*, 46, 1–19.

Koop, G. (1994), "Recent Progress in Applied Bayesian Econometrics," *Journal of Economic Surveys*, 8, 1–34.

——— (1995), "Parameter Uncertainty and Impulse Response Analysis," *Journal of Econometrics*, 72(1–2), 135–150.

Lindley, D.V. (1957), "A Statistical Paradox," *Biometrika*, 44, 187–192.

Litterman, R.B. (1986), "Forecasting with Bayesian Vector Autoregressions – Five Years of Experience," *Journal of Business and Economic Statistics*, 4, 25–38.

McCulloch, R.E., N.G. Polson, and P.E. Rossi (1995), "A Bayesian Analysis of the Multinomial Probit Model with Fully Identified Parameters," University of Chicago Graduate School of Business Working paper.

McCulloch, R.E. and P.E. Rossi (1991), "A Bayesian Approach to Testing the Arbitrage Pricing Theory," *Journal of Econometrics*, 49, 141–168.

——— (1995), "An Exact Likelihood Analysis of the Multinomial Probit Model," *Journal of Econometrics*, 64, 207–240.

McCulloch, R.E. and R.S. Tsay (1993a), "Analysis of Threshold Autoregressive Processes with a Random Number of Regimes," in M. Tarter and M. Lock (eds.), *Proceedings of the 25th Symposium on the Interface between Computing Science and Statistics*, Fairfax, VA: Interface Foundation.

——— (1993b), "Bayesian Inference and Prediction for Mean and Variance Shifts in Autoregressive Time Series," *Journal of the American Statistical Association*, 88, 968–978.

——— (1994), "Statistical Analysis of Economic Time Series via Markov Switching Models," *Journal of Time Series Analysis*, 15, 523–540.

Min, C. (1995), "Forecasting the Adoptions of New Consumer Durable Products," George Mason University, School of Business Administration, Working paper.

Nerlove, M., D.M. Grether, and J.L. Carvalho (1979), *Analysis of Economic Time Series*, New York: Academic Press.

Newton, M.A. and A.E. Raftery (1994), "Approximate Bayesian Inference by the Weighted Likelihood Bootstrap" (with discussion), *Journal of the Royal Statistical Society*, Series B, 56, 3–48.

Peron, P. (1989), "The Great Crash, the Oil Shock, and the Unit Root Hypothesis," *Econometrica*, 57, 1361–1401.

Phillips, P.C.B. (1998), "Impulse Response and Forecast Error Variance Asymptotics in Nonstationary VARs," *Journal of Economics*, 83, 21–56.

Poirier, D.J. (1998), "Frequentist and Subjectivist Perspectives on the Problem of Model Building in Economics" (with discussion), *Journal of Economic Perspectives*, 2, 120–170.

——— (1995), *Intermediate Statistics and Econometrics: A Comparative Approach*, Cambridge, MA: MIT Press.

Raftery, A.E. (1996), "Hypothesis Testing and Model Selection" in W.R. Gilks, S. Richardson, and D.J. Spiegelhalter, eds., *Markov Chain Monte Carlo in Practice*, London: Chapman and Hall, chapter 10.

Rozanov, Y.A. (1967), *Stationary Random Processes*, San Francisco: Holden-Day.

Runkle, D.E. (1987), "Vector Autoregressions and Reality," *Journal of Business and Economic Statistics*, 5, 437–442.

Shao, J. (1989), "Monte Carlo Approximations in Bayesian Decision Theory," *Journal of the American Statistical Association*, 84, 727–732.

Sims, C.A. (1980), "Macroeconomics and Reality," *Econometrica*, 48, 1–48.

——— (1986), "Are Forecasting Models Usable for Policy Analysis?" *Federal Reserve Bank of Minneapolis Quarterly Review*, 10, 2–15.

Sims, C.A. and T. Zha (1999), "Error Bands for Impulse Responses," *Econometrica* 67, 1113–1156.

Smith, A.A. (1991), "Solving Stochastic Dynamic Programming Problems using Rules of Thumb," Queen's University Department of Economics Discussion Paper No. 816.

Taylor, S. (1986), *Modeling Financial Time Series*, New York: Wiley.

Tierney, L. (1991), "Exploring Posterior Distributions Using Markov Chains," in E.M. Keramaidas (ed.), *Computing Science and Statistics: Proceedings of the 23rd Symposium on the Interface*, Fairfax: Interface Foundation of North America, 563–570.

——— (1994), "Markov Chains for Exploring Posterior Distributions" (with discussion and rejoinder), *Annals of Statistics*, 22, 1701–1762.

Tong, H. (1978), "On a Threshold Model," in C.H. Chan (ed.), *Pattern Recognition and Signal Processing*, Amsterdam: Sijthoff and Noordhoff.

——— (1983), *Threshold Models in Non-linear Time Series Analysis*, New York: Springer-Verlag.

Tong, H. and K.S. Lim (1980), "Threshold Autoregression, Limit Cycles and Cyclical Data," *Journal of the Royal Statistical Society*, Series B, 42, 245–292.

Weiss, A.A. (1991), "Multi-step Estimation and Forecasting in Dynamic Models," *Journal of Econometrics*, 48, 135–149.

Weiss, A.A. and A.P. Andersen (1984), "Estimating Forecasting Models Using the Relevant Forecast Evaluation Criterion," *Journal of the Royal Statistical Society*, Series A, 137, 484–487.

West, M. and J. Harrison (1990), *Bayesian Forecasting and Dynamic Models*, Berlin: Springer-Verlag.

Whittle, F. (1983), *Prediction and Regulation by Linear Least-Square Methods* (2nd edn.), Minneapolis: University of Minnesota Press.

Zellner, A. (1962), "An Efficient Method of Estimating Seemingly Unrelated Regressions and Test of Aggregation Bias," *Journal of the American Statistical Association*, 57, 500–509.

    (1971), *Bayesian Inference in Econometrics*, New York: Wiley.

Part IV

Other areas of application and technical issues

Introduction

Roberto S. Mariano

The common denominator in simulation-based inference (SBI) is the use of simulations for inference when dealing with econometric models which contain expectations that are intractable numerically and analytically. Here, we take inference to cover not only model parameter estimation and hypothesis testing, but also other facets of statistical analysis such as model validation, forecasting, and statistical properties of procedures.

Stochastic simulation for multiple integral evaluation is indeed a standard technique in numerical analysis. In econometrics, it has found direct application in various distinguishable directions. One of the earlier econometric applications dealt with Monte Carlo techniques for the analysis of exact sampling distributions of econometric estimators and test statistics in models beyond standard linear regression. A prominent example which received a great deal of attention in the early 1960s is the linear simultaneous equations model, where finite-sample properties of least squares and likelihood-based estimators and tests were investigated through stochastic simulations. In this area of application, model estimators, such as two-stage least squares and more general instrumental variable methods for simultaneous equations models, can be calculated with ease. However, an analytical study of their finite-sample properties is mostly intractable because the estimators depend on sample observations in a complicated way. Monte Carlo experimentation presents a viable approach toward approximating the exact sampling distributions of these estimators and evaluating expectations of functions of these estimators. Hendry (1984) provides an excellent survey.

A second area of application is prediction and specification testing in non-linear econometric models, where stochastic simulations are used to obtain unbiased forecasts and appropriate prediction regions. In addition to standard Monte Carlo simulations, efficiency and robustness considerations lead to bootstrap procedures as well as simulation variance reduction techniques through the use of antithetic and control variates. For example,

303

see Brown and Mariano (1984, 1989, 1997), and Mariano and Brown (1983).

Lerman and Manski (1981), McFadden (1989), and Pakes and Pollard (1989) ushered in another major area of application, in a way, more basic than those mentioned above – namely, tractable calculation of model parameter estimates themselves. Dealing with the multinomial probit model, Lerman and Manski introduced the naive frequency simulator for choice probabilities in implementing numerical maximization of the likelihood function. Technical problems with this procedure, arising from non-differentiability and the inordinately large number of replications required in simulation, led to the development of smooth simulators and their asymptotic properties in McFadden and in Pakes and Pollard.

Since then, these papers have spawned numerous research on simulation for estimation – an area to which one interpretation of the phrase "simulation-based inference" has been applied. Models of application also have expanded – from high-dimensional qualitative response models, which Lerman and Manski, McFadden, and Pakes and Pollard addressed, to Bayesian analysis, non-linear state space models and other time series models covered in the earlier parts of this volume.

This part of the book goes into other areas of application and some technical aspects of stochastic simulations: specifically, treatment of unobservables, Bayesian analysis of customer satisfaction survey data, use of simulations to validate calibrated models, simulation efficiency in the bootstrap, and small sample properties and the relation to the bootstrap of indirect inference estimators.

In the first chapter, Bradlow utilizes simulation to implement a Bayesian analysis of hierarchical models for customer satisfaction survey data. Here, in dealing with binary data with a hierarchical structure, Bradlow overlays a random effect probability model on an underlying logistic probability structure. Stochastic simulations overcome computational difficulties arising from non-conjugate likelihood and priors. To implement posterior inference, the author uses three approaches: maximum likelihood empirical Bayes, grid approximation, and Gibbs sampling with a metropolis step. In his analysis of data from the Dupont Corporation 1992 Customer Satisfaction Packaging Division Survey, Bradlow makes two conclusions. First, the Bayesian methods do not differ much from each other. Second, the Bayesian methods improve on standard maximum likelihood methods.

In the following chapter, Gourieroux, Renault, and Touzi discuss the small sample properties of the indirect inference procedure. This method has been proposed in the literature (e.g., Smith (1993), and Gourieroux, Montfort, and Renault (1993)) for complicated models with the following characteristics:

(a) the likelihood function cannot be written out explicitly,

(b) the maximum likelihood estimate cannot be calculated directly, with or without the use of simulations, and

(c) the model can be simulated stochastically, given model parameter values and initial conditions.

In such cases, the indirect inference procedure requires the investigator to perform the following steps:

1 specify a criterion function which depends on sample observations and some auxiliary parameters. Optimize this criterion function, given the available sample, to obtain estimates of the auxiliary parameters. In many applications, such as Ohanian *et al.* in this volume, the criterion function is an approximation to the conditional or exact likelihood function implied by the model;

2 calibration by simulation. Here, the investigator simulates a pseudo-sample at given model parameter values, estimates the criterion parameters at each pseudo-sample, and chooses as his indirect estimate of the model parameter that value in this step which gives the criterion parameter estimate "closest" to that obtained in step 1.

This simulation-based estimator has been studied mostly from the asymptotic point of view. In this chapter, the authors utilize Edgeworth expansion to show that the indirect inference estimator, just like the bootstrap, automatically operates a second-order bias correction.

The chapter by Ohanian, Violante, Krusell, and Rios-Rull, applies SBI techniques to the estimation of an aggregate non-linear production function with latent input variables – namely, the quality of skilled and unskilled labor. The authors utilize three alternative SBI procedures – stochastic integration, extended Kalman filtering with indirect inference correction, and simulated pseudo-maximum likelihood. Using Monte Carlo experiments, the authors assess the reliability of these techniques in small samples and in trending latent variables. The authors' estimates of the production function parameters point to two important factors for the recent increases in the wage of skilled workers relative to unskilled workers: capital–skill complementarity and the recent drop in relative prices of equipment.

The chapter by Canova and Ortega uses simulation-based approaches in testing calibrated general equilibrium models and compare these simulation procedures with more standard methods of testing the fit of non-linear dynamic equilibrium models. The authors provide a concrete example where simulation-based diagnostics are used to assess the ability of a calibrated model to reproduce second-order properties of saving and investment in an open economy.

In the final chapter, Brown studies the stochastic error and computational demands arising from the use of simulated bootstrap in parametric and semiparametric models. In applying bootstrap, one needs to generate enough replications to keep simulation error from dominating the approximation refinements being sought through the procedure. Brown shows that bootstrap implementation can be enhanced, in the sense that simulation replication requirements can be reduced considerably through a control variate approach based on limiting distributions.

References

Brown, B.W. and R.S. Mariano (1984), "Residual-Based Stochastic Prediction and Estimation in a Nonlinear Simultaneous System," *Econometrics*, 52, 321–343.
  (1989), "Asymptotic Behavior of Predictors in Dynamic Nonlinear Simultaneous Systems," *Economic Theory*, 5, 430–452.
  (1997), "Reduced Variance Prediction in Dynamic Nonlinear Models," University of Pennsylvania Discussion Paper.
Gourieroux, C.A.A., A. Montfort, and E. Renault (1993), "Indirect Inference," *Journal of Applied Econometrics*, 8, S85–S118.
Hendry, D. (1984), "Monte Carlo Experiments in Econometrics," in Z. Griliches and M.D. Intriligator (eds.), *Handbook of Econometrics*, vol. II, Amsterdam: North-Holland, chapter 16, pp. 937–976.
Lerman, S. and C. Manski (1981), "On the Use of Simulated Frequencies to Approximate Choice Probabilities," in C. Manski and D. McFadden (eds.), *Structural Analysis of Discrete Data with Econometric Applications*, Cambridge, MA: MIT Press.
Mariano, R.S. and B. Brown (1983), "Asymptotic Behavior of Predictors in a Nonlinear Simultaneous System," *International Economic Review*, 24, 995–1026.
McFadden, D. (1989), "A Method of Simulated Moments for Estimation of Discrete Response Models with Numerical Integration," *Econometrica*, 57, 995–1026.
Pakes, A. and D. Pollard (1989), "Simulation and the Asymptotics of Optimization Estimators," *Econometrica*, 57, 1027–58.
Smith, A.A. (1993), "Estimating Nonlinear Time-Series Models Using Simulated Vector Autoregressions," *Journal of Applied Econometrics*, 8, S63–S84.

12 A comparison of computational methods for hierarchical models in customer survey questionnaire data

Eric T. Bradlow

1 Introduction

Hierarchical models for binary outcome data have many areas of practical application. Consider the case where a business surveys J customers on K items yielding binary satisfaction matrix $\mathbf{Y} = (y_{jk})$, $j = 1,\ldots,J$, $k = 1,\ldots,K$ where $y_{jk} = 1$ if customer j is satisfied on item k and 0 otherwise. If we define a probability matrix $\mathbf{P} = (p_{jk})$, with $p_{jk} = \text{prob}(y_{jk} = 1)$, then

$$[\mathbf{Y}|\mathbf{P}] = \prod_{j=1}^{J} \prod_{k=1}^{K} p_{jk}^{y_{jk}} (1 - p_{jk})^{1-y_{jk}} \tag{1}$$

is a product of Bernoulli probabilities where $[A|B]$ denotes the conditional density of A given B. This chapter will use a model for the p_{jk} originally suggested by Rasch (1960) for educational tests. The Rasch model

$$\text{logit}(p_{jk}) = t_{jk} = \mu + \alpha_j + \gamma_k \tag{2}$$

is an additive logistic model for the p_{jk}. If we define $\vec{\alpha} = (\alpha_1,\ldots,\alpha_J)$, $\vec{\gamma} = (\gamma_1, \ldots,\gamma_K)$, and $\vec{\theta}_1 = (\vec{\alpha}, \vec{\gamma}, \mu)$, we have a standard form of the logistic regression likelihood

$$[\mathbf{Y}|\vec{\theta}_1] = \prod_{j=1}^{J} \prod_{k=1}^{K} \frac{e^{t_{jk}y_{jk}}}{1 + e^{t_{jk}}}. \tag{3}$$

The interpretation of the parameter vector $\vec{\theta}_1$ is that the αs account for the satisfaction probabilities of the individual respondents, the γs for the questionnaire items, and μ for the overall baseline level of satisfaction. Many statistical software packages (SAS, BMDP, SY-STAT, etc.) contain routines to perform maximum likelihood calculations based on $[\mathbf{Y}|\vec{\theta}_1]$ via a

This research was inspired by applied problems seen by the author while working as marketing statistician at the DuPont Corporation, Wilmington DE. This research was supported in part by AHCPR, Proposal No. 1R01HS07118-01. "Hierarchical Statistical Modeling in Health Policy Research".

Newton–Raphson (NR) algorithm. Using NR or some other iterative algorithm is necessary in this case because the system of equations

$$\frac{\partial}{\partial \theta_{1t}} \ell(\vec{\theta}_1 \mid Y) = 0 \quad t = 1, \dots, J + K + 1 \tag{4}$$

with $\vec{\theta}_1 = (\vec{\alpha}, \vec{\gamma}, \mu) = (\theta_{11}, \dots, \theta_{1, J+K+1})$, and $\ell(\vec{\theta}_1 \mid Y) = \log(\text{likelihood}(\vec{\theta}_1 \mid \mathbf{Y}))$ cannot be solved in closed form. Drawing inferences for $\vec{\theta}_1$ via asymptotic normal approximations for the maximum likelihood estimate (MLE) based on $(\mathbf{Y} \mid \vec{\theta}_1)$ alone suffers from the following limitations, however:

(i) Responses for a person (or item) which contains all 1s (entirely satisfied) or all 0s (entirely dissatisfied) will have inestimable parameters since the estimated logits of their probabilities will tend to $\propto$ and $- \infty$ respectively

(ii) Not considering another level of variability in the αs (γs) would ignore the relationship among the persons (items) and could yield asymptotic standard errors which are too large. If the hierarchical structure is "unnecessary" then the data will speak to that and MLEs and their associated standard errors would result anyway.

To overcome these limitations, a set of priors for the parameters $\vec{\alpha}, \vec{\gamma}$, and μ (now to be considered random effects) are proposed to model the common source of variability in the logistic probabilities where

$$\vec{\alpha} \mid \sigma^2 \sim \mathrm{MVN}_J(0, \sigma^2 I_{J \times J}) \tag{5}$$

$$\vec{\gamma} \mid \tau^2 \sim \mathrm{MVN}_K(0, \tau^2 I_{K \times K}) \tag{6}$$

$$[\mu] \propto c \tag{7}$$

with $\vec{\alpha} \perp \vec{\gamma} \perp \mu \mid \sigma^2, \tau^2$. If we define $\vec{\theta}_2 = (\sigma^2, \tau^2)$ to have improper priors such that $[\sigma^2] \propto c, [\tau^2] \propto c$, then we have specified the distributions in the left-hand column of the Bayesian hierarchical diagram shown in figure 12.1. The left-hand side is called the specification side because these are the probability models specified by the analyst. The right-hand side is called the inferential side because these distributions are used to make posterior inferences about $\vec{\theta}_1$ and $\vec{\theta}_2$. In this setting however, computational difficulties arise in making exact posterior calculations owing to the non-conjugate form of the likelihood and prior. This chapter discusses three different methods for obtaining posterior inferences for $\vec{\theta}_1$ and $\vec{\theta}_2$. These methods will be demonstrated on a data set taken from a DuPont Corporation 1992 Customer Satisfaction Survey. The methods are described briefly here and in more detail in subsequent sections.

To obtain posterior inferences for $\vec{\theta}_1$ we need to integrate out the second stage parameter as follows

	Specification	Inferential
Data	$[Y|\vec{\theta}_1]$	$[Y]$
Stage 1	$[\vec{\theta}_1|\vec{\theta}_2]$	$[\vec{\theta}_1|Y]$
Stage 2	$[\vec{\theta}_2]$	$[\vec{\theta}_2|Y]$

Figure 12.1 Hierarchical diagram

$$[\vec{\theta}_1|\mathbf{Y}] = \int [\vec{\theta}_1|\mathbf{Y}, \vec{\theta}_2][(\vec{\theta}_2|Y]d\vec{\theta}_2. \tag{8}$$

Because this integral cannot be calculated in closed form, some approximation is necessary. In MLEB inference, we obtain an approximation for $\tilde{\theta}_1$, the posterior mode, by first maximizing $[\vec{\theta}_2|\mathbf{Y}]$ yielding $\tilde{\theta}_2$, and then finding the mode of $[\vec{\theta}_1|\mathbf{Y}, \tilde{\theta}_2]$. The Maximum Likelihood Empirical Bayes (MLEB) inference will be done via an approximate EM algorithm (Dempster, *et al.* (1977)) based on a normal approximation to the likelihood of $\vec{\theta}_1$ given $\mathbf{Y}$ and $\vec{\theta}_2$. If the posterior for $\vec{\theta}_2$ is concentrated around the mode $\tilde{\theta}_2$, the MLEB step, replacing $[\vec{\theta}_2|\mathbf{Y}]$ by a degenerate distribution at the mode, is likely to be a good approximation. In that case the approximation of the posterior mode $\tilde{\theta}_1$ using MLEB methods will be similar to the mode calculated from fully Bayesian methods.

Another approach to posterior inference about $\vec{\theta}_1$ involves making a grid approximation to $\ell(\vec{\theta}_2|\mathbf{Y})$. In this method we first sample from the grid approximation to $\vec{\theta}_2|\mathbf{Y}$; call this draw θ_2^*. Since samples from $\vec{\theta}_1|\mathbf{Y}, \theta_2^*$ cannot be drawn directly, we sample from an approximation to $\vec{\theta}_1|\mathbf{Y}, \theta_2^*$ and then use importance weighting to "fix-up" the sample. From this method we obtain draws from the posterior distribution of $\vec{\theta}_1|\mathbf{Y}$. Various approximating distributions for $\vec{\theta}_1|\mathbf{Y}, \theta_2^*$ (i.e., multivariate normal and multivariate t with various degrees of freedom) are considered.

A third approach, Gibbs sampling (Gelfand and Smith (1990)) can be used to draw samples from the joint posterior distribution of $\vec{\theta}_1, \vec{\theta}_2|\mathbf{Y}$. To apply this method we alternate between draws from $[\vec{\theta}_1|\mathbf{Y}, \vec{\theta}_2]$ and $[\vec{\theta}_2|\mathbf{Y}, \vec{\theta}_1]$. Since we cannot sample from $[\vec{\theta}_1|\mathbf{Y}, \vec{\theta}_2]$ directly, draws are taken from an approximating distribution and a metropolis algorithm (Hastings (1970)) is employed which yields draws from the correct joint posterior distribution.

2   An application to a 1992 Customer Satisfaction Survey

To demonstrate the benefits and techniques of the hierarchical models, we use a subset of a 1992 DuPont Corporation Customer Satisfaction Survey. This survey had $J = 189$ respondents and $K = 20$ questionnaire items. The 20 questions involved five major categories: product quality, technical support, marketing support, supply/delivery and innovation. For purposes of this analysis we will ignore these categories and treat all 20 questions as exchangeable. Since maximum likelihood is used as a basis of comparisons for the Bayesian methods, 14 out of 189 respondents who had given responses either all 1s or all 0s were removed from the data set to avoid infinite ML parameter estimates (*note*: if we include these the comparison will be more favorable to Bayesian versus ML methods since the latter have no finite estimates). Of the remaining 175 respondents, a random sample of 30 respondents was selected (yielding **Y**, a 30×20 satisfaction matrix); this sample size is large enough to mimic the high dimensionality of the full data set but small enough so that computation time is reasonable (computation time grows linearly with the sample size).

Although, in theory we would like **Y** to be fully observed, there are many questions certain respondents are either unwilling or unable to answer. For example if a CEO is asked "How is the technical support your company receives?" he or she may have no information about this issue and choose not to respond to the item. Missing survey items, coded as NAs, are treated as dissatisfied responses

$$y_{jk} = \begin{cases} y_{jk} \text{ if } y_{jk} \text{ is observed} \\ 0 \text{ otherwise.} \end{cases}$$

Subsequent models will incorporate a model for the non-response mechanism. For this particular data set, the percent of NAs among the 600 entries was modest (36), and were not wholly concentrated in one person or one question. Covariate information was collected for the survey respondents but will not be included in any of the models considered here.

2.1   *Maximum likelihood analysis*

As a baseline for comparison of the Bayesian models, a maximum likelihood analysis was performed based on the product Bernoulli likelihood given in (3). To make this model identifiable two constraints, $\sum_{j=1}^{J} \alpha_j = 0$ and $\sum_{k=1}^{K} \gamma_k = 0$, were added. Maximum likelihood was performed via NR using a convergence criterion of $\max |\vec{\theta}_1^{(n+1)} - \vec{\theta}_1^{(n)}| < 0.0001$ where $\vec{\theta}_1^{(n)}$ is the nth iterate from the algorithm. This criterion corresponds to a very small difference on the logit scale and assuming the algorithm has converged, differences of this magnitude would have no practical effects on the inferences for $\vec{\theta}_1$.

To obtain starting values for the algorithm we note the following from (2)

$$\sum_j \sum_k \text{logit}(p_{jk}) = JK\mu + K\sum_j \alpha_j + J\sum_k \gamma_k$$
$$= JK\mu. \tag{9}$$

Solving for μ suggests the starting value $\mu^{(0)} = \text{logit}(\bar{y}...)$ where $\bar{y}...$ is $\frac{\sum_j \sum_k y_{jk}}{JK}$. Similarly $\vec{\alpha}^{(0)} = (\text{logit}(\bar{y}_1.),\dots,\text{logit}(\bar{y}_J.)) - \mu^{(0)}$ and $\vec{\gamma}^{(0)} = (\text{logit}(\bar{y}_{.1}), \dots,\text{logit}(\bar{y}_{.K})) - \mu^{(0)}$ are obtained as initial estimates of $\vec{\alpha}, \vec{\gamma}$.

A program written in S-PLUS was run on a Sun SPARCstation 2, taking 70 seconds to converge in seven iterations. Associated asymptotic standard errors can be obtained from the inverse second derivative matrix of the log likelihood evaluated at the mode. For $\alpha_1,\dots,\alpha_{J-1}$ and $\gamma_1,\dots,\gamma_{K-1}$ this corresponds to the square root of associated diagonal elements of the second derivative matrix. For α_J and γ_K using the constraints we have that:

$$\text{var}(\alpha_J) = \text{var}(-\sum_{j=1}^{J-1} \alpha_j)$$

$$= \sum_{j=1}^{J-1} \text{var}(\alpha_j) + 2\sum_{j_0 < j_0'} \text{cov}(\alpha_{j_0}, \alpha_{j_0'})$$

$$= \sum_{s=1}^{J-1}\sum_{t=1}^{J-1} -\ell''(\vec{\theta}_1|\mathbf{Y})_{st}^{-1}|_{\hat{\theta}_1^{mle}}$$

and similarly

$$\text{var}(\gamma_K) = \sum_{k=1}^{K-1} \text{var}(\gamma_k) + 2\sum_{k_0 < k_0'} \text{cov}(\gamma_{k_0}, \gamma_{k_0'})$$

$$= \sum_{s=J}^{J+K-2}\sum_{t=J}^{J+K-2} -\ell''(\vec{\theta}_1|\mathbf{Y})_{st}^{-1}|_{\hat{\theta}_1^{mle}}$$

the sums of the appropriate block submatrices from the inverse second derivative matrix. Maximum likelihood estimates for $\vec{\alpha}$ and $\vec{\gamma}$ are in table 12.1; $\hat{\mu} = 0.675$ (SE $= 0.111$). Some interesting things to note are:

Table 12.1. *MLEs, standard errors, row and column percentages for αs and γs*

Person #	$\hat{\alpha}$	SE of $\hat{\alpha}$	$\bar{y}_{i.}$	Item #	$\hat{\gamma}$	SE of $\hat{\gamma}$	$\bar{y}_{.j}$
19	−3.238	0.768	0.10	19	−1.811	0.437	0.300
18	−2.727	0.657	0.15	17	−1.621	0.427	0.333
14	−1.998	0.555	0.25	14	−1.260	0.415	0.400
24	−1.701	0.529	0.30	5	−0.913	0.410	0.467
10	−1.429	0.511	0.35	9	−0.913	0.410	0.467
27	−1.171	0.499	0.40	18	−0.913	0.410	0.467
23	−0.677	0.490	0.50	7	−0.388	0.416	0.567
4	−0.677	0.490	0.50	1	−0.018	0.429	0.633
3	−0.432	0.492	0.55	13	−0.018	0.429	0.633
28	−0.432	0.492	0.55	6	−0.018	0.429	0.633
25	−0.432	0.492	0.55	8	−0.018	0.429	0.633
30	−0.183	0.498	0.60	10	0.178	0.439	0.667
6	−0.183	0.498	0.60	2	0.386	0.451	0.700
12	0.076	0.509	0.65	20	0.386	0.451	0.700
17	0.076	0.509	0.65	4	0.607	0.467	0.733
11	0.351	0.526	0.70	12	0.607	0.467	0.733
15	0.649	0.553	0.75	11	1.111	0.514	0.800
16	0.649	0.553	0.75	3	1.111	0.514	0.800
7	0.649	0.553	0.75	15	1.752	0.596	0.867
22	0.649	0.553	0.75	16	1.752	0.596	0.867
26	0.649	0.553	0.75				
9	0.649	0.553	0.75				
1	0.984	0.591	0.80				
2	0.984	0.591	0.80				
20	0.984	0.591	0.80				
21	0.984	0.591	0.80				
29	0.984	0.591	0.80				
5	1.381	0.652	0.85				
8	1.893	0.762	0.90				
13	2.690	1.023	0.95				

(i)   The $\hat{\alpha}$s vary from a low of −3.238 for person 19 to a high of 2.690 for person 13.

(ii) The $\hat{\gamma}$s vary from a low of −1.811 for item 19 to a high of 1.752 for questions 15 and 16.

(iii) The lowest predicted probability is $\hat{p}_{19,19} = 0.012$ and the highest is $\hat{p}_{13,15} = \hat{p}_{13,16} = 0.994$.

(iv) The SEs for the γs are lower than those for the αs owing to the larger number of observations, 30, available for estimating each γ.

(v) Since this is a logistic model, the SE are minimized when $p(1-p)$ is maximized which occurs when the row (column) percentages are equal to 0.5.

(vi) The ordering of the αs (γs) is identical to the ordering of the row (column) percentages. This result is a property of the Rasch model; the row (column) sums are jointly sufficient for estimating the parameters $\vec{\alpha}$ and $\vec{\gamma}$ respectively.

2.2 Bayesian models

Incorporation of another level of variability via probabilistic models for $\vec{\alpha}$, $\vec{\gamma}$ and μ reflect a belief in a common source of variability among the responses for persons and questions. The prior distributions given in (5), (6), and (7) specify one reasonable set of first-stage priors for $\vec{\theta}_1$. Flat second-level priors were chosen for $\vec{\theta}_2$ for three reasons. First, there is no prior information about realistic values of σ^2 and τ^2 since no historical data or analyses exist. Secondly, a flat prior on σ^2, τ^2 will yield proper posteriors, whereas commonly chosen $[\sigma^2] \propto \sigma^{-1}$ and $[\tau^2] \propto \tau^{-1}$ does not because the data, and in fact any conceivable data set, are consistent with $\sigma^2 = 0$, $\tau^2 = 0$. Thirdly, if the data set contains a lot of information about σ^2 and τ^2 yielding fairly precise estimates, inferences will not be affected by this choice of prior. Moreover if the data set contains little information about these parameters, we should not allow inferences to be distorted or give a false sense of security by adding prior information which has no substantiation.

Posterior inferences for the unknown parameter vectors $\vec{\theta}_1$, $\vec{\theta}_2$ will be made from the posterior distributions $[\vec{\theta}_1|\mathbf{Y}]$ and $[\vec{\theta}_2|\mathbf{Y}]$ respectively. Since as previously stated these distributions cannot be maximized or sampled from directly we will discuss a variety of different approaches to posterior inference.

2.3 Maximum likelihood empirical Bayes (MLEB)

A MLEB approach is one way to approximate the intractable integral for $[\vec{\theta}_1|\mathbf{Y}]$ given in (8). A good introduction to these methods is given in Efron and Morris (1975) and Maritz and Lwin (1989). MLEB inference involves maximizing the posterior distribution of $[\vec{\theta}_2|\mathbf{Y}]$ yielding $\tilde{\theta}_2$ and then maximizing $[\vec{\theta}_1|\mathbf{Y}, \tilde{\theta}_2]$ as a function of $\vec{\theta}_1$. The first difficulty in the current problem is that $[\vec{\theta}_2|\mathbf{Y}]$ cannot be maximized directly. Following the approach of Stiratelli, Laird, and Ware (1984), we use an approximate EM algorithm (Dempster, Laird, and Rubin (1977)). The idea is that if we knew $\vec{\alpha}$, $\vec{\gamma}$, and μ then standard maximum likelihood theory treating the αs as a sample from $N(0, \sigma^2)$, and the γs as a sample from $N(0, \tau^2)$ yields

$$\hat{\sigma}^2 = \frac{\Sigma_j \alpha_j^2}{J} \tag{10}$$

$$\hat{\tau}^2 = \frac{\Sigma_k \gamma_k^2}{K}. \tag{11}$$

Because the αs and γs are truly unknown, we replace the sufficient statistics for estimating $\hat{\sigma}^2$ and $\hat{\tau}^2$ ($\Sigma_j \alpha_j^2, \Sigma_k \gamma_k^2$) by their posterior expectations. So the M-step of the EM algorithm is:

M-step

$$\hat{\sigma}^{2(n+1)} = \frac{E(\Sigma_j \alpha_j^2 | \mathbf{Y}, \vec{\theta}_2^{(n)})}{J}$$

$$= \frac{\Sigma_j (E(\alpha_j | \mathbf{Y}, \vec{\theta}_2^{(n)}))^2 + \Sigma_j \mathrm{var}(\alpha_j | \mathbf{Y}, \vec{\theta}_2^{(n)})}{J} \tag{12}$$

$$\hat{\tau}^{2(n+1)} = \frac{E(\Sigma_k \gamma_k^2 | \mathbf{Y}, \vec{\theta}_2^{(n)})}{K}$$

$$= \frac{\Sigma_k (E(\gamma_k | \mathbf{Y}, \vec{\theta}_2^{(n)}))^2 + \Sigma_k \mathrm{var}(\gamma_k | \mathbf{Y}, \vec{\theta}_2^{(n)})}{K} \tag{13}$$

where $\vec{\theta}^{(n)}$ represents the nth iterate for $\vec{\theta}$. In the E-step we compute these posterior expectations based on the new value of $\vec{\theta}_2$. We alternate E- and M-steps until convergence.

The expectations and variances which come from $[\vec{\theta}_1 | \mathbf{Y}, \vec{\theta}_2]$ cannot be calculated directly since

$$[\vec{\theta}_1 | \mathbf{Y}, \vec{\theta}_2] \propto [\mathbf{Y} | \vec{\theta}_1][\vec{\theta}_1 | \vec{\theta}_2] \tag{14}$$

is the product of Bernoulli likelihoods and a non-conjugate multivariate normal prior. Our strategy is to approximate the likelihood $(\vec{\theta}_1 | \mathbf{Y})$ (denoted $\mathrm{lik}(\vec{\theta}_1 | \mathbf{Y})$) by a multivariate normal. A multivariate Taylor series approximation to $\ell(\vec{\theta}_1 | \mathbf{Y}) = \log(\mathrm{lik}(\vec{\theta}_1 | \mathbf{Y}))$ around $\tilde{\theta}$ is given by

$$\ell(\vec{\theta}_1 | \mathbf{Y}) = (\vec{\theta}_1 - \tilde{\theta})\ell_{\tilde{\theta}}^{\prime t} + \frac{1}{2}(\vec{\theta}_1 - \tilde{\theta})\ell_{\tilde{\theta}}^{\prime\prime}(\vec{\theta}_1 - \tilde{\theta})^t \tag{15}$$

where $\ell_{\tilde{\theta}}^{\prime}$ and $\ell_{\tilde{\theta}}^{\prime\prime}$ are respectively the $1 \times (J + K + 1)$ vector of first derivatives and $(J + K + 1) \times (J + K + 1)$ matrix of second derivatives of $(\mathbf{Y} | \vec{\theta}_1)$ evaluated at $\vec{\theta}_1 = \tilde{\theta}$. Then using (14), combining the approximation to $\ell(\vec{\theta}_1 | \mathbf{Y})$ and the multivariate normal prior for $[\vec{\theta}_1 | \vec{\theta}_2]$ we have that

$$\ell(\vec{\theta}_1 | \mathbf{Y}, \vec{\theta}_2) \approx c + (\vec{\theta}_1 - \tilde{\theta})\ell_{\tilde{\theta}}^{\prime t} + \frac{1}{2}(\vec{\theta}_1 - \tilde{\theta})\ell_{\tilde{\theta}}^{\prime\prime}(\vec{\theta}_1 - \tilde{\theta})^t - \frac{1}{2}(\vec{\theta}_1 \Sigma^{-1} \vec{\theta}_1^t) \tag{16}$$

where

$$\Sigma^{-1} = \begin{pmatrix} \sigma^{-2}I_{J\times J} & 0 & 0 \\ 0 & \tau^{-2}I_{K\times K} & 0 \\ 0 & 0 & 0 \end{pmatrix}$$

is the prior precision matrix. We note that the uniform prior $[\mu] \propto c$ is equivalent to a normal with mean 0 and precision 0. Rewriting (16) with $\Omega_{\tilde{\theta}}^{-1} = -\ell_{\theta}''$ and then completing the square for $\vec{\theta}_1$ we obtain

$$\ell(\vec{\theta}_1 | \mathbf{Y}, \vec{\theta}_2) \approx c + (\vec{\theta}_1 - \mu^*)S_{\tilde{\theta}}^{-1}(\vec{\theta}_1 - \mu^*)^t \tag{17}$$

with

$$\mu^* = (\tilde{\theta}\Omega^{-1} + \ell_{\theta}')S_{\tilde{\theta}}$$
$$S_{\tilde{\theta}}^{-1} = \Omega_{\tilde{\theta}}^{-1} + \Sigma^{-1}$$

a standard normal quadratic form.

Because we want the approximation of $\ell(\vec{\theta}_1 | \mathbf{Y}, \vec{\theta}_2)$ given in (17) to be around its posterior mode and not an initial guess $\tilde{\theta}_0$, we initially approximate $\ell(\vec{\theta}_1 | \mathbf{Y}, \vec{\theta}_2)$ around some $\tilde{\theta}_0$, calculate μ^*, reapproximate $\ell(\vec{\theta}_1 | \mathbf{Y}, \vec{\theta}_2)$ around μ^*, and cycle until convergence. This is equivalent to a NR algorithm for finding the mode of this log likelihood, which is an approximation to $E(\vec{\theta}_1 | \mathbf{Y}, \vec{\theta}_2)$. Once the mode $\tilde{\theta}$ is obtained to find $E(\vec{\theta}_1 | \mathbf{Y}, \vec{\theta}_2)$ and $E(\vec{\theta}_1^2 | \mathbf{Y}, \vec{\theta}_2)$, the expectation of the sufficient statistics described in (12) and (13), we use the center of the quadratic form and the diagonal elements of $S_{\tilde{\theta}}^{-1}$ given in (17) evaluated at the current value of $\vec{\theta}_2$ yielding:

E-step

$$E(\vec{\theta}_1 | \mathbf{Y}, \vec{\theta}_2^{(n)}) = (\ell_{\vec{\theta}_1^{(n)}}' + \vec{\theta}_1^{(n)}\Omega_{\vec{\theta}_1^{(n)}}^{-1})S_{\vec{\theta}_1^{(n)}, \vec{\theta}_2^{(n)}} \tag{18}$$

$$E(\vec{\theta}_1^2 | \mathbf{Y}, \vec{\theta}_2) = E(\vec{\theta}_1 | \mathbf{Y}, \vec{\theta}_2^{(n)})^2 + \vec{1} \cdot S_{\tilde{\theta}}^{-1} \tag{19}$$

where $E(\vec{\theta}_1 | \mathbf{Y}, \vec{\theta}_2)$ and $E(\vec{\theta}_1^2 | \mathbf{Y}, \vec{\theta}_2)$ are $J + K + 1$ dimensional vectors. To summarize the EM algorithm employed:
(1) Choose some starting value $\vec{\theta}_1^{(0)}, \vec{\theta}_2^{(0)}$; set $n = 1$.
(2) Obtain $E(\vec{\theta}_1 | \mathbf{Y}, \vec{\theta}_2^{(n)})$ and $E(\vec{\theta}_1^2 | \mathbf{Y}, \vec{\theta}_2)$ from (18) and (19) respectively (E-step).
(3) Obtain $\vec{\theta}_2^{(n)}$ using equations (12) and (13) (M-step).
(4) If $\max (|\vec{\theta}_1^{(n)} - \vec{\theta}_1^{(n-1)}|) < 0.0001$ STOP.
(5) Let $n = n + 1$; go to (2).
A nice feature of this EM algorithm is that although its original purpose was to find the posterior mode of $[\vec{\theta}_2 | \mathbf{Y}]$, a by-product of the algorithm from the E-step is the MLEB solution $E(\vec{\theta}_1 | \mathbf{Y}, \vec{\theta}_2)$.

Table 12.2. *Shrinkage factors for the αs and γs*

i	$\hat{\alpha}_i^{mle}$	$\hat{\alpha}_i^{mleb}$	$B_{\alpha i}$	$\hat{\gamma}_i^{mle}$	$\hat{\gamma}_i^{mleb}$	$B_{\gamma i}$
1	0.984	0.696	0.293	−0.018	−0.016	0.090
2	0.984	0.696	0.293	0.386	0.287	0.256
3	−0.432	−0.297	0.313	1.111	0.722	0.351
4	−0.677	−0.477	0.296	0.607	0.426	0.298
5	1.381	0.934	0.324	−0.913	−0.603	0.340
6	−0.183	−0.114	0.379	−0.018	−0.016	0.090
7	0.649	0.477	0.265	−0.388	−0.234	0.398
8	1.893	1.196	0.368	−0.018	−0.016	0.090
9	0.649	0.477	0.265	−0.913	−0.603	0.340
10	−1.429	−1.017	0.288	0.178	0.152	0.149
11	0.351	0.271	0.228	1.111	0.722	0.351
12	0.076	0.075	0.018	0.607	0.426	0.298
13	2.690	1.492	0.445	−0.018	−0.016	0.090
14	−1.998	−1.396	0.301	−1.260	−0.846	0.329
15	0.649	0.477	0.265	1.752	1.046	0.403
16	0.649	0.477	0.265	1.752	1.046	0.403
17	0.076	0.075	0.018	−1.621	−1.091	0.327
18	−2.727	−1.813	0.335	−0.913	−0.603	0.340
19	−3.238	−2.045	0.368	−1.811	−1.216	0.328
20	0.984	0.696	0.293	0.386	0.287	0.256
21	0.984	0.696	0.293			
22	0.649	0.477	0.265			
23	−0.677	−0.477	0.296			
24	−1.701	−1.204	0.293			
25	−0.432	−0.297	0.313			
26	0.649	0.477	0.265			
27	−1.171	−0.836	0.286			
28	−0.432	−0.297	0.313			
29	0.984	0.696	0.293			
30	−0.183	−0.114	0.379			

This algorithm was applied to the same 30×20 DuPont data set analyzed via maximum likelihood in section 2.1. Starting values chosen for the algorithm were $\vec{\theta}_1^{(0)} = 0$, $\sigma^2 = 0.1$, $\tau^2 = 0.1$. The algorithm was also run on a Sun SPARCstation 2 and converged in 85 seconds in 16 iterations. The estimates of the αs and γs from the analysis are given in table 12.2 and table 12.3 along with a comparison to the ML estimates. B is defined as the amount of shrinkage of the MLE toward 0, the prior mean for $\vec{\theta}_1$, by the equation

Table 12.3. *Estimates of μ, σ^2, τ^2*

	$\hat{\mu}$	$\hat{\sigma}^2$	$\hat{\tau}^2$
MLE	0.675	–	–
MLEB	0.582	0.961	0.574

$$(1 - B) \cdot \hat{\theta}^{mle} + B \cdot 0 = \hat{\theta}^{mleb} \tag{20}$$

or

$$B = 1 - \frac{\hat{\theta}^{mleb}}{\hat{\theta}^{mle}}. \tag{21}$$

The average shrinkage of the αs is 28.5 percent and for the γs is 27.6 percent. The effects of this shrinkage can be seen most dramatically when we compare the estimated probability of person 19 being satisfied on question 19 obtained via the MLEs versus the MLEB estimates. From maximum likelihood $\hat{p}_{19,19} = 0.012$ and from the MLEB estimates it is 0.064. On the opposite extreme $\hat{p}_{13,15}$ from MLEs is 0.994 and it is 0.958 from MLEB estimates. Secondly, the shrunken estimates of the αs and γs have considerably less variability than the MLEs. Thirdly, since $\hat{\sigma}^2$ is 0.961 compared to $\hat{\tau}^2 = 0.574$ in this data set there is more variability in the person effects than the item effects.

Although the MLEB estimates have lower variability than the unshrunken MLEs, this does not guarantee that the actual estimates are "better" using a squared error loss function (or others). To explore this, a simulation experiment was performed based on data generated from the distribution $[\mathbf{Y} | \vec{\theta}_2]$. Specifically:

(i) Draw $\alpha_1^*, \ldots, \alpha_{30}^*$ independently from $N(0, \hat{\sigma}^2)$, $\gamma_1^*, \ldots, \gamma_{20}^*$ from $N(0, \hat{\tau}^2)$ and set μ^* equal to $\hat{\mu}$ yielding $\vec{\theta}_1^*$.

(ii) Draw a 30×20 satisfaction matrix $\mathbf{Y}^*$ from $[\mathbf{Y} | \vec{\theta}_1^*]$ based on probability matrix $\mathbf{P}^*$ defined by the inverse logit of $\mu^* + \alpha_j^* + \gamma_k^*$.

(iii) Analyze $\mathbf{Y}^*$ via ML and MLEB methods, yielding $\hat{\theta}_1^{mle}$ and $\hat{\theta}_1^{mleb}$.

(iv) Compute the error sum of squares for both estimates equal to

$$SS_{mle} = (\hat{\theta}_1^{mle} - \vec{\theta}_1^*)'(\hat{\theta}_1^{mle} - \vec{\theta}_1^*)$$
$$SS_{mleb} = (\hat{\theta}_1^{mleb} - \vec{\theta}_1^*)'(\hat{\theta}_1^{mleb} - \vec{\theta}_1^*).$$

(v) Repeat steps (i)–(iv) 100 times

This analysis will give us 100 data sets similar to the observed one in that the variability in the person effects and the item effects are fixed at the MLEB estimates yet the persons and items themselves are treated as

Table 12.4. *Simulation results, averages based on 100 trials*

	MLE	MLEB
Total SS	15.7	14.6
SS_α	10.2	9.8
SS_γ	5.5	4.8

random. From the 100 generated data sets, we can estimate to a reasonable level of precision the predictive distribution of any statistic. The simulation results, shown in table 12.4, imply a modest improvement for MLEB estimates over MLEs.

Improvement would be more substantial when σ^2 and τ^2 are small as the MLEB solution would provide a more accurate estimate of the true posterior $[\vec{\theta}_1 | Y]$.

2.4   Grid approximation to $[\vec{\theta}_2 | \mathbf{Y}]$

Another approach to dealing with the intractability of calculating $[\vec{\theta}_1 | \mathbf{Y}]$ in (8) is to approximate $[\vec{\theta}_2 | \mathbf{Y}]$ by a discrete distribution over a grid of values. We can obtain this approximation as follows. The marginal posterior distribution of $\vec{\theta}_2$ can be written as

$$[\vec{\theta}_2 | \mathbf{Y}] = \int [\vec{\theta}_1, \vec{\theta}_2 | \mathbf{Y}] d\vec{\theta}_1$$

$$\propto \int [\mathbf{Y} | \vec{\theta}_1][\vec{\theta}_1 | \vec{\theta}_2] d\vec{\theta}_1 \tag{22}$$

where $[\vec{\theta}_1 | \vec{\theta}_2]$ is normal. By making the same normal approximation to $\ell(\vec{\theta}_1 | \mathbf{Y})$ used in the MLEB analysis (see (15)) this integral becomes tractable in closed form. Combining the approximation to $\ell(\vec{\theta}_1 | \mathbf{Y})$ with $[\vec{\theta}_1 | \vec{\theta}_2]$ and completing the square as before in (18), but in this case keeping all terms which are a function of $\vec{\theta}_2$, we get

$$\text{lik}(\vec{\theta}_2 | \mathbf{Y}) \approx |\Sigma^{-1} S|^{\frac{1}{2}} \exp(\hat{\theta}_1^{mleb} \Omega^{-1} S(\hat{\theta}_1^{mleb} \Omega^{-1})^t + \ell'(\vec{\theta}_1 | \mathbf{Y})$$

$$[(\hat{\theta}_1^{mleb} \Omega^{-1} S)^t + \frac{1}{2} S\ell'(\vec{\theta}_1 | \mathbf{Y})^t])$$

where Ω^{-1}, S (which is a function $\vec{\theta}_2$ as shown in (17)), and ℓ' are all evaluated at the mode $\hat{\theta}_1^{mleb}$. A 20×20 grid of values for σ^2 and τ^2 was chosen to cover most of the mass of the distribution, where σ^2 varied from 0.01 to 2.5

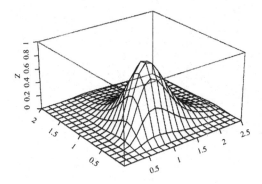

Figure 12.2 Likelihood grid for $\vec{\theta}_2 | Y$

and τ^2 from 0.01 to 2. A three-dimensional plot of the likelihood on the grid is shown in figure 12.2.

Posterior inference based on this grid approximation is done in the following manner.

(i) Draw 100 pairs $\vec{\theta}_{2,i} = (\sigma_i^2, \tau_i^2)$ from the grid approximation to likelihood $(\vec{\theta}_2 | \mathbf{Y})$.

(ii) For each pair $\vec{\theta}_{2,i}$ draw a $\vec{\theta}_{1,i}$ from an approximation to $[\vec{\theta}_1 | \mathbf{Y}, \vec{\theta}_{2,i}]$ since the true $[\vec{\theta}_1 | \mathbf{Y}, \vec{\theta}_{2,i}]$ cannot be sampled from directly because the likelihood and prior are non-conjugate.

Several different approximations to $[\vec{\theta}_1 | \mathbf{Y}, \vec{\theta}_{2,i}]$ were tried including the multivariate normal previously discussed, an overdispersed normal, and the multivariate student's-t distribution with various degrees of freedom (3, 8, 20 were used). For the overdispersed normal instead of letting S^{-1} the posterior precision matrix equal $(\Omega^{-1} + \Sigma^{-1})$ we let $S^{-1} = (k\Omega^{-1} + \Sigma^{-1})$ where $k = 0.8$. The form of the multivariate t distribution used here is

$$t(\hat{\theta}_1^{mleb}, S) = \hat{\theta}_1^{mleb} + S^{\frac{1}{2}} Z \lambda^{-\frac{1}{2}} \tag{23}$$

where $\hat{\theta}_1^{mleb}$ is computed from equation (18), $S = (\Omega^{-1} + \Sigma^{-1})^{-1}$ evaluated at the mode, $Z \sim MVN(0, I_{(J+K+1) \times J+K+1})$ and $\lambda = \frac{\chi_n^2}{n}$. The diagnostics for determining whether the approximating distribution is a good fit to the true $[\vec{\theta}_1 | \mathbf{Y}, \vec{\theta}_2]$ are the importance weights w_i, $i = 1, \ldots, 100$ where

$$w_i \propto \frac{\text{true}[\vec{\theta}_{1,i} | \mathbf{Y}, \vec{\theta}_{2,i}]}{\text{approximation}[\vec{\theta}_{1,i} | \mathbf{Y}, \vec{\theta}_{2,i}]}. \tag{24}$$

If the approximation is a good fit to the true density we would expect to see uniformity in the importance weights. If the true density has mass in places where the approximate density has very little, this would lead to weights

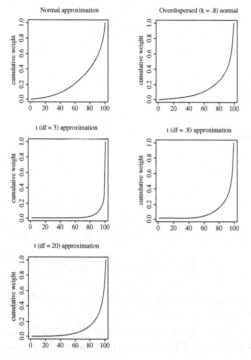

Figure 12.3 Cumulative plot of (w_i) for approximations to $[\vec{\theta}_1 | Y, \vec{\theta}_2]$

greater than 1 indicating that the approximate density would not have enough draws from those areas. If the reverse happens where the approximate density has more mass than the true, the weights will be very small for some draws and large for others yielding a large variance for posterior estimates. Although points would be sampled from every part of the true distribution, this would be a very inefficient sampling scheme. A plot of the cumulative density function is shown in figure 12.3 for the various approximate distributions.

From the plots we can see that the multivariate normal approximation appears to do the best (i.e., has the most uniform weights) and therefore it will be used for the remainder of this chapter. Three thousand draws, not including the previous 100, were taken from the multivariate normal approximation. If we take a large number of draws, even though the weight distribution is skewed, our effective sample size may still be large enough to yield accurate estimates. Posterior estimation of $\vec{\theta}_1$ is based on the weighted mean

$$\hat{\theta}_1^{grid} + \mathbf{D}^t \cdot \mathbf{w} \tag{25}$$

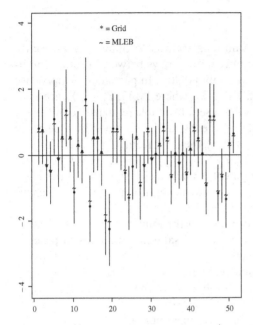

Figure 12.4 95% posterior intervals for $\vec{\theta}_1$ based on the normal approximation

where $\mathbf{D}$ is the 3000×51 dimensional matrix of draws from the approxima-
tion to $[\vec{\theta}_1 | \mathbf{Y}, \vec{\theta}_2]$ and $w = (w_1, \ldots w_{3000})$ is the vector of importance weights
(normalized to have sum 1). A plot of 95 percent posterior intervals for $(\theta_{1,1},
\ldots \vec{\theta}_{1,51}) = (\vec{\alpha}, \vec{\gamma}, \mu)$ is shown in figure 12.4 with the location of $\hat{\theta}^{mleb}$ and $\hat{\theta}^{grid}$
indicated on the interval.

From this plot we notice that (1) $\hat{\theta}^{mleb}$ and $\hat{\theta}^{grid}$ are fairly close, (2) $\hat{\theta}^{mleb}$ is
shrunken toward 0 more than $\hat{\theta}^{grid}$, and (3) the posterior intervals for $\vec{\theta}_1$ are
fairly wide implying predictions with fairly large standard errors. Result (1)
is not that surprising because a large amount of data are available to estimate σ^2 and τ^2 so substituting a point estimate does fairly well. Result (2)
occurs because the grid method uses the posterior means for $\vec{\theta}_2$ instead of
the mode used in MLEB analysis. In particular, since the posterior means
for σ^2 and τ^2 are larger than the corresponding modes, the grid estimates
will be shrunk less toward zero owing to the larger prior variance. Result
(3) is also expected because there are not a lot of data available to estimate
each α or each γ individually. In the next section another method, Gibbs
sampling (Gelfand and Smith (1990)), which does not rely on a grid
approximation to $[\vec{\theta}_2 | \mathbf{Y}]$ will be used to generate posterior samples.

2.5   Gibbs sampling

Gibbs sampling is an iterative sampling method to obtain draws from a posterior distribution based on alternating draws between a set of conditional distributions (Gelfand and Smith (1990)). In particular, suppose we want a set of draws from $[Y_1, Y_2, Y_3, \ldots, Y_V]$ where $Y_1, Y_2, Y_3, \ldots, Y_V$ are arbitrary random variables. Then under a set of suitable regularity conditions, draws from the joint distribution of the Ys can be obtained by repeatedly drawing $Y_1^{(n)}$ from $[Y_1 \mid Y_2^{(n-1)}, \ldots, Y_V^{(n-1)}]$, then $Y_2^{(n)}$ from $[Y_2 \mid Y_1^{(n)}, Y_3^{(n-1)}, \ldots, Y_V^{(n-1)}], \ldots$, and $Y_V^{(n)}$ from $[Y_V \mid Y_1^{(n)}, Y_2^{(n)}, \ldots, Y_{V-1}^{(n)}]$ for $n = 1, \ldots, N$. Once these N draws are obtained some judgment is made as to when and if the algorithm has converged. If we define m to be the iteration number at which we deem the algorithm to have converged, then the draws $(Y_1^{(m)}, \ldots, Y_V^{(m)}), \ldots, (Y_1^{(N)}, \ldots, Y_V^{(N)})$ are considered draws from the joint posterior distribution $[Y_1, \ldots, Y_V]$. Open issues in applying Gibbs sampling methods in practice involve determining the necessary N to have precise posterior estimates, and also the method to determine m, the point at which the draws are considered draws from the true joint distribution. In this problem, draws from $[\vec{\theta}_1, \vec{\theta}_2 \mid \mathbf{Y}]$ are obtained in the following manner

(i)   Initialize $\vec{\theta}_1^{(0)}, \vec{\theta}_2^{(0)}$ to some starting values; let $n = 1$.

(ii)   Draw $\vec{\theta}_1^{(n)}$ from $[\vec{\theta}_1 \mid \mathbf{Y}, \vec{\theta}_2^{(n-1)}]$.

(iii)   Draw $\vec{\theta}_2^{(n)}$ from $[\vec{\theta}_2 \mid \mathbf{Y}, \vec{\theta}_1^{(n-1)}]$.

(iv)   Let $n = n + 1$; go to step (ii) if $n < \text{cutoff} = N$.

One difficulty in using this algorithm for our model is that we cannot sample from $[\vec{\theta}_1 \mid \mathbf{Y}, \vec{\theta}_2^{(n-1)}]$ directly. Therefore, instead of implementing step (ii) we draw from an approximation to $[\vec{\theta}_1 \mid \mathbf{Y}, \vec{\theta}_2^{(n-1)}]$ in conjunction with a metropolis step (Hastings (1970), Roberts and Smith (1993)) as follows:

(iia)   Drawing $\vec{\theta}_1^*$ from an approximation to the true $[\vec{\theta}_1 \mid \mathbf{Y}, \vec{\theta}_2^{(n-1)}]$

(iib)   let

$$\vec{\theta}_1^{(n)} = \begin{cases} \vec{\theta}_1^* \text{ with probability } \min\left(1, \dfrac{w(\vec{\theta}_1^*)}{w(\vec{\theta}_1^{(n-1)})}\right) \\ \vec{\theta}_1^{(n-1)} \text{ otherwise.} \end{cases}$$

where $w(\vec{\theta}_1^{(n-1)})$ is defined in (24) as the importance ratio evaluated at $\vec{\theta}_1 = \vec{\theta}_1^{(n)}$. To implement step (iii) we note that

$$\sigma^{2(n)} \sim J s_{\vec{\alpha}^{(n)}}^2 \cdot \chi_J^{-2}$$

$$\tau^{2(n)} \sim K s_{\vec{\gamma}^{(n)}}^2 \cdot \chi_K^{-2}$$

where $s_{\vec{\alpha}^{(n)}}^2$ and $s_{\vec{\gamma}^{(n)}}^2$ are the sample variance of the αs and γs at the nth iteration and χ_g^{-2} is an inverse chi-square random variable with g degrees of freedom (Box and Tiao (1973)). The Gibbs sampler was run in five parallel series of length 1,000 each on a Sun SPARCstation 2

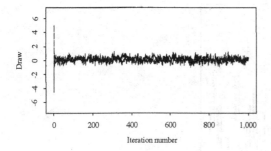

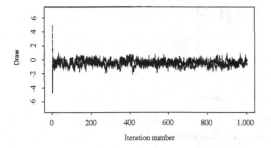

Figure 12.5 Gibbs sampler for σ^2 (top) and γ^2 (bottom), 3 series of 1,000 iterations

taking 18 seconds per iteration for each of the 5,000 iterations. The starting values chosen were overdisposed for $\vec{\theta}_2$ in the spirit of Gelman and Rubin (1992) to help assess convergence of the sampler. Specifically, $\vec{\theta}_1^{(0)}$ equaled $\hat{\theta}^{grid}$ for all five series and $\vec{\theta}_2^{(0)} = (\tau^{2(0)}, \tau^{2(0)})$ was initialized to $(0.01, 0.01)$, $(0.50, 0.50)$, $(1, 1)$, (e^3, e^3), and (e^5, e^5) for the first through fifth series respectively. For purposes of showing an uncluttered plot, only the first, third, and fifth series for σ^2 and τ^2 are shown (on the log scale) in figure 12.5. We see that the Gibbs sampler appears to converge very quickly, in fewer than ten steps, even for overdispersed starting values as extreme as 0.01 and e^5. To be conservative, draws 51 through 1,000 were used to do posterior calculations. with five series this yields us 4,750 draws from the joint posterior distribution of $\vec{\theta}_1, \vec{\theta}_2 | \mathbf{Y}$. Since these draws are correlated a random sample of size 1,000 out of 4,750 was used to make posterior inferences. Ninety-five percent posterior intervals for $\vec{\theta}_1$ and $\vec{\theta}_2$ were calculated and compared with the intervals computed using the grid approximation. The intervals seem to align themselves fairly well (see

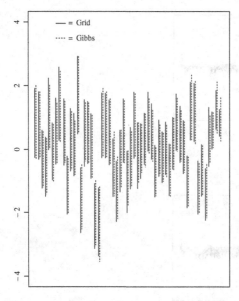

Figure 12.6 Comparison of 95% posterior intervals for $\alpha_1, \ldots, \alpha_{30}, \gamma_1, \ldots, \gamma_{20}, \sigma^2, \gamma^2$ based on the grid approximation and Gibbs sampling

figure 12.6), with the one noticeable difference being the wider intervals using Gibbs for $\vec{\theta}_2$. This result may be due to the fact that the discrete grid for $[\vec{\theta}_2|\mathbf{Y}]$ did not cover the tails of the distribution well enough or that the sample of 3,000 from the discrete grid is not large enough to get draws from far out in the tails.

2.6   Comparison of inferences

A comparison of the various methods, when utilized for decision making, should entail a contrast of the inferences derived. The Bayesian methods, which all provide inferences from the same posterior will provide identical inferences as long as the estimation error is kept minimal. However, the ML methods would not necessarily provide the same inferences, and in particular when ranking individuals and/or items is desired the shrinkage provided by Bayesian methods will likely alter the obtained ranking or at least make extreme cases look less extreme (as in table 12.2 and figure 12.4 for cases 18 and 19). This adjustment would be more extreme in other data sets where the number of items answered per individual (hence the amount of information) is likely to vary substantially.

3   Future work

Many issues remained untouched in this chapter that will have to be addressed to make this technology more useful from a practical sense and more rigorous from a statistical sense. The general areas of future research include:

(i)   Instead of setting $y_{jk} = 0$ if the rating is unobserved, probability models for y_{jk} being observed as a function of covariance $\vec{x}_j$ can be built. The rationale behind the improvement is that whether someone can answer a question about a particular item (e.g., product quality) may be a function of a set of covariates for that person (e.g., their job type, age, etc.). Furthermore, the mechanism itself by which people do not respond may be of intrinsic interest as well. This research issue is partially addressed in Bradlow (1994), and Bradlow and Zaslavsky (1999).

(ii)   Although this chapter only detailed the analysis for one business within the DuPont Corporation, there are many data sets from the corporate wide 1992 CS study. From a statistical point of view, however, analyzing each of these businesses separately would not be appropriate given the nested hierarchical corporate structure. Probability models will be extended to include this additional level of randomness. Instead of looking just at the y_{jk}, we will consider y_{jkl}, $l = 1, \ldots, 230$ where l indexes businesses. From this type of analysis we can get business level estimates which borrow strength from similar businesses and similarly for the person and item effects.

(iii) The probability models suggested in this chapter need to be checked in some way to see if they are an adequate description of the phenomena. One way to do this is via the posterior predictive distribution $[Y^*$ $| Y]$ where Y^* is a future hypothetical satisfaction matrix. To do this type of analysis we could choose some statistic of interest, say the maximum estimated probability of a person being satisfied on a particular item, and calculate this for a large number of Y^*s. To generate Y^*s we need to be able to sample from $[\vec{\theta}_1, \vec{\theta}_2 | Y]$ obtaining $(\vec{\theta}_1^*, \vec{\theta}_2^*)$ and then $[Y | \vec{\theta}_1^*, \vec{\theta}_2^*]$ yielding Y^*. Then by comparing the observed statistic from $\mathbf{Y}$ to a histogram of this statistic based on the Y^*s we get some idea of the model fit.

(iv)   The model proposed in this chapter assumes homogeneity of variance from the αs and γs. Whether this assumption holds can be assessed to some degree from the data. One possible remedy would be to postulate more than one variance for the αs (or γs), and consider this a missing data problem because we do not know the group indicator for each α which specifies what its variance would be (i.e., $\alpha_j \sim N(\vec{x}_j \beta'$,

$\sum_{g=1}^{G} \sigma_g^2 V_{jg})$ where V_{jg} is an indicator for person j being in group $g = 1$, $\ldots, G)$.

4   Conclusions

The 30×20 satisfaction matrix introduced in this chapter was analyzed using maximum likelihood, MLEB, grid approximation, and Gibbs sampling methods. While the results did not turn out dramatically different for the Bayesian methods, analyzing the problem in a Bayesian framework was an interesting exercise in applying Bayesian computational methods and comparing how Bayesian posterior inferences differ from standard ML results. Future data sets incorporating missing values and respondents who give all 1s or 0s should yield analyses where the different Bayesian methods also have varying results. Certainly, since these methods have easily interpretable output, are relatively inexpensive to run, and yield more sensible answers than exploratory methods, it seems worthwhile to implement them in the future.

Bibliography

Albert, J.H. and S. Chib (1993), "Bayesuian Analysis of Binary and Polychotomous Response Data," *Journal of the American Statistical Association*, 88(422), 669–679.

Andrich, D. (1978), "A Rating Formulation for Ordered Response Categories," *Psychometrika*, 43(4), 561–573.

Belin, T.R., G.J. Diffendal, S. Mack, J.L. Schafer, D.B. Rubin, and A.M. Zaslavsky (1993), "Hierarchical Logistic Regression Models for Imputation of Unresolved Enumeration Status in Undercount Estimation," *Journal of the American Statistical Association*, 88(423), 1149–1166.

Bickel, P.J. and K.A. Doksum (1977), *Mathematical Statistics: Basic Ideas and Selected Topics*, Holden-Day.

Box, G.E.P. and G.C. Tiao (1973), *Bayesian Inference in Statistical Analysis*, Addison-Wesley.

Bradlow, E.T. (1994), "Analysis of Ordinal Survey Data with 'No Answer' Responses," Harvard University Department of Statistics, doctoral dissertation.

Bradlow, E.T. and A.M. Zaslavsky (1999), "A Hierarchical Latent Variable Model for Ordinary Survey Data with 'No Answer' Responses," *Journal of the American Statistical Association*, March 1999 (forthcoming).

Conaway, M.R. (1992). "The Analysis of Repeated Categorical Measurements Subject to Non-ignorable Nonresponse," *Journal of the American Statistical Association*, 87(419), 817–824.

(1989), "Analysis of Repeated Categorical Measurements With Conditional Likelihood Methods," *Journal of the American Statistical Association*, 84(405), 53–62.

Cressie, N. and P.W. Holland (1983), "Characterizing the Manifest Probabilities of Latent Trait Models," *Psychometrika*, 48(1), 129–141.

Dempster, A.P., N.M. Laird, and D.B. Rubin (1977), "Maximum Likelihood from Incomplete Data via the EM Algorithm," *Journal of Statistical Studies*, Series B, 39, 1–38.

Efron, B. and C. Morris (1975), "Data Analysis Using Stein's Estimator and its Generalizsations," *Journal of the American Statistical Association*, 70(350), 311–319.

Gelfand, A.G. and A.F.M. Smith (1990), "Sampling-based Approaches to Calculating Marginal Densities," *Journal of the American Statistical Association*, 85, 398–409.

Gelman A. and D.B. Rubin (1992), "Inference from Iterative Simulation Using Multiple Sequences," *Statistical Science*, 7(4), 457–511.

Hastings, W.K. (1970), "Monte-Carlo Sampling Methods Using Markov Chains and their Applications," *Biometrika*, 57, 97–109.

Holland, P.W. (1990a), "On the Sampling Theory Foundations of Item Response Theory Models," *Psychometrika*, 55(4), 577–601.

(1990b), "The Dutch Identity, A New Tool for the Study of Item Response Models," *Psychometrika*, 55(1), 5–18.

Lindsay, B., C.C. Clogg, and J. Grego (1991), "Semiparametric Estimation in the Rasch Model and Related Exponential Response Models, Including a Simple Latent Class Model for Item Analysis," *Journal of the American Statistical Association*, 86(413), 96–107.

Little, R.J.A. and D.B. Rubin (1987), *Statistical Analysis with Missing Data*, New York: Wiley.

Maritz, J.S. and T. Lwin (1970, repr. 1989), *Empirical Bayes Methods*, Chapman and Hall.

Masters, G.N. (1982), "A Rasch Model for Partial Credit Scoring," *Psychometrika*, 47(2), 149–174.

McCullagh, P. and J.A. Nelder, (1983), *Generalized Linear Models*, Chapman and Hall.

Meng, X.L. and D.B. Rubin (1993), "Maximum Likelihood Estimation via the ECM Algorithm: A General Framework," *Biometrika*, 80(2), 267–278.

Rasch, G. (1960), "Probablistic Models for Some Intelligence and Attainment Tests," Copenhagen: Nielson and Lydiche (for Danmarks Paedagogiske Institut).

Roberts, G.O. and A.F.M. Smith (1993), "Bayesian Computation via the Gibbs Sampler and Related Markov Chain Monte Carlo Methods," *Journal of Statistical Studies*, Series B, 55(1), 3–23.

Rosenbaum, P.R. (1984), "Testing the Conditional Independence and Monotonicity Assumptions of Item Response Theory," *Psychometrika*, 49, 425–436.

Stiratelli, R., N. Laird., and J.H. Ware (1984), "Random-Effects Models for Serial Observations with Binary Response," *Biometrics*, 40, 961–971.

13 Calibration by simulation for small sample bias correction

Christian Gourieroux, Eric Renault, and Nizar Touzi

In this chapter we study the finite sample properties of the indirect inference procedure, introduced by Smith (1993) and generalized independently by Gallant and Tauchen (1996) and Gourieroux, Monfort, and Renault (1993). This statistical procedure can be seen as an extension of the simulated method of moments in the sense that the information contained in the data is summarized by a general instrumental criterion rather than a given number of empirical moments. Under usual regularity conditions, the indirect inference estimator has been shown to be consistent and asymptotically normal. In practice, this method has been implemented on simulated or real data, and appeared to perform well (see Pastorello, Renault, and Touzi (1993), Kouki and Renault (1994)). In this chapter, we provide some additional properties of the indirect inference for small samples.

First, we relate the median-bias correction procedure, suggested by Andrews (1993) for first-order autoregressive models (AR(1)), to the general indirect inference procedure. Andrews' procedure is an exact bias correction for the least squares (LS) estimator in the sense of the median indicator, and can be described as follows: if the LS estimator of the autoregressive parameter α for a sample size T is $\hat{\beta}_T$ then, the estimator $\hat{\alpha}_T^U$, defined as the value of α that yields the finite sample distribution of the LS estimator to have a median of $\hat{\beta}_T$, is exactly median unbiased. The intuition behind the choice of the median-unbiasedness criterion for small sample accuracy seems to be the important skewness of the finite sample distribution of the LS estimator, especially when the AR parameter is close to 1, which makes the median a better measure of central tendency than the mean.

In this chapter, Andrews' procedure is shown to be closely related to the indirect inference approach. Therefore, we generalize such a bias correction procedure to a general class of dynamic models. A comparison by simulations between the median-bias correction procedure and the indirect inference for $AR(p)$ models is provided in section 3.

However, the most popular bias correction procedures rely on the computation of the bias. In some simple cases, an explicit formula for the small sample bias is available, as for the maximum likelihood estimator of the variance parameter in a sample of independent variables distributed as a normal $\mathcal{N}(\mu, \sigma^\epsilon)$. Such a characterization of the bias can be exploited to define an unbiased estimator from the initial biased one.

In general, an explicit formula for the small sample bias is not available. If the first terms of the bias expansion in powers of $\frac{1}{T}$ can be computed, then a new estimator can be defined such that the bias is reduced up to some order $\frac{1}{T^a}$. For instance, Orcutt and Winokur (1969) showed that the first term in the expansion of the bias of the LS estimator of the AR parameter in an $AR(1)$ model is of order $\frac{1}{T}$, and thus a second-order unbiased estimator can be computed (see e.g. Rudebusch (1993)). A generalization of the results of Orcutt and Winokur to the $AR(p)$ case is provided by Shaman and Stine (1989)).

In most cases of interest, even the first terms of the expansion of the bias are difficult to compute explicitly. The bootstrap estimator, introduced by Efron (1979), presents the valuable advantage of operating a second-order correction of the bias automatically, thanks to simulations. For an infinite number of simulations, we show that the indirect inference also operates a second-order bias correction. However, in contrast with the bootstrap methods, this result does not hold for a finite number of replications. A precise comparison between both estimators up to the third order of an Edgeworth expansion is provided in the case of an infinite number of simulations; we find no evidence for the dominance of one of these methods.

The chapter is organized as follows. In section 1, we define and compare the goals of three simulation-based procedures of bias reduction: median-bias correction à la Andrews (1993), parametric bootstrap, and indirect inference. We stress both the similarities between the three approaches (including iterated versions of bootstrap and indirect inference) as well as their general differences. In section 2, we use Edgeworth expansions in order to examine the second-order bias of the indirect inference estimator, and we provide a precise comparison with the bootstrap estimator. Section 3 presents some simulation results for $AR(1)$ and $AR(2)$ models, and compares the indirect inference estimator to the median-bias correction procedure of Andrews.

1   Small sample properties of indirect inference

1.1   The indirect inference principle

In this subsection we provide a brief review of the indirect inference procedure introduced by Smith (1993) and generalized independently by Gallant and Tauchen (1996) (GT hereafter) and Gourieroux, Monfort, and Renault (1993) (GMR hereafter). (For a complete review, see Gourieroux and Monfort (1995).) It is well known that the estimators of GT and GMR are asymptotically equivalent (see GMR), and that they coincide in the special case where the auxiliary model and the true one have the same number of parameters ($p = d$ in the following notations). The results derived in this chapter concern essentially the latter case, and therefore we only present GMR's approach. Consider the general model

$$Z_t = \varphi(Z_{t-1}, u_t; \theta) \tag{1}$$

$$Y_t = r(Y_{t-1}, Z_t; \theta) \tag{2}$$

where $\{u_t, t = 1, \ldots, T\}$ is a white noise process with known distribution G_0, $\{Z_t, t = 0, \ldots, T\}$ is an unobservable stationary state variable whose dynamics is characterized by the transition equation (1), for a given unknown value θ^0 of the vector θ of parameters, lying in an open bounded subset $\Theta \subset \mathbb{R}^p$ and a given function φ. $\{Y_t, t = 0, \ldots, T\}$ is a stationary process whose dynamics is defined by the measurement equation (2), for the value θ^0 of the parameters and a given function r.

The important feature that the dynamic model (1)–(2) has to satisfy is that one can draw simulated paths according to it, given a value θ of the parameters and an initial condition $(\tilde{Y}_0, \tilde{Z}_0)$. This is achieved by drawing independent simulated disturbance paths $\{u_t^h, t = 1, \ldots, T\}$, $h = 1, \ldots, H$, in the distribution G_0, and computing simulated paths $\{Y_t^h(\theta), t = 0, \ldots, T\}$ according to the recursive system

$$Z_t^h(\theta) = \varphi(Z_{t-1}^h(\theta), u_t^h; \theta)$$

$$Y_t^h(\theta) = r(Y_{t-1}^h(\theta), Z_t^h(\theta); \theta)$$

with initial values $Y_0^h(\theta)$ and $Z_0^h(\theta)$ drawn for instance in the stationary distribution of (Y, Z) with the value θ of the parameters, or taken as initial fixed values $\tilde{Y}_0, \tilde{Z}_0$. The main idea of indirect inference is to match simulated data with observed ones in order to estimate the parameters of the model. Let Q_T be a given function mapping $\mathbb{R}^T \times B$ into $\mathbb{R}$ for some open bounded subset B of $\mathbb{R}^d$ with $d \geq p$, and define

$$\hat{\beta}_T = \arg\max_{\beta \in B} Q_T(Y_T, \beta)$$

$$\tilde{\beta}_T^h(\theta) = \arg\max_{\beta \in B} Q_T(Y_T^h(\theta), \beta), \quad h = 1, \dots, H \tag{3}$$

where $Y_T = \{Y_t, t = 1, \dots, T\}$ and $Y_T^h(\theta) = \{Y_t^h(\theta), t = 1, \dots, T\}$. Q_T can be interpreted as the estimation criterion corresponding to an instrumental model which is a good approximation of the true model, and which allows for classical estimation procedures. The pseudo-maximum likelihood of Gourieroux, Monfort, and Trognon (1989) is an example of such an instrumental criterion. As defined, $\hat{\beta}_T$ summarizes the information given by the sample path Y_T. For instance, if we choose as instrumental criterion $Q_T = -\|\bar{k}_T - \beta\|^2$, where $\bar{k}_T$ is a vector of d empirical moments of Y, then the sample path Y_T is summarized by these d empirical moments.

The indirect-inference estimator in the sense of GMR is defined by

$$\hat{\theta}_T^H = \arg\min_{\theta \in \Theta} \left\| \hat{\beta}_T - \frac{1}{H} \sum_{h=1}^{H} \tilde{\beta}_T^h(\theta) \right\|_{\Omega_T}^2$$

$$= \arg\min_{\theta \in \Theta} \left[\hat{\beta}_T - \frac{1}{H} \sum_{h=1}^{H} \tilde{\beta}_T^h(\theta) \right]' \Omega_T^{-1} \left[\hat{\beta}_T - \frac{1}{H} \sum_{h=1}^{H} \tilde{\beta}_T^h(\theta) \right] \tag{4}$$

where Ω_T is a symmetric positive definite matrix which converges almost surely to a symmetric positive definite matrix Ω. For instance, for $Q_T = -\|\bar{k}_T - \beta\|^2$, $\hat{\theta}_T^H$ defined in (4) is the MSM (method of simulated moments) estimator of θ (Duffie and Singleton (1993)), and the indirect inference procedure appears as a natural generalization of the MSM.

As the number H of simulated sample paths goes to infinity, the limit indirect inference estimator is

$$\hat{\theta}_T = \arg\min_{\theta \in \Theta} \|\hat{\beta}_T - E[\tilde{\beta}_T(\theta)]\|_{\Omega_T}^2 \tag{5}$$

where the expectation is with respect to the distribution G_0 of the error term. While the indirect inference procedure is presented as an asymptotic estimation methodology, we focus in this chapter on its finite sample properties asymptotic (for fixed T) in the case where the instrumental and the true models have the same number of parameters, i.e., $p = d$; under this condition, the asymptotic properties of this estimator are independent of the weighting matrix Ω_T. Let us define the function b_T mapping Θ into $b_T(\Theta)$ by

$$b_T(\theta) = E[\tilde{\beta}_T(\theta)] \tag{6}$$

which is the binding function in the finite sample context, and assume the usual identifiability condition:

Assumption 1.1 *The finite sample binding function b_T, mapping Θ into $b_T(\Theta)$, is uniformly continuous and one-to-one.*

In contrast with the usual asymptotic analysis, the distribution of the auxiliary estimator $\hat{\beta}_T$ may recover some values of $\mathbb{R}^p$ which are not attained by the function b_T, and the minimum in (5) may be positive. In order to simplify the presentation, we therefore make the following additional assumption:

Assumption 1.2 *The support of the distribution of $\hat{\beta}_T$ is included in* $b_T(\Theta)$.

Under the last assumption, for an infinite number of replications, the indirect inference estimator is simply given by

$$\hat{\theta}_T = b_T^{-1}(\hat{\beta}_T). \tag{7}$$

In the general case, an expression of the indirect inference estimator in the form (7) can always be obtained by considering an (asymptotically equivalent) modification of the estimator (5). Thanks to the uniform continuity of b_T on the open bounded set Θ, a continuous extension of b_T to the closure of Θ exists. This allows us to construct an extension $\bar{b}_T$ of b_T, which is one-to-one on the whole space $\mathbb{R}^p$. We can therefore define the slightly modified inference estimator $\hat{\theta}_T = \bar{b}_T^{-1}(\hat{\beta}_T)$ for which the results of subsection 1.3 can be stated in terms of the extension $\bar{b}_T$.

Before studying the finite sample properties of the indirect estimator (7), let us recall some related bias correction procedures that have appeared in the literature on autoregressive models.

1.2   Median-bias correction in autoregressive models

Andrews (1993) suggested an exact median-unbiased estimator for the autoregressive coefficient of an AR(1) model. Extensions of this methodology to the AR(p) case have been proposed by Andrews and Chen (1994) and Rudebusch (1992); in the case $p > 1$ the estimators are only approximately median unbiased since the median is not suitable for vector variables. The purpose of this section is to provide a presentation of these procedures which highlights the analogy with the indirect inference methodology.

Consider the following latent AR(p) time series $\{ Y_t^*, t = 0, \ldots, T \}$

$$\phi(L) Y_t^* = u_t, \text{ for } t = p, \ldots, T \tag{8}$$

where L is the lag operator, $\phi(L) = 1 - \sum_{j=1}^{p} \alpha_j L^j$ is the lag polynomial whose roots are assumed to lie on or outside the unit circle and $\{u_t, t = 1, \ldots, T\}$ is a Gaussian white noise with variance σ^2; $Y_0^*, ..., Y_{p-1}^*$ are drawn from the stationary distribution of the process Y^*, if all the roots of $\phi(L)$ lie outside the unit circle, and are arbitrary constant otherwise. We denote by Θ^p the set of vectors $\alpha \in \mathbb{R}^p$ such that the roots of the polynomial $1 - \sum_{j=1}^{p} \alpha_j x^j$ lie outside the unit circle. In the AR(1) context it is known that $\Theta^1 = (-1, 1)$. More generally, it is shown in appendix 1 that Θ^p is an open bounded subset of $\mathbb{R}^p$.

Next, we consider the following models for the observed process $\{Y_t, t = 0, ..., T\}$

model 1: $Y_t = Y_t^*, t = 0, ..., T,$

model 2: $Y_t = \mu + Y_t^*, t = 0, ..., T,$

model 3: $Y_t = \mu + \gamma t + Y_t^*, t = 0, ..., T,$ (9)

where μ and γ are two unknown parameters. Now, let $\hat{\beta}_T$ be the (unconstrained) LS estimator of the AR parameters $\alpha = (\alpha_1, ..., \alpha_p)'$ corresponding to one of the previous models. If the model used is well specified the estimator $\hat{\beta}_T$ is consistent. However it is biased in finite samples because of the presence of lagged dependent variables which violates the assumption of non-stochastic regressors in the classical linear regression model. In particular, for estimating the sum of the AR coefficients $\sum_{j=1}^{p} \alpha_j$, which is useful in the study of the long-run persistence properties, the bias tends to be downward and quite large. For estimating the time trend coefficient γ, the bias is upward and quite large. For an AR(1) model, we refer to table 2 of Rudebusch (1993) which shows that the probability to underestimate the AR parameter when the latter is 0.9 equals 0.89 and still increases for values of the AR parameter closer to 1. In practice, the latter case appears very frequently; in financial applications for instance, interest rates or asset price volatilities are usually modeled by a latent continuous time Ornstein–Uhlenbeck process (see, e.g., Vasicek (1977) and Scott (1987)), which time discretization yields to an AR(1) process with AR parameter converging to 1 as the time space between observations goes to zero.

The bias correction procedure, suggested by Andrews in the AR(1) framework, and generalized to the AR(p) one by Rudebusch (1992) and Andrews and Chen (1994), relies on the pivotal property of the LS estimator of the AR parameter α whose probability distribution does not depend on the other parameters of the model. Therefore, given a value of the AR parameter α, one can define a unique distribution corresponding to the LS estimator $\tilde{\beta}_T(\alpha)$ induced by a sample of length T, when the true value of the AR parameter is α.

In the AR(1) framework, one can define the function $m_T(\alpha)$, as the median of the random variable $\tilde{\beta}_T(\alpha)$, and the estimator $\hat{\alpha}_T^U$ by

$$\hat{\alpha}_T^U = \arg \min_{\alpha \in [-1,1]} |\hat{\beta}_T - m_T(\alpha)|. \tag{10}$$

Assuming that the function $m_T(.)$ is increasing (which was checked by Andrews (1993) thanks to a Monte Carlo study) the last estimator can be written as

$$\hat{\alpha}_T^U = \begin{cases} 1 & \text{if } \hat{\beta}_T > m_T(1), \\ m_T^{-1}(\hat{\beta}_T) & \text{if } m_T(-1) < \hat{\beta}_T \le m_T(1), \\ -1 & \text{if } \hat{\beta}_T \le m_T(-1) \end{cases} \tag{11}$$

where $m_T(\pm 1) = \lim_{\alpha \to \pm 1} m_T(\alpha)$. The estimator defined in (11) is median unbiased since, by the increasing property of the function $m_T(.)$, we have $\hat{\alpha}_T^U \ge \alpha^0$ if $m_T(\hat{\alpha}_T^U) \ge m_T(\alpha^0)$, and from the definition of $\hat{\alpha}_T^U$, this is equivalent to $\hat{\beta}_T \ge m_T(\alpha^0)$, where α^0 is the true value of the parameter. Therefore, we get $P[\hat{\alpha}_T^U \ge \alpha^0] = 1/2$. Note that the median-unbiasedness property of $\hat{\alpha}_T^U$ does not depend on the values assigned to $\hat{\alpha}_T^U$ when $\hat{\beta}_T$ is outside the bounds $m_T(-1)$ and $m_T(1)$ since the median of a distribution does not depend on the values taken from both sides of the median; these values have just to be larger than α^0 if $\hat{\beta}_T > m_T(1)$ and vice versa, and, since α^0 lies in $(-1,1)$, the values outside the bounds in (11) are well suited.

The practical implementation of this procedure requires the computation of the median function m_T. By drawing simulated paths $\{\tilde{y}_t^h(\alpha), t = 0, ..., T\}$, $h = 1, ..., H$, and computing the LS estimator for each path, we get H independent and identically distributed realizations $\tilde{\beta}_T^h(\alpha)$, $h = 1, ..., H$. An approximation of $m_T(\alpha)$ can thus be obtained as the median of the $\tilde{\beta}_T^h(\alpha)$s. For an infinite number of simulated paths, such an approximation converges toward the required limit $m_T(\alpha)$. Therefore, the median-unbiased estimator suggested by Andrews (1993) is nothing but an application of the indirect inference where the binding function defined in (6) is replaced by the median of the auxiliary estimator. An important feature of this application of indirect inference is that the instrumental model coincides with the true model.

The problem in generalizing the median-bias correction procedure to the AR(p) case is that the median indicator is not suited for vector variables. However, defining the median of the vector variable $\hat{\beta}_T(\alpha)$ as the vector of medians of each component, Rudebusch (1993) and Andrews and Chen (1994) suggested a direct generalization of the last procedure for the AR(p) framework. Unfortunately, such estimators are only approximately median unbiased for two reasons:

On the one hand, the joint fit of medians for all the components is impossible in general.

On the other hand, the probability distribution (and therefore the

median) of a given component depends on the true unknown value of
the other components.
In the sequel, we study the finite sample properties of the indirect inference
estimator which handles with any vector variable since it is based on the
mean indicator.

1.3 Mean-bias correction by indirect inference

We have stressed in the previous subsection the formal analogy between
"median-bias correction" à la Andrews and indirect inference methodology. Indeed, the corresponding finite sample property of indirect inference
is a "mean-bias correction" according to the following proposition.

Proposition 1.1
*(i) Suppose that the true and instrumental models have the same number of
parameters ($p = d$). Then, under assumptions 1.1 and 1.2, the indirect inference estimator $\hat{\theta}_T$ defined in (5) is b_T mean unbiased, i.e.*

$$b_T^{-1}\{E[b_T(\hat{\theta}_T)]\} = \theta^0$$

where θ^0 is the true value of the parameters.

*(ii) Suppose that the instrumental model coincides with the true one, and
that the first-step estimator $\hat{\beta}_T$ is mean unbiased, i.e., $E(\hat{\beta}_T) = \theta^0$. Then the
indirect inference estimator $\hat{\theta}_T$ coincides with the first-step estimator, i.e.,
$\hat{\theta}_T = \hat{\beta}_T$.*

Proof. (i) From the expression (7) of the indirect inference estimator,
$E[b_T(\hat{\theta}_T)] = E[\hat{\beta}_T] = E[\tilde{\beta}_T(\theta^0)] = b_T(\theta^0)$, and the result follows from the one-
to-one property of the function $b_T(.)$.
(ii) The result is obvious since b_T is the identity function under the
unbiasedness condition. □

The second part of the proposition says that if the first-step estimator is
mean unbiased, then the indirect inference procedure does not make it
worse. Part (i) is the counterpart of the median-unbiasedness property in
the Andrews bias correction procedure. In particular, if the bias of the estimator is an affine function of the unknown parameter, i.e., b_T is affine, then
the indirect inference estimator is exactly mean unbiased. But, since b_T is
unknown in general, we cannot conclude from this property that indirect
inference will reduce the bias of the first-step estimator.

In order to understand the result of the first part of the last proposition
consider the following iterative procedure. Define the function $b_T^{(1)}$ from the
estimator $\hat{\theta}_T$ as b_T has been defined from $\hat{\beta}_T$, i.e., $b_T^{(1)}(\theta) = E_\theta(\hat{\theta}_T)$, for $\theta \in \Theta$.

We can therefore define the estimator $\hat{\theta}_T^{(1)} = b_T^{(1)-1}(\hat{\theta}_T)$. More generally, we define the sequence of estimators

$$\hat{\theta}_T^{(k)} = b_T^{(k)-1}(\hat{\theta}_T^{(k-1)}), \text{ with: } b_T^{(k)}(\theta) = E_\theta(\hat{\theta}_T^{(k-1)}), \ \theta\epsilon\Theta \tag{12}$$

assuming that the functions $b_T^{(k)}$ and the estimators $(\hat{\theta}_T^{(k-1)})$ satisfy assumptions 1.1 and 1.2. Then, if this procedure converges, i.e., if the limits $b_T^{(\infty)} = \lim_{k\to\infty} b_T^{(k)}$ and $\hat{\theta}_T^{(\infty)} = \lim_{k\to\infty} \hat{\theta}_T^{(k)}$ exist, then the limit estimator $\hat{\theta}_T^{(\infty)}$ is mean unbiased. To see this, notice that for such a limit point, we have $b_T^{(\infty)}(\hat{\theta}_T^{(\infty)}) = \hat{\theta}_T^{(\infty)}$, which means that $b_T^{(\infty)}$ equals the identity function on $\hat{\theta}_T^{(\infty)}(\Theta)$, the set of values which might be taken by the estimator $\hat{\theta}_T^{(\infty)}$ when the true value of the parameter θ varies in Θ. It then follows from the definition of $b_T^{(\infty)}$ that $E_{\theta_0}[\hat{\theta}_T^{(\infty)}] = b_T^{(\infty)}(\theta^0) = \theta^0$, where the last equality follows from the fact that $\theta^0 \epsilon \hat{\theta}_T^{(\infty)}(\Theta)$.

1.4   *Examples*

Example 1 Consider independent and identically $\mathcal{N}(\updownarrow, \sigma^\epsilon)$ distributed observations $Y_1, ..., Y_T$, and take as a first-step (auxiliary) estimator the maximum likelihood one. Then it is well known that the variance estimator

$$\hat{s}_T^2 = \frac{1}{T}\sum_{t=1}^{T}(Y_t - \bar{Y}_T)^2, \text{ with } \bar{Y}_T = \frac{1}{T}\sum_{t=1}^{T}Y_t \tag{13}$$

is biased in finite samples. The expectation of this first-step estimator can be computed explicitly in this simple example

$$E(\hat{s}_T^2) = \sigma^2 - \frac{1}{T}\sigma^2$$

and the finite sample binding function $E[\hat{s}_T^2(.)]$ is thus linear in the variance parameter σ^2. Therefore the indirect inference estimator (7) (corresponding to an infinite number of replications) is unbiased, and is equal to

$$\hat{\sigma}_T^2 = \frac{T}{T-1}\hat{s}_T^2 \tag{14}$$

Example 2 In the previous example, we pointed out the fact that the indirect inference estimator is mean unbiased if the bias of the auxiliary estimator is an affine function of the true value of the parameter. We now give an example where the (finite sample) binding function is a power of the true value of the parameter. Consider the model

$$Y_t = \theta u_t$$

and the estimator

$$\hat{\beta}_T = \bar{Y}_T^k = \left(\frac{1}{T}\sum_{t=1}^{T} Y_t\right)$$

for a given integer k. The expectation of this estimator is

$$b_T(\theta) = \mu(T,k)\theta^k, \text{ where: } \mu(T,k) = E\left[\left(\frac{1}{T}\sum_{t=1}^{T} u_t\right)^k\right]$$

so that the indirect inference estimator is given by

$$\hat{\theta}_T = b_T^{-1}(\hat{\beta}_T) = [\mu(T,k)]^{-1/k}\bar{Y}_T.$$

The expectation of this estimator is

$$b_T^{(1)}(\theta) = [\mu(T,k)]^{-1/k}\mu(T,1)\theta.$$

Since $b_T^{(1)}$ is linear function of the parameter θ, the next-step estimator $\hat{\theta}_T^{(1)} = b_T^{(1)-1}(\hat{\theta}_T)$ is unbiased and for any $p \geq 2$, $\hat{\theta}_T^{(p)} = \hat{\theta}_T^{(1)}$.

1.5 Indirect inference versus bootstrap

As far as we are concerned by a simulation-based procedure of bias correction, a direct competitor of indirect inference is of course the bootstrap methodology first introduced by Efron (1979). While it was first defined as a non-parametric methodology for *iid* observations, we are now able to define a "parametric bootstrap" as "resampling from the hypothesized distribution, with parameters estimated" (Hall (1994), even for dynamic models, through "recursive sampling": "resample error terms recursively to preserve the serial relationships in the error terms" (Jeong and Maddala (1993).

In other words, for an initial estimator $\hat{\beta}_T$, a bootstrap sample path of index h, $h = 1, ..., H$, is defined recursively by

$$Z_t^h(\hat{\beta}_T) = \varphi(Z_{t-1}^h(\hat{\beta}_T), u_t^h; \theta)$$

$$Y_t^h(\hat{\beta}_T) = r(Y_{t-1}^h(\hat{\beta}_T), z_t^h(\hat{\beta}_T); \theta) \tag{15}$$

from H independent simulated disturbance paths $\{u_t^h, t = 1, ..., T\}$ drawn in the distribution G_0 and with initial values $Y_0^h(\hat{\beta}_T)$ and $Z_0^h(\hat{\beta}_T)$, $h = 1, ..., H$ independently drawn in the stationary distribution of (Y,Z) with the value $\hat{\beta}_T$ of the parameters, or taken as initial fixed values $\tilde{Y}_0$, $\tilde{Z}_0$.

Of course, such a recursive drawing is conformable to our model if and only if $\tilde{\beta}_T$ is itself interpreted as an estimator of the vector θ of parameters of interest (once more, instrumental model and structural model coincide).

In such a case, bootstrap sampling is nothing but a particular occurrence of the indirect inference sampling defined above for the value $\hat{\beta}_T$ of the vector of parameters.

But the so-called bootstrap estimator and its approximation $\tilde{\theta}_T^H$ (for a finite number H of replications) do not coincide in general with their indirect inference competitors $\hat{\theta}_T$ and $\tilde{\theta}_T^H$, since according to Hall (1994), they are defined by

$$\tilde{\theta}_T = \hat{\beta}_T - [b_T(\hat{\beta}_T) - \hat{\beta}_T] \tag{16a}$$

$$\tilde{\theta}_T^H = \hat{\beta}_T - \left[\frac{1}{H}\sum_{h=1}^{H}\tilde{\beta}_T^h(\hat{\beta}_T) - \hat{\beta}_T\right]. \tag{16b}$$

In general they do not solve the non-linear systems in θ, that define $\hat{\theta}_T$ and $\tilde{\theta}_T^H$, respectively

$$\hat{\beta}_T = b_T(\theta) \tag{17a}$$

and

$$\hat{\beta}_T = \frac{1}{H}\sum_{h=1}^{H}\tilde{\beta}_T^h(\theta). \tag{17b}$$

There is however one way to see $\tilde{\theta}_T$ (resp. $\tilde{\theta}_T^H$) as a proxy of $\hat{\theta}_T$ (resp. $\hat{\theta}_T^H$); we will now demonstrate this point when $H = \infty$ for notational convenience (but for the finite case H can be described in the same way).

When we face the non-linear equation

$$\hat{\beta}_T = b_T(\theta)$$

with the idea that $\hat{\beta}_T$ is not a bad estimator of θ, we may hope that the binding function $b_T(.)$ is sufficiently close to identify to imply that

$$g_T^1(\theta) = \theta + (\hat{\beta}_T - b_T(\theta))$$

is a strong contraction with respect to θ. In such a situation, we may solve the non-linear equation

$$\hat{\beta}_T = b_T(\theta)$$

or equivalently look for a fixed point θ of $g_T^1(\theta)$ by considering the limit of the sequence

$$\theta^{n+1} = g_T^1(\theta^{(n)})$$

for a given initial value $\theta^{(1)}$. Moreover, it is worthwhile to note that a solution of the equation (17a) may also be looked for as the limit of a sequence

$$\theta^{(n+1)} = g_T^\lambda(\theta^{(n)}) \tag{18}$$

where

$$g_T^\lambda(\theta) = \theta + \lambda(\hat{\beta}_T - b_T(\theta))$$

for a given scalar λ between 0 and 1.[1] The interpretation of this procedure is appealing since

$$\theta^{(n+1)} = \theta^{(n)} + \lambda(\hat{\beta}_T - b_T(\theta^{(n)}))$$
$$= (1 - \lambda)\theta^{(n)} + \lambda(\hat{\beta}_T - \text{bias}) \tag{19}$$

where $b_T(\theta^{(n+1)}) - \theta^{(n)})$ is seen as an evaluation at step n of the bias of $\hat{\beta}_T$. $\theta^{(n+1)}$ is a convex combination of the previous step estimator $\theta^{(n)}$ and of the initial estimator $\hat{\beta}$ **bias corrected** at step n.

To summarize, as soon as we are able to find λ such that $g_T^\lambda(.)$ is a strong contraction, we have defined an algorithm which is appealing for at least two reasons:

First, it converges toward the indirect estimator.

Second, each step of the algorithm is a natural bias correction that **does not require additional simulations**. Indeed, once H independent simulated paths $\{u_t^h, t = 1, \ldots, T\}$, have been drawn the recursive system

$$\begin{cases} Z_t^h(\theta) = \varphi(Z_{t-1}^h(\theta), u_t^h, \theta) \\ Y_t^h(\theta) = r(Y_{t-1}^h(\theta), Z_t^h, (\theta), \theta) \end{cases}$$

may be used for each value $\theta^{(n)}$, $n = 1, 2, \ldots$, of θ.

With respect to this algorithm, it is astonishing to observe that the usual bootstrap procedure performs **only the first step of the algorithm** for the particular choice: $\theta^{(1)} = \hat{\beta}_T$ and $\lambda = 1$, since

$$\theta^{(2)} = \bar{\theta}_T = g_T^1(\hat{\beta}_T). \tag{20}$$

One might argue that an iterated procedure

$$\theta^{(3)} = g_T^1(\bar{\theta}_T)$$
$$\theta^{(4)} = g_T^1(\theta^{(3)}) \tag{21}$$

will improve the estimator since, at each stage, we perform a better evaluation of the bias used to correct $\hat{b}_T$.

Of course, the bootstrap literature suggests also an improvement of $\bar{\theta}_T$ (or $\bar{\theta}_T^H$) by the so-called iterated bootstrap

---

[1] In an independent posterior work, MacKinnon and Smith (1995) propose the same procedure with the following comment: "Larger values of λ are likely to result in a lower probability that the sequence will converge, but faster convergence if it does so. In practice, it may be desirable to try $\lambda = 1$ and then try lower values of λ if the procedure does not seem to be converging."

$$\bar{\theta}_T^{(1)} = \bar{\theta}_T = \hat{\beta}_T - [b_T^{(1)}(\hat{\beta}_T) - \hat{\beta}_T]$$

$$\bar{\theta}_T^{(2)} = \bar{\theta}_T^{(1)} - [b_T^{(2)}(\bar{\theta}_T^{(1)}) - \bar{\theta}_T^{(1)}]$$

and more generally

$$\bar{\theta}_T^{(n+1)} = \bar{\theta}_T^{(n)} - [b_T^{(n+1)}(\bar{\theta}_T^{(n)}) - \bar{\theta}_T^{(n)}].$$

But it is important to bear in mind that if we use a large number H^1 of replications to obtain a correct proxy of the binding function $b_T^{(1)}(.)$ associated with the preliminary estimator $\hat{\beta}_T$, we also need H^2 replications to characterize $b_T^{(2)}(.)$ and more generally H^n replications to characterize $b_T^{(n)}(.)$. Indeed, we need H drawings of $\bar{\theta}_T^{(1)}$ to characterize the proxy of $b_T^{(2)}(.)$ but each drawing of (a proxy of) $\bar{\theta}_T^{(1)}$ itself requires H drawings to characterize $b_T^{(1)}$. This makes the iterated bootstrap (as the iterated indirect inference defined in subsection 1.3) quickly infeasible. At the opposite the iterative procedure (21) appears as a feasible and natural improvement of the bootstrap estimator. In this respect, the indirect inference estimator seems to be preferred to the usual bootstrap estimator, at least when its interpretation as limit of a sequence (18) is correct.

2   Edgeworth expansions

When the bias of a given estimator can be computed, as in the case of the variance parameter of a linear regression, a mean-unbiased estimator can be defined from the initial estimator. However, the bias cannot be computed explicitly in general. Another approach consists in computing explicitly the first terms of the expansion of the bias in $\frac{1}{T}$, so as to define a new estimator with reduced bias. This is a usual practice in autoregressive models, where the expansion up to the first order has been provided by Orcutt and Winokur (1969) for AR(1) models and by Shaman and Stine (1989) for general AR(p) models. However, even this methodology requires the explicit computation of the expansion up to some order, which is very difficult in general.

Bootstrap methods have been proposed (see Efron, 1979) to operate the latter correction automatically: the bias of order $\frac{1}{T}$ disappears in the bootstrap estimator. In the following sections, we show that the indirect inference estimator presents the same property and we compare both estimation methodologies by focusing on the next term of the expansion.

2.1   Second-order bias correction by indirect inference

We suppose again that the instrumental and the true models have the same number of parameters, and that the auxiliary estimator $\hat{\beta}_T$ is a consistent estimator of the parameter θ^0. The following analysis relies on the assumption that the auxiliary estimator admits an Edgeworth expansion

$$\hat{\beta}_T = \theta^0 + \frac{A(v,\theta^0)}{\sqrt{T}} + \frac{B(v,\theta^0)}{T} + \frac{C(v,\theta^0)}{T^\alpha} + o\left(\frac{1}{T^\alpha}\right) \tag{22}$$

where $\alpha \in \{\frac{3}{2}, 2\}$, $A(v,\theta^0)$, $B(v,\theta^0)$, $C(v,\theta^0)$, are random vectors depending on some asymptotic random term v, and the expansion is to be understood in the probability sense (see, e.g., Hall (1992, chapter 2)). The next order after the $\frac{1}{T}$ one is $\frac{1}{T^2}$ in most situations; in order to deal with the general case we introduce the order $\frac{1}{T^\alpha}$, where α could be $\frac{3}{2}$ or 2. Such an Edgeworth expansion exists in many cases of interest where the statistic under consideration has a limiting standard normal distribution (see Hall (1992, paragraph 2.3, p. 46)).

Under some regularity conditions on the random coefficients A, B, and C of the Edgeworth expansion (22), we can show that the indirect inference estimator also has an Edgeworth expansion which can be fully characterized:

Proposition 2.1 *Under some regularity conditions, the indirect inference estimator $\hat{\theta}_T^H$, given in (4), has the following Edgeworth expansion*

$$\hat{\theta}_T^H = \theta^0 + \frac{A_H^*}{\sqrt{T}} + \frac{B_H^*}{T} + \frac{C_H^*}{T^{3/2}} + o(T^{-3/2}) \tag{23}$$

where the coefficients A_H^*, B_H^*, and C_H^*, are deduced from A, B, and C by

$$A_H^* = A(v,\theta^0) - \frac{1}{H}\sum_{h=1}^{H} A(v^h,\theta^0), \tag{24}$$

$$B_H^* = B(v,\theta^0) - \frac{1}{H}\sum_{h=1}^{H} B(v^h,\theta^0) - \left[\frac{1}{H}\sum_{h=1}^{H} \frac{\partial A}{\partial \theta'}(v^h,\theta^0)\right]A_H^* \tag{25}$$

$$C_H^* = \left[C(v,\theta^0) - \frac{1}{H}\sum_{h=1}^{H} C(v^h,\theta^0)\right]1_{\{\alpha=3/2\}}$$

$$- \left[\frac{1}{H}\sum_{h=1}^{H} \frac{\partial B}{\partial \theta'}(v^h,\theta^0)\right]A_H^* - \left[\frac{1}{H}\sum_{h=1}^{H} \frac{\partial A}{\partial \theta'}(v^h,\theta^0)\right]$$

$$B_H^* - \frac{1}{2}A_H^{*\prime}\left[\frac{1}{H}\sum_{h=1}^{H} \frac{\partial^2 A}{\partial \theta \partial \theta'}(v^h,\theta^0)\right]A_H^* \tag{26}$$

where the random variables v, v^h, $h = 1, ..., H$ are independent and identically distributed.

Proof. See appendix 2.

Let us first consider the limit case of an infinite number of replications. We get

$$A_\infty^* = \lim_{H\to\infty} A_H^* = A(v,\theta^0) - E[A(v,\theta^0)],$$

$$B_\infty^* = \lim_{H\to\infty} B_H^* = B(v,\theta^0) - E[B(v,\theta^0)] - E\left[\frac{\partial A}{\partial \theta'}(v,\theta^0)\right]\{A(v,\theta^0)$$
$$- E[A(v,\theta^0)]\}$$

and we can deduce the following result:

Corollary 2.1 *The indirect inference estimator $\hat{\theta}_T$, corresponding to an infinite number of simulations is unbiased up to the second order, i.e., the terms of order $\frac{1}{\sqrt{T}}$ and $\frac{1}{T}$ in the Edgeworth expansion satisfy:* $E(A_\infty^*) = E(B_\infty^*) = 0.$

For a fixed number of replications H, the last property is not valid. We still have $E(A_H^*) = 0$ and the first-order bias vanishes. In contrast with the auxiliary estimator, the second-order bias of the indirect inference estimator does not depend on the coefficient B, and is determined by

$$E(B_H^*) = -E\left\{\frac{1}{H}\sum_{h=1}^{H}\frac{\partial A}{\partial \theta'}(v^h,\theta^0)\left[A(v,\theta^0) - \frac{1}{H}\sum_{h=1}^{H}A(v^h,\theta^0)\right]\right\}$$

$$= -\sum_{j=1}^{p}E\left\{\frac{1}{H}\sum_{h=1}^{H}\frac{\partial A}{\partial \theta_j}(v^h,\theta^0)\left[A_j(v,\theta^0) - \frac{1}{H}\sum_{h=1}^{H}A_j(v^h,\theta^0)\right]\right\}$$

$$= -\sum_{j=1}^{p}\text{cov}\left\{\frac{1}{H}\sum_{h=1}^{H}\frac{\partial A}{\partial \theta_j}(v^h,\theta^0); A_j(v,\theta^0) - \frac{1}{H}\sum_{h=1}^{H}A_j(v^h,\theta^0)\right\}$$

$$= \frac{1}{H^2}\sum_{j=1}^{p}\sum_{h=1}^{H}\text{cov}\left\{\frac{\partial A}{\partial \theta_j}(v^h,\theta^0); A_j(v^h,\theta^0)\right\}$$

$$= \frac{1}{H}\sum_{j=1}^{p}\text{cov}\left\{\frac{\partial A}{\partial \theta_j}(v,\theta^0); A_j(v,\theta^0)\right\} \tag{27}$$

where the equalities follow from the independence between the random variables v and v^h, $h = 1, ..., H$. Therefore the second-order bias of the indirect inference estimator is smaller than that of the auxiliary estimator as soon as

$$\frac{1}{H}\left|\sum_{j=1}^{p}\text{cov}\left\{\frac{\partial A}{\partial \theta_j}(v,\theta^0); A_j(v,\theta^0)\right\}\right| \le |E[B(v,\theta^0)]| \tag{28}$$

which provides the minimum number of replications required to improve the second-order bias of the estimator.

2.2   Comparison with the bootstrap bias correction

The important result of corollary 2.1 is a well-known property of the bootstrap estimators, which are also based on simulations. We first recall briefly the expansion of the bootstrap estimator $\bar{\theta}_T$ and of its approximation $\bar{\theta}_T^H$ before comparing then with the indirect inference ones.

According to (16b)

$$\bar{\theta}_T^H = \hat{\beta}_T - \left[\frac{1}{H}\sum_{h=1}^H \tilde{\beta}_T^h(\hat{\beta}_T) - \hat{\beta}_T\right]. \tag{29}$$

As in the previous section, if we assume that the first-step (auxiliary) estimator has an Edgeworth expansion, the bootstrap estimator defined in (29) also has an Edgeworth expansion (under some regularity conditions)

$$\bar{\theta}_T^H = \theta^0 + \frac{A_H^b}{\sqrt{T}} + \frac{B_H^b}{T} + \frac{C_H^b}{T^{3/2}} + o(T^{-3/2}) \tag{30}$$

where the coefficients A_H^b, B_H^b, C_H^b are deduced from A, B, and C by

$$A_H^b = A(v,\theta^0) - \frac{1}{H}\sum_{h=1}^H A(v^h,\theta^0), \tag{31}$$

$$B_H^b = B(v,\theta^0) - \frac{1}{H}\sum_{h=1}^H B(v^h,\theta^0) - \left[\frac{1}{H}\sum_{h=1}^H \frac{\partial A}{\partial \theta'}(v^h,\theta^0)\right]A(v,\theta), \tag{32}$$

$$C_H^b = \left[C(v,\theta^0) - \frac{1}{H}\sum_{h=1}^H C(v^h,\theta^0)\right]1_{\{\alpha=3/2\}}$$

$$- \left[\frac{1}{H}\sum_{h=1}^H \frac{\partial B}{\partial \theta'}(v^h,\theta^0)\right]A(v,\theta^0) - \left[\frac{1}{H}\sum_{h=1}^H \frac{\partial A}{\partial \theta'}(v^h,\theta^0)\right]B(v,\theta^0)$$

$$- \frac{1}{2}A'(v,\theta^0)\left[\frac{1}{H}\sum_{h=1}^H \frac{\partial^2 A}{\partial \theta \partial \theta'}(v^h,\theta^0)\right]A(v,\theta). \tag{33}$$

As for the indirect inference estimator, the first-order bias is zero, i.e., $E(A_H^b) = 0$. The second-order bias is given by

$$E(B_H^b) = -\frac{1}{H}\sum_{h=1}^H E\left[\frac{\partial A}{\partial \theta'}(v^h,\theta)A(v,\theta)\right]$$

$$= E[A(v,\theta^0)]E\left[\frac{\partial A}{\partial \theta'}(v,\theta^0)\right] \tag{34}$$

where the last equality follows from the independence of the random variables v and v^h, $h = 1, \ldots, H$. Equation (34) shows that:

If $E[A(v,\theta^0)] \neq 0$, then, even for an infinite number of simulations, the bootstrap estimator presents a second-order bias; from this viewpoint, the indirect inference estimator is preferred since its second-order bias vanishes for an infinite H.

If $E[A(v,\theta^0)] = 0$, then the second-order bias of the bootstrap estimator vanishes for a finite number of replications H, i.e., $E(B_H^b) = 0$, from this viewpoint, the bootstrap estimator dominates the indirect inference one.

In the case $H = \infty$ and $E[A(v,\theta^0)] = 0$, both estimators correct from the second-order bias. We therefore examine the third-order bias. We denote by $C_\infty^* = \lim_{H\to\infty} C_H^*$ and $C_\infty^b = \lim_{H\to\infty} C_H^b$; using again the independence between v and the v^h, $h = 1, \ldots, H$, and the fact that $E[A(v,\theta^0)] = 0$, we obtain the third-order bias of the indirect inference estimator

$$E(C_\infty^*) = -\frac{1}{2}E\left[A(v,\theta^0)'E\left(\frac{\partial^2 A}{\partial\theta\partial\theta'}(v,\theta^0)\right)A(v,\theta^0)\right] \tag{35}$$

and that of the bootstrap estimator

$$E(C_\infty^b) = -E\left[\frac{\partial A}{\partial\theta'}(v,\theta^0)\right]E[B(v,\theta^0)]$$

$$-\frac{1}{2}E\left[A(v,\theta^0)'E\left(\frac{\partial^2 A}{\partial\theta\partial\theta'}(v,\theta^0)\right)A(v,\theta^0)\right]. \tag{36}$$

Clearly, the two expressions (35) and (36) cannot be compared in general, and the indirect inference and bootstrap estimators are competitors for an infinite number of simulations.

2.3   Examples

To illustrate these results, we consider again the first example of subsection 1.4: $Y_1, \ldots, Y_T$ are independent and identically distributed $\mathcal{N}(\mathbb{1},\sigma^\epsilon)$, and the first-step (auxiliary) estimator is the maximum likelihood one

$$\hat{m}_T = \frac{1}{T}\sum_{t=1}^T Y_t \quad \text{and} \quad \hat{s}_T^2 = \frac{1}{T}\sum_{t=1}^T (Y_t - \hat{m}_T)^2.$$

By drawing H replications, we can compute

$$\tilde{s}_T^{2^h}(m,\sigma^2) = \frac{1}{T}\sum_{t=1}^{T}[Y_t^h(m,\sigma^2) - \tilde{m}_T^h(m,\sigma^2)]^2.$$

Recalling that $Y_t^h(m,\sigma^2) = m + \sigma u_t^h$, where u_t^h, $h = 1, \ldots, T$, are drawn independently in the standard normal distribution, the last expression can be written as

$$\tilde{s}_T^{h^2}(m,\sigma^2) = \sigma^2\frac{1}{T}\sum_{t=1}^{T}(u_t^h - \bar{u}_T^h)^2, \text{ with } \bar{u}_T^h = \frac{1}{T}\sum_{t=1}^{T}\bar{u}_t^h.$$

Therefore, by equating $\hat{s}_T^2$ with $\frac{1}{H}\sum_{h=1}^{H}\tilde{s}_T^{2^h}(m,\sigma^2)$, we obtain the indirect inference estimator of σ^2

$$\hat{\sigma}_T^{2^H} = \sigma^{0^2}\frac{\sum_{t=1}^{T}(u_t - \bar{u}_T)^2}{\frac{1}{H}\sum_{h=1}^{H}\sum_{t=1}^{T}(u_t^h - \bar{u}_T^h)^2}.$$

The finite sample distribution of the indirect inference estimator is such that

$$\frac{\hat{\sigma}_T^{2^H}}{\sigma^{0^2}} \rightsquigarrow F[T-1, H(T-1)]$$

where $F(p,q)$ stands for the Fisher distribution, and in the limit case $H = \infty$, we have

$$(T-1)\frac{\hat{\sigma}_T^2}{\sigma^{0^2}} \rightsquigarrow \chi^2(T-1).$$

For fixed H, the bias of the indirect inference estimator is given by

$$E(\hat{\sigma}_T^2) - \sigma^{0^2} = \frac{2\sigma^{0^2}}{H(T-1)-2} \tag{37}$$

while the bias of the first-step estimator is

$$E(\hat{s}_T^2) - \sigma^{0^2} = -\frac{1}{T}\sigma^{0^2}.$$

We can thus conclude that the indirect inference estimator bias is smaller than that of the first-order estimator as soon as

$$H > 2\frac{T+1}{T-1}.$$

3 Simulation results

In this section, we examine the empirical content for AR(p) models of the theoretical results of sections 1 and 2. Indeed, unbiasedness of the indirect inference estimators does not give direct intuition on their performance. Section 3.1 gives simulations results for the AR(1) case and compares the median-unbiased estimator of Andrews (1993) to the indirect inference estimator. Then, section 3.2 presents an application to the AR(2) model and compares the indirect inference methodology to the approximate median-bias correction procedures suggested by Rudebusch (1992) and Andrews and Chen (1994).

As stated previously, we do not present any application for the general model (1)–(2), and we refer to Pastorello, Renault, and Touzi (1993) for an application of indirect inference to the estimation of the volatility process parameters, from option prices data in stochastic volatility models which are popular in option pricing literature. More precisely, these authors compare the estimators obtained by a consistent approximation of the maximum likelihood estimator (including Andrews' bias correction) to the indirect inference estimator. Their results show that the latter estimators perform as well as the former ones even though no (apparent) bias correction is performed.

3.1   Application to AR(1) models

As in Andrews (1993), assumption 1.1 is not justified by an analytic proof and we use simulations to check its validity for different sample sizes T. Simulations are performed as described in section 2 for model 2 of (9) without time trend and taking $\sigma^0 = 0.5$. Values of $b_T(\alpha^0)$ and $m_T(\alpha^0)$ for $\alpha^0 = -0.995 + 0.005k$, $k = 0, ..., 399$, are computed by Monte Carlo simulations without using any numerical trick to improve the efficiency of the algorithm: $b_T(\alpha^0)$ and $m_T(\alpha^0)$ are simply approximated by their finite sample counterparts with finite large enough H.

Table 13.1 and figure 13.1 present our simulation results with $H = 15,000$, which provides very close values for the function m_T to those of Andrews' table 2, and show clearly the increasing feature of m_T and b_T.

Comparing the functions b_T and m_T, we see that there exists some $\alpha_T^*(\approx 0.06$, for $T = 50$) such that the median of the LS estimator is larger than its mean if and only if the true value of the AR parameter is larger than α_T^*, i.e., the distribution of the LS estimator for the AR parameter is skewed to the right for values of α larger than α_T^*, and to the left for values of α smaller than α_T^*. A direct consequence is that, when the LS estimator of the AR parameter $\hat{\beta}_T$ lies in $m_T([-1,1]) \cap \varepsilon_T([-1,1])$

$$\text{if } \hat{\beta}_T > \alpha_T^*, \text{ then } \hat{\alpha}_T > \hat{\alpha}_T^U,$$
$$\text{if } \hat{\beta}_T < \alpha_T^*, \text{ then } \hat{\alpha}_T < \hat{\alpha}_T^U,$$
$$\text{if } \hat{\beta}_T = \alpha_T^*, \text{ then } \hat{\alpha}_T = \hat{\alpha}_T^U.$$

Table 13.1. *Mean and median of the LS estimator of the AR parameter in an AR(1) model without time trend*

$$(H = 15,000)$$

	T = 40		T = 50		T = 80	
α	Mean	Median	Mean	Median	Mean	Median
−0.999	−0.937	−0.950	−0.989	−0.997	−0.964	−0.973
−0.80	−0.727	−0.750	−0.780	−0.789	−0.761	−0.771
−0.60	−0.545	−0.560	−0.586	−0.596	−0.570	−0.578
−0.40	−0.363	−0.371	−0.397	−0.404	−0.381	−0.385
−0.20	−0.181	−0.184	−0.208	−0.212	−0.191	−0.191
0.00	−0.000	−0.002	−0.022	−0.023	−0.001	−0.000
0.10	0.091	0.095	0.072	0.073	0.094	0.095
0.20	0.181	0.187	0.166	0.169	0.189	0.191
0.30	0.272	0.280	0.260	0.265	0.284	0.287
0.40	0.362	0.372	0.354	0.361	0.379	0.384
0.50	0.452	0.465	0.452	0.461	0.474	0.480
0.60	0.542	0.556	0.545	0.556	0.569	0.576
0.70	0.631	0.647	0.638	0.651	0.664	0.673
0.80	0.719	0.736	0.730	0.745	0.759	0.769
0.85	0.762	0.782	0.775	0.792	0.805	0.816
0.90	0.805	0.824	0.819	0.836	0.852	0.863
0.93	0.829	0.849	0.845	0.862	0.879	0.890
0.97	0.860	0.880	0.877	0.895	0.913	0.925
0.99	0.874	0.893	0.892	0.910	0.929	0.941
1.00	0.880	0.899	0.899	0.916	0.936	0.947

As suggested by Andrews for computing the median-unbiased estimator, the indirect inference estimator can be determined by linear interpolation in table 13.1. Figure 13.1 justifies the linear approximation of the functions m_T and b_T. Table 13.2 provides some comparative results for indirect inference and median-unbiased estimators, and shows that there is no important difference between them in practice. Hence, we can conclude that the indirect inference estimator suggested in this chapter performs as well as the median-unbiased one suggested by Andrews (1993). Finally, figure 13.2 plots the kernel estimates of the densities of the LS estimator $\hat{\beta}_T$ and the indirect inference estimator $\hat{\alpha}_T$ for a sample size $T = 50$ and values of the AR parameter $\alpha = 0.75, 0.85$.

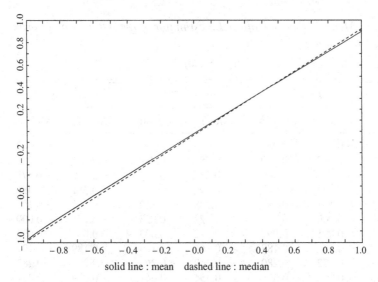

solid line : mean   dashed line : median

Figure 13.1 Median and mean of the LS estimator of the AR parameter in AR(1) models

3.2   *Application to AR(2) models*

First, we characterize the set Θ^2 of autoregressive coefficients $\alpha = (\alpha_1, \alpha_2) \in \mathbb{R}^2$ such that the latent process Y^*, with convenient initial values, is stationary, i.e., the roots of the lag polynomial operator $\phi(x) = 1 - \alpha_1 x - \alpha_2 x^2$ are outside the unit circle. Let $\Delta = \alpha_1^2 + 4\alpha_2$ be the discriminant of the lag polynomial operator.

Case A: $\Delta \geq 0$, then, since $\phi(0) = 1 > 0$, the roots of $\phi(.)$ are outside the unit circle iff $\phi(-1) > 0$ and $\phi(1) > 0$, i.e., $1 - \alpha_1 - \alpha_2 > 0$ and $1 + \alpha_1 - \alpha_2 > 0$.

Case B: $\Delta < 0$, then ϕ has two conjugate complex roots which are outside the unit circle iff $\alpha_2 \in (-1, 0)$.

We thus conclude that

$$\Theta^2 = \{(\alpha_1, \alpha_2) \in \mathbb{R}^2 \,|\, \alpha_1^2 + 4\alpha_2 \geq 0, \, 1 + \alpha_1 - \alpha_2 > 0, \, 1 + \alpha_1 - \alpha_2 > 0\}$$
$$\cup \{(\alpha_1, \alpha_2) \in \mathbb{R}^2 \,|\, \alpha_1^2 + 4\alpha_2 < 0, \, -1 < \alpha_2 < 0\}$$

which can be written in

$$\Theta^2 = \{(\alpha_1, \alpha_2) \in \mathbb{R}^2 \,|\, \alpha_1 + \alpha_2 < 1, \, \alpha_1 - \alpha_2 > -1, \, \alpha_2 > -1\}. \tag{38}$$

In contrast with the application (38), the finite sample binding function b_T is now charging a subset of $\mathbb{R}^2$, and verification of assumption 1.1 through Monte Carlo simulations is much more time consuming. By defini-

Table 13.2. *Some comparative results between median-unbiased and indirect inference estimators*

$$(T = 50)$$

$\alpha = -0.8$			$\alpha = 0.2$			$\alpha = 0.9$		
LS $\hat{\beta}_T$	MU $\hat{\alpha}_T^U$	II $\hat{\alpha}_T$	LS $\hat{\beta}_T$	MU $\hat{\alpha}_T^U$	II $\hat{\alpha}_T$	LS $\hat{\beta}_T$	MU $\hat{\alpha}_T^U$	II $\hat{\alpha}_T$
-0.746	-0.755	-0.765	0.222	0.255	0.260	0.817	0.878	0.897
-0.859	-0.871	-0.888	0.109	0.138	0.139	0.843	0.908	0.928
-0.592	-0.596	-0.607	0.322	0.359	0.366	0.681	0.732	0.747
-0.768	-0.779	-0.793	0.034	0.059	0.064	0.814	0.875	0.894
-0.779	-0.790	-0.805	0.324	0.361	0.368	0.807	0.867	0.885
-0.823	-0.834	-0.850	0.184	0.216	0.219	0.811	0.871	0.890
-0.756	-0.766	-0.778	0.087	0.115	0.116	0.647	0.696	0.710
-0.710	-0.718	-0.732	0.110	0.139	0.141	0.589	0.635	0.648
-0.830	-0.842	-0.857	-0.036	-0.017	-0.022	0.816	0.877	0.896
-0.879	-0.892	-0.909	0.246	0.280	0.285	0.910	0.990	1.000

tion, given the LS estimator $\hat{\beta}_T$, the indirect inference estimator $\hat{\alpha}_T$ is the unique solution to the equation $\hat{\beta}_T = \bar{b}_T(\alpha)$, where $\bar{b}_T$ is an extension of b_T, as described in section 1. Since no explicit expression of the function $\bar{b}_T^{-1}$ is available, we have to use numerical methods in order to solve for $\hat{\alpha}_T$, which usually require numerical evaluation of the gradient of the finite sample binding function.

For the present AR(2) model, we use the algorithm defined in subsection 1.5 which is likely to avoid such time-consuming numerical procedures. The basic idea behind our procedure, is that the finite sample binding function in the AR(1) framework is close to the identity function (up to a constant), according to figure 13.1. Therefore, we can hope that such a property is still valid for the AR(2) case so that the function

$$g_T^1(\alpha) = (\alpha) + \hat{\beta}_T - \bar{b}_T(\alpha) \tag{39}$$

is a strong contraction, and the indirect-inference estimator $\hat{\alpha}_T$ is its unique fixed point. Thus, for a given $\hat{\beta}_T$ we construct the sequence $(\hat{\alpha}_T^{(n)})_{n \geq 0}$ by

$$\hat{\alpha}_T^{(0)} = \hat{\beta}_T \text{ and } \hat{\alpha}_T^{(n+1)} = g_T^1(\hat{\alpha}_T^{(n)}). \tag{40}$$

If g_T^1 is a strong contraction, this sequence converges toward the unique fixed point $\hat{\alpha}_T$.

For our application, we consider $\alpha_1 = 1.2$ and $\alpha_2 = -0.4$ as true values of the AR parameters, and we fix $\sigma = 0.5$ and $\mu = 1$. The sample size is set to

α = 0.75

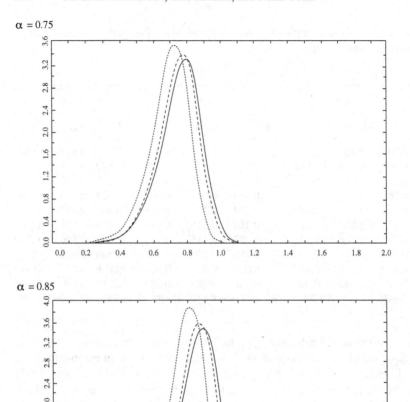

α = 0.85

Figure 13.2 Kernel estimates of the density of the estimators of the AR parameter in an AR(1) model

$T = 40$ and the number of simulations in the indirect inference procedure is fixed at $H = 5,000$, i.e., $b_T(\alpha)$ is approximated by its sample moment counterpart with 5,000 observations. We perform 1,000 experiments by simulating the AR(2) process, computing the corresponding LS and indirect inference estimators, and we construct (Gaussian) kernel estimates of the density of each estimator.

Table 13.3. *Estimators of the AR coefficients ($\alpha_1 = 1.2$ and $\alpha_2 = -0.4$)*
$\mu = 1$, $\sigma = 0.5$, $T = 40$, $H = 5,000$, $1,000$ *experiments*

	α_1		α_2	
Procedure	Mean	Median	Mean	Median
LS $\hat{\beta}_T$	0.936	0.947	-0.191	-0.215
MU $\hat{\alpha}_T^U$	1.191	1.213	-0.396	-0.430
II $\hat{\alpha}_T$	1.202	1.229	-0.406	-0.444

The algorithm described above appears to perform well since convergence of the procedure, up to an error of 10^{-4}, is achieved for a maximum of 6 iterations.[2] However, for some simulated paths, the LS estimator happens to be close to the frontier of the set $b_T(\Theta^2)$ and the algorithm fails to be contracting. In such cases, we define the sequence

$$\hat{\alpha}_T^{(0)} = \hat{\beta}_T \text{ and } \hat{\alpha}_T^{(n+1)} = g_T^\lambda(\hat{\alpha}_T^{(n)})$$

where

$$g_T^\lambda(\alpha) = \alpha + \lambda(\hat{\beta}_T - \bar{b}_T(\alpha))$$

and λ is chosen so as g_T^λ is a strong contraction. In our application, we obtain convergence in all cases with $\lambda = 0.2$.

We also wish to compare the performance of indirect inference to the approximately median-unbiased procedure suggested by Rudebusch (1992). We therefore compute for the same experiments the associated approximately median-unbiased estimators and we construct kernel estimates of their density functions. Figure 13.3 presents plots of kernel estimates of the density functions of the different estimators and shows clearly the bias correcting feature of both indirect inference and approximately median-unbiased procedures; the mean and the median of the different estimators are reported in table 13.3. Another important conclusion that we can draw from figure 13.3 is that the indirect inference and the approximately median-unbiased estimators are very close, as already noticed in the AR(1) context of section 4.1, and there is no significant difference between their mean and median. Therefore, we conclude that the $\bar{b}_T$-mean indicator of central tendency is a good measure which takes into account the asymmetry of the LS estimator distribution.

---

[2] More precisely, let $\bar{b}_T(\alpha) = (\bar{b}_{1,T}(\alpha), \bar{b}_{2,T}(\alpha))'$ and $\hat{\beta}_T = (\hat{\beta}_{1,T}, \hat{\beta}_{2,T})'$; by convention, convergence of the algorithm occurs when $\sum_{j=1}^2 |\bar{b}_{j,T}(\hat{\alpha}_T) - \hat{\beta}_{j,T}| \leq 0.0001$.

Estimators of α_1

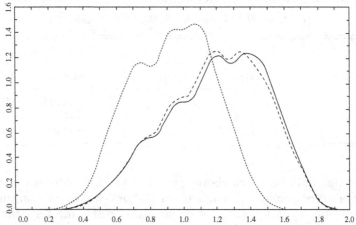

Estimators of α_2

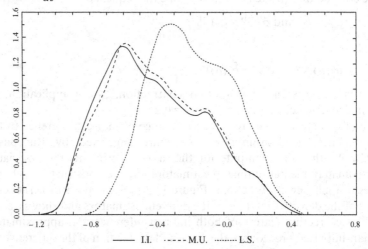

——— I.I.   - - - - M.U.   ········ L.S.

Figure 13.3 Kernel estimates of the density of the estimators of the AR
parameters in an AR(2) model (regular regression form)

Next, we compare the indirect inference procedure to the approximately
median-unbiased procedure of Andrews and Chen (1994). These authors
suggested a generalization of Andrews' (1993) methodology to the AR(p)
case in the same way as Rudebusch (1992), but using a Dickey–Fuller
regression form for the AR(p) model

$$Y_t^* = \gamma_1 Y_{t-1}^* + \gamma_2 \Delta Y_{t-1}^* + \dots + \gamma_p \Delta Y_{t-p+1}^* + u_t, \; t = p, \dots, T \qquad (41)$$

where: $\Delta Y_{t-i}^* = Y_{t-i}^* - Y_{t-i-1}^*$, $\gamma_1 = \sum_{i=1}^{p} \alpha_i$ and $\gamma_i = -\sum_{j=i}^{p} \alpha_j$ for $i = 2 \ldots p$. In our AR(2) context, we have $\gamma_1 = \alpha_1 + \alpha_2$ and $\gamma_2 = -\alpha_2$, and the set Θ^2 in terms of this new parameterization can be deduced from (38).

$$\Theta^2 = \{(\gamma_1, \gamma_2) \in \mathbb{R}^2 \mid \gamma_1 < 1, \ \gamma_2 < 1, \text{ and } \gamma_1 + 2\gamma_2 > -1\}. \tag{42}$$

Indirect inference and approximately median-unbiased estimators are simultaneously computed according to the same numerical procedure as above. Figure 13.4 contains plots of kernel estimates of the density function for the different estimators of the AR coefficients, and shows clearly the bias correcting feature of both indirect inference and approximately median-unbiased procedures; the mean and the median of the different estimators are reported in table 13.4. As noted before, the two procedures produce very close estimators and the difference between their mean and median is very small.

Finally, we compare estimators of the sum of the AR coefficients obtained in the regular form and the Dickey–Fuller regression form of the AR(2) model. Figure 13.5 presents kernel estimates of the density function of each estimator and shows that these estimators are very close, as noted by Andrews and Chen (1994).

Appendix 1
Θ^p is an open bounded subset of $\mathbb{R}^p$

In this appendix, we prove that Θ^p is an open subset of $\mathbb{R}^p$.

Let Θ^p be the set of parameters $(a_1, \ldots, a_p) \in \mathbb{R}^p$ such that the roots of the associated polynomial $P(X) = 1 - \sum_{i=1}^{P} a_i X^i$ are strictly outside the unit circle, i.e.

$$\Theta^p = \left\{ a \in \mathbb{R}^p : 1 - \sum_{i=1}^{P} a_i z^i \neq 0, \ \forall z \in \mathbb{C}, \ |z| \leq 1 \right\}.$$

Let $a \in \Theta^p$ and let us prove the existence of some $r > 0$ such that $B(a,r) = \{b \in \Theta^p, \|a - b\| < r\} \subset \Theta^p$.

If such an r does not exist then for all $n \in \mathbb{N}$, $\{n \neq 0\}$, there exists $a^{(n)} \in B\left(a, \dfrac{1}{n}\right)$ such that $a^{(n)} \notin \Theta^p$. This means that there exists $z_n \in \mathbb{C}$ with $|z_n| \leq 1$ and $1 - \sum_{i=1}^{P} a_i^{(n)} z_n^i = 0$.

Estimators of γ_1

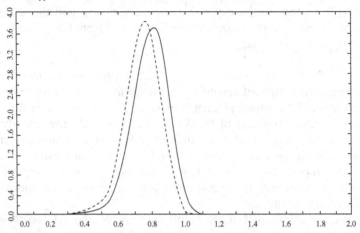

Estimators of γ_2

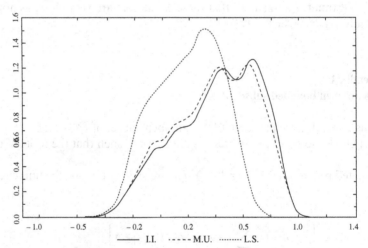

Figure 13.4 Kernel estimates of the density of the estimators of the AR
parameters in an AR(2) model (Dickey–Fuller regression form)

Now, since the sequence (z_n) is bounded in $\mathcal{C}$, there exists some z with
$|z| \leq 1$ such that $z_n \to z$ as $n \to \infty$, possibly along a subsequence. Moreover

$$1 - \sum_{i=1}^{P} a_i z^i = 1 - \sum_{i=1}^{P} a_i^{(n)} z_n^i + \sum_{i=1}^{P} (a_i^{(n)} - a_i) z_n^i + \sum_{i=1}^{P} a_i (z_n^i - z^i)$$

Table 13.4. *Dickey–Fuller regression form* ($\gamma_1 = 0.8$ *and* $\gamma_2 = 0.4$)
$\mu = 1$, $\sigma = 0.5$, $T = 40$, $H = 5,000$, $1,000$ *experiments*

Procedure	γ_1		γ_2	
	Mean	Median	Mean	Median
LS $\hat{\beta}_T$	0.743	0.752	0.194	0.210
MU $\hat{\alpha}_T^U$	0.783	0.796	0.388	0.416
II $\hat{\alpha}_T$	0.794	0.807	0.410	0.446

and taking limits as $n \to \infty$, we get

$$|\sum_{i=1}^{P}(a_i^{(n)} - a_i)z_n^i| \leq \sum_{i=1}^{P}|a_i^{(n)} - a_i| \to 0$$

$$|\sum_{i=1}^{P}a_i(z_n^i - z^i)| \leq \sum_{i=1}^{P}|a_i|\|z_n^i - z^i\| \to 0$$

and therefore $1 - \sum_{i=1}^{P}a_iz^i = 0$ which cannot happen since $|z| \leq 1$ and $a \in \Theta^P$.

Appendix 2
Edgeworth expansion of the indirect inference estimator

The Edgeworth expansion (22) may be applied both to the auxiliary estimator

$$\hat{\beta}_T = \theta^0 + \frac{A(v,\theta^0)}{\sqrt{T}} + \frac{B(v,\theta^0)}{T} + \frac{C(v,\theta^0)}{T^\alpha} + o\left(\frac{1}{T^\alpha}\right)$$

and to the estimators based on the simulated values

$$\tilde{\beta}_T^h(\theta) = \theta + \frac{A(v^h,\theta)}{\sqrt{T}} + \frac{B(v^h,\theta)}{T} + \frac{C(v^h,\theta)}{T^\alpha} + o\left(\frac{1}{T^\alpha}\right), h = 1, \dots, H$$

where v and v^h, $h = 1 \dots, H$ are independent with identical distribution. Now the indirect inference estimator is the solution $\hat{\theta}_T^H$ of

$$\hat{\beta}_T^H = \frac{1}{H}\sum_{h=1}^{H}\tilde{\beta}_T^h(\hat{\theta}_T^H).$$

By plugging the Edgeworth expansions of $\hat{\beta}_T$ and $\tilde{\beta}_T^h$ we get

$$\theta^0 + \frac{A(v,\theta^0)}{\sqrt{T}} + \frac{B(v,\theta^0)}{T} + \frac{C(v,\theta^0)}{T^\alpha} + o(T^{-\alpha})$$

Approximately median unbiased (M.U.) estimators

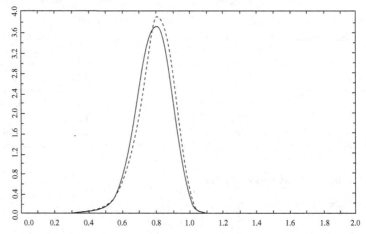

Indirect inference (I.I.) estimators

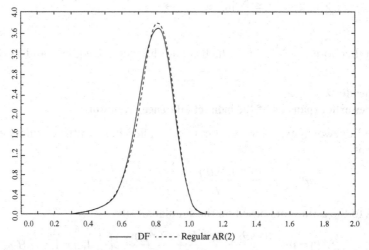

——— DF · · · · · Regular AR(2)

Figure 13.5 Estimation of the sum of the AR coefficient in an AR(2) model: regular versus Dickey–Fuller regression form

$$= \frac{1}{H} \sum_{h=1}^{H} \left[\hat{\theta}_T^H + \frac{A(v^h, \hat{\theta}_T^H)}{\sqrt{T}} + \frac{B(v^h, \hat{\theta}_T^H)}{T} + \frac{C(v^h, \hat{\theta}_T^H)}{T^\alpha} + o(T^{-\alpha}) \right]$$

which provides the form of the Edgeworth expansion for $\hat{\theta}_T^H$ as follows. Let:

$$\hat{\theta}_T^H = \theta^0 + \frac{A_H^*}{\sqrt{T}} + \frac{B_H^*}{T} + \frac{C_H^*}{T^{3/2}} + o(T^{-3/2})$$

be the Edgeworth expansion of $\hat{\theta}_T^H$. Then by Taylor expansion of $A(v^h, \hat{\theta}_T^H)$, $B(v^h, \hat{\theta}_T^H)$ and $C(v^h, \hat{\theta}_T^H)$ around θ^0 and keeping only terms of order lower than $T^{-\alpha}$ we get:

$$\theta^0 + \frac{A(v, \theta^0)}{\sqrt{T}} + \frac{B(v, \theta^0)}{T} + \frac{C(v, \theta^0)}{T^\alpha} + o(T^{-\alpha})$$

$$= \theta^0 + \frac{A_H^*}{\sqrt{T}} + \frac{B_H^*}{T} + \frac{C_H^*}{T^{3/2}} + o(T^{-3/2})$$

$$+ \left\{ \frac{1}{\sqrt{T}} \frac{1}{H} \sum_{h=1}^{H} A(v^h, \theta^0) + \frac{1}{T} \frac{1}{H} \sum_{h=1}^{H} \frac{\partial A}{\partial \theta'}(v^h, \theta^0) A_H^* \right.$$

$$+ \frac{1}{T^{3/2}} \frac{1}{H} \sum_{h=1}^{H} \frac{\partial A}{\partial \theta'}(v^h, \theta^0) B_H^* + \frac{1}{2} \frac{1}{T^{3/2}} \frac{1}{H} \sum_{h=1}^{H} A_H^{*\prime} \frac{\partial^2 A}{\partial \theta \partial \theta'}(v^h, \theta^0) A_H^* + o(T^{-3/2}) \right\}$$

$$+ \left\{ \frac{1}{T} \frac{1}{H} \sum_{h=1}^{H} B(v^h, \theta^0) + \frac{1}{T^{3/2}} \frac{1}{H} \sum_{h=1}^{H} \frac{\partial B}{\partial \theta'}(v^h, \theta^0) A_H^* + o(T^{-3/2}) \right\}$$

$$+ \frac{1}{T^\alpha} \frac{1}{H} \sum_{h=1}^{H} C(v^h, \theta^0) + o(T^{-\alpha}).$$

Identifying both sides of the equality provides the result announced in proposition 2.1.

References

Andrews, D.W.K. (1993), "Exactly Median-Unbiased Estimation of First Order Autoregressive/Unit Root Models," *Econometrica*, 61(1), 139–165.

Andrews, D.W.K. and H.Y. Chen (1994), "Approximately Median-Unbiased Estimation of Autoregressive Models with Application to US Macroeconomic and Financial Time Series," *Journal of Business and Economic Statistic*, 12(2).

Duffie, D. and K.J. Singleton (1983), "Simulated Moments Estimation of Markov Models of Asset Prices," *Econometrica*, 61(3), 929–952.

Efron, B. (1979), "Bootstrap Methods: Another Look at the Jackknife," *Annals of Statistics*, 7, 1–26.

Gallant, R.A. and G. Tauchen (1996), "Which Moments to Match," *Econometric Theory*, 12, 657–668.

Gourieroux, C. and A. Monfort (1995), "Simulation Based Estimation Methods", CORE Lecture Series, Oxford University Press.

Gourieroux, C., A. Monfort, and E. Renault (1993), "Indirect Inference," *Journal of Applied Econometrics*, 8, S85–S118.

Gourieroux, C., A. Monfort, and A. Trognon (1989), "Pseudo-Maximum Likelihood Methods" Theory," *Econometrica*, 52, 681–700.

Hall, P. (1992), "The Bootstrap and Edgeworth Expansion," *Springer Series in Statistics*, Springer-Verlag.

(1994), "Methodology and Theory for the Bootstrap," *Handbook of Econometrics*, vol. IV, Amsterdam: North-Holland, chapter 39, pp. 2341–2381.

Jeong, J. and G.S. Maddala (1993), "A Perspective on Application of Bootstrap Methods in Econometrics," *Handbook of Statistics*, vol. XI, Elsevier Science.

Kouki, M. and E. Renault (1994), "A Structural Approach to Determining Scale Economies in the Banking Industry," Presented at ESEM, Maastricht, August 1994.

MacKinnon, J. and A. Smith (1995), "Approximate Bias Correction in Econometrics," discussion paper, Queen's University, Kingston, Ontario.

Orcutt, G.H. and H.S. Winokur Jr. (1969), "First Order Autoregression: Inference, Estimation and Prediction," *Econometrica*, 37, 1–14.

Pastorello, S., E. Renault, and N. Touzi (1993), "Statistical Inference for Random Variance Option Pricing," discussion paper CREST and GREMAQ.

Rudebusch, G.D. (1992), "Trends and Random Walks in Macroeconomic Time Series: A Re-examination," *International Economic Review*, 33, 661–680.

(1993), "The Uncertain Unit Root in Real GNP," *American Economic Review*, 83(1), 264–272.

Scott, L. (1987), "Option Pricing when The Variance Changes Randomly: Theory, Estimation and Application," *Journal of Financial and Quantitative Analysis*, 22, 419–438.

Shaman, P. and R.A. Stine (1989), "A Fixed Point Characterization for Bias of Autoregressive Estimators," *Annals of Statistics*, 17(3), 1275–1284.

Smith, A.A. (1993), "Estimating Nonlinear Time-Series Models Using Simulated Vector Autoregressions," *Journal of Applied Econometrics*, 8, S63–S84.

Vasicek, O. (1977), "An Equilibrium Characterization of the Term Structure," *Journal of Financial Economics*, 5, 177–188.

14 Simulation-based estimation of a non-linear, latent factor aggregate production function

Lee Ohanian, Giovanni L. Violante, Per Krusell and Jose-Victor Rios-Rull

1   Introduction

The purpose of this chapter is to explore in detail a number of econometric issues associated with the specification and estimation of a non-linear, latent variable aggregate production function developed in Krusell, Ohanian, Rios-Rull, and Violante (1995) (hereafter KORV). In particular, we discuss how different simulation-based methods can be used to address a number of difficult problems associated with our particular model, and evaluate the relative performance of these methods. Since some of these issues have not been analyzed in much detail using simulation-based methods, the findings reported here may be of use to other researchers working in similar environments.

In our earlier paper, we developed an aggregate production function that differs substantially from the standard production function used in macroeconomic analysis. The development of our alternative model was motivated by a key fact of the US economy. In the last 30 years, a substantial difference has emerged in the growth rates of wages for workers with different educational levels. John, Murphy, and Pierce (1993) report that the median wage earner among college graduates experienced a 15 percent increase in inflation-adjusted wages between 1964 and 1988, while the median wage earner among high school graduates experienced a 5 percent decline in real wages over the same period. The widening gap in the relative wage of skilled or unskilled labor is commonly referred to as the "wage premium" or "skill premium."

This observation has a number of important economic and social

Krusell, University of Rochester, Ohanian, University of Minnesota and Universtiy of Pennsylvania, Rios-Rull, Federal Reserve Bank of Minneapolis and University of Pennsylvania, and Violante, University of Pennsylvania. We would like to thank Filippo Altissimo, Frank Diebold, John Geweke, and Roberto Mariano for helpful comments and suggestions, and Daniel Houser for excellent research assistance. Violante acknowledges the *Ente per gli Studi Monetari, Bancari e Finanziari "L. Einaudi"* for financial support.

implications. First, not only do these data represent a striking change from the past, but the trend in wage disparity seems to be accelerating, suggesting the possibility of even *greater* economic inequality in the future. While individuals with higher educational attainment historically have received higher wages, the wage premium to education was relatively constant over time, and in fact narrowed considerably in the 1940s. Increased wage inequality is a relatively new phenomenon, and has increased substantially in the last 15 years. Moreover, these observations are at variance with standard economic theory, which predicts that factor price differentials in the long run will tend to narrow as producers substitute away from relatively expensive factors into cheaper factors. These observations also have a number of key implications for government policy. For example, they play a central role in current discussions of redistribution, welfare, and social insurance reform, since the extent to which aid recipients can be moved successfully into employment depends in an important way on the wages they can earn.

Given these implications, a number of economists have tried to account empirically for the main factors responsible for the growing wage gap between skilled and unskilled workers. Despite substantial research on this topic, no consensus explanation for these observations has been established. Perhaps the most comprehensive work in this area is by Bound and Johnson (1992) who empirically evaluate four popular explanations for these changes: (1) the loss of high wage manufacturing jobs associated with the US trade deficit, (2) the decline in the ability of labor unions to negotiate high wages, (3) changes in technology, and (4) a slowdown in the growth rate of the college-educated population. Using regression methods, they find that these potential explanations account for only a fraction of the observed changes. Instead, most of the growth in the wage premium is explained by a regression-residual category, which they summarize as "*a combination of skill-biased technical change and changes in unmeasured labor quality.*"

Our theory can be used to interpret structurally the empirical findings of Bound and Johnson, and others. The main premise of our theory is based on the economic interactions between the behavior of the wage premium and two other key observations. First, there has been a rapid decline in the relative price of capital equipment over the past 25 years (Gordon (1990)). Associated with this falling price of capital equipment has been rapid growth in the stock of business capital equipment. Second, there is considerable empirical evidence (Hamermesh (1993) lists several references) that suggests *unskilled* labor and physical capital are relatively good substitutes, while *skilled* labor and physical capital are relatively complementary. Our theory proposes the following explanation for the change in the wage premium: the rise in the relative wages of skilled labor reflects the sharp increase in the stock of physical capital equipment given that they are relative complements in production. Moreover, the secular decline in the price of equipment puts downward pressure on the competitive price of unskilled labor, since they are relatively good substitutes.

To implement this theory empirically, we developed an aggregate production function with four inputs. This production technology differs considerably from the standard model in macroeconomics in that it explicitly distinguishes between skilled and unskilled labor, and between capital structures and capital equipment. We estimate the parameters of the production function, and study quantitatively the extent to which differences in complementarities between the two types of labor and capital equipment can account for the increase in wage inequality. This strategy allows us to interpret and understand the main empirical findings of Bound and Johnson within the context of a fully articulated model. In particular, it allows us to separate the effects on the wage premium of the two main factors cited by Bound and Johnson: (1) technical improvement in capital equipment, and the different ways in which skilled and unskilled labor interact with equipment, and (2) changes in unmeasured quality of the two types of labor.

While the focus of our initial paper was on the development of the theory, data construction, and economic interpretation of the empirical findings, the main theme of this chapter is a detailed analysis and presentation of the specification and estimation of the parameters of the four-input non-linear production function.

There are a number of challenging and interesting econometric issues associated with estimating the parameters of this production function. The three main issues are:

1   unmeasured labor quality of both skilled and unskilled workers enters the production function *non-linearly* as a *latent* variable,
2   we recognize that labor efficiency has changed over time, so we model the unobservable state as a *non-stationary* stochastic process,
3   the sample size we will work with is relatively small.

In particular, we will consider two different stochastic specifications for labor efficiency (which could be interpreted as human capital). The first specification is a trend stationary latent state and the second is a first-difference stationary latent state with drift. Across these two specifications, we contrast three different procedures for estimating the parameters of interest. The first method is based on the exact likelihood of the model which is obtained by integrating out the unobservable state. The second method is based on a simpler, but misspecified auxiliary model subsequently corrected by indirect inference, and the third method is based on a simulated pseudo ML estimator. We provide Monte Carlo evidence on the performance of these estimators in non-stationary environments and in small samples and discuss their computational efficiency.

By providing a detailed analysis of the issues associated with parameter estimation in our specific model, we hope that our findings will be useful to other researchers analyzing problems that share some of the characteristics of our environment.

The remainder of the chapter is organized as follows. In section 2, we describe the aggregate production function, and summarize the data used in the analysis. In section 3 we present the alternative specifications of the model that differ according to the way we deal with unmeasurable labor quality. In section 4, we outline the possible estimation methods when labor efficiency is assumed to be stochastic and compare their performance in a Monte Carlo analysis. Section 5 presents the results of the estimation, and the economic interpretation. Section 6 presents a summary and our conclusions.

2   The model and data

2.1   The production function

To develop the production function, we consider two categories of labor input: skilled workers, and unskilled (or less-skilled) workers. The two categories are different from the point of view of production. The skill level is assumed to be exogenous, i.e., we do not model the individual's choice of skill level. We disaggregate the capital stock into two components, structures and equipment, because the most striking changes in the relative price of capital have occurred in the equipment category.

We choose to represent the production technology with a general nested CES functional form. This function is relatively simple and parsimonious, and allows for different substitution possibilities across factors. The production function is

$$y_t = A_t k_{st}^\alpha [\mu u_t^\sigma + (1-\mu)(\lambda k_{et}^\rho + (1-\lambda)s_t^\rho)^{\frac{\sigma}{\rho}}]^{\frac{1-\alpha}{\sigma}}.$$

This technology has several distinguishing features. The technology has (stochastic) neutral technical progress A_t and is a CRS Cobb–Douglas function with two inputs: (i) capital structures, k_s, and (ii) the composite term $[\mu u_t^\sigma + (1-\mu)(\lambda k_{et}^\rho + (1-\lambda)s_t^\rho)^{\frac{\sigma}{\rho}}]^{\frac{1}{\sigma}}$. This second term is a CES aggregate over unskilled labor, u, with share parameter μ, and a *second* CES aggregate (with share parameter $1-\mu$) over capital equipment, k_e, and skilled labor, s (the relevant share parameters within this second CES term are λ and $1-\lambda$, respectively). The parameter α measures structures' share of income. The parameters σ and ρ are the key elements from the standpoint of our theory, since they govern the amount of substitutability between (i) unskilled labor and the CES aggregate of capital equipment and skilled labor, and (ii) skilled labor and capital equipment, respectively. To satisfy regularity conditions, both σ and ρ are restricted to lie in $(-\infty, 1)$. Higher values of σ or ρ than zero correspond to more substitutability than Cobb–Douglas for the corresponding aggregate. The elasticity of substitution between equipment (or skilled labor) and unskilled labor is $\frac{1}{1-\sigma}$, and the elasticity of substitution between equipment and skilled labor is $\frac{1}{1-\rho}$. For simplicity, we assume that neutral technical progress A_t is an *iid* random variable, with mean normalized to 1.

The labor inputs are measured in efficiency units: each input type is a product of the number of labor hours and an hourly efficiency index. In particular, $s \equiv H_s n_s$ and $u \equiv H_u n_u$, where n_i is the number of hours and H_i the quality per hour of type $i = s, u$. It is clear that H_i can be given two distinct interpretations: it could be human capital, accumulated by the individual, or it could represent a skill-specific technology level, which may have come about by research and development activity. In the absence of direct measures of these two, they cannot be distinguished. Given our *iid* restriction on neutral technological change, we implicitly assume that all the technical progress in the economy is factor specific.

The wage premium, π, is defined as the ratio of skilled wages to unskilled wages. Assuming that factor prices are equal to marginal products, we have

$$\pi_t = \frac{(1-\mu)(1-\lambda)}{\mu}\left[\lambda\left(\frac{k_{et}}{S_t}\right)^{\rho} + (1-\lambda)\right]^{\frac{\sigma-\rho}{\rho}}\left(\frac{n_{ut}}{n_{st}}\right)^{1-\sigma}\left(\frac{H_{st}}{H_{ut}}\right)^{\sigma}.$$

The main premise of our theory regarding the relative complementarity of skilled labor and capital equipment, and the relative substitutability between unskilled labor and equipment corresponds to the case in which $\sigma > \rho$. In this case, as argued in KORV, the wage premium necessarily rises in response to an increase in the amount of equipment, *ceteris paribus*. Thus, the extent to which our theory featuring capital–skilled labor complementarity is useful to interpret the behavior of the wage premium can be evaluated by estimating the parameters of the production function, specifically the substitutability parameters σ and ρ.

2.2   The data

2.2.1 Data on labor input
This section presents a summary of the data construction procedures.[1] The sources of our data on labor input and wages are **CPS Annual Demographic**

---

[1] A detailed data appendix is available upon request.

March Files for the years 1964–1993. We have restricted our attention to all persons between 16 and 70 years old, excluding the self-employed. The procedure for constructing the series for skilled and unskilled labor input and wages consists of two steps. In the *first step* we generate a partition of the sample into more than 200 demographic groups constructed on the basis of age, race, gender, and educational level. For each one of these groups, we have a measure of average labor input and labor earnings. Hourly wage is simply the ratio between yearly labor income and yearly measure of labor input in terms of hours worked. The *second step* consists of sorting these groups into two categories: skilled workers and unskilled workers, and computing measures of total annual labor input for skilled workers n_{st} and of their hourly wage w_{st}, as well as total annual labor input for the unskilled n_{ut} and their hourly wage w_{ut}. Since there are no generally accepted definitions of skilled and unskilled (or less skilled) labor input, in KORV we explored several different methods to perform this aggregation, some based on education and others on the distribution of labor income across demographic groups. In this chapter we will focus on one particular education-based criterion that defines unskilled workers as those individuals with less than 12 years of schooling (high school graduate). In order to aggregate group-specific measures into the broad class of skilled and unskilled defined by the above criterion, we assume that the groups within a class are perfect substitutes (they simply add). Moreover, for the aggregation we use as weights the group wages of a given base year (1980, for consistency with the construction of the capital series) in very much the same way as real GDP is computed in National Income and Product Accounts (**NIPA**).[2] Panels (a) and (b) of figure 14.1 report the labor input ratio and the wage premium implied by our definition of skills.

2.2.2 Data on capital
We have two types of capital in our model: producers' durable equipment (PDE) and non-residential structures. A key aspect of the data is that the relative price of capital equipment had declined secularly. Since in the data the behavior of the prices of structures and personal consumption has been similar, we treat them identically, deflating by the price index for consumer non-durables and services.

The measurement of capital equipment is more difficult, since we are interested in *efficiency units* of equipment entering the production function. To obtain efficiency units, we need to compute the relative price of equipment. Because of the enormous improvement in the quality of equipment

---

[2] Note that we have CPS data for the period 1964–1993, but since wages and labor input data in the survey refer to one year earlier, our sample spans the period 1963–1992.

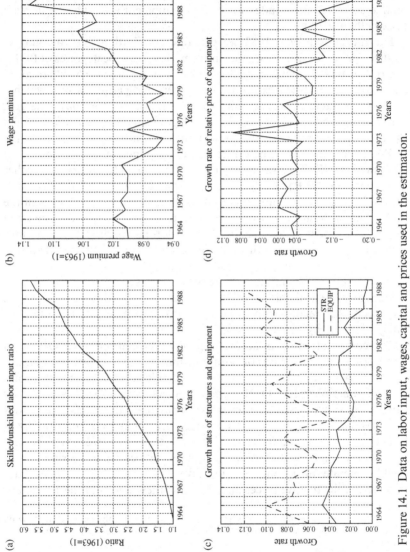

Figure 14.1 Data on labor input, wages, capital and prices used in the estimation.

goods that has occurred in the last 15 years, especially for information technologies, quality-adjusted price indexes are needed for a meaningful measure of this relative price. The method we have used to aggregate all the quality-adjusted prices for the different categories of PDE and to obtain a unique corrected price index for capital equipment is simply the implicit price deflator (IPD).

For the period 1963–1983 we can rely on Gordon's (1990) quality-adjusted prices for what he defines as the *primary* 16 subcategories of PDE.[3] For the post-1983 sample period, we are not aware of any existing quality-adjusted series of PDE, except for computers and peripherals on which a fairly large literature of quality-adjustment procedures has emerged. Therefore, we have aggregated the 16 categories used by Gordon through the IPD with base year 1980 into the four main categories classified in the NIPA: office and information processing equipment (OIP), industrial equipment (INDEQ), transportation equipment (TRANSP), and other equipment (OTHER). The price indexes for the INDEQ, TRANSP, and OTHER categories did not appear to experience dramatic changes in the 1980s, and we assume that the relationship between quality-adjusted and official price indexes documented by Gordon has been stable over time. This allows us to estimate this relation using Gordon's adjusted data as a dependent variable and the official series as regressors in a VAR on the levels for 1963–1983, and then to use the estimates and the exogenous variables, which are available up to 1992, to forecast the adjusted-price series. We specify the relationship in levels to take advantage of potential cointegration among variables.[4]

The computation of an accurate quality-adjusted series for OIP is an important issue, since this is the group within PDE that recorded the largest change in price and relative share. We first divided the OIP group into computer and peripherals (COMP), and all others. For all the OIP categories other than computers and peripherals, we have used the official price index series. We do this for two reasons. First, we are not aware of any attempt at quality-adjustment of the series which covers the 1984–1992 sample period. Second, it is our view that using the forecasting technique described above could generate misleading results, given that dramatic changes have occurred in the relative prices and shares of these goods in the 1980s. For

---

[3] See appendix B.18 in Gordon (1990). His quality adjustment involves a detailed study on more than 100 specific products and the use of hedonic regressions and matching model procedures.

[4] We estimated a VAR(1) on q_t^a augmented with the exogenous variables $DCOINC_{t-1}$ and q_{t-1}, where q^a is the vector of quality-adjusted prices for INDEQ, TRANSP, and OTHER obtained from Gordon's data, q is the vector of the corresponding official NIPA price indexes and $DCOINC$ is a coincident indicator of the business cycle. The latter two sets of variables are available until 1992.

instance, the NIPA official price index of communication equipment[5] grew at an increasing rate in the 1960s and 1970s, but in the 1980s this rate decreased steadily. These observations suggest that the relation between official and quality-adjusted indexes for these goods may have changed structurally in the 1980s.

Substantial research has been done on computing quality adjusted price indexes for computers and peripherals. We distinguished between PCs, mainframes (a broad category that includes also supercomputers, workstations and midrange computers) and peripherals, and derived quality-adjusted measures of prices for these three groups from the existing literature. Berndt, Griliches, and Rappaport (1995) provide an hedonic price index for PCs, Brown and Greenstein (1995) compute a price index for mainframes, and Cole, et al. (1986) compute one for peripherals. We then constructed the series for the quality-adjusted price index for COMP by aggregating these prices through an IPD for the period 1984–1990.[6]

We then aggregated the price indexes for the four main categories of PDE with the IPD procedure. The relative price of equipment is constructed by dividing the aggregate IPD price series through the price index for consumption. Investment in capital equipment in efficiency units is constructed by deflating the nominal series of investment in equipment from NIPA through our quality-adjusted price index for equipment and then it is used together with a given depreciation rate and an initial value for the stock to construct a series for capital equipment. Table 14.1 summarizes the average growth rates of the relative price and the capital stock equipment in efficiency units in the three decades of the sample.

Panel (c) in figure 14.1 reports the growth rates of structures and equipment over time and panel (d) presents the decline of the relative price of equipment, especially sharp in the 1980s.

3   Unobserved labor efficiency and model specifications

To estimate the parameters of the production function, we will use the first-order necessary conditions of a competitive profit maximizing firm. We assume that the firm observes the efficiency factors $\{H_{st}, H_{ut}\}$ of its labor inputs and the relative price of equipment p_t before making its choice on the quantities of the four inputs to hire but does not observe the *iid* neutral technical change A_t. On the other hand, only p_t is observed by the econometrician.

---

[5] This price index is computed as the ratio between the series in current dollars GIPCE and the series in constant (1987) dollars GIPCEQ.

[6] As we could obtain data on COMP only up to 1990, this will be our endpoint of the sample in the estimation.

Table 14.1. *Capital equipment*

Growth rate	1963–1972	1973–1982	1983–1992
Relative price	− 0.023	− 0.028	− 0.139
Efficiency units	0.070	0.069	0.114

For the labor efficiency terms, we distinguish three cases that provide a benchmark to evaluate the performance of different estimation techniques. Define h_t as $\log(H_t)$. In the first case (denoted as DT) the log of labor efficiency is simply a deterministic trend. In the second case (TS) h_t is a trend stationary process with no autocorrelation. In the third case (FDS) it is assumed to follow a first difference stationary process with drift. These three specifications imply the following laws of motion for the unobservable states

(DT): $h_t = h_0 + \gamma t$
(TS): $h_t = h_0 + \gamma t + \omega_t$
(FDS): $h_t = \gamma + h_{t-1} + \omega_t$.

Here ω_t is a (2×1) vector of disturbances distributed as $N(0,\Omega)$, h_0 is a (2×1) vector of constants, and γ is a (2×1) vector which specifies the (constant) growth rates of the two efficiency factors. We treat H_t as a latent variable, but only in the two latter specifications does it evolve stochastically.

We exploit three restrictions to estimate the parameters of the production function. The first restriction is that the ratio of the wage bill of skilled to unskilled workers be equal to that observed in the data

$$\frac{w_{st}N_{st}}{w_{ut}N_{ut}} = wbr_t(H_t, X_t; \phi). \tag{1}$$

The left-hand side of the equation is the ratio of the wage bill in the data, and the right-hand side is the wage bill ratio from the model, which has as arguments the marginal products of the two types of labor, the vector of efficiency factors, a vector of exogenous observable variables $X_t = \{K_{et}, K_{st}, n_{ut}, n_{st}\}$ and a vector of structural parameters, ϕ.

The second restriction is that aggregate labor's share of income in the model (lsh_t) be equal to that observed in the data

$$\frac{w_{st}N_{st} + w_{ut}N_{ut}}{Y_t} = lsh_t(H_t, X_t; \phi). \tag{2}$$

The data for the LHS of this restriction is the ratio of unambiguous labor income – defined as wages, salaries, and benefits – divided by the sum of the numerator and unambiguous capital income, which includes corporate profits, depreciation, rental income, and interest payment, following the methodology illustrated in Cooley (1995).

The third restriction is an equal rates of return condition that equates the expected gross rates of return of the two types of capital

$$(1 - \delta_s) + mpks_t(H_t, X_t; \phi) = (1 - \delta_e) \frac{E_t(p_{t+1})}{p_t} + \frac{1}{p_t} mpke_t(H_t, X_t; \phi). \quad (3)$$

The left-hand side of the equation is the net of depreciation return to capital structures, while the right-hand side of the equation is the expected net of depreciation return to capital equipment. The terms *mpke* and *mpks* denote "marginal product of capital equipment" and "marginal product of capital structures," respectively. δ_s and δ_e are the depreciation rates for structures. In the estimation, the expression $(1 - \delta_e)\frac{p_{t+1}}{p_t} + \varepsilon_t$ replaces the first term on the right-hand side, where ε_t is an *iid* forecast error which is assumed to have the Gaussian structure $\varepsilon_t \sim N(0, \eta_\varepsilon)$. Note that the A_t term drops out of the first two conditions, and does not appear in the third one as the *iid* assumption allows us to integrate it out.

Given the relatively small sample and the large number of parameters, we have reduced the dimensionality of the parameter space by adopting values for those parameters that have been estimated or calibrated in prior studies. Following Greenwood, Hercowitz, and Krusell (1997) we calibrated δ_s, δ_e and α. Furthermore, we used data on the relative price of equipment to estimate the standard deviation of the one-step forecast error η_ε. This was accomplished by fitting to the deviations of $\frac{p_{t+1}}{p_t}$ from a linear trend an $ARMA(1,1)$ model;[7] we then measured the standard deviation of the residuals and we multiplied it by $(1 - \delta_e)$. The number obtained – which is quite robust to different specifications for the linear conditional mean – is the calibrated counterpart of η_ε. The results of the calibration for these parameters are in table 14.2.

Since we calibrate these parameters, it is worth noting that we do not take into account this parameter uncertainty in the estimation. However the use of this procedure increases considerably the degrees of freedom.

$$\pi_t = 0.95 - 0.008t + 0.75\pi_{t-1} - 0.95\varepsilon_{t-1} + \varepsilon_t$$
$$\text{with } \bar{R}^2 = 0.57, DW = 2.3, \hat{\sigma}_\varepsilon = 0.035.$$

---

[7] The results of the estimation were (call $\pi_{t+1} = \frac{p_t + 1}{p_t}$)

$$\pi_t = 0.95 - 0.008t + 0.75\pi_{t-1} - 0.95\varepsilon_{t-1} + \varepsilon_t$$
$$\text{with } \bar{R}^2 = 0.57, DW = 2.3, \hat{\sigma}_\varepsilon = 0.035.$$

Table 14.2. *Calibrated parameters*

$\alpha = 0.11$	$\delta_s = 0.05$	$\delta_e = 0.125$	$\eta_\varepsilon = 0.03$

4   Estimation and inference with stochastic labor efficiency

Although attractive for its simplicity, the deterministic approach to the estimation of our model has the crucial shortcoming that some error terms need to be "artificially" added to the wage bill and the labor share equations for the model to be estimated. But these error terms have no structural economic interpretation. Sargent (1981), among others, has argued that the practice of adding error terms to equations is not a legitimate procedure. This is not an issue, however, for the stochastic specifications of labor efficiency, since the shocks enter into the exogenous laws of motion of the unobservable labor efficiency factors.

The model with stochastic labor efficiency is a relatively difficult one to estimate in that the latent variables – the (2×1) vector of labor efficiency factors H_t – are embedded within a non-linear function. Given this complication, the model becomes a non-linear latent variable (or state-space) model of the following form

$$\text{ME: } Z_t = f(X_t, H_t; \phi) + \varepsilon_t$$

$$\text{SE: } \begin{cases} h_t = h_0 + \gamma t + \omega_t \\ \text{or} \\ h_t = \gamma + h_{t-1} + \omega_t \end{cases} \tag{4}$$

where ME indicates the three measurement equations, and SE stands for state equations. The function f contains the three non-linear observational equations (1), (2), and (3) obtained as restrictions from the model. Z_t and X_t are respectively the (3×1) and (4×1) vectors of dependent and exogenous variables described in section 3, h_t is the (2×1) vector of the logs of the latent labor efficiency factors, ε_t and ω_t are respectively (3×1) and (2×1) vectors[8] of *iid* multivariate normal disturbance terms with mean zero and covariance η_ε and Ω. Define $\phi \equiv \{\delta_s, \delta_e, \alpha, \mu, \lambda, \sigma, \rho, \eta_\varepsilon\}$ as the (8×1) vector of parameters of the measurement equation, and define $\varphi \equiv \{h_0, \gamma, \Omega\}$ as the (7×1) vector of parameters of the state equations. Again, for notational simplicity call $\theta = \{\phi, \varphi\}$. Since we have only 28 observations, we chose to reduce the dimensionality of the parameter vector to be estimated using *a priori* information from the calibration of δ_s, δ_e, α, and η_ε and described above and some additional restrictions. First we

---

[8] Since ε_t enters only the third ME, the first two components of this vector are identically zero.

assume that the innovations to the log of skilled and unskilled labor efficiency do not covary and have the same standard deviation, hence we can rewrite $\Omega = \eta^2_h I_2$. Second, we fix the initial level of skilled labor efficiency h_{0s} as a scaling factor. This latter restriction is needed as our model does not have any implications on the *levels* of variables. It actually turns out that given a value for the initial quality index of skilled labor h_{0s}, then the other parameters λ, μ, and h_{0u} are identified and can be estimated, but all four parameters together are not identified. The dimensionality of the parameter vector to be estimated, θ, is therefore reduced to eight.

Given the non-linear state-space representation of our model, as in (4), there is a variety of techniques that in principle could be used to estimate the parameters of the production function. The source of the difficulties in estimating our model originates exactly from the *joint presence* of the non-linearity and the unobservability of some key endogenous variables. In fact, the non-linearity of the measurement equations prevents us from using the classical Kalman filter methods to integrate out the latent variable. The Kalman filter in this case still yields the *best linear predictor*, but the best predictor need not be linear and more in general, as Meinhold and Singpurwalla (1989) emphasize, may not be close to the linear one. The Kalman filter estimator is therefore *non-robust* to non-linear perturbations of the model, which makes it particularly unsuitable for our case.[9]

Indicating with the superscript T the vector of all sample observations, the joint p.d.f. of our model is $\psi(Z^T, H^T | X^T; \theta)$. Since H_t is latent, we can only observe $\psi(Z^T | X^T; \theta)$, therefore in the structural estimation it is necessary to collapse the first p.d.f. into the second in order to map the model into the data.

There are several simulation-based approaches that can be used to address this problem. A necessary condition for the implementation of all of them is that there be no feedback from the endogenous variables to the exogenous variables (or, the exogenous variables must be *strongly exogenous*). This is an issue in our analysis because capital and labor are kept fixed throughout the simulation, while in equilibrium they will tend to respond to variations in H_t. The only way of dealing with this problem explicitly would be to extend the model to a dynamic general equilibrium setting, in which one could solve for the decision rules for capital accumulation and labor supply. In this case, capital and labor could be simulated based on the draws of the error terms. Of course, this would be a much more complicated model without an analytic solution, and would also involve a higher number of parameters in the estimation. The basic set-up of our environment suggests that the scope of this problem may not be very large.

---

[9] For further evidence on this point, see Mariano and Tanizaki in this volume.

First, the disturbance terms are *iid*, so that shocks today to labor efficiency or the relative price of capital equipment are not expected to persist. Second, while shocks may affect investment, which is a flow, the overall effect on the *stock* of capital will be relatively small, since on average business equipment investments are about 8 percent of the capital stock in the US. Finally, if the innovation variance of the shocks is fairly small, this will tend to limit the range of values the shocks can take. We have indeed found that the innovation variance is quite small, and is discussed in more detail in section 5.

The simulation-based methods we consider in this chapter are stochastic integration of the state vector (which we contrast with a numerical integration algorithm), estimation of an auxiliary model with indirect inference correction, and simulated pseudo-maximum likelihood. In what follows we will outline these three methods, run some Monte Carlo experiments, and, in the last part of this section, compare their performance in our environment.

4.1   Numerical and stochastic integration

The first way to attack the estimation problem described above is integrating out the latent state vector to obtain the likelihood solely as a function of observable variables and parameters. This requires in principle performing an integral of dimension $(T \times 2)$,[10] precisely $\int \psi(Z^T, H^T | X^T; \theta) dH^T$. When maximizing the criterion function for the estimation, the integral has to be computed each time the hill-climbing algorithm evaluates the function in the parameter space. For this reason, finding an efficient (but sufficiently precise) way of computing multimensional integrals is the crucial step in this approach to the estimation of non-linear state-space models.

The two specifications (trend stationary and first difference stationary) have very different implications in terms of the best strategy to adopt, given that one wants to follow the approach of integrating out the latent state and construct the exact observable likelihood. The trend stationary specification does not have autocorrelation in the labor efficiency factor, therefore the integration in greatly simplified as it reduces to a sequence of T two-dimensional integrals. For this latter case we have compared two integration methods: numerical quadrature and stochastic simulation.

Quadrature is a numerical method that approximates the integral on the state vector at time t as follows

---

[10] More generally, the dimension of the integral is the number of elements in the state vector multiplied by the sample size.

$$\int \psi(Z_t, H_t | X_t; \theta) dH_t \simeq \sum_{j=1}^{N} \psi(Z_t^j | H_t^j, X_t; \theta) \psi_\omega(H_t^j; \theta) w^j \qquad (5)$$

where the N quadrature points $\{H_t^j\}_{j=1}^N$ and their respective weights $\{w^j\}_{j=1}^N$ are deterministically preassigned in the given quadrature rule. Z_t^j is the vector of values of the dependent variables implied by the jth node of the latent state vector. Note that in our case both $\psi_\omega(H_t; \theta)$ and $\psi(Z_t^j | H_t^j, X_t; \theta)$ are normal p.d.f. Obviously, the approximation error in the computation of the integral will be smaller, the larger is the number of nodes N.

The second approach is the stochastic simulation of the integral. We can write

$$\int \psi(Z_t, H_t | X_t; \theta) dH_t \simeq \frac{1}{S} \sum_{i=1}^{S} \psi(\tilde{Z}_t^i | \tilde{H}_t^i, | X_t; \theta) \qquad (6)$$

where the equality holds exactly as $S \rightarrow \infty$. Here $\tilde{H}_t^i$ denotes the ith draw of the state from $\psi_\omega(H_t; \theta)$ and $\tilde{Z}_t^i$ and implied vector of endogenous variables obtained from $f(\cdot)$. Once we are able to compute the integral in (5) or (6), the exact likelihood function for the model can be constructed and evaluated at each point in the parameter space attained by the numerical optimization algorithm. This procedure will deliver, respectively, a quadrature-based MLE (QUAD) and a simulated MLE (SMLE). Note that for the SMLE case, throughout all the maximization of the objective function the *same* set of $(T \times S)$ random numbers must be used to prevent the likelihood from becoming a random function.

It is important to indicate that the methodology of integrating out the state requires to specify some additional error terms to the measurement equations for the maximized likelihood not to be degenerate. As we discussed earlier, we are not comfortable with the specification of additive arbitrary error terms to the first two equations. An alternative would be to introduce measurement error explicitly in one of the series, but this would generate a (generally) non-Gaussian model with an unknown distribution that, together with the non-linearity of the measurement equation, becomes fairly untractable. In the Monte Carlo experiment that follows we have simply attached additively a Gaussian error term to each equation, so that the likelihood – once the state is integrated over – is a correctly specified Gaussian density. Given the shortcoming of the specification of this model, we present the Monte Carlo results for heuristic purposes, and will not use this procedure when formally estimating the model parameters from US data.

We have compared across 200 Monte Carlo trials the Gauss–Legendre quadrature method with $N = 256$ quadrature points in the two-dimensional space of the latent state vector against stochastic simulation based on

Table 14.3. *Quadrature trend stationary case (percentage bias)*

	N = 256		
	Mean	Median	S.D.
σ	− 1.62	− 1.72	1.31
ρ	1.01	1.01	1.98
γ_u	− 6.43	− 6.51	9.68
γ_s	0.23	− 0.13	8.35

Table 14.4. *Simulated MLE: trend stationary case (percentage bias)*

	S = 10			S = 50			S = 100		
	Mean	Median	S.D.	Mean	Median	S.D.	Mean	Median	S.D.
σ	− 2.30	− 2.32	1.62	− 2.32	− 2.40	1.46	− 2.31	− 2.40	1.41
ρ	1.37	1.39	2.13	1.34	1.28	2.03	1.36	1.39	1.99
γ_u	− 11.17	− 10.08	12.22	− 11.47	− 12.19	10.98	− 11.20	− 11.56	10.70
γ_s	1.38	0.94	9.73	1.19	0.65	8.81	1.29	0.95	8.76

$S = 10, 50, 100$. We only estimate the key parameters from the perspective of our theory σ, ρ, γ_u, γ_s and we set to the remaining four parameters to the values used in the DGP. The appendix to this chapter contains a detailed description of all the Monte Carlo experiments we have performed.

Comparing results from tables 14.3 and 14.4 which summarize the empirical distribution of the percentage bias in figure 14.2, it emerges that all coefficients except γ_u show very little mean and median bias. It is interesting to note how the smoothed empirical distribution in the quadrature case and in the SMLE (especially with $S = 100$) show a strikingly similar shape for all four parameters. In general, the quadrature method dominates the stochastic simulation in terms of mean bias. It is quite remarkable however, that computing the stochastic integration with only ten draws delivers such a small estimation bias. Note that there is little improvement in going from $S = 10$ to $S = 100$ in terms of mean bias, while a non-negligeable reduction in the standard deviation (S.D.) of the bias is obtained. Even in terms of standard deviation, the quadrature method is superior. For S above 100 only very marginal improvement was noticed in the stochastic

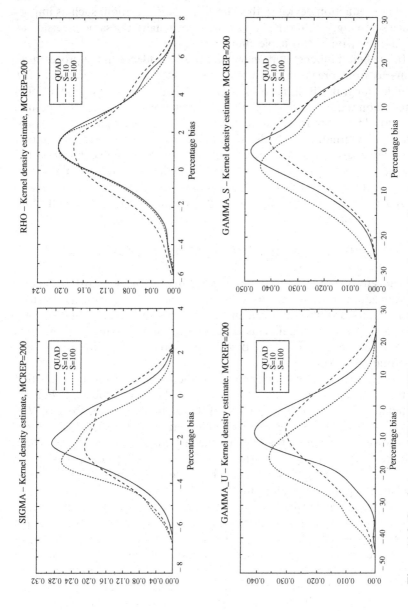

Figure 14.2 Quadrature and SMLE − (TS) case: empirical distribution of percentage bias

integration-based maximum likelihood estimator, at the expense of a large increase in computational time. It appears that only by associating some variance reduction device to the Monte Carlo integration, such as importance sampling,[11] could the latter procedure achieve the same precision as quadrature with a reasonable number of draws.

In the first difference stationary case the dependence in the process prevents us from breaking down the $(T \times 2)$ integral into a sequence of T double integrals. It is clear that performing such a multidimensional integration requires a huge number of simulations (or quadrature points) that would tremendously slow down the underlying optimization algorithm, so alternative methods are required. An alternative technique that provides an exact solution and in principle is implementable in this particular case is the Gibbs sampler associated with the simulated EM algorithm. In the EM method (see Ruud (1991) for a survey) the function to be maximized with respect to θ^{j+1}, for a given θ^j computed at the jth step of the hill-climbing algorithm is

$$Q(\theta^{j+1}; \theta^j) = \int \log \psi(Z^T | H^T, X^T; \theta^{j+1}) \psi_\omega(H^T | Z^T; \theta^j) dH^T.$$

The advantage of this method compared to a standard likelihood maximization is that the objective function, when maximized, strictly increases toward the maximum and can be very fast in reaching the neighborhood of the optimum. This is because the state is integrated out with respect to a more informative density (compared to the SMLE) which is conditional also on Z^T.

In the simulated version of the EM, the integral of the $Q(\cdot)$ function cannot be computed analytically and it is therefore simulated. For the simulation one needs to draw paths of the latent state vector from $\Psi_\omega(H^T | Z^T; \theta^j)$. These draws are more complicated as this density is *a priori* unknown and therefore they require the implementation of Markov chain Monte Carlo techniques. Carlin, Polson, and Stoffer (1992) describe a method which is suitable for our case based on a single move Gibbs sampler and an acceptance–rejection step.

This approach which couples the Gibbs sampler and the simulated EM, however, has three major drawbacks. First, the process for h_t in first differences does not have stationary distribution, hence the Gibbs sampler would never achieve convergence. Even if one is willing to transform this specification into a very persistent stationary process in levels, the algorithm will be extremely slow to reach convergence as the Carlin, Polson, and Stoffer method is based on a single-move sampler. Second, the accep-

---

[11] See Geweke (1989) and Danielsson and Richard (1993).

tance–rejection step embedded in the Carlin, Polson, and Stoffer procedure further slows down the algorithm, especially when the parameter values are far from the true ones. Finally, it is well known that the EM algorithm is very inefficient once in the neighborhood of the maximum and to our knowledge there is no proof of convergence for its simulated counterpart.[12] Our initial experience with this method proved to be extremely slow and inefficient.

4.2 *Auxiliary model and indirect inference*

The second method we used is a two-step procedure. In the first step an auxiliary model which provides an approximation to the more complex structural model is estimated. This allows one to sidestep the problem of multidimensional integration. In the second step, one can recover consistent estimates of the parameters by a standard application of indirect inference methods. The auxiliary model we chose to work with is the extended Kalman filter (EKF) (see Anderson and Moore (1979)). A first-order Taylor series approximation of the true model is made around the predicted value of the latent factors at each point in time and the standard Kalman recursion is run on the linearized model.

First, define $h_{t|t-1}$ as the one-step ahead linear predictor of the (log of the) latent state vector, changing according to the specification (trend or first differences) that we choose. Denote also $Z_{t|t-1} = \frac{\partial f(X_t, h_t; \theta)}{\partial h'_t}\big|_{ht=ht|t-1}$ and $f_{t|t-1} = f(X_t, h_{t|t-1}; \theta)$. It follows that $Z_t = f_{t|t-1} + Z_{t|t-1}(h_t - h_{t|t-1}) + \tilde{\varepsilon}_t$. The main source of approximation is that the error term $\tilde{\varepsilon}_t$ no longer necessarily has zero mean, in general is correlated with h_t, and is not normal, while in the EKF it will be treated as a Gaussian white noise.[13] The linearization above justifies the EKF recursion which runs as follows:

$$P_{t|t-1} = P_{t-1|t-1} + \Omega,$$

$$k_t = P_{t|t-1}Z'_{t|t-1}(Z_{t|t-1}P_{t|t-1}Z'_{t|t-1} + \Sigma)^{-1},$$

$$P_{t|t} = P_{t|t-1} - k_t(Z_{t|t-1}P_{t|t-1}Z'_{t|t-1} + \Sigma)k'_t,$$

$$h_{t|t} = h_{t|t-1} + k_t(Z_t + f_{t|t-1})$$

where Σ is the covariance matrix of the errors to the measurement equations (non-zero only in the equal rates of return condition) and $P_{t|t-1}$ (respectively $P_{t|t}$) is the mean square error associated with the predicted (updated) linear projection of h_t.

---

[12] Chan and Ledolter (1995) show that it is only possible to prove that after a certain number of iterations the SEM with high probability will get close to the maximizer of the likelihood of the observed data. Experience with the SEM seems to suggest that at some point the algorithm starts fluctuating randomly around a constant value but does not converge.

[13] No approximation is needed on the state equations, since they are linear.

Table 14.5. *Extended Kalman filter (percentage bias)*

| | Trend stationary case | | | | | | I(1) case | | |
| | Low variance | | | High variance | | | Low variance | | |
	Mean	Median	S.D.	Mean	Median	S.D.	Mean	Median	S.D.
σ	0.10	0.12	1.08	0.34	0.20	2.52	-0.19	-0.30	0.89
ρ	-0.26	-0.50	1.94	-0.59	-0.60	3.65	-0.06	0.31	4.74
γ_u	-0.07	-0.35	7.42	1.80	1.47	18.61	28.13	-1.29	114.31
γ_s	-0.65	-1.01	8.44	1.31	2.30	17.30	-3.59	14.33	135.36

In terms of initialization of the filter, $h_{1|0}$ was started through a randomization, i.e., by drawing from $N(h_0, P_{0|0})$, where $P_{0|0}$, was set to $\eta_\infty^2 I_2$. The innovation form of the likelihood function for the time t observation was constructed as

$$\ell(Z_t; X_t, \theta) = -\frac{1}{2}\ln|\Lambda_{t|t-1}| - \frac{1}{2}(Z_t - f_{t|t-1})'\Lambda_{t|t-1}^{-1}(Z_t - f_{t|t-1})$$

where $\Lambda_{t|t-1} = Z_{t|t-1} P_{t|t-1} Z_{t|t-1} + \Sigma$ and it was maximized over θ.

We expect that this approximation will generate biased estimates, as the auxiliary linearized model is misspecified except for a neighborhood of the conditional mean of the states. The bias we will obtain is in principle a combination of the small sample bias and the misspecification bias, but the two components cannot be distinguished. In general, for a given sample size, the error is higher the larger is the difference between the first and second moments of the structural model and their respective approximations $f_{t|t-1}$ and $\Lambda_{t|t-1}$.

To evaluate the magnitude of this bias, we performed a Monte Carlo experiment on both specifications. Table 14.5 collects the main results about the mean, median percentage bias and its empirical standard deviation and figures 14.3 and 14.4 depict the smoothed empirical distributions of the percentage bias of the parameter estimates. Here we distinguished two cases: the first with low standard deviation and the second with high standard deviation (larger by a factor of 2.5) in the unobservable states.

Unexpectedly, in the trend stationary specification for all the parameter estimates the mean bias is always below 2 percent. The empirical distribution of the bias is somewhat less concentrated for the growth rate parameters, indicating the danger of a potential high bias. The mean bias is larger for the specification with high variance, but still extremely small (both estimates of σ and ρ exhibit less than 0.6 percent bias on average), although the standard deviation doubles as is evident from figure 14.3. This result is very

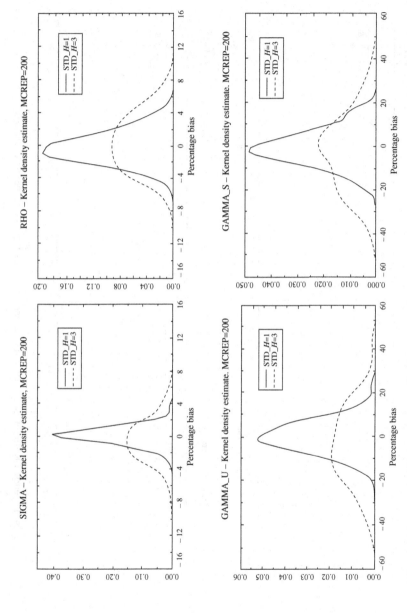

Figure 14.3 Extended Kalman filter – (TS) case: empirical distribution of percentage bias

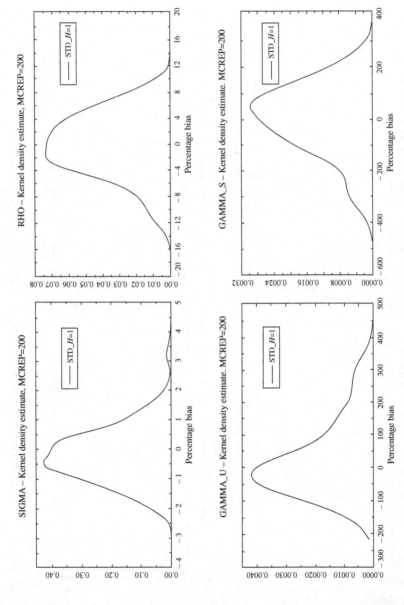

Figure 14.4 Extended Kalman filter – (FDS) case: empirical distribution of percentage bias

surprising given that the model is quite non-linear and the EKF it is just a linear approximation around the predicted value of the state. The reason for this result might reflect the fact that in the presence of the deterministic trend which allows forecasting the state very accurately, so the EKF is indeed a good approximation.

In the I(1) case there is a marked difference between the mean bias of the substitution parameters, in line with that of the trend stationary model, and the bias of the drift parameters which is more than 30 times higher on average. The direction of the median bias for all four parameters is the same as in the trend stationary case. For the drift terms, a huge standard error of the bias was recorded which indicates that estimates with very large distortions are probable. Also, as is clear from figure 14.4, the empirical densities, especially for the drift parameters, show large skewness.

Although the bias we found in the trend stationary specification and for the σ and ρ parameters in the $I(1)$ model is extremely small, the EKF is, in principle, inconsistent. As a result, it seems appropriate to implement an indirect inference correction. Denote by $\hat{\theta}_T$ the EKF inconsistent estimator lying in the parameter space Θ and denote the "true" parameter vector β_0 lying in B. We can define a bias function $b: B \to \Theta$ which maps "true values" β_0 into biased estimates $\hat{\theta}_T$. This function is obtained by simulating the endogenous variables $\{Z^{Ti}(\beta)\}_{i=1}^{M}$ from the model for any given parameterization β in B and re-estimating a vector $\hat{\theta}_{MT}(\beta)$, where M is the number of simulations used for the estimation. The premise of the indirect inference correction is exactly to use these simulations in order to correct the initial EKF estimate $\hat{\theta}_T$. The indirect inference estimator of β_0 is simply:

$$\hat{\beta}_{MT}(\Lambda) = \arg\min_{\beta \in B} (\hat{\theta}_{MT}(\beta) - \hat{\theta}_T)' \Lambda (\hat{\theta}_{MT}(\beta) - \hat{\theta}_T)$$

where Λ is a symmetric negative-definite matrix, defining a metric. The indirect inference algorithm therefore searches for that value of β which minimizes the distance, taken in the Λ-metric, between the estimate of the auxiliary model when data are generated under that β-parametrization of the model and the original estimate $\hat{\theta}_T$. Gourieroux, Monfort, and Renault (1993) and Gourieroux and Monfort (1994) develop the asymptotic theory of the indirect inference estimator and derive the form for the optimal weighting matrix Λ. Gourieroux, Renault, and Touzi (1995) investigate its small sample properties through Edgeworh expansions. Since the asymptotic theory and the small sample characterization exist only for stationary cases, we believe it is useful to perform some Monte Carlo experiments to assess the properties of the indirect inference correction in the type of non-stationary environment we consider.

Figure 14.5 shows the results of a series of 50 Monte Carlo trials where the model in the trend stationary specification was first estimated by EKF

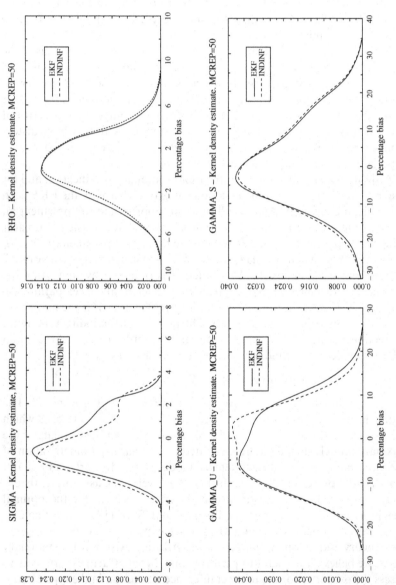

Figure 14.5 Extended Kalman filter and Ind. Inf. – (TS) case

Table 14.6. *EKF and indirect inference (percentage bias): I(1) case*

	Mean		Median		S.D.	
	EKF	INDINF	EKF	INDINF	EKF	INDINF
σ	-6.84	-6.04	-6.58	-6.02	1.49	2.08
ρ	-3.19	-3.73	-4.75	-4.92	6.35	5.94
γ_u	-19.70	-0.16	-12.25	1.25	41.29	21.57
γ_s	-1.37	-10.51	-2.66	-9.66	11.22	12.59

and then by indirect inference with EKF as auxiliary model. The indirect inference estimator was based on $M = 15$ and $S = 50$. The weighting matrix was set to the identity matrix, but as the numbers of parameters to be estimated are the same in the auxiliary and structural model, this is the optimal choice. Perhaps not surprisingly, since the bias of the EKF is so small, the indirect inference correction is often indistinguishable from its first-step counterpart and for some cases it even tends to worsen the initial estimate but this may be due to the low number of trials that were performed.

In the first difference stationary case (table 14.6), although the mean bias of the EKF is larger than in the trend stationary case, the indirect inference is not always effective. Only for the drift term of unskilled labor it provides a non-negligible adjustment of the estimate towards the true value. These results are based on 50 Monte Carlo trials, but we think that even once the simulation uncertainty is substantially reduced, the pattern of our findings will not change dramatically.

4.3 Simulated pseudo-MLE

An alternative method of bypassing the multidimensional integration problem is the use of simulation techniques jointly with a pseudo-maximum likelihood estimation (PMLE). The theory of PMLE was developed by White (1982) and Gourieroux, Monfort, and Trognon (1984). The extension to the simulated case is due to Laroque and Salanié (1989, 1993, 1994). The main premise of the PMLE method is that one can approximate the unknown and untractable distribution on which the "observable" likelihood is based with a simpler, but possibly misspecified, objective function constructed only from some empirical moments of the dependent variables. When these moments cannot be obtained analytically, under fairly general conditions they can be simulated. The simulated version of the PMLE or simulated PMLE (SPMLE) reduces the computational burden from one $(T \times 2)$-dimensional integral to T different two-dimensional integrals, since the moments of the dependent variables are simulated at each period t to construct the likelihood. In particular, given our distributional assumptions on the error terms, we generate S realizations of the dependent variables each indexed by i, by following these two steps

$$\text{step 1: } \begin{cases} h_t^i = h_0 + \gamma t + \omega_t^i \\ \text{or} \\ h_t^i = \gamma + h_{t-1}^i + \omega_t^i \end{cases}$$

$$\text{step2: } Z_t^i = f(X_t, H_t^i, \varepsilon_t^i; \phi).$$

In step 1 a realization of ω_t is drawn from its distribution and used to construct a time t value for h_t. In step 2 this realization of h_t, together with a draw of ε_t allows to generate a realization of Z_t. As mentioned for the SMLE method, the set of $(T \times S)$ draws must be kept fixed during the optimization of the objective function. We chose to work with the SPMLE based on the first and second simulated moments of the unknown distribution, respectively

$$m_S(X_t; \theta) = \frac{1}{S} \sum_{i=1}^{S} f(X_t, H_t^i(\varphi), \varepsilon_t^i; \phi),$$

$$V_S(X_t; \theta) = \frac{1}{S-1} \sum_{i=1}^{S} (Z_t^i - f(X_t^i, H_t^i(\varphi), \varepsilon_t^i; \phi))(Z_t^i - f(X_t^i, h_t^i(\varphi), \varepsilon_t^i; \phi))'.$$

The simulated pseudo-likelihood as a function of $\theta \equiv \{\phi, \varphi\}$ becomes

$$\ell_S(Z^T; X^T, \theta) = \frac{1}{2T} \sum_{t=1}^{T} \{[Z_t - m_S(X_t; \theta)]' V_S(X_t; \theta)^{-1}[Z_t - m_S(X_t; \theta)]$$

$$+ \log \det(V_S(X_t; \theta))\} \tag{7}$$

and the SPMLE estimator $\hat{\theta}_{ST}$ is defined as the maximizer of the function in (7).

The SPMLE has in principle three sources of approximation to the correctly specified model. The first one comes from the potential misspecification in the objective function. Instead of the untractable exact likelihood, we use a simpler loss function. The second source of approximation originates from the fact that the true moments are replaced by the simulated ones, inducing an error due to the finiteness of the number of simulations S. In addition to finite number of simulations bias and misspecification bias, there is a third source of potential bias, which is finite sample bias.

Laroqur and Salanié (1994) proved that in a stationary environment, as $S \to \infty$, $T \to \infty$ and $\frac{\sqrt{T}}{S} \to o$, the SPLME has the same asympotic properties of the PMLE, hence the SPMLE estimator converges to the pseudo-true value and it is asymptotically normal. Gourieroux, Monfort, and Trognon (1984) proved that if the pseudo-distribution belongs to the quadratic exponential family, as in our specification, then there is no misspecification bias and the PMLE is consistent and asymptotically normal. This gain in the robustness of the estimator comes at the cost of a loss in efficiency compared to the MLE. As far as the simulation bias is concerned, Laroque and Salanié (1994) prove that this bias has the order of $\frac{1}{S}$ and according to their Monte Carlo experiments, for $S = 20$ the bias is already quite small.

The theory underlying the use of SPMLE is asymptotic and for stationary environments, but in our analysis, the regressors and the unobservable variables have trends and the sample size is small. Therefore, to evaluate the performance of SPMLE in our setting, we conducted a Monte Carlo analysis. In the first specification the latent variables were trend stationary. In the second specification they were random walks with drift.

The results of the Monte Carlo experiment are presented in figures 14.6–14.7 and tables 14.7–14.8. These figures show the empirical distributions of the percentage bias of the key coefficients for $S = 10$, $S = 20$, and $S = 50$ where S is the number of simulations used to generate the empirical moments in the simulated pseudo-likelihood in (7).

For the trend stationary case, figure 14.6 and table 14.7 show that in general there is very little mean and median bias in the estimation even for $S = 10$, which is a very encouraging result. For $S = 50$ the mean bias is essentially zero. The bias of the substitution parameters σ and ρ is never larger than 6 percent and averages respectively 0.06 percent and -0.16 percent. Although still roughly symmetric in a neighborhood of zero, the distribution of the bias in the estimators of the trend growth rate coefficients for the labor efficiency factors is more spread with substantial mass for values in the bias distribution between 10 percent and 20 percent.

The performance of SPMLE is more disappointing when the latent states are integrated, however. This evidence is summarized in table 14.8. Although the mean bias for the substitution parameters is still very small, it increases enormously on the estimates of the drift terms. Another surprising feature of these estimates is that as S increases, the mean bias does not seem to be reduced, rather it seems to be larger. The same surprising pattern emerges for the standard deviation of the drift parameters. As shown in figure 14.7, the empirical distribution of the estimators is remarkably skewed which involves the danger of a severe bias in the estimates. Recall that the same type of skewness (although less pronounced) was found in the EKF estimator, hence skewness seems to be a feature of the small distribution of the estimators in the first difference stationary case.

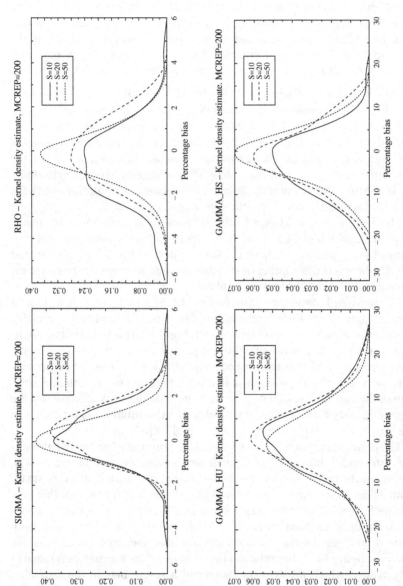

Figure 14.6 Simulated pseudo MLE – (TS) case: empirical distribution of percentage bias

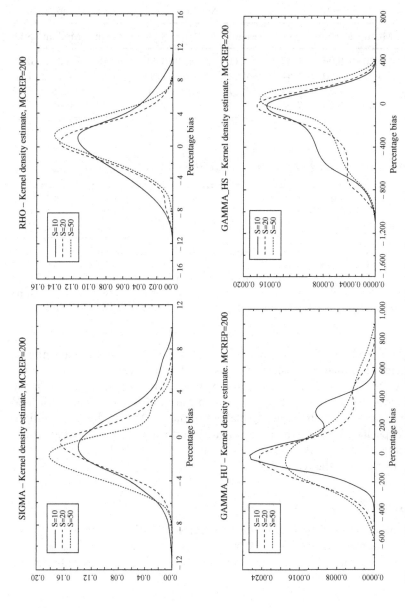

Figure 14.7 Simulated pseudo MLE – (FDS) case: empirical distribution of percentage bias

Table 14.7. *SPMLE: trend stationary case (percentage bias)*

	S = 10			S = 20			S = 50		
	Mean	Median	S.D.	Mean	Median	S.D.	Mean	Median	S.D.
σ	0.20	0.09	1.05	0.11	0.09	0.93	0.06	0.03	0.92
ρ	−0.33	−0.20	1.54	−0.22	−0.34	1.26	−0.16	−0.17	1.10
γ_u	0.85	1.21	7.45	0.27	0.09	6.61	−0.16	−0.38	7.19
γ_s	−1.09	−0.70	7.64	−1.01	−1.10	7.18	−0.73	−0.65	5.75

Table 14.8. *SPMLE: first difference stationary case (percentage bias)*

	S = 10			S = 20			S = 50		
	Mean	Median	S.D.	Mean	Median	S.D.	Mean	Median	S.D.
σ	−0.41	−0.65	2.90	−0.61	−0.705	2.48	0.89	−1.01	2.23
ρ	0.17	0.54	3.58	0.52	0.786	3.17	0.77	1.14	2.79
γ_u	77.60	27.87	168.04	102.72	68.350	199.54	190.49	153.58	223.22
γ_s	−214.35	−144.87	251.40	−224.02	−125.050	285.85	−295.48	188.47	291.02

One could in principle improve on the SPMLE by running an indirect inference estimation with SPMLE as a first step. This procedure, given the consistency of the first-step estimator would provide a correction for the potential small-sample bias, as pointed out in Gourieroux, Renault, and Touzi (1995). Given the negligible bias of the SPMLE in the trend stationary specification, and the unsatisfactory performance of indirect inference in the random walk case obtained for the EKF, we do not pursue this correction in either case.

4.4   A comparison of the methods

In order to make a meaningful comparison of the performance of the different methods we outlined in this section, it is necessary to assess also their computational efficiency. We have standardized the speed by setting to 1 the time needed for the fastest method, the SMLE with $S = 10$, which takes about 7 seconds for one complete estimation.

The numbers above suggest that for the simulation-based estimators evaluated in our paper, time increases approximately linearly with the

Table 14.9 *Numerical efficiecy: trend stationary case*

QUAD	SMLE		EKF	IND.INF.	SPMLE	
$N = 256$	$S = 10$	$S = 100$		$S = 50$, $M = 15$	$S = 10$	$S = 50$
22	1	9.5	1.5	290	7	38

number of simulations. As our results did not suggest the existence of huge deficiencies when S is low compared to a high S, an efficient strategy in estimation seems to be starting to explore the parameter space with a small S, and only when sufficiently good initial conditions are found increase S so as to reduce the simulation uncertainty.

Note also that the EKF method is obviously very fast, as for every iteration of the hill-climbing algorithm it has just to compute the derivative of the measurement equations at the value of the conditional mean for the state and then run the Kalman filter recursion to construct the likelihood. Unfortunately, since it is inconsistent it should always be coupled with indirect inference, which is on the contrary extremely slow. This reduces substantially the speed advantage of EKF.

Taking into account both bias and computational efficiency, our Monte Carlo analysis suggests the following observations:

1   In the (FDS) specification, the EKF performs better than SPMLE, since for the latter we found a huge bias in the drift term of the labor efficiency factors and higher variability of estimates. Moreover the SPMLE surprisingly shows higher bias when S is larger.

2   The performance of the estimators in terms of mean and median bias seems largely superior in the (TS) case compared to the (FDS) model. This is particularly true for the growth rate parameters, where the high mean biases we recorded potentially put a heavy burden on working with this specification. For all parameters, the different methods – when analyzed with the (FDS) specification – generate estimates with much higher variability.

3   All methods in the (TS) specification show very little mean and median bias. The standard deviation of the percentage bias is in general larger for the growth rate parameters γ_u and γ_s.

4   The quadrature-based MLE is superior to the simulated MLE when no variance reduction technique is associated with the latter.

5   In the (TS) case both EKF and SPMLE show less bias and less variability in the estimates than the numerical and stochastic integration methods. This holds true particularly for estimates of γ_u. Moreover, the

integration procedure depends crucially on the specification of additive error terms to the measurement equations which, as we argued already, are of difficult interpretation.

6   Indirect inference does not make any improvement upon the inconsistent first-step EKF estimator in the (TS) case, most likely because of the very small bias of the EKF, but even in the (FDS) case, where the bias of the first-step estimator is larger, indirect inference is not effective.

7   In the (TS) case, SPMLE is comparable to EKF, in that the small sample bias is practically absent, but it is superior as it has two advantages over the EKF. First, by increasing S the mean bias and its variance (the latter already smaller than in the EKF) of the SPMLE can be further reduced. Second, although SPMLE is slower for S large enough to give reliable results, it is a consistent estimator and does not need any correction by indirect inference which, in our experience, dramatically slows down the whole estimation.

Based on these findings, we conjecture that the negligible small sample bias in the trend stationary case may reflect an analog to "super-consistency" of the estimators of coefficients associated with regressors which have a deterministic trend. When we simulate the labor efficiency vector to generate the moments needed in the pseudo-likelihood function and perform the estimation, we introduce a deterministic trend non-linearly in the measurement equation. As all the parameters of interest interact in some way with the latent states, the speed of convergence of the estimates may benefit from the trend.

Second, it is possible that when latent states are modeled as integrated processes, the population objective function based on simulated estimators (such as SPMLE and indirect inference) becomes a random function, generating inconsistent estimates.[14] This would explain the very large variance that we found for some of the parameter estimates and the surprising finding that the bias does not decline and sometimes increases with higher number of simulations. The higher reliability of the EKF estimator in the random walk specification is probably due to the fact that its objective function is based on the conditional first and second moments of the state which, even in the I(1) specification, exist and that they are finite. On the other hand, the simulated pseudo-likelihood function is based on moments of the endogenous variables constructed from simulated paths of the latent vector, hence they are affected by the unconditional moments of the latter, which are not finite.

To conclude, from the evidence we have accumulated the specification with trend-stationary labor efficiency seems much more reliable and, for

---

[14] This point was also made in an example by Laroque and Salanié (1993).

this specification, estimation by SPMLE is accurate and relatively fast. In section 5 we will present the results of the SPMLE method of our model for the trend stationary case.

5   Results of the estimation

Based on our analysis described earlier, we have estimated by SPMLE the model described by the (TS) state equations and the measurement equations in (1), (2), and (3). Recall that there are eight parameters to estimate: σ defines the elasticity of substitution between unskilled labor and equipment $\frac{1}{1-\sigma}$, ρ defines that of skilled labor with equipment $\frac{1}{1-\rho}$, γ_u and γ_s are the growth rates of labor efficiency, λ and μ are the weights in the CES nestings of the production function, h_{0u} is the initial value for unskilled labor efficiency, and η_ω^2 is the variance of both efficiency factors. In what follows we will discuss only the estimates of the two elasticity parameters, the two growth rates of labor efficiency and their variance, which are all the parameters of economic interest. The model has been estimated from 1963 to 1990, using the time series on labor input, wages, capital, and relative prices described in the section on data construction.

An important choice in the analysis is the number of simulations, S. The estimation algorithm was run with $S = 500$. We chose this number, since at this point changes in the estimated parameter vector due to simulation uncertainty were negligible.

The main difficulty encountered in the estimation procedure was to pin down the variance of the latent state. In fact, when η_ω was estimated together with the other parameters, the algorithm would always tend to increase quickly the estimated variance generating an implausibly high variability in the implied simulated path of labor efficiency. Moreover, owing to this high variance in the latent states, the growth rate coefficients were extremely difficult to estimate precisely. Therefore, we conducted the estimation in two steps. We fixed a very fine grid of values over a realistic[15] range for η_ω and for each of these points; we estimated the rest of the parameter vector. The maximum of the pseudo-likelihood function across these grid points delivered the final estimates.

When dealing with such a large parameter space and with simulation-based estimation techniques there is uncertainty on whether the maximum found is local or global. To assess the global nature of the optimum, we used Veall's (1990) test based on the asymptotic confidence interval for the

---

[15] We simulated the model with different values of the variance of the efficiency factors and set a range for which the model generated data showed approximately the same variance as in our sample.

first-order statistics computed by De Haan (1981). Call ℓ the value of the objective function at the optimum, ℓ^1 and ℓ^2 the highest two values of a vector of M random evaluations of the likelihood in the parameter space. We reject the null hypothesis that the optimum is not a global maximum at $(1-p)$ level of confidence if $\ell^p > \ell$, where $\ell^p = \ell^1 + (\ell^1 - \ell^2) / \left(p^{\frac{-2}{k}} - 1\right)$ and k is the dimension of the parameter space. We performed $M = 60{,}000$ random evaluations of the likelihood in our 8-dimensional parameter space.[16] We found that we could reject the null hypothesis only at a level of $p = 0.185$. Therefore at conventional confidence levels, the hypothesis is not rejected.

In addition we used the information collected through these random evaluations in a subsequent analysis by identifying points far from our estimate where the likelihood was relatively high and re-started the maximization routine at those new initial guesses, but only lower local maxima were found. Moreover these alternative extrema predict almost perfect substitution between either of the two labor inputs and equipment, which is difficult to accept from the viewpoint of economic theory. This further evidence confirms the global nature of our estimate.

Table 14.10 shows the SPMLE estimates and standard deviations and also reports the indirect inference correction for small-sample bias for the parameters which are economically most interesting ($\sigma, \rho, \gamma_u, \gamma_s$). Standard deviations of the SPMLE estimator were computed on the basis of the asymptotic covariance matrix $\frac{1}{T}\left(J_0^{-1}I_0 J_0^{-1}\right)$ where

$$I_0 = E_0\left\{\frac{\partial\ell(Z_t;X_t,\theta_0)}{\partial\theta}\frac{\partial\ell(Z_t;X_t,\theta_0)}{\partial\theta'}\right\}$$

$$J_0 = E_0\left\{-\frac{\partial^2\ell(Z_t;X_t,\theta_0)}{\partial\theta\partial\theta'}\right\}.$$

E_0 denotes the expectation with respect to Z_t and X_t taken under θ_0. The sample counterparts of I_0 and J_0 are

$$\hat{I}_{ST} = \frac{1}{T}\sum_{t=1}^{T}\left\{\frac{\partial\ell(Z_t;X_t,\hat\theta_{ST})}{\partial\theta}\frac{\partial\ell(Z_t;X_t,\hat\theta_{ST})}{\partial\theta'}\right\} \text{ and}$$

$$\hat{J}_{ST} = \frac{1}{T}\sum_{t=1}^{T}\left\{-\frac{\partial^2\ell(Z_t;X_t,\hat\theta_{ST})}{\partial\theta\partial\theta'}\right\}. \tag{8}$$

In the last row of table 14.10 the implied net average rate of return on capital r in the economy is reported. This latter number was computed as the sample mean of the average, for each year, between the model predic-

---

[16] It is not clear what should be the optimal ratio M/k. Veall finds that in some cases with three parameters, ten random draws would deliver satisfactory results in terms of test power, but other examples with only one parameter needed at least 200 draws.

Table 14.10. *Estimation results*

Parameter	SPML	Ind. Inf.
σ	0.486	0.487
	(0.048)	—
ρ	-1.172	-1.179
	(0.110)	—
γ_u	-0.041	-0.040
	(0.016)	—
γ_s	0.033	0.032
	(0.003)	—
η_ω	0.086	—
	(0.013)	—
r	0.072	—

tion of rates of return on structures and on equipment, weighted by their respective share of total capital in efficiency units. We found r to be about 7.2 percent, which is very close to the 6.9 percent calibrated in Cooley (1995).

It is striking that the indirect inference estimates[17] are extremely close to the initial SPLE estimates, which provided evidence for our conjecture based on the Monte Carlo experiments in section 4.3. These results are consistent with our theory, in that they indicate much stronger complementarity between skilled labor and equipment than between unskilled labor and equipment. The elasticity of substitution in the latter two inputs is more than four times higher. These estimates are also broadly in line with the existing literature that is surveyed in Hamermesh (1993).

The growth rate of unskilled labor efficiency is estimated to be negative but its statistical significance is low, while the efficiency of skilled labor grew at an average rate of 3.2 percent, according to the estimates. We need to note that as the unobservable states and some of the exogenous variables have trends, the convergence rate of the SPMLE estimator might be higher than $\sqrt{T}$ at least for some of the parameters. The evidence from the Monte Carlo experiment points in this direction, as the empirical standard deviations were found to be smaller than the asymptotic standard deviations reported in table 14.10.

In any case a negative value for γ_u should not be surprising. Recall that in our classification, unskilled individuals are those who did not receive a high-school diploma. In the last 25 years the average level of education has

---

[17] In the indirect inference estimation we set $S = 200$ and $M = 10$. The matrix Λ is simply the identity matrix.

increased dramatically and therefore it is not unreasonable to presume that, as a matter of composition, the average quality of workers without a high-school degree has worsened over time.

Figure 14.8 reports the fit of the three equations used in the estimation and the implied wage premium versus the data. The rate of return differentials are quite small for the whole sample, although their variability tends to increase slightly toward the end of the sample. The labor share in the model has the same long-term movements as those in the data, decreasing in the 1970s and increasing after 1984. The model does not capture the increase in the first five years of the sample, but looking at the scale, the discrepancy between model and data is very small. Perhaps the most striking result is that the predicted wage premium (which is not estimated as a dependent variable, but generated from the estimated parameter values) matches the data extremely well, tracking very closely all three swings in the data: the increase of the 1960s, the decline in the 1970s and the sharp acceleration in the 1980s.

6   Summary and conclusions

In this chapter, we explored in detail a number of issues associated with the estimation of a latent variable, non-linear aggregate production function, and used the estimated parameters to evaluate the extent to which different substitution possibilities between skilled labor and capital, and unskilled labor and capital, in conjunction with recent declines in the relative price of equipment, could account for variations in the wage gap between skilled and unskilled workers over the last 30 years. Our model involved a number of complications from the perspective of identification and estimation, in particular, a small sample, trending regressors, and non-stationary latent variables that entered the function non-linearly. We examined three types of estimation procedures for this problem: (i) numerical and stochastic integration, (ii) the extended Kalman Filter with indirect inference correction, and (iii) simulated pseudo-maximum likelihood.

Our Monte Carlo evidence clearly shows that the simulation-based estimation procedures that we have compared perform much better when latent variables are trend stationary rather than integrated. Under the first difference stationary specification, SPMLE was found to have very large bias for the drift parameters and the bias did not tend to fall with the number of simulations. Indirect inference, even when in the I(1) case the first step estimator showed substantial bias, did not prove useful in adjusting the estimates toward their true value. The extended Kalman filter on the contrary showed good properties even when the unobservable variables were modeled as first difference stationary processes. In the trend

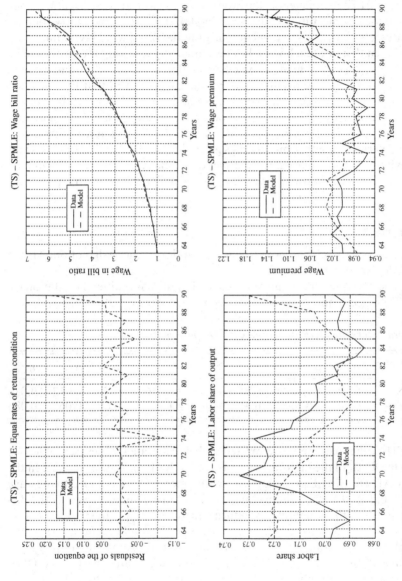

Figure 14.8 Data and predictions from the estimated model

stationary specification, all methods showed very little bias, but the SPMLE based on the first two moments was judged to be superior to numerical and stochastic integration and to the EKF. Finally, the estimated (by SPMLE) parameters of the production function are consistent with our theoretical conjecture on the role of capital–skill complementarity coupled with the extensive growth in equipment in the rising wage premium.

Given that not much work has been done in evaluating the performance of these types of simulation-based estimation procedures in non-standard environments, these results are of particular interest in that they indicate that these methods can be useful in estimating models for certain types of non-stationarity and in small samples but also they point at the potential dangers in using the same methods with other types on non-stationarities. To determine whether our findings generalize to other types of models and environments, additional work along these lines will prove fruitful in providing researchers with new tools to attack difficult econometric problems.

Appendix

This appendix provides a complete description of the design of our Monte Carlo experiments.

The DGP for the trend stationary (TS) and first difference stationary (FDS) specifications are summarized in the following table:

Parameters for DGP in Monte Carlo experiments

Model	σ	ρ	γ_u	γ_s	h_{0u}	h_{0s}	μ	λ	η_ω
TS	0.50	-1.15	-0.04	-0.03	2.1	6.0	0.77	0.012	0.086
FDS	0.50	-0.40	-0.04	-0.03	2.1	6.0	0.60	0.060	0.086

The other parameters were fixed at their calibrated values (see table 14.2 in the text). In the high variance case of the EKF, η_ω was set to 0.22. In the QUAD and SMLE procedures, a measurement error was added to the wage bill and to the labor share equation with same standard error as the disturbance in the equal rates of return equation, i.e., $\eta_\varepsilon = 0.03$.

For every Monte Carlo trial, $T = 30$ observations of the endogenous variables were generated. Only four parameters were estimated – σ, ρ, γ_u, γ_s – while all the other parameters were fixed at their value used in the DGP. The number of replications for each experiment was set to 200 except for the experiments involving indirect inference which were based on 50 trials in the (TS) case and on 25 in the (FDS) case. The 200 sample paths of data generated from the (TS) or the (FDS) model are the same across all estimation methods, to minimize simulation uncertainty.

The starting values for the estimates of the parameter vector were drawn randomly at each Monte Carlo trial in the admissible region of the parameter space. From the point of view of economic theory, both σ and ρ are constrained to be less than 1, but γ_u and γ_s are in principle unconstrained, although very high positive or negative values are economically implausible. Moreover, high negative values for these growth rates can generate a negative labor share or wage bill ratio, which are clearly meaningless. For this reason, we constrained the absolute value of the growth rates of labor efficiency to be less than 25 percent per year in the initial draws.

Call θ_0 the parameter set of the DGP and $\hat{\theta}$ the estimates with any of the methods above, then the percentage bias is computed as: $\frac{\hat{\theta} - \theta_0}{|\theta_0|} \times 100$.

For the kernel estimates of the empirical distributions of the percentage bias in parameter estimates, we used a Gaussian kernel with smoothing parameter fixed according to Silverman's "rule of thumb" (see Silverman (1986, p. 45)).

The codes for QUAD MLE, SMLE, EKF, and SPMLE were written in GAUSS 3.1 with extensive use of the OPTMUM library and were run on a Dell XPS P100, 16Mb RAM. The convergence criteria was always set to 10e-4. The code for indirect inference was written in FORTRAN (and made use of the IMSL libraries) optimally compiled with IBM AIX XL FORTRAN Compiler/6000 and run on a IBM SPARC 10.

References

Anderson, B.D.O. and J.B. Moore (1979), *Optimal Filtering*, Englewood-Cliffs, NJ: Prentice-Hall.

Berndt, E., Z. Griliches, and N. Rappaport (1995), "Econometric Estimates of Price Indexes for Personal Computers in the 1990s," *Journal of Econometrics*, 68, 243–268.

Bound J. and G. Johnson (1992), "Change in the Structure of Wages in the 80s; An Evaluation of Alternative Explanations," *American Economic Review*, 78(2), 124–128.

Brown, K. and S. Greenstein (1995), "How Much Better is Bigger, Faster and Cheaper? Buyer Benefits from Innovation in Mainframe Computers in the 1980s," NBER Working Paper No. 5138, May 1995.

Carlin, B., N. Polson, and D. Stoffer (1992), "A Monte-Carlo Approach to Non-normal and Nonlinear State-Space Modeling," *Journal of the American Statistical Association*, 87, 493–500.

Chan, K.S. and J. Ledolter (1995), "Monte Carlo Estimates for Time Series Involving Counts," *Journal of the American Statistical Association*, 90, 242–251.

Cole, R., Y. Chen, J. Barquin-Stolleman, E. Dulberger, N. Helvacian, and J. Hodge (1986), "Quality-adjusted Price Indexes for Computer Processors and Selected Peripherals Equipment," *Survey of Current Business*, January.

Cooley, T. (ed.) (1995), *Frontiers of Business Cycle Research*, Princeton, NJ: Princeton University Press.

Danielsson J. and J.F. Richard (1993), "Accelerated Gaussian Importance Sampling," *Journal of Applied Econometrics*, 8, S153–S173.

De Haan, L. (1981), "Estimation of the Minimum of a Function Using Order Statistics," *Journal of the American Statistical Association*, 76, 467–469.

Geweke, J. (1989), "Bayesian Inference in Econometrics Using Monte-Carlo Integration," *Econometrica*, 57, 1317–1340.

Gordon, R. (1990), *The Measurement of Durable Goods Prices*, Chicago: University of Chicago Press.

Gourieroux, C. and A. Monfort (1994), "Simulation Based Econometric Methods," manuscript.

Gourieroux, C., A. Monfort, and E. Renault (1993), "Indirect Inference," *Journal of Applied Econometrics*, 8, 85–118.

Gourieroux, C., A. Monfort, and A. Trognon (1984), "Pseudo-Maximum Likelihood Methods: Theory," *Econometrica*, 52, 681–700.

Gourieroux, C., E. Renault, and N. Touzi (1995), "Calibration by Simulation for Small Samples Bias Correction," manuscript.

Greenwood, J., Z. Hercowitz, and P. Krusell (1997), "Long-Run Implications of Investment-Specific Technological Change," *American Economic Review*, 87(3), 342–362.

Hamermesh, D.S. (1993), *Labor Demand*, Princeton, NJ: Princeton University Press.

Juhn, C., K.M. Murphy, and B. Pierce (1993), "Wage Inequality and the Rise in the Returns to Skill," *Journal of Political Economy*, 101, 410–442.

Kim, S. and N. Shephard (1994), "Stochastic Volatility: Likelihood Inference and Comparison with ARCH Models," manuscript.

Kitagawa, G. (1987), "Non-Gaussian State-Space Modeling of Nonstationary Time-Series" (with discussion), *Journal of the American Statistical Association*, 82, 1032–1063.

Krusell P., L. Ohanian, J. Rios-Rull, and G. Violante (1995), "Capital-Skilled Labor Complementarity and Inequality," manuscript, University of Minnesota.

Laroque, G. and B. Salanié (1989), "Estimation of Multi-Market Fix-Price Models: An Application of Pseudo Maximum Likelihood Methods," *Econometrica*, 57, 831–860.

(1993), "Simulation Based Estimation of Models with Lagged Dependent Varibales," *Journal of Applied Econometrics*, 8, 119–133.

(1994), "Estimating the Canonical Disequilibrium Model: Asymptotic Theory and Finite Sample Properties," *Journal of Econometrics*, 62, 165–210.

Meinhold, R.J. and N.D. Singpurwalla (1989), "Robustification of Kalman Filter Models," *Journal of the American Statistical Association*, 84, 479–486.

Ruud, P. (1991), "Extensions of Estimation Methods Using the EM Algorithm," *Journal of Econometrics*, 49, 305–341.

Sargent, T. (1981), "Interpreting Economic Time Series," *Journal of Political Economy*, 89(2), 213–248.

Silverman, B.W. (1986), *Density Estimation*, London: Chapman and Hall.

Veall, M.R. (1990), "Testing for a Global Maximum in an Econometric Context," *Econometrica*, 58, 1459–1465,

White, H. (1982), "Maximum Likelihood Estimation of Misspecified Models," *Econometrica*, 50, 1–28.

15 Testing calibrated general equilibrium models

Fabio Canova and Eva Ortega

1 Introduction

Simulation techniques are now used in many fields of applied research. As shown elsewhere in this book, they have been employed to compute estimators in situations where standard methods are impractical or fail, to evaluate the properties of parametric and non-parametric econometric estimators, to provide a cheap way of evaluating posterior integrals in Bayesian analysis and to undertake linear and non-linear filtering with a computationally simple approach.

The task of this chapter is to describe how simulation-based methods can be used to evaluate the fit of dynamic general equilibrium models specified using a calibration methodology, to compare and contrast their usefulness relative to more standard econometric approaches and to provide an explicit example where the various features of the approach can be highlighted and discussed.

The structure of this chapter is as follows. First, we provide a definition of what we mean by calibrating a model and discuss the philosophy underlying the approach and how it differs from standard dynamic time series modeling. Second, we discuss various approaches to the selection of model parameters, how to choose the vector of statistics used to compare actual with simulated data and how simulations are performed. Third, we describe how to formally evaluate the model's approximation to the data and discuss alternative approaches to account for the uncertainty faced by a simulator in generating time paths for the relevant variables. Although we present a general overview of alternative evaluation techniques, the focus is on simu-

We have benefitted from the comments of John Geweke, Frank Diebold, Jane Marrinan and of the participants of the conference "Simulation Based Inference in Econometrics" held in Minneapolis, USA. The financial support of a DGICYT grant is gratefully acknowledged. Part of the work was conducted when the second author was visiting the IMF and the University of Pennsylvania.

lation-based methods. Finally, we present an example, borrowed from Baxter and Crucini (1993), where the features of the various approaches to evaluation can be examined.

2 What is calibration?

2.1 A definition

Although it is more than a decade since calibration techniques emerged in the mainstream of dynamic macroeconomics (see Kydland and Prescott (1982)), a precise statement of what it means to calibrate a model has yet to appear in the literature. In general, it is common to think of calibration as an unorthodox procedure to select the parameters of a model. This need not to be the case since it is possible to view parameter calibration as a particular econometric technique where the parameters of the model are estimated using an "economic" instead of a "statistical" criteria (see, e.g., Canova (1994)). On the other hand, one may want to calibrate a model because there is no available data to estimate its parameters, for example, if one is interested in studying the effect of certain taxes in a newly born country.

Alternatively, it is possible to view calibration as a cheap way to evaluate models. For example, calibration is considered by some as a more formal version of the standard back-of-the-envelope calculations that theorists perform to judge the validity of their models (see, e.g., Pesaran and Smith (1992)). According to others, calibration is a way to conduct quantitative experiments using models which are known to be "false", i.e., improper or simplified approximations of the true data generating processes of the actual data (see, e.g., Kydland and Prescott (1991)).

Pagan (1994) stresses that the unique feature of calibration exercises does not lie so much in the way parameters are estimated, as the literature has provided alternative ways of doing so, but in the particular collection of procedures used to test tightly specified (and false) theoretical models against particular empirical facts. Here we take a more general point of view and identify six steps which we believe capture the essence of the methodology. We call calibration a procedure which involves:

(i)   Formulating an economic question to be addressed.
(ii) Selecting a model design which bears some relevance to the question asked.
(iii) Choosing functional forms for the primitives of the model and finding a solution for the endogenous variables in terms of the exogenous variables and the parameters.
(iv) Choosing parameters and stochastic processes for the exogenous

variables and simulating paths for the endogenous variables of the model.

(v) Selecting a metric and comparing the outcomes of the model relative to a set of "stylized facts."

(vi) Doing policy analyses if required.

By "stylized facts" the literature typically means a collection of sample statistics of the actual data such as means, variances, correlations, etc., which (a) do not involve estimation of parameters and (b) are self-evident. More recently, however, the first requirement has been waived and the parameters of a VAR (or the impulse responses) have also been taken as the relevant stylized facts to be matched by the model (see, e.g., Smith (1993), Cogley and Nason (1994)).

The next two subsections describe in detail both the philosophy behind the first four steps and the practicalities connected with their implementation.

2.2   Formulating a question and choosing a model

The first two steps of a calibration procedure, to formulate a question of interest and a model which bears relevance to the question, are self-evident and require little discussion. In general, the questions posed display four types of structure (see, e.g., Kollintzas (1992) and Kydland (1992)):

Is it possible to generate Z using theory W?

How much of the fact X can be explained with impulses of type Y?

What happens to the endogenous variables of the model if the stochastic process for the control variable V is modified?

Is it possible to reduce the discrepancy D of the theory from the data by introducing feature F in the model?

Two economic questions which have received considerable attention in the literature in the last ten years are the so-called equity premium puzzle, i.e., the inability of a general equilibrium model with complete financial markets to quantitatively replicate the excess returns of equities over bonds over the last hundred years (see, e.g., Mehra and Prescott (1985)) and how much of the variability of GNP can be explained by a model whose only source of dynamics is technology disturbances (see, e.g., Kydland and Prescott (1982)). As is clear from these two examples, the type of questions posed are very specific and the emphasis is on the numerical implications of the exercise. Generic questions with no numerical quantification are not usually studied in this literature.

For the second step, the choice of an economic model, there are essentially no rules except that it has to have some relevance with the question asked. For example, if one is interested in the equity premium puzzle, one can choose a model which is very simply specified on the international and the government side, but very well specified on the financial side so that it is possible to calculate the returns on various assets. Typically, one chooses dynamic general equilibrium models. However, several authors have used model designs coming from different paradigms (see, e.g., the neo-Keynesian model of Gali (1994), the non-Walrasian models of Danthine and Donaldson (1992) or Gali (1995), and the model with union bargaining of Eberwein and Kollintzas (1995)). There is nothing in the procedure that restricts the class of model design to be used. The only requirement is that the question that the researcher formulates is quantifiable within the context of the model and that the theory, in the form of a model design, is fully specified.

It is important to stress that a model is chosen on the basis of the question asked and not on its being realistic or being able to best replicate the data (see Kydland and Prescott (1991) and Kydland (1992)). In other words, how well it captures reality is not a criterion to select models. What is important is not whether a model is realistic or not but whether it is able to provide a quantitative answer to the specific question the researcher poses.

This brings us to discuss an important philosophical aspect of the methodology. From the point of view of a calibrator all models are approximations to the DGP of the data and, as such, false. This aspect of the problem has been appreciated by several authors even before the appearance of the seminal article of Kydland and Prescott. For example, Hansen and Sargent (1979) also concede that an economic model is a false DGP for the data. Because of this and in order to test the validity of the model using standard statistical tools, they complete the probabilistic structure of the model by adding additional sources of variability, in the form of measurement errors or unobservable variables, to the fundamental forces of the economy.

For calibrators, the model is not a null hypothesis to be tested but an approximation of a few dimensions of the data. A calibrator is not interested in verifying whether the model is true (the answer is already known from the outset), but in identifying which aspects of the data a false model can replicate and whether different models give different answers because they are false in different dimensions. A calibrator is satisfied with his effort if, through a process of theoretical respecification, a simple and highly stylized model captures an increasing number of features of the data (confront this activity with the so-called normal science of Kuhn (1970)).

Being more explicit, consider the realization of a vector of stochastic processes y_t (our data) and some well-specified theoretical model $x_t = f(z_t, \gamma)$ which has something to say about y_t, where z_t are exogenous and predetermined variables and γ is a parameter vector. Because the model does not provide a complete description of the phenomenon under investigation we write

$$y_t = x_t + u_t \tag{1}$$

where u_t is an error representing what is missing from $f(z_t, \gamma)$ to reproduce the stochastic process generating y_t and whose properties are, in general, unknown (it need not necessarily be mean zero, serially uncorrelated, uncorrelated with the xs, and so on). Let B_y and B_x be continuous and differentiable functions of actual and simulated data, respectively. Then standard econometric procedures judge the coherence of the model to the data by testing whether or not $B_x = B_y$, given that the difference between B_x and B_y and their estimated counterpart $\hat{B}_x = \hat{B}_y$ arise entirely from sampling error. While this is a sensible procedure when the null hypothesis is expected to represent the data, it is less sensible when it is known that the model does not completely capture all aspects of the data.

The third step of a calibration exercise concerns the solution of the model. To be able to obtain quantitative answers from a model it is necessary to find an explicit solution for the endogenous variables of the model in terms of the exogenous and predetermined variables and the parameters. For this reason it is typical to parameterize the objective function of the agents so that manipulation of the first-order conditions is analytically tractable. For example, in general equilibrium models, it is typical to choose Cobb–Douglas production functions and constant relative risk-aversion utility functions. However, although the main objective is to select simple enough functional forms, it is well known that almost all general equilibrium models and many partial equilibrium models have exact analytical solutions only in very special situations.

For general equilibrium models, a solution exists if the objective function is quadratic and the constraints linear (see, e.g., Hansen and Sargent (1979)) or when the objective function is log linear and the constraints linear (see, e.g., Sargent (1987, chapter 2)). In the other cases, analytical expressions relating the endogenous variables of the model to the "states" of the problem do not exist and it is necessary to resort to numerical techniques to find solutions which approximate equilibrium functionals either locally or globally. There has been substantial theoretical development in this area in the last few years and several solution alogorithms have appeared in the literature (see, e.g., the special January 1990 issue of the *JBES* or Marcet (1994)).

The essence of the approximation process is very simple. The exact solution of a model is a relationship between the endogenous variables x_t, the exogenous and predetermined variables z_t, and a set of "deep" parameters γ of the type $x_t = f(z_t, \gamma)$, where f is generally unknown. The approximation procedures generate a relationship of the type $x_t^* = g(z_t, \theta)$, where $\theta = h(\gamma)$ and where $\|f - g\| < \epsilon$ is minimal for some local or global metric. Examples of these types of procedures appear in Kydland and Prescott (1982), Coleman (1989), Tauchen and Hussey (1991), Novales (1990), Baxter (1992), and Marcet (1992), among others. The choice of a particular approximation procedure depends on the question asked. If one is concerned with the dynamics of the model around the steady state, local approximations are sufficient. On the other hand, if one is interested in comparing economic policies requiring drastic changes in the parameters of the control variables, global approximation methods must be preferred.

2.3 Selecting parameters and exogenous processes

Once an approximate solution has been obtained, a calibrator needs to select the parameters γ and the exogenous stochastic process z_t to be fed into the model in order to generate time series for x_t^*. There are several approaches to the choice of these features of the model. Consider first the question of selecting z_t. This choice is relatively uncontroversial. One either chooses it on the basis of tractability or to give the model some realistic connotation. For example, one can assume that z_t is an AR process with innovations which are transformations of a $N(0, 1)$ process and draw one or more realizations for z_t using standard random number generators. Alternatively, one can select the Solow residuals of the actual economy, the actual path of government expenditure or of the money supply. Obviously, the second alternative is typically preferred if policy analyses are undertaken. Note that while in both cases z_t is the realization of a stochastic process, in the first case the DGP is known while in the second it is not and this has implications for the way one measures the uncertainty in the outcomes of the model.

Next, consider the selection of the vector of parameters γ. Typically, they are chosen so that the model reproduces certain observations. Taking an example from physics, if one is interested in measuring water temperature in various situations it will be necessary to calibrate a thermometer for the experiments. For this purpose a researcher arbitrarily assigns the value of $0°C$ to freezing water and the value $100°C$ to boiling water and interpolates values in the middle with, say, a linear scale. Given this calibration of the thermometer, one can then proceed to measure the results of the experiments: a value close to $100°C$ indicates "hot" water, a value close to $30°C$ indicates "tepid" water, and so on. To try to give answers to the economic question he poses, a calibrator must similarly select observations to be used to calibrate the model thermometer. There are at least three approaches in the literature. One can follow the deterministic computable general equilibrium (CGE) tradition, summarized, for example, in Showen and Whalley (1984), the stochastic dynamic general equilibrium tradition pioneered by Kydland and Prescott (1982), or employ more standard econometric techniques. There are differences between the first two approaches. The first one was developed for deterministic models which do not necessarily possess a steady state while the second one has been applied to dynamic stochastic models whose steady state is unique. Kim and Pagan (1995) provide a detailed analysis of the differences between these two approaches. Gregory and Smith (1993) supplement the discussion by adding interesting insights in the comparison of the first two approaches with the third.

In CGE models a researcher solves the model linearizing the system of equations by determining the endogenous variables around a hypothetical equilibrium where prices and quantities are such that there is no excess demand or excess supply. It is not necessary that this equilibrium exists. However, because the coefficients of the linear equations determining endogenous variables are functions of these equilibrium values, it is necessary to measure this hypothetical equilibrium. The main problem for this literature is therefore to find a set of "benchmark data" and to calibrate the model so that it can reproduce these data. Finding this data set is the most complicated part of the approach since it requires a lot of judgment and ingenuity. The process of specification of this data set leaves some of the parameters of the model typically undetermined, for example, those that describe the utility function of agents. In this situation a researcher either assigns arbitrary values or fixes them to values estimated in other studies in the literature. Although these choices are arbitrary, the procedure is coherent with the philosophy of the models: a researcher is interested in examining deviations of the model from a hypothetical equilibrium, not from an actual economy.

In stochastic dynamic general equilibrium models, the model is typically calibrated at the steady state: parameters are chosen so that the model, in the steady state, produces values for the endogenous variables which match corresponding long-run averages of the actual data. In both this approach and the CGE approach, point estimates of the parameters used to calibrate the model to the equilibrium are taken to be exact (no standard deviations are typically attached to these estimates). As in the previous set-up, the steady state does not necessarily pin down all the parameters of the model. Canova (1994) and Gregory and Smith (1993) discuss various methods to select the remaining parameters. Briefly, a researcher can choose parameters *a priori*, pin them down using values previously estimated in the literature, can informally estimate them using simple method of moment conditions, or formally estimate them using procedures like generalized method of moments (GMM) (see, e.g., Christiano and Eichenbaum (1992)), simulated method of moments (see, e.g., Duffie and Singleton (1993)) or maximum likelihood (see, e.g., McGratten, Rogerson, and Wright (1993)). As pointed out by Kydland and Prescott (1991), choosing parameters using the information contained in other studies imposes a coherence criterion among various branches of the profession. For example, in the business cycle literature one uses stochastic growth models to examine business cycle fluctuations and checks the implications of the model using parameters typically obtained in micro studies, which do not employ data having to do with aggregate business cycle fluctuations (e.g. micro studies of labor markets).

If one follows a standard econometric approach, all the parameters are chosen by minimizing the MSE of the error u_t in (1), arbitrarily assuming that the error and the model designs are orthogonal, or by minimizing the distance between moments of the actual data and the model or maximizing the likelihood function of the data given the model design. As we already pointed out, this last approach is the least appealing one from the point of view of a calibrator since it makes assumptions on the time series properties of u_t which are hard to justify from an economic point of view.

To clearly understand the merits of each of these procedures it is useful to discuss their advantages and their disadvantages. Both the CGE and the Kydland and Prescott approach where some of the parameters are chosen *a priori* or obtained from a very select group of studies are problematic in several respects. First, there is a selectivity bias problem (see Canova (1995)). There exists a great variety of estimates of the parameters in the literature and different researchers may refer to different studies even when they are examining the same problem. Second, there is a statistical inconsistency problem which may generate very spurious and distorted inference. As Gregory and Smith (1989) have shown, if some parameters are set *a priori* and others estimated by simulation, estimates of the latter may be biased and inconsistent unless the parameters of the former group are the true parameters of the DGP or consistent estimates of them. Third, since any particular choice is arbitrary, extensive sensitivity analysis is necessary to evaluate the quality of the results. To solve these problems Canova (1994, 1995) suggests an approach for choosing parameters which allows, at a second stage, the drawing of inferences about the quality of the approximation of the model to the data. The idea is very simple. Instead of choosing one set of parameters over another he suggests calibrating each parameter of the model to an interval, using the empirical information to construct a distribution over this interval (the likelihood of a parameter given existing estimates) and conducting simulation by drawing parameter vectors from the corresponding joint "empirical" distribution. An example may clarify the approach. If one of the parameters of interest is the coefficient of constant relative risk aversion of the representative agent, one typically chooses a value of 2 and tries a few values above and below this one to see if results change. Canova suggests taking a range of values, possibly dictated by economic theory, say [0, 20], and then over this range constructing a histogram using existing estimates of this parameter. Most of the estimates are in the range [1, 2] and in some asset pricing models researchers have tried values up to 10. Given this information, the resulting empirical distribution for this parameter can be very closely approximated by a $\chi^2(2)$, which has the mode at 2 and about 5 percent probability in the region above 6.

The selection of the parameters of theoretical models through statistical estimation has advantages and disadvantages. The main advantage is that these procedures avoid arbitrary choices and explicitly provide a measure of dispersion for the estimates which can be used at a second stage to evaluate the quality of the approximation of the model to the data. The disadvantages are of various kinds. First of all, to undertake a formal or informal estimation it is typically necessary to select the moments one wants to fit, and this choice is arbitrary. The standard approach suggested by Kydland and Prescott can indeed be thought of as a method of moment estimation where one chooses parameters so as to set only the discrepancy between the first moment of the model and the data (i.e., the long-run averages) to zero. The formal approach suggested by Christiano and Eichenbaum (1992), or Fève and Langot (1994) on the other hand, can be thought of as a method of moment estimation where a researcher fits the discrepancies between model and data first and second moments to zero. The approach of choosing parameters by setting to zero the discrepancy between certain moments has the disadvantage of reducing the number of moments over which it will be possible to evaluate the quality of the model. Moreover, it is known that estimates obtained with the method of moments or GMM may be biased. Therefore, simulations and inference conducted with these estimates may lead to spurious inference (see, e.g., Canova, Finn and Pagan (1994)). In addition, informal SMM may lead one to select parameters even though they are not identifiable (see Gregory and Smith (1989)). Finally, one should note that the type of uncertainty which is imposed on the model via an estimation process does not necessarily reflect the uncertainty a calibrator faces when choosing the parameter vector. As is clear from a decade of GMM estimation, once the moments are selected and the data given, sample uncertainty is pretty small. The true uncertainty is in the choice of moments and in the data set to be used to select parameters. This uncertainty is disregarded when parameters are chosen using extremum estimators like GMM.

Finally, it is useful to compare the parameter selection process used by a calibrator à la Kydland and Prescott and the one used by a traditional econometric approach. In a traditional econometric approach parameters are chosen so as to minimize some **statistical** criteria, for example, the MSE. Such criteria do not have any economic content, impose stringent requirements on the structure of u_t, and are used, primarily, because there exists a well-established statistical and mathematical literature on the subject. In other words, the parameter selection criteria used by traditional econometricians does not have economic justification. On the other hand, the parameter selection criteria used by followers of the Kydland and Prescott methodology can be thought of as being based on **economic** criteria. For example, if the model is calibrated so that, in the steady state, it matches the long-run features of the actual economy, parameters are implicitly selected using the condition that the sum (over time) of the discrepancies between the model and the data is zero. In this sense there is an important difference between the two approaches which has to do with the assumptions that one is willing to make on the errors u_t. By calibrating the model to long-run observations a researcher selects parameters assuming $E(u) = 0$, i.e., using a restriction which is identical to the one imposed by a GMM econometrician who chooses parameters using only first moment conditions. On the other hand, to conduct classical inference a researcher imposes restrictions on the first and second moments of u_t.

The comparison we have made so far concerns, obviously, only those parameters which enter the steady state conditions of the model. For the other parameters a direct comparison with standard econometric practice is not possible. However, if all parameters are calibrated to intervals with distributions which are empirically determined, the calibration procedure we have described shares a tight connection with Bayesian inferential methods such as consensus analysis or meta-analysis (see e.g., Genest and Zidak (1986) or Wolf (1986)).

Once the parameters and the stochastic processes for the exogenous variables are selected and an (approximate) solution to the model has been found, simulated paths for x_t^* can be generated using standard Monte Carlo simulation techniques.

3   Evaluating calibrated models

The questions of how well a model matches the data and how much confidence a researcher ought to give to the results constitute the most critical steps in the calibration procedure. In fact, the most active methodological branch of this literature concerns methods to evaluate the fit of a model selected according to the procedures described in section 2. The evaluation of a model requires three steps: first, the selection of a set of stylized facts;

second, the choice of a metric to compare functions of actual and simulated data; and, third, the (statistical) evaluation of the magnitude of the distance. Formally, let S_y be a set of statistics (stylized facts) of the actual data and let $S_{x^*}(z_t, \gamma)$ be a set of statistics of simulated data, given a vector of parameters γ and a vector of stochastic processes z_t. Then model evaluation consists of selecting a function $\psi(S_y, S_{x^*}(z_t, \gamma))$ measuring the distance between S_y and S_{x^*} and assessing its magnitude.

The choice of which stylized facts one wants to match obviously depends on the question asked and on the type of model used. For example, if the question is what is the proportion of actual cyclical fluctuations in GNP and consumption explained by the model, one would choose stylized facts based on variances and covariances of the data. As an alternative to the examination of second moments, one could summarize the properties of actual data via a VAR and study the properties of simulated data, for example, by comparing the number of unit roots in the two sets of data (as in Canova, Finn, and Pagan (1994)), the size of VAR coefficients (as in Smith (1993)), or the magnitude of certain impulse responses (as in Cogley and Nason (1994)). Also, it is possible to evaluate the discrepancy of a model to the data by choosing specific events that one wants the model to replicate, e.g., business cycle turning points (as in King and Plosser (1994) or Simkins (1994)) or variance bounds (as in Hansen and Jagannathan (1991)).

Classical pieces in the calibration literature (see, e.g., Kydland and Prescott (1982) or (1991)) are typically silent on the metric one should use to evaluate the quality of the approximation of the model to the data. The approach favored by most calibrators is to gloss over the exact definition of the metric used and informally assess the properties of simulated data by comparing them to the set of stylized facts. In this way a researcher treats the computational experiment as a measurement exercise where the task is to gauge the proportion of some observed statistics reproduced by the theoretical model. This informal approach is also shared by cliometricians (see, e.g., Summers (1991)) who believe that rough reproduction of simple sample statistics is all that is needed to evaluate the implications of the model ("either you see it with naked eyes or no fancy econometric procedure will find it").

There are, however, alternatives to this informal approach. To gain some understanding of the differences among approaches, but at the cost of oversimplifying the matter, we divide evaluation approaches into five classes:
(i) Informal approaches.
(ii) Approaches which do not consider sampling variability of actual data or the uncertainty in simulated data, but instead use the statistical properties of u_t in (1) to impose restrictions on the time series properties of

ψ. This allows them to provide an R^2-type measure of fit between the model and the data (see Watson (1993)).

(iii) Approaches which use the sampling variability of the **actual** data (affecting S_y and, in some cases, estimated γ) to provide a measure of the distance between the model and the data. Among these we list the GMM-based approach of Christiano and Eichenbaum (1992), Cecchetti, Lam, and Mark (1993) or Fève and Langot (1994), and the frequency domain approaches of Diebold, Ohanian, and Berkowitz (1995) and Ortega (1995).

(iv) Approaches which use the uncertainty of the **simulated** data to provide a measure of distance between the model and the data. Among these procedures we can distinguish those who take z_t as stochastic and γ as given, such as Gregory and Smith (1991), Söderlind (1994), or Cogley and Nason (1994) and those who take both z_t and γ as stochastic, such as Canova (1994, 1995).

(v) Finally, approaches which consider the sampling variability of the **actual** data and the uncertainty in **simulated** data to evaluate the fit of the model. Once again we can distinguish approaches which, in addition to taking S_y as random, allow for variability in the parameters of the model (keeping z_t fixed), such as DeJong, Ingram, and Whiteman (1995) from those which allow for both z_t and γ to vary, such as Canova and De Nicoló (1995).

Because the emphasis of this book is on simulation techniques, we will only briefly examine the first three approaches and discuss in more detail the last two, which make extensive use of simulation techniques to conduct inference. Kim and Pagan (1994) provide a thorough critical review of several of these evaluation techniques and additional insights on the relationship among them.

The evaluation criterion that each of these approaches proposes is tightly linked to the parameter selection procedure we discussed in the previous section.

As mentioned the standard approach is to choose parameters using steady state conditions. Those parameters which do not appear in the steady state are selected *a priori* or with reference to existing literature. Also, since S_y is chosen to be a vector of numbers and no uncertainty is allowed in the selected parameter vector, one is forced to use an informal metric to compare the model to the data. This is because, apart from the uncertainty present in the exogenous variables, the model links the endogenous variables to the parameters in a deterministic fashion. Therefore, once we have selected the parameters and we have a realization of S_y, it is not possible to measure the dispersion of the distance $\psi(S_y, S_{x*}(z_t, \gamma))$. From the point of view of the majority of calibrators this is not a problem. As emphasized by

Kydland and Prescott (1991) or Kydland (1992), the trust a researcher has in an answer given by the model does not depend on a statistical measure of discrepancy, but on how much he believes in the economic theory used and in the measurement undertaken.

Taking this as the starting point of the analysis Watson (1993) suggests an ingenious way to evaluate models which are known to be an incorrect DGP for the actual data. Watson asks how much error should be added to x_t^* so that its autocovariance function equals the autocovariance function of y_t. Writing $y_t = x_t^* + u_t^*$ where u_t^* includes the approximation error due to the use x_t^* in place of x_t, the autocovariance function of this error is given by

$$A_{u*}(z) = A_y(z) + A_{x*}(z) - A_{x*y}(z) - A_{yx*}(z).$$ (2)

To evaluate the last two terms in (2) we need a sample from the joint distribution of (x_t^*, y_t) which is not available. In these circumstances it is typical to assume that either u_t^* is a measurement error or a signal extraction noise (see, e.g., Sargent (1987)), but in the present context neither of the two assumptions is very appealing. Watson suggests choosing $A_{x*y}(z)$ so as to minimize the variance of u_t^* subject to the constraint that $A_{x*}(z)$ and $A_y(z)$ are positive semidefinite. Intuitively, the idea is to select $A_{x*y}(z)$ to give the best possible fit between the model and the data (i.e., the smallest possible variance of u_t^*). The exact choice of $A_{x*y}(z)$ depends on the properties of x_t^* and y_t, i.e., whether they are serially correlated or not, scalar or vectors, full rank processes or not. In all cases, the selection criteria chosen imply that x_t^* and y_t are perfectly linearly correlated where the matrix linking the two vectors depends on their time series properties and on the number of shocks buffeting the model. Given this framework of analysis, Watson suggests two measures of fit, similar to a $1 - R^2$ from a regression, of the form

$$r_j(\omega) = \frac{A_{u*}(\omega)_{jj}}{A_y(\omega)_{jj}}$$ (3)

$$R_j(\omega) = \frac{\int_{\omega \in Z} A_{u*}(\omega)_{jj} d\omega}{\int_{\omega \in Z} A_y(\omega)_{jj} d\omega}$$ (4)

where the first statistic measures the variance of the jth component of the error relative to the variance of the jth component of the data for each frequency and the second statistic is the sum of the first over a set of frequencies. This last measure may be useful to evaluate the model, say, at business cycle frequencies. It should be stressed that (3) and (4) are lower bounds. That is, when $r_j(\omega)$ or $R_j(\omega)$ are large, the model poorly fits the data. However, when they are small, it does not necessarily follow that the model is appropriate since it may still fit the data poorly if we change the assumptions about $A_{x*y}(z)$.

To summarize, Watson chooses the autocovariance function of y as the set of stylized facts of the data to be matched by the model, the ψ function as the ratio of A_{u^*} to A_y and evaluates the size of ψ informally (i.e., if it is greater than one, between zero and one, or close to zero). Note that, in this approach, γ and z_t are fixed, and A_{x^*} to A_y are assumed to be measured without error.

When a calibrator is willing to assume that parameters are measured with error because, given an econometric technique and a sample, parameters are imprecisely estimated, then model evaluation can be conducted using measures of dispersion for simulated statistics which reflect parameter uncertainty. There are various versions of this approach. Christiano and Eichenbaum (1992), Cecchetti, Lam, and Mark (1993), and Fève and Langot (1994) use a version of a J-test to evaluate the fit of a model. In this case S_y are moments of the data while ψ is a quadratic function of the type

$$\psi(S_y, S_{x^*}(z_t, \gamma)) = [S_y - S_{x^*}(\gamma)]V^{-1}[S_y - S_{x^*}(\gamma)]' \tag{5}$$

where V is a matrix which linearly weights the covariance matrix of S_{x^*} and S_y, and S_{x^*} is random because γ is random. Formal evaluation of this distance can be undertaken following Hansen (1982): under the null that $S_y = S_{x^*}(z_t, \gamma)$ the statistic defined in (5) is asymptotically distributed as a χ^2 with the number of degrees of freedom equal to the number of overidentifying restrictions, i.e., the dimension of S_y minus the dimension of the vector γ. Note that this procedure is correct asymptotically, that it implicitly assumes that $x_t = f(z_t, \gamma)$ (or its approximation x_t^*) is the correct DGP for the data and that the relevant loss function measuring the distance between actual and simulated data is quadratic.

The methods proposed by Diebold, Ohanian, and Berkowitz (DOB) (1995) and Ortega (1995) are slightly different but can be broadly included into this class of approaches.

For DOB the statistic of interest is the spectral density matrix of y_t and, given a sample, this is assumed to be measured with error. They measure the uncertainty surrounding point estimates of the spectral density matrix employing (small sample) 90 percent confidence bands constructed using parametric and non-parametric bootstrap approaches and Bonferroni tunnels. On the other hand, they take calibrated parameters and the realization of z_t as given so that the spectral density matrix of simulated data can be estimated without error simply by simulating very long time series for x_t^*. Ortega (1995) also takes the spectral density matrix as the set of stylized facts of the data to be matched by the model. Unlike DOB, she considers the uncertainty in actual and simulated data by jointly estimating the spectral density matrix of actual and simulated data and constructs measures of uncertainty around point estimates of the spectral density matrix using asymptotic distribution theory.

In both cases, the measure of fit used is generically given by

$$C(\gamma, z_t) = \int_0^{\pi} \psi(F_y(\omega), F_{x*}(\omega, \gamma, z_t)) W(\omega) d\omega \qquad (6)$$

where $W(\omega)$ is a set of weights applied to different frequencies and F are the spectral density matrices of actual and simulated data.

DOB suggest various options for ψ (quadratic, ratio, likelihood type) but do not construct a direct test statistic to examine the magnitude of ψ. Instead, they compute a small sample distribution of the event that $C(\gamma, z_t)$ is close to a particular value (zero if ψ is quadratic, 1 if ψ is a ratio, etc.). Ortega, on the other hand, explicitly uses a quadratic expression for ψ and uses an asymptotic χ^2 test to assess whether the magnitude of the discrepancy between the model and the data is significant or not. The set of asymptotic tools she develops can also be used to compare the fit of two alternative models to the data and decide which one is more acceptable.

If a calibrator is willing to accept the idea that the stochastic process for the exogenous variables is not fixed, she can then compute measures of dispersion for simulated statistics by simply changing the realization of z_t while maintaining the parameters fixed. Such a methodology has its cornerstone in the fact that it is the uncertainty in the realization of the exogenous stochastic process (e.g. the technology shock), an uncertainty which one can call extrinsic, and not the uncertainty in the parameters, which one can call intrinsic, which determines possible variations in the statistics of simulated data. Once a measure of dispersion of simulated statistics is obtained, the sampling variability of simulated data can be used to evaluate the distance between statistics of actual and simulated data (as, e.g., Gregory and Smith (1991, 1993)).

If one uses such an approach, model evaluation can be undertaken with a probabilistic metric using well-known Monte Carlo techniques. For example, one may be interested in finding out in what decile of the simulated distribution the actual value of a particular statistic lies, in practice, calculating the "size" of calibration tests. This approach requires two important assumptions: that the evaluator takes the model economy as the true DGP for the data and that differences between S_y and S_{x*} occur only because of sampling variability. To be specific, Gregory and Smith take S_y be a set of moments of the data and assume that they can be measured without error. Then, they construct a distribution of $S_{x*}(z_t, \gamma)$ by drawing realizations for the z_t process from a given distribution, given γ. The metric ψ used is probabilistic, i.e., they calculate the probability $Q = P(S_{x*} \leq S_y)$, and judge the fit of the model informally, for example measuring how close Q is to 0.5.

An interesting variation on this set-up is provided by Söderlind (1994) and Cogley and Nason (1994). Söderlind employs the spectral density matrix of the actual data while Cogley and Nason choose a "structural" impulse response function as the relevant statistics to be matched. Söderlind maintains a probabilistic metric and constructs the empirical rejection rate for the event that the actual spectral density matrix of y_t lies inside the asymptotic 90 percent confidence band for the spectral density matrix of the simulated data. Such an event is replicated by drawing vectors x_t for a given distribution. Cogley and Nason choose a quadratic measure of distance which, under the null that the model is the DGP for the data, has an asymptotic χ^2 distribution and then tabulate the empirical rejection rates of the test, by repeatedly constructing the statistic drawing realizations of the z_t vector. To be specific, the ψ function is in this case given by

$$\psi_{k,j}(\gamma) = [IRF^k_{x*}(z^j_t,\gamma) - IRF^k_{y}]V^{-1}[IRF^k_{x*}(z^j_t,\gamma) - IRF^k_{y}]' \qquad (7)$$

where j indexes replications and k steps, IRF^k is the impulse response function, and V is its asymptotic covariance matrix at step k. Because for every k and for fixed j $\psi_{k,j}(\gamma)$ is asymptotically χ^2, they can construct (a) the simulated distribution for $\psi_{k,j}$ and compare it with a χ^2 and (b) the rejection frequency for each model specification they examine.

In practice, all three approaches are computer intensive and rely on Monte Carlo methods to conduct inference. Also, it should be stressed that all three methods verify the validity of the model by computing the "size" of the calibration tests, i.e., assuming that the model is the correct DGP for y_t.

The approach of Canova (1994, 1995) also belongs to this category of methods, but, in addition to allowing the realization of the stochastic process for the exogenous variables to vary, he also allows for parameter variability in measuring the dispersion of simulated statistics. The starting point, as discussed earlier, is that parameters are uncertain not so much because of sample variability, but because there are many estimates of the same parameter obtained in the literature, since estimation techniques, samples, and frequency of the data tend to differ. If one calibrates the parameter vector to an interval, rather than to a particular value, and draws values for the parameters from the empirical distribution of parameter estimates, it is then possible to use the intrinsic uncertainty, in addition to or instead of the extrinsic one, to evaluate the fit of the model. The evaluation approach used is very similar to the one of Gregory and Smith: one simulates the model repeatedly by drawing parameter vectors from the empirical "prior" distribution and realizations of the exogenous stochastic process z_t from some given distribution. Once the empirical distribution of the statistics of interest is constructed, one can then compute either the size of calibration tests or the percentiles where the actual statistics lie.

The last set of approaches considers the uncertainty present in the statistics of both actual and simulated data to measure the fit of the model to the data. In essence what these approaches attempt to formally measure is the degree of overlap between the (possibly) multivariate distributions of S_y and S_x using Monte Carlo techniques. There are differences in the way these distributions have been constructed in the literature. Canova and De Nicoló (1995) use a parametric bootstrap algorithm to construct distributions for the statistics of the actual data. DeJong, Ingram and Whiteman (DIW) (1996), on the other hand, suggest representing the actual data with a VAR and a computing posterior distribution estimates for the moments of interest by drawing VAR parameters from their posterior distribution and using the AR(1) companion matrix of the VAR at each replication. In constructing distributions of simulated statistics, Canova and De Nicoló take into account both the uncertainty in exogenous processes and parameters while DIW only consider parameter uncertainty. The two approaches also differ in the way the "prior" uncertainty in the parameters is introduced in the model. The former paper follows Canova (1995) and chooses empirical-based distributions for the parameter vector. DIW use subjectively specified prior distributions (generally normal) whose location parameter is set at the value typically calibrated in the literature while the dispersion parameter is free. The authors use this parameter in order to (informally) minimize the distance between actual and simulated distributions of the statistics of interest. By enabling the specification of a sequence of increasingly diffuse priors over the parameter vector, such a procedure illustrates whether the uncertainty in the model's parameters can mitigate differences between the model and the data.

Finally, there are differences in assessing the degree of overlap of the two distributions. Canova and De Nicoló choose a particular contour probability for one of the two distributions and ask how much of the other distribution is inside the contour. In other words, the fit of the model is examined very much in the style of the Monte Carlo literature: a good fit is indicated by a high probability covering of the two regions. To describe the features of the two distributions, they also repeat the exercise varying the chosen contour probability, say, from 50 percent to 75 percent, 90 percent, 95 percent, and 99 percent. The procedure allows them to detect anomalies in the shape of the two distributions due to clustering of observations in one area, skewness, or leptokurtic behavior. In this approach actual data and simulated data are used symmetrically in the sense that one can either ask whether the actual data could be generated by the model or, vice versa, whether simulated data are consistent with the distribution of the empirical sample. This symmetry allows the researcher to understand much better the distributional properties of error u_t in (1). Moreover, the symmetry with which the two distributions are treated resembles very much the process of switching the null and the alternative in standard classical hypothesis testing.

DeJong, Ingram, and Whiteman take the point of view that there are no well-established criteria to judge the adequacy of a model's "approxima-tion" to reality. For this reason they present two statistics aimed at synthet-ically measuring the degree of overlap among distributions. One, which they call confidence interval criterion (CIC) is the univariate version of the contour probability criteria used by Canova and De Nicoló and is defined as

$$CIC_{ij} = \frac{1}{1-\alpha} \int_a^b P_j(s_i) ds_i \qquad (8)$$

where s_i, $i = 1, \dots, n$ is a set of functions of interest, $a = \frac{\alpha}{2}$ and $b = 1 - a$ are the quantiles of $D(s_i)$, the distribution of the statistic in the actual data, $P_j(s_i)$ is the distribution of the simulated statistic where j is the diffusion index of the prior on the parameter vector and $1 - \alpha = \int_a^b D(s_i) ds_i$. Note that, with this definition, CIC_{ij} ranges between 0 and $\frac{1}{1-\alpha}$. For CIC close to zero, the fit of the model is poor, either because the overlap is small or because P_j is very diffuse. For CIC close to $\frac{1}{1-\alpha}$ the two distributions overlap sub-stantially. Finally, if $CIC > 1$, $D(s_i)$ is diffuse relative to $P_j(s_i)$, i.e., the data are found to be relatively uninformative regarding s_i.

To distinguish among the two possible interpretations when CIC is close to zero, DeJong, Ingram, and Whiteman suggest a second summary measure analogous to a t-statistic for the mean of $P_j(s_i)$ in the $D(s_i)$ distrib-ution, i.e.

$$d_{ji} = \frac{EP_j(s_i) - ED(s_i)}{\sqrt{\text{var } D(s_i)}}. \qquad (9)$$

Large values of (9) indicate that the location of $P_j(s_i)$ is quite different from the location of $D(s_i)$.

The final problem of the DIW methodology is to choose α. DeJong, Ingram, and Whiteman fix a particular value ($\alpha = 0.01$) but, as in Canova and De Nicoló, varying α for a given j is probably a good thing to do in order to describe the feature of the distributions. This is particularly useful when we are interested in partitions of the joint distributions of s_i because graphical methods or simple statistics are not particularly informative about distributions in high dimensional spaces.

4   Policy analyses

Although it is not the purpose of this chapter to discuss in detail how calibrated models can be used for policy analyses, it is useful to describe the implications of the procedure for questions which have policy implications and how policy experiments can be undertaken. As we have already mentioned, a model is typically calibrated to provide a quantitative answer to very precise questions and some of these questions have potential policy implications. To forcefully argue the policy implications of the exercise one needs to be confident in the answer given by the model and to do this it is necessary to undertake extensive sensitivity analysis to check how results change when certain assumptions are modified.

As we have seen, the answers of the model come in the form of continuous functions $h(x_t^*) = h(g(z_t, \gamma))$ of simulated data. In theory, once g has been selected, the uncertainty in h is due to the uncertainty in γ and in z_t. Since in standard calibration exercises the γ vector is fixed, it is therefore typical to examine the sensitivity of the results in the neighborhood of the calibrated values for γ. Such experiments may be local, if the neighborhood is small, or global, in which case one measures the sensitivity of the results to perturbations of the parameters over the entire range. This type of exercise may provide two types of information. First, if results are robust to variations of a parameter in a particular range, its exact measurement is not crucial. In other words, the uncertainty present in the choice of such a parameter does not make the answers of the model tenuous and economic inference groundless. On the other hand, if results crucially depend on the exact selection of certain parameters, it is clearly necessary to improve upon the existing measurement of these parameters.

A local sensitivity analysis can be undertaken informally, replicating the experiments for different values of the parameters (as in Kydland and Prescott (1982)) or more formally, calculating the elasticity of h with respect to γ (as in Pagan and Shannon (1985)). A global sensitivity analysis can be efficiently undertaken with Monte Carlo methods or numerical semideterministic techniques (see, e.g., Niederreiter (1988)) if the function g is known and the distribution of the γ vector is specified. If g is only an approximation to the functional linking x to z and γ, one can use techniques like importance sampling (see Geweke (1989)) to take into account this additional source of uncertainty. Clearly the two types of sensitivity analysis are not incompatible and should both be undertaken to assess the degree of trust a researcher can attach to the answer given by the model. Finally, one should note that the type of sensitivity analysis one may want to undertake depends also on the way parameters are selected and models evaluated. For example, if one uses the approach of Canova

(1994, 1995) or DeJong, Ingram, and Whiteman (1996), the evaluation procedure automatically and efficiently provides sensitivity analysis to global perturbations of the parameters within an economically reasonable range.

Once model answers to the question of interest have been shown to be robust to reasonable variations in the parameters, a researcher may undertake policy analyses by changing the realization of the stochastic process for z_t or varying a subset of the γ vector, which may be under the control of, say, the government. Analyses involving changes in the distribution of z_t in the g function are also possible, but care should be exercised in order to compare results across specifications.

5   An example

In the field of international economics, robust stylized facts are usually hard to obtain. One of the most stable regularities observed in the data is the high correlation of national saving and domestic investment, both in time series analysis of individual countries and in cross-section regressions where the average over time of these variables is treated as a single data point for each country. High saving and investment correlations are observed in small economies as well as large ones, although the correlation tends to be lower for smaller countries. These findings were originally interpreted as indicating that the world economy is characterized by a low degree of capital mobility. Yet most economists believe that the world is evolving toward an increasingly higher degree of international capital mobility. Baxter and Crucini (1993) forcefully turned this initial interpretation around by providing a model in which there is perfect international mobility of financial and physical capital but which generates high time series correlations of national saving and investment. Their evaluation of the model lies entirely within the standard Kydland and Prescott approach, i.e., parameters are fixed at some chosen values, no uncertainty is allowed in actual and simulated statistics and the metric used to compare actual and simulated data is informal.

The task of this section is threefold. First, we want to study whether the time series properties of simulated saving and investment do indeed reproduce those of the actual data when the model is formally examined with the tools described in this article. To this end we provide several measures of fit which can be used to gauge the closeness of the model to the data using variants of the simulation-based procedures described in the previous section. Second, we wish to contrast the outcomes obtained with various evaluation procedures and compare them with those obtained using more standard techniques. This will shed further light on the degree of approximation of the model to the data, and point out, when they emerge, unusual features of the model. Finally, we wish to provide a few suggestions on how to fine tune the model design so that undesirable features are eliminated while maintaining the basic bulk of the results.

5.1   *The model*

We consider a model with two countries and a single consumption good. Each country is populated by a large number of identical agents and labor is assumed to be immobile across countries and variables are measured in per capita terms. Preferences of the representative agent of country $h = 1,2$ are given by

$$U \equiv E_0 \sum_{t=0}^{\infty} \frac{\beta^t}{1 - \sigma} [C_{ht}^{\mu} L_{ht}^{(1-\mu)}]^{1-\sigma} \tag{10}$$

where C_{ht} is private consumption of the single composite good by the representative agent of country h and L_{ht} is leisure, β is the discount factor, σ the coefficient of relative risk aversion, and μ the share of consumption in utility. Leisure choices are constrained by

$$0 \leq L_{ht} + N_{ht} \leq 1 \quad \forall h \tag{11}$$

where the total endowment of time in each country is normalized to 1 and N_t represents the number of hours worked. The goods are produced with a Cobb–Douglas technology

$$Y_{ht} = A_{ht}(K_{ht})^{1-\alpha}(X_{ht}N_{ht})^{\alpha} \quad h = 1,2 \tag{12}$$

where K_t is the capital input, α is the share of labor in GDP, and where $X_{ht} = \theta_x X_{ht-1} \forall h$ with $\theta_x \geq 1$. X_{ht} represents labor-augmenting Harrod-neutral technological progress with deterministic growth rate equal to θ_x. Production requires domestic labor and capital inputs and is subject to a technological disturbance A_{ht} with the following properties

$$\begin{bmatrix} A_{1t} \\ A_{2t} \end{bmatrix} = \begin{bmatrix} \bar{A}_1 \\ \bar{A}_2 \end{bmatrix} + \begin{bmatrix} \rho & \nu \\ \nu & \rho \end{bmatrix} \begin{bmatrix} A_{1t-1} \\ A_{2t-1} \end{bmatrix} + \begin{bmatrix} \epsilon_{1t} \\ \epsilon_{2t} \end{bmatrix}$$

where $\epsilon_t = [\epsilon_{1t} \epsilon_{2t}]' \sim N\left(0, \begin{bmatrix} \sigma_{\epsilon}^2 & \psi \\ \psi & \sigma_{\epsilon}^2 \end{bmatrix}\right)$ and $[\bar{A}_1, \bar{A}_2]'$ is a vector of constants. The parameter ψ controls the contemporaneous spillover while ν is the lagged spillover of the shocks.

Capital goods are accumulated according to

$$K_{ht+1} = (1 - \delta_h)K_{ht} + \phi(I_{ht}/K_{ht})K_{ht} \quad h = 1,2 \tag{13}$$

where $\phi(\frac{I_{ht}}{K_{ht}}) > 0$ is concave and represents the costs of adjusting capital. As explained by Baxter and Crucini (1993), there is no need to choose a functional form for ϕ; it is sufficient to describe its behavior near the steady state. We do this by specifying two parameters: $\frac{1}{\phi'}$, which corresponds to Tobin's Q – i.e., the price of existing capital in one location relative to the price of new capital – and $\xi_{\phi'}$, the elasticity of the marginal adjustment cost function with respect to the investment–capital ratio.

Governments finance their consumption purchases, G_{ht}, by taxing national outputs with a distorting tax and transferring what remains back to domestic residents. For simplicity we assume that $G_{ht} = G_h$, $\forall t$. The government budget constraint is given by

$$G_h = TR_{ht} + \tau_h Y_{ht} \quad \forall h \tag{14}$$

where τ_h are tax rates and TR_h are lump-sum transfers in country h.

The economy-wide resource constraint is given by

$$\pi(Y_{1t} - G_{1t} - C_{1t} - I_{1t}) + (1 - \pi)(Y_{2t} - G_{2t} - C_{2t} - I_{2t}) \geq 0 \tag{15}$$

where π is the fraction of world population living in country 1.

Finally, following Baxter and Crucini (1993), we assume complete financial markets and free mobility of financial capital across countries so that agents can write and trade every kind of contingent security.

To find a solution to the model we first detrend those variables which drift over time by taking ratios of the original variables with respect to the labor augmenting technological progress, for example, $y_{ht} = \frac{Y_{ht}}{X_{ht}}$, etc. Second, since there are distortionary taxes in the model, the competitive equilibrium is not Pareto optimal and the competitive solution differs from the social planner's solution. As in Baxter and Crucini (1993) we solve the problem faced by a pseudo-social planner, modifying the optimality conditions to take care of the distortions. The weights in the social planner problem are chosen to be proportional to the number of individuals living in each of the countries. The modified optimality conditions are approximated with a log linear expansion around the steady state as in King, Plosser, and Rebelo (1988). Time series for saving and investment in each of the two countries are computed analytically from the approximate optimality conditions. The second-order properties of saving and investment of actual and simulated data are computed eliminating from the raw time series a linear trend.

The parameters of the model are $\gamma = [\beta, \sigma, \alpha, \theta_x, \delta, \rho, \nu, \sigma_e, \psi, \pi, \xi_{\phi'}, \phi', \tau]$ plus steady state hours and the steady state Tobin's Q which we set equal to 1. The exogenous processes of the model are two productivity disturbances so that $z_t = [A_{1t}\ A_{2t}]'$.

The actual data we use are per capita basic saving (i.e., computed as $S_t = Y_t - C_t - G_t$) and investment for the period 1970:1–1993:3 for the US and for Europe in real terms, seasonally adjusted, and are from OECD Main Economic Indicators. Plots of the detrended series appear in figure 15.1.

The statistics we care about are the diagonal elements of the 4×4 spectral density matrix of the data and the coherence between saving and investment of the two "countries." Spectral density estimates at each frequency are computed smoothing with a flat window 13 periodogram ordinates. Figure 15.2 plots these statistics.

In the benchmark experiment the vector γ is the same as in Baxter and Crucini (1993) except for σ_ϵ which they normalize to 1, while we set it equal to the value used in Backus, Kehoe, and Kydland (1995), and reported in the first column of table 15.1. When we allow for parameters to be random we take two approaches: the one of Canova (1994) and the one of DeJong, Ingram, and Whiteman (1996). In the first case empirical-based distributions are constructed using existing estimates of these parameters or, when there are none, choosing *a priori* an interval on the basis of theoretical considerations and imposing a uniform distribution on it. The distributions from which the parameters are drawn and their features are displayed in the second column of table 15.1. In the second case distributions for the parameters are assumed to be normal, with means equal to the basic calibrated parameters presented in column 1, while dispersions are *a priori* chosen. The third column of table 15.1 reports these distributions.

We generate samples of 95 observations to match the sample size of actual data. Because the initial conditions for the capital stock are set arbitrarily, the first 50 observations for each replication of the model are discarded. The number of replications used for each exercise is 500.

5.2   The results

Table 15.2 summarizes the results obtained using four different evaluation approaches. Each row reports how the model fares in reproducing the spectral densities of saving and investment and the saving–investment coherence for the US and Europe on average at business cycle frequencies (cycles of 3–8 years).

As a reference for comparison, the two first rows report the average spectral densities and coherence at business cycle frequencies for actual and simulated data when parameters are fixed (Kydland and Prescott approach). National saving is highly correlated with domestic investment but the average coherence at business cycle frequencies is higher for Europe than for the US. The variability of both US series is also higher and US investment are almost two times more volatile than European ones. This

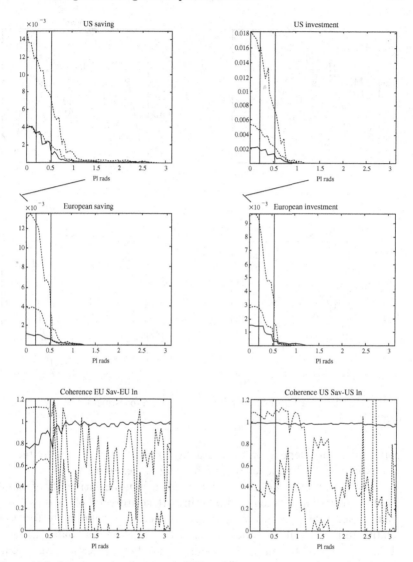

Figure 15.2 Spectra and coherences of US and European per capita saving and investment (linearly detrended logs of the series). 95% asymptotic confidence interval of estimated spectral densities and coherences for actual data displayed in dashed lines, spectra and coherences of simulated data for one draw in solid lines. Vertical lines indicate the frequencies associated to cycles of 8 and 3 years.

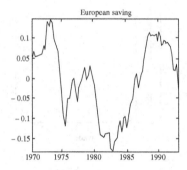

Figure 15.3 US and European per capita saving and investment: linearly detrended logs of the series

pattern does not depend on the averaging procedure we choose; in fact, it is present at every frequency within the range we examine.

Given the symmetry of the model specification, the variability of simulated saving and investment is similar in both continental blocs, it is somewhat lower than the actual data for Europe, but definitively too low relative to the actual US series. Moreover, as in the actual data, the variability is higher for national savings than for domestic investment. Consistent with Baxter and Crucini's claims, the model produces high national saving and investment correlations at business cycle frequencies. In fact, the model coherences for the US are higher than those found in the actual data.

The following rows of table 15.2 check whether the above results persist when the performance of the model is evaluated using some of the procedures described in this chapter.

The first approach, which we use as a benchmark, is the one of Watson

Table 15.1. *Parameter values used in the simulations*

Parameter	Basic	Empirical density	Prior normal
Steady state hours (H)	0.20	Uniform [0.2, 0.35]	Normal (0.2, 0.02)
Discount factor (β)	0.9875	Trunc. Normal [0.9855, 1.002]	Normal (0.9875, 0.01)
Risk aversion (σ)	2.00	Truncated $\chi^2(2)$ [0, 10]	Normal (2, 1)
Share of labor in output (α)	0.58	Uniform [0.50, 0.75]	Normal (0.58, 0.05)
Growth rate (θ_x)	1.004	Normal (1.004, 0.001)	1.004
Depreciation rate of capital (δ)	0.025	Uniform [0.02, 0.03]	Normal (0.025, 0.01)
Persistence of disturbances (ρ)	0.93	Normal (0.93, 0.02)	Normal (0.93, 0.025)
Lagged spillover of disturbances (ν)	0.05	Normal (0.05, 0.03)	Normal (0.05, 0.02)
Standard deviation of technology innovations (σ_ϵ)	0.00852	Truncated $\chi^2(1)$ [0, 0.0202]	Normal (0.00852, 0.004)
Contemporaneous spillover (ψ)	0.40	Normal (0.35, 0.03)	Normal (0.4, 0.02)
Country size (π)	0.50	Uniform [0.10, 0.50]	0.5
Elasticity of marginal adjustment cost function ($\xi_{\phi'}$)	-0.075	-0.075	-0.075
Steady state Tobin's Q ($\frac{1}{\phi}$)	1.0	1.0	1.0
Tax rate (τ)	0.0	0.0	0.0

Notes:
"Empirical density" refers to distributions for the parameters constructed using either existing estimates or *a priori* intervals as in Canova (1994). "Prior normal" refers to distributions for the parameters which are *a priori* chosen as in DeJong, Ingram, and Whiteman (1996). The range for the parameter is reported inside the brackets. The mean and the standard deviation for the distribution are reported inside the parentheses.

Table 15.2. Fit of the model at business cycle frequencies

	US Spectra		Europe Spectra		US coherence	Europe coherence
	S	I	S	I	S-I	S-I
Actual data	0.75	0.88	0.68	0.49	85.41	93.14
Simulated data	0.36	0.18	0.35	0.18	94.04	93.00
Watson approach						
Identification 1	0.02	0.05	0.20	0.23	0.04	0.13
Identification 2	0.24	0.21	0.05	0.04	0.20	0.15
Probability covering						
Fixed parameters	46.46	8.63	55.71	43.57	98.99	92.91
Normal distribution	35.30	23.40	32.89	37.00	98.17	90.34
Empirical distribution	19.63	18.60	21.11	20.20	94.71	95.69
Critical value						
Fixed parameters	90.80	99.89	82.16	93.91	15.60	49.04
Normal distribution	71.80	89.90	66.00	76.60	19.80	51.89
Empirical distribution	62.50	79.70	73.30	74.60	33.46	29.60
Error						
Fixed parameters	0.25	0.55	0.30	0.28	-9.17	0.37
Normal distribution	0.19	0.56	0.29	0.28	-9.01	0.81
Empirical distribution	0.13	0.58	0.42	0.35	-6.07	-2.86

Notes:

Actual and simulated data are linearly detrended and logged, in real per capita terms. Simulations are undertaken using 500 draws. All rows except the third and the fourth report numbers in percentage terms. "Watson approach" reports the average statistic (4) at business cycle frequencies. "Probability covering" reports the average covering at business cycle frequencies of the theoretical 95 percent range. "Critical value" the percentile where the actual data lies on average at business cycle frequencies, and "Error" the median error across simulations on average at business cycle frequencies. S refers to saving and I to investment.

(1993). Given the spectral density matrix of the actual saving and investment for the two economic blocs, we calculate the spectral density matrix of the approximation error and compute the measure of fit (4) where Z includes frequencies corresponding to cycles of 3–8 years. Since in the model there are two technology disturbances, the spectral density matrix of simulated saving and investment for the two countries is singular and of rank equal to two. Therefore, to minimize the variance of the approximation error we consider two different identification schemes: in "identification 1" we jointly minimize the error term of the saving and investment of the first country (row 3 of table 15.2) and in "identification 2" we jointly minimize the saving and investment errors of the second country (row 4 of table 15.2). Note that to generate $R_j(\omega)$ we make two important assumptions: (i) that the spectral density matrix of the actual and simulated data can be measured without error and (ii) that the parameters of the model can be selected without error.

The results suggest that the fit of the model depends on the identification scheme used. On average, the size of the error at business cycle frequencies is between 2 percent and 5 percent of the spectral density of those variables whose variance is minimized and between 20 percent and 30 percent of the spectral density of other variables, suggesting that "some" error should be added to the model to capture the features of the spectral density matrix of the data. Overall, we find small differences in the fit for the two continental blocs, and within continental blocs between the two variables of interest. Changes in the coherences across identifications are somewhat relevant and the model appears to fit coherences much better when we minimize the variance of US variables.

To show how the Monte Carlo techniques discussed in this chapter can be used to evaluate the quality of the model's approximation to the data we compute three types of statistics. First, we report how many times on average, at business cycle frequencies, the diagonal elements of the spectral density matrix and the coherences of model generated data lie within a 95 percent confidence band for the corresponding statistics of actual data. That is, we report $T_1 = \int_{\omega_1}^{\omega_2} \int_{S_1(\omega)}^{S_2(\omega)} p_\omega(x) dx d\omega$ where $S_1(\omega)$ and $S_2(\omega)$ are the lower and upper limits for the asymptotic 95 percent band for the spectral density of actual data, ω_1 and ω_2 are the lower and upper limits for the business cycle frequencies and $p_\omega(x)$ is the empirical distribution of the simulated spectral density matrix for the four series at frequency ω.

If the spectral density matrix of the actual data is taken to be the object of interest to be replicated, T_1 reports the *power* of a test which assumes that the model is the correct DGP for the actual data. If we are not willing to assume that the model is the correct DGP for the actual data, these numbers judge the quality of the approximation by informally examining the magnitude of the probability coverings. No matter which interpretation we take, a number close to 95 percent would indicate a "good" model performance at a particular frequency band.

We compute 95 percent confidence bands for the actual data in two ways: using asymptotic distribution theory (as in Ortega (1995)) and using a version of the parametric bootstrap procedure of Diebold, Ohanian, and Berkowitz (1995). In this latter case, we run a four variable VARs with six lags and a constant, construct replications for saving and investment for the two countries by bootstrapping the residuals of the VAR model, estimate the spectral density matrix of the data for each replication and extract 95 percent confidence bands after ordering the replications, frequency by frequency.

Replications for the time series generated by the model are constructed using Monte Carlo techniques in three different ways. In the first case we simply randomize on the innovations of the technology shocks, keeping their distribution fixed (as in Gregory and Smith (1991)), and use the basic parameter setting displayed in the first column of table 15.2. In the second and third cases parameters are random and drawn from the distributions listed in the second and third columns of table 15.2. The results appear in rows 5–7 under the heading "Probability covering." To economize on space and because simulated results are similar when the 95 percent confidence bands for actual data are computed asymptotically or by bootstrap, row 5 presents the probability covering using an asymptotic 95 percent band when only the stochastic processes of the model are randomized, row 6 presents the probability covering using an asymptotic 95 percent band when we randomize on the stochastic processes of the model and parameters are drawn from normal prior distributions, and row 7 when parameters are drawn from empirically based distributions.

The results obtained with this testing approach highlight interesting features of simulated data. With fixed parameters, the average percentage of times the model's spectra are inside the 95 percent band of the actual spectra is, in general, much smaller than 95 percent, its magnitude depends on the series and it is highest for European saving. When we randomize the parameters using the DIW approach, results are more uniform across series and the probability covering is always of the order of 30 percent while when we randomize using empirical-based distributions, the average percentage of times the model's spectra are inside the 95 percent confidence band is somewhat lower. These results occur because with random parameters, simulated distributions are shifted and stretched: the model produces a wider range of variabilities than those possibly consistent with the data and this reduces the percentage of times simulated data are inside the asymptotic 95 percent band for each frequency. For coherence the results are very similar across the three rows: in this case, adding parameter variability does not change the outcomes. This is because parameter variability increases the volatility of saving and investment and their covariance by the same factor and this factor cancels out in the computation of coherences. In general, we find that the model slightly "overfits" US coherences, i.e., on average too many simulations fall inside the asymptotic 95 percent band, while the opposite is true for European coherences. However, with empirical-based priors, the coverage in both cases is close to 95 percent.

In sum, this evaluation procedure confirms that the model is better suited in matching coherences than volatilities at business cycle frequencies and that the covering properties of the model do not improve when we allow the parameters to be random.

To gain further evidence on the properties of the simulated distributions of the data, we next compute a second statistic: the percentile of the simulated distribution of the spectral density matrix of saving and investment for the two countries, where the value of the spectral density matrix of actual data (taken here to be estimated without an error) lies on average, at business cycle frequencies. Implicitly, this p-value reports, over the selected frequency band, the proportion of replications for which the simulated data are less than the historical value. In other words, if $\bar{S}_y(\omega)$ is the spectral density matrix of the actual data at frequency ω we report $T_2 = \int_{\omega_1}^{\omega_2} \int_{-\infty}^{\bar{S}y(\omega)} p_\omega(x) dx d\omega$ where all variables have been previously defined. Seen through these lenses the spectral density matrix of the actual data is treated as a "critical value" in examining the validity of the theoretical model. Values close to 0 percent (100 percent) indicate that the actual spectral density matrix is in the left (right) tail of the simulated distribution of the spectral density matrix of simulated data at that particular frequency band, in which case the model is poor in reproducing the statistics of interest. Values close to 50 percent, on the other hand, suggest that the actual spectral density matrix at those frequencies is close to the median of the distribution of the spectral density matrix of simulated data so the model is appropriate at those frequencies. Note also that values of the statistics in the range $[\alpha, 100 - \alpha]$, where α is a chosen confidence percentage, would indicate that the model is not significantly at odds with the data. We report the results of this exercise in rows 8–10 of table 15.2 under the heading "Critical value." Row 8 presents results when only the innovations of the technology disturbances are randomized, row 9 displays results when the parameters are drawn for normal priors, and row 10 when parameters are drawn from an empirical-based distribution.

As expected, the model with fixed parameters is unable to match the variabilities of the four series at business cycle frequencies. For all variables the statistics of actual data are in the right tail of the simulated distribution of the statistics at each frequency, i.e., a large proportion of simulations generate average values for the spectral density at business cycle frequencies which are lower than those found in the actual data. For European variables, however, the picture is less dramatic. With parameter variability the picture changes. For all variables it is still true that actual variability exceeds the median of the simulated distribution on average at business cycle frequencies, but, at least with empirical priors, it is now within the interquartile range of the simulated distribution for three of the four variables. This is because parameter variability pushes the median of the simulated distribution close to the actual value, shifting the location to the left (less variability is generated). In essence, with parameter variability the model generates two features which improve its overall distributional fit: a wider range of variabilities at business cycle frequencies (with a somewhat larger percentage of more extreme values) and a less concentrated and less skewed distribution.

For coherences the results are somewhat different. With fixed parameters the model generates average coherences at business cycle frequencies which are much higher than in the data for the US but close to the median for Europe (actual values are in the 15th and 50th percentile). With random parameters (and empirical-based priors), the situation improves for the US (actual coherence moves up to the 33rd percentile) but worsens for Europe. Once again, parameter variability enhances the range of possibilities of the model but it fails to tilt the distribution so as to more adequately reproduce the data.

Taken together, the results of these two exercises suggest that with fixed parameters the model generates a distribution for variability which is skewed to the left and only partially overlapping with a normal asymptotic range of variabilities for the data. For coherence the opposite occurs: the overlapping is high but also the skewness within the band is high. Parameter uncertainty, by tilting and stretching the shape of the simulated distribution, ameliorates the situation and in terms of the distributions of certain statistics used, actual and simulated data are almost indistinguishable.

To complete the picture, we finally compute the distributional properties of the approximation error by Monte Carlo methods, i.e., we compute the distribution of the error needed to match the spectral density matrix of the actual data given the model's simulated spectral density matrix. To compute the distributional properties of the log of the error, we draw, at each replication, parameters and innovations from the posterior distribution of the VAR representation of the actual data, construct time series of interest following the procedure of DeJong, Ingram, and Whiteman (1996), and estimate the spectral density matrix of the four series. At each replication, we also draw parameters and innovations from the distributions presented in table 15.2, construct the spectral density matrix of simulated data and compute $S_u^i(\omega) = S_y^i(\omega) - S_x^i(\omega)$, i.e., the error in matching the spectral density matrix of the data $S_y^i(\omega)$ at replication i. By drawing a large number of replications we can construct a non-parametric estimate of this distribution (using, for example, kernels) and compute moments and fractiles at each frequency. If the model is the correct DGP for the data, the distribution for this error would be degenerate at each frequency. Otherwise the features of this distribution (median value, skewness, kurtosis, etc.) may indicate what is missing from the model to capture the features of interest in the data. The last three rows in table 15.2 present the median (across replications) of the average error across business cycle frequencies for the six statistics of interest under the heading "Error." Once again, we performed the calculations randomizing both on the stochastic processes of the model and the parameters of the model. Row 11 reports the results when parameters are fixed and rows 12 and 13 when the simulated time series incorporate uncertainty in both stochastic processes and parameters.

The results are quite similar in the three cases for the diagonal elements of the spectral density matrix. The model fails to generate enough variability at business cycle frequencies for US investments while for the other three variables the error is much smaller. The magnitude of the difference is, however, significant. For example for US savings and keeping parameters fixed, the error is about one-third of the actual variability at business cycle frequencies. The results for coherences depend on which of the two countries we consider. For US variables the model generates systematically higher coherences (negative spectral errors) while for Europe the opposite is true. Relatively speaking, the magnitudes of these errors are smaller than those obtained comparing spectra. Adding parameter variability as in DeJong, Ingram, and Whiteman does not change the results too much. However, when parameters are drawn from empirical-based priors, the model generates higher coherences in both cases.

5.3 What did we learn from the exercise?

Our exercise pointed out several important features of the model used by Baxter and Crucini (1993). As claimed by the authors, we find it generates high coherences between national saving and investment at business cycle frequencies which are of the same magnitude as the actual ones for European saving and investment. However, we also saw that the model tends to generate coherences which are uniformly higher than those observed in US data and this is true regardless of whether we use fixed or random parameters. In particular, we show that in only about 20 percent of the simulations is the simulated coherence smaller than the actual one and that there is tendency for the model to cluster saving and investment correlations in the vicinity of 1. Nevertheless, also in this case, the magnitude of the error is small. The model performance is worse when we try to account for the variability of saving and investment for the two continental blocs at business cycle frequencies. With fixed parameters, the simulated distribution at business cycle frequencies is skewed toward lower than toward actual values for all variables of interest and the degree of overlap of simulated and actual distributions varies between 8 percent and 50 percent. Parameter variability helps but it does not represent a complete solution to the problem. This is clearly demonstrated by the size of the median value of the spectral error at business cycle frequencies which is sometimes larger than the error obtained with fixed parameters and always positive.

These results suggest that if one is interested in replicating the distributional properties of the statistics of the data (rather than their point estimates), it is necessary to respecify the model, at least for the US. What is primarily needed are two types of features. First, we need some real friction, maybe by adding a new sector (non-traded goods) which uses capital to produce goods. This modification is likely to reduce the median value of the distribution of correlation of saving and investment at business cycle frequencies. Second, we need an additional propagation or variability enhancing device, maybe in the form of a lower adjustment cost of capital or higher elasticity of investment to technology innovations. For the US this can bring simulated variabilities at business cycle frequencies more in the range of the values we found in the data.

6   Summary and conclusions

The task of this chapter was to illustrate how simulation techniques can be used to evaluate the quality of a model's approximation to the data, where the basic theoretical model design is one which fits into what we call a calibration exercise. In section 2 we first provided a definition of what calibration is and then described in detail the steps needed to generate time series from the model and to select relevant statistics of actual and simulated data. In section 3 we overviewed four different formal evaluation approaches recently suggested in the literature, comparing and contrasting them on the basis of what type of variability they use to judge the closeness of the model's approximation to the data. In section 4 we described how to undertake policy analysis with models which have been calibrated and evaluated along the lines discussed in the previous two sections. Section 5 presented a concrete example, borrowed from Baxter and Crucini (1993), where we designed four different simulation-based statistics which allowed us to shed some light on the quality of the model approximation to the data, in particular, whether the model is able to reproduce the main features of the spectral density matrix of saving and investment for the US and Europe at business cycle frequencies. We showed that, consistent with Baxter and Crucini's claims, the model qualitatively produces a high coherence of saving and investment at business cycle frequencies in the two continental blocs but it also has the tendency to generate a highly skewed simulated distribution for the coherence of the two variables. We also showed that the model is less successful in accounting for the volatility features of US and European saving and investment at business cycle frequencies and that taking into account parameter uncertainty helps in certain cases to bring the properties of simulated data closer to those of the actual data.

Overall, the example shows that simulation-based evaluation techniques are very useful to judge the quality of the approximation of fully specified general equilibrium models to the data and may uncover features of the model which are left hidden by more simple but more standard informal evaluation techniques.

References

Backus, D., P. Kehoe, and F. Kydland (1995), "International Business Cycles: Theory and Evidence," in T. Cooley (ed.), *Frontiers of Business Cycle Analysis*, Princeton, NJ: Princeton University Press.

Baxter, M. (1991), "Approximating Suboptimal Dynamic Equilibria: An Euler Equation Approach," *Journal of Monetary Economics*, 27, 173–200.

Baxter, M. and M. Crucini (1993), "Explaining Saving-Investment Correlations," *American Economic Review*, 83, 416–436.

Canova, F. (1994), "Statistical Inference in Calibrated Models," *Journal of Applied Econometrics*, 9, S123–S144.

(1995), "Sensitivity Analysis and Model Evaluation in Simulated Dynamic General Equilibrium Economies," *International Economic Review*, 36, 477–501.

Canova, F., M. Finn, and A. Pagan (1994), "Evaluating a Real Business Cycle Model," in C. Hargreaves (ed.), *Nonstationary Time Series Analysis and Cointegration*, Oxford University Press.

Canova, F. and G. Nicoló (1995), "The Equity Premium and the Risk Free Rate: A Cross Country, Cross Maturity Examination," CEPR Working Paper No. 1119.

Cecchetti, S.G., P. Lam, and N. Mark (1993), "The Equity Premium and the Risk Free Rate: Matching Moments," *Journal of Monetary Economics*, 31, 21–45.

Christiano, L. and M. Eichenbaum (1992), "Current Business Cycle Theories and Aggregate Labor Market Fluctuations," *American Economic Review*, 82, 430–450.

Cogley, T. and J.M. Nasom (1994), "Testing the Implications of Long-run Neutrality for Monetary Business Cycle Models," *Journal of Applied Econometrics*, 9, S37–S70.

Coleman, W. (1989), "An Algorithm to Solve Dynamic Models," Board of Governors of the Federal Reserve System, International Finance Division, Discussion Paper No. 351.

Danthine, J.P. and X.X. Donaldson (1992), "Non-Walrasian Economies," Université de Lausanne, Cahiers de Recherche Economique No. 9301.

DeJong, D., B. Ingram, and C. Whiteman (1996), "A Bayesian Approach to Calibration," *Journal of Business and Economic Statistics*, 14(1), 1–9.

Diebold, F., L. Ohanian, and J. Berkowitz (1995), "Dynamic Equilibrium Economies: A Framework for Comparing Models and Data," NBER Technical Working Paper No. 174.

Duffie, D. and K. Singleton (1993), "Simulated Moments Estimation of Markov Models of Asset Prices," *Econometrica*, 61, 929–950.

Eberwein, C. and T. Kollintzas (1995), "A Dynamic Model of Bargaining in a Unionized Firm with Irreversible Investment," *Annales d'Economie et de Statistique*, 37–38, 91–116.

Fève, P. and F. Langot (1994), "The RBC Models through Statistical Inference: An Application with French Data," *Journal of Applied Econometrics*, 9, S11–S37.

Gali, J. (1994), "Monopolistic Competition, Business Cycles and the Composition of Aggregate Demands," *Journal of Economic Theory*, 63, 73–96.

(1995), "Non Walrasian unempoloyment Fluctuations," NBER Working Paper No. 5337.

Genest, C. and M. Zidak (1986), "Combining Probability Distributions: A Critique and an Annotated Bibliography," *Statistical Science*, 1, 114–148.

Geweke, J. (1989), "Bayesian Inference in Econometric Models Using Monte Carlo Integration," *Econometrica*, 57, 1317–1339.

Gregory, A. and G. Smith (1989), "Calibration as Estimation," *Econometric Reviews*, 9(1), 57–89.

(1991), "Calibration as Testing: Inference in Simulated Macro Models," *Journal of Business and Economic Statistics*, 9(3), 293–303.

(1993), "Calibration in Macroeconomics," in G.S. Maddala (ed.), *Handbook of Statistics*, vol XI, Amsterdam, North-Holland.

Hansen, L. (1982), "Large Sample Properties of Generalized Method of Moment Estimators," *Econometrica*, 50, 1029–1054.

Hansen, L. and R. Jagannathan (1991), "Implications of Security Market Data for Models of Dynamic Economies," *Journal of Political Economy*, 99, 225–262.

Hansen, L. and T. Sargent (1979), "Formulating and Estimating Dynamic Linear Rational Expectations Models," *Journal of Economic Dynamic and Control*, 2, 7–46.

Kim, K. and A. Pagan (1995), "The Econometric Analysis of Calibrated Macroeconomic Models," in H. Pesaran and M. Wickens (eds.), *Handbook of Applied Econometrics*, vol. I, Oxford: Blackwell, chapter 7, pp. 356–390.

King, R. and C. Plosser (1994), "Real Business Cycles and the Test of the Adelmans," *Journal of Monetary Economics*, 33, 405–438.

King, R., C. Plosser, and S. Rebelo, (1988), "Production, Growth and Business Cycles: I and II," *Journal of Monetary Economics*, 21, 195–232 and 309–342.

Kollintzas, T. (1992), "Comment to J.P. Danthine: Calibrated Macroeconomic Models: What and What For," manuscript, Athens University, GA.

Kuhn, T. (1970), *The Structure of Scientific Revolution*, Chicago: Chicago University Press.

Kydland, F. (1992), "On the Econometrics of World Business Cycles," *European Economic Review*, 36, 476–482.

Kydland, F. and E. Prescott (1982), "Time To Build and Aggregate Fluctuations," *Econometrica*, 50, 1345–1370.

(1991), "The Econometrics of the General Equilibrium Approach to Business Cycles," *Scandinavian Journal of Economics*, 93(2), 161–178.

Marcet, A. (1992), "Solving Nonlinear Stochastic Models by Parametrizing Expectations: An Application to Asset Pricing with Production," Universitat Pompeu Fabra, Working Paper No. 5.

(1994), "Simulation Analysis of Stochastic Dynamic Models: Applications to Theory and Econometrics," in C. Sims (ed.), *Advances in Econometrics, Sixth World Congress of the Econometric Society*, Cambridge University Press.

McGratten, E., B. Rogerson, and R. Wright (1993), "Estimating the Stochastic Growth Model with Household Production," Federal Reserve Bank of Minneapolis manuscript.

Mehra, R. and E. Prescott (1985), "The Equity Premium: A Puzzle," *Journal of Monetary Economics*, 15, 145–162.

Niederreiter, H. (1988), "Quasi Monte Carlo Methods for Multidimensional Numerical Integration," *International Series of Numerical Mathematics*, 85, 157–171.

Novales, A. (1990), "Solving Nonlinear Rational Expectations Models: A Stochastic Equilibrium Model of Interest Rates," *Econometrica*, 58, 93–111.

Ortega, E. (1995), "Assessing and Comparing Multivariate Dynamic Models," European University Institute, manuscript.

Pagan, A. (1994), "Calibration and Econometric Research: An Overview," *Journal of Applied Econometrics*, 9, S1–S10.

Pagan, A. and X. Shannon (1985), "Sensitivity Analysis for Linearized Computable General Equilibrium Models," in J. Piggott and J. Whalley (eds.), *New Developments in Applied General Equilibrium Analysis*, Cambridge University Press.

Pesaran, H. and R. Smith (1992), "The Interaction Between Theory and Observation in Economics," University of Cambridge manuscript.

Sargent, T. (1987), *Dynamic Macroeconomic Theory*, Cambridge, MA: Harvard University Press.

Showen, J. and J. Whalley (1984), "Applied General Equilibrium Models of Taxation and International Trade: An Introduction and Survey," *Journal of Economic Literature*, 22, 1007–1051.

Simkins, S.P. (1994), "Do Real Business Cycle Models Really Exhibit Business Cycle Behavior?" *Journal of Monetary Economics*, 33, 381–404.

Smith, T. (1993) "Estimating Nonlinear Time Series Models Using Simulated VAR," *Journal of Applied Econometrics*, 8, S63–S84.

Söderlind, P. (1994), "Cyclical Properties of a Real Business Cycle Model," *Journal of Applied Econometrics*, 9, S113–S122.

Summers, L. (1991), "Scientific Illusion in Empirical Macroeconomics," *Scandinavian Journal of Economics*, 93(2), 129–148.

Tauchen, G. and R. Hussey (1991), "Quadrature Based Methods for Obtaining Approximate Solutions to Integral Equations of Nonlinear Asset Pricing Models," *Econometrica*, 59, 371–397.

Watson, M. (1993), "Measures of Fit for Calibrated Models," *Journal of Political Economy*, 101, 1011–1041.

Wolf, F. (1986), *Meta-Analysis: Quantitative Methods for Research Synthesis*, Beverly Hill, CA: Sage.

16   Simulation variance reduction for bootstrapping

Bryan W. Brown

1   Introduction

The bootstrap and related techniques have received widespread application in the applied statistics and econometric literature. The bootstrap has been used to estimate the distribution function, bias, and standard errors of statistics of interest. The reasons for the widespread use of the bootstrap are twofold. First, the bootstrap can sometimes provide distribution or variance estimates upon which to base asymptotic inferences in cases where the asymptotic variances are difficult or impossible to obtain in the usual way. Second, and more importantly, the inferences based on the bootstrap are perceived to be more accurate in finite samples than those based on standard asymptotic approaches.

In the estimation of the distribution function, there is sound basis for the second reason. The bootstrap distribution function of a statistic can be narrowly defined as the exact finite sample distribution function evaluated at estimates of the parameters. In models with sufficient regularity, asymptotically pivotal statistics, which have a limiting distribution that does not depend on unknown parameters, the standard bootstrap will yield an approximation that is closer to the true distribution, in terms of orders of probability, than the usual limiting distribution. By nesting the original bootstrap within another bootstrap, the approximation error for non-pivotal statistics can be similarly reduced. Likewise, nested bootstraps can conceivably be used to further reduce the approximation error in pivotal statistics.

The limitation to this otherwise rosy picture is the fact that, as narrowly defined, the bootstrap requires knowledge, up to unknown and estimable parameters, of the exact finite sample distribution of the statistic of interest. Since this distribution is seldom available, the typical approach has been to simulate the distribution using the postulated underlying parametric distribution with estimated parameters. The problem that arises with this approach is that the Monte Carlo simulations introduce an additional source of approximation error that must be considered relative to the bootstrap approximation error. Obviously, with sufficiently numerous simulation replications this will not be a problem. If, however, the number of simulation replications is roughly the same order as the sample size, as is frequently the case, then the simulation approximation error can be significant and conceivably even dominate the bootstrap approximation error. For procedures involving nested simulated bootstraps, we have reason to be doubly concerned since each nest introduces a simulation approximation error.

The purpose of this chapter is to carefully study the role of the number of simulation replications in the approximation error resulting from simulated bootstraps. In the next section, the simulated bootstrap is formally considered and the number of replications required to assure that the simulation approximation error does not dominate the bootstrap approximation error is determined. A control variate variance reduction approach for bootstrap estimation of distribution functions is developed, in the third section, and compared, in terms of replication requirements, to the usual approaches. In the fourth section, the control variate approach is extended to the estimation of moments of the statistic of interest and an antithetic variate variance reduction technique is also introduced. A set of sampling experiments for a very simple model is presented in the fifth section to assess the small-sample behavior and feasibility of the new procedures.

Among the major findings of this chapter are the following. For the most common pivotal statistics, the number of bootstrap simulation replications must be of order n^2 in order for the simulation approximation error to not dominate the bootstrap approximation error, where n is the sample size. In a nested bootstrap, the number of inner bootstrap replications must, similarly, be n^2 but the number of outer bootstrap replications must be n^3. For the control variate bootstraps, the requirements are reduced to n, for the non-nested case and the inner loop of the nested case, and n^2, for the outer loop of the nested case. The antithetic variate approach is shown to yield similar gains in bootstrapping the moments of statistics, when the underlying disturbances are symmetrically distributed. The sampling experiments demonstrate that the control variate approach is quite feasible for both nested and non-nested parametric bootstraps and can yield impressive results even in very small samples.

2   Basic concepts

In this section, we consider the motivation for using the simulated bootstrap to study the properties of statistics and discuss the computational burden that results. We only consider *iid* models since the bootstrap is considerably complicated by the presence of non-*iid* conditions. Specifically, we assume

$$z_i \overset{iid}{\sim} f_z(\cdot, \theta) \tag{1}$$

with the density $f_z(\cdot, \theta)$ known up to the parameter vector θ. It is sometimes convenient to partition the parameter vector as $\theta = (\beta', \eta')'$ where β are the structural parameters of interest and η are nuisance parameters. The statistic in question is denoted

$$T_n(\theta) = T(z_1, z_2, \ldots, z_n) \tag{2}$$

where the argument θ reminds us of the dependence on parameters through the generating distribution. This statistic will typically, but not always, be standardized as in the *t*-ratio $(\bar{x}_n - \mu_0)/(s_n^2/n)^{1/2}$ for the sample mean or the quadratic form $n(\hat{\beta}_n - \beta_0)' \hat{V}_\beta^{-1}(\hat{\beta}_n - \beta_0)$ for the regression estimator. The properties of the statistic studied in this chapter can be represented by the expectation

$$\Gamma_n(\theta, t) = E_\theta[G(T_n(\theta), t)] \tag{3}$$

where $E_\theta[\cdot]$ denotes the exact finite sample expectation using the density $f_z(\cdot, \theta)$. This approach is very general and includes the distribution function of $T_n(\theta)$ when $G(T_n(\theta), t) = 1(T_n(\theta) \leq t)$ and moments when $G(T_n(\theta), t) = T_n(\theta))'$.

Following Beran (1989), we use the "bootstrap" estimator of the target expectation.

$$\Gamma_n(\hat{\theta}_n, t) = E_{\hat{\theta}_n}[G(T_n(\hat{\theta}_n), t)] \tag{4}$$

as the basis for inference regarding $T_n(\theta_0)$, where $\hat{\theta}_n$ is an estimator of the true value θ_0. This is just the exact finite sample expression for the expectation evaluated at estimates of the parameters. Suppose that the expectation function $\Gamma_n(\theta, t)$ converges in probability to the limiting functional $\Gamma_\infty(t)$, then the usual approach is to base inferences on this function. Under fairly general limiting behavior, $\Gamma_n(\hat{\theta}_n, t)$ will give a better approximation to the expectation $\Gamma_n(\theta_0, t)$ than the asymptotic approach based on $\Gamma_\infty(t)$. Specifically we have:

Lemma 1 (Beran, 198?) *Suppose* $\hat{\theta}_n = \theta_0 + O_p(n^{-1/2})$, $\Gamma_n(\theta, t) = \Gamma_\infty(t)$ $+ n^{-m/2} R_n(\theta, t) + O(n^{-(m+1)/2})$, $R_n(\cdot)$ *Lipshitz uniformly in* θ. *Then* $\Gamma_n(\hat{\theta}_n, t)$ $= \Gamma_n(\theta_0, t) + O_p(n^{-(m+1)/2})$.

Aside from the smoothness imposed on the remainder term $R_n(\theta, t)$, the most salient feature of the preconditions is that the limiting functional $\Gamma_\infty(t)$

does not depend on unknown parameters. Under these conditions, $\Gamma_n(\hat{\theta}_n,t)$ is closer to $\Gamma_n(\theta_0,t)$ than $\Gamma_\infty(t)$ by a factor $O_p(n^{-1/2})$.

The limitation of the approach suggested in the previous paragraph is the requirement of knowledge of the exact finite sample expectation functional $\Gamma_n(\theta,t)$, which is usually not available. Given knowledge of the underlying density function and estimates of its parameters, the obvious solution is to approximate the expectation functional through Monte Carlo simulation. Specifically, we generate the new random variables

$$z_i^{(j)} \overset{iid}{\sim} f_z(\cdot,\hat{\theta}_n) \tag{5}$$

for $i = 1,2, ..., n; j = 1,2, ...S$ and the new statistics

$$T_n^{(j)}(\hat{\theta}_n) = T(z_1^{(j)}, z_2^{(j)}, ..., z_n^{(j)}). \tag{6}$$

Now, taking $\hat{\theta}_n$ as given, we approximate $\Gamma_n(\hat{\theta}_n,t) = E_{\hat{\theta}_n}[G(T_n,t)]$ with the sample average

$$\Gamma_{nS}(\hat{\theta}_n,t) = S^{-1}\sum_{j=1}^{S} G(T_n^{(j)}(\hat{\theta}_n),t). \tag{7}$$

Applying a central limit theorem to this sample average yields the following, rather obvious, expansion result, which enables a comparison of the stochastic error introduced from the original sample with the stochastic error introduced from the Monte Carlo pseudo-samples.

Theorem 1 *Suppose the preconditions of the Lemma are satisfied and $\Gamma_n(\theta,t) = E_\theta[G(T_n(\theta),t)]$ and $V_n(\theta,t) = \mathrm{var}_\theta[G(T_n(\theta),t)]$ exist and bounded uniformly in θ. Then $\Gamma_{nS}(\hat{\theta}_n,t) = \Gamma_n(\theta_0,t) + O_p(n^{-(m+1)/2}) + O_p(S^{-1/2})$.*

The additional conditions introduced for the theorem are assured when we are estimating the distribution function of $T_n(\theta_0)$, since $G(\cdot,t) = 1(\cdot \leq t)$.

We define the statistic $T_n(\theta)$ to be pivotal with respect to the functional $\Gamma_n(\theta,t)$ if the component of the latter's expansion depending on θ is asymptotically negligible. In terms of the expansion given in the preconditions of the theorem this means that $m \geq 1$. In most cases of interest, such as distribution estimation, the leading term in the approximation error from using the asymptotic functional $\Gamma_\infty(t)$ is $O_p(n^{-1/2})$, whereupon $m = 1$ and the second term above becomes $O_p(n^{-1})$. In this case, the third term, resulting from Monte Carlo simulation, will dominate unless $S \geq n^2$ as n grows large. In some cases, such as estimating the non-normalized bias of estimators with limiting zero mean normal behavior, the leading term in the approximation error is $O_p(n^{-1})$, whereupon $m = 2$ and the second term becomes $O_p(n^{-3/2})$. In this case, the approximation error resulting from Monte Carlo simulation will dominate unless $S \geq n^3$. If n is small neither of these cases may present a problem. When n is large, however, as in the

complex analysis of large cross-sectional data sets, either of these cases
might present a substantial computational burden.

If $T_n(\theta)$ is non-pivotal with respect to $\Gamma_n(\theta,t)$, then the component
depending on θ is asymptotically non-negligible. In our current notation,
this can be represented by $\Gamma_\infty(t) = 0$ and $m = 0$, whereupon the expansion
simplifies to $\Gamma_n(\theta,t) = R_n(\theta,t) + O_p(n^{-1/2})$ and the leading term $R_n(\theta,t)$
depends on θ. In this case, the second term in the expansion for the simulated bootstrap given above becomes $O_p(n^{-1/2})$ and we need only require
that $S \geq n$ to assure that the simulation error does not dominate. Of course,
we could have used the usual asymptotic approximation to obtain the same
degree of precision. Accordingly, unless the asymptotic approximation is
particularly difficult to compute, the motivation for using the usual bootstrap is not compelling for the non-pivotal case.

An approach that has been recommended for obtaining higher-order
refinements in the approximation of the distribution function, for both the
pivotal and non-pivotal cases, is the use of nested bootstraps. Ignoring
simulation error for the moment, we take $T_n^1(\theta) = \Gamma_n(\hat\theta_n(\theta), T_n(\theta))$ as the statistic of interest to be bootstrapped, where $\hat\theta_n(\theta)$ indicates the dependence
of $\hat\theta_n$ on the parameters θ of the generating distribution. Note that this statistic will be pivotal, even when the original statistic is non-pivotal, since
$T_n^1(\theta) = \Gamma_n(\theta, T_n(\theta)) + O_p(n^{-(m+1)/2})$ and $\Gamma_n(\theta, T_n(\theta)) \sim U(0,1)$, by the properties of a c.d.f. evaluated at a realization of the random variable. Let
$\Gamma_n^1(\theta, t^1) = E_\theta[1(T_n^1(\theta) \leq t^1)]$ denote the exact finite sample distribution of
$T_n^1(\theta)$ and $\Gamma_n^1(\hat\theta_n, t^1)$ its bootstrap, then it is reasonable to write the expansion

$$\Gamma_n^1(\theta, t^1) = t^1 + n^{-(m+1)/2} R_n^1(\theta, t^1) + O(n^{-(m+2)/2}) \tag{8}$$

since the first non-uniform term should be $O(n^{-(m+1)/2})$. If the remainder
terms in this expansion satisfy the conditions of lemma 1 then we have
$\Gamma_n^1(\hat\theta_n, t^1) = \Gamma_n^1(\theta_0, t^1) + O_p(n^{-(m+2)/2})$. Thus the bootstrap of the bootstrap
yields a (further) refinement in the approximation to the distribution of the
original statistic.

Unfortunately, the nesting of bootstraps only compounds the problems
pointed out above that arise from using simulations to approximate the
expectations involved. In simulating $\Gamma_n(\theta, T_n)$, we found

$$\begin{aligned}T_{nS}^1(\theta_0) &= \Gamma_{nS}(\hat\theta_n(\theta_0), T_n(\theta_0)) \\ &= \Gamma_n(\theta_0, T_n(\theta_0)) + O_p(n^{-(m+1)/2}) + O_p(S^{-1/2})\end{aligned} \tag{9}$$

where S denotes the number of Monte Carlo replications in the inner boot-
strap. Similarly, for $\Gamma_{nS_1}^1(\hat\theta_n, t_1) = \sum_{k=1}^{S_1} 1(T_n^{1(k)}(\hat\theta_n) \leq t_1)$, application of the
theorem yields

$$\Gamma_{nS_1}^1(\hat\theta_n,t^1) = \Gamma_n^1(\theta_0,t^1) + O_p(n^{-(m+2)/2}) + O_p(S_1^{-1/2}) \tag{10}$$

where S_1 denotes the number of Monte Carlo replications in the outer bootstrap.

As above, these results can be used to determine the number of Monte Carlo simulations required to assure that the simulation error is no larger in stochastic magnitude than the estimation error. For the case where the original statistic is non-pivotal ($m = 0$), we will need the number of simulations in the inner bootstrap S to be no smaller than n and in the outer bootstrap S_1 to be no smaller than n^2, which means the total number of simulations of the model $S \cdot S_1$ must be no smaller than n^3. For the usual case of a pivotal statistic ($m = 1$), we will need $S \geq n^2$ for the inner bootstrap and $S_1 \geq n^3$ for the outer bootstrap, whereupon the total number of simulations of the model must satisfy $S \cdot S_1 \geq n^5$. If n is even moderately large, we begin to see the limitation in implementing nested bootstraps is going to be the number of replications needed to obtain the desired accuracy. In particular, the feasibility of further nesting of the bootstraps to obtain even higher-order refinements is not promising.

Although writing the expansion in Lemma 1 in terms of powers of $n^{1/2}$ is quite natural, less pessimistic results can be given under weaker conditions. Specifically, suppose the smallest remainder term in the expansion for $\Gamma_n(\theta,t)$ is $o(n^{-m/2})$ rather than $O(n^{-(m+1)/2})$, then the simulation error in the non-nested bootstrap will not dominate if $n^m/S = o(1)$ and in the nested bootstrap if $n^{m+1}/S_1 = o(1)$ and $n^m/S = o(1)$. For the most common case of $m = 1$, we have $n/S = o(1)$ required for the non-nested bootstrap and $n^2/S_1 = o(1)$ for the nested bootstrap. Thus the total number of simulations in both the inner and outer bootstrap $S \cdot S_1$ of the nested approach must exceed n^3. The approach introduced below, to reduce the required number of bootstrap simulations, will yield similar gains, however, whether the remainder is $o(n^{-m/2})$ or $O(n^{-(m+1)/2})$.

It is informative to discuss how one might conduct a one-sided hypothesis test using either the nested or non-nested bootstrap to obtain corrected size. Owing to monotonicity of the estimated distribution functions, extreme (large) values of the statistic $T_n(\theta)$ translate into extreme values of $\Gamma_{nS}(\hat\theta_n(\theta),T_n(\theta))$ and $\Gamma_{nS_1}^1(\hat\theta_n,\Gamma_{nS}(\hat\theta_n(\theta),T_n(\theta)))$. Accordingly, for the non-nested approach, one rejects the null if the approximate right-hand prob-value $1 - \Gamma_{nS}(\hat\theta_n(\theta),T_n(\theta))$ exceeds the α-value chosen. Likewise, for the nested approach, one rejects if $1 - \Gamma_{nS_1}^1(\hat\theta_n,\Gamma_{nS}(\hat\theta_n(\theta),T_n(\theta)))$ exceeds α. For a two-sided test, the procedure is identical except it is conducted for both $T_n(\theta)$ and $-T_n(\theta)$ and comparison is made to $\alpha/2$. Note that the two-sided approach does not necessarily impose symmetry so the right- and left-hand tail areas may differ.

The problems arising from Monte Carlo approximation to the expectation function pointed out above occurred because, given $\hat{\theta}_n$, we were averaging the *iid* random variable $G(T_n^{(j)}(\hat{\theta}_n),t)$ and $G(T_n^{(j)}(\hat{\theta}_n),t) - \Gamma_n(\hat{\theta}_n,t)$ $= O_p(1)$. The approach taken in the sequel is to find a related *iid* random variable, say $\tilde{G}_n(\hat{\theta}_n,t) = \tilde{G}(z_1^{(j)}, z_2^{(j)},\ldots, z_n^{(j)};\hat{\theta}_n,t)$, such that $E_{\hat{\theta}_n}[\tilde{G}_n(\cdot)]$ $= E_{\hat{\theta}_n}[G_n(\cdot)]$ but $\tilde{G}_n(\hat{\theta}_n,t) - \Gamma_n(\hat{\theta}_n,t) = o_p(1)$, and average it instead. Since it has the same expectation, the average of the new random variable will converge to the same value but will do so more quickly as a result of the smaller variability. Specifically, suppose that $\tilde{G}_n(\theta,t) - \Gamma_n(\theta,t) = O_p(n^{q/2})$, for $q > 0$, then the following extension of theorem 1 may be applied to compare the simulation and estimation error to determine the number of simulations required.

Theorem 2 *Suppose the preconditions of lemma 1 are satisfied and $\Gamma_n(\theta,t) = E_\theta[\tilde{G}_n(\theta,t)]$ and $V_n(\theta,t) = \mathrm{var}_\theta[n^{q/2}(\tilde{G}_n(\theta,t) - \Gamma_n(\theta,t))]$ exist and are bounded uniformly in θ. Then $\tilde{\Gamma}_{nS}(\hat{\theta}_n,t) = \Gamma_n(\theta_0,t) + O_p(n^{-(m+1)/2}) + O_p(n^{-q/2}S^{-1/2})$.*

Of course, the outstanding issue is how to design functions such as $\tilde{G}_n(\theta,t)$ that have simulation variability improvements of the order indicated. The most widely used techniques for reducing simulation variability are control variates, where we subtract off a zero mean component with negative correlation, and antithetic variates, which exploits symmetry of the disturbance distribution. Most of our attention in this chapter will focus on the use of control variates although the antithetic approach will be used in the estimation of moments. In both cases, we will use the large-scale asymptotic distribution of the statistic in question to construct the reduced variance estimator.

3   Distribution estimation

In this section, we examine the specific problem of distribution estimation. Although we restrict our attention to pivotal statistics, the same approach can be used in bootstrapping the distribution of non-pivotal statistics. In the notation of the previous section, the distribution function is given by $\Gamma_n(\theta,T_n(\theta)) = E_\theta[1(T_n(\theta) \le t)]$, so the function of interest is $G(T_n(\theta),t)$ $= 1(T_n(\theta) \le t)$. In order to implement the general scheme outlined in the previous paragraph, we need to assume limiting behavior on $T_n(\theta)$ with finite sample knowledge of the leading term. Specifically, we assume

$$T_n(\theta) = w(z_1,z_2, \ldots, z_n;\theta) + O_p(n^{-q/2}) \tag{11}$$

with $w_n(\theta) = w(z_1,z_2, \ldots, z_n;\theta)$ and $F_w(\theta,t) = E_\theta[1(w_n(\theta) \le t)]$ known up to the parameters. Note that since the statistic is pivotal, $F_w(\theta,t) = F_w(t)$ does not depend on θ for $q = 1$. A number of important examples satisfy this condition, including t-ratios and quadratic forms involving all the least squares estimators (OLS, 2SLS, 3SLS, LIML, FIML, NLS, NL2SLS, NL3SLS) under normal disturbances independent of the exogenous variables.

We will now use our knowledge of the limiting distribution of T_n and hence $G(T_n(\theta),t)$ to form a control variate that eliminates the leading stochastic term in $G(T_n(\theta),t)$ and then simulate the remainder. Given θ and knowledge of $w_n(\theta)$, we generate $z_i^{(j)} \overset{iid}{\sim} f_z(\cdot,\theta)$, form $T_n^{(j)}(\theta)$ and $w_n^{(j)}(\theta) = w(z_1^{(j)}, z_2^{(j)}, \ldots, z_n^{(j)}; \theta)$, and define

$$\tilde{G}(T_n^{(j)}(\theta), w_n^{(j)}(\theta), t) = 1(T_n^{(j)}(\theta) \le t) - 1(w_n^{(j)}(\theta) \le t) + F_w(\theta, t). \quad (12)$$

By construction, this functional has the same expectation as $G(T_n^{(j)}(\theta), t) = 1(T_n^{(j)}(\theta) \le t)$, but is $O_p(n^{-q/2})$ about the expectation. This function can be averaged over the Monte Carlo replications, evaluated at $\theta = \hat{\theta}_n$, and theorem 2 applied to obtain

$$\begin{aligned}\tilde{\Gamma}_{nS}(\hat{\theta}_n, t) &= S^{-1} \sum_{j=1}^{S} \tilde{G}(T_n^{(j)}(\hat{\theta}_n) w_n^{(j)}(\hat{\theta}_n), t) \\ &= \Gamma_n(\theta_0, t) + O_p(n^{-(m+1)/2}) + O_p(n^{-q/2} S^{-1/2}). \end{aligned} \quad (13)$$

In general, we require $S \ge n^{m+1-q}$ to ensure that the Monte Carlo error does not dominate. For the most common case of $q = m = 1$, we find that S need only be at least as large as n.

The control variate approach can also be applied to the outer bootstrap of a nested bootstrap to obtain further refinements but reduced simulation requirements. We now take $\tilde{T}_n^1(\theta) = \tilde{\Gamma}_{nS}(\hat{\theta}_n(\theta), T_n(\theta))$ as our statistic of interest to be bootstrapped. Suppose $S \ge n^{m+1-q}$, as required by the results of the previous paragraph, then we find $\tilde{T}_n^1(\theta) = \Gamma_n(\theta, T_n(\theta)) + O_p(n^{-(m+1)/2})$, where $\Gamma_n(\theta, T_n(\theta)) \sim U(0,1)$. Moreover, for $q < m+1$, we have $\tilde{T}_n^1(\theta) = F_w(w_n) + O(n^{-q/2})$, since $\Gamma_n(\theta, T_n(\theta)) = F_w(w_n) + O(n^{-q/2})$ is also implied by the previous paragraph. Let $\tilde{\Gamma}_n^1(\theta, t^1) = E_\theta[1(\tilde{T}_n^1(\theta) \le t^1)]$ be the exact finite sample distribution of $\tilde{T}_n^1(\theta)$ and $\tilde{\Gamma}_n^1(\hat{\theta}_n, t^1)$ its bootstrap. It follows from the uniformity noted above that $\tilde{\Gamma}_n^1(\theta, t^1) = t^1 + O(n^{-(m+1)/2})$.

Given θ and knowledge of $w_n(\theta)$, we generate $z_i^{(k)} \overset{iid}{\sim} f_z(\cdot, \theta)$ and form $\hat{\theta}_n^{(k)}(\theta)$, $T_n^{(k)}(\theta)$, and $w_n^{(k)}(\theta) = w(z_1^{(k)}, z_2^{(k)}, \ldots, z_n^{(k)}; \theta)$ in each of S_1 replications of the outer bootstrap. Taking $\hat{\theta}_n^{(k)}(\theta)$ and $T_n^{(k)}(\theta)$ as given, we conduct S replications of an inner bootstrap, as outlined above (13), to obtain $\tilde{T}_n^{1(k)}(\theta) = \tilde{\Gamma}_{nS}^{(k)}(\hat{\theta}_n^{(k)}(\theta), T_n^{(k)}(\theta))$ for each outer replication. We now define the control variate

$$\tilde{G}^1(\tilde{T}_n^{1(k)}(\theta), w_n^{(k)}(\theta), t^1) = 1(\tilde{T}_n^{1(k)}(\theta) \le t^1) - 1(F_w(w_n^{(k)}(\theta)) \le t^1) + t^1 \quad (14)$$

which has the same expectation as $1(\tilde{T}_n^{1(k)}(\theta) \le t^1)$ but is $O_p(n^{-q/2})$ about the expectation. Averaging this function over the outer replications, evaluated at $\theta = \hat{\theta}_n$, and applying theorem 2 yields

$$\tilde{\Gamma}^1_{nS_1}(\hat{\theta}_n, t^1) = S_1^{-1}\sum_{j=1}^{S_1}\tilde{G}^1(\tilde{T}^{1(j)}_n(\hat{\theta}_n), w_n^{(j)}(\hat{\theta}_n), t^1)$$

$$= \tilde{\Gamma}^1_n(\theta_0, t^1) + O_p(n^{-(m+2)/2}) + O_p(n^{-q/2}S_1^{-1/2}). \tag{15}$$

In general, we need $S_1 \geq n^{m+2-q}$ to guarantee that the simulation error in the outer bootstrap does not dominate. For the usual $m = q = 1$, we need $S_1 \geq n^2$, so the total number of replications $S \cdot S_1$ must be no smaller than n^3.

In order to give content to the nature of $w_n(\theta)$, we apply the approach introduced above to a non-trivial example: the non-linear least squares (NLS) model. The model is given by

$$y_i = g(x_i, \beta) + \epsilon_i \tag{16}$$

where $\epsilon_i \overset{iid}{\sim} N(0, \sigma^2)$, independent of x_i. Let $\theta = (\beta', \sigma^2)'$, $g_i(\beta) = g(x_i, \beta)$, and $\nabla g_i(\beta) = \partial g_i(\beta)/\partial\beta$, then the NLS estimator $\hat{\beta}_n$ is given as the solution to

$$0 = n^{-1}\sum_{i=1}^{n}\nabla g_i(\hat{\beta}_n) \cdot (y_i - g_i(\hat{\beta}_n)) \tag{17}$$

and under general assumptions has the limiting behavior $n^{1/2}(\hat{\beta}_n - \beta_0) \overset{d}{\rightarrow} N(0, V(\theta_0))$, where $V(\theta_0) = \sigma_0^2[\text{plim}_{n\rightarrow\infty}n^{-1}\sum_{i=1}^{n}\nabla g_i(\beta_0)\nabla g_i(\beta_0)']^{-1}$. For this example, we will estimate the distribution of the-ratio

$$T_n = e'_\ell(\hat{\beta}_n - \beta_0) \cdot [e'_\ell(\hat{V}_n/n)e_\ell]^{-1/2}$$

where $\hat{V}_n = \hat{\sigma}_n^2[n^{-1}\sum_{i=1}^{n}\nabla g_i(\beta_n)\nabla g_i(\beta_n)']^{-1}$, $\hat{\sigma}_n^2 = n^{-1}\sum_{i=1}^{n}(y_i - g_i(\hat{\beta}_n))^2$, and e_ℓ is a zero vector except for unity in element ℓ.

In our Monte Carlo simulations, we need only simulate ϵ since it is independent of x. Given our estimates $\hat{\beta}_n$ and $\hat{\sigma}_n^2$, for replication j, observation i, we draw $\epsilon_i^{(j)}$ from $N(0, \hat{\sigma}_n^2)$ and hence form $y_i^{(j)} = g_i(\hat{\beta}_n) + \epsilon_i^{(j)}$, $\hat{\beta}_n^{(j)}$, $V_n^{(j)}$, and

$$T_n^{(j)} = e'_\ell(\hat{\beta}_n^{(j)} - \beta_0) \cdot [e'_\ell(\hat{V}_n^{(j)-1}/n)e_\ell]^{-1/2}. \tag{18}$$

Given x_i and $\hat{\theta}_n$, it is straightforward to show that

$$w_n^{(j)}(\hat{\theta}_n) = e'_\ell\{(\hat{V}_n^{-1}) \cdot [n^{-1/2}\sum_{i=1}^{n}\nabla g_i(\hat{\beta}_n) \cdot (y_i^{(j)} - g_i(\hat{\beta}_n))]\} \cdot$$

$$[e'_\ell(\hat{V}_n^{-1}/n)e_\ell]^{-1/2} \tag{19}$$

is *iid* $N(0,1)$ and differs from $T_n^{(j)}(\hat{\theta}_n)$ by terms $O_p(n^{-1/2})$. Substituting the last two eqations and $F_w(t) = \Phi(t)$ into $\tilde{G}(T_n^{(j)}, w_n^{(j)}, t)$, as given by (12), and averaging, defines our improved non-nested bootstrap estimator of the distribution function of the t-ratio. In a similar fashion, these same definitions can be used in an outer bootstrap to obtain the components of $\tilde{G}^1(T_n^{1(k)}, w_n^{(k)}, t^1)$, as given by (14), and averaged to yield an improved nested bootstrap estimator of the distribution function.

Beran (1989) has also proposed the mixing of analytic approximations and simulation in a nested bootstrap to obtain refined approximations to the distribution function. Suppose we have the higher-order Edgeworth-type approximation

$$\Gamma_n(\theta,t) = \Gamma_\infty(t) + n^{-1/2}R_n(\theta,t) + O(n^{-1}), \tag{20}$$

as given in lemma 1, but $R_n(\theta,t)$ is known up to the parameters θ. Beran proposes that we bootstrap $T_n^1(\theta) = \Gamma_\infty(T_n(\theta)) + n^{-1/2}R_n(\hat{\theta}_n(\theta),(T_n(\theta)))$ via simulation. Since this statistic will be uniform up to $O_p(n^{-1})$, its bootstrap will yield an approximation correct to $O_p(n^{-3/2})$. In order for the simulation error to not dominate the expansion we will need in $S \geq n^3$ in the simulated outer bootstrap. It is still possible in this approach to reduce the number of required simulations through the use of control variates. Specifically, we can reduce the number of required simulations, in the outer bootstrap, to $S \geq n^2$.

The procedures introduced in this section allow for refined estimation of the distribution function when the underlying distribution of the observed variables is parametrically specified. It is tempting to try to extend the approach to semi-parametric models, such as the non-linear regression model with the distribution of the disturbances ϵ unrestricted except for independence of x, zero mean, and constant variance. Rather than drawing $\epsilon_i^{(j)}$ from $N(0,\hat{\sigma}_n^2)$ we draw from the empirical distribution $\hat{F}_\epsilon(c)$ $= n^{-1}\Sigma_{i=1}^n 1(\hat{\epsilon}_i \leq c)$, of the residuals. The complication arises in finding $F_w(\theta,t) = E_\theta[1(w_n(\theta) \leq t)]$ when ϵ has the discrete distribution $\hat{F}_\epsilon(\cdot)$. Although, in principle, it should be possible to work out the expectation it would likely be as computationally intensive as a number of additional Monte Carlo replications.

4   Moment estimation

In this section, we consider the estimation of moments of the statistic of interest. Examples of moments of statistics that have been bootstrapped include bias and standard error estimates of parameter estimates. In terms of the notation of this chapter the function whose expectation is of interest is

$$G(T_n(\theta),t) = T_n(\theta)^t \tag{21}$$

As in the previous section, we need to assume some finite sample knowledge of the leading term in the expansion for $T_n(\theta)$. Specifically, we again assume

$$T_n(\theta) = w(z_1,z_2,\ldots,z_n;\theta) + O_p(n^{-q/2}) \tag{22}$$

but now with $E_\theta[w(z_1,z_2,\ldots,z_n;\theta)^t]$ known up to the parameters. The leading examples given in the previous section that satisfied this condition would also be likely candidates for the procedure introduced below. Note that it is sometimes possible that the moments being estimated do not exist, as in certain cases of the simultaneous equation estimators, whereupon the procedures proposed below may need reinterpretation.

Our knowledge of the limiting behavior of $T_n(\theta)$ can again be used to form control variates. Specifically, given θ and knowledge of $w_n(\theta)$, we generate $z_i^{(j)} \sim iid\ f_z(\cdot,\theta)$, form $T_n^{(j)}(\theta)$ and $w_n^{(j)}(\theta) = w(z_1^{(j)},z_2^{(j)},\ldots,z_n^{(j)};\theta)$, and define

$$\tilde{G}(T_n^{(j)}(\theta),w_n^{(j)}(\theta),t) = (T_n^{(j)}(\theta))^t - (w_n^{(j)}(\theta))^t + E_\theta[w^t] \tag{23}$$

which is *iid*, and $O_p(n^{-q/2})$ about the same expectation as $(T_n^{(j)}(\theta))^t$. Averaging this function, evaluated at $\theta = \hat{\theta}_n$, over the Monte Carlo replications, yields

$$\tilde{\Gamma}_{nS}(\hat{\theta}_n,t) = S^{-1}\sum_{j=1}^{S}\tilde{G}(T_n^{(j)}(\hat{\theta}_n),(w_n^{(j)}(\hat{\theta}_n),t$$

$$= \Gamma n(\theta,t) + O_p(n^{-(m+1)/2}) + O_p(n^{-q/2}S^{-1/2}). \tag{24}$$

For the pivotal statistics considered in this section, we would usually have $q=m$ and either $m=1$ or $m=2$. In either case, we find that only $S \geq n$ is required to ensure that the Monte Carlo error is not dominated.

We now study the estimation of both odd and even moments. For the odd moment case, we would typically have $T_n(\theta) = n^{-1/2}(\hat{\beta} - \beta)$ with $w(z_1,z_2,\ldots,z_n;\theta) \sim N(0,V_n(\theta))$ whereupon $\Gamma_\infty(t)=0$ for t odd. Thus the statistic is pivotal for the odd moment in question and there is no need to standardize. The leading term in the even moments of this statistic will, in general, depend on θ and hence be non-pivotal. As was pointed out above, using the bootstrap to estimate in non-pivotal cases is no more accurate than the usual asymptotic approximations. Accordingly, we should examine the even moments of the pivotal analogue $T_n(\theta) = (\hat{V}\beta)^{-1/2}(\hat{\beta} - \beta)$ which has $w(z_1,z_2,\ldots,z_n;\theta) \sim N(0,I)$ and $E_\theta[w(z_1,z_2,\ldots,z_n;\theta)^t] = k(t)$. Rather than directly estimating the variances or standard errors of our estimated parameters using a bootstrap and comparing to the asymptotic estimates, we would estimate the variances of the standardized t-ratios and compare them to unity.

With the introduction of a little more structure, we can utilize the antithetic variates approach to reduce simulation variability for the estimation of odd moments. Specifically, we suppose the model takes the form

$$\rho(y_i,x_i;\beta) = \epsilon_i \tag{25}$$

where $\epsilon_i \overset{iid}{\sim} N(0,\sigma^2)$ independent of x_i and the inverse function $y_i = \pi(\epsilon_i,x_i;\beta)$ exists. This model would include all the linear and non-linear least squares models as special cases. For all of the least squares estimators, we find $T_n(\theta)$ $= n^{1/2}(\hat{\beta} - \beta) = w(z_1, z_2, \ldots, z_n; \theta) + O_p(n^{-m/2})$ with

$$w(z_1, z_2, \ldots, z_n; \theta) = n^{-1/2} \sum_{i=1}^{n} q(x_i; \theta) \epsilon_i. \tag{26}$$

In our bootstrap replications, we generate the pseudo-observations $y_i^{(j)} = \pi(\epsilon_i^{(j)}, x_i, \hat{\beta})$ and $\tilde{y}_i^{(j)} = \pi(-\epsilon_i^{(j)}, x_i, \hat{\beta})$ where $\epsilon_i^{(j)} \overset{iid}{\sim} N(0, \hat{\sigma}^2)$. We then form $T_n^{(j)}(\theta)$ based on $z_i^{(j)} = (y_i^{(j)}, x_i)$, in the usual fashion, and $\tilde{T}_n^{(j)}(\theta)$ from $\tilde{z}_i^{(j)} = (\tilde{y}_i^{(j)}, x_i)$. These can now be combined to obtain the antithetic combination

$$\tilde{G}(T_n^{(j)}(\theta), (\tilde{T}_n^{(j)}(\theta), t)) = [T_n^{(j)}(\theta)^t + (\tilde{T}_n^{(j)}(\theta))^t]/2 \tag{27}$$

which, due to the asymptotic linearity in ϵ and t odd, is $O_p(n^{-m/2})$. Averaging this component yields

$$\tilde{\Gamma}_{nS}(\hat{\theta}_n, t) = S^{-1} \sum_{j=1}^{S} G(T_n^{(j)}(\hat{\theta}_n), \tilde{T}_n^{(j)}(\hat{\theta}_n), t)$$
$$= \Gamma_n(\theta, t) + O_p(n^{-(m+1)/2}) + O_p(n^{-m/2} S^{-1/2}) \tag{28}$$

which is essentially the same, in terms of orders of magnitude, as the control variate approach. The disadvantage of the antithetic approach is that it does not work at all for even moments and not well for non-linear functions such as those used for the distribution function.

For the more restricted models introduced for the antithetic approach, it is possible to extend the estimation of moments to the semiparametric case where the distribution of the disturbances ϵ is unrestricted except for independence of x, zero mean, and constant variance. Under these relaxed assumptions, we draw from the empirical distribution $\hat{F}_\epsilon(c) = n^{-1} \sum_{i=1}^{n} 1(\hat{\epsilon}_i \leq c)$, of the residuals. The control variate approach would proceed as before, except that $E_\theta[(w_n(\theta))^t]$ would have to be evaluated using the discrete empirical distribution $\hat{F}_\epsilon(\cdot)$ and $\hat{\theta}_n$ as the truth. If we are willing to add the assumption that ϵ has a symmetric distribution, then the antithetic procedure discussed above can also be applied to the semiparametric estimation of odd moments.

The complication in these semiparametric extensions is that they add an additional term to the approximation since we are now approximating the distribution with a multinomial discrete distribution. Specifically, we now have the following expansion for the reduced variance bias estimator:

$$\Gamma_{nS}^*(\hat{\theta}_n, t) = \Gamma_n(\theta, t) + \underbrace{O_p(n^{-(m+1)/2})}_{\text{Bootstrap Approx.}} + \underbrace{O_p(n^{-(m/2)} S^{-1/2})}_{\text{Monte Carlo Approx.}} + \underbrace{O_p(?)}_{\text{Discrete Approx.}}. \tag{29}$$

Of course, the discrete approximation error would be present even if we were using the standard bootstrap approach. So, in cases where the standard bootstrap is known to work under semiparametric assumptions, the reduced variance approaches should also work. Examples where the discrete approximation error has been shown to be no larger than the bootstrap approximation error include the least squares model under independence (see Hall (1985)), the least squares model with conditional mean zero disturbances (see Mammen (1993)), and the GMM model (see Hall and Horowitz (1996)).

The variance reduction approaches proposed in this section are closely related to those proposed by Hendry and Harrison (1974) for estimating, by Monte Carlo techniques, the finite sample moments of estimators in the linear simultaneous equations. They proposed a control variate approach which subtracted off the leading term in the limiting distribution and thereby averaged terms that were $O_p(n^{-1/2})$ rather than $O_p(1)$ about the expectation of the estimators moment. They also proposed an antithetic approach that averages the usual function with an evaluation at the negative of the disturbances to obtain similar gains in precision. The basic difference is that they were conducting their exercise in the confines of a classical Monte Carlo experiment and knew the exact values of the parameters and sought to estimate exact moments. Here we must use estimated parameters and seek to estimate the moments evaluated at the estimates.

5   Sampling experiments

In this section, we present the results of some very simple Monte Carlo sampling experiments. The simplicity of the model and statistics to be bootstrapped is at least partially dictated by the fact that the bootstrap procedures under examination themselves utilize Monte Carlo simulation. Moreover, some of the bootstrap estimators of interest involve nested Monte Carlo simulations with the number of replications exponential in the sample size. Consequently, even for simple statistics and moderate sample size, a prohibitive amount of computer time can be required. In any event, our objective in these experiments is to determine how well the procedures proposed in this chapter work in small and moderate sample sizes. Aside from the simplicity of the model and statistics, the analysis of this section is subject to all the qualifications that usually apply to Monte Carlo studies of finite sample properties of estimators. Nonetheless, the experiments should be suggestive as to how we might expect the new procedures to perform relative to the usual asymptotic inference and also illustrate the feasibility of the approach.

The statistic studied is a non-linear transformation of the sample mean of a normally distributed random variable. The purpose of the non-linearity is to introduce non-normalities in the statistic of interest, whereupon the asymptotic approach might be expected to perform less favorably in small samples. Specifically, for $z_i \overset{iid}{\sim} N(\mu_0, \sigma_0^2)$ and $\bar{z}_n = n^{-1}\sum_{i=1}^{n} z_i$, we consider the quadratic form

$$T_n(\theta_0) = n \cdot (\hat{\beta}_n - \beta_0)^2 / \hat{V}_n \tag{30}$$

where $\beta_0 = 1/(1 + \mu_0^2)$ and $\hat{\beta}_n = 1/(1 + \bar{z}_n^2)$. The variance estimator is obtained using standard techniques and is given by

$$\hat{V}_n = 4 \cdot \beta_0^4 \cdot \mu_0 \cdot \hat{\sigma}_n^2 \tag{31}$$

where $\hat{\sigma}_n^2 = n^{-1}\sum_{i=1}^{n} (z_i - \bar{z}_n)^2$. It is straightforward to show this statistic is asymptotically $\chi^2(1)$ and that $m = 1$ for this statistic. In each experiment, $\sigma_0^2 = 1$ is used in generating the original data.

We first examine the estimation of the distribution function for this statistic. Specifically, we estimate the sizes of the asymptotic (Asy.), standard bootstrap (Std. Boot.), reduced variance nested bootstrap (C.V. Boot.), nested bootstrap (Nest. Boot.), and reduced variance bootstrap (C.V. Nest.). For this experiment, the null hypothesis value $\mu_0 = 1$ (and hence $\beta_0 = 0.5$) is used in generating the original data and the bootstrap replications. The number of bootstrap replications in the non-nested approaches and the inner bootstrap of the nested approaches S is given to equal the sample size n. The number of bootstrap replications in the outer bootstrap of the nested approaches S_1 is set equal to the square of the sample size.

The rejection frequencies from 10,000 Monte Carlo replications for ostensible sizes of 10 percent, 5 percent, and 1 percent and sample sizes of 10, 25, and 100 are presented in table 16.1. Note that results are not reported for the bootstraps for the smaller ostensible sizes at smaller sample sizes. This is because there can be a problem of granularity when S is small. Specifically, how do we establish the 1 percent point when we only have ten bootstrapped observations? For this reason we might want to use a moderate value for S, even though it need not grow large faster than n. Also note that results have not been reported for the nested bootstrap approaches for the largest sample size of 100. This is because of the enormous computational requirements involved in doing 10,000 replications of $(n^2 =)10,000$ outer bootstrap replications of $(n =)100$ inner bootstrap replications.

Several features of table 16.1 are worthy of comment. The asymptotic approach over-rejects, particularly in the tails, except for the largest sample size, which is a reflection of the non-linearity. The standard bootstrap over-rejects even more dramatically for all ostensible sizes and sample sizes when $S = n$. Neither of these results is surprising since our analysis above shows the approximation error for both distribution estimators to be $O_p(n^{-1/2})$, in this case. Although the reduced variance bootstrap estimator significantly over-rejects in the smallest sample, it is much closer to the ostensible size than the alternatives and seems to work well in the larger samples. The

Table 16.1. *Transformed mean model: size 10,000 Monte Carlo replications*

n	S	S_1	Method	10%	5%	1%
10	—	—	Asy.	0.1391***	0.0898***	0.0387***
	10	—	Std. Boot.	0.1835***	—	—
	10	—	C.V. Boot.	0.1117***	—	—
	10	100	Nest. Boot.	0.1599***	0.1005***	0.0911***
	10	100	C.V. Nest.	0.1020	0.0531***	0.0137***
25	—	—	Asy.	0.1109***	0.0629***	0.0199***
	25	—	Std. Boot.	0.1084**	—	—
	25	—	C.V. Boot.	0.1039	—	—
	25	625	Nest. Boot.	0.1120***	0.0700***	0.0351***
	25	625	C.V. Nest	0.0992	0.0498***	0.0099
100	—	—	Asy.	0.1052	0.0574*	0.0133
	100	—	Std. Boot.	0.1126***	0.0647***	0.0211***
	100	—	C.V. Boot.	0.1029	0.0558	0.0126

Notes:
  *Significant at 0.05 level.
  **Significant at 0.01 level.
  ***Significant at 0.001 level.

nested bootstrap over-rejects the most of all, which reflects the fact that we have not met the requirements for the simulation error not to dominate with this approach. The reduced variance nested bootstrap works best of all, with a slight over-rejection in the tails for the smallest sample. In terms of correcting for size, both the nested and non-nested reduced variance bootstraps are attractive, feasible alternatives.

We next study the possible power of the alternative approaches. This is accomplished by imposing $\mu = 1.5$ in generating the original data, but $\mu = 1.0$ in the null hypothesis imposed in forming the statistic and the bootstrap replications. The outcome of this experiment is presented in table 16.2. We are particularly interested in whether the additional simulation error from using less than the recommended number of replications in the standard bootstrap and nested bootstrap results in loss of power. The outcome of 10,000 replications of this experiment is also presented in table 16.2. Obviously, the over-rejection when the null is correct that was found above carries over to even larger rejections under a misspecified null. On the other hand, the smaller (correct) sizes for the reduced variance bootstraps under a correct null is reflected in much smaller power under a misspecified null. There are really no surprises here.

We now examine the performance of bias estimators for the transformed

Table 16.2. *Transformed mean model: power 10,000 Monte Carlo replications*

n	S	S_1	Method	10%	5%	1%
10	—	—	Asy.	0.3068	0.1731	0.0470
	10	—	Std. Boot.	0.3681	—	—
	10	—	C.V. Boot.	0.2395	—	—
	10	100	Nest. Boot.	0.3179	0.2003	0.1804
	10	100	C.V. Nest.	0.2104	0.0976	0.0349
25	—	—	Asy.	0.6899	0.5111	0.1778
	25	—	Std. Boot.	0.6337	—	—
	25	—	C.V. Boot.	0.6210	—	—
	25	625	Nest. Boot.	0.6400	0.4677	02682
	25	625	C.V. Nest	0.6044	0.3612	0.0726
100	—	—	Asy.	0.9988	0.9975	0.9784
	100	—	Std. Boot.	0.9990	0.9973	0.9651
	100	—	C.V. Boot.	0.9993	0.9966	0.9030

mean model. Since we are dealing with an odd moment, we will deal with the unstandardized statistic $T_n(\theta) = (\hat{\beta}_n - \beta_0)$. For this experiment, the value $\mu_0 = 1$ is used in generating the original data but the estimate $\bar{z}_n$ is used in the bootstrap replications. The results of 10,000 Monte Carlo replications of the alternative bootstrap estimators of the bias for this model are reported in table 16.3. Estimated standard errors are given in parentheses.

Now $n^{1/2}(\hat{\beta}_n - \beta_0) \xrightarrow{d} N(0, V_\beta)$, so the unnormalized statistic $\hat{\beta}_n - \beta_0$ has bias and variance $O(n^{-1})$. It follows that the variance of the standard bootstrapped bias would be $O(n^{-2})$ and the standard error $O(n^{-1})$, for $S = n$. This relationship is roughly reflected in the bias estimates and their standard errors, both of which are monotonically declining with the sample size. There seems to be very little difference between the average levels of the bias estimates using the standard bootstrap and the reduced variance bootstrap. This is hardly surprising, since they both have the same expectation. The big difference is in the variability which is shown by the estimated standard errors. For $S = n$, we would expect the reduced variance estimator to have an approximation error that is smaller by the factor $n^{-1/2}$. This relationship is roughly reflected in the standard errors.

Finally, we examine the performance of the bias estimators for the transformed mean model under semiparametric assumptions. The bootstrap replications in this case are based on draws from the empirical distribution

Table 16.3. *Parametric bias estimation: 10,000 Monte Carlo replications*

n	S	Std. Boot.	Red. Boot.
10	10	0.01084 (0.04648)	0.01076 (0.02003)
25	25	0.00773 (0.01979)	0.00756 (0.00414)
100	100	0.00237 (0.00505)	0.00236 (0.00049)

of the original sample. The underlying random variable is given by $z_i = \mu_0 + \sigma_0(1/3)^{1/2}w_i$, where w_i is an *iid* draw from the student-t distribution with three degrees of freedom, whereupon z_i is *iid* (μ_0, σ_0^2). The results of 10,000 Monte Carlo replications are reported in table 16.4.

The results of this experiment are roughly the same as for the parametric case except for sample size 10, in which case the bias estimates are smaller than before and there is less difference between the standard bootstrap and the reduced variance bootstrap. More generally, the advantage of the reduced variance estimator relative to the standard bootstrap is still clear but less pronounced. Doubtless, the approximation error from using the discrete empirical distribution, which is common to both, draws them closer together.

6   Concluding remarks

In this chapter, the stochastic error and computational demands introduced from the use of Monte Carlo simulations to approximate bootstraps of expectations of statistics are studied. For pivotal statistics, the stochastic error resulting from simulation is shown, in the second section, to dominate the stochastic error introduced by the bootstrap unless $S \geq n^2$, where n denotes the sample size and S the number of simulation replications. In a simulated nested bootstrap, the number of replications in the inner bootstrap is similarly shown to require $S \geq n^2$ but the number of replications in the outer bootstrap must satisfy $S_1 \geq n^3$, where S_1 denotes the number of simulation replications in the outer loop. Thus the total number of replications in a nested bootstrap of a pivotal statistic must be n^5 to insure that the simulation stochastic error is no larger than the bootstrap stochastic error. This computational requirement can be prohibitive even in simple models with moderate samples.

A control variate approach is introduced, in the second section, for parametric bootstrapping of the distribution function of the statistic of interest. This approach utilizes the leading term in the asymptotic expansion for the

Table 16.4. *Semiparametric bias estimation: 10,000 Monte Carlo replications*

n	S	Std. Boot.	Red. Boot.
10	10	0.00642 (0.04880)	0.00652 (0.03437)
25	25	0.00604 (0.02145)	0.00589 (0.01246)
100	100	0.00212 (0.00547)	0.00219 (0.00203)

statistic and its expectation to form a function that has the same expectation but smaller variance than the original statistic. For the most common pivotal statistics, the number of simulation replications required in a non-nested bootstrap and the inner loop of a nested bootstrap are reduced to $S \geq n$. The number of replications required in the outer loop of a nested bootstrap is reduced to $S_1 \geq n^2$. Thus the total number of replications required in a nested bootstrap is reduced to n^3. Although the computational requirements involved in the latter result can still be substantial, it is an enormous improvement over the requirements for a standard nested bootstrap.

The control variate approach is extended to parametric and semiparametric bootstrap estimation of moments of statistics in the fourth section. In the parametric case, the control variate approach is shown to reduce the number of replications required in bootstrapping moments of pivotal statistics (and odd moments for many others) from $S \geq n^2$ to $S_1 \geq n$. An antithetic variate approach is shown to yield similar improvements in the bootstrapping of odd moments of the usual estimators when the underlying disturbances are symmetrically distributed. Both the control variate and antithetic approaches are extended to the distribution-free case. For models where the usual distribution-free bootstrap yields asymptotic refinements, the reduced variance moment bootstraps can be expected to work equally well, but with fewer replications.

In the fifth section a sampling experiment was conducted to ascertain the feasibility and small sample behavior of the new reduced-variance bootstrap approaches relative to the usual approach. A simple transformed mean model was utilized due to the immense computational requirements involved in a Monte Carlo simulation of the nested bootstrap approaches. A simple squared t-ratio was the statistic of interest in the bootstrapping of distribution functions. The usual asymptotic approach did not work well in small samples for this approach, even when the underlying disturbances were normal, owing to the non-linearity. The usual non-nested and nested bootstrap estimates of the distribution based on $S=n$ and $S_1=n^2$ performed even more poorly in small samples. The non-nested and nested control-variate bootstrap estimators, based on the same replication sizes, fared much better, particularly the latter. The results for bootstrapping the bias of the same statistic were quite similar.

The results of this chapter, while quite encouraging, are subject to several limitations. First, with respect to bootstrapping moments, is the requirement that we know the leading term in the asymptotic expansion of the statistic and its expectation. This is fairly straightforward in the least square-type models but can be complicated elsewhere. Second, with respect to bootstrapping distributions, is the further requirement that we know the exact finite sample distribution of the leading term. For practical purposes, this means we can only apply the results to the least squares models with normal disturbances. Finally, is the *iid* assumption for the variables. Although the same concept of the use of control-variates is likely to be fruitful in the dependent or *iid* cases, the specific implementation will probably be somewhat different. For example, in the dependent case, we must deal with issues such as gathering the data into blocks to preserve the dependence characteristics. Fortunately, these limitations leave room for further substantive work along similar lines.

Appendix

Proof of Lemma 1 By substitution, $\Gamma_n(\hat{\theta}_n,t) = \Gamma_\infty(t) + n^{-m/2}R_n(\hat{\theta}_n,t) + O(n^{-(m+1)/2})$ and

$$\Gamma_n(\hat{\theta}_n,t) - \Gamma_n(\theta_0,t) = n^{-m/2}[R_n(\hat{\theta}_n,t) - R_n(\theta_0,t)] + O(n^{-(m+1)/2})$$

$$= n^{-m/2}O_p(\|\hat{\theta}_n - \theta_0\|) + O(n^{-(m+1)/2})$$

$$= O_p(n^{-(m+1)/2}). \quad \square$$

Proof of Theorem 1 See proof of theorem 2, below, for $G_n^*(\theta,t) = G(T_n,t)$ and $q = 0$. $\square$

Proof of Theorem 2 By the uniform boundedness of the first two moments of $n^{q/2}(G_n^*(\theta,t) - \Gamma_n(\theta,t))$ and the *iid* property of $z^{(j)}$ given $\hat{\theta}_n$, a uniform CLT applies for $n^{q/2} S^{1/2}[S-1\sum_j^{S=1} G_n^*(\hat{\theta}_n,t) - \Gamma_n(\hat{\theta}_n,t)]$ and $\Gamma_{n,S}^*(\hat{\theta}_n,t) = \Gamma_n(\hat{\theta}_n,t) + O_p(n^{-q/2}S^{-1/2})$. Substitution from lemma 1 yields the desired result. $\square$

References

Beran, R. (1987), "Prepivoting to reduce level error of confidence sets," *Biometrika*, 74, 457–468.

  (1988), "Prepivoting Test Statistics: A Bootstrap View of Asymptotic Refinements," *Journal of the American Statistical Association*, 83, 687–697.

Brown, B. and W. Newey (1995), "Bootstrapping for GMM," Department of Economics, Massachusetts Institute of Technology, mimeo.

Efron, B. (1978), "Better Bootstrap Confidence Intervals," *Journal of the American Statistical Association*, 82, 171–185.

  (1979), "Bootstrap Methods: Another Look at the Jacknife," *Annals of Statistics*, 7, 1–26.

Efron, B. and R.J. Tibshirani (1983), *An Introduction to the Bootstrap*, New York: Chapman and Hall.

Hall P. (1985a), "Resampling a Coverage Process," *Stochastic Process Applications*, 19, 259–269.

  (1985b), *The Bootstrap and Edgeworth Expansion*, New York: Springer-Verlag.

  (1986), "On the Bootstrap and Confidence Intervals," *Annals of Statistics*, 14, 1431–1452.

  (1988), "Theoretical Comparison of Bootstrap Confidence Intervals," *Annals of Statistics*, 16, 927–983.

Hall P. and J.L. Horowitz (1996), "Bootstrap Critical Values for Tests Based on Generalized-Method-of-Moments Estimators," *Econometrica*, 64, 891–916.

Hall P., J.L. Horowitz, and B.-Y. Jing (1995), "On Blocking Rules for the Bootstrap with Dependent Date," *Biometrika*, 82, 561–574.

Hendry, D.F. (1984), "Monte Carlo Experiments in Econometrics," in Z. Griliches and M. Intrilligator (eds.), *Handbook of Econometrics*, vol. II, Amsterdam: North-Holland, chapter 16, pp. 937–976.

Hendry, D.F. and R.W. Harrison (1974), "Monte Carlo Methodology and the Finite Sample Behavior of Ordinary and Two-Stage Least Squares," *Journal of Econometrics*, 2, 151–174.

Horowitz, J.L. (1997), "Bootstrap-Based Critical Values for the Information-Matrix Test," *Journal of Econometrics*, 61, 395–411.

  (1995), "Bootstrap Methods in Econometrics: Theory and Numerical Performance," Department of Economics, University of Iowa, Working Paper No. 95–10.

Maddala G.S. and J. Jeong (1993), "A Perspective on Application of Bootstrap Methods in Econometrics," in G.S. Maddala, C.R. Rao, and H.D. Vinod (eds.), *Handbook of Statistics*, vol. XI, Amsterdam: North-Holland, pp. 573–610.

Mammen, E. (1993), "Bootstraps and Wild Bootstraps for High Dimensional Linear Models," *Annals of Statistics*, 21, 255–285.

Mikhail, W.M. (1972), "Simulating the Small-Sample Properties of Econometric Estimators," *Journal of the American Statistical Association*, 62, 620–624.

Politis, D.N. and J.P. Romano (1994), "Large Sample Confidence Regions Based on Subsamples Under Minimal Assumptions," *Annals of Statistics*, 22, 2031–2050.

Singh, K. (1981), "On The Asymptotic Accuracy of Efron's Bootstrap," *Annals of Statistics*, 9, 1187–1195.

Vinod, H.D. (1983), "Bootstrap Methods: Applications in Econometrics," in G.S. Maddala, C.R. Rao, and H.D. Vinod (eds.), *Handbook of Statistics*, vol. XI, Amsterdam: North-Holland, pp. 573–610.

Wu, C.F.J. (1986), "Jackknife, Bootstrap, and Other Resampling Methods in Regression Analysis," *Annals of Statistics*, 14, 1261–1295.

Index